# Nestorian Question On The Administration Of The Eucharist, By Isho'yabh IV

# NESTORIAN QUESTIONS ON THE ADMINISTRATION OF THE EUCHARIST, BY ISHO'YABH IV

*A CONTRIBUTION TO THE HISTORY OF THE EUCHARIST IN THE EASTERN CHURCH*

**PROEFSCHRIFT**

TER VERKRIJGING VAN DEN GRAAD VAN

**DOCTOR IN DE GODGELEERDHEID**

AAN DE RIJKSUNIVERSITEIT TE LEIDEN

OP GEZAG VAN DEN RECTOR-MAGNIFICUS

DR J. A. J. BARGE

HOOGLEERAAR IN DE FACULTEIT DER GENEESKUNDE

VOOR DE FACULTEIT DER GODGELEERDHEID

TE VERDEDIGEN

OP VRIJDAG 26 NOVEMBER 1937

DES NAMIDDAGS TE VIER UUR

DOOR

**WILLEM CORNELIS VAN UNNIK**

GEBOREN TE HAARLEM

GORGIAS PRESS

2006

First Gorgias Press Edition, 2006.



**ISBN 1-59333-409-5**

This edition is based on digitized images kindly provided by Mr. David Malick

GORGIAS PRESS
46 Orris Ave., Piscataway, NJ 08854 USA
www.gorgiaspress.com

Printed in the United States of America

*Materterae piae memoriae*
*Parentibus*

Gaarne grijp ik de gelegenheid, mij door de academische traditie geboden, aan om in het openbaar mijn zeer hartelijken dank uit te spreken aan allen, die mij door hun onderwijs, voorbeeld en aanmoediging gevormd en tot zelfstandig onderzoek gebracht hebben.

In zeer bijzonderen zin geldt dit van de Leidsche Faculteit der Godgeleerdheid. Dat ik den professoren De Graaf en Windisch, die uit den kring der onderzoekers heengingen, niet meer persoonlijk kan danken, doet mij zeer leed. Hun colleges zal ik niet licht vergeten.

Bij hen, die te vroeg naar ons inzicht werden opgeroepen, moet ik helaas ook den naam schrijven van professor Eekhof. Hoeveel ik aan hem verplicht ben, laat zich moeilijk vertolken. Van zijn enthousiasme voor de kerkgeschiedenis, van zijn nauwkeurigheid, die wist slechts in het groote getrouw te kunnen zijn, als het kleine niet verwaarloosd was, van zijn toegewijde liefde te mogen genieten is mij een onwaardeerbaar voorrecht geweest en nog dagelijks tot zegen!

Met groote dankbaarheid gedenk ik Uwe lessen, hooggeleerde Eerdmans en Kristensen, waarin steeds diepe eerbied jegens het voorwerp van Uwe studiën zich paarde aan scherpzinnigheid en onafhankelijkheid van oordeel.

Al sta ik nog niet volledig in het ambt van onze Ned. Herv. Kerk, waarvoor Gij ons opleiddet, hooggeleerde Knappert en Van Nes, toch ben ik U dankbaar voor de liefde voor de kerk en haar arbeid, die Gij bij ons hebt aangewakkerd.

Uw onderwijs te volgen, hooggeleerde Van Holk, Bakhuizen van den Brink, Korff en Sevenster, was mij niet gegeven. Wel ben ik erkentelijk voor de vriendelijkheid, die Gij mij bij onderscheidene gelegenheden hebt bewezen.

Door Uw propaedeutische colleges en privatissima, door vele persoonlijke gesprekken, vooral door Uw vertrouwen mij als Uw assistent bewezen, en door Uw groote persoonlijke belangstelling, hooggeleerde Thierry, hebt Gij mij ten zeerste aan U verbonden.

Met dankbaarheid gedenk ik ook de groote bereidwilligheid van U, hooggeleerde Van Groningen en zeergeleerde De Buck, om mij in te leiden in de vakken, die U zijn toevertrouwd.

Deze dissertatie zou niet geschreven zijn, zoo Gij, hooggeleerde Wensinck, niet vele uren van Uw kostbaren tijd hadt willen afstaan om mij het Syrisch te leeren en bij mij de liefde te wekken en te versterken voor het Oostersch Christendom. Mogen de volgende bladzijden U toonen, dat dit niet geheel en al tevergeefsch is geweest. Het zou mij een voldoening zijn, zoo ik U met dezen arbeid eenig genoegen bereid had.

Wat ik U te danken heb, hooggeschatte Promotor, hooggeleerde De Zwaan, kan ik eigenlijk niet onder woorden brengen. Van meet af aan hebt Gij mij

*Uw hartelijke vriendschap geschonken. Door Uw schitterende colleges hebt Gij de studie van het Nieuwe Testament en het oudste Christendom voor mij een vreugde doen worden. Met raad en daad hebt Gij mij steeds willen steunen; in zeer vele gesprekken met mij vragen betreffende de studie en praktijk willen bespreken. Bij dat alles hebt Gij mij nooit gebonden aan Uw opvattingen; maar mij telkens weer in vrijheid zelf laten zoeken. Het stemt mij tot blijdschap te mogen weten dat het Uw volle instemming had, toen mijn studie zich wendde tot het gebied van Uw „oude liefde". Ook hierin liet Gij mij de vrije hand. Ik hoop van harte, dat de uitkomst daarvan U niet heeft teleurgesteld en dit boek U een klein bewijs zij van mijn dankbaarheid voor het vele, dat Gij mij hebt willen schenken.*

*Uw warme belangstelling, hooggeleerde Thiel en zeergeleerde Spoelder, heeft mij sedert mijn Gymnasiumjaren begeleid; ik wil niet nalaten U daarvoor oprecht te danken.*

*En zou ik het dispuut „Quisque Suis Viribus" niet met blijdschap gedenken? Veel heb ik daar mogen leeren door de lezingen en door de straffe critiek. Der broederen vriendschap was mij een groote schat. Onvergetelijke uren heb ik in dien kring mogen doorbrengen. Van harte groet ik hen allen, waar ook heen verstrooid!*

*In het buitenland eenigen tijd te mogen studeeren, is een groot voorrecht. Hoe dankbaar ik ben, dat ik dit in "Woodbrooke" heb mogen doen, zullen zij beseffen, die daar, evenals ik, genoten hebben van ernst en humor, van diepte van geloof en wijdte van blik. "Woodbrooke", de plaats, waar Rendel Harris het stempel van zijn fijnen geest zoo sterk op gedrukt heeft. De omgang, die ik daar mocht hebben met Prof. H. G. Wood en met den gast Prof. Henry J. Cadbury van Harvard, U.S.A., is voor mij zeer vruchtbaar geweest. Onverbrekelijk verbonden aan het werk voor mijn proefschrift is mij de figuur van Dr. Mingana. De gastvrijheid in zijn Collectie van handschriften en in zijn huis, de bereidwilligheid, waarmee hij mij ter zijde heeft gestaan bij het bewerken van mijn dissertatie door bespreking van verschillende vragen en door het beschikbaar stellen van boeken en handschriften, de wijze, waarop deze Westersch-Oostersch geleerde mij het Oosten heeft nabijgebracht, hebben ten zeerste bijgedragen tot mijn studie van het Oostersch Christendom in het algemeen en van de texten, die hier onderzocht worden in het bijzonder. Voor dit alles hen te danken is aangename plicht.*

*Gaarne spreek ik mijn diepgevoelde erkentelijkheid uit aan allen, die mij de studie, zooals ik ze heb mogen volbrengen, mogelijk maakten, in het bijzonder aan de Beheerders van het „Fonds Noorthey", die mij op ruime wijze in staat stelden om langer te studeeren dan ik zelf had kunnen denken, en aan het Bestuur van het „Oostersch Genootschap" te Leiden voor het bewilligen van een ondersteuning bij het uitgeven van dit proefschrift.*

*De moeite, die Prof. Post van Nijmegen en Prof. Lietzmann van Berlijn zich hebben willen getroosten om mij facsimile's van eenige handschriften van de Vaticaansche en Berlijnsche bibliotheek te bezorgen, heeft mij zeer aan hen verplicht. De voorkomendheid, waarmee het personeel van de Universiteitsbibliotheek te Leiden mij steeds heeft geholpen, vermeld ik met dankbaarheid.*

*De beteekenis, die het materiaal, dat in dit proefschrift is verwerkt, bezit, ook voor Orientalisten en Liturgiologen buiten onze landsgrenzen, heeft mij den moed gegeven om dit werk in het Engelsch uit te geven. Het feit, dat deze taal mijn moedertaal niet is, heeft natuurlijk eigenaardige moeilijkheden met zich meegebracht. Mej. S. C. de Land, leerares te Haarlem, heeft de groote moeite genomen om de gansche copie met het oog op het Engelsch nauwkeurig door te lezen. Voor deze haar bereidwilligheid ben ik haar zeer grooten dank verschuldigd. Zoo hoop ik ten zeerste, dat dit boek geen "double Dutch" geworden is. Waar zich·toch nog onjuistheden tegen de Engelsche taal en stijl mogen bevinden, koester ik den wensch, dat ze de lezers niet te veel zullen storen en hen niet zullen verhinderen om van den inhoud kennis te nemen. Want ik zou het betreuren, als onnauwkeurigheden van den vorm den inhoud zouden schaden.*

*Voor de buitengewoon aangename wijze, waarop de firma Joh. Enschedé en Zonen de uiterlijke verzorging van dit werk heeft willen behartigen, wil ik haar zeer danken.*

ܒܬܘܕܝܬܐ ܕܝܫܘܥ ܡܫܝܚܐ ܫܠܡܬ ܟܬܒܬܐ ܗܕܐ: ܡܪܢ ܢܥܕܘܪ ܠܢ
ܒܨܠܘܬܐ ܘܕܡܪܬܝ ܒܚܘܒܗ ܕܢܫܡܥܘܢܝܗ: ܘܫܘܒܚܐ ܠܐܠܗܐ ܠܥܠܡ
ܠܥܠܡܝܢ ܐܡܝܢ ܀

# TABLE OF CONTENTS

# LIST OF ABBREVIATIONS

'Abdisho', *Catalogue*, in: *B.O.*, iii 1.

'Abdisho', *Nomocanon*, ed. et tr. Mai.

'Addai': Liturgy of the Apostles Addai and Mari.

Badger: G. P. Badger, *The Nestorians and their Rituals*, London, 1849–1852, 2 volumes.

Bar Hebraeus, (*Chr. Eccl.*): Bar Hebraeus, *Chronicum ecclesiasticum*, ed. J. B. Abbeloos-Th. J. Lamy, Lovanii, 1877, Tomus iii.

Bar Hebraeus, *Nomocanon*, ed. P. Bedjan, Parisiis, 1898, translation in: Mai (2nd part).

A. Baumstark, *L.G.*: A. Baumstark, *Geschichte der syrischen Literatur*, Bonn, 1922.

Bingham: J. Bingham, *Origines Ecclesiasticae, Antiquities of the Christian Church*, London, 1856, 2 volumes (reprint from the original edition 1708–1722).

*B.O.*: J. S. Assemani, *Bibliotheca Orientalis Clementino-Vaticana*, Romae, 1719–1728, 3 volumes in 4 parts.

J. Braun, *Lit. Handlex.*: J. Braun, *Liturgisches Handlexicon*[2], Regensburg, 1924.

O. Braun, *Synhados*: O. Braun, *Das Buch des Synhados*, Stuttgart-Wien, 1900.

Browne-Maclean: A. J. Maclean and W. H. Browne, *The Catholicos of the East and his people*, London, 1892.

*Budge, B. G.*: E. A. Wallis Budge, *The Book of the Governors, The Historia Monastica of Thomas, Bishop of Marga A.D.* 840, London, 1893, 2 volumes.

*Canon* (without addition): of John bar Abgare, see p. 133–135.

*C.S.C.O.*: *Corpus Scriptorum Christianorum Orientalium*, ed. J. B. Chabot-I. Guidi e.a., Parisiis, 1903 sqq., Scriptores Syri.

*D.A.C.L.*: F. Cabrol-H. Leclercq, *Dictionnaire d'Archéologie Chrétienne et de Liturgie*, Paris, 1903–. . . , (if the author of an article is not mentioned, it is always Dom. Leclercq).

*D.C.A.*: W. Smith-S. Cheetham, *Dictionary of Christian Antiquities*, London, 1875–1880, 2 volumes.

*D. Th. C.*: A. Vacant-E. Mangenot-E. Amann, *Dictionnaire de Théologie catholique*, Paris, 1909–. . . .

Diettrich, *Taufllit.*: G. Diettrich, *Die nestorianische Taufliturgie*, Giessen, 1903.

Elias Nisib., *Beweis*: Elias von Nisibis, *Beweis der Wahrheit des Glaubens*, übers. von L. Horst, Colmar, 1886.

*E.R.E.*: J. Hastings c.s., *Encyclopedia of Religion and Ethics*, Edinburgh, 1908–1926, 12 vols.

*E.S.D.O.*: A. J. Maclean, *East Syrian Daily Offices, translated from the Syriac*, London, 1894.

*Expos.* i–ii: *Anonymi Auctoris Expositio Officiorum Ecclesiae Georgio Arbelensi vulgo adscripta*, ed. et interpr. R. H. Connolly, in: *C.S.C.O.*, ii 91–92, Parisiis, 1911–1915, 2 volumes in 4 parts (the translation is quoted).

Gismondi i–ii: Maris, Amri et Slibae, *De Patriarchis Nestorianorum Commentaria*, ed. et tr. H. Gismondi, Pars prior, *Maris versio latina*, Romae, 1899; Pars altera, *Amri et Slibae versio latina*, Romae, 1897 (cf. A. Baumstark, *L.G.*, S. 6).

Hanssens ii–iii: J. M. Hanssens, *Institutiones Liturgicae de ritibus orientalibus*, Tomus ii, *De Missa rituum orientalium* Pars prima, Romae, 1930; Tomus iii, *De Missa rituum orientalium* Pars altera, Romae, 1932.

*J. Th. St.: The Journal of Theological Studies.*

Jugie, *Theol. Dogm.:* M. Jugie, *Theologia Dogmatica Christianorum Orientalium ab Ecclesia catholica dissidentium*, t. v, *De theologia dogmatica Nestorianorum et Monophysitarum*, Parisiis, 1935.

Kaufmann, *Handbuch:* C. M. Kaufmann, *Handbuch der christlichen Archaeologie* [3], Paderborn, 1922.

Kayser: C. Kayser, *Die Canones Jacob's von Edessa übers. und erläutert*, Leipzig, 1886.

Labourt, *Christianisme:* J. Labourt, *Le Christianisme dans l'Empire perse sous la dynastie sassanide* (224–632) [2], Paris, 1904.

Lamy: Th. J. Lamy, *Dissertatio de Syrorum fide et disciplina in re Eucharistica, accedunt veteris ecclesiae Syriacae monumenta duo: unum Joannis Tellensis Resolutiones canonicae . . . alterum Jacobi Edesseni Resolutiones canonicae . . .*, Lovanii, 1859.

*L.E.W.:* F. E. Brightman, *Liturgies Eastern and Western*, i *Eastern Liturgies*, Oxford, 1896.

Lietzmann, *Messe:* H. Lietzmann, *Messe und Herrenmahl*, Bonn, 1926.

*L.O.C.:* E. Renaudot, *Liturgiarum Orientalium Collectio* [2], Francofurti ad Moenum, 1847, 2 vols.

*L.O.O.:* I. E. Rahmani, *Les Liturgies Orientales et Occidentales, étudiées séparement et comparées entre elles*, Beyrouth, 1929.

Mai: A. Mai, *Scriptorum Veterum Nova Collectio*, Tomus x, Romae, 1838.

*M.S.G.:* J. P. Migne, *Patrologiae cursus completus, series graeco-latina*, Parisiis, 1857 sqq.

*M.S.L.:* J. P. Migne, *Patrologiae cursus completus, series latina*, Parisiis, 1844 sqq.

Narsai, tr. Connolly: R. H. Connolly, *The liturgical Homilies of Narsai*, Cambridge, 1909.

'Nest': Liturgy of Nestorius.

Nöldeke, *Syrische Gramm.:* Th. Nöldeke, *Kurzgefasste syrische Grammatik* [2], Leipzig, 1898.

*O.C.: Oriens Christianus.*

Payne Smith, *Dictionary:* J. Payne Smith (Mrs. Margoliouth), *A compendious Syriac Dictionary founded upon the Thesaurus Syriacus of R. Payne Smith*, Oxford, 1903.

Pitra, *Monumenta*, i: J. B. Pitra, *Juris Ecclesiastici graecorum historia et monumenta*, vol. i, Romae, 1864.

*P.O.: Patrologia Orientalis*, ed. R. Graffin-F. Nau, Paris, 1903 sqq.

*P.R.E.* [3]*:* J. Herzog-A. Hauck, *Realencyklopädie für protestantische Theologie und Kirche*, Leipzig, 1896–1913, dritte Auflage, 24 vols.

*R.G.G.* [2]*:* H. Gunkel-L. Zscharnack, *Die Religion in Geschichte und Gegenwart*, [2] Tübingen, 1927–1932, 5 vols. + Registerband.

Riedel: W. Riedel, *Die Kirchenrechtsquellen des Patriarchats von Alexandrien*, Leipzig, 1900.

*Synod. Arab.* (or: *Nomocanon Arab.*): see: p. 121-122.

*T.: Takhsa = Liturgia sanctorum Apostolorum Adaei et Maris, cui accedunt duae aliae in quibusdam festis et feriis dicendae: necnon Ordo Baptismi*, Urmiae, 1890.

'Theod': Liturgy of Theodorus of Mopsuestia.

Villecourt, *Observances:* L. Villecourt, *Les observances liturgiques et la discipline du jeûne dans l'église copte*, in: *Le Muséon*, 1924, p. 201–280; 1925, p. 261–320 (french translation of the liturgical parts of the *Livre de la Lampe des Ténèbres et de l'exposition (lumineuse) du service (de l'Eglise)* par Abu 'l Barakat, not yet in the edition of the arabic text in: *P.O.* xx, ed. Villecourt-Tisserant-Wiet).

*W.S.: Woodbroke Studies, christian documents edited and translated with a critical apparatus*, by A. Mingana, Cambridge, 1927 sqq.

## LIST OF MANUSCRIPTS

Vaticanus Syriacus 150 (p. 64–66).
Vaticanus Arabicus 147 (p. 121).
Berolinus Syriacus 38 (text of 'Addai').
Mingana Syriacus 13 (Exposition of Timothy ii).
Mingana Syriacus 121 (p. 134, n. 1.).
Mingana Syriacus 566 (p. 66–67).
Mingana Syriacus 586 and 587 (Letters of Isho'Barnun; p. 130).

Syriac texts are always quoted in translation for the convenience of the liturgiologists who do not know Syriac.

## i. PRELIMINARY OBSERVATIONS

Immutable and traditional; these two adjectives are generally used to characterize the Near East.

Much has changed in the course of long ages in Greece, Asia Minor, Syria, Palestine, Egypt etc. One reign superseded the other. Many places were destroyed and their ruins offered the materials for another civilization. Hellenism, Islam and Mongolian invasions gave these countries a different aspect with regard to culture, religion and science. And yet, in reading the records of people who travelled in this part of the world one is struck by the words written at the beginning of this chapter. It is true, the Western business-spirit has also affected these countries and effaced much characteristic detail. And yet, the atmosphere of the Bible is still round these ancient places, though it was not specially guarded as a relic in a museum. Eastern people were the same in their manners and thoughts as centuries ago. Seeing them was a living commentary upon many passages of the Scripture and of the Churchfathers.

This was not the result of a retrogressive development; but the superstructure had changed while the basis had remained the same. The judgement we summarized is not based on the superficial observations of people who "did" the East and who were deceived by the romantic idea of being in the lands of the Bible. No, scholars who had made an intensive study of the history of these countries in various times, and travelled there with critical sense, declared that such a journey threw fresh light upon their studies and elucidated many points without all sorts of constructions of a Western studyroom. Meeting an Oriental man or woman makes many interpretations offered by a Western scholar simply impossible.[1]

The book we propose to publish on the following pages belongs to a certain time and a certain department of the Christian East, viz. the Nestorian Church of the 11th cent. The Christian East does not belie its nature. It is and wants to be traditional. Almost every comprehensive study of this field of research stresses this point. Oriental Christianity forms a special type along with Roman Catholicism and Protestantism. It has a history of its own and because of that a particular connection with the ancient church.

(1) From a long array of such witnesses we quote: A. Deissmann, *Licht vom Osten*[4], Tübingen, 1923, S. 1 and passim; H. Th. Obbink, *Op bijbelschen bodem*[2], Amsterdam, 1927, blz. 7–8, 13–16.

It lies outside the scope of this book to prove this verdict by a number of illustrations. It is sufficient for the present moment to refer to the judgement of some very competent scholars who have clearly brought to light the characteristic differences between Eastern and Western Christendom. The famous German scholar, Prof. Ad. von Harnack, formulated his opinion in this way: "Die morgenländische Kirche ist in kultureller, philosophischer und religiöser Hinsicht das versteinerte 3. Jahrhundert".[1] In somewhat different words it was repeated by one of the best connoisseurs of the Christian East in its various aspects, Prof. A. Baumstark. His word is based upon a larger first-hand knowledge of the sources as that of Von Harnack and is therefore the more significant. He speaks of "der Greisenhaftigkeit des Morgenlandes in dem Haften an der Vergangenheit"; he calls it: "der christliche Antike".[2]

These words were spoken with regard to the whole complex of Oriental Churches, Russia and Abessynia, Persia and Greece. We need not to examine here the question whether it is right to view all these churches as a unit. For the particular church of the Nestorians in Mesopotamia does not form an exception to this rule. Two quotations of experts, one Roman Catholic and one Evangelical, lead us on the same track. Dom. H. Leclercq makes in passing the following remark: "Si le donatisme avait duré jusqu'à nos jours, sans l'épreuve de la législation des empereurs et de l'invasion des Arabes, il nous offrirait probablement un phénomène archéologique infiniment precieux, comparable à celui de l'Église nestorienne. Celle-ci s'est *cristallisée dans l'immobilité disciplinaire et liturgique* et nous présente l'état antérieur à sa rupture avec l'Église comme une stratification aussi rare qu'intéressante".[3] The conclusion of Prof. Heiler reads as follows: "Mag diese Kirche auch von ihrer einstigen geistigen Höhe herabgesunken sein, so hat sie doch... ihre reichen altchristlichen Schätze fast unversehrt erhalten".[4]

(1) A. v. Harnack, *Der Geist der morgenländischen Kirche im Unterschied von der abendländischen*, in: *Aus der Friedens- und Kriegsarbeit, Reden und Aufsätze*, N.F. iii, Giessen, 1916, S. 129–130 (the whole article: S. 101–140) and cf. his: *Lehrbuch der Dogmengeschichte*[4], ii, Tübingen, 1910 passim. (2) In his important series of lectures, A. Baumstark, *Grundgegensätze morgenländischen und abendländischen Christentums*, Rheinau, 1932, S. 37, 41 and passim.–Cf. C. M. Kaufmann, *Handbuch der altchristlichen Archäologie* [3], Paderborn, 1922, S. 6: "Zumal im Orient wird mit einem noch ungleich verlängerten Nachwirken der Antike zu rechnen sein gegenüber dem Abendlande". (3) *D.A.C.L.*, s.v. *Donatisme*, t. iv, col. 1457; italics are mine. (4) F. Heiler, *Urkirche und Ostkirche*, München, 1936, S. 453.

It is a matter of course that the varying fates of history have changed here several things; there was growth and decline; the emphasis has altered. Yet all the authors quoted before suggest this question: *is it not possible to expect in this way fresh details for our study of the New Testament and the history of the ancient church?*[1] Does this tradition begin at the 3rd and 4th cent. or already before? For if these churches have retained the aspect of christian antiquity, it will enable us by studying their present state and history to solve many problems which are still open by defect of details. Some interesting observations on this line have been made about 25 years ago by Prof. de Zwaan in his inaugural address on: "the importance of historical study of Greek-Eastern Christendom".[2]

Before giving some examples I wish to make two remarks. The first one is concerned with the problem of the relation between idea and phenomenon. It is not right to suppose that if the spirit remains the same, its expression in the visible world does not alter, for other influences, too, determine its formation.[3] Although a certain church proclaims its traditional character, it is not advisable to conclude that all its forms of theology and cultus are identical with those of thousand years ago. This consideration warns us to be careful in making "Rückschlüsse" from the present condition. We can admit the unity of Eastern Christianity as against the West, and yet: every church has had his own origin and history and this is the reason why we observe unity in spirit and great differences in form between them. Only by a critical and comparative study of the facts we can fix what is ancient and what is of recent date.–Secondly the study of Eastern Christendom is still in its very beginning. It may be somewhat bold to express this opinion in view of the long series of publications from Byzantine, Syriac, Coptic, Ethiopic,

(1) O. Linton, *Das Problem der Urkirche in der neueren Forschung*, Uppsala, 1932, S. 195: "Es muss der Versuch gemacht werden, das Recht der alten Kirche genetisch aus dem orientalischen Recht, *regressiv aus dem Recht der anatolischen Kirchen zu verstehen*. So ist das geschichtliche Problem über Recht und Urchristentum zu lösen". (italics are mine). (2) J. de Zwaan, *De beteekenis van de historische studie van het Grieksch-Oostersch Christendom*, Haarlem, 1912. (3) One example will suffice to illustrate this point. The well-known controversy of Russian Church history, called Raskol (cf. N. Bonwetsch, *Raskolniken*, in: *P.R.E.*[3], xvi, S. 436–443; B. Raptschinsky, *Russisch Christendom*, Zutphen, 1935, blz. 130–162) shows us a schism, cause of great hatred, originating from some small corrections of the liturgy. Yet nobody will deny that the two parties were not animated by the same spirit. This is an extreme case of what is seen elsewhere; though the different churches show the same "spirit", they have not developed along the same lines.

Arabic, Armenian and Georgian sources and the great number of papers and books devoted to this research especially during the last 50 years. But if we see the vastness of this field, the result is comparatively small. The idea expressed in the foregoing quotations may have repelled many people; the interest was more directed to the fortunes of the Church in the West, which can easily be explained since its sources were nearer at hand and not written in many obscure languages, and since its study offered aspects which are of importance for the questions of to-day.[1] What could be expected from "dead" churches?[2] The publication of sources, the higher oecumenical interest; liturgical movements made many Western churchmen turn to the East and get a better understanding for the living forces of Eastern Christianity. And last not least, the discovery of a good many books lost in Western tradition but preserved in the East awakened the sense that from this side some more light upon the ancient church could be expected. But we are still at the beginning.

I cannot develop the thoughts expressed in the foregoing sentences more fully here, but they might not been forgotten in order to avoid too hasty conclusions.

It is a remarkable fact, as Prof. von Harnack once observed, that the history of the ancient church has been exclusively written from Western sources.[3] Although it can easily be accounted for, as the first investigators met first with the Greek and Latin authors, while the East was inaccessible. But it must be emphasized that the Eastern Churches have had a seperate existence with another connection with the early church than the West. From this point of view the invaluable merit of Prof. Felix Haase consisted in collecting the data scattered over so many publications.[4] It is true that his book contains merely the outward history, not that of dogma, litterature, worship etc.; the materials must be critically sifted, but at any rate he has laid an indispensable basis. It is premature to decide in what respect the previous opinions must be revised, but it may be considerable, e.g. with regard to some heretics.[5] However it may be, historical research must consider all the materials

(1) Cf. e.g. P. Wernle, *Einführung in das theologische Studium* [2], Tübingen, 1912, S. 183–184. (2) This has often and for a long time been and is still the judgement of very many Western students of theology. (3) Cf. F. Haase, *Altchristliche Kirchengeschichte nach orientalischen Quellen*, Leipzig, 1925, S. ix–x. (4) In his book quoted in the previous note. (5) E.g. Nestorius, cf. F. Loofs, *Nestorius*, in: *P.R.E.* [3], xxiv, S. 239–244 who said: „Mehrere Publikationen haben seit dem

available; and who would deny that additions are not very welcome?

The study of this part of Christendom does not only broaden the basis for our judgment, but it makes us discover lines which had once existed within the christian communities, but were left by the great masses and fell into oblivion. Some examples may suffice. The complete text of the book of Henoch would not be known unless by the canon of the Ethiopic Church.[1] Think of the many oriental versions of the so-called Churchorder of Hippolytus with its many problems of liturgy and order;[2] the Odes of Solomon[3] which show a spirit very much akin to Gospel of John and the letters of Ignatius; the Epistula xi Apostolorum.[4] Many fragments of lost works are contained in the commentaries written after many centuries; a striking case are those of Hippolytus' "Heads against the presbyter Gaius" found in the works of Dionysius bar Salibi (12th cent.).[5]

As to the study of the New Testament itself it is superfluous to show the importance of Eastern versions and Fathers for the textual criticism. Although scholars agree upon this point, it cannot be said that everything worth doing has been done here. On the other hand it seems to be often forgotten that the Eastern Church had a very rich exegetical tradition in its commentaries and scholia, not only of allegorical interpretation. The generally accepted rule for right exegesis is that it must be done "e mente auctoris". But the application of this rule supposes correspondence between the "mens auctoris" and the "mens explicatoris", and it is hard to realize this in practice. Psychology is very instructive and warning

Erscheinen des A(rtikels) die Forschung auf eine neue Basis gestellt" (S. 239) and: "Nestorius hat nur gewonnen durch die Erweiterung des Materials zu seiner Beurteilung" (S. 243).–F. Haase, *a.a.O.*, S. 377–387.

(1) E. Schürer, *Geschichte des jüdischen Volkes im Zeitalter Jesu Christi*[4], iii, Leipzig, 1909, S. 268–290; although large Greek fragments are known (S. 269 and several papyri) which offer a better text, only the Ethiopic version is complete and has been discovered first. (2) R. Lorentz, *De Egyptische Kerkorde en Hippolytus van Rome*, Haarlem, 1928, blz. 5–14.–Some of these Eastern versions were used for our Commentary, but I did not enter into an investigation of their mutual relations, since they have also a value of their own, as lawbooks for later ages in the particular churches which have transmitted them. (3) J. Rendel Harris and A. Mingana, *Odes and Psalms of Solomon*, Manchester, 1916–1920, 2 vols. (4) One of great discoveries of Prof. Carl Schmidt, *Gespräche Jesu mit seinen Jüngeren nach der Auferstehung*, Leipzig, 1919, and: J. de Zwaan, *The date and origin of the Epistle of the eleven Apostles*, in: *Amicitiae Corolla*, London, 1933, p. 344–355. (5) Cf. O. Bardenhewer, *Geschichte der altkirchlichen Literatur*[2], ii, Freiburg i. Br., 1913, S. 569–570.

in this respect. If one gets acquainted with the history of the exegesis of the N.T., it will be seen that various scholars trying to find an "objective" interpretation react differently upon the same text. This reaction depends not only upon the amount of knowledge, but also upon philosophical, psychological and theological structure. Nobody can totally break away from this, although he can be corrected by others. Because of its identity with the men of the ancient world the strange Eastern world anno 400 A.D. or 800 can be of some help. Knowledge of the reactions of these people, quite different from those of the Western religious and scholarly traditions, is far from worthless. At any rate it will help us to read the New Testament in eastern light.

But is it allowed to use such young sources since so many changes have altered the face of the Eastern world? Except by those who accept the exegesis of the Fathers as authoritative, it is hardly done, probably because of the great number of "zeitgenossische" sources and since the changes are so clear. Yet if one observes the freedom of the "Religionsgeschichtler" in explaining the N.T. from sources which date from centuries before or after it,[1] it is only making a similar use of the Christian sources. And if one rejects the latter method, the former, too, must be abandoned.

In realizing the many problems which are raised by the study of the N.T. and history of the ancient church, it would be certainly a mistake if the data which may be given by the Eastern church were too rashly neglected. Of course, the present writer is quite aware that this is an ideal at the moment, since so little has been done to study the life of the Eastern Church itself. But it should always be remembered.[2]

(1) One of the latest and most striking examples is the use of the Mandaean books. (2) I have only spoken of the importance of this study for the first ages of Christianity. But I do not overlook that it has also an aim in itself to fill a great gap in many books on the history of the Christian Church (cf. J. B. Kidd, *The Churches of Eastern Christendom from A. D. 451 to the present time*, Londen, 1927, Prefatory note). One has only to remember the fact that these churches faced the great problem which has not lost its interest, Christianity and Islam. It goes without saying that this is a condition for right execution of the former task. At present most of this study is made from a different point of view viz. that of the "Konfessionskunde" (which describes the present situation of the various churches and studies the history only in so far it has some bearing upon the problems of to-day; cf. F. Kattenbusch, *Lehrbuch der vergleichenden Confessionskunde*, Freiburg i. Br. 1892, S. 5: „Alles das [fällt] aus dem Rahmen unserer Disciplin heraus, was im Laufe der Zeit zur blossen Episode geworden ist. Was nicht mehr wirksam ist, das geht uns auch nichts an u.s.w."); in which

A very appropriate example of the above considerations will be found in the study of the early christian liturgy, especially in that of the Eucharist.[1] This is not an arbitrary choice, since the book we are about to publish, is concerned with "Questions on the Service of the Altar". It is impossible to investigate or even to sum up in a few lines the whole complex of questions which arise if one says: early christian eucharist. But we should mention some of them.

"Do this in remembrance of me." The whole church has been faithful to this command of the Lord given at the last Supper (according to the earliest witness Paul, 1 Cor. xi 24). This remembrance formed the centre-part of the liturgy and of the faith of all Christians throughout the ages.[2] Because it has been instituted by Jesus Christ some hours before and in view of His death, it is natural to assume that this act was preserved as purely as possible. No wonder that it contains a large part of tradition, since it is easier to hand down a rite than a thought without changing it.

This central sacrament of the Church can be studied from various points of view. One can ask: how should it be administrated at the present moment; and the answer will be found in various handbooks for the use of the ministers of the different parts in which the "Body of Christ" has been divided. The historical questions are only touched upon in so far they bear upon the present-day-liturgy.[3] Since the history has often brought loss and gain in particular cases, it is quite another thing to ask: what was the structure and idea of the liturgy at a certain date in a certain place? For out of the meal in the upper room of Jerusalem has developed a long

the Eastern Orthodox Church occupies most space while the lesser Eastern churches, such as Copts, Nestorians, Jacobites etc. are treated in a few pages. This proportion is right for the centuries after 1453 A.D., but it should be reversed, if one is concerned about the historical situation and importance before that date.

(1) J. Braun, *Liturgisches Handlexicon* [2], Regensburg, 1924, S. 196–197, gives the following definition of liturgy: "1) im weitesten Sinn jeder von der zuständigen Authorität od. durch Brauch u. Gewohnheit geregelte gemeinschaftl. öffentl. Gottesdienst . . . 2) im engeren Sinne die von der K. im Namen u. Auftrag Christi durch eigens von ihr dazu berufene u. bevollmächtigte Amstpersonen gemäss den von ihr geschaffenen od. anerkannten Formularen u. Regeln zur Verherrlichung Gottes u. zum Heile ihrer Angehörigen ausgeübte stellvertretende u. mittlerische Gebetstätigheit (viz.: "Spendung der Sakr., die Weihe u. Segnung, die Prozessione u. Exorzismen; Messefeier–Stundengebet"); 3) im engesten u. vorzüglichsten Sinn die euchar. O-feier . ." (2) Whether it kept the original meaning or not (cf. a.o. H. Lietzmann, *Geschichte der alten Kirche*, Berlin, 1935, ii, S. 120) does not matter here. (3) Cf. the definition of L. Eisenhofer, *Handbuch der katholischen Liturgik*, Freiburg i. Br., 1932, i, S. 53.

series of various rites. Every part of the Church has its own. In the Western Church the Roman rite prevailed over the Milanese, Gallican and Gothic rites.[1] In the East the churches of Alexandria, Antioch, Jerusalem etc. had their own liturgy which was guarded and enriched within the Eastern Orthodox Church or within the seperate communities such as Copts, Syrians and Nestorians.[2] A survey of the materials is found in Lietzmann's study on "Messe und Herrenmahl".[3] Besides the liturgical manuscripts we have a good number of incidental references in the Fathers. The task of liturgical research is formulated in this way by Prof. Baumstark who devoted a large part of his study to it and is a great authority:[4] "Die Sammlung und das Verhör dieser (äussern) Zeugnisse (über Dinge der liturgischen Entwicklung)–die auf ältern Stufen der Entwicklung stehenden liturgischen Urkunden selbst . . . in befriedigender Ausgabe zu erschliessen, wo nötig zu erklären und den Zusammenhang der einzelnen untereinander zu bestimmen–Spuren ihres Werdeprozesses (which are shown by the liturgies) . . . sorgfältigst zu verfolgen und mit den äussern Quellenzeugnissen vergleichend zu verbinden." If this laborious work has been done, the question arises if all those types cann be reduced to a common "Grundform"; what was the cause of those changes; what is the connection with the Eucharist in the New Testament. The evidence of the N.T. is interpreted in many opposite directions[5] and the chain which links it up with the evidence of the 3rd and 4th cent. is thin. Generally it is assumed that the surrounding world had a good deal of influence ("hellenization"); was it on Paul or later? These are the great questions on which the discussion turns. If one reads

(1) Cf. L. Duchesne, *Origines du culte chrétien*[5], Paris, 1923, and: *D.A.C.L.*, s.v.v.–For our purpose we can leave aside the difference in structure between Eastern and Western liturgies. (2) Introduction of F. E. Brightman, *Liturgies Eastern and Western*, Oxford, 1896, i.–The Western Church had a tendency to uniformity; the Eastern to diversity. Only in the 12th cent. we find a case of "Gleichschaltung" of the Alexandrian rite to that of Byzance, *D.A.C.L.*, s.v. *Alexandrie (liturgie)*, t. i., col. 1188. (3) H. Lietzmann, *Messe und Herrenmahl*, Bonn, 1926, S. 1–24. (4) In his little introduction: *Vom geschichtlichen Werden der Liturgie*, Freiburg i. Br., 1923, S. 3–4.–A good survey in: Y. Brilioth, *Eucharistic Faith and Practice*, London, 1930, p. 1–92. (5) The book of L.D.T. Poot, *Het oud-christelijk Avondmaal en zijn historische perspectieven*, Wageningen, 1936, is disappointing in this respect. He discusses with the "Religionsgeschichtler", tries to find the original meaning of the texts of the Gospels and Paul by a survey of the opinions of various scholars, but he neglects to take into account the great lines which divide Roman Catholic, Greek Orthodox, Anglican and Protestant exegesis. The second part of the title is dealt with in an extremely poor way.

the modern books on them, it will be seen that the later Eastern rites play a great part.[1]

The importance of this study is not only that we get an idea of the Christian cult at a certain date. Prof. Baumstark and Lietzmann have drawn attention to the fact that by the way of comparison certain facts of relation between several churches are detected which are not known from elsewhere.[2] But greater weight must be attached to the fact that the liturgy is an expression of christian faith and life; it has been made to thank God for His salvation in Christ Jesus and it led many people in its ancient forms to a deeper apprehension of the christian truth. On the other hand the thoughts connected with these obsolete forms were not always the same, and it is worth while to study this change of ideas. "The study of the Liturgy whatever else it may be, must also be a study in religious psychology"[3] and it is a valuable way to understand the religious life of a church.[4]

There exists a great difference between the Eastern and Western form of the liturgy, along with an agreement in words, and in its conception. Did the traditional character of the East retain here the early-christian idea?

It cannot be denied that much has already been done to elucidate the many problems of criticism, relation etc. of the liturgical sources, especially of the West,[5] but the real idea of the structure of this study has been discovered during the last 50 years. Prof. Lietzmann[6] calls his book "ein erster Versuch . . , einen Richtweg durch den Urwald zu schlagen". The oldest interest in this study was merely controversial. The Protestant theologians combatted the Mass as a medieval invention; the Roman Catholic scholars

(1) G. P. Wetter, *Altchristliche Liturgien i, Das christliche Mysterium*, Göttingen, 1921, S. 1–4, has pointed out some very important lines with regard to the bearing of liturgical study upon the problems of early church history (though I believe that his method of tackling the problems is not sound). (2) H. Lietzmann, *Messe*, S. vi–vii, and: A. Baumstark, *Festbrevier und Kirchenjahr der syrischen Jakobiten*, Paderborn, 1910, S. 25. (3) E. Bishop, *Liturgica Historica*, Oxford, 1918, p. 123. (4) Cf. A. C. Headlam: "There are no books which show more accurately the historical and doctrinal position of a Church than its Liturgies and other services", in: A. J. Maclean, *East Syrian Daily Offices*, London, 1894, p. vii– A. Baumstark, *Festbrevier*, S. 25: "Die Liturgie einer Kirche darf im allgemeinen als das treueste Spiegelbild ihrer geschichtlichen Individualität gelten". (5) Cf. *Liturgiewissenschaft*, in: H. Gunkel–L. Zscharnack u. A., *die Religion im Geschichte und Gegenwart* [2], iii, Tübingen, 1929: O. Casel–katholisch, Sp. 1689–1691; P. Glaue–evangelisch, Sp. 1691–1693.–More detailed in: L. Eisenhofer, *Handbuch*, i, § 15–18, S. 118–148. (6) H. Lietzmann, *Messe*, S. vi.

defended it as the pure institution of our Lord. In the course of this debate the Eastern liturgies were published to show that the mass was not medieval and that the Roman Church was in accordance with the primitive one. This was the aim of Goar and Renaudot in editing their famous collections[1] though they contain so much stuff in their texts and notes which makes them still indispensable and which can serve a more objective purpose. When the polemical stimulus flagged, the liturgical study became mainly a part of Pastoral Theology, more studied by Roman Catholics and Anglicans because of their rich liturgical life than by Protestants. The Western forms stood in front. But there was a weakness, "a certain sterility of liturgical work in the last century; namely, that it has been in the main a study in ritual rather than a study in religion; as a consequence it has seemed to be in touch rather with professionalism than with life, and appears in its general character to be predominantly of clerical interest".[2] During the last half of a century the deeper understanding of liturgical life, finding its expression in liturgical movements in all branches of the Church, the increasing importance of the study of the Eastern church and the discovery of many valuable documents have cooperated to an enhanced interest in the research of the liturgy of the ancient church.

Nevertheless it would be premature to think that everything is already clear. Much material is still waiting to be sifted. Liturgy is an expression and possession of the masses; it is quite different from the writings of certain persons belonging to a certain time. "Still und geräuschlos vollzog sich allgemein bis zum 16. Jahrhundert und vollzieht sich heute noch im Orient aller liturgische Einzelfortschritt."[3] This makes it often impossible to fix the date and origin of a particular prayer or action. The method of reconstructing an older stage by comparison of certain prayers and actions within various groups, will often give us a clue (although room must be left for the assumption of an original growth on both sides). At any rate it is impossible at the present state of affairs to draw long lines. The task of the moment is to publish, to estimate the sources as completely as possible and to fix their importance

(1) J. Goar, *Euchologion*, Lutetiae Parisiorum, 1647 (², Venetiis, 1730); E. Renaudot, *Liturgiarum Orientalium Collectio* ², Francofurti ad Moenum, 1847 (1st ed. of 1716). (2) E. Bishop, *l.c.*, p. 106. (3) A. Baumstark, *Vom geschichtlichen Werden*, S. 132, in a chapter: "Grenzen des Wissenkönnens".-Cf. the careful words of E. Bishop, written after a lifetime of study in this field, *l.c.*, p. ix.

for a certain liturgical group. If this is done, one can go on to trace older layers, to reconstruct the liturgy of a former period and to answer the main questions formulated before.

Having this in view I publish this xith century writing of the Nestorians. The special Introduction and Commentary must help to fix its date, and investigate the traditional background. It must certainly be of some use to study this liturgy of the Nestorians, since competant authorities[1] pointed out the great traditional value of the Nestorians and their writings. A survey of the research of their liturgy will form a proper introduction, as it helps us to find out the problems of this group and the bearing of their answer.

(1) Cf. p. 6 and: F. Cabrol, *D.A.C.L.*, s.v. *hérétiques*, t. vi, col. 2256: "Les nestoriens peuvent être cités parmi les rares hérétiques qui firent exception à la règle. Ils conservèrent avec soin, en se séparant de l'Église, leur liturgie qui est en substance celle du ve siècle . . . . Aussi leurs livres liturgiques ont-ils à ce point de vue une spéciale valeur".

## ii. THE NESTORIANS AND THE RESEARCH OF THEIR LITURGY

i. In his book on the "Churches of Eastern Christendom" written for the general reader, Dr. Kidd did not pay very much attention to the "internal life"[1] of these various churches. His only remark about the liturgy of the Nestorians was that they "held to the common standard of Christendom".[2] Therefore it is the more striking that he gives the following extensive quotation from a book of Fortescue's (from 1911) on the other Syriac church of the Jacobites: "They produced a 'brilliant school of liturgical science'; and Dionysius bar Salibi († 1171), Bishop of Amida (Diabekr) is famous as the author of a treatise (the Liturgy of St. James) *such as no other church could show in the Middle Ages. The result of this is that we know more about the history of the Jacobite rite than of any other*".[3] Some grave objections must be made against this statement. In the first place (what could not possibly be known to Fortescue), that the exposition of Dionysius mentioned before[4] is for a great deal nothing but plagiarism, as is also found in several of his works. This appears when it is compared with the texts published in 1913 by Dom. Connolly, the expositions of George of the Arabs and Moses Bar Cepha.[5] Dionysius was a remarkable author of the Jacobite Renaissance but a very traditional one (this fact gives him some importance), more excelling in voluminosity than in originality. Secondly one wonders where this "brilliant school" comes from; it cannot be founded on this writing alone and we do not know more about it, for the fact that several authors on liturgical matters lived in the course of many ages does not permit us to speak of a "school". In the third place (and this is important for our investigation): this wording ignores absolutely that liturgical activity was not in the least confined to the Jacobite Syrians. It lies outside the scope of this work to show this in detail

(1) By this I mean specially: Doctrine, Cult and Ethics. (2). B. J. Kidd, *The Churches of Eastern Christendom*, p. 419. We are justified to take his book as a starting-point for the following exposition, since it aims at giving a comprehensive survey of the history of Eastern Christendom, based upon the research of the last fifty years. (3) B. J. Kidd, *l.l.*, p. 437, from: A. Fortescue, *Lesser Eastern Churches*, London, 1913, p. 331 (italics are mine). (4) Published by H. Labourt: Dionysius Bar Salibi, *Expositio liturgiae*, in: *C.S.C.O.*, ii 93, Parisiis, 1903.-About the life and works of Dionysius, cf. A. Baumstark, *L.G.*, S. 295–298. (5) R. H. Connolly–H. W. Codrington, *Two Commentaries on the Jacobite Liturgy*, Londen, 1913, p. 2.

with regard to the other churches. As to the Nestorians[1] the rest of this book will form a sufficient refutation, I hope.

His opinion can largely be explained[2] from ignorance; for the Nestorians did not attract the attention of scholars in the same measure as the Jacobites. Though J. S. Assemani devoted two of the four volumes of his "Bibliotheca" to them and gave extensive extracts from their writings, it lasted one century and a half before further studies and publications were made. It seemed as though people were quite satisfied with what he had published. The reasons are obvious. The rise of the study of Syriac literature coincides with the acquisition of a great part of the treasures of the Library of the Syriac-Jacobite "Monastery of the Mother of God" in Scete (Egypt) by the British Museum. This new era was inaugurated by Dr. Cureton (the Vatican Library, which contained a good many Nestorian Mss. from which Assemani got his information, was practically inaccessible). These writings were all of Jacobite origin, or at least transmitted by the Monophysites. All the large collections of Syriac Mss. in Europe were in the same position. But this was not the only reason, for there were Nestorian Mss. In the first place the attention of editors was attracted by works written in Greek before the confessional division, and lost in the original language, but preserved in Syriac; and moreover these sources gave a clearer picture of an important part of churchhistory, such as the time of Justinian and the rise of Monophysitism.[3] The Jacobites had always been in contact with the Greek Church and were nearer to Europe than the Nestorians who lived in the plains of Mesopotamia or mountains of Kurdistan.

The interest for the Nestorians came later (± 1890). Various reasons worked together: several libraries enlarged their fund of Nestorian Mss.; important publications were made (Gismondi's Chronicles, the "Book of the Governors"). The adherents of this creed came out their refuges in the mountains round about Lake

(1) It is not impossible that they even influenced the later Jacobites: Bar Hebraeus quotes Persian Canons in his: *Nomocanon* iv 2, culled from John Bar Abgare (see p. 133–135); Dionysius copied much from Isho'Dad of Merw; the same holds good for the mystics. (2) Not as a whole; for an impression of the Nestorian activity is given by the list of *L.E.W.* p. lxxx, and by A. Baumstark, *L.G.*, passim which, I do not know for what reason, remained unknown to Dr. Kidd. (3) An important remark is made by A. J. Maclean, *Syrian Christians*, in: *E.R.E.*, xii, p. 167: "The history of many of these Christians has usually been considered in Europe only as far as it affects their relations with certain heresies, *i.e.* only from one episode (however important) of their annals.

Van and Urmia and the neighbourhood of Mosul where they had hidden themselves before the persecutions of the Turcs and Kurds. The Roman Catholic and Anglican Missions tried to come into touch with them, and this created the practical need for books. Of the Roman Catholics it will be sufficient to mention the name of P. Bedjan who provided the Chaldeans (Uniates) with numerous editions of their ancient authors for devotional purposes (Acta Martyrum et Sanctorum etc.) this literature serving at the same time scientific research. The mission of the Arch-Bishop of Canterbury printed especially liturgical books (Maclean). Since that time the number of publications of works of Nestorian origin increased steadily; we do not need to register them as it has been excellently done by Prof. Baumstark in his "Geschichte der syrischen Literatur" A. ii, B. i and iii. His pages give a clear impression of the bulk of this literature. He registered, too, the Mss. that had once been found in the East but got lost in the World War. What was left by that disaster was collected by Dr. Mingana on his travels in the Near East and incorporated in his collection (at the Selly Oak Colleges' Library, Birmingham).

But is that impression right? Are we not the victim of an optical illusion? If one makes a list of the eight centuries during which the Nestorian Church had its flourishing time and if one takes into account the expansion made by its mission far into Asia and realizes the number of books, it must be confessed that it is somewhat poor! *Startling gaps make it almost impossible to compose something that looks like a history in the modern sense of the word.* These gaps cannot be bridged over by generalizing a statement about one century and assuming that it remained the same in another age or place. Nor can we say that everything is traditional if sources are wanting.

We cannot think of writing even a short history of the Nestorian church. Yet it seems to be necessary to give a short characteristic of some sources that are of fundamental importance for its history and which will constantly be used in the following pages. We pass by publications from the hand of a particular person like exegetical works, poems, books with letters (such as those of Isho'yabh iii and Timothy i), books dealing with the School of Nisibis or Chronicles of a particular city such as that of Seërt and of Arbela, important though they may be (liturgical expositions etc. will be discussed later on) because they do not deal with the Church as a whole. In general we may say, that their importance for the study of the liturgy is next to nothing. This is due to two reasons. In the first place to a certain habit of the Syrians in general which was formulated by Prof. Burkitt in relation to Ephraim in this way: "(Ephraim) whose works are excessively voluminous and well preserved, cannot help affording us many curious glimpses into the life and thought of the Church to which he belongs. But it is a weary task, gleaning the grains of wheat among the chaff. Ephraim is extraordinarily prolix, he repeats himself again and again, and for all the immense mass of material there seems very little to take hold of."[1] Secondly it finds its origin in the nature of the liturgical development itself: "still und geräuschlos vollzog sich allgemein bis zum 16. Jahrhundert, vollzieht sich heute noch im Orient aller liturgische Einzelfortschritt,"[2] while it is also true that we do not hear what was selfevident to the people themselves.[3]

We begin our summary of these general sources of the Nestorian churchlife by mentioning the Chronicles of Mari, Amr and Sliba, published by Gismondi.[4] They give the history of the church of the East from its beginning up to their time (12th and 14th century) in a list of the Patriarchs. The dates of them are given together with a short characteristic in fairly general terms; some facts, which the compilers thought outstanding are mentioned. They do not give a clear insight into the times recorded, but because they form the only source of first rate knowledge, we must be thankful for them. Based upon them is the third part of the "Chronicon Ecclesiasticum" of the Jacobite Bar Hebraeus[5] who deals with the Nestorian patriarchs in describing the life and works of the Metropolitans of the Eastern Jacobites. It is also written in the typical style of Chroniclers (cf. the style of the biblical Books of Kings and Chronicles).

More promising for the study of our theme may seem the reading of the "Synodicon Orientale", first published in a German translation by Oscar Braun[6] and some years later in the original together with a French translation by J.B. Chabot.[7] This work con-

(1) F. C. Burkitt, *Early Eastern Christianity*, London, 1904, p. 96. (2) A. Baumstark, *Vom geschichtlichen Werden der Liturgie*, S. 132. (3) Cf. A. Baumstark, *a.a.O.*, S. 134. (4). H. Gismondi, *Maris, Amri et Slibae de patriarchis Nestorianorum commentaria*, Romae, 1897–99, 3 vols. (5) Bar Hebraeus, *Chronicon Ecclesiasticum*, ed. J. B. Abbeloos – Th. J. Lamy, Lovanii, 1877, Tomus iii. (6) O. Braun, *Das Buch des Synhados*, Stuttgart-Wien, 1900. (7) J. B. Chabot, *Synodicon Orientale*, Paris, 1903 (through an unhappy coincidence I was not able to consult this edition, but had to rely upon the German translation only.

cludes with a piece from the hand of Ḥenanisho' ii (773–74/779–80)[1] so that it is very probable that this work was compiled during his reign or shortly after. It contains a number of decisions and edicts of a great many Nestorian Synodes and Patriarchs from the first Synode of the Persian Church in 410 onward in chronological order. This work has a great importance for the study of the church in general, but it does not afford much information about liturgical matters, in spite of a statement of Labourt.[2] The documents which are of importance for the liturgy will be mentioned in ch. vi. We read about many admonitions to Priests who do not perform their duty and therefore need reproof, and more of that kind. The Synodicon gives us a picture of the life of the church, but we must remember that it is always dangerous to use judicial decisions as sources of the *real state of a church.* On a whole the greater part of these canons is merely canonical in nature. We record here (because it will be of some use later on, p. 121), that there exist of this Synodicon two Arabic translations. These have not been considered in preparing the above editions. There is only one statement about the interrelation of these three texts given by Prof. I. Guidi and quoted by all other authors.[3] Guidi wrote: "Ich habe die Borgianische Handschr. mit den arabischen Uebersetzungen des Elias und des Ibn aṭ–Ṭayyib verglichen und gesehen, dass dieselben weit davon entfernt sind, uns das alte Synodicon treu zu repräsentieren. Ibn aṭ–Ṭayyib's Buch ist sehr regelmässig und gut geordnet, aber vieles, dass nicht nothwendig oder praktisch nützlich schien, ist getilgt und zum Teil ausgelassen worden . . . ja selbst die Canones sind zwar inhaltlich wiedergegeben, aber nicht selten stark abgekürzt. Bei Elias dagegen ist die alte Form oft bewahrt, sehr vieles aber gänzlich ausgelassen".[4] It is not quite certain when these translators lived; the common opinion is: Elijah of Damascus (893) and Ibn aṭ–Ṭayyib († 1043), to which Dr. Riedel objected assigning them to the 14th century.[5] These collections are remarkable since they are often quoted by the Coptic canonist Abu 'l

(1) Cf. A. Baumstark, *L.G.*, S. 54–55; 215. (2) J. Labourt, *Le Christianisme dans l'Empire Perse* [2], Paris, 1904, p. 339, who gives the impression that it contains a good number of liturgical regulations. (3) R. Duval, *Littérature Syriaque*[3], Paris, 1907, p. 166; W. Riedel, *Kirchenrechtsquellen des Patriarchats von Alexandrien*, Leipzig, 1900, S. 152; G. Graf, *Die christlich-arabische Literatur bis auf die frankische Zeit*, Strassburg, 1908, S. 39, N.1. (4) I. Guidi, *Ostsyrische Bischöfe und Bischofssitze im* V., VI. *und* VII. *Jahrhundert*, in: *Zeitschrift der deutschen morgenländischen Gesellschaft*, 1889, S. 389–390. (5) W. Riedel, *a.a.O.*, S. 148–152.

Barakat and seem to have had some influence on these Alexandrian collections![1]

The Synodicon was continued in the following ages with a great collection of letters and other canonical decisions, only a part of which has been published by Prof. Sachau.[2]

The "Nomocanon" of 'Abdisho' published by A. Mai in 1838[3] brought together the civil and ecclesiastical laws arranged in a systematical order; in it have been preserved a good number of canons which otherwise would have been lost. This became the official lawbook of the church since its composition at the end of the 13th century.[4]

Though the "Book of the Governors" of Thomas of Marga[5] deals professedly with the history of the Monks until the middle of the 9th century it gives us much insight in churchlife in general, so that it may be counted among the chief sources.

Some points from this history which may elucidate the importance of the study of the Nestorians and furnish a background to that of their liturgy in particular must be given here. For it was rightly pointed out by Prof. Baumstark, that "nur von dem Hintergrunde eines kirchlich-kulturgeschichtlichen Gesamtbildes vermag sich die liturgiegeschichtliche Einzelerscheinung im richtigen Lichte abzuheben".[6] This remains true even if we are concerned only with a small field for it is linked up with many essential threads of ecclesiastical history. But it is premature to give more than some points since a critical history belongs still to the *pia vota*. Assemani's big volumes contain much stuff and afforded the material for study of many generations, but it is, especially in part iii 2, arranged according to a wrong standard of criticism. Our

(1) It can be shown by a careful comparison of the texts, printed or analysed by Dr. Riedel, with the Nestorian canonical literature. The Alexandrian canonists had a profound knowledge of the lawbooks of the other churches, as is proved by the remark of an Arabic Ms. (Bodleian 40), quoted by G. Horner, *Statutes of the Apostles*, London, 1904, p. xxxviii. (2) E. Sachau, *Syrische Rechtsbücher*, Berlin, 1908, 3 Bde; and cf. A. Baumstark, *L.G.*, S. 287 and Ak 1. (add to the Mss: Mingana Syr. 586 and 587). (3) A. Mai, *Scriptorum veterum nova collectio*, Tom. x, Romae, 1838; about 'Abdisho' cf. A. Baumstark, *L.G.*, S. 323–325. (4) This is the smaller Sunhadus mentioned by W. H. Browne – A. J. Maclean, *The Catholicos of the East and his People*, London, 1892, p. viii. (5) Thomas of Marga, *The Book of Governors*, ed. E. A. Wallis Budge, London, 1893, 2 vols. (6) A. Baumstark, *Festbrevier und Kirchenjahr der syrischen Jakobiten*, Paderborn, 1910, S. 2.

century produced some rather minute sketches in some encyclopaedia's;[1] regarding the history before the conquest of the Arabs, the books of Labourt and Wigram are still the right guides, supplemented by Sachau's translation and use of the chronicle of Arbela.[2] But all these books important though they are give only the outward history of the Nestorian Church. So none of them gives more than superficial remarks about the subject that interests us here; and one misses a clear discussion of the wider questions of historical and dogmatical interest.[3] Nevertheless the history of the Church in Mesopotamia before the rise of Islam is pretty clear compared with that after the fall of the Sassanide-empire. The Arabic period is still waiting for a thorough investigation. There are two short monographs about Sahdona and Timothy i; the "Literaturgeschichte" of Baumstark shows some pathways. Browne has worked up much material (also from Arabic sources) in discussing the question of the "Eclipse of Christianity in Asia",[4] but nevertheless it cannot be called a historiography of that age. The picture can and must be more detailed than this; its outlines should be marked sharper, the "internal" history of the church should be brought to light and the characters of the leading churchmen should be made clearer. The frame work of the geographical expansion is furnished in a succinct form in the papers of Dr. Mingana.[5]

The history of the Nestorian church properly speaking begins with the year 410 when at a Synod at Seleucia-Ctesiphon this See was made independent by the Persian Bishops and put on the same

(1) E. g. J. Petermann-K. Kessler, *Nestorianer*, in: *P.R.E.*[3], xiii, S. 723-736. A. J. Maclean, *Nestorianism*, and: *Syrian Christians*, in: *E.R.E.*, ix, p. 321–322, and: xii, p. 176–177; E. Tisserant–E. Amann, *Dictionaire de Théologie catholique*, s.v. *Nestorienne (l'Eglise)*, t. xi, col. 157–323. The last article of 1932 is by far the most detailed and is at present the best general history of this church. (2) E. Sachau, *Die Chronik von Arbelā*, in: *Abhandlungen der preusischen Akademie der Wissenschaften* (Berlin), 1915; *Vom Christentum in der Persis*, in: *Sitzungsberichte der preusischen Akademie u.s.w.*, 1916; *Zur Ausbreitung des Christentums in Asien*, in: *Abhandlungen u.s.w.*, 1919. (3) H. Labourt, *Le Christianisme dans l'Empire Perse* [2], Paris, 1904; W. A. Wigram, *An Introduction to the History of the Assyrian Church*, London, 1910. A short summary will be found in: K. Müller, *Kirchengeschichte*, i [2], Tübingen, 1929, S. 441–449; 770–775. (4) L. E. Browne, *The Eclipse of Christianity in Asia*, Cambridge, 1933.–While my book was in the press I saw an advertisement of: A. R. Vines, *The Nestorian churches, a concise history of Nestorian Christianity in Asia from the Persian schism to the modern Assyrians*, London, 1937. I was unable to use it for the present work; so this note must suffice. (5) A. Mingana, *The early spread of Christianity in Central Asia and the Far East*, Manchester, 1925; *The early spread of Christianity in India*, Manchester, 1926. (I used the separate reprints).

rank with the great Patriarchates. As a matter of fact this was largely influenced by the king. Dogmatically one stood on the Nicene-Creed; discipline was largely the same as in the rest of the Eastern churches. It was through the labours of Barsauma that Nestorianism definitely conquered Persia.[1] Before 410 this area had been spiritually dependent on Edessa which itself had a strong connection with Antioch. The Patriarch of the latter See was the head of those churches and it was the centre both for the Government of the state and for learning and culture, fundamentally Greek. But as far as the older history of Edessa and its hinterland is concerned, a genuinely Aramean mission and christianity had sprung up very early,[2] which only at a later date was covered by Greek influences.[3] The exact nature of this process escapes our observation; but from the writings of the Persian Sage Afrahat it may be seen how a Christianity outside the trend of the Greek world developed (he wrote after Nicaea); "it was possible to hold the Christian position with different watchwords from those which the Church borrowed from her refractory sons Tertullian and Origen".[4] It is a widespread opinion that the origin of this development was for a good deal Jewish.[5] It is well known that there were large Jewish colonies in the cities of Mesopotamia.[6] On the other hand travellers in the 19th and 20th cent. have noticed various usages among the Christians of Kurdistan that found their parallels in the Old Testament and seemed to be derived from Jewish origin; the same was found in some books of law of the Syrian Christians.[7] But it is rather dangerous to draw this conclusion from these facts, for in the years that lay between these two poles, the O.T. had a growing influence upon the whole Christian life;[8] besides that those usages find their parallels on the Greek soil too, where any possi-

(1) The details will be found in the books mentioned before. (2) F. C. Burkitt, *l.l.*, passim; A. von Harnack, *Mission und Ausbreitung des Christentums in den ersten drei Jahrhunderten*[4], Leipzig, 1924, ii, S. 678–698; a very important collection of materials in: F. Haase, *Altchristliche Kirchengeschichte*, S. 70–111. (3) Remarkable symptomes form the titles of the Ministers; the names of the old offices are genuinly Syriac: ܩܫܝܫܐ = presbyter, ܡܫܡܫܢܐ = deacon, while the title of Hypodiakonos a.o. was simply taken over from Greek. (4) F. C. Burkitt, *l.l.*, p. 95. (5) Cf. H. Lietzmann, *Geschichte der alten Kirche*, Berlin, 1936, ii, S. 273. (6) E. Schürer, *Geschichte des jüdischen Volkes im Zeitalter J.C.*[4], Leipzig, 1909, iii, S. 6–10. (7) C. Kayser, *Die Canones Jacob's von Edessa*, Leipzig, 1886, S. 80–81, 89 a.e. – This problem is different from that discussed by W. O. E. Oesterley, *The Jewish Background of the Christian Liturgy*, Oxford, 1925. (8) A. von Harnack, *Lehrbuch der Dogmengeschichte*, [5], Tübingen, 1931, ii, S. 84, N 1, and S. 469.

bility of Jewish influence is excluded. It may not be overlooked, that they are often common Eastern habits, that survived on one place longer than on an other. The possibility of a contra-distinction against the Jews did also exist!

In connection with our theme we must mention here also the "Acts of Thomas", that document that most of all N.T.ical Apocrypha gave rise to long discussions. I do not dare to give a well-founded opinion about the all-important question: Gnostic or Catholic; this decides about the value of the accounts of a kind of Eucharist in Ch. 27, 29, 49–50, 133 in which bread is the sole element.[1] However this may be, no line seems to lead to the later Nestorian liturgy which has bread and wine and quite a different structure, in accordance with all the Greek liturgies. A research of the facts afforded by the Acts of the Martyrs and the writings of Ephraim, enabling us to get a better idea of the pre-Greek times is badly wanted.[2] We have shown some lines of which it must be asked whether they have found their continuation in the later Persian theology etc. and survived as an undercurrent of the official teaching;[3] or has the overflowing Greek movement pushed away all what was ancient? Has e.g. the Nestorian church kept the Agape for long ages while it had vanished in the other churches (we find a notice that it was celebrated in the 12th century);[4] is this old or a revival without connection with the práctice of the early church?

The school of the Persians in Edessa had followed and propagated the Doctrines of the great Antiochene School and by that way this particular Christology came to Persia. In the Christological struggles of the 5th century which are related in every book on the History of Dogma, it receded to this country where it had the preference of being politically undangerous, as it was not the religion of the Byzantine Emperors. But in spite of that the struggle with the State and with the Magians occupies an important place.

(1) Cf. H. Lietzmann, *Messe*, S. 243–245; on the *Acta Thomae* in general cf. the Introduction of W. Bauer, in: E. Hennecke, *Neutestamentliche Apokryphen* [2], Tübingen, 1924, S. 256–258, and the literature quoted there. (2) While remembering what was said by Burkitt, *l.l.*, p. 100. (3) See e.g. the P<sup>e</sup>shita which was recasted from older translations. (4) Gismondi i, p. 4: "Porro (after the death of the Apostel Mari) Madainae fideles e gente magorum conveniebant ad convivium post liturgiam, secundum praeceptum charitatis, a pravis moribus abhorrentes, quod et servant qui montes incolunt". J. M. Hanssens, *Institutiones*, ii, p. 293 refers to *Expos.* ii, p. 83.

Nevertheless the church flourished under the spiritual leadership of men as Narsai and Babai the Great, who established for ever the Antiochene traditions in the Persian church. The following time brought about a definite separation from the Greek church.[1] It is a matter of course that this cannot be taken absolutely. We hear that Mar Thomas of Edessa and Mar Abba travelled in the West and brought with them a translation of the liturgy of Nestorius;[2] there are some rather similar traditions about a mission of the Persians to the Emperor of which the Patriarchs Isho'yabh i and ii participated and during which they celebrated the Mass with the Byzantine Emperor who was astonished that their liturgies were almost identical. But except for merchants the contact does not seem to have existed. Yet the fact may not be overlooked that the Monks played a great part in this church (a good many of the Bishops were taken from them) and that they found their spiritual ideal among the Egyptian Fathers of Scete; they had this in common with the Greeks and the Jacobites and it would be worth while to investigate what actual and spiritual relations have existed between the different departments of the Christian Church.[3] The Nestorian character was endangered by some men as Ḥenana[4] who tried to introduce the Alexandrian theology which was forcibly opposed by the other leaders and reinforced the position of the Antiochians by canonizing Theodore of Mopsuestia as the "Interpreter". In later ages some deviations from this position may be found in the exegesis of Isho'dadh of Merw.[5] This shows that a clear knowledge of what was really Nestorian is wanting. More than is done so far, future investigations will have to determine what is the exact relation between the position of Theodore and his companions and of the Nestorians and whether there is a development in dogmatics[6]. Sahdona tried to get the

(1) Nestorians were practically not found in the West, cf. J. Pargoire, *l'Eglise Byzantine de* 527 *à* 847 ³, Paris, 1923, p. 27.– "Avec elle [sc. the Church of the Roman Empire] on n'avait aucune relation officielle; mais c'était toute la dissidence car aucun anathème n'avait été lancé ni d'un côté, ni de l'autre", said L. Duchesne, *L'église au vime siècle*, p. 326, quoted by Kidd, *Churches of Eastern Christendom*, p. 516. (2) Cf. A. Baumstark, *L.G.*, S. 120 and Ak. 1–3. (3) The contact with the Monophysites was closer than with the Greeks. To characterize it as "Todfeindschaft" (see p. 40) is too strong. The relations were often friendly, even while one condemned each other's doctrinal position as heretical. Unfortunately, they have never been properly studied. (4) A. Baumstark, *a.a.O.*, S. 127. (5) G. Diettrich, *Die Stellung Isho'dad's in der Auslegungsgeschichte*, Giessen, 1902. (6) Leading up to a state in which the particular Nestorian theology is not

Chalcedonian Creed acknowledged by the church in the time of Isho'yabh iii, but he was condemned as a heretic. Mysticism flourished in the 7th century with men as Isaac of Nineveh and Dadisho' and it has been observed that it had many points of resemblance with the other churches and even with Mohammedanism.[1] Though it did not last long, its influence was considerable. The same may be said about philosophy and medicine; the place of Nestorian physicians at the court of the Sassanides and Chalifs is well known; it is a striking fact, that several Patriarchs had studied medicine which was also taught at the schools (cf. the rule for the schools of Theodosius 853–858, in: 'Abdisho', *Nomocanon*, vi 3). In all these departments the Nestorians passed the learning of the Greeks on to the Arabs by whom it was cultivated and became influential on the development of these studies in Western Europe in the Middle Ages.[2] The Nestorians were a separate body from the political point of view in the same way as other subjected communities: their Patriarch was both their religious and civil head. They were all treated in the same way, that is to say periods of spiritual power alternated with those of severe persecution, which often found their cause in the over-boldness of the Christians. From the fact that the Patriarch was also the civil leader, it followed that he had also to give canons about all kind of secular matter which are also incorporated in the churchbooks. This juridical tradition has never been systematically investigated as far as I know; a comparison with the Lawbooks of other churches would show that this tradition is rather complicated, but that there exists a definite relationship,[3] possibly parallel with the liturgical affinities, a relation about which we do not get information from other sources. Right from the beginning a great

even known as is found in the present time; A. J. Maclean, *Nestorianism*, in: *E.R.E.*, ix, p. 332.

(1) A thorough study of this subject is still a desideratum; for the present, see the Introduction of Prof. A. J. Wensinck, to his translation of Isaac of Nineveh, Amsterdam, 1923, and the small book by the same author: *Oostersche Mystiek, Christelijke en Mohammedaansche*, Amsterdam, 1930; and: A. Mingana, *W.S.* vii, *Early Christian Mystics*, Cambridge, 1934, passim. (2) A. Baumstark, *Ostsyrisches Christentum und ostsyrischer Hellenismus*, in: *Römische Quartalschrift für christliche Altertumskunde und für Kirchengeschichte*, 1908, ii, S. 17–35 shows in an essay "für weitere Kreise" the influx of Western ideas into the East as a counterpart of Strygovski's well-known thesis of the oriental influence upon the West. (3) A beginning of it was made by W. Riedel, *Kirchenrechtsquellen des Patriarchats von Alexandrien*, Leipzig, 1900, who shows that Nestorian books were used in Alexandria.

missionary expension has taken place even to India and China.[1] We have but very little indications about its nature. At any rate it is sure, that it was simply a transplantation of the Persian church-life; the services were all held in Syriac (so among the Thomas-Christians in India[2]); although some traces of translation of liturgical books were found among the documents discovered by expeditions in Central Asia.[3] All these mission-fields were subjected to the Patriarch at home. This mission, too, has had its ups and downs and the contact with the motherchurch was not always strong. Some very interesting documents from the 13th century are the history of Yabhallaha and the travelstory of the Franciscan William of Rubruc; they give a clear picture of the great extension, but also of the low standard in respect of churchlife of the Nestorian church of that time. It is difficult to say whether this expansion has taken place at the cost of the intensity of religious life of the home-church itself. In any case it is true that the sources do not show us a glorious picture of spiritual life: intrigues at every choice of a Patriarch and intervening of the state; simony; slackening of discipline; several officers ignorant themselves of the traditions of the church, etc. Many attempts to lift the standard were undertaken, e.g. by reorganizing the schools (Sabarisho'; Theodosius, etc.). But the recurrence of these efforts show that it was extremely necessary. At the same time we hear of apostasy to Islam. Further investigations will have to determine whether this picture is too dark and to consider the question why there have always been people who stuck to the faith of their fathers in spite of the persecutions in the centuries that came with Timur Lenk. It will show, I believe, that the vital forces of Christianity were still living among much superstition. Fetichism alone is too easy an answer.

What questions do result from this history? 1) Seclusion from

(1) Details about this missionary efforts were given by Dr. Mingana in his books on Christianity in Central Asia and the Far East and about India, see p. 22 note 5.–About the Nestorians in China see: P. Y. Saeki, *The Nestorian Documents and Relics in China*, 1937. (2) We do not need to enter into the history of this church nor into that of their liturgy, as the latter was nothing but the Nestorian rite; literature about them in: A. Mingana, *Early Spread of Christianity in India*, Manchester, 1926; R. H. Connolly–E. Bishop, *The work of Menezes on the Malabar Liturgy*, in: *J. Th. St.*, 1914, p. 396–425, 569–593; F. C. Burkitt, *The Old Malabar Liturgy*, in: *J. Th. St.*, 1928, p. 155–157; *D.A.C.L.*, s.v. *Malabar*, t. x, col. 1260–1277, and: Hanssens, ii, p. 389–393. (3) A. Mingana, *Central Asia*, p. 42–44.

the other churches and struggles with the ruling non-christian powers. 2) Maintaining of pre-Greek traditions and of Antiochene Theology (they preserved important works of Nestorius and Theodore of Mopsuestia); not only as a special Christological doctrine, but as a special conception of christianity as a whole.[1] 3) Passing on of mysticism. 4) Connection with other churches in doctrine and discipline; monasticism. 5) Expansion. Only when these points are sufficiently made clear, the time will come to write a history according to critical standards, and to determine the position of the Nestorians historically, theologically, religiously.

One further point may be mentioned which is of special interest for the study of the New Testament. During the last fifteen years a good deal has been made of the Mandeans and their religion. It was thought that they are the true followers of John the Baptist, and that their books (dating from the 9th century and later!) give us an insight into the world of Eastern "Gnosis" which had influenced the beginnings of Christianity to a very large extent.[2] A strong blow against this theory was given in an article of Prof. Lietzmann,[3] who showed that the Mandeans were totally dependent on the Nestorians and that the Nestorian ritual of Baptism was the pattern on which the most conspicuous rite of the Mandeans was made.

All the points mentioned above tend to show the importance of the investigation of the liturgy; for it is different from that in other churches; preserved traditions from the ancient church of

(1) Cf. A. Baumstark, *Die nestorianische Schriften "de Causis Festorum"*, in: *O.C.*, 1901, S. 341–342. (2) For our purpose it is not necessary to mention the great mass of books and articles in which the statement made in the text was debated, nor to discuss the points involved. It will be sufficient to refer the readers to the article of K. Kessler (1903), *Mandäer*, in: *P.R.E.*[3], xii, S. 155–183 for the older literature, while the discussions we have in view are summarized by H. Schlier, *Zur Mandäerfrage*, in: *Theologische Rundschau*, 1933, S. 1–34; 69–92, and: J. Thomas, *Le mouvement baptiste en Palestine et Syrie* (150 *av. J.-C.*– 300 *ap. J.-C.*), Gembloux, 1935, p. 184–267. (3) H. Lietzmann, *Ein Beitrag zur Mandäerfrage*, in: *Sitzungsberichte der Akademie der Wissenschaften zu Berlin*, phil.-hist. Klasse, 1930, S. 596–608.–As it is our sole aim to draw attention to the part which the Nestorians play in this discussion, we do not examine the question whether Prof. Lietzmann's case is sound or that of his critic Schlier, *a.a.O.*, S. 84–90; cf the mediating position of J. Thomas, *l.c.*, p. 217, n. 2; 218 and p. 221, n. 2: "nous ne nions pas que les Mandéens aient emprunté à la liturgie syrienne; ce que nous nions, c'est qu'on puisse expliquer par là toute le complexe de leur rituel baptismal."

Mesopotamia and of the Antiochene teachers (in the Mystagogy); mysticism was often connected with liturgy; and the Canons about it were often the same in various churches; while being the centre of religious life it was spread all over Asia and formed the heart of christianity, even its single expression for many people during several ages.[1]

ii. A short summary of what has been written about the Nestorian liturgy will be useful to become acquainted with the questions that are under discussion and the material that is at our disposal.[2] We pointed out before, that it was not before 1890 that the Nestorians came to the fore in scientific literature. In general this statement is true, but it must be modified with regard to their liturgy. For at the very beginning of the comparative study of the liturgy the classical work of *E. Renaudot* made known the three Eucharistic formularies used by the Nestorians, viz. that of the Apostles Addai and Mari, of Theodore of Mopsuestia and of Nestorius,[3] in a latin translation with notes (which are, however, not so complete as those on the Coptic and Jacobite rite).[4] He made a "Dissertatio"[5] precede which is as always full of good remarks. He begins by telling that these translations have been made from real nest. Mss., but these authorities were not many

(1) We do not deal with the history and liturgical pratices of the so-called Chaldaeans = Nestorians, united with Rome. Their history begins at 1552. Their liturgy is practically identical with that of the true Nestorians; some slight differences are found; see: Badger ii, p. 241–243, and: *L.E.W.*, p. lxxxi, referring to: G. Bickel, *Der katholische Orient*, Münster, 1874, no. 6. But they cannot be considered as maintaining the Nestorian traditions, for all that was inconsistent with the Roman doctrine, was expurged; cf. L. Duchesne, *Origines de Culte chrétien* [5], Paris, 1925, p. 72, n. 2: "Ceux qui servent aux communautés catholiques ont subi de nombreuses retouches inspirées par un zèle qui n'a pas toujours été selon la science"; and: A. Mingana, *India*, p. 167. See about the Chaldaeans, R. Janin, *Les églises orientales et les rites orientaux* [2], Paris, 1926, p. 513–522. (2) We do not propose to give a complete bibliography, but only those works which contain observations of some special importance for our subject; neither did we register all translations. (3) The ordo communis of these formularies is the same. The Anaphora of 'Theod.' is used from the First Sunday of Annunciation or Advent till Palmsunday; 'Nest.' is used five times a year, viz. on Epiphany, Jan. 6th; Friday of John the Baptist (first Friday after Epiphany); Memorial of the Greek Doctors (Friday after the 4th Sunday of the Epiphany); Thursday of the Rogation of the Ninevites (cf ad Q. 11); Passover (cf. ad Q. 50). 'Addai' is the anaphora during the rest of the year. (4) E. Renaudot, *Liturgiarum Orientalium Collectio*, 2 volumes; 1st edition, Parisiis, 1716; 2nd ed., Francofurti ad Moenum, 1847.–The translations mentioned in the text: ii, p. 578–642. (5) *L.O.C.*, ii, p. 561–577.

nor were they old; on the other hand they agreed practically in every thing.[1] His argument is directed against the Italian missionaries who had treated the venerable rite of the Indian Christians in such a miserable way at the Synod of Diamper (1599) and had introduced several new ceremonies instead of leaving to the Thomas-christians (cf. p. 27, n. 2) their own liturgy without heretical names (the ordinary Roman Catholic way of treating the Uniates). As a matter of course it is also against the Protestants to prove the correctness of the R.C. attitude regarding the Eucharist (this is the aim of both volumes). Therefore this introduction deals with two points: *a.* the Nestorian ritual is old; *b.* it is not infected by stains of nest. heresy. 'Addai' is called after the Apostles who according to the common Syriac tradition won these countries for Christianity, and the Jacobites and Greeks have never blamed them for making a Nestorian liturgy on their own hand; consequently Renaudot is inclined to affirm the first part of the question whether this is the old Mesopotamian liturgy or imported from the heretics, though he acknowledges that it is rather difficult to decide. The fact that its prayers are generally, compared with those of other rituals, simple and not verbose, is a proof of their age. This cannot be said about the rubrics as these were generally not inserted, but handed down in other books.[2] Besides the other liturgies refer to the former and not the other way round. It goes back to the time before the division. Nothing particularly Nestorian will be found in them except some places in 'Nest.' (as opposed to the Daily Office that is full of it). The words of the Institution (which are missing in 'Addai') are the same as in other eastern liturgies, and are followed by an Epiclesis.[3] These liturgies contain all the elements of a "valid" liturgy. The words of the Institution are not found in the older codex, but some pages of it are missing on which they might have been written, for it is impossible that they should have been omitted and they are also

(1) He used one MS. that was mutilated and repaired; one written by the Chaldaean Patriarch Joseph in Rome 1697 (corrected after R.C. Missals) while some help could be derived from the translation of the liturgy found in India by the Missionaries mentioned in the text. (2) *L.O.C.*, ii, p. 563: "De ritibus etiam certa conjectura duci non potest: cum in plerisque Missalibus libris cujuscumque linguae, non semper adscripti sint, nam aliunde peti solent. Aliquos ex aliis Ecclesiasticis monumentis agnoscimus, quorum Codices in Oriente scripti mentionem nullam faciunt, de quibus tamen dubitare non possumus, quamvis notitia illorum satis obscura sit, quia libri Nestorianorum prae caeteris rarissimi sunt." (3) Cf. ad Q. 15.

found in 'Theod.' and 'Nest.'. 'Addai' has also an Epiclesis before the words of Christ (in an ordinary scheme of liturgy), but not in the usual place for which Renaudot gives some parallels; he assumes that there was a double Epiclesis. It does not matter that the breaking and signing of the host is the same as found elsewhere; on the contrary it proves its unity with the rest in the doctrine of transubstantiation. With regard to his translation he says that it is as literal as possible, but that the Syriac style does not allow a verbal one in latin. At the end he says that the Greek authors do not betray any knowledge of the Nest. liturgy. Leontius of Byzance is the only one, but his statement cannot be pressed and he tells only that there was a liturgy known as that of Theodore. If this was true that it was full of blasphemy, it is different from that called 'Theod.' by the Nestorians.[1] Summing up we find that here is given a publication of the texts that falls short of its own requirements; that questions about origin, words of the Institution and Epiclesis are put; that the Greek evidence is negative and that the Nestorian doctrine of the Euch. agreed with the Roman Catholic. On the other hand nothing is said about historical development of the formularies.

About ten years later *J. S. Assemani* published his famous "Bibliotheca Orientalis", iii 1 (1725) giving in it several new texts (Canons and Letter of John Bar Abgare–excerpts from the expositions of George of Arbela and Timothy ii), and 2 (1728) containing a systematical survey "De Syris Nestorianis". He dealt with the Eucharist in § 12 of Chapter vii[2] that tells about "Nestorianorum veterum et recentiorum errores". This title is eloquent! Its aim is controversial by nature; it does not clear the historical questions. It does not contain a discussion of the questions raised by the liturgy (had this sufficiently been done by Renaudot?), but of liturgical usages and Eucharistic teaching in which the Nestorians seemed to deviate from the Catholic doctrine. All utterances of

(1) As this text is used over and over again in the discussions I shall give it here in full: Leontius Byzantinus, *adversus incorruptiocolas et Nestorianos*, iii 19, in: *M.S.G.*, 86, 1, p. 1368c: τολμᾷ καὶ ἕτερον κακὸν τῶν εἰρημένων οὐ δεύτερον. ἀναφορὰν γὰρ σχεδιάζει ἑτέραν παρὰ τὴν πατρόθεν ταῖς ἐκκλησίαις παραδιδομένην, μήτε τὴν τῶν ἀποστόλων αἰδεσθεὶς μήτε τὴν τοῦ μεγάλου Βασιλείου ἐν τῷ αὐτῷ πνεύματι συγγραφεῖσαν λόγου τινὸς; κρίνων ἀξίαν εν ᾗ ἀναφορᾷ βλασφημιῶν (οὐ γὰρ εὐχῶν) τελετὴν ἀπεπλήρωσεν. Since this statement has no bearing upon the questions discussed in the main part of this thesis we do not need to give an exact interpretation of these words.
(2) *B.O.*, iii 2, p. ccxc–cccxviii.

the Nestorians (Babai, George of Arbela, Timothy ii, 'Abdisho') are placed on the same level, though he points out at various occasions that the older Nestorians were closer to the Catholic truth than their posterity ± 1700. We may summarize his argument in the following way: The Nestorians adhered to the doctrine of their spiritual father who taught: "In sacramentis vivificantibus nos hominis simplicis corpus et sanguinem sumere", though they confessed the real presence of Christ in the Eucharist. Their teaching is the same as that of the R.C. but in explaining it there are two opinions "Plerosque quidem confiteri, in Eucharistia vere ac realiter existere idem corpus Christi, quod est in coelo; nonnullos vero asserere, Eucharistiam nil aliud esse, quam corpus mysticum, idest, unitum vero et naturali corpori Christi, non ipsum Christi corpus". Next comes a discussion of the rebukes of Joseph ii,[1] the uniate Patriarch, about the preparing of the Euch. bread from the ferment, called Malcha, about the use of grapes instead of wine, about the omission of the words of the Institution, about the consecration effected by the Epiclesis, about the offering of a host in honour of the Virgin which is supposed to be her body, about the fact that the Patriarch officiates with his head covered. In connection with the first point he mentions the apocryphal story about the particle of the Eucharistic bread of the Lord's Supper itself, which was handed down to the Eastern churches whose tradition goes right back to the Lord himself.[2] The belief that the elements are changed by the Holy Spirit is a later intrusion, the words of the Institution must be supplied from the other formularies. The other points are of minor importance, e.g. the objections against the Nestorians by a certain Thomas about their receiving the Eucharist in their hands and the "Communio sub utraque". Assemani accuses the Nestorians of the following mistakes: some of them think that "Communio sub utraque" is absolutely necessary, which he denies by pointing to the children's communion, and that of the sick; they condemn the use of the Greeks of the intinct bread and of putting hot water into the chalice; they do not practise the reservation of the Eucharist; some of them forbid the Eucharist to be taken to the sick; they forbid to hold mass twice a day on the same altar; they do not know private masses; they think the bread and wine are polluted by various occurrences;[3]

(1) Joseph ii lived ± 1700. (2) See ad Q 52. (3) In this connection Assemani uses our "Questions".

they do not read the scriptures in ferial offices; and according to some people they celebrate the liturgy on Maundy Thursday after sunset. All these points are extensively discussed. A grave defect, however, consists in the fact that this part is really controversial and that the texts quoted are not historically arranged, but systematically. Consequently we cannot say, that his work helps much towards the solution of the questions connected with the history of the rite. The texts he published had some importance. But unfortunately the subsequent writers used these excerpts without recurring to the original texts. It goes without saying that their interpretation was often wrong, because the contexts were missing.

Within the scope of his great work on the "History of the Holy Eastern Church" Dr. *J. M. Neale*, one of the leading liturgiologists of the middle of last century, said some words about the origin of the Nest. Liturgies (the Nestorians are not treated separately). He argued that a part of 'Nest.' was older than 431 since the Nestorians did not borrow from Constantinople anything after that date, and that 'Nest.' has its origin in Byzance is proved by an addition to the Epiclesis. Because 'Addai' formes the pro-anaphorical part of the other two, this must be considerably older. The names show Persian origin. Neale puts this dilemma: Seleucia had little contact with the Roman Empire; "they (the Nestorians) must therefore either have had the liturgy of S. James, and after the time of their separation have rejected it, and formed an other office from their own fancy; or they must have had a primitive liturgy from their own apostles, to which they stead-fastly clung". The first supposition is excluded by the School of Edessa, neither does the liturgy contain Nestorianism nor were they ever blamed for changing it. Conclusion: the last assumption is right! Sign of its old age is its simplicity; the structure cannot be deduced from Cesarea or Jerusalem.[1] So he argues for a higher estimation of this particular liturgy that has always been neglected; it "is one of the earliest, and perhaps the very earliest of the many formularies of the Christian Sacrifice".[2] The latter statement is right, I think;

(1) Palmers argument against its old age, viz. that Ephraim Syrus shows a variation, if compared with all three Nest. liturgies, since they have the Intercessions before the Epiclesis and Ephraim after it, is dismissed by pointing to other transpositions of prayers in other liturgies (2) J. M. Neale, *Introduction to the History of the Holy Eastern Church*, London, 1849, i, p. 319-323.–On the

but the way in which it is reached cannot be approved of from the historical point of view; his way of arguing is untenable in view of the evidence which could not be known to him. That the Apostles have entrusted a complete liturgy to every one of their churches is a fundamental idea of Neale[1] that is inspired by his dogmatical view, but cannot possibly be held. Besides that his discussion only deals with the origin of the Nestorian liturgy, but leaves aside its subsequent history in the church. The texts published by Assemani have not been used.

In the same time, Rev. *G. P. Badger* published the results of two travels in the East which he had made to see what could be done by the English to help the Nestorians. He wrote his well-known "The Nestorians and their rituals". The second part is of special interest and it marked a new step forward, because it had collected a great number of liturgical texts in an English translation. As to the Eucharist he gave 'Nest.' and elucidated some dogmatical points by quotations from the Daily Offices and 'Abdisho's book "The Pearl". His method consisted in following the 39 Articles of the Anglican Church and comparing the Nestorian doctrine with them.[2] About the Lord's Supper they believe in the real presence: the Lord distributes Himself to the worthy recipient and seals to him the forgiveness of sins and strengthens the grace of God; they believe that the elements are changed by the Epiclesis; the wicked do not eat Christ's body, therefore there are strong admonitions to humbleness; they communicate "sub utraque" though under Roman Catholic influence some ignorant priests(!)[3] practise the "communio sub una"; as to the sacrifice the Nest. know only one real sacrifice of Christ upon the Cross, that upon

omission of the words of the Institution, see p. 485–487. Mr. Neale considered it to be late.

(1) As to the liturgies of James, Marc, Basilius and Chrysostomus he simply takes over the results of such witers as Renaudot, Le Brun, Le Quien, Bona, Palmer and others; he assumes "that these Liturgies, though not composed by the Apostles whose names they bear, were the legitimate development of their unwritten tradition, respecting the Christian Sacrifice; the words, probably, in the most important parts, the general tenor in all portions, descending unchanged from the Apostolic authors." (2) G. P. Badger, *The Nestorians and their Rituals*, London, 1852, 2 volumes; about his method cf. ii, p. 28.–The Eucharist is dealt with in chapter xxxii–xxxv and xlii; the discussion was based upon Oriental Mss.; the text of 'Abdisho' was already published by A. Mai, *Veterum Scriptorum Nova Collectio*, x, Romae, 1838 with a latin translation. (3) The same words as found in our treatise, cf. ch. vi.

the altar is commemorative; there are no solitary masses; the prayers for the dead are only for those departed in righteousness. Quite rightly his book was qualified by Dr. Baumstark[1] as "für seine Zeit höchst verdienstvoll", but he adds that it is only concerned with the final result of the development, while it does not say anything about the other documents which may throw some light upon this development. This is exactly the right estimation of the value and defect of this book. For its importance lies in the fact that it had collected so many different formularies and as such it has done service to many scholars.

The "Dissertatio" of *Th. J. Lamy*[2] (1859) does not possess any value of its own (this judgement does not affect the main part of the book, being the publication and commentary of two important Jacobitic writings, but the pages on the Nestorians). It depends on the texts published by Assemani. He is only concerned with the dogmatical and controversial question; the first part of his writing tries to prove from Syriac sources that the Protestant opinion about the Eucharist is wrong and that the R.C. position is strengthened by the evidence, even of these heretics. He concludes that: "Realem autem Praesentiam a Nestorianis negari nullus Syrorum hucusque, quod sciam, dixit. Semper itaque in admittendo eo dogmate cum catholicis convenerunt Nestoriani sive antiqui sive recentiores, etsi in explicatione illius mysterii saepe hallucinati sunt, et in re disciplinari merito reprehensi" (p. 59) though he admitted that some Nestorian authors held an other view (but they, he thinks, were not of importance); the same result as that of Assemani.

*Dr. Steitz* who wrote a long series of articles on the Eucharistic teaching of the Greek church which were of great influence,[3] stands in the same relation to Assemani. He formulated his conclusion after a reproduction of some of Assemani's texts, in this way:[4] "Dass die Nestorianer dem symbolisch-dynamischen Standpunkte in der Abendmahlslehre treu geblieben sind, wie er in den Jahrhunderten

(1) A. Baumstark, *Festbrevier und Kirchenjahr*, S. 2. (2) Th. J. Lamy, *Dissertatio de Syrorum fide et Disciplina in re Eucharistica; accedunt veteris ecclesiae syriacae monumenta duo*, Lovanii, 1859, Art. vii, p. 44–59. (3) F. Kattenbusch, *Lehrbuch der vergleichenden Confessionskunde*, Freib. i. Br., 1892, i, S. 413 ff. based his paragraph on the Eucharist upon them; and A. von Harnack, *Lehrbuch der Dogmengeschichte*[5], Tübingen, 1931, ii, S. 457 ff. constantly refers to him as the great authority. (4) G. Steitz, *Die Abendmahlslehre der griechischen Kirche*, in: *Jahrbücher für deutsche Theologie*, xiii (1868), S. 58–66, § 46 *Die Nestorianer des Mittelalters.*

der grossen christologischen Kämpfe der Kirche übereinstimmend festgehalten wurde." This could be compared with the Christology "in ähnlicher Weise namen sie zwar das in seiner natürlichen Integrität unverändert fortbestehende Brot als Bild des zum Himmel erhöhten Christus, bekannten aber gleichwohl *einen* Leib im Abendmahl und im Himmel vermöge der Identität der versöhnenden Kraft und Wirkung. Diese Ansicht hat vermöge des dynamischen Symbolismus, von dem sie ausgeht eine unverkennbare Verwandtschaft mit der monophysitischen" though their christologies were totally different (S. 58). He does not accept the double line of Assemani-Lamy; all texts are, in his opinion, explained by the theory formulated above.

This paper was the last in which the dogmatical position of the Nestorians regarding the Eucharist was discussed. After that time this question rested and this was right, I think. The mistake was that the discussions were held 1) with insufficient survey and criticism of the sources; the difference that exists between the nature of various books quoted, was overlooked; all utterances were thought to be of equal importance and the possibility of historical and dogmatical change was not taken into account; 2) with questions and arguments determined by Western controversies: R.C.-Anglican-Calvinistic-Lutheran. The fact was not considered that the Nestorians, like the Eastern Church in general, might have had an opinion that did not fit in with Western categories, that their approach to "Sacrament" was different. Though these discussions were not so heated as those regarding the Greeks and other liturgical families that were better known[1], yet it was fortunate that it came to an end, since it was hopeless because of the scarcity of texts. Yet the publication of Renaudot had a lasting value and Assemani had shown that the information about the history of the Nest. liturgy could be enlarged. But the problems concerning the fate of the liturgy during some 15 or more centuries had not yet been detected. The second phase in which the texts were published is marked by an absolute change of interest. This change coincided with and was the result of the great development of the historical investigation of Christianity and of the growing understanding of the meaning of "Liturgy".

(1) Cf. Neale, *l.l.*, p. 319: "It (the Nestorian liturgy) is generally passed over as of very inferior importance"; and: F. E. Brightman, *L.E.W.*, p. x.

This new era[1] began already in 1871 when *Dr. Bickel* edited two leaves of the MS. Brit. Mus. Add. 14669 exhibiting an anaphora-text of the sixth century in a very mutilated state.[2] This anaphora was clearly of an East-Syrian type. But for the moment nothing could be made of it as the historical background was wanting. The same scholar once prepared "eine auf dem gesammten Quellenmateriale beruhende Entwickelungsgeschichte und Darstellung der ostsyrischen L." But, unfortunately, this book has never been issued and I do not know what was the state of his investigations or what has become of his notes. The article he contributed to the encyclopaedia of Prof. Kraus[3] must take its place. This rite existed before the Nestorians came to Persia; this older formulary has been treated by Isho'yabh iii in the same way as the Roman Mass by Gregory i. He gives a survey of the various texts: 'Fragment' is typically Persian ("memento" before the Epiclesis); it is "ein Uebergangsstadium von der gemeinsamen Grundlage zu der spätern nestorianischen Form"; probably it represents a rest of the normal liturgy before its curtailment by I. iii.–'Addai' is "wohl im Folge jener Abkürzung im Kanon, arg zerrütet und der Berichtigung durch die beiden andern nestorianischen Anaphoren

(1) We pass by the books on "Konfessionskunde", such as: F. Kattenbusch, *a.a.O.*; F. Loofs, *Symbolik*, i, Tübingen, 1902, and: H. Mulert, *Konfessionskunde*, Giessen, 1927, as their sections on the Nestorians are very small and do not furnish details.–R. Janin, *Les églises orientales et les rites orientaux*[2], Paris, 1926, p. 478–496 has much about it, but only the present usages; he assumes influence of Antioch (Palestine) upon the Persian rite, revision by Isho'yabh iii, and enriching in later times, p. 479. The historical apparatus and proofs for these statements are wanting.–A most excellent and up-to-date first part of a "Konfessionskunde" was published this year by Prof. F. Heiler, *Urkirche und Ostkirche*, München, 1937. As to the Nestorians it does not embody original research, but is a comprehensive survey based upon the best authorities. He does not speak about the history of the rite (S. 446–450) but only mentions the fact that 'Addai' is the liturgy of Seleucia and got its present form through Isho'yabh i and iii (byzantine influence); the main part consists of a description of 'Addai'–the words of the Institution are omitted because of the holiness of the words. He sums up the other anaphora-texts and the days in which they are said. In dealing with the Nestorian doctrine of the Euch. he uses the texts of Jugie (cf. p. 55), but without their Roman-Cath. interpretation (S. 441). –S. Salaville, *Les Liturgies Orientales*, Paris, 1932, deals exclusively with the Greek rite; what is said about the Nestorians is extremely poor and without value.
(2) G. Bickel, in his: *Conspectus rei syrorum literariae*, Münster, 1871, p. 71–73; a reprint in: Appendix L of *L.E.W.*, p. 511–518. A revision of it made from a fresh collation of the manuscript was given by Dom. R. H. Connolly, *Sixth Century Fragments of an East-Syrian Anaphora*, in: *O.C.*, 1925, S. 99–128.
(3) G. Bickel, *Liturgie* iv, in: F. X. Kraus, *Real-Encyklopädie der christlichen Alterthümer*, Freiburg i. Br., 1886, ii, S. 321–323.

bedürftig" (it misses the words of the Institution, though they are usually said)–'Theod.' and 'Nest.' are not written by these heretics. Next he offers a survey of the text as he thinks it had been fixed by I. iii, a reconstruction from the texts in Mss. and printed books controled by the older nestorian liturgists. In spite of a number of additions "stimmt die ostsyrische L. auf das Genaueste in ihrer ganzen Anordnung mit der vornicänischen gemeinschaftlichen uebercin wie sie denn auch in ihre Diction und Anschauungsweise einen höchst alterthümlichen Charakter bewahrt hat". He describes the Roman Catholic editions of the Missale for Mesopotamia and India and refers to his own critical edition in: "der katholische Orient" 1874, based upon some printed texts and one London MS.–I have summarized this article, partly in his own words, because it is an excellent piece of work which shows in every line the great knowledge of its author on this subject. It makes us regret the more that death prevented him to publish the book he promised.

To this we join the book of the well-known liturgiologist at the end of last century Prof. *Probst.*[1] In his usual manner he had collected from the latin translation of the Ephraim-edition of the Assemani's those places that seemed to him to contain reminiscences of the liturgy of 'Addai'. They show according to Probst that this liturgy was known to Ephraim from beginning to end and that the Nestorian tradition that it had been composed by the Apostles themselves was right. No further use is made of this argument. We cannot think of discussing all the places he adduces, but we may point out that he often gives the text a meaning that cannot be taken for an unprejudiced exegesis. He overlooked that it is not certain that the 'Addai' was the liturgy of Edessa. (For the use that can be derived from Ephraim's writings see p. 19; many of the works of Ephraim are spurious and a critical sifting is necessary before using them.[2])

The complete Syriac text of the Liturgy had been published some years before by the Anglican Missionaries in Mesopotamia, in the: "Liturgia Sanctorum Apostolorum Adaei et Maris, etc."[3]

(1) F. Probst, *Die Liturgie des 4. Jahrhunderts und deren Reform*, Münster, 1896, S. 308–318; (2) Cf. O. Bardenhewer, *Geschichte der altkirchlichen Literatur* 1-2, Freib. i. Br., 1924, iv, S. 346–349. (3) *Liturgia Sanctorum Apostolorum Adaei et Maris, cui accedunt duo aliae in quibusdam festis et feriis dicendae: Necnon Ordo Baptismi*, Urmiae, Typis Missionis Archiepiscopi Cantuariensis, 1890 (the volume I used had only one title-page; in: *L.E.W.*, p. lxxvii it is said that it was published in two parts, resp. 1890 and 1892).

With regard to the Eucharist this Missal contained besides the Ordo Communis and the three Anaphoratexts, the formulary for the renewal of the Holy Leaven and for the Preparation of the Elements. 27 Canons containing "Admonitions of the Altar" were joined to it. An introduction dealing with the Mss. etc. has not been prefixed, as this book was destined for practice. Something about it, though in an other form than is wanted in a scientific edition, was given by Dean Maclean who had helped to prepare it: "In the preparation of this edition of the Takhsa several comparatively modern manuscripts, the only ones available, were collated from different districts inhabited by the East Syrians. The oldest of these, written at Alqosh about 1500 A.D., was taken as the basis, and all matter taken from other manuscripts was included in brackets. We must specially notice that these printed books aim rather at representing the present use of the East Syrians than at reproducing the most ancient text, and are published for practical rather than antiquarian purposes."[1] Nothing is said about the canons. It seemed as though it had escaped the attention of the editors that they are the same as those of John B. Abgare published by Assemani.[2]

The section on the Eucharist given by *Browne* and *Maclean* in their book on the East Syrians, is mainly a description of the Lord's Supper as celebrated by the Nestorians. It is based upon these texts and their personal impressions. They wrote their book to excite interest in their missionary efforts, not to give a critical exposition of the history of Nestorianism; so it describes the state of this church ± 1890. They were of opinion, that 'Theod.' and 'Nest.' did not originate from Mopsuestia and Constantinople; but that the latter certainly was composed by using a Constantinopolitan liturgy (St. Basil) though the heretical traces are of Syrian origin.[3] Dean Maclean was also assisting in preparing the translation of the Persian rite in *Brightman's* collection,[4] that is made upon the Takhsa-text. The Introduction (p. lxxvii-lxxxi) gives in its usual way much bibliographical information. Dr. Brightman mentions

(1) A. J. Maclean, *East Syrian Daily Offices*, London, 1894, p. xxviii-xxix.-I do not see what is meant by J. M. Hanssens, *Institutiones Liturgicae*, ii, p. 310: "ratione tamen habita additionum quas editores in ordinem istius missae induxerunt". The Ordo Praeparationis was derived from one manuscript of Jilu, *L.E.W.*, p. lxxvii. (2) *B.O.*, iii 1, p. 238-248; cf. p. 133. (3) W. H. Browne-A. J. Maclean, *The Catholicos of the East and his People*, London, 1892, p. 243-266; the reference in the text is to p. 245-246. (4) F. E. Brightman, *Liturgies Eastern and Western*, i *Eastern Liturgies*, Oxford, 1896, p. 245-305.

the liturgical books and their printed texts (including the Chaldean ones); the Mss. known to him; and he gives the sources for the history of the rite, though this is not tabulated in an Appendix. He sums up: three other Anaphoratexts, viz. of Barsauma and Narsai, mentioned by 'Abdisho' (*B.O.*, iii, p. 66, 65) and of Diodore of Tarsus, mentioned in the account of the Synod of Diamper of which Renaudot (*L.O.C.*, ii, p. 569) questioned the existence and of which nothing else is known. As to 'Theod.' he points to the evidence of Leontius Byzantinus. The assigning of Bickel's text to Diodore by Dr. Wright[1] was groundless. For further information he refers to the "Commentators, of whom the works of the following are extant": Isho'yabh i, George of Arbela, Yabhallaha ii, Questions found in Vat. Syr. 150; George of Arbela, Exposition of the ecclesiastical offices; 'Abdisho', the Pearl; Timothy ii, On the seven causes of the Mysteries; the Book of the heavenly Intelligences. The following he enumerates as lost: an exposition by Narsai, by Hannana of Hedhaiyabh and by Isho'barnun. He has omitted the canons of John v.; 'Fragment' has been reprinted in an appendix (cf. p. 37 n. 2). An examination of this summary must be postponed until the moment when we make out what problems result from the discussions.[2]

In his popular book "die Messe im Morgenland"[3] Dr. *Baumstark* associated himself with Dr. Brightman to a large extent; he gives the flesh to the skeleton of his predecessor. He points out, that the West-Syrian mass (Jerusalem type) could not supersede the East-Syrian one, because this had become the Nestorian formulary to which the Jacobite stood "im Verhältniss der Todfeindschaft". Christianity in Edessa c.a. had been purely Aramean, thus a liturgy must have coincided "mit der ersten erfolgreichen Predigt" (S. 48; where does B. know this from?). The indications of Ephraim are scarce and rather unimportant, though his writings like those of James of Sarug and Philoxenos of Mabbug (Jacobites) need a closer

(1) W. Wright, *Syriac Literature*, London, 1894, p. 28. (2) The article of Mr. H. W. Codrington, on the Nestorian liturgy of the Presanctified., in: *J. Th. St.* 1904, will be found summarized in the Commentary ad Q 16. (3) A. Baumstark, *Die Messe im Morgenlande*, Kempten, 1906 (1921), S. 48–51.– Dr. Baumstark wrote in 1922 about this former book: "Ein ohne Vorwissen des Verfassers veranstalteter Neudruck der infolge vieler und hochbedeutsamer Funde heute naturgemäss vielfach völlig veralteten Arbeit, erschien 1921" in: *Vom geschichtlichen Werden der Liturgie*, Freib. i. Br. 1922, S. 139. But this declaration affects other parts, but not so much that on the East-Syrians, for the discoveries which gave many problems a new aspect were not in this field.

investigation from the liturgical point of view which may yield some result. The expositions of Barsauma and Narsai were still known in the 13th–14th century, they may have reflected the use of Nisibis. He mentions the fragment of Bickel as the sole survival of the old East-Syrian lit. 'Addai' must be considered as the liturgy of Seleucia-Ctesiphon which was extended all over Asia. Its previous history may be found in some places of the Acts of the Persian Martyrs and the "Synodicon Orientale". The activity of Isho'yabh i was of extreme importance and that of Isho'yabh iii was conclusive. The latter had been in the West and some traces of Byzantine influence may go back to his time.[1] The edition of Takhsa has no historical value, since it is based upon Mss. not older than the 15th century. The history must be found in the expositions, of which he mentions the same as Brightman (but not 'Abdisho'). As his work was destined for general readers, these facts are only stated, but not proved by references to the sources.

The contribution of the same author to the "Χρυσοστόμικα" does not belong, properly speaking, to the works discussed here.[2] For it aimed at showing that in 'Nest.' the liturgy of Constantinople before the 9th century has been preserved, though it had undergone various changes and was modeled after the East-Syrian pattern. This was done by Mar Abba and Mar Thomas, who translated it after their visit to the West (cf. the texts S. 777–781). Baumstark tries to prove that this liturgy is a neglected source for the history of the Byzantine rite previous to 'Chrysostomus'. It is noteworthy that B. pointed out that the dogmatical retouches are not of "Nestorian" (in the heretical sense) origin, but are

(1) Cf. A. Baumstark, *Ostsyrisches Christentum und ostsyrischer Hellenismus*, in: *Römische Quartalschrift*, 1908, ii S. 24: "Im 7. Jahrhundert ist der Schöpfer der endgiltigen Ordnung nestorianischen Gottesdienstes (Isho'yabh iii) in Konstantinopel gewesen, und man braucht nur das von Bedjan zum Druck besorgte *Brevarium Chaldaicum* aufmerksam durchzugehen, um zu empfinden, wie bedeutungsvoll die Reise nach der byzantinischen Kaiserstadt für das Lebenswerk des Mannes geworden sein muss." (2) A. Baumstark, *Die Chrysostomosliturgie und die syrische Liturgie des Nestorios*, in: Χρυσοστόμικα, Roma, 1908, S. 771–857. His results were disputed by Th. Schermann, in: *Theologie und Glaube*, 1913, S. 299–313, 392–395. (I have not seen this paper.)–This discussion is important for the history of the Greek liturgy, but does not really affect that of the Nestorian liturgy. Therefore it has been mentioned by the great investigator of the Byzantine rite, Dom. Pl. de Meester, in: *D.A.C.L.*, s.v. *Grecques* (*liturgies*), t. vi, col. 1602 [1924]. He expresses his judgement in these words: "M. A. Baumstark n'enlèvera pas la conviction que ses études restent entachées d'un *a priorisme* indéfendable".

anti-pneumatological. He says that 'Theod.' was the liturgy of Mopsuestia treated in the same way (p. 850; 848).[1]

In the large "Dictionnaire" of Dom. F. Cabrol-Dom. H. Leclercq a very short and unsatisfactory article is written by *V. Ermoni.*[2] It says something about the title of 'Addai' and about the mission in Edessa which has no connection with the liturgy. It is pointed out, that the Nestorian tradition ascribes the definite formulation "dans la forme abrégée" to Isho'yabh iii. Then a survey of the service is given (according to Renaudot). The pecularities of it are 1. the great intercession is placed before the Epiclesis and after the Anamnese; 2. bread and wine are covered by a separate cloth and then by a common one, called Anaphora; 3. at the beginning they use incense; 4. there are two fractions, during the first the bread is broken into two parts, during the second into more for the communion. Nothing more is said and no effort is made to solve the riddles, nor to give a survey of the problems connected with this liturgy and its history. The points he mentions, are not of great importance.[3]

The knowledge of the sources was greatly enhanced by two publications of Dom. *R. H. Connolly*. In 1905 Dr. Mingana had published two volumes with poems of the "Harp of the Holy Spirit" Narsai.[4] Among them some were of special interest for the study of the liturgy in general, viz. the numbers xvii, xxi, xxii and xxxii; and the first two for the Eucharist in particular. These four were translated by the well-known Syriac scholar into English, and so readily accessible. Hom. xvii contains a mystagogical exposition of the complete service without the Mass of the Catechumens (corresponding to: *L.E.W.*, p. 267–304); xxi some very short references, the Eucharist being treated here only as a sequence to Baptism. The former is by far the more complete and important. For in its extra-anaphorical part it runs parallel with 'Addai' (cf. the Table

(1) A Greek reconstruction of what he thought to be the original, is given in: A. Baumstark, *Die konstantinopolitanische Messliturgie vor dem ix. Jahrhundert*, in: *Kleine Texte* 35, Bonn, 1909. (2) V. Ermoni, *D.A.C.L.*, s.v. *Addée et Maris* (*Liturgie d'...*), t. i, col. 519–523. (3) Indispensable though *D.A.C.L.* is for the beginnings of Christianity and for the Western part of the Church, it is extremely disappointing to notice that the East has been treated in a very insufficient, and sometimes absolutely deficient manner. An article on the Nestorian liturgy is missing. It may be found in very few words s.v. *Orientales* (*liturgies*), t. xii, col. 2659 (9 lines!!). (4) A. Mingana, *Narsai homiliae et carmina*, Mosul, 1905, 2 vols. – R. H. Connolly, *The liturgical homilies of Narsai*, in: *Texts and Studies*, viii 1, Cambridge, 1909.

of Connolly, p. l–lxii) which would prove its age (the plus in 'Addai' is "elaboration"). If it were genuine! This is not absolutely certain. The homily is not found in the Mss. that formed the basis for the edition; it is ascribed by some authors to 'Abdisho' of Elam (13th century) and contains elements that are certainly of a later date than Narsai. Dr. Mingana[1] pointed out that the authorship of a 13th century-writer is impossible, as it is written in a non-riming style, while all verses of the 13th century are riming; but that it had been brought up to date by a man living some centuries after Narsai. The greater part of Connolly's introduction discusses this genuineness: the internal evidence of metre, the use of words and similarity of ideas with the homilies that are undisputed show to him that Narsai was the writer. Comparison with 'Addai' showed that it "runs parallel with the Liturgy of the Apostles except in the Anaphora portion", the deviations in the anaphora consisting in: shorter form of the Sanctus, a short prelude to the Institution, an Intercession in the same place, but much longer (agreement with 'Nest.' and 'Theod.'); an apparently different invocation. Connolly suggested that Narsai who is credited with a "Qudasha" by 'Abdisho', used here his own work that agreed with 'Nest.' in the intercession (Connolly assumed that Anaphora's of Barsauma and Narsai once existed, p. lxx). With regard to the anaphora of 'Addai' we have no answer that was older than N. As to 'Nest.' and 'Theod.' he holds the usual opinion. He has an important "Additional note" in which he compares the underlying liturgies of Narsai and George of Arbela;[2] the latter stands between N. and the present rite. He discusses interpolations viz. the Lord's Prayer (as to the Litany p. 24–25, cf. *Expos.* l. iv, c. 25, he does not consider it spurious); he shows that George knew 'Theod.' and 'Nest.' (a.o. with regard to the words of the Institution). A very valuable appendix was added by Mr. *E. Bishop*. It contains a storehouse of comparative material, inserting the information furnished by N. into the history of the liturgy of the ancient church. We may note the following observations: Narsai does not seem to know altarveils, the faithful could see everything (p. 90–91); N. stresses the feeling of "Awe and Fear" towards the Eucharist, like Chrysostomus (Antioch), contrasted with the Cappadocians whose feelings are different, 'Addai' is reticent and more on the side of

(1) See: Connolly, *l.l.*, p. xiii, where a letter of Dr. Mingana is quoted. (2) Cf. p. 44.

the latter (p. 94–97); he thinks that the "diptychs" were introduced into the mass in the East in the course of the 4th century (p. 113); that the canon was said in a voice not audible to the congregation in the 5th century in Persia in the same way as in Constantinople in the 8th (p. 126); about the moment of consecration he suggests that Narsai used an earlier East-Syrian terminology in which our Lord Himself is designated in the Eucharist as "the Spirit" (p. 148).

Some years later the exposition, generally ascribed to George of Arbela, was published by the same Benedictine together with a latin translation.[1] The fourth book explains the Eucharistic service, including the Missa Catechumenorum, in a mystagogical way.[2] It does not contain many historical references. In a very short introduction Connolly showed that it was baseless to assign it to George as there is no evidence in the Mss. In 1913 he thought 'Abdisho' B. Nahriz (beginning 11th century) was the writer; two years later he changed his opinion and then his conclusion was, that it was written probably in the 9th century by an unknown author (ii, p. 3).[3] Connolly did not add any investigation; only a sketch of an Nestorian church based upon these treatises was given (i p. 195–97).[4]

The second volume also contained the text of Abraham Bar

(1) *Anonymi Auctoris Expositio Officiorum Ecclesiae Georgio Arbelensi vulgo adscripta*, ed. R. H. Connolly, in: *C.S.C.O.*, ii 91–92, 1911–1915, 4 volumes.–About its contents, see p. 127. (2) Cf. *Expos.* ii, p. 2: (mysteria) "figuram alicuius rei praeteritae vel futurae depingunt" viz. the history of the world, culminating in the death and resurrection of the Lord, and its future till the second-coming of Jesus and the fulfilment of the Kingdom of Heaven.–Some remarks on "Mystagogy" will be found on p. 61, n. 3. (3) That it was not written by George (so since Assemani every author) is the prevailing opinion at the present moment, see: A. Baumstark, *L.G.*, S. 239 and: J. B. Chabot, *La Litérature Syriaque*, Paris, 1934, on the authority of Dom. Connolly. – I think his conclusion is right, though his arguments are absolutely wrong. (4) Not for its intrinsic value but because it has not been mentioned by Connolly and because A. Baumstark has a long note upon it, we state that the Ms. of which G. Diettrich saw the beginning, the rest being missing, was identical with *Expos.*, see: G. Diettrich, *Bericht über neu entdeckte handschriftliche Urkunden zur Geschichte des Gottesdienstes in der nestorianischen Kirche*, in: *Nachrichten von der kgl. Gesellschaft der Wissenschaften zu Göttingen*, phil. -hist. Klasse, 1909, S. 160–218, Ms. ii, described on: S. 170–182. A. Baumstark, *L.G.*, S. 200, Ak. 14, asked whether this writing had been identical with that in five books of Gabriel of Beth Qatraja though this is impossible if the agreement with George of Arbela must be explained by dependence of the former on the latter. The extracts from the text given by Diettrich are: S. 176 = *Expos.* i, p. 25, 23–26, 29 (text); 178 = 28, 18–30, 13; 180–181 = 31, 6–32, 5; the list of chapters is the same, expect ch. ix (Con.). The only difference was that Con.'s text was divided into seven books, the other into nine.

Lipheh's Exposition. This one seems to be incomplete; for Abraham b. Lipheh is quoted in the *Expos.* at various occasions in which these sentences can not be traced in the present edition. It is not sure when its author lived; Connolly decided for the 7th or certainly 8th century (ii, p. 150), but this supposition is extremely weak. The greater part of this work forms a Mystagogical explanation of the Eucharist in very short words.

Dr. *J. H. Srawley* dealt with the Eucharist before 431 A.D.; so a discussion of the Nestorian evidence did not fall within the scope of his book. Yet he thinks that 'Addai' is older than that date and has importance, as it comes from a region that "was not affected so early or to so great an extent as other regions in Eastern Christendom by the developments which were taking place in Greek-speaking lands during the fourth century". As characteristics he gives: no words of Institution; no parallel to the Anamnese; the Invocation has something in common with that of the Ethiopic Churchorder; the prayers before the communion prepare for the communion; there is no correspondence with the intercession for the dead.[1]

It is a matter of course that the history of Syriac literature of Prof. *Baumstark* contains a good many references, that are of importance for the history of the liturgy too. We need not register all the places where he mentions it. Of special interest are the following. 1) Giving his opinion about the authorship of Homily xvii of Narsai he says that it is impossible to find here a work of this Father as the underlying liturgy seems to suppose knowledge of 'Nest.' which was translated after his time;[2] it may be that he was the redactor of 'Addai' or made himself an anaphora. As to the "Qudasha" of Barsauma he thinks that this was not a lost Eucharist-formulary, but the prayer ascribed to him in the ritual of altar-consecration.[3] 2) The fragment of Bickel is important because it gives us an insight into the peculiar nature of the Eucharistic prayer of the Monophysites in Mesopotamia. Its structure is much akin to that of the Nestorian 'Addai'.[4] 3) His most important remarks are of course about the great reformer of the liturgy Isho'yabh iii. It is generally supposed by later writers, that he reformed the ritual of Baptism and Reconciliation that bear his

(1) J. H. Srawley, *The early History of the Liturgy*, Cambridge, 1913, p. 127–128.
(2) A. Baumstark, *L.G.*, S. 112 and S. 348 (the latter is the more important).
(3) A. Baumstark, *L.G.*, S. 108. (4) A. Baumstark, *L.G.*, S. 140.

name, as well as the Eucharist. It is said that he forbade to use any other anaphora besides the three and that he shortened a very long text, probably that of 'Addai' that gives really the impression of being handled in that way.[1] Baumstark gives a list of the Mss., none of them being older than the 14th century. Most of them give a normal text that cannot be traced earlier than the 15th century, while two of them show that there existed even in the 13th century a text different from the normal one (Ms. Seërt 38, lost; Berlin 38=Sachau 167, 1496 A.D.).[2] We pass over all the other names of those who have written anything about the liturgy and whose works are indicated with Baumstark's well-known carefulness; most of them will be adduced in the sequence of our book.[3]

Though[4] his remarks about the Nestorians as well as those on the Oriental Liturgies in general are very poor the name of Mgr. *L. Duchesne* justifies to summarize his opinion.[5] He distinguishes between the usage in Edessa (Roman territory) and Seleucia-Ctesiphon (Persian); about the former he says we are "médiocrement" informed (this is a rather mild expression!); the Nestorians have preserved much of the latter for us. A particularity is the place of the "Memento" before the Anamnese. The oldest literary documents are the four homilies of Narsai (xvii is considered genuine);

(1) For details see p. 126. (2) A. Baumstark, *L.G.*, S. 199–200. (3) See the many references in the footnotes which show how much the present writer is indebted to this safe and accurate guide through the complicated history of Syriac literature.–The same author's: *Vom geschichtlichen Werden der Liturgie*, Freiburg i, Br., 1922, does not deal with the Eucharist in particular. (4) G. P. Wetter, *Altchristliche Liturgien*, Göttingen, 1921–1922, 2 vols., can be omitted. His studies are in many respects very interesting and stimulating, but he "prends son bien où il le trouve", and mixes all liturgies without distinguishing the various centres and their history. What he thinks to be old, is put together. Consequently the Nestorians are not specially mentioned. The only point that is worth while to notice is his suggestion that the omission of the words of the Institution in 'Addai' and 'Fragment' is a very ancient characteristic (he refers to "Canones Hippolyti" and the exposition of Cyrillus Hieros.; i, S. 61). As a matter of fact they do not fit in with the conception which Welter supposed to be the oldest.– A reaction on this idea is given by Prof. Y. Brilioth, *Eucharistic Faith and Practice, Evangelical and Catholic*, London, 1930, p. 41 (the sole place in which he mentions the Nestorians), it may represent an ancient type, but "then it is a lingering relic, in a backwater of the church".–This book discusses in an admirable clear and succinct way the general idea of the Christian liturgy, but does not offer a detailed study of the separate types and their growth. Accordingly, it is not necessary to refer it in detail. (5) L. Duchesne, *Origines du Culte chrétien* [5], Paris, 1925, p. 70–72, (the first edition is of 1889; I think that the impression I used was made ± 1910 and that that of 1925 was a mere reprint).

he mentions the names of the various formularies saying that Renaudot's text was "imparfaitement éditée". The omission of the words of the Institution seems to be a "particularité, évidemment très importante", though they are found in the Malabar-rite and Narsai; it has not yet been explained. 'Addai' is the work of Isho'yabh iii, according to the Nestorian tradition, "dans la forme abrégée où nous la présente le texte attribué aux saints Addée et Maris". It does not give us any other information.

Prof. *Lietzmann* used as a basis for his masterly study in "Messe und Herrenmahl" the Urmia-text (and Brightman's translation) and the 'Fragment'. He paid no attention to the other sources and did not mention anything that can contribute to the history of the rite. He studied first the separate parts of the anaphora: 1) the words of the Institution are omitted from fear of profanation; because the Liturgy contains an Anamnese, the words must always have been spoken, even if they were not written down; 'Fragm.' points to the place of the Holy Words, but that is a "sekundären Formulierung" (S. 33–35); 2) the Anamnese is not separated from the missing words of Institution by a number of intercessions, which usually follow after the Epiclesis; this is a secondary formation and Lietzmann suggests that it happened after the time when the Institution was thought to effect the consecration instead of the Epiclesis; transition to the idea of offering is not found and this fact, as some other defects that seem to point to antiquity, makes it probable that it is a shortened edition of an older text (S. 54); 3) the Epiclesis of 'Addai' may contain a number of very old features (S. 72); 4) about the Euch. prayer, he judges as follows: "Als Ganzes betrachtet ist somit die Praefatio der Nestorianer ein spätes und überarbeitetes Mosaik aus bekannten Stücken (S. 148, cf. S. 145–149). Summarizing his work and marking its general results, he says that the Antiochene liturgy of the 4th century was built upon the text of 'Hippolytus' and that from this Ant. Lit. descend: Byz. (Bas. and Chrys.)–James (with several other Anaphoras); "möglich, dass die nestorianische Apostelliturgie eine ältere Form repräsentiert oder wenigstens Spuren davon erhalten hat: aber auch dann ist ihre wurzelhafte Verbindung mit dem antiochenischen Typ unbezweifelbar. Möglich ist freilich auch, dass sie einen ganz sekundären Charakter trägt" (S. 261–262). After the foregoing expositions of Lietzmann this conclusion or better: dilemma seems somewhat strange; and it seems as though he tends to prefer the second part. At any rate the wording shows that a definite answer cannot yet be given; this result is in contrast with that about the other liturgies, because his opinion about them seems fairly settled. In other words a reopening of the investigation does not seem to be superfluous. In connection with the use of the sources already referred to an examination of what the history of this rite may teach us, must precede.[1]

The year 1929 yielded two very important contributions. The famous bishop of the Uniate Jacobites Mgr. *Rahmani* who, a Syrian himself, was well known for his books on Eastern liturgies, published the results of a lifetime of study in this field.[2] Though this work betrays on every page the wide knowledge of its learned author, it cannot be denied that it contains many too rash conclusions, nor can it be called exhaustive. Many books and problems are clearly overlooked. As a matter of fact, time has not yet come for such comparative studies, as the necessary preliminary investigations have not yet been made. A special chapter deals with "la Liturgie des Syriens orientaux",[3] though its treatment was not so full as that of St. James. We summarize here his argument. The case whether the Apostles Addai and Mari converted the East, is left undecided. He mentions by the way the expansion and separation of the Persian Church. "Les Syriens orientaux se sont distingués des autres chrétiens par leurs rites et leurs cérémonies." According to the Nestorian tradition the Eucharistic Formulary, made by the Apostles, was abridged by Isho'yabh iii[4]; he observes that no trace whatever has been preserved from this abridged original. Next he gives a survey of the sequence and a reproduction of various prayers (French translation; syriac original in the footnotes) of the 'Fragment'. This shows no similarity neither in form nor contents with 'Addai'. An important witness of the prior history of the ritual is the Hymn xxi of Narsai (follows survey), for it contains a testimony of the great antiquity of some ceremonies and prayers in the Missa Fidelium.[5] He denies that Hom. xvii can be regarded

(1) H. Lietzmann, *Messe und Herrenmahl*, Bonn, 1926, *a.a.O.* (2) I. E. Rahmani, *Les liturgies orientales et occidentales*, Beyrouth, 1929. (3) Rahmani, *l.c.*, p. 335–376. (4) See below p. 126. (5) As such he mentions: a) Disposition of bread and wine on the altar; b) the presence of two deacons near the alter, one with a fan; c) the officiant addresses his prayers on behalf of the congregation to the Father; d) the Sursum Corda and its response; e) commemoration of living and dead; f) the preface ending with the Sanctus; g) the Epiclesis; h) the fraction of the host and its signing; i) the formel "the Love of God the Father

as genuine, external arguments (consult the survey of Connolly's book, p. 43) militate against it and ceremonies and prayers are mentioned that were introduced into the Nestorian liturgy in the course of the 7th and 9th century (their origin was mostly, he thinks, Byzantine).[1] Some specially Nestorian usages he sums up next: they have had for long a piece of leather instead of a sacred stone (he does not say since what time); he mentions some particulars of the clerical garments, based on George of Arbela, Expos., l. ii, c. 6; the response after the Sursum Corda: "Unto thee, o God of Abraham etc." (*L.E.W.*, p. 283), and: "The offering is being offered unto God the Lord of all" (*ibidem*); the response of the people: "And with thee and with thy spirit" (*L.E.W.*, p. 275); the prayers after the Sanctus are addressed to the Son. Byzantine influences may be seen in the following acts: making the sign from the right shoulder to the left, reciting secret prayers ending with an ecphonesis (said in a loud voice), the dialogue between the officiant and the deacon, the litany *L.E.W.*, p. 262–266, a translation of the Greek. Then he surveys the whole mass and his conclusion is: "qu'on ne peut faire remonter au dela du ixe siècle la liturgie nestorienne, dite des *apôtres*, étant donné que c'est le catholicos Jésus-jab qui l'a rédigée dans sa forme abrégée, et que ses successeurs jusqu'à Timothée ier († 823) y ont introduit des additions empruntées au rit byzantin." (p. 363). It is not of apostolic origin because its Euch. prayer is not addressed to the Father, contrary to the other liturgies of the Apostolic Sees and

etc."; j) the preface to the Lord's Prayer; k) the elevation of the host and the profession of faith; Holy is the Father; l) the communion "sub utraque" and a special formula for each of them.

(1) His arguments seemed to be convincing to a scholar as Prof. A. Rücker, see his review of the book, in: *O. C.*, 1928-1929, S. 281.–Dom. Leclercq (in his article in: *D.A.C.L.*, s.v. *Narsai*, t. xii, col. 884–888) simply reproduces the conclusions of Dom. Connolly and Mr. Bishop (see p. 43) and does not say a word on R's objections.–In this connection an article of Prof. F. C. Burkitt, *the Mss. of "Narsai on the Mysteries"*, in: *J. Th. St.*, 1928, p. 269–275, must also be mentioned. He drew attention to the difficult manuscript-tradition and added to Baumstark's list: Br. Mus. Add. 18716 with the same text as Cambridge Add. 2818, where Narsai's homily (the authorship has been proved by Dom. Connolly) is preceded by an "Editors Introduction to a 'classic'." The Mss. give an "edition of the ancient Homily on the greatness of the Mysteries, prepared by 'Abdisho', Metropolitan of Elam about A.D. 1222. The edition consisted in a set of prefaces, the insertion of rubrics in the text and also some additions which were almost entirely in prose" (p. 274). It may be that these new points give us the clue to solve the problem.

Justin, (an exception is made by the Coptic Lit. of St. Gregory). Nevertheless there are some expressions and ceremonies "de la plus haute antiquité": the dismissal not only of the catechumenes but also of the non-communicants; the allusion to the Eucharist without mentioning it in that formula; not: the Holy Things to the Holy Ones, but the Holy Thing (cf. Matth. vii 6; and Test. Domini, Ephraim Syrus, James of Sarug, p. 290); the officiant kisses the host at the elevation; he gives the communicants a part in their right hand; he distributes the remnants among the children after the communion. The omission of the words of the Institution is a "grave défaut" of the Mss., but found in the Nestorian authors and in the Maronitic liturgy of St. Peter.[1] Some remarks about the Uniate Missal of Mosul which follow do not concern us here. The 'Theod.' and 'Nest.' were translated by Mar Abba and Thomas as is written in the best Mss., but as the Greek originals are lost we do not know in how far this translation was an accurate one; at any rate the tradition was known in the 10th century. There are a number of places which are tabulated by Rahmani, showing the similarity of 'Theod.' and 'Nest.' with 'Bas.' and 'Chrys.' (p. 368–374). He ends by pointing out that the formula of consecration in 'Nest.' agrees with traditions of Irenaeus (adversus haereses v 33) and Ephraim (quoted by Rahmani on p. 207) about the Lord eating and drinking His own body and Blood. Resuming the arguments of Rahmani we find that: *a.* 'Addai' in its present form dates from the 9th century; *b.* it has some very old features; *c.* we do not know anything about this ancient liturgy; *d.* it is largely influenced by Byzantine elements. It would be right to accept these conclusions, if they were based on a study of the whole history of the liturgy in the Nestorian Church. This has not been done.[2] Nevertheless it must be admitted that these pages form one of the most profound investigations of the subject and its results must be seriously weighed by a future student.

The second contribution of the year 1929 was an article by Mr. *E. C. Ratcliff* on: "The original form of the anaphora of Addai

(1) In a special paragraph Rahmani pointed out the affinity between 'Addai' and the Maronitic liturgy of St. Peter, p. 322–332. "Cette ressemblance peut s'expliquer par deux hypothèses, ou bien les deux liturgies proviennent d'une source commune, ou l'une des deux dérive de l'autre", p. 332; R. adopts the latter possibility: the Maronites being the borrowers. (2) Ad Q. 105–116, it will be shown that this leads to mistakes which can prove fatal for the whole construction.

and Mari", called by the writer himself: "A suggestion".[1] After an introduction in which he points out the fact, that this church of the East was cut off from the rest of the church and had a development of its own, he says that 'Theod.' and 'Nest.' belong in their present form probably to the middle of the 6th century, "are examples of 'Jerusalemization', and are not representative of the earlier East Syrian tradition of Liturgy" (p. 24). Some words are said about the lack of Mss. and the relation of 'Addai' and the Malabar-liturgy. Then he goes on arguing that Narsai was deeply influenced by the Greek spirit; "the Eucharistic outlook of his xvii and xxi Homilies is in complete harmony with the spirit of Jerusalem" (p. 26). He is probably commenting upon his own anaphora that must have been of 4th century Greek, Jerusalem type. For while the framework is that of 'Addai', he leaves this text in the anaphora, because its prayers were not sufficiently developed to suit a mind acquainted with those Greek liturgies. This anaphora contains an Institution. The simplicity of 'Addai' is favourable to its priority. "There is no doubt that embedded in the present anaphora of Addai and Mari, there is to be found the Eucharistic prayer of the old Edessene Church" which was connected with Antioch (p. 26). Narsai has no place for ܟܘܫܦܐ; these have been interpolated. There remains: 1. an expanded Eastern form of "Sursum mentes"; 2. address of praise to the Trinity, the Maker and Saviour of men, leading up to the Sanctus; 3. thanksgiving; 4. intercession and oblation; 5. prayer expressing the significance of the rite including an Epiclesis. The place of the intercession does not form part of the oldest stratum: it consists of two parts ܟܘܫܦܐ and ܓܗܢܬܐ; the former is not found in George of Arbela, the latter is earlier, but without any connection: "we should note that with it disappears the only mention in the anaphora of the offering of Body and Blood of Christ by priest and people" (p. 27). Mr. Ratcliff tries to show that the Sanctus is an intrusion and the Epiclesis as well, because they have no links with the sequence of the foregoing and following thoughts and he suggests that they were a consequence of Hellenization. The result of this manupulation is: *a.* an address of praise to the name of the Creator and Redeemer; *b.* a thanksgiving for what has been done for us; *c.* a solemn following of Christ's example and a special commemoration

(1) E. C. Ratcliff, *The original form of the anaphora of Addai and Mari, a suggestion*, in: *J. Th. St.*, 1929, p. 23–32.

of His redemptive death and resurrection for which thanks are offered. "This is a εὐχαριστία pure and simple . . . The rite has no necessary connexion with the Last Supper; the connexion is rather with the Emmaus Supper"; it is not simply an Agape, but a δρᾶμα cf. Did. x. The prayers are addressed to the Son; this may be late, but may have some connection with early East Syrian tradition, cf. Acta Thomae.

Of course these are mere hypotheses, so is rather difficult to criticize them. It is not quite certain what Mr. R. understands by "Jerusalemization". It is remarkable that the result of this analysis brings out a type of liturgy that has some striking resemblance with the type analysed by Prof. Lietzmann in his "Messe und Herrenmahl" who called it the "Serapion-type". But these suggestions can only be made fruitfull, if we possess a critical edition of the text. Before that time it is useless to discuss them.

The most comprehensive collection of materials concerning the Eucharist in the Eastern Churches after the publications of Renaudot and Dr. Brightman, are the "Institutiones" of Prof. *Hanssens.*[1] He has not reedited the old texts nor brought to light unknown liturgical sources. But he has registered every detail found in the printed texts (formularies, canons, passing references) in an admirable way. He deals with the elements, preparation and administration of the Eucharist; describes the "usus praesens" and the history. He compared all the liturgical groups for every act seperately. Yet, it is not a history in the true sense, but a storehouse of facts.–It is a matter of course that all points of Eucharistic practices are also illustrated by Nestorian quotations. It is unnecessary to tabulate all these places as they can easily be found with the help of the index. Yet we may draw attention to the survey of the sources of the history of the liturgy during the 4th–8th century (p. 458–470) and of those of the 9th century till the present time (p. 501–502). He points out that we do not know anything of this rite before the 5th century, but probably it was not very unlike that of Edessa. He quotes the Canons 9, 13, 15 of the Synode of 410 A.D. He thinks that the 'Fragment' was an anaphora from the time before the introduction of Nestorianism and draws some parallels between this one and that of 'Nest.'. Next he gives an extract of Narsai's Hom. xxi, exhibiting a reformed ordo. Hom. xvii

(1) J. M. Hanssens, *Institutiones Liturgicae*, Tomus ii, *De Missa Rituum Orientalium* Romae, 1930; Tomus iii, 1932; *Appendix ad T. ii et iii*, Romae, 1932.

he thinks dubious, for the reasons referring to his critical bibliography (this has not yet appeared). He mentions the tradition about 'Theod.' and 'Nest.' and infers from Canon 14 of Ezechiel i (576) that everywhere the same liturgy was celebrated in Mesopotamia.[1] Then follow the Canons 1, 2, 3 and reference to 5 of Isho'yabh i to James Bishop of Darai. The account of Isho'yabh iii and his reformation is mainly extracted from the "Expositio"[2] (summing up the pages where I. is *mentioned*) with the other references (ch. vi, ii c) Next comes the survey of Abraham Bar Lipheh. The importance of the "Expositio" is mentioned, but it is not summarized. The "Responsiones" of George of Arbela in Vat. Syr. 150 are still inedited. Further he mentions a book "De Divinis Officiis" written by Ibn at-Tayyib and refers to the schoollaw of Sabarisho' ii (831–825). This list is not quite complete, for why has Timothy ii been omitted and other books registered already by Brightman; the Canons of John v are not described either. The third part consists for the larger part of a discussion: "De singulis missae orientalis ritibus"–Ch. xvi (p. 622–632) gives a complete list of the editions of the texts; of the names of the Anaphora's ('Addai'; Barsauma [lost]; Diodore of Tarses [lost; suppressed by Isho'yabh iii, but found in India at the end of xvith cent.]; Ephraim [lost; cf. p. 126]; Narses [lost]; 'Nest.'; 'Theod.'; 'Fragment'[?]); of the expositions; he mentions the work of Isho'yabh (cf. ch. vi, ii c); the origin of 'Addai' is Edessa and Leontius Byzant. refers to it (p. 31, n. 1); the origin of 'Theod.' and 'Nest.' is made known by the colophons in the Mss. (translated by Mar Abba and Thomas Edess. [± 550]); Prof. Hanssens refers to the opinion of Rahmani and the discussion of Baumstark without a further decision.

In a small paper[3] Prof. *Brightman* tried to show that the liturgy of Theodore of Mopsuestia mentioned by Leontius of Byzance is really 'Addai'; his argument is mainly based upon similarity in ideas, but I cannot find among them anything that is conclusive.

(1) This interpretation of the text is wrong. (2) Hanssens says, *l.l.*, p. 465: "In istis autem constitutionibus condendis, Iesuiabus earum rerum praesertim sollicitus fuerat, quae mysteria exprimerent; minus vero ei curae fuit, utrum omnia quae scripsisset diligenter perficerentur necne". This seems to be a reflex of *Expos.* ii, p. 33, cf. p. 109, but the last clause does not express the exact sense for in the text it is stated that he was silent about those which did not express a type. This makes a difference! Moreover, this is clearly the idea of the author of *Expos.*, and cannot be taken as the exact reproduction of the thoughts of I. iii. (3) F. E. Brightman, *The Anaphora of Theodore*, in: *J. Th. St.*, 1930. p. 160–164.

Mgr. *Tisserant* in his detailed history of the Nestorians [1] has only a very short note on their liturgy. The present Nestorian rite must have some connection with Antioch, "mais le développement s'en est fait d'une façon tellement indépendante qu'il n'y a plus grand' chose de commun au point de vue liturgique, entre les deux branches de l'Église de la langue syriaque" (col. 314). The words of the Institution have no importance for them, the real presence in which they believe being effected by the Epiclesis. Further he gives some information on their manner of communicating and the preparation of the Malkha (col. 315–316). With regard to the details of the Mass (which he did not discuss) he referred to an article "Orientales (messes)", by I. Ziadé, [2] an extremely poor contribution (at least about the Nestorians). The Persian rite has been simply incorporated with that of Antioch. As to its history he repeats the contents of R. Janin (see p. 37, n. 1; Col. 1436). He does not say a word on the commentaries or Mss. and the main part of it consists of a survey of the course of the liturgie in the different rites belonging to the groups of Antioch, Alexandria, Byzance. Of course the fact that the words of the Institution are missing is mentioned; several explanations are offered. Mr. Z. himself does not know where they should be said properly, but: "il semble impossible que le rite nestorien se serve pour la messe normale d'une anaphore ne possédant pas l'essentiel".

In 1932 Dom. *Engberding* [3] published a paper in which he pursued a clue given by Mgr. Rahmani, viz. the comparison of 'Addai' with the Liturgy of Peter of the Maronites. This study is a model of its kind from the point of view of method. His conclusion, reached after a careful collation, was: "Das gegenseitige Verhältniss der beiden Bearbeitungen muss dahin bestimmt werden, dass *m* durchweg die ältere und damit die ursprünglichere Gestalt bietet"; it has "grundlegende Bedeutung" since it exhibits the text of the old Patriarchate of Antioch before 430 A.D. which reigned over Mesopotamia and the Libanon. In passing it may be observed that the author does not believe that Isho'yabh iii curtailed the older texts.

Though it does not belong to the Nestorian Church properly speaking, we may mention here the find of Dr. *Mingana*, who dis-

(1) E. Tisserant, *D.Th.C.*, s.v. *Nestorienne*, t. xi, cf. p. 22, n. 1. (2) I. Ziadé, *D.Th.C.*, s.v. *Orientales (messes)*, t. xi, col. 1434–1487. (3) H. Engberding, *Urgestalt, Eigenart und Entwickelung eines altantiochenischen Eucharistischen Hochgebet*, in: *O. C.*, 1932, S. 32–48.–Its conclusion is opposite to that of Mgr. Rahmani, p. 50, n. 1.

covered the "Book of the Mysteries" or "Liber ad Baptizandos" of Theodore of Mopsuestia.[1] For it is well known that this book has not only been preserved by the Nestorians, but has also deeply influenced their ideas about the liturgy.[2] In his preface the learned Editor quotes the first half of Prof. Lietzmann's conclusion, pointing to the antiquity of the Nestorian rite, which is exactly his own opinion too and in favour of which he quotes also an arabic book of the late Archbishop Joseph David, entitled *Kuṣāra.* He states that "the Liturgy commented upon by Theodore has nothing in common with the Liturgy ascribed to him, in the East Syrian Church" (p. xiii).[3] The discussion of this liturgy which has been commented upon by Theodore, by Prof. Lietzmann[4] shows that it has the same structure as the ordinary Antiochene type.

The doctrinal aspect of the Nestorian Eucharist was considered by Mr. *M. Jugie.*[5] He has used all sources available and exposes their doctrine of the "presentia realis" (which all teachers have held though their statements about it were not always sound according to Jugie); of the "materia eucharistiae" (Malkha); of the "forma eucharistiae" and Epiclesis (the older Nestorians held the conversion by the words of Institution, but some of them as the present people attribute the consecration to the Epiclesis–we may quote here a typical sentence [p. 316]: "Inde colligere potes sacerdotes nestorianos, quoties hac liturgia utentur, revera non consecrare; quod Deus accidere ideo fortasse permisit, quod fideles nestoriani sine

(1) A. Mingana, *Commentary of Theodore of Mopsuestia on the Lord's Prayer and on the Sacraments of Baptism and the Eucharist, W. S. vi,* Cambridge, 1933. (2) Dr. Mingana mentioned only the quotations found in the Greek and Latin Church. It does not seem to be out of place to give the following Nestorian writers who quoted him: Narsai (xvii, once he is introduced by the author's name, but also the parallels given by Connolly from Cyrillus Hieros. are his); Abraham Bar Lipheh (*Expos.* ii, p. 165); Dadisho' (in: *W. S.* vii, p. 94–96); and in the statute for the schools of Sabarisho' ii quoted by 'Abdisho', *Nomocanon,* vi 3, the reading of this book is obligatory even for those who are studying medicine, cf. p. 147. (3) Against H. B. Swete, in: *Dictionary of Christian Biography,* s.v. *Theodore,* London, 1887, iv, p. 943, and: O. Bardenhewer, *Geschichte der altkirchlichen Literatur*[2], Freiburg i. Br., 1923, iii, S. 321, who states that 'Abdisho' in his catalogue does not mention it, but he thinks no reason to doubt the Nestorian tradition and Leontius. (4) H. Lietzmann, *Die Liturgie des Theodor von Mopsuestia,* in: *Sitzungsberichte der preussischen Akademie der Wissenschaften,* 1933. (5) M. Jugie, *Theologia Dogmatica Christianorum Orientalium ab ecclesia catholica dissidentium,* t. v, *De theologia dogmatica Nestorianorum et Monophysitarum,* Parisiis, 1935, p. 295–318.–A short, but convenient sketch of Nestorian literature will be found on p. 27–38! A remarkable statement of it is the following about Abraham bar Lipheh: "scripsisse videtur ante reformationes liturgicas Iso'yabhi iii" (p. 33). I do not know what are his reasons.

praevia peccatorum confessione ad sacram mensam accedere solent"); of the eucharist as sacrifice and mentions some (very few) practices. It should be said, that it is not a history of the Eucharist but only a small part of it. Its collections and comments must be used with caution, as the learned author uses the roman-catholic schemes and doctrines as a standard which prevents him and his readers to grasp exactly the Nestorian point of view.

What is the result of this variety of opinions? For this word expresses the impression left by reading the books quoted before, In spite of the fact that according to most authors the Nestorian liturgy is of great antiquity and forms a class of its own, a complete monograph of it does not exist, has not even been tackled.[1] Except for the mentioning of editions the above books and articles have not so much in common; the only point that often recurs is the omission of the words of Institution. It is of course impossible to submit all these pages to a thorough criticism; for this would compel us to go outside the Nestorian area and it seems to the present writer that many of the problems touched upon are not yet "spruchreif". Besides that many of the previous authors worked with insufficient knowledge of the sources. Therefore we will only try to form a clear idea of the points at issue. The formulation of the questions is in itself a criticism, as it shows where the learned authors who have written on this subject, fall short.

1) Direct sources: Three liturgies appointed by Isho'yabh iii; not one of the Mss. known so far goes back beyond the 13th century (this fact is not changed by the Mss. of the Mingana collection). 'Addai' was perhaps shortened by I.; 'Theod'. and 'Nest.' were translated from the Greek in the 6th century.[2] The question is: Have we in our Mss. and editions the unchanged tradition of I. before us? In other words have the 6–7 centuries not influenced their texts? Two forms of the texts are at our disposal: Urmia (Brightman) and Renaudot but a critical edition is wanting. They are not in all respects similar. Takhsa has the longer one. Which is the more original? Baumstark gives the impression as though Cod. Berl. 38 shows a totally different recension of 'Addai'; a

(1) Except by Bickel, cf. p. 37. The publisher Aschendorf, Münster i. W. announces a forthcoming volume of the: *Liturgische Quellen und Forschungen*, written by Prof. A. Rücker, *Die ostsyrische Messliturgien*, but without any indication of its character. (2) This is certain by manuscript-evidence.

perusal of this Ms.[1] and comparison with T. has not convinced me. Before speaking about *the* Nestorian Liturgy it must be fixed which text is the purest and oldest. The greatest difference may be found in the rubrics; generally those in T. surpass the rubrics of the others in length. 'Fragment' is practically useless, as it does not show historical connections, and everything that is said about it is mere conjecture; for the present it can only be used as a separate type but without great authority.

2) These questions lead us directly to the history of this rite: indirect sources. It can be divided into two periods: by the activity of Isho'yabh iii. It is good to take the chronologically reversed order: *a*) What changes has the liturgy undergone in the time from I. till our Mss.? *b*) What was the character of the reformation of I.? *c*) What was the pre-Ish. 'Addai' and its connection with the old liturgy of Persia and Edessa?

The answer to *a*) can be given, as the list of Brightman seems to give us help. Yet it must be cleared. It has become known that the exposition of George of Arbela (?) enables us to get a survey of the liturgy of his time (but see p. 127–128); the same may be said about the older one of Bar Lipheh (not mentioned by Brightman). The commentary of Narsai, which he stated to be lost, has been recovered in Hom. xvii according to some people, which would be an important evidence to the antiquity (pre-Ish.) of the parts of 'Addai' outside the anaphora, this latter being probably his own work; though interpolations are not to be excluded. Other scholars disputed this view and credited later times with this exposition. The question is still *sub-judice*. As to the "exposition of the services" by Isho'Bar Nun that was thought by Brightman to be a Eucharistic document (lost), this may have been a reform of the Daily Offices (Baumstark).[2] The ܩܘܕܫܐ of Bar Sauma is designated by a word of too vague a meaning to apply this without further comment to the Eucharist, since it means simply "Consecration" which may be said of various liturgical practices. Brightman also mentions an anaphora of Diodorus which is said to be referred to in the Acts of the Synod of Diamper; the Ms. Berlin 39 styles 'Theod.' as "of the interpreters Diodorus and Theodorus".[3] It might be that the

(1) I used a facsimile through the kind offices of Prof. Lietzmann of Berlin.
(2) A. Baumstark, *L. G.*, S. 220; – Or was this the *Expositio*, ed. Connolly, as seems to be the opinion of Assemani, *B.O.*, iii 1, p. 166 (apparently this has escaped the attention of Connolly). (3) Cf. A. Baumstark, *L.G.*, S. 120, Ak. 3.

same is the case in the Acts, so that we need not suppose it was a lost anaphora. 'Abdisho' ascribes[1] to Isaac of Nineveh a book "De divinis Mysteriis"; it is not known what this means; it may have been simply an ascetical work.[2] We may point to some books mentioned by Baumstark that seem to be lost or have not been examined yet: S. 218, Ephraim of Elam, a letter against the reception of the communion from the hand of Greeks and Jacobites; S. 240, Elias of Kashkar, a book on the "Mysteries of the Church" (nothing of it is known; is it too bold to venture that this book is the same as the "Expositio"?); S. 287, 'Abdisho' Bar Bahrîz, also an exposition (this was first identified by Connolly with his exposition; afterwards he retracted it and came to the conclusion referred to before); S. 311, John Bar Zô'bî, an other explanation in poetical form (preserved in several Mss.); S. 324, Ak. 5, a short exposition of the Daily Office and the Mass by 'Abdisho'. The "Pearl" of 'Abdisho' does not contain anything that is of interest for the history of the rite; it is dogmatical and shows the Nestorian doctrine about this sacrament in the 13th cent.

So we find that there are left from Br.'s list: the items of Vat. Syr. 150 and the book of Timothy ii. The latter has not found an editor yet.[3] We read the 4th book which deals with the liturgy, in: Codex Mingana Syriacus 13. It appeared that the analysis given by Assemani is not unsatisfactory. The questions do not contain any information that is actually of importance for the better knowledge of the history (the proper names mentioned by Assemani are the only ones occurring). In ch. 15 a commentary of the liturgy is given occupying nearly half the treatise; the explanation is very short. Of course it furnishes us with the outline of the liturgy of his days (as far as I could see it does not deviate very much from the ordinary form in T.; it goes without saying that this form is also of importance in collating Codex Berlin 38). At any rate it gives an interesting insight into the questions that were discussed in his time in the Nestorian church, e.g. 14: "Ad Patrem dirigi Orationes in Liturgia" (cf. the remark of Rahmani, p. 48–49). Some of them may be traditional, as appears from 16: "De Consignationibus", in which the same point is discussed that was treated some centuries before (it is cited ad Q. 89). Vat. Syr. 150 is left; nothing about it is

(1) *Ap.* Assemani, *B.O.*, iii 1, p. 104. (2) A. Baumstark, *L.G.*, S. 223. (3) A good number of Mss. contain it, cf. A. Baumstark, *L.G.*, S. 325, Ak. 8.

known except some information scattered in the "Bibliotheca Orientalis" (see p. 65). It is needless to dwell any longer about it as it will be the subject of the next chapters of our introduction.

We asked: what is the value of these writings for the "History of the rite"? Beforehand it must be fixed what is the exact meaning of "rite"; it can contain prayers and indications of liturgical actions. In most cases only the former category is examined but the latter also belong to the liturgy and these are susceptible of expansion. Besides that the liturgy is encircled by usages such as: Communion, Preparation of the Elements, etc. It is not advisable to give it too narrow a meaning. In this connection the Canons of John v Bar Abgare get their importance.

*b*) We are very badly informed about the character of the reformation of I. iii concerning the Eucharist. A provisional discussion of it will be given afterwards (p. ch. vi, ii c). A definite investigation of the subject must try to detect I.'s liturgical texts. If this has been done, one can test the opinion of Baumstark (copied by Heiler) that he acted under Byzantine influence (it may be asked whether this traces of Byzantine influence are real or merely due to the same origin, or are of a later date than I. iii).

*c*) Hardly anything based on facts (!) can be stated about it; some information may be derived from the Synodicon Or. along with the Hom. xxi of Narsai. At this point a decision about the genuinity of Hom. xvii is urgent. In how far is Rahmani right with his "ancient features"? Must one be satisfied with hypotheses? What is the relation between the opinion that 'Addai' is the ancient liturgy of Seleucia-Ctesiphon and the statement of Isaac, Canon xiii (quoted p. 118)? Is it possible to reconstruct an original form by comparison with other formularies? This is the more important for 'Addai' which is a complete liturgy while the others are merely anaphora-texts.

3) Not before a careful examination of these points has brought about what is the value of the printed texts and what can be separated as later intrusions, one may go in for an investigation into the filiation with other liturgical groups.[1] It is natural to do

(1) As to the study of the liturgical relation between the Nestorians and their neighbours, one should keep in mind that the Nestorian Church had a development of its own, but that churches were not in watertight compartments: there was intercourse between the Nestorians and the Jacobites (cf p. 17, n. 1, and p. 25, n. 1). A very interesting symptom of it is offered in our treatise Q 108. This relation must be taken into account and it seems to the present writer that the

so with 'Theod.' and 'Nest.', since it has been handed down that they originate from the Greek church. 'Nest.' was already subjected to a discussion between Prof. Baumstark and Prof. Schermann. As to 'Theod.' a careful comparison with the liturgy underlying Theodore's commentary must be recommended in spite of the verdict of Dr. Mingana who nevertheless left the final decision to professional liturgiologists. Are they really the liturgies of respectively Constantinople and Mopsuestia? In case of the latter it seems advisable to break away for the present from the statement of Leontius Byzant.; every interpretation of what he meant by "Blasphemies" was mere guessing. It is possible that Leontius who lived a century later[1] has made a mistake and it should not be overlooked, that he was a polemist! Perhaps "Blasphemies" must not be limited to wrong teaching about the dogmas; everything called by Theodore "Prayer" was *eo ipso* blasphemous for his opponent; what mattered was the interpretation of the same statements.[2] The case of 'Addai' is not so easy; it must undoubtedly be considered as the oldest, as was seen already by Renaudot, and provisionally as a separate type. Here we get back the dilemma formulated by Prof. Lietzmann. Perhaps it cannot be solved before more is known about the liturgical history of the Nestorians and the rival churches.

This concerns the *prayers* of the liturgy (in Lietzmann's book only those of the anaphora). Besides them there are the *acts*. These too must be submitted to a comparative research, keeping in view three questions: is this spontaneous development; or borrowing; or descent from common ancestors? In so far as I can see, the answer to these problems will be different from that mentioned before and will not corroborate it; other filiations and links will appear. At any rate it is wrong to neglect this growth of the rubrics etc. especially as these acts had a dogmatical meaning for later generations.

The Homilies of Narsai, the "Expositio" etc. were valued before

formula of Dom. H. Engberding, *Altantiochenisches Eucharistisches Hochgebet*, in: *O.C.*, 1932, S. 47: "der methodische Grundsatz der vergleichenden Liturgiegeschichte (ist): Wo in getrennten Kirchengemeinschaften ein gemeinsamer Text sich findet, ragt dieser in seinem Alter bis in die Zeit vor der Trennung hinauf" though right in many cases, should not be applied in a too simple or too doctrinaire manner.

(1) O. Bardenhewer, *Geschichte der altkirchlichen Literatur*, Freiburg i. Br., 1932, v, S. 9–13. (2) Compare for instance the totally opposite conclusions drawn from the same Nicene Creed by Nestorians and Jacobites.

only as sources to reconstruct the liturgy in use at a certain date. As a rule this is the only use made of these books. But it is not the end which their authors had in view (see e.g. the quotation on p. 127).

4) In this way we come to more dogmatical positions with regard to the Eucharist, viz. to the question: what is the meaning of all these actions and prayers? Does there exist a special doctrine about essence, aim and working of the Sacrament? What is the relation with the Mystagogy, i.e. the exposition of Eucharist? Is there a connection with Mysticism? The point must be considered whether additions have been made for dogmatical reasons. It is a matter of course that these questions must also be dealt with by way of comparison. This will explain much that is obscure.[1] The study of the Mystagogy or explanation of the liturgy is still waiting. Yet it should not be neglected as it reveals the feelings of the believers during the celebration.[2] From these sources it is obvious that the Nestorian teaching has not been so traditional as it is often thought[3] and that it changed through the ages (read: Narsai, Hom. xvii[?] and xxi; Abraham b. Lipheh; *Expos.*; and Timothy ii). The influence of Theodore (see p. 55, n. 2) and of Dionysius Areopagita, who is generally considered as the great teacher in these matters,[4] can be examined here. Then arises the question about the

(1) Cf. *Expos.* ii, p. 4, about this obscurity. (2) Cf. R. H. Connolly, *Two Commentaries*, p. x: "... commentaries on the whole Liturgy, which give a more lively picture of the manner in which the Holy Eucharist was celebrated by the Syrian Jacobites in the Middle Ages than the manuscripts, with their brief rubrics and limited scope can afford. In these commentaries we have, moreover, the ideas and sentiments connected with the celebration of the Christian Mysteries in the minds of living men."–Many Greek and Syriac commentaries are left which have never been investigated. Something of it in: F. Kattenbusch, *Mystagogische Theologie*, in: *P.R.E.*[3], xiii, S. 612–622 (*D.Th.C.* and *D.A.C.L.* do not contain an article; A. Wilmart, *D.A.C.L.*, s.v. *Expositio Missae*, t.v, col. 1014–1027 treats the Western church alone, a defect which is often found in this indispensable and magnificant work). (3) There is a marked difference between the Nestorians and the Jacobites. The latter have a strong chain of tradition as will be seen in reading Codrington–Connolly, *Two Commentaries* as compared with the Exposition of Dionysius b. Salibi (ed. Labourt). Of the former everyone has his own view (the same will be found in another department, p. 136, n. 1.); *Expos.* ii, p. 34 dares to say about his predecessor Abraham b. Lipheh: "Ab. in dementia sua"! (4) A. Ehrhard, ap. K. Krumbacher, *Geschichte der byzantinischen Literatur*[2], München, 1897, S. 141, says about Dionysius' influence on the Byzantine Church: "Den Ausgangspunkt derselben (Mysticism) bilden die mystischen Schriften des Dionysius Pseudoareopagites von denen sie ihre Eigenart, ihre kultisch-symbolische Richtung empfangen haben".–Dionysius was known in the Nestorian church (see: Timothei i Patriarchae, *Epistula* xvi, ed.

connection with Christology as discussed in several places of Babai, "Liber de Unione",[1] and others. In this borderland of liturgy and dogmatics one must always keep in mind the links with both.[2] For in the life of the church the one could not be thought of without the other. Practically nothing has been done so far in this field! The knowledge of liturgical hymns is connected with it. It will enable us to answer what is typically Nestorian,[3] what is the relation with the Antiochene school, and in what respect we may speak of a common "fond" with the other churches. By combining 3 and 4 the omission of the words of Institution can only be fruitfully discussed (it has also been omitted in Theodore's explanation).

We see several diverging sets of problems arising from the evidence, which cross each other in the study of the liturgy. Reviewing what has been done to solve them permits us to say that it is still the "least known of Eastern rites" (Brightman).[4] It is out of question to examine all these subjects in one book though we must be aware that all these problems are linked up with each other. We must begin at the beginning. Our attention is drawn by the question: *what are the contents, nature and meaning of the treatises con-*

O. Braun, p. 120 (in: *C.S.C.O.*, ii 67); xxxiii, p. 156; *W.S.* vii, p. 13–15; Isaac of Nineveh, tr. A. J. Wensinck, p. 114; but I do not believe that he had a far-reaching influence upon the liturgical explanation; in that connection he is never quoted.

(1) Babai Magni, *Liber de Unione*, ed. A. Vaschalde, in: *C.S.C.O.*, ii 61, Parisiis, 1915. (2) Dom. H. Engberding, *Die Kirche als Braut Christi in der ostsyrischen Liturgie*, in: *Orientalia Christiana Periodica*, Roma, iii, 1937, S. 5: "Man kan nicht behaupten, dass die wissenschaftliche Forschung das Gebiet der ostsyrischen Liturgie stiefmütterlich behandele. Im Gegenteil, die letzte Jahrzehnte haben manche, z. T. recht wertvolle Arbeit, herausgebracht (on S. 44–48 he gives a bibliography of the work of the last century; it contains all sorts of liturgical editions and studies, not only eucharistic.–With regard to the great task I cannot help thinking that these words of Dom. E. give too favourable a representation of the results attained). Und doch lässt sich nicht leugnen, dass alle diese Arbeiten, eine einzige ausgenommen, einen Bereich fast vollständig ausser Acht lassen: den der Theologie, d.i. *der systematischen Aufarbeitung und Untersuchung des in der genannten Liturgie niedergelegten religiösen Gedankengutes*". (3) Cf. this judgment of Renaudot, *L.O.C.*, ii, p. 565: "Liturgiae illae, prima ('Addai') praesertim, etiam in codicibus non admodum vetustis, inter multas, variique generis orationes vix ullam habent, quae Nestorianae doctrinae particulam aliquam repraesentet, una Nestorii excepta", and of A. J. Maclean, *E.S.D.O.*, p. xxv: "The infrequent occurrence of Nestorian language will perhaps surprise the reader .... we shall find no trace of heterodoxy in the following pages.... On the other hand, we find much that is quite inconsistent with true Nestorianism." (4) *L.E.W.*, p. x.

*tained in Vat. Syr.* 150. For we must first have a profound knowledge of the materials that can be disposed of, before we come to other questions, because otherwise the uncertainty will remain whether this unknown source will interfere with the results reached. In the following pages we propose to publish and comment upon the first part of them, the "Special Introduction" will discuss the problems involved. The plan to do so is evident. We must try to determine the exact date of the writing and after that ask whether its form or contents enable us to consider the whole book as a piece of evidence of the practice of some centuries before. The commentary will discuss the same for the separate questions and special points. Although the first part will be published, it is a matter of course that the author examined the other parts too, as will be seen from many places in which they are quoted.

## iii. DESCRIPTION AND COMPARISON OF THE MANUSCRIPTS

The text of the Nestorian treatise we are publishing here is based upon two manuscripts. One of these is deposited in the Vatican Library, where it is known as *Codex Vaticanus Syriacus* 150; the other manuscript lies in the Mingana-Collection at the Selly Oak Colleges' Library in Birmingham. Its class-mark is: *Mingana Syriacus* 566.

Before we pass to a description and comparison of these codices, we record for the sake of completeness that a third manuscript is known to have existed at one time at the Archiepiscopal Library of Seërt.[1] A short description from the hand of Mgr. Addai Scher has been incorporated by Dom. R. H. Connolly in his edition of the "Interpretatio Officiorum" of Abraham bar Lipheh. This MS. was designated by him as codex i.[2] It was a: "Codex chartaceus, saeculo ut videtur decimo sexto exaratus". It contained among various other items on different subjects: "Quaestiones de Eucharistia". They were anonymous and the same as the tract that is published here, as Dr. Mingana kindly informed me.[3] Together with the whole collection of which it formed a part this codex was burnt in the Worldwar in 1916.

*Description.* We now turn to those manuscripts which did not suffer the fate of so many oriental books, that were destroyed in the calamaties which befell Eastern Christendom at so many occasions, or perished through the carelessness of their owners. For the reader's convenience we may give the contents of the two manuscripts, so far as it is of interest for the present investigation. We follow their description as given in the respective Catalogues of their collections.

The beginning of the *Vatican* MS. was analysed by the Assemani's as follows[4]: "Codex in 8., bombycinus, foliis 215 constans, strongulis Syriacis exaratus, inter Orientales Codices ab Andrea Scandar in Vaticanam Bibliothecam inlatos, olim Tertius.

i. Georgii Arbelae et Mosuli Episcopi, Quaestiones de ministerio

(1) A. Scher, *Catalogue des manuscripts syriaques et arabes conservés dans la bibliothèque épiscopale de Séert*, Mosul, 1905. (2) *Expos.* ii text, p. 162, n. 1. (3) *Letter*, Birmingham, 9-3-1935. (4) St. Ev. Assemani et J. S. Assemani, *Bibliothecae Apostolicae Vaticanae Codicum Manuscriptorum Catalogus*, Pars i, Tomus iii, Romae, 1759 (reprint: Paris, 1927), p. 280-281.

Altaris . . . Quaesita et Responsa circa Consecrationem Ecclesiae, et Chrismatis: circa sacram Liturgiam, et Communionem Corporis et Sanguinis Domini, circa Panis Eucharistici confectionem, et Vini praeparationem: circa Officium Divinum, vespertinum, nocturnum, et matutinum: circa Sponsalia, et Benedictionem Sponsorum; et circa Exequias Defunctorum.

ii. Ejusdem Georgii Quaestiones de Baptismo fol. 39$^{b}$.

iii. Jaballahae Magni Patriarchae Chaldaeorum qui olim Nuhadrae Episcopus fuerat, Quaestiones de Baptismo, de Sacris Ordinationibus fol. 56.

iv. Ejusdem Jaballahae . . . Quaestiones de Sponsalibus, de Nuptiis, et de Sacra Liturgia fol. 66.

v. Jesujabi Arzunitae . . . Quaestio, an Eucharistia extra Ecclesiam sit deferenda fol. 93.[1]

vi. Georgii Metropolitae Arbelae et Mosuli, Quaesita de Communione in Paschate, fol. 94.

It appears from the Colophon (fol. 215) that this MS. was written Anno Graecorum 2020 (A.D. 1709). In the "Bibliotheca Orientalis" iii 1 and 2 various parts of this codex were extracted by Assemani:[1] from i: 1, p. 240, 242, 243, 244, 245, 248, 251, and a reproduction of several regulations (without quoting them) in 2, p. cccxvi, § 7; from ii: many sentences in his description of the Nestorian Rite of Baptism, in 2, p. cclxi-cclxx; from v: 1, p. 244.

Through the kind offices of Dr. R. R. Post, formerly of the "Nederlandsch Historisch Instituut te Rome", now Professor at Nijmegen University, it was made possible for me to study those parts of this codex in facsimile which are concerned with my subject and still unpublished, viz. foll. 1-40 and 65-94. The same scholar was so kind as to write me, that the state of this manuscript is very bad, and that it has been pasted over to save it from perishing. Except for a number of places which are absolutely ruined and where nothing is left but a hole, the codex is still very legible.[2] Some places where the reading was doubtful were collated for me upon the MS. itself by Prof. Georg Graf, to whom I wish to express my sincerest thanks for his kindness.

On closer examination one finds, that the codex has eighteen

(1) In: *B.O.* iii 1, p. 111–Assemani gives a better summary: „Fragmentum de modo Eucharistiae infirmis administrandae; de confectione hostiae Eucharisticae; de Baptismo in Ecclesia, ubi Baptisterium desideratur, conferendo; deque Liturgia a solo Sacerdote minimae celebranda". (2) *Letter*, Rome, 3-6-1934.

lines to the page, and that Assemani's statement, regarding the first four treatises at least, needs a small but extremely important addition. It is a fact (which is impossible to infer from his report) that the authors' names, both of George of Arbela and of Yaballaha were added in the margin by a later Maronitic hand, as Prof. Baumstark already observed with regard to the first item.[1] These names, therefore, are suspect from the point of view of textual criticism. As to the following two treatises, here the proper name forms part of the text itself.

The account of Assemani does not shed any light on the origin of this codex. So we are at a loss about its ancestry.

The codex *Mingana Syriacus* 566 has been analysed by Dr. Mingana in the Catalogue of his collection.[2] In this case too it is not necessary for our purpose to quote his description in full. The contents of this manuscript (size 236 × 177 mm with 199 leaves and 18 lines to the page) are rather miscellaneous. The items our study is concerned with, are the following:

*A*. Ff. 1b-34a: Questions and Answers dealing with the Eucharistic elements and with liturgical subjects . . . The questions are asked by a young scholar and answered by a venerable teacher.

*B*. Ff. 34a-46a. Theological Questions and Answers dealing with baptism.

*C*. Ff. 46a-66b. Theological and liturgical questions and answers dealing with baptism and liturgy and attributed to the Patriarch[3] Isho'yabh the Great who had been Bishop of Nuhadrāyé.

*D*. Ff. 66b-67b. Similar questions and answers by Georg, Metropolitan of Arbel and Mosul. (At the end of all the above questions and answers is the following subscription [fol. 67b]: ܫܠܡ ܒܥܘܕܪܢܗ ܡܪܢ ܘܒܪ̈ܚܡܘܗܝ ܥܘܗ̈ܕܢܐ ܕܬܫܡܫܬܐ ܕܡܕܒܚܐ ܘܫܪܟܐ [The description of] the observances of the service of the alter and the rest is brought to a close through the help and mercy of our Lord.)

"Dated (fol. 198b) 17th June 1931, and written for me (through the deacon Matthew, son of Paul) by the deacon Joseph, son of Thomas, son of the deacon Sīpa, of the family of Baith Abūna, of the small town of Alkosh, in the time of Pope Pius xi and of the

(1) A. Baumstark, *L.G.*, S. 239. (2) A. Mingana, *Catalogue of the Mingana Collection of Manuscripts*, Vol. i, Syriac and Garshūni Manuscripts, Cambridge, 1933, Col. 1070-1076. (3) Lit.: the Catholicos, an East-Syrian name of the Primate; cf. *D.A.C.L.*, s.v. *Katholicos*, t. viii, col. 686—689.

Chaldaean . . . Patriarch Emanuel ii. Copied from a MS. of the monastery of our Lady, which is dated 1994 of the Greeks (A.D. 1683) and which was written in the monastery of Rabban Hormizd by the priest 'Abdīsho' . . . Bold East Syrian hand. Fully voweled. Headings in red. Profusely rubricated. Fairly broad margins" (col. 1076).

For a clear apprehension of this Colophon it is necessary to know that Dr. Mingana had a manuscript very carefully copied by the mentioned deacon Joseph in cases he could not acquire the manuscript itself, so that he got "a faithful copy".[1] The codex which is meant is no. 93 in the list of Mgr. A. Scher.[2] A copy of a certain part of it was used by Dom. Connolly as codex ii of his edition mentioned before.[3] Nothing else of this manuscript has been published, as far as I know.[4] Although we have in codex Mingana Syr. 566 a very young manuscript, its text is certainly older than that of the Vatican one.

Henceforth these manuscripts will be designed by the symbols V. and M.

The first thing to do is to make a *comparison between these two codices*. From the full analyses as given in the Catalogues it does not seem likely as though they have much in common. There is only one striking conformity viz. V. ix = M. S.[5] The other names are totally different and the divisions show that V. is not a direct copy of the "Vorlage" of M.[6] We are obliged to recognize the existence of two manuscripts which have not been copied from the same original. Although it is possible that there exists a conformity in the other treatises in spite of the differences in names and divisions (which may be due to copyists), this fact has no further importance for the investigation with which we are concerned in this book. Henceforth we shall deal only with the parts mentioned before which treat of *Questions about the Eucharist*. We find these in V.: i-vi = M.: A.-D. On collating these texts in both codices it becomes apparent that they are for the greater part the same, a result not

(1) Cf. A. Mingana, *Catalogue etc., Introductory Note*, p. vi. (2) A. Scher, *Notice sur les manuscripts Syriaques conservés dans la bibliothèque du Couvent de Notre-Dame-des-Sémences*, in: *Journal Asiatique* 10, 8, p. 55-82. (3) *Vide* p. 44, n. 1. (4) We cannot speak here with certainty in view of the fragmentary character of tradition which has generally not much respect for the names of authors. (5) Cf. A. Baumstark, *L.G.*, S. 220 Ak. 2. (6) Thus the Exposition of Abraham b. Lipheh is wanting in V. (but was contained in the Seërt MS. which, however, has no further relation with the others).

to be expected from the descriptions of the catalogues. First we start upon a careful comparison of these parts as far as the contents are concerned (A), afterwards we shall ask whether the part we propose to publish might offer some special text-critical points (B).

*A*. For the sake of clearness a list of the names in the headings had to be made:

| | V. | | M. |
|---|---|---|---|
| i. | anonymous; in margin: George of Arbela | = | anonymous. |
| ii. | ,, ,, ,, ,, ,, ,, | = | ,, |
| iii. | ,, ,, ,, Yabhallaha the Great, bishop of Nuhadra | = | Isho'yabh the Great, Bishop of Nuhadrāyé |
| iv. | ,, ,, ,, ditto | = | |
| v. | Isho'yabh i of Arzun | = | |
| vi. | George of Arbela | = | George of Arbela |

The last and the first two items (not taking into account what is written in the margin of V, though it needs to be asked whether this addition is right or not) agree in both MSS. They deviate from each other in the rest where only the *names* of Isho'yabh and "the Great, Nuhadra" are points of contact. Presently, viz. in the next parts of our investigation we shall answer this question regarding the authors. For the present moment we are only concerned with the differences between the two manuscripts.

We may say a word on the note contained in M. after item D. What is the meaning of this reference? The easiest explanation of "Observances of the Service of the Altar" is that these words were culled from M. fol. 1b, and that "the rest" includes Baptism, marriage etc. as a matter of minor importance. The result would be that in (one of) the ancestor(s) of M. these subjects were reckoned as a unit by a copyist, not formally but materially.[1]

We may register in i the following external differences:

*A*. The reversion of the order of the questions 10-13, as follows: M. 10-11-12-13 and V. 12-13-11-10.

*B*. Q. and A. 24 is omitted in V.

*C*. V. has in Q. 41: "Question" instead of "Solution", and goes on with this change until Q. 44 after which he returns to the right track.

(1) The possibility that the Canons of John b. Abgare once stood in this place (as in M. viii), but were left out, seems to be less probable, as their name was: "Canons and Observances of the Altar".

*D.* In Q. 46 V. has not the "Solution" but puts this in the place of Q. 47.

*E.* V. omits the Solution of Q. 47 and Q. and S. 48; consequently we get a very queer change for V. goes on to write "Solution" instead of "Question" etc.

*F.* Something similar has happened elsewhere: fol. 29b18–30a1 (Q. 112). Here the contents of the Q. and "Solution" have been omitted and the word "Question" is immediately followed by the "Answer" and consequently the text is unintelligible.

*G.* The concluding rubric of the treatise at page 34a is omitted.

We pass ii and iii as irrelevant for the present investigation. Questions about the Eucharist return in V. foll. 66–93 = M. 51–66. V. shows in these pages a considerable plus over M., viz. *twelve* questions. These additions do not give the impression of being interpolations. On the contrary they fit in very well in the preceding context at least so far as one may venture to affirm about this Quaestiones-Literature [1], its structure being always loose. Yet the possibility cannot be ruled out that a reader at some later time should have provided his copy with some new questions in places which seemed to him wanting a further explanation. But still, the former suggestion seems more probable. I am inclined to the view that M. omitted these pieces which seemed superfluous. I may refer to the fact that M. or his "Vorlage" obviously changed the text of V. fol. 93b in such a way that not only the inscription of V. was left out, perhaps because the name of Isho'yabh was found already at the beginning of iii, but that also a part of its first Q. was affected. Consequently the text in M. was thrown into confusion and its sense destroyed, while V. has kept the right order.[2] In view of the present material it cannot be settled what reason compelled the copyist. Dogmatical corrections[3] (the writer of M. is, as appears from the colophon, a Uniate = Chaldean = a Nestorian, subject to the See of Rome) are out of the question. The choice remains between carelessness of the copyists or the possibility that the first author himself should have given at one time a revised edition.

In surveying these two parts we observe the remarkable fact that

(1) About the Questions *vide* ch. v. (2) This regards only the collation of V. and M.; but this is not sufficient as the Arabic tradition is different, cf. p. 121–122. (3) They are very often found but almost exclusively in dogmatical statements and names, cf. e.g.: A. J. Wensinck, *Mystic Treatises of Isaac of Nineveh*, Amsterdam, 1923, p. xvii, and: A. Mingana, *Early Christian Mystics*, *W.S.* vii, Cambridge, 1934, p. 74-75.

while i shows only very unimportant changes, those of ii are of a different nature and contain a certain amount of new information. This may be due to the two treatises having once circulated independently. Their union may have taken place at a later date. In this connection it should be remembered that each of them has its own conclusion and that codex-Seërt contained only the first group. But all these suggestions are merely hypothetical.

*B.* I have given the text of the best written manuscript M. in facsimile[1]. This text has served as a basis for my translation. This procedure was justified by the following reasons: 1. It is a copy of the elder codex; 2. According to the result reached in *A.* it seems that M. has the better text, for this part at least; 3. A detailed study of the variants as found in V. and M. cannot be decisive in favour of one, only two codices being at our disposal, but M. seems in most cases to have the text that should be preferred.

This last point needs some further explanation. Appendix i shows a table of the places where V. deviates from the standard-text. Whatever was of some importance for the translation has been referred to the foot-notes.

This list does not register the fact that V. often has "Answer" where M. uses the word "Solution" or the reverse, this change being of rather small importance. Yet we may mention these places here:

| | |
|---|---|
| V.: Answer<br>M.: Solution: | 28× at the questions: 27, 28, 29, 38, 49, 53, 63, 65, 66, 67, 69, 73, 74, 75, 76, 78, 80, 86, 88, 89, 90, 91, 97, 98, 99, 100, 102, 103. |
| V.: Solution:<br>M.: Answer | 4× at the questions: 16, 17, 105 and 117. |

In overlooking this series one cannot say that either manuscript has a preference for a certain terminology. Both seem to use these terms at random and I have been unable to detect a reason for these variations. It appears that both words were considered to be interchangeable. In the next paragraph some works of Greek origin will be dealt with; the same change, viz. between ἀποκρίσις and λύσις will be found there.

Still another kind of differences has not been specially noted. V. (and this fact is not a favourable presumption for the text of this

(1) Words of the MS. in red have been underlined.

manuscript) seems to have been written, especially in the second part, by an untrained copyist. Consequently there are many places in which he began a word on one line, but having written two letters he saw that the space did not suffice. He then wrote the word on the next line and marked the preceding letters by a circle of dots. He records this for the sake of completeness, though it is of no further importance.

That the text of V. is not very good, is proved by a number of mistakes in which Syriac words were written, that have no meaning in the sentence, cf. e.g. Q. 69, 84, 105 ܫܪܝ in stead of ܫܘܪܝ, "end" in stead of "beginning".[1] The number of mistakes in M., see: $2^{b}1$, $9^{b}14$ is considerably smaller.

In one instance I ventured to go against the unanimous witness of V. and M., viz. in Q. 83-84; the context shows clearly that "Answer" and "Question" have been left out. It may be that something of the same character happened in Q. 37 where we should add: "Question" before "I saw", and "Answer" before "This"; but in this case one cannot say that the sequence of thought is confused. The text of the manuscripts gives a sufficient sense. These facts raise the question of the origin of our MSS. Both copies might possibly descend from one and the same codex. The evidence, however, is too small for certainty on this point. The common source lies further back than the direct fathers of the present manuscripts; perhaps it was due to the author.

We have arranged our list of variants under some heads giving now a few illustrations for each of them:

1. A number of places show a reversion of the order of the words, such as is common in many manuscripts: M. $4^{b}6$, $6^{a}3$, $8^{a}8$-9 etc. (not marked in the foot-notes).

2. At some places an accusative is expressed in M. by ܠ which has been neglected in V.: $17^{a}8$, $21^{b}4$, this use of the preposition being facultative.[2] In several places the reading of either manuscript

(1) Have we a similar case in ܡܬܚܫܝܢ instead of ܡܬܚܫܚܝܢ M. $25^{b}13$ and $29^{a}18$; this form as it stands can only be derived from ܚܫ to suffer, pt. Ethpe'el; but this has nothing to do with "to use" which is required by the sentence. Unless a verb ܚܫܐ is not registered in the Dictionaries, as is the case with ܟܡܝܪܬܐ M. $20^{b}9$–V. variant reading in $15^{b}6$; ܬܢܘܪܬܐ M. $19^{a}3$ where V. has the ordinary ܬܢܘܪܐ. (2) Th. Nöldeke, *Kurzgefasste syrische Grammatik* [2], Leipzig, 1898, § 288.

varies only orthographically: 8a2, M. ܒܪܬܗܢܘܬܐ–V. ܒܪܬܗܢܘ;[1] 8a10, M. ܡܠܟܬܝ–V. ܡܠܟܬܐ;[2] 8b 15, M. ܠܐܢܛܠ–V. ܢܛܠ;[3] 16b12, M. ܡܚܙܝܬܐ–V. ܐܦܝܬܐ.[4] In other cases one manuscript has the object-suffix immediately with the verb while the other writes it separately (or with the substantive itself): 11b1 (not marked in the footnotes).

3. Likewise we did not mention in the footnotes the differences in the use of conjunctions such as ܐܦ, ܕܝܢ, ܐܘ, ܘ; it being well known how easily such words are inserted or left out in copying. Both manuscripts vary here without a chance of some characteristic of private or peculiar style. The same holds good for the change of prepositions having the same meaning.

4. Various places show differences in the use of synonyms. For examples see: M. 33b17 ܢܣܝܢܐ = V. ܐܦܣܩܘܦܐ; M. 16a4 ܦܘܪܩܢܐ = V. ܫܘܬܦܘܬܐ; M. 11b4 ܗܦܟ = V. ܐܬܐ; M. 10a7, b1 ܫܡܫ = V. ܫܡ; M. 8a14 ܢܦܫ = V. ܦܓܪ; M. 22a12 ܦܘܪܫܢܐ = V. ܦܘܪܩܢܐ; M. 32a2 ܟܠܗ = V. ܡܠܬܐ. We choose some very conspicuous instances, some of which may have exegetical consequences. It is important that these cannot be derived from the same original MS.

5. Next comes a number of places where either M. or V. have a surplus. All these cases are marked in the footnotes. Some of them are but extensions of the quotations from prayers. This is a characteristic of V. This MS. often quotes extensively where M. has only the first two words (cf. M. 5a13, 31a3) and in some cases it offers a text which is not found in "Takhsa". This fact is only remarkable because it shows the variety existing even in the 10th cent. The same is found in the Office of Baptism.[5] The reverse, however, is also found; V. omits in several places: "and in the name of the Son etc."

The value of these variants for the text is but slight. In contrast with the greater part of the cases of the former category,[6] it requires notice that V. has a number of additions in the beginning but that the number of omissions compared to M. was growing as it went on. These omissions do not generally effect a change in the meaning of the sentences because the lost words merely repeated things already said. It is, therefore, often difficult to decide about the original text. Yet we are justified in saying that the rule: "lectio brevior potior" does not hold good here. There are a number

(1) *Ibid.*, § 202 I 7. (2) *Ibid.*, § 202 D. (3) *Ibid.*, § 155. (4) Cf. J. Payne Smith, *Dictionary*, s.v. (5) Cf. G. Diettrich, *Taufliturgie*, S. 65–66, and elsewhere. (6) Cases mentioned sub 3 are not taken into account.

of places in V. which show clearly that this codex has left out typical Syriac epithets (e.g. $2^{b}15$). One might quote evidence from other Syriac manuscript copies showing omissions of one half of a paralellism of words for the sake of brevity. This tendency is evident in V. in various places, e.g. M. $13^{a}18$-$b1$; $15^{b}9$-10; I think almost everyone of V.'s omissions (as far as they are not mere mistakes) should be explained in this way. It is not so easy to decide, whether the same is true for M.; the possibility, however, (see Q. 100) should not be rulled out. At any rate, I could not find any other reason for the origin of these variant readings.

6. Finally V. has in some places (viz. Q. 10 end, Q. 16, Q. 17, Q. 52) extensive stretches of "varia lectio" or rather additions. Their origin has not become clear to me.

In surveying this matter and carefully weighing its critical implications the choice of M. as the leading manuscript may certainly be justified, *as long as a third independent witness cannot be found.* The origin of variants like those sub 4 and 6 remains a problem. Did they arise from dictation? One might prefer this guess, as it could also serve as an explanation of those sub 3 and 5.

## iv. THE WRITER AND HIS TIME

We observed in the previous chapter that neither of the manuscripts of the treatise has an author's name prefixed, but that George of Mosul and Arbela was mentioned as its author by a later Maronitic hand on the margin of V.

The first author who published some information about our treatise was, as has been said before (p. 65), J. S. Assemani.[1] In his "Bibliotheca Orientalis" and in his "Catalogue" he accepted the above tradition concerning the writer without any criticism. His opinion has been generally received. Dr. Wright has borrowed it from him,[2] so did Prof. Brightman[3], Dom. Connolly[4] and some time ago J. B. Chabot[5] and Prof. Hanssens.[6] Prof. Duval is silent about this question, since he did not include liturgical writings in his History of Syriac Literature.[7] In his exhaustive handbook of Syriac Literature Prof. Baumstark uttered some doubts. He expressed himself as follows: "Dafür dass er (George) sich in gelehrter Arbeit mit demselben (liturgical study) beschäftigt habe, bieten, da er als Autor nur von einer späten maronitischen Hand bezeichnet wird, Beantwortungen von 'Fragen über den Dienst des Altares' so wie von solchen über Taufe und Osterkommunion keinen sicheren Beleg", referring to V.[8]

Having reproduced the current opinions on the author of our treatise as found in the handbooks we must try to settle this question. The obvious questions are: What is known about this George of Arbela? What are the external witnesses except the doubtful note in the margin? What is the internal testimony of the treatise itself?

i. All the sources on George of Arbela have been brought together and analysed by Prof. Baumstark.[9] He was ordained a bishop of the well-known See of Mosul and Arbela by the Catholicos Emmanuel (938-960). Twice (in 963 and 987)[10] he was a candidate for the highest office of the Nestorian Church, but he never issued victoriously from the intrigues during these choices (we may note

(1) Cf. about this family L. Petit, in: *D.A.C.L.*, t. i, col. 2973-2981. (2) W. Wright, *A short History of Syriac Literature*, London, 1894, p. 231, n 3. (3) F. E. Brightman, *L.E.W.*, p. lxxx. (4) R. H. Connolly, *Expos.*, II b, p. 2 (though this applies to V ii). (5) J. B. Chabot, *Littérature syriaque*, Paris, 1934, p. 116; he does not consider the *Expos.* to be a work of George. (6) J. M. Hanssens i, p. 501. (7) R. Duval, *La Littérature Syriaque*[3], Paris, 1907, p. xvi; at least I think this is the reason though he mentions, *l. l.*, p. 393, the *Expos.* as a work of George. (8) A. Baumstark, *L. G.*, S. 239; Ak. 6: iii° should be corrected in vi°. (9) A.

that this intriguing was usual under these circumstances). He died probably in 987. Further, he is mentioned by the Nestorian writer 'Abdisho' and in several MSS. as an expert in ecclesiastical law, redactor of the Daily Office of 6th August[1] and compiler of some prayers and hymns. The quotation from Baumstark puts the "Questions about Easter-communion and Fasting" among the "dubia". But there is, to our view, no sufficient reason to do so. We have been unable to detect any internal grounds against his authorship. Both manuscripts tell us that follow: "ܡܢ ܫܘܐ̈ܠܐ ܕܡܪܝ ܓܝܘܪܓܝܣ ܡܝܛܪܘܦܘܠܝܛܐ ܕܐܪܒܝܠ ܘܡܘܨܠ = (Some) of the questions of Mar George Metropolitan of Arbela and Mosul" and this is part of the text, and not: in *one* manuscript, and by a later hand in margine! It follows from this heading that we find here an extract from a larger collection.–We have already mentioned (p. 44, n. 3), that the authorship of the extensive and important "Expositio Officii Ecclesiastici" is no more ascribed to him since its publication by Dom. Connolly. These are the facts known thus far.

ii. Consulting 'Abdisho' one discovers that this author has mentioned him in his "Catalogue" among the Canonists (§ 192 Collectores Canonum).[2] This passing glance does not mean much as A. does not say a word about George's other, undoubtedly genuine, writings. J. S. Assemani treated George in his "Appendix ad Catalogum Ebedjesu Sobensis". This "Appendix" contains more than one well-known name which 'Abdisho' had skipped over. But Assemani only gives a detailed analysis of the "Exposito"[3] and does not speak about our treatise. This did not happen intentionally for in his "Catalogue" of the Vatican MSS., at a later date, Assemani shows no doubt about the authorship. My investigation

Baumstark, *L.G.*, S. 239. (10) Dr. Wright, *Syriac Literature*, p. 230-231 wrongly says that he was also a candidate in 961 (three times altogether); but *B.O.*, ii, p. 452, to which he refers, does not contain a word about it.

(1) In Ak. 3 of Baumstark it must be added that it also is found in the manuscript that was examined by G. Diettrich, *Bericht u.s.w.* (cf. p. 44, n. 4), S. 268 and N. 1. With all probability he is meant in the *Letter* of Elias of Nisibis (cf. p. 83, n. 7), in: *O.C.*, 1913, S. 259 as the man who changed prayer during the consecration of a Katholikos. cf. p.. (2) Ed. *B.O.*, iii 1, p. 279.–About this 'Abdisho' see: A. Baumstark, *L.G.*, S. 323-325. (3) *B.O.*, iii 1, p. 518-540; that on Baptism is not mentioned either; this fact probably induced G. Diettrich, *Die nestorianische Taufliturgie*, Giessen, 1903, S. 61, to mix up the *Expositio* (written in questions) and the *Quaestiones*. But the criticism of Dom. Connolly, *Expos.* ii, p. 3, is too severe, as the critic himself is liable to a grave mistake ascribing the *Quaestiones* to George of Arbela.

has not provided me with any external witness to throw light upon this matter. So we have to consult the writing itself.

iii. In its *Introduction* something is told about the origin of this work. The information furnished by it is as follows: The person who answers the questions is an "Old man" who may be counted among the teachers of a school since he is confronted with a student. The starting point is that the service of the church is neglected and not administered according to the tradition of the Ancients, because many people have lately become priests who were not sufficiently qualified, and did not possess the indispensable knowledge of the Canons and Formularies in question. Every one is doing what seems good to him and nobody takes care. Ignorance and arrogance are the characteristics of these priests, as another place tells us (cf. Q. 119). The author has been summoned to cope with this evil as he has acquired a sound knowledge of the exact liturgical tradition which he has received from the Ancients. He will surely stop the mockery of the ignorant. Though acknowledging his own unworthiness and stupidity, he is willing to tell what he saw from the Ancients with whom he once performed the service of the altar.

Some points are clear from this, yet in reading this preface we are struck by its very traditional tone. This complaint about the low standard of the present clergy compared with the excellence of the past is one that is found over and over again in Nestorian and other literature: the race of the "laudatores temporis acti" never dies. The modesty of the author is also a typical and indispensable part of such a preface. Arrogance and ignorance are generally imputed to opponents.[1] Does the schematical character of this framework invalidate this information? This is one question. But there remain other points to consider.

*Proper names* are generally fit to give a clue. The names Ḥazza and Nineveh in Q. 116 do not yield more than that our treatise must have been written before A.D. 1200, since Arbela which took the place of Ḥazza was founded at that time.[2] – The Tigris (Q. 78, 79) is specially mentioned among the rivers into which dust and ashes are thrown; in V. it is even the only one. So it is obvious to assume that the writer and his pupil lived near this river. – The books quoted are only the "Canons" (preface, Q. 48) or "Admonitions"

(1) For details cf. the Commentary on this place. (2) Cf. the Note ad Q. 116.

(Q. 49) which the author has also in view elsewhere without naming them. These Canons may be identified with those given by John v bar Abgare (900-905)[1].—The persons which our text mentions are the Catholici Timothy (i ± 800, cf. Q. 108) and 'Abdisho' (Q. 7). The latter must be the first of this name.[2] He reigned from 963-987, and is known as a contemporary and rival of George of Arbela. A liturgical addition ordered by him is quoted here with approval. We notice that this 'Abdisho' was a pupil of the "High Monastery" near Mosul; the importance of this fact will become clear afterwards[3] (p. 148).

This last name gives a *terminus a quo* though it does not affect the question about which we are concerned here, namely whether George was the writer, since he outlived 'Abdisho' (and the text does not say plainly whether 'Abd. is still alive or not) and was candidate for the Catholicate after 'Abd.'s death.—The name of Ḥazza fixes the *terminus ad quem* on 1200 A.D.

More information enabling us to fix its date between 987 and 1200 A.D. cannot be gathered from this treatise. We must attain our end by a roundabout way. This will have the advantage that it puts us in a position to answer the question which arose at page 68 with regard to the writers of the other treatises.

iv. In Q. 108 the writer happens to speak about reciting the Lord's Prayer in the Ritual of Baptism. He says: "We have spoken at some length about Baptism and shown that it is necessary that the Lord's Prayer should be recited in that service . . . three times . ." and in Q. 109 he is asked to specify them, as it said only twice. Nothing relating to this question is found in the preceding part, as one would expect. We must turn, therefore, to the second tract dealing *ex professo* with Baptism. In fact we find something of the kind discussed there (M. fol. $35^b$-$36^a$): On account of the Question why formerly the Baptismal Service began with: "We confess and adore . . ."[4] and now with the Lord's Prayer,[5] it is said that formerly Baptism was immediately joined to the Evening Service of the

(1) *Vide* p. 133–135. (2) The Nestorian Church had 3 Patriarchs of that name, viz. i 963–986; ii 1074–1090; iii 1138-1147. At this state of discussion it is impossible to decide who is the right one. But from the facts brought together in the next pages it will be seen that the choice made in the text is the only one possible. (3) All the sources of his life are compiled and analysed in: A. Baumstark, *L.G.*, S. 239; and cf. the note of Dr. Mingana in: *W.S.* vii, p. 145, n. 1. (4) T., p. 61 (after the preparations). (5) As is done in the present formulary, T., p. 55.

Resurrection; so they began with the said Prayer of: "We confess etc." as the Lord's Prayer had been recited already twice. So the opinion prevailed, that this was the proper beginning. But now the Priests have understood, that no sacramental action can be performed without the Lord's Prayer.[1] *This correspondence shows conclusively that our treatise and that on Baptism are at any rate by the same author.*

Now we turn to the third tract. This includes M. fol. 46a-65b; the end does not belong to it, but are questions by Isho'yabh of Arzun.[2] In V. it runs from fol. 56-93 (there is no reason for dividing it into two parts, as is done in V.)–That its author[3] is the same as that of i is proved by M. fol. 53a. He writes there: "I have asked you before about the Gemurta which falls from the paten of the Sacraments on the ground; is it right to return it to the paten; and you answered: No! Now I want to ask you etc." To this subject the author reverts some pages later (M. fol. 55a). Here we meet with a clear reference to Q. 41 of our book: "*Q.*: What must be done with the Gemurta that falls from the paten on the altar? *S.*: They must carry it with care and give it to one of the people, and add another one to it, but it should not be returned to the paten". This is in fact not a literal quotation, but its contents do agree exactly with the above (cf. ad Q. 41). His references, both here and in Q. 108 (see before), are more paraphrasing than literal.

A further proof is found in M. fol. 58a where a decision *a minori ad maius* is given from Q 11 and 59 (cf. the Commentary).

We notice from such references that the treatises V. 1, ii, iii (+ iv) = M. *A-C* belong together and have the same author.[4] A corroboration is also found in the fact that only the first one has an introduction while ii and iii start immediately with their questions. It may be that the remark in M. fol. 67 (cf. p. 66) has some importance in this connection, the author including the Q Q. of Isho'yabh in his work since they deal with the same matters.

Up to this point we have established the following facts: the

(1) The text is not important enough to justify its publication in full; this summary of the argument will suffice. We want readers to observe that two more Lord's Prayers are said in this Service (cf. ad Q. 109) about which no question existed; making altogether *three* times. (2) About the disorder of its beginning in M. cf. p. 69 and 120. (3) The question of the different author's names in M. and V. will be left aside for the present moment. It will be discussed at the end of this section. (4) Codex Seërt contained only the first item. But this seems to have been a MS. drawn from different sources without any idea leading this choice; so its witness cannot count against the other two.

writer was a teacher living in the neighbourhood of the Tigris, between A.D. 987-1200. As to the sequence of publishing his writings this is not identical with that of our MSS. but: i on Baptism; ii on the Eucharist 1st part; iii on Ordination and the Eucharist 2nd part.[1]–This result is still somewhat poor, but the unity of authorship we have observed puts us in a position to go further. It is really a fact of fundamental importance since iii offers a number of highly interesting data.

v. The new data furnished by iii are the following:

*a.* In M. fol. 52b we read: "Q.: I have seen in the town Mosul in a big church in the days etc." This shows that the conversation described in our treatise was *not* held in this city.

*b.* In an Answer M. fol. 59a it is said: "It happened in the days of the right reverend Mar George, Metropolitan of Mosul, while I was a deacon etc." From this it appears that the writer's identity with George of Arbela, suggested by V. in the margin, is excluded.[2] He must be a, probably younger, contemporary of his. The tract seems to have been written after the dead of George 987. But as it is not said when he obtained his office, we cannot say anything about his age; nothing can be derived from the fact that he is styled "a venerable old man", for it is not clear what is the exact meaning of this name.

*c.* With some hesitation we quote the Question of the same page: "The bishop has authority over his diocese (country), cathedral (church) and residence (town). But if to us happens something like this, how must we do?" The Questioner seems to be exempt from the jurisdiction of a bishop; so he was probably a monk. We draw this conclusion with hesitation since we do not know how this point was exactly regulated.[3]–i 49 is not sufficiently clear (monasteries–churches of laymen). In this connection we may

(1) The definition of the contents of our tract by Assemani is not right; see ch. v. N.B. *In the sequence i and ii are always referring to the tracts on the Eucharist, ii beginning with M. fol.* 51*b* 11 = *V. fol.* 66. (2) I have not found any indication pointing to the origin of Assemani's statement. (3) J. Labourt, *Christianisme*, 1904, p. 324 says: "Cette soumission absolue à l'épiscopat est un des traits caractéristiques du monachisme oriental". – He knows only of two cases of exemption "pour l'époque qui nous occupe" *(ibid.*, n.); in later ages exemption was the rule, as appears from 'Abdisho', *Nomocanon*, vii 6: "on the privilegies of the monasteries and their exemption from the jurisdiction of the bishops". – *D.A.C.L.*, s. v. *Exemption monastique*, t. v, col. 951–962 deals exclusively with the West. *D.C.A.* i, p. 643 s. v. *Exemption* mentions one case of the 7th century in the East (emperor Mauricius).

point to the formula: "Your Brotherhood" and "Venerable old man" in the Introduction, which are typical for monks circles.[1]

*d.* The time is definitively fixed by the last and most important quotation. Its interest will justify the literal translation of the full text, long though it be. M. fol. 46b-48b (Syriac text in facsimile at the end of this book).[2]

"*Question:* There was once a dispute between the Catholicos Mar Mari and Mar George, Metropolitan of Mosul, the matter of dispute being how the signing of the Ordination must be signed over the head of the Ordinand (of all ranks) from the Reader up to the Catholicos. Mar Mari said: From his back he must begin with the signing to his forehead, and from his right ear to his left one. But George said: From the forehead of the Ordinand he must begin to his back, and from his right ear to his left one. Which of these two is right? What clear demonstration is brought forward by everyone of those who hold either view? How did you see that the Ancients signed, tell us clearly. Because in the lifetime of the Catholicos Mar Mari the sign was made according to his command; but after that they followed the practice of Mar George. When we asked them: Why have you left your rule and reverted from it? they answered: This rule was a wilfulness of his; but the rule of Mar George is the right one.[3] But this Catholicos of our days, Mar John signs according to the rule of Mar Mari, and he said (in defence of this practice): By this rule I was signed a Bishop and Metropolitan, and I do not deviate from it. But others do not follow it. And you, how did you see the former generations signing? *Answer:* I do not remember to have seen it done by the heads of the church from the day on which I entered into the service of the Church and the School in a way different from that of Mar George. It happened once upon a time in the High Monastery, that Priests and Deacons were consecrated according to the precepts of the Scholars. I saw they were signing according to that of Mar George. Besides that in the time of his trouble with the Catholicos, Mar George asked the old men, older than he himself: How did you see the Metro-

(1) Cf. e. g. Budge, *B.G.* i, p. xxxiii n. 1, and on many other places; and almost every book dealing with Monasticism, not only in Syriac. (2) It was superfluous to reproduce fol. $48^b$, since only one word of that page belongs to this extract. Therefore ܒܓܒܝܢܗ should be added at the end of fol. $48^a$. (3) In the Officebook the rule of Mar George is found, cf. G. P. Badger ii, p. 324 rubric. – Timothy ii, *Liber de Sacramentis*, I 12, mentions this question in dealing with the form of the cross in the ordination, in: *B.O.*, iii 1, p. 573.

politans Israel and Luke[1] making this sign? The old men answered: We do not remember nor know how they signed. *Question:* What led Mar Mari to this change? *Answer:* Because in the time of the Catholicos 'Abdisho', that is to say after his death, the Metropolitans and Bishops came together to elect a Catholicos. Mari of Persia was present with them, though it was not habitual that the faithful came together with them, and by royal assistance he was made Patriarch. Having finished his election the Bishops came before him that he might confirm them, and he signed them according to the rule he had ordained. But when Mar George saw the change made by Mar Mari in the signing he said to his fellow Metropolitans: "Behold that Catholicos you made Patriarch over you, does not even know how to sign! When the Patriarch heard this, he became angry but hid it in his heart. After a month he convoked the Fathers and they made a Synod; and the Fathers subscribed that his way of signing was valid; even Mar George did so and professed but without his will that it was valid". This paragraph is followed by an exposition of the liturgical reasons of the Fathers (fol. 48b-49a) and the argument of Mar George in support of his opinion, (fol. 49a-b) which have nothing to do with the point discussed here.

This piece is valuable for several reasons. In the first place it contains information about the author. He was in the service of Church and School. Once he lived in the High Monastery (cf. p. 148); at least, the way in which this fact is mentioned, proves that he is there no more. The proper names are all of the end of the 10th century. (Mar George vide supra p. 74–75; the other names will be found in the next paragraph). He wrote in the days of a Catholicos named John. All this information squares with what we have found before.

Next to this we see that Georg of Arbela, as was partly known from other sources, has been much interested in the exact main-

(1) This Israel may be the Patriarch of that name, see below p. 86. In this connection it is worth while to notice that he is styled as redactor of the formulary of Ordination (not in: A. Baumstark, *L.G.*), cf. Badger, *l.l.*, p. 322: "The ordering of Readers, Sub-deacons, Deacons, and Presbyters, drawn up by Mar Kiprianus Metropolitan of Nisibis, by Mar Yeshua-yau Catholicos and Patriarch, and by the learned Mar Israel". About Cyprian of Nisibis (± 750) see: A. Baumstark, *L.G.*, S. 213 and Ak. 10; Iso'yabh is iii, A. Baumstark, *L.G.*, S. 200 Ak. 5 (about the Israel mentioned in: A. Baumstark, *L.G.*, S. 334 see ad Q. 16).– Luke was probably the predecessor of George on the See of Arbela 930–950, cf. *B.O.*, iii 2, p. dccxxi.

tenance of liturgical traditions which came to him by oral transmission. As such he might have been the champion of the strict party as against Mari who was ignorant of the Traditions of the Nestorian Church.

Here it is the right place to discuss the external facts, after the internal evidence viz. the author's names in the MSS. In V. the tract is ascribed to "Yabhallaha *the Great, the Patriarch* who was once *bishop of Nuhadra*" (in the margin)–in M. to "*the Patriarch* Isho'yabh *the Great* who was *bishop of Nuhādrayē*". These titles have in common the words in italics. Nuhadraye means inhabitants of Nuhadra.[1] (Beit) Nuhadra is a district between the Tigris and Zab north of Alqosh.[2] But the proper names are not identical. The preliminary question is: who can be meant by these names?

*a.* The Nestorian Church has had three Patriarchs of the name Yabhallaha. The first one reigned A.D. 415–420;[3] nothing is known about his liturgical activities. – The second was Patriarch 1190–1222; he is praised as a good leader of the Church and it is known that he occupied himself with liturgical poems; he had been bishop of Maipherkat. According to Assemani and Prof. Brightman[4] he was the author of these Q Q (on what authority, I do not know). Prof. Baumstark[5] does not mention this fact. – The last one of this name is well known for his journal; he reigned 1281–1317. His lifestory, interesting though it may be, cannot be told here.[6] He had not been bishop of Nuhadra. As far as I know nothing has been found which marks him as a great liturgical teacher. For though G. Diettrich[7] credits him with a redaction of the Baptismal Rite according to a Berlin MS., he does not give any reason for assigning it to him, and it is safer to follow Prof. Baumstark[8] who leaves it open ("ungewiss welcher" S. 368).

However this may be, it is of no weight for the present investigation. For a comparison between the established facts of p. 81 and these dates shows that none of the three Yabhallaha's answers to the requirements.

(1) Cf. Nöldeke, *Grammatik*, § 135. (2) The exact frontier in: Budge, *B.G.* ii, p. 111 n. 2; cf. a map of the country, e. g. in: J. Labourt, *Christianisme*.–But in the time of our treatises Nuhadra was a bishop's see on the borders of the Euphrates, cf. A. R. Vine, *The Nestorian Churches*, London, 1937, p. 115 and map, p. 121. (3) J. Labourt, *Christianisme*, and: W. A. Wigram, *Introduction*, 1910, Index s. v. (4) *L.E.W.*, p. lxxx. (5) A. Baumstark, *L.G.*, S. 304. (6) Cf. A. Baumstark, *L.G.*, S. 325-326 and: E. Nestle, *Jahballaha iii*, in: *P.R.E.*[3], viii, S. 523-524. (7) G. Diettrich, *Taufliturgie*, S. xiii, N. 1. (8) A. Baumstark, *L.G.*, S. 199, 351.

*b.* When the Nestorians are speaking of Isho'yabh the Great, especially with regard to liturgical matters, the thoughts turn immediately to the third Patriarch of that name.[1] He was the great reformer of the liturgy and as such he had won his fame. He lived in the middle of the 7th century. So he cannot be taken into account for our treatises nor can, of course, the foregoing Patriarchs of his name. – Assemani[2] mentions one bishop of Nuhadra, named Isho'yabh living in the time of the Patriarch Machicha 1091–1108; but he is so obscure that the epitheton "the Great" which is incontestable by the witness of the two MSS. is impossible, and his lifetime does not agree with that of our author.

How can we solve this riddle? I venture to suggest that the real name of our writer written in top of the treatise was: Isho'yabh.[3] Well, *we find in the history of the Nestorian Church a man of that name in the time of 'Abdisho' and John, who became Patriarch, viz. Isho'yabh iv*, the immediate successor of John vii. Whatever we know about his life[4] agrees very well with the data of our treatises. He studied at the School of Mar Mari in Dorkoni, a small village on the borders of the Tigris;[5] he became a priest and after a short time he enjoyed a great reputation owing to his integrety (not usual in his days, see below) and chastity. The text of Mari is worth being quoted in full: "Morum integritate et castimoniae ac doctrinae laude inclaruit. Eum 'Ebedjesu ('Abdisho') episcopum praeposuit sedi Qaṣr et Nuharwânârum,[6] constituitque doctorem ac procuratorem, mox praeclara eius fama circumquaque divulgata est. Scholam rexit reliquis diebus 'Ebedjesu, ac tempore Mâr Mâris, Joannis et Joannis. Aufugit autem ab oppressione Ibn Gâbri". He was ordained a Patriarch in 1021[7] and reigned till 1026.

(1) Cf. ch. vi, ii c. (2) *B.O.*, ii, p. 455–456. (3) It may be somewhat bold; but I would point for this substitution of J. by Y. (meaning practically the same) to the following parallels (which are, however, not quite sure): A. Baumstark, *L.G.*, S. 304 (thinks that a writing of Isho'yabh b. Malkon is ascribed to Yabhallaha b. M.) and the MS. of Berlin, mentioned in the text, (all other MSS. ascribe the ritual of Baptism to I. iii; the text of this MS. cannot be called "revised"). (4) Gismondi i, p. 103–104; ii, p. 56. (5) *B.O.*, iii 2, p. cmxxx; this school was named after Mar Mari, the Apostle of Persia who was said to have died there (the Acts of Mari, in: P. Bedjan, *Acta Martyrum et Sanctorum*, Parisiis-Lipsiae, 1890, i p. 92. (6) Cf. *B.O.*, iii 2, s.v. Kosra: "urbs Episcopalis in Babylonia ad Provinciam Patriarchalem pertinens". – This conflicts with "Nuhadra" in the heading of MSS. (p. 68). I suggest a variation between the Syriac and Arabic names. (7) His choice was considered uncanonical by Elias of Nisibis (because of the reading of a wrong word in the liturgy and simony), in a *letter* translated by B. Vandenhof, *Ein*

Of course, we cannot control how far we are justified in combining the statements of our tracts with those of the Chronicles since they are not identical in all particulars. But at any rate it is a highly probable suggestion explaining various data which otherwise should remain unexplained. He is not called: "the Great", but ܪܒܐ has also the meaning of "Teacher";[1] so it is not necessary to stick to the translation of Assemani and Dr. Mingana as the only one possible. Whatever may be the true rendering, both meanings of the epithet may justly be applied to him, according to the testimony of Mari.

In this way a very conspicuous figure would be added to the list of Nestorian authors in which he is missing up to the present time (a matter of little weight owing to the fragmentary state of tradition); and the shadowy name of Isho'yabh iv would get a more pregnant meaning.

vi. The names mentioned in the preceding paragraph may guide us in a research concerning the lifetime of our author and the state of affairs in the Church during that period. Our sources are those parts of the "Liber Turris" of Mari and Amr, which were published by Gismondi and a portion of the "Chronicum Ecclesiasticum" of Bar Hebraeus which is based upon them.[2] As has been observed these Chronicles are of a rather fragmentary character. They relate many anecdotes but do not attempt to draw a truly historical picture. We shall only quote what seems necessary for our subject; but in doing so one is largely handicapped by the nature of these books.

We make our starting point in the beginning of the 10th century. The first year of this century is also the first of the reign of the Patriarch *John v bar Abgare* (900-905).[3] His choice to the patriarchal See raised the usual contentions. John was chosen under the influence of the Caliph but without bribing, a point which is marked in our sources as a very striking one. He is characterized as: "excelling in knowledge and ascetism".[4] At the very beginning of

*Brief des Elias bar Šinaja über die Wahl des Katholikos Iso'yabhs iv*, in: *O.C.* 1913, S. 56–81, 236–262.

(1) Cf. J. Payne Smith, *Dictionary*, s.v.–This title is also used in the *Responsa Canonica* of John of Tella (ed. Lamy.) (2) For the titles see p. 19; cf. *B.O.*, iii 1, p. 617-618 with his cross-references; for the writers of that time, see: A. Baumstark, *L.G.*, S. 235-242, 285-288. (3) Cf. A. Baumstark, *L.G.*, S. 235. (4) Bar Hebraeus, col. 227.

his reign he made a vow and professed his ideals of his duty which he made obligatory for his successors: (a) maintenance of the true doctrine and (b) care for the Church by building churches and finally: "Eas (ecclesias) piis viris commissurum, presbyterum aut diaconum non ordinaturum nisi secundum canones, presbyterum quidem post lectionem novi testamenti, diaconum vero post lectionem psalterii, nec divitem ad ordines promoturum qui minime sit idoneus, nec pauperem reiecturum qui sit idoneum".[1] This quotation shows what seemed to be a grave defect of the Church at that time: office and rank varied with the sum of money one was ready to pay, simony being the rule. He restaured the old rule requiring knowledge in stead of money (cf. p. 75). On several occasions he gave directions how the service ought to be conducted by answering questions and by promulgating "Canones" that since have formed part of the Officebooks (cf. p. 134). The summary of his Patriarchate was: "Optimo regimine ecclesiam gubernavit".[2]

He was succeeded by *Abraham iii* (905-937), whose reign seems to have been a flourishing-period for his church: "tot floruerunt sapientes viri insignes ac scientiarum doctores, quot hic diserte memorare longum esset" (we cannot but regret that Mari has restrained his eloquence just here). Not so much characteristic for this time, as important for the history of the liturgy is the fact that an addition was made to the liturgy because some ecclesiastic had turned to the Melchites as he thought he was not sufficiently honoured by the Nestorians; "ipsius causa compositus est uterque canon qui in liturgia recitatum de eo qui in sua fide divisus est: 'qui anceps in sua fide haeret . . . Abeat qui non amat' ".[3]

During the office of *Emmanuel* (938-960) the church had a time of further peaceful development and was not troubled by Mohammedan riots. His knowledge of the future, his skilful interpretation and his eloquence are praised but unfortunately he was very avaricious, a fact which was not profitable for the Church.[4]

(1) Gismondi i, p. 78; ii p. 48 added after the reading of the Psalms: "et quae iis adjecta sunt (ex hymnis aliisque)". (2) Gismondi i, p. 79. (3) Gismondi i, p. 81.–This is probably an addition to the words at the beginning of the Offertory (*L.E.W.*, p. 267); but it is found nowhere in the MSS. and editions of T. which I consulted.–About Abraham, Gismondi i, p. 79–84; ii, p. 48–49. The latter tells us, 'Ab. wrote a "liber admonitionum", but we do not hear anything else about the nature of this book; so we do not know if it is liturgical (not in: A. Baumstark, *L.G.*). (4) Emmanuel: Gismondi i, p. 84–87; ii, p. 49.

*Israel* whose name we mentioned before, reigned but one year (963). He owed his elevation to the Chalif whose victory he had foretold. He had been a teacher in the school of Mar Mari (cf. p 83) and was "castimonia ac pietate illustris".[1] From the fragment given above it appears that he was held to be an expert in liturgical tradition.

Now we come to the time immediately preceding our writings. The name of the successing Patriarch viz. *'Abdisho'* has been mentioned several times.[2] He was educated in the High Monastary and Bar Hebraeus tells us that he was "expert in the ecclesiastical sciences and trained in logic by Bar Nesicha, a pupil of the holy Moses bar Cepha of ours".[3] This is a very interesting remark as this Moses was one of the most famous Fathers of the Jacobites. Moses bar Cepha died in 903 and wrote many books on exposition of the Bible and of the liturgical Offices.[4] 'Abdisho' was the author of some prayers and probably of several sermons. Changes in the liturgical order and building of churches are also referred to him. About his character we hear that he was conspicuous for his sanctity and doctrine and gifted with an excellent intellect but rather irascible. As a matter of fact people could bear him only because of his holy living, for there was much reason for complaint. Personally he was in no wise able to administer the church in the right way.[5] This task was left for others who were "wicked people". They embezzled money received for assistance of the poor, and for that reason he had even to dismiss one of his friends called 'Abdisho'. On the other hand he stirred up bad feelings by inflicting excommunication on several occasions. From all this information we can easily guess that his time was not a culminating-point in the life of the church.

During the vacancy of the See a certain *Elias of Cascar* looked after it. He was designated his successor but died before his inthronization.[6] The death of this man who is highly praised proved fatal to the church. The *Mari* mentioned in the foregoing fragment now ascended the throne (987-1001).[7] He was a man of noble birth

(1) Israel: Gismondi i, p. 87-88. (2) *Vide* p. 77. (3) Bar Hebraeus, col. 251. (4) All sources about his life are found in: A. Baumstark, *L. G.*, S. 281-282, and S. 360 where the important explanation of his on the Eucharist is mentioned (ed. R. H. Connolly-H. W. Codrington, *Two Commentaries on the Jacobite Liturgy*, London, 1913, p. 16–86 [text] = p. 24–90 [tr.]). (5) His reign was taken as an example by Elias of Nisibis in contrast with his ownt imes (*Letter*, ed. B. Vandenhof, in: *O.C.*, 1913, S. 65–66). (6) Cf. A. Baumstark, *L. G.*, S. 240. (7) Gismondi i, p. 92-97; ii p. 55.

and had filled a high office. Afterwards he became a monk and was appointed inspector by 'Abdisho'. At a later date he became Bishop of Persia and discharged his office very well. His choice was as usual accompanied by various contentions, but he was acknowledged by the Chalif as head of the Christians, and Bar Hebraeus tells us that as a matter of fact he was thrusted upon the church by the Chalifs. We saw from the fragment that there were troubles between him and the other priests at his ordination, since he made a liturgical mistake in the signing and we are also told that he read the Gospel but did not expose it; he held Mass but did not preach at the entrance of the altar as had been the use of his predecessors. It should not be forgotten that George of Arbela, one of his leading opponents, had been a candidate himself. That accounts for some jealousy. His personal character is praised for his compassion and modesty. But he missed the qualities of a good governor and moreover he was reputed to be ignorant of the teaching of the Church and of its services and orders ("eius regimen viri potius erat opulenti sane ad gubernandum idonei ob divitias quam regimen patriarchae statuendi praescripta juris studiosi: nec religionis doctrina pollebat"). His financial management was not so bad but in spite of that some instances are told of selling church property,[1] and, worst of all, he ordained many unqualified persons "haud excultos nec idoneos qui Deum nequaquam verebantur, nec de ecclesiastica disciplina quidquam noverant". This, for our subject extremely important, testimony[2] throws a glaring light upon the situation of the Church during his reign. We can hardly expect better from a leader that was not instructed himself, and though his reign lasted only fourteen years, the church was saddled with these bad functionaries. Our writer looking back upon this time knows that in his days things have not changed. At this time *John* was patriarch, probably the one who follows next in the list, viz. the 6th of his name (1001-1011).[3] That he is meant in the fragment quoted before (p. 80), seems to follow from the fact that he did not wish to leave the practice of Mari which is easy to understand, if he was his immediate predecessor.

(1) This bad habit is often combatted in the Synodical Canons but it seems to have been an inveterate evil of all ages not specially of his time. (2) Cf. the Introduction of our tract: "... all the priests, our colleagues took recently possession of the churches and were not instructed, and so did not follow the Canons and Orders of the service of the altar". (3) Gismondi i, p. 97-100; ii, p. 55-56; Bar Hebraeus, col. 261, 272-278, 281-283.

His former life had not been the best preparation for his high office; he had been rather wicked. Having been ordained Bishop by Mari he became afterwards Metropolitan of Persia, but he was not popular among his correligionists being rather self-conceited and arrogant. He took openly profits from the ordinations and instead of building churches he ruined them; he closed schools and prevented the giving of alms. Moreover he was rather inclined to anathematize his opponents. We can gather from this that things went in the same bad way as under his predecessor.

We assumed before that this John vi was intended as "our patriarch" but one might defend also the view that his successor *John vii* (1011-1020) is meant.[1] This ecclesiastic had been Bishop of Hirta. He was famous for his intellect and tolerance, though he was not free from avarice. In his time the threats of pogroms of which we hear also in the decades before became a bitter reality. Christianity in those countries was badly smitten by persecution. A vivid description of the dreadful manner in which they were usually executed is found in several places of Mari's Chronicle.[2] In this time the Christians were forced to wear a distinct dress and we are told that many apostasized from the faith because of the contumely and the stoning to which they were exposed. The consequences were naturally felt in the performance of public worship: "cuius rei causa exstitit hominum in sua religione relaxatio ac sacerdotum pessima agendi ratio in altari et ecclesiis ac oratoriis". In several places churches were destroyed.

Surveying the history of the internal state of affairs in the Nestorian church during the 10th century, we find that its standard was very low, partly by the lax discipline and administration of its highest officers who were often haughty, corrupt and ignorant, partly by the menace of the persecutions and the apostasy or at least the weakening of faith among the masses. *This is exactly the background that suits the features we found on page* 76. These facts answer us the question we have put before, viz. whether the traits of the introduction were not traditional; our conclusion is: they are not. The church at the author's time was in sore need of restauration in various respects and one of the most urgent measures

(1) Gismondi i, p. 100–103; ii, p. 56; Bar Hebraeus, col. 283–285. (2) Cf. Gismondi i, p. 69-70, and in his history of Mari and his successors; this has been the same during all ages; the slaughters of the Armenians in our century are still fresh in mind.

was to stop the liturgical disorder, since the liturgy was of such a great importance. This was his aim in writing his treatises.[1]

vii. *Conclusion:* Resuming the facts about the author, they are the following: he was Isho'yabh, who afterwards became the fourth Patriarch of that name, but at the time he was bishop of Nuhadra and a Schoolmaster of very high repute (the name of the School is not mentioned, but was probably in his diocese). He wrote his tracts on liturgical matters in the two first decades of the 11th century about 1010, in order to restaure the awful state of affairs in his church which had arisen during the bad government of the last Patriarchs, especially *in liturgicis*. He had been at the High Monastery and deacon in Mosul, in touch with George of Arbela and 'Abdisho', both of whom he followed.

Having thus fixed the name of the author and the time of our writing we may insist on *its importance* both for our knowledge of the history of that time and for the liturgy in general. In giving a chronological survey in the second part of his "La Littérature Syriaque", Prof. R. Duval says about the 10th and 11th century: "Ce siècle est aussi terne que le précédent; la décadence littéraire ne subit plus que de rares arrêts. Après de longs intervalles apparait quelque savant docteur qui s'efforce de ranimer le feu des études près de s'éteindre, mais ses efforts tourneront le plus souvent au profit de la science arabe".[2] This judgment is very much to the point, though he did allow that the Nestorians kept the first place. Our treatises enable us to fill this gap to a certain extent. They have been written by a prominent teacher and clergyman of the Nestorians, a doctor of the type mentioned by Prof. R. Duval. But even when taking these books into account, it must be allowed that our sources for the history of the Church in Asia in this period are very scarce and

(1) It is interesting to read the picture drawn by Elias of Nisibis in his *Letter* (ed. Vandenhof, in: *O.C.*, 1913) as it agrees in many respects with the facts mentioned in the text. He wrote in 1021 and described the sad state of the church in that time as compared with that of 'Abdisho' i; the decline was manifested by the manner of worship and the study of the schools.–It was the result of despising the Canons of the Church (S. 65–66). Formerly one choose pious and orthodox men to be Patriarch, "jetzt aber fragt man nach dem, der schön ist an Gestalt, einen langen Bart hat, reich ist an Geld, keck, erfahren in (allen) weltlichen Händeln, während man nach der Lehre der Kirche und nach dem was oben geschrieben steht (Canons) nicht fragt" (S. 259).–These sentences were directed against Isho'yabh iv! (2) R. Duval, *La Littérature Syriaque*[3] p. 394.

poor. Concerning the internal ecclesiastical life they are almost deficient. This lamentable fact does not only apply to this age. We do know very little about the daily life of the Churches. One is at a loss to say exactly, how the priests performed their services in the churches of Mesopotamia and Middle Asia. In such a case those sources that are still at our disposal, obtain a greater importance. The tracts edited here give us at least some insight into the life of those churches and into various liturgical practices and difficulties of a place and a time of which too much is unknown. We should like to know more, but we must make the most of the little that is left.

From the liturgical point of view our treatises have, of course, some importance of their own. Besides that we know that about 1000 A.D. some interesting liturgical movements were on foot in other oriental churches.[1] The question may be posed, if the liturgical revival in the Nestorian Church, from which these documents resulted, had any connection with that movement. The answer must be, I think, in the negative. It appeared from the sources that the revival was sufficiently justified by the whole state of affairs in this particular church itself. On the other hand it is not probable since the Nestorians were not in close touch with the Jacobites and even less with Western (Byzantine) Christendom. For several reasons (historical, geographical solation) all great movements in Christianity passed by the Persian Church.

To estimate more precisely the value of this book it will be necessary to investigate in what degree the form in which this information have come down to us should be traditional, and what was the actual background of the study of liturgical matters within the Nestorian church. The next chapters are devoted to this end.

(1) A. Baumstark, *Festbrevier und Kirchenjahr der syrischen Jakobiten*, Paderborn, 1910, S. 43: "Wir werden auch in anderem Zusammenhang der Nähe der Jahrtausendwende als einer in der Geschichte der jakobitischen Liturgie nicht weniger als in derjenigen der syrisch-byzantinischen Kunstverhältnisse wichtigen Epoche begegnen, die durch ein neues Sichbegegnen orientalischer Elemente des Ostens und ursprünglich hellenistischer Elemente des Westens ihr eigentümliches Gepräge erhällt, sei es nun, dass im einzelnen Falle mehr Östliches nach dem Westen oder Westliches nach dem Osten zuvordringt".

## V. THE FORMAL CHARACTERISTICS OF THIS WRITING: QUAESTIONES

Before passing on to a research of the style and form of this book it will not be superfluous to give a survey of its contents. We informed the readers already of the description given by Assemani in his "Catalogue" (cf. p. 64–65). But comparing his analysis with the treatise itself one will find that actually the subjects mentioned by him are found there, but that his statement prevents us from getting an exact idea of the nature of the matters under discussion; and this may be expected from such a report. We will give another one, more in accordance with its contents. Fullness of detail is inevitable because of the great number of questions raised.

*Introduction:* p. 1–2: The writer is asked to give the exact liturgical rules according to tradition concerning various points, because many people deviate from them at the present moment. Reluctantly since he does not think himself the right man to do so, he promises to reproduce what he saw the previous generations doing.

i. Q. 1–7[1] *Consecration of the altar:* where the right practice is found (1–2); how many signs of the Cross and Gehanta's must be made over the oil (3–5); how the sign of the Cross should be made over holy vessels (6); an addition to one of the Gehanta's (7).

ii. Q. 8–51. *Violation of the holiness of the altar or of the Eucharistic elements* in the liturgy through various mistakes:

8–9 Closing of the curtains of the Apse.

10 Placing of a wrong chalice on the altar.

11–14 Falling down of Eucharistic elements on the altar.

15 Consequences of wrongly mixing the chalice.

16–17 Consecration while Eucharistic bread is reserved or left by accident.

18 Eating Eucharistic bread during the ablutions.

19 The Sacristan takes the Eucharistic bread to distribute among the people before the proper time.

20–22 Touching or kissing of paten and chalice by laymen.

(1) The numbers refer to the questions in my translation, but are not found in the Syriac text.

23–25 Communion of paten (23) and chalice (25) the officiant being without girdle or while the communicants do not kiss nor ask for forgiveness.

26 Difference in solution between 23 and 25.

27 Censing by a priest who is not fasting.

28 Entering the altar without girdle.

29–31 Entering of the altar by a pagan or a Christian child.

32 An angry communicant returns the Sacrament.

33 Cooked food next to the Eucharistic bread on the paten.

34 Drinking at the ablutions in the altarplace.

35 The altar without Cross or Gospel.

36 Communion by a single priest.

37 Leaving of Eucharistic bread.

38 Ordering of the Sacrament by a single priest.

39 Entering the altar without sandals.

40–41 Eucharistic elements touching the ground.

42 A pagan receives a host.

43 Communion of wine only.

44–45 Desecration by a flood.

46–48 Mixing the chalice in cases of lack of wine.

49–50 Taking more pieces at the ablutions than is allowed; exception on Maundy Thursday.

51 Carrying the Eucharist outside the church.

iii. Q. 52-86. *Preparation of the Eucharistic elements for Consecration.*

52 Baking of the Eucharistic bread.

53–55. Impure oil in the dough.

56 Dough falling to the ground.

57 Water on the dough.

58 The bread touched by a layman after baking.

59 Water on the bread.

60 A small particle is the same as the whole bread.

61 Offering a piece that had fallen on the altar.

62–63 Unlawfully entering the altar at the Prothesis without girdle or sandals.

64 How much of the unconsecrated bread may be distributed.

65–67 How and how much bread should be offered on the altar.

68–69 What must be done if too small a quantity is offered and the punishment of the priest.

70–71 Eucharistic bread damaged.

72–75 A mistake in composing a chalice.

76 Adding afterwards Eucharistic bread in cases one thinks there is too little.

77 What must be done with the bread that is not destined for the altar but is put upon it.

78–79 Cleaning of altar and censer.

80–81 Difference between bread for the altar and the Eulogia.

82–84 Mistake in kneeding the dough.

85–86 Desecration of the oven after baking.

iv. Q. 87–104. *Some acts and objects in the mass.*

87–89 How many times and where should the sign of the Cross be made over the elements in the liturgy and deviation from it.

90–93 The whole number of signs, which and where.

94–95 The habit of deacons to say "Bless, o my Lord" in receiving the chalice.

96 A wrong way of making the sign of the Cross.

97–99 Cross and Gospel; censer, and elements on the altar on the right- or lefthandside of the priest.

100 Mystagogical meaning of the fans beside the altar.

101 Difference between Cross and Gospel.

102 How many times the priest says "Peace be with you".

103 Place of the Cross beside the Bishop.

104 Mystagogical meaning of the "Throne".

v. Q. 105–116. Why *the Lord's Prayer* should be said at the beginning of all services except Betrothal and Marriage and Funeral, while in former times it was never said.

117 Connection of Evening-service and Funeral-service.

vi. Q. 118–123. *Place of Cross and Gospel* beside Bishop, priest and altar in the mass.

We have summed up in this table the great variety of questions under some heads to get a survey. But it is apparent that this book does not provide a systematic unity neither in the main sections nor in the sequence of the particular questions though some questions actually belong together. The questions are posed pell-mell about various difficulties which may occur or have really taken place in the practical preparation and execution of the liturgy by the officiants. As to the third part (V. iii = M.C) it is even impossible to give the slightest order. Here one is struck by finding more a narrative and it is on the whole more extensive in its questions and answers.

We observed already that the form of our writing is that of Question and Answer or Solution.[1] Besides that we notice a certain uniformity of the questions. Generally they are very short: A question is posed how a certain act should be performed *rite;* after having received the answer the questioner goes on with: "I have seen people who . . .", telling a different way of performing it, and asking whether this is right. Sometimes the introduction is: "It happened once that . . .", then it is simply recording a case with the request to tell precisely what should be done. Many times the student begins with: "If such or such a case occurs, how must it be dealt with?"[2] It is superfluous to give examples; by far the greater part of the questions are treated in this way. Besides that, there are some questions asking information about the meaning of certain objects in the cult (Q. 100 and 104); dogmatical (101) and a long series about the Lord's Prayer, a subject to which so much attention has been devoted since it raised a good deal of dust in the Nestorian church (cf. ad Q. 105–116). The answers are generally very concise, a single time only a reason is given and there is only one place in the questions where the Bible is quoted (Q. 60 in M., omitted in V.).

*The whole book gives by the tone of its writing the strong impression that they are real questions about occurrences in the practice of the church.* This impression is corroborated if it is noticed that many cases are reactions upon the canons divulgated by the Patriarch John v (e.g. Introduction, Q. 48, 49). The preface fits in very well with the state of affairs in the Nestorian church about 1000 A.D. as was shown before. Are these impressions right?

It is not without importance to study this question more closely

(1) On p. 70 we saw that the latter indications are used interchangeable.
(2) This last clause is often omitted, and the sentence has an elliptical character.

since we are concerned about the value of these documents for our knowledge of the liturgical life of the Nestorians. On account of V. x Mr. Bensly pointed out "that other instances of the catechetical method of conveying instruction may be seen in Cod. Vat. CL under the remaining titles, and also in one of the Syriac MSS. preserved in the British Museum (cf. Dr. Wright's catalogue, p. 985a)".[1] This shows that there existed a certain type of literature of Quaestiones dealing with various subjects (V.: liturgical, biblical, dogmatical). It is worth while to examine this form somewhat closer. *The question arises whether the form of this book allows us to find here traditional material, literary fiction or freshly formulated questions.* The observations of some scholars quoted below point to tradition. It is also suggested by some indications of the treatise itself: the introduction is largely traditional in its expressions; the writer refers over and over to the Fathers; several questions are dealt with elsewhere.

The best way to discuss this matter is by giving a succinct survey of works that have been written in this form and by ascertaining the observations made by various scholars on this point. We confine ourselves within the limits of the ancient-christian, Byzantine and Syriac literature, while keeping in mind that the method of Questions and Answers has remained a favourite one up to now especially for catechetical instructions both in eastern and western Christendom.

Yet we must protest against styling these books "catechisms", for these suppose a systematically arranged whole of notions in which gradual progress of thought is made by the way of Questions and Answers. But this is not the case here. The questions stand without any connection side by side. If some questions are linked up, the author wants to investigate some possibilities arising from the same situation. But the survey on p. 91–93 shows sufficiently that a logical development of ideas was not aimed at.

Prof. Jordan whose "Geschichte der altchristlichen Literatur" as

(1) R. L. Bensly, *ap.* H. B. Swete, *Theodori . . . Mopsuesteni . . . Commentarii*, Cambridge, 1880, i, p. xii n.–G. P. Badger, ii, p. 164, n. quotes, in discussing the Nestorian opinion about the influence of an unworthy priest on the administration and efficacy of the Eucharist, a "Query" and "Answer" from "an ancient manuscript in the possession of Kasha Mendu of Amedia. The book appears to be *a sort of general catechism*, but is so much mutilated that I was unable to discover the title of the work or the author's name" (I could not trace elsewhere the quotation he gives).–Likewise Th. J. Lamy, p. 62, n. 1, says that there exists such a form and gives some examples, but he did not go further into the matter; he styles it catechetical; cf. the quotation of Bardenhewer below p. 97.

a whole is built upon the principle of the formal characteristics of the writings under discussion, and Prof. O. Bardenhewer in the summaries at the head of the 3rd and 4th part of his "Geschichte der altkirchlichen Literatur" have concerned themselves with this class of books and ordered the material falling within the limits of their works.[1] The first scholar referring to the researches of Prof. Heinrici[2] pointed out that there had come into being among the Greeks a kind of exposition "welche schwierige Stellen griechischer Autoren dadurch erklärte, dass man Widersprüche . . . aufdeckte und dann löste, and das literarisch in der Form fingierter Gespräche, in Rede und Antwort... mit dem Titel ἐρωτήσεις πεύσεις καὶ ἀποκρίσεις, ἀπορίαι καὶ λύσεις, lateinisch quaestiones und ähnlich". The Jewish philosopher Philo was the first to apply this method to the Bible; several times it is found in the commentaries of Origen and the Homilies of Chrysostom. The first among the Christian scholars who published a whole book in this form was the churchhistorian Eusebius in his: "On the Discrepancies of the Gospels" in two volumes.[3] Besides that this kind of literature was used in the works of Theodoretus of Cyrus and in various pseudo-athanasian and -augustinian, anonymous writings; later on by Byzantine authors. Jordan observes in a footnote that this form seems to be specially used in the well-known Antiochene School who applied it to dogmatical and similar subjects, e.g. the four pseudo-justinian tracts.[4] He concludes saying that it is important to see "*dass im diesen Aporien sich eine lebendige Tradition geltend machte, sodass 'Frage' und 'Lösung' von einem bis zum anderen weitergegeben wurden* und dann gesammelt oft hinsichtlich ihres Autors nicht mehr bestimmt werden können" (italics are mine).

Bardenhewer has taken this over in substance though he re-

(1) H. Jordan, *Geschichte der altchristlichen Literatur*, Leipzig, 1911, S. 409–411, § 69 Die Aporienliteratur. – O. Bardenhewer, *Geschichte der altkirchlichen Literatur*, Freiburg i. Br., iii², 1923, S. 29–30, and S. 667; iv ¹⁻², 1924, S. 12–13. (2) G. Heinrici, *Scholien*, in: *P.R.E.*³, xvii, S. 736–738, and: *Zur patristischen Aporienliteratur*, in: *Abhandlungen der k. sächsischen Gesellschaft der Wissenschaften*, phil.-hist. Klasse, 1909, S. 841–860. (3) It dealt with the various traditions about the Birth- and Resurrectionstories; nothing but fragments are left, cf. O. Bardenhewer, *a.a.O.*, iii, S. 257, and: G. Beyer, *Die evangelischen Fragen und Lösungen des Eusebius in jakobitischer Überlieferung und deren nestorianischen Parallelen*, in: *O.C.*, 1927, S. 80–97 and 284–292 (he does not say anything about the form). (4) O. Bardenhewer, *a.a.O.*, i², 1913, S. 240–246 (a mixture of exegetical, apologetical, dogmatical, cosmological and other questions); they are well known because A. von Harnack thought to have discovered in them the lost writings of Diodorus of Tarsus.

cognized in it an "autochthones Gebilde" of the Christians built up from real questions. He added a number of titles, mainly latin, and pointed out that the Greeks afterwards used this form for dogmatical and ascetical purposes. Next to this kind of literature which is essentially exegetical occurs this form of questions in an other category of writings, viz. "Schriften populär-didaktischer, kathechismusartiger Tendenz" as the two Monksrules of St. Basil. "Hier sind die Fragen reine Fiktionen". Ten years later he distinguished this form sharply from the dialogue; the latter consists of a discussion of a central theme, while the Quaestiones contain a variegated series of different topics. It is allotted to exegetical literature.[1]

As a matter of fact most of the books written as "Quaestiones et Responsiones" deal with the Holy Scripture. In an extensive series of articles M. G. Bardy has carefully investigated this form. It is not necessary for our purpose to give an exact account of them all. But it is worth while to give his, what seems to me, undisputable result: "Encore pouvons-nous distinguer deux catégories de questions. Les premières sont purement artificielles: c'est l'exégète lui même qui les pose, afin d'avoir l'occasion de les résoudre, et, s'il suit, comme il est fréquent, l'ordre même des livres saints, nous nous trouvons en présence d'un commentaire plus ou moins suivi . . . Les autres sont vraies questions: elles ont été posées à un interprète en renom, à un savant évèque, à un ami, par des correspondants réèls, et l'exégète n'a rien autre chose à faire qu'à fournir la solution des problèmes soulevés par son correspondant".[2] He points out that there are many standing questions; that afterwards they become absolutely traditional; he draws a parallel with the Florilegia and Catenae from which they are only distinguished by their form. Actually this last observation is a very suggestive one. For these commentaries in Florilegia and Catenae[3] have been made to collect the authoritative exposition of the Fathers about certain places in Scripture and they are a marked feature of the Byzantine

(1) Besides those categories mentioned before I should like to draw attention to the "Responsa Canonica" of Timothy of Alexandria (381–385) in the same form (O. Bardenhewer, *a.a.O.*, iii, S. 104); it is not clear to what class they belong according to Bardenhewer. This writer does not say a word about the genuinity. (2) G. Bardy, *La litérature patristique des "Quaestiones" et "Responsiones" sur l'Écriture sainte*, in: *Revue Biblique*, 1933, p. 351 (the whole series in the volumes of 1932 and 1933). (3) G. Heinrici, *Catenen*, in: *P.R.E.*[3], iii, S. 754–767; xxiii, S. 295–296, gives a short but clear summary. Of course some more work has been done in this field during the last twenty years; but it is superfluous for the present purpose to cite more titles.

Theology. It is well known that these writings have been drawn up from various sources and that their tradition and filiation is extremely complicated: in copying, names have been omitted, quotations shortened or left out. But they are very important since they contain many fragments of Churchfathers (even heretics) which would otherwise have been lost. Here we have a case where older traditions have been preserved through later compilations! Are we right in saying: the same holds good for these "Quaestiones"? We saw before that the traditional element is stressed both by Prof. Jordan and M. Bardy. If the "Quaestiones" are traditional in the same way as the Catenae, the result would be very important. For in that case we might find in them a witness of a stage of the liturgy some ages before the actual compilation, e.g. in this book of the 11th century rules of the 5th century or of Isho'yabh iii. Before entering upon an investigation of this, we will see the result of the study of some other examples. But at the outset we must keep in mind that the two cases compared before are not quite parallel. For the text of a Bible is a fixed subject without any change. But the liturgy though it is fixed is dependent on different factors from outside when it is performed.

The *Byzantine literature* has continued the methods of their fore-fathers, in accordance with the highly traditional character of that Church. It was observed by Ehrhardt that this form needed further investigation;[1] he gives as specimens the "Quaestiones et Responsiones" of Anastasius Sinaita and Maximus Confessor dealing with exegetical, dogmatical and moral questions;[2] Photius' "Amphilochia" discussing without any systematical order all kind of theological and profane subjects showing the state of knowledge at the time of its writer;[3] besides that dogmatical, ascetical and liturgical works.[4] As far as the study of these writings allows a judgement, it seems that the Byzantines did not hesitate to copy their predecessors, as usual.

(1) A. Ehrhardt, *ap.* K. Krumbacher, *Geschichte der byzantinischen Literatur*², München, 1897, S. 65. (2) The printed text is not that of Anastasius, *a.a.O.*, S. 65, cf. O. Bardenhewer, *a.a.O.*, v, 1932, S. 45. (3) *a.a.O.*, S. 75, cf. F. Kattenbusch, *Photius*, in: *P.R.E.*³, xv, S. 386–387. (4) E. g. on theology and incarnation by Nikolaos of Methone, *a.a.O.*, S. 87 = Theodore of Raithu (cf. O. Bardenhewer, *a.a.O.*, v, S. 13); several of Symeon of Thessalonica, *a.a.O.*, S. 113.–Some of the Apocryphal Books of the N.T. are Questions to and Answers of the Lord. "The Byzantines were fond of this form of writing", says Dr. M. R. James, *The Apocryphal New Testament*, Oxford, 1924, p. 504, cf. p. 187. As this category is a group of its own with a special development, we may leave it aside in this discussion.

Without repeating what is contained in Vat. Syr. 150 (liturgical, exegetical, canonical, grammatical questions) we find in *Syriac literature*[1] books giving answers to biblical questions, among others the "Book of Scholia" of Theodore Bar Koni who also treats grammatical, apologetical and anti-heretical points.[2] Many examples of all these sorts may be found scattered in Baumstark's "Geschichte".

As distinct from the former groups it is extremely difficult to demonstrate dependency and imitation here. Even if this can be done in a certain case, it does not necessarily apply to the others. On the other hand it may be and is very likely (since the Nestorians and Jacobites were as traditional as the other Churches) that several writers have largely quoted others now lost so that it is impossible to trace the degree of their plagiarism. We are allowed, I think, to state that tradition as such is not inherent to the literary form of the questions, but that this must be determined for every category in particular and that it depends upon the subject matter.

One more kind of writings was omitted, important though it may be since it is of the utmost value to know whether we have to do here with traditional materials. This is that of the Questions and Answers about the canonlaw and liturgy (the latter subject is often subsumed under the former), for here we are concerned about the question, how in a certain time such or such a priest or Patriarch of a certain oriental church judged, how a certain rite had to be administered. For this decides to what time these books really belong. Are they living questions, or merely copied from former ages, but without connection with the present liturgy? We know that liturgies that were out of date, were still copied by some people who had literary or historical interest to preserve them.[3]

Besides that the Eastern books of Canon Law are simply large

(1) The *Christian Arabic literature* offers some examples (biblical, dogmatical, diverse), cf. G. Graf, *Catalogue de manuscripts arabes chrétiens conservés au Caire*, Citta del Vaticana, 1934 (*Studi e Testi*, 63), p. 309, Index s.v.–Quotations from the *Responsa Ecclesiastica* of Michael on points of the ritual in: *L.O.C.*, i, p. 176–177. –But the present state of our knowledge makes it impossible to decide the question whether they are composed of older traditions or not. (2) Cf. A. Baumstark, *L.G.*, S. 60, 116, (not preserved), 127 (idem), 129 and Ak. (idem), 218-219, 200 (not preserved), 286 (published), 295 (preserved), 310. Ascetical works e.g. in: A. J. Wensinck, *Mystic Treatises of Isaac of Nineveh*, chapter xxxv, p. 152-180. *W.S.* vii, p. 165–168, cf. p. 146. (3) Th. Schermann, *Aegyptische Abendmahlsliturgien des ers'.n Jahrtausends*, Paderborn, 1912, S. 7; cf. the interesting question in: A. Rücker, *Das dritte Buch der Memrē des Kyriakos von Antiochien und seine Väterzitate*, in: *O.C.*, 1934, S. 114, about the question, why the "Testament of our Lord" is not used any more.

collections of older material. They are totally different from Western "Corpora Juris Canonici". They consist of canons and decisions of Synods and Patriarchs brought together in chronological order, but without much system (sometimes under special headings). Consequently comparatively young books contain ancient material (cf. e.g. Riedel, Bar Hebraeus' "Nomocanon", "Synodicon Orientale").

In the ancient church only the Responsa of Timothy of Alexandria can be compared, but nothing special is said about their origin. But a parallel is offered in the 2 Regulae Monasticae of Basil. We heard that Bardenhewer called them fictitious. Against this statement a severe objection is that these rules are *not* in systematical order, what should be expected in this case. On the contrary the subjects are very loosely connected. Quite rightly Mr. Clark observed in his examination of the ascetical writings of St. Basil: "This very lack of order is a strong proof that we have before us a *bona fide* record of real answers to real questions".[1] We can safely stick to this opinion as long as the proof of the opposite has not been given. Bardenhewer fails to show that it is a fiction.

We return to the Syrians. We find that there existed a translation of Timothy of Alexandria.[2] An offspring of the Syriac church itself are both the "Resolutiones Canonicae" of John of Tella (519–538)[3] where questions put by a disciple Sergius are answered, and those of James of Edessa (7th–8th century).[4] The first editor Th. J. Lamy remarks that this literary form exists, but he did not go further into the matter.[5] The translator of the latter work Kayser[6] facing the question whether they were written by James himself, leaves it open. He thinks that it is not certain that this form of tradition is genuine, as the MSS. show variations and Bar Hebraeus has incorporated them in another form in his "Nomocanon", the big collection of all previous canonical work of the Jacobite church.[7] "Es fragt sich nun, hat Jakob selbst diese Zusammenstellung gemacht, oder hat erst ein Späterer nach den Entscheidungen und Anordnungen dieses Bischofs, die er in seinen Briefen und Akten fand, unsere Sammlung veranstaltet und dabei die Fragen zu

(1) W. K. L. Clark, *St. Basil the Great*, Cambridge, 1913, p. 73, cf. p. 69–74.
(2) Cf. A. Baumstark, *L.G.*, S. 263; it is preserved in the MS. of Paris 63 containing several canonical works. (3) A. Baumstark, *L.G.*, S. 174. (4) One of the most famous Jacobites, cf. A. Baumstark, *L.G.*, S. 248–256. (5) Th. J. Lamy, p. 62, n. 2. (6) C. Kayser, S. 74–78. (7) Bar Hebraeus, *Nomocanon*, ed. P. Bedjan, Parisiis, 1898.

Grunde gelegt, welche in den Klosterschulen mit den jungen Geistlichen gewöhnlich verhandelt wurden" (S. 76). He considers it certain that real questions are at any rate the basis. The heading of the book is rather explicit on this point: "Fragen, die der Presbyter Addai Philoponus an den Bischof Jakob von Edessa richtete und auf welche derselbe (nachstehende) Antworten gab. Einige von diesen Fragen regten zwar Andere bei dem besagten Presbyter an, andere aber warf er von selbst auf..." (Kayser, S. 11). I cannot see why this reference to a later schoolmaster is necessary (perhaps it is the outcome of a certain type of historical and literary criticism of the end of the 19th century). The deviations of the manuscripts cannot possibly militate against the authorship of James. Why is it impossible that James himself should have answered these questions and that Bar Hebraeus, the great compiler, should have made an extract from them? A similar case may be found in Bar Hebraeus' treatment of George, Bishop of the Arabs.[1] He wrote several letters on liturgical matters. Prof. Ryssel, the editor of his works, said that the Canons of his were not culled from a special book of churchlaw, but "wahrscheinlich solche Stellen aus seinen Schriften... welche Entscheidungen über Fragen des Kultus und des Kirchenrechts enthalten und die von Späteren, eventuell sogar erst von Bar Hebraeus, der sie in seinem Nomokanon aufgenommen hat, in die für Kanones nötige präcise Form gebracht wurden".[2] So we may safely conclude that there is no reason to throw doubt upon the authorship of James who gave in it real questions of the practice of the church. We have discussed this in such a detailed form because we meet with the same question on the Nestorian side.[3]

(1) Cf. A. Baumstark, *L.G.*, S. 257-258. (2) V. Ryssel, *Georg der Araberbischof*, in: *P.R.E.*[3], vi, S. 529. (3) As to their outward form, their expression and their "atmosphere" the QQ. of John Tell. and James Edess. are exactly parallel to our book; in this respect they are useful to illustrate the point at issue. But it is not out of place to remark that a great difference in contents exists between the Jacob. and Nest. books under discussion, though they all deal with liturgical Questions. The former group gives resolutions about the treatment of the host and other subjects outside the Liturgy, about the intercourse with heretics, magicians, the duties of a deaconess, burial, conditions for admission to the Eucharist etc. (for this reason the title of Lamy's book, *Dissertatio de Syrorum Fide et Disciplina in re Eucharistica*, is somewhat misleading since the two documents published are for the minor part Eucharistic. A Nestorian parallel to them may be found e.g. in the letter of Isho' Barnun to Macarius, cf. p. 131–133). They do not discuss points of the Liturgy proper, as is done in our treatises. In the formergroup we find juridical questions, in the latter ritual questions.

The "Synodicon Orientale" has preserved a letter of the Patriarch Isho'yabh i (581-596)[1] to James, Bishop of Darai, in which various points of the liturgy and of its requirements are dealt with. This is a reply to questions put by the said Bishop as appears sufficiently from the introduction: "Und wir, von der Bitte deiner Liebe gezwungen, antworten der Wahrheit gemäss ohne Zögern, wenn auch kurz, auf deine Fragen über die priesterlichen Ordnungen und kirchlichen Kanonen des Dienstes des geistigen Lebens".

Some centuries later we find that the famous Catholicos Timothy i (780-823)[2] gave the Canons of his first Synod in the form of questions and answers; and some other works about the Canonlaw are divided in the same way. Among those published by Prof. E. Sachau, dealing with the law of succession and other secular questions, since the Catholicos was also the head of the Christians in their civil relations, is one about the Reservation of the host.[3] In this case too the variety of subjects makes it highly probable that they answered real needs which were generally the cause of convoking a Synod. The same was done by his successor Isho'barnun,[4] both in his decisions edited by Sachau[5] as in his replies to letters which were inserted in the part of the "Synodicon Orientale" that has not yet published. Another specimen of this manner of codification of canonlaw may be found in the "Quaestiones Ecclesiasticae" of John Bar Abgare to which a letter is prefixed in which he wrote to his correspondent: "Quod porro spectat ad Quaestiones, quas proposuisti, cupiens discere, quid ad singula quae rettulisti, nostrorum canonum leges praescribant; id vero ad praesentium literarum calcem a me expositum accipies, ubi ad singulas quaestiones tuas plane distincteque respondeo".[6]

The Exposition of the Liturgy, ascribed to George of Arbela, is also written in questions and answers. But there is a difference; for they give explanations of what is found in the liturgical books, while the category we have in view tries to solve difficulties arising

(1) A. Baumstark, *L.G.*, S. 126; the letter in: O. Braun, *Das Buch des Synhados*, Stuttgart-Wien, 1900, S. 237-277. (2) Sources and Literature collected in: A. Baumstark, *L.G.*, S. 217–218. (3) E. Sachau, *Syrische Rechtsbücher*, Berlin, 1908, ii, S. 68–69, Kanon 14. (4) Cf. A. Baumstark, *L.G.*, S. 219–220.–Are there two letters to Macarius, viz. in V., fol. 175 *b*–180 *b*. = M., fol. 149 *a*–152 *a* and in Mingana Syr. 587 = Vt. B. 81 (K. vi) or are their identical, cf. p. 132? (addition to Baumstark, S. 220, Ak. 1). (5) E. Sachau, *a.a.O.*, S. 119–147. (6) They are published in: *B.O.* iii, 1, p. 249–254, the quotation is from p. 249.

from the performance of the liturgy since theory of the books and practice of the Church were often different; and many cases were not provided for in the liturgical books.[1] In Expos. we find the logical order that is missing in our treatises. It may safely be ranked with the Catechisms.

Surveying the questions mentioned in the last sections the thought suggests itself that we have to do with real questions.[2] The preceding words always suppose an actual questioner; the variation of the subjects[3] shows that these collections are not treatises adorned with a proper name as dedication which is merely a literary fiction.

What reasons may have caused the compilation of these questions in general? What was their "Sitz im Leben"? Besides the facts that can be taken from the introductions to the letters quoted before, some very interesting accounts may be given showing how these various categories came into existence.

In the big collection of stories about Monks of Thomas of Marga it is told that a certain Narses was asked what was the origin of the answers inserted in the Paradise of Palladius. He said: "The holy Fathers were accustomed to sit down with the novices before them and scribes wrote down the questions which were asked and the explanations of them, and counsels, and answers, and they placed them in writing for their own benefit and for the benefit of those who should come after them".[4] It may be that this statement is not true in regard to the time of Palladius; but at any rate it shows how people imagined that it had happened and this imagination was probably a picture of their own methods.

One example may suffice to show at what ancient date the treatment of ritual questions which necessarily arise through the expansion of the ritual, came into being. Hieronymus replied to a correspondent: "De sabbatho quod quaeris utrum ieiunandum sit, et de eucharistia an accipienda quotidie . . . scripsit quidem et

(1) The "Questions du patriarche Timothée sur l'office", mentioned in: A. Baumstark, *L.G.*, S. 325, Ak. 8, are the same as his book on the Mysteries and not real questions, as Dr. Mingana kindly informed me, *Letter*-Birmingham, 9-3-1935.
(2) For only in very few cases Canons of former churchmen are quoted, while the Nestorians, too, were used to cite them, if possible, cf. e.g. Elias of Nisibis, *Letter*, tr. Vandenhof, in: *O.C.*, 1913, who fills several pages with a long array of rules against simony; Isho'yabh i, *Letter to James of Darai*, *Can.* iii (O. Braun, *Synhados*, S. 243) quotes Nicaea, *Can.* xviii; the compilations in: 'Abdisho', *Nomocanon.*
(3) The various topics are not systematically exposed, but only casually (the next chapter § ii offers a good many examples). (4) Budge, *B.G.*, ii, p. 547-548.

Hippolytus vir disertissimus et carptim diversi scriptores e variis auctoribus edidere".[1]

With regard to the subsequent history we confine ourselves to some examples from the Syrians. In 538 some eastern Jacobites asked their co-religionists in Constantinople for information and the answer is still extant; it was edited by Mgr. Rahmani.[2] Another instance of this kind is found in the correspondence of Isho'yabh iii (as a matter of fact this is the only one in all his letters).[3]

The history of the Patriarch John vi (cf. p. 87–88) furnishes another example. In his time a king of the Turks had been converted to Christianity since he had been saved in a wonderful way by a Christian saint when he had gone astray. His people lived on milk and meat. The question which the Bishop of Merw wanted to be answered, was: what must be done by these people in Lent as the ordinary regulations for fasting were impossible in this case. The Patriarch decided that they should abstain from meat and if they were used to drink sour milk they should take sweet milk as a change of habit.[4] This shows clearly how all kind of difficulties arose form practice. Certain conditions, laid down by the lawbooks, are or cannot be fulfilled; the decision built upon these conditions cannot be applied and the question is: what should be done?

*Mutatis mutandis* we find the same case in our treatises. In the second part (V. iii and iv = M. C.) the author mentions several times the origin of these questions. So ii 15 deals with a sacristan who finds crumbs and now goes to ask a priest what he should do. The questioner is not satisfied with the priest's answer and wishes the decision of our author. ii 23 informs us that by accident something

(1) Hieronymus, *Epistula* 71, 6, in: *M.S.L.* 22, col. 672. Some interesting parallels may be found in the Old Testament, cf. Haggai ii 12 and 13 with the note of E. Sellin, *Das Zwölfprofetenbuch*[2-3], Leipzig, 1930, S. 463: "Der Prophet soll die Priesterschaft um eine das kultische Leben betreffende Thora angehen; man sieht, dass die mündliche Thoraerteilung durch ihre schriftliche Fixierung noch nicht verdrängt war, vgl. Mal. 2, 7; Hos. 4, 6; Deut. 17, 9. 11 usw." (2) I. E. Rahmani, *Vetusta Documenta Liturgica*, in: *Studia Syriaca* iii, Sharfeh, 1908, p. 5-23 (text) = p. 30-48 (transl.).–The text we read here is only the Answer in the form of Canons, without the Questions. The heading and ending in a codex of the Library in Sharfeh informs us about the authors of the questions and of the answer, published p. 27 (tr.); the codex Paris-Sang. 62 followed by Rahmani in his edition of the text misses it. (3) Isho'yabh iii, *Liber Epistularum*, ed. R. Duval, *C.S.C.O.*, ii 64, p. 244 (t. = 177 versio). (4) Gismondi, p. 100; Bar Hebraeus, *Chr. Eccl.*, col. 279-281; A. Mingana, *Early Spread of Christianity in Central Asia*, p. 16–17.

was poured over the altar and people went to ask the Bishop about it. The teachers as authorities in these matters are mentioned in ii 17 and 35; they were asked for instruction but their answer seemed to be highly disputable.[1] The same is supposed in the Introduction, when it is said that everyone speaks about all the events according to his own knowledge (cf. also ch. vi, i). These statements give us an insight into the church-practice and show vividly how they used to act. These questions were put in the school; but they arose when in a certain church the conditions necessary for performing the Eucharist were not fulfilled because of the ignorance or negligence of the priests. What has been done in the Nestorian church with regard to these subjects? What part did the schools play in them? These questions form the theme of the next chapter.

To this it may be added that it appears very clearly that we have not to do with fictions of the writer. See e.g. Q. 85: a case is told; but the answer cannot be given properly as the author has never heard of such a thing from the Ancients. In ii 24 he says that he will record what he has seen, concerning the consecration of the altar, and a story follows from the time that he was a deacon. All this shows what meaning must be attached to his "I have seen or heard". It implies real facts.

Their treatment seems sometimes to tend to casuistry when a solution is followed by: "But if . . .". But it is not absolute casuistry, since it gives so many examples from real life which are not specially constructed. Besides that we find only comparatively few instances of it, and we may make the same remark as is done on p. 95 about the catechisms.

From the foregoing investigation we may conclude that there existed a type of literature in the form of questions dealing with various subjects. In many cases Q. and A. were handed down from generation to generation. But the Questions of practical Theology go back to real questions unless the opposite is definitly stated (it will be shown in the next paragraph, that "Ancients", "Fathers" etc. are not a sufficient warrant to date these QQ. some centuries before the actual time of their publication ± 1005–1015). But it goes without saying that this fact does not exclude the existence of

(1) These questions will be found quoted in the commentary ad Q. 15, Q. 17, Q. 24 and Q. 35.–ii is throughout this book: V. iii + iv = M.C.; my numbering begins at M. fol. 51 b. 11.–Cf. Isho'Barnun, quoted in: *B.O.* iii 1, p. 224: "Many teachers do not allow it at all and some of them . . . ."

parallels in other liturgical sources which will be quoted in the commentary. But they are not of a nature to necessitate the supposition that our author merely copies predecessors. The similarity must be explained by the fact that the author wished to maintain the traditions of former times. Besides that it is quite probable that the same case took place several times in the course of some ages! *It cannot be concluded from the mere form of these writings that it contains older layers.*

This does not preclude the possibility of a certain tradition in regard to the shaping of these questions. Both in the Jacobite questions of John of Tella and these of James of Edessa as in our Nestorian ones is found a particular way of putting the questions. ܐܪܐ or ܡܛܠܡܢ at the beginning (their meaning will be discussed later on) is frequently occurring. The Greek aequivalent is found in those of Timothy of Alexandria. This shows the same form of expression in the course of six centuries (these are not the only (formal) resemblances, see p. 114, n. 1 and: commentary, passim). Nevertheless this does not prove anything about the contents, for it should not be forgotten that this material is canonical which reveals a strong traditional form as is also found in every juridical expression. The same is true for other words that are often found in these treatises, e.g. to qualify the actions of opponents as stupidity which is typical for antiheretical treatises.

It remains a noteworthy fact that proofs from Scripture are missing, the more so as this occurs in other replies to liturgical questions (so in Timothy i and Isho'Bar Nun).[1] It is possible that this was omitted because the purpose of the writer was only to give the heritage of the Fathers without their foundation.

As to the style this is on the whole very abrupt, sometimes obscure, especially for those who are not well informed about the Nestorian liturgical usage, though this was naturally no drawback for its first hearers or readers. On the other hand it is somewhat verbose so that V. shortens by omitting epithets etc. (p. 73). After all it shows a kind of style which is typically Syrian. Whether it has some pecularities of its own or is characteristic for a special time, I do not dare to decide.

(1) A very striking example of the use of Scriptural prooftexts may be found in: W. Riedel-W. E. Crum, *The Canons of Athanasius of Alexandria*, London, 1904 (since this book will be quoted in the Commentary at several occasions, and has such an illustrious author's name, it is not out of place to refer to O. Bardenhewer, *Geschichte der altkirch. Lit.*, iii, S. 68–69 who considers it spurious. "Sicher aber ist, dass diese Kirchenordnung aus Ägypten stammt, und wahrscheinlich, dass sie der Zeit des Athanasius nicht fernsteht").

## vi. THE "QUESTIONS ON THE EUCHARIST" OF ISHO'YABH IV AND THEIR RELATION WITH THE LITURGICAL TRADITION OF THE NESTORIANS

We discussed in the previous chapter the formal side of our writing, and saw that its form did not answer the question whether the materials contained in it were traditional; on the contrary, everything pointed to assuming here real questions arising out of the liturgical practice of ± 1000 A.D. But to estimate more exactly its value for the knowledge of the history of the liturgy, it is necessary to examine the contents of the book. We must face this problem: *do these questions and answers transmit the substance of the instruction of previous generations, of some centuries ago?*[1] In other words: is it allowed to use this work as a witness of the liturgical practice not only of the 10–11th, but also of the 7th or even 5th century?

The solution of this problem can only be tried by the way of an exact interpretation of the information given by the author about the kind of difficulties which threatened the liturgical life of his church and about the sources of his knowledge which enabled him to give this (right) answer.

i. Some sentences at the very beginning of the "Introduction"[2] form the obvious starting-point. The Questioner describes the bad state of the church in his days because of the priests who are not instructed and do not follow the "Canons and Orders of the Service of the Altar". If something happens during the performance of the liturgy, they do not care for it but they act as they like it (commentary). But this young priest himself comes to his teacher to learn the rules of the old men, in order that he might be right according to the standard of the church. These words may seem somewhat enigmatical. If they are read in the light of the whole work they become perfectly clear.

(1) We speak of the special regulations as given in our Q. Q. It is a matter of course that the elements from which they are made existed centuries before; e.g. the Lord's Prayer dates from the very beginning of Christianity, but Q. 105 sqq. are only possible after the time of Timothy i; the same is true for the altar, Eucharistic Bread etc. But we ask here when the special rules of our Q. Q. have been made. (2) The Introduction is an integral part of the book. There are no reasons to consider it spurious.

In the "Commentary on the Liturgy", written by the Jacobite Father Moses bar Kepha (cf. p. 86, n. 4) some similar tones are heard. He blames "many untrained and ill-instructed priests" because of an improper addition.[1] He tells us, that some people say a "Gloria" in the Anaphora, although it "does not belong to the Qurrābhā, but has been introduced by the presbyters. This appears from the fact that the service-books of the presbyters are written according to the pleasure of each one and there is no agreement between them: for whereas the lectionaries of the Old and New (Testaments) do not vary in a single place, thou seest that the service-books of the presbyters contain frequent and considerable variations"[2]–a statement which seems to me to be of the utmost importance for the (textual) criticism of the Jacobite liturgy. He uses the same qualification for those who "strike their hands upon their foreheads" at the "Kyrie". They who break the Coal "are uninstructed and ignorant of the Mysteries of the Christians".[3] In reading these words one should remember that Moses is exposing the spiritual meaning of the prayers and actions of the liturgy. But the latter are only mentioned in passing, and this book has a positive aim and not the negative one to correct those priests; so the notes upon them are rather incidental. At any rate the quotations show priests who had peculiarities both in their prayers and acts because of their ill-instruction while the service-books exhibited great variations.

Our treatise has been written about a century later. Does it combat the same irregularities, viz. changing of prayers and actions of the divine liturgy itself? What is the character of the events?

The ill-instruction of the priests, i.e., not following the "Canons and Orders" and giving a wrong solution of various occurrences, is evident from the questions. This definition implies that the right order is indicated in the books mentioned. They will be found in the "Takhsa" (cf. p. 38–39). This service-book contains the "Canons" of John bar Abgare which will be discussed later on in this chapter.[4]

(1) Moses bar Kepha, in: *Two Commentaries on the Jacobite Liturgy*, ed. R. H. Connolly–H. W. Codrington, p. 36; cf. the quotation from John of Tella, p. 142. (2) *Ibid.*, p. 39–40 (quoted by Dionysius b. Salibi, *Expositio*, ed. H. Labourt, *C.S.C.O.* ii 93, Parisiis 1903, p. 61).–He uses the same word ܦܘܪܣܬܐ = service-book as our author (Q. 1 and fol. 34a; cf. p. 125). (3) *Ibid.*, p. 61–69 ("coal"–cf. commentary). (4) Cf. p. 133–135; it is clear that the present edition is a composition which contains several formularies which are much later than the time of Isho'yabh iii.

The "Orders" dealing with the matters of our Q.Q. are the Liturgy of the holy Apostles Addai and Mari[1] for the liturgy proper; the Formularies for signing of the Altar with or without oil in cases of consecration or desecration, and the Order of Mixing (which was prefixed by Dr. Brightman to 'Addai' in *L.E.W.* but is not found before it in the MSS.). From the present edition it is quite clear what should be done. Many questions are, from this point of view, merely asking what one knows already; and the answer repeats simply what may be read in T. on various places.[2] Yet it seems as though the Questioner was himself not quite sure in referring to the service-books since he is afraid of being mocked at and asks for exact indications. Besides this it is not superfluous to remark that there exists some difference between the 19th and the 10th century, between the printed text of T. which incorporates everything mentioned in various MSS. and the MSS. themselves as used in the churches.

It is a well-known fact that the oldest liturgical texts such as Serapion, Apostolical Constitutions[3] etc. contain hardly any direction for the right performance of the liturgy besides the prayers. It is true: they are not service-books in the strict sense, but the lack of "rubrics" (the indication of the actions, generally written in red characters) is striking, the more because they are not found in the oldest MSS. either. These copies are generally very young, mostly after the 10th century. The rubrics as given in *L.E.W.* are not old, but actually modern.[4] With regard to the Western Church Dom. J. Baudot wrote: "Chaque église particulière possédait ses ordinaires ou coutumiers (in which the regulations for a solemn performance of the Mass are found); ces sortes de directoires semblent s'être répandues surtout à partir du xi^e^ et du xii^e^ siècle."[5] The same freedom and variety seem to have ruled in the Eastern Church and among the Nestorians.

It was pointed out before (p. 57) that the Nestorian MSS.

(1) It is natural for the parts outside the Anaphora; but in the Anaphora, too, he follows 'Addai', as appears from Q. 89 sqq.–see Commentary. (2) The Commentary gives sufficient proofs for this. (3) The *Euchologium* of Serapion, in: G. Wobbermin, *Altchristliche liturgische Stücke aus der Kirche Ägyptens*, Leipzig, 1898 (*Texte und Untersuchingen* 17,3); the other texts in: *L.E.W.* (4) *L.E.W.* p. viii–ix; cf. *L.O.C.* ii, p. 563 (quoted on p. 30, n. 3) and: J. Braun, *Liturgisches Handlexicon*, S. 301: "In der vorkarol. Zeit gab es in den lit. Büchern nur sehr wenige Rubriken . . . Im späten Malt. sind sie ihnen meist bereits in sehr erheblichem Ausmass eingefügt." (5) J. Baudot, *D.A.C.L.*, s.v. *Cérémonial*, t. ii, col. 3296.

show variants in the prayers, but mainly in the rubrics. Even in the 15th century there were not uniformly ordered; while the prayers are practically the same, the directions they contain are different. There are additions (see ad Q. 94 and ad Q. 24). This fact is in accordance with the general rule that the prayers had been fixed before the rubrics (cf. also p. 127). The liturgy underlying the "Expos." follows in the main the present text of 'Addai', but not in every detail. An exact collation of the existing MSS. of the Eucharist has not yet been made.[1] To compensate this defect to a certain extent we may refer to the critical study of the text of the Nestorian baptismal rite published by Dr. G. Diettrich in 1903[2] since this formulary offers a good parallel. A glance through his book shows the growth of the formularies and the insertion of various ceremonial notes. This ritual is generally ascribed to the great reformer Isho'yabh iii. But the actual situation of some centuries after his death is very well illustrated by the following notice. The MS. J² which often exhibits remarkable and, for our purpose, illuminating additions, draws attention to a varying practice.[3] This makes Diettrich observe: "Aus diesem Verhör der Zeugen ist soviel gewiss, dass Iso'yabh III keine bindenden Bestimmungen über die Krönung der Getauften und ähnliche damit verbundene Ceremonien gegeben hat. Beachte das völlige Schweigen der Codd. J¹ Jahbh mal β und das: 'wenn es beliebt'–auch jenes: 'das sei nach der Gewohnheit des Ortes' bei J²." There is a stock to which all sorts of expansions are added and it seems that each church or country had its own specialities. This offers a good parallel to the situation in the time of our QQ.

From these facts it is clear that the service-books in the time of our author varied in their rubrics. The rubrics were not the more important part of the liturgy. But at the same time the danger was not imaginary that the differences in practice would become greater and that every priest would perform his task on his own hand. The unity of the liturgy is threatened, a matter of great importance for a church of that type[4] (cf. commentary). This diversity of the MSS.

(1) I compared the texts of T.; *L.O.C.;* Berol. 38 and various Nestorian Expositions. The result cannot be published here. (2) G. Diettrich, *Die nestorianische Taufliturgie*, Giessen, 1903. (3) G. Diettrich, *a.a.O.*, S. 87. The additions are scattered over the whole formulary. (4) Cf. the state some ages before (time of Babai): "Each country, and town, and monastery and school had its own hymns and songs of praise and tunes, and sang it in its own way, and if a teacher of a scholar happened to be away from his own school he was obliged to stand

is one reason for the uncertainty. It is caused by another one. These variations in the MSS. show that they do not go back to the same archetype; and secondly that the common ancestor of the prayers did not contain such detailed rubrics as the present books. This is in accordance with the general observation made before and is made highly probable too by the way in which "*Expos.*" speaks about the service-book which had been made obligatory for the Nestorian churches by Isho'yabh iii (see below ii c). Not everything had been regulated in them. Besides that it happened that a former practice was neglected or substituted by another one (cf. ad Q. 87). The QQ. reveal the dangerous places. *It is noteworthy that the formulary of 'Addai' with its prayers is not under discussion.* The difficulties came from the outside; by certain circumstances the matter becomes so complicated that it has not been provided for in the service-books. For they can prescribe what the Officiant must do, what vessels are required, what Elements must be used for the Eucharist. But they can not know what hindrances are possible. It is to a certain extent always ideal, and it supposes the knowledge of many practical questions. So the "Formulary of Mixing" says that wine and water must be mixed in the chalice, but does not indicate the quantity; 'Addai' that everything must be ordered at the end, but not what must be done with the remaining particles. Some directions were given in the "Admonitions" or "Canons", but in spite of them there remained a great number of uncertainties and it is doubtful if the Canons were generally accepted (cf. p. 137–138).

From other sources it can be seen that *these Q. Q. are linked up with the state of affairs in the Nestorian Church* ± 950–1000 *A.D.*, not only with regard to the outward circumstances (cf. ch. iv), but also to their contents. Q. 87 sqq. are a clear proof. If compared with T. it seems as though they are rather superfluous, since they agree exactly with T. They cannot be explained but by assuming that the matter had not been fixed in that time. This turns out to be the right solution. Timothy ii mentions a controversy about this very point in the 13th century. He writes,[1] after having indicated that they must be signed as is done in our book: "We practise according to

[silent] like an ignorant man", in: Budge, *B.G.* ii, p. 293–Babai (± 700; A. Baumstark, *L.G.*, S. 212–213) brought unity in singing as Isho'yab iii (p. 125) had done for the services.–At the time of our treatises other divergencies were dangerous. But in all cases we observe local varieties which ask for uniformity.

(1) The full text is quoted in the Commentary *in loco*.

the prevailing Law (ܢܡܘܣܐ) and the given Commandment (ܦܘܩܕܢܐ). This is according to the opinion of the Catholici and Patriarchs Mar Abraham and Mar Emanuel." The other opinion is that of the Catholici Isho'yabh, Seliba Zakha and Isho'Barnun. The wording of Timothy shows that he recurs to tradition of the 10th century in which Mar Abraham and Mar Emanuel reigned (p. 85) and that this tradition had replaced an older one. I does not become clear whether it formed already a part of the liturgy. But probably it was not so.

When the groups of questions as divided in the table p. 91-93 are examined, it becomes sufficiently apparent that they were not yet fixed. In the first group the "cardo quaestionis" is found in Q. 5, and it seems in Q. 6 as though the signing with oil is not generally known (see ii), while the Addition of 'Abdiso' is of the author's time. The second group deals with cases which cannot be provided for; as to the reconsecration of the altar difference is made between "with or without oil". Some of these cases are mentioned in the rubric T. p. 119, but not all (cf. ad Q. 1) and it is not certain when this rubric has made been. There is a formulary, ascribed to Isho'yabh iii, to do it "with oil"; another one "without" is anonymous. Prof. Baumstark assumed that this one was probably made bij Elias i (1028–1049) who is credited with a regulation of altar-consecration.[1] This would fit in very well with the fact that in the time of our writing it was not fixed and that the regulation was made by the Catholicos after the discussion in the school, because the need was felt. In the third group the preparation of the Elements is discussed. It is stated expressedly by the "Expos."[2] that no such formulary had been given by Isho'yabh iii. It may be that the first one who laid down the rules for it was John v in his Canons which were not strictly followed (p, 137–138) and left a large playing ground. The date of the Formulary is absolutely unknown; but it is not incorporated in the MSS. of T., but drawn by the editors from a special source.[3] An investigation into the matter of Q. 96 shows that the regulation such as it stands in T. and is given in this Q. has been decided by Elias of Nisibis († after 1049);[4] once more a case which was open in the time of our author and required a definite rule. The question of the Lord's Prayer had divided the church into

(1) A. Baumstark, *L.G.*, S. 286. (2) *Expos.* ii, p. 36. (3) "a MS. of the district of Jilu", *L.E.W.*, p. 246; another MS. and oral tradition is mentioned, *ibid.*, p. 249, n.b. (4) Cf. ad Q. 96.

two camps, one following the commandment of Timothy i, the other party sticking to the old regulation of I. iii. It is mentioned in "*Expos.*" and in that time it had not yet been decided (cf. ad Q. 105). The place that must be taken by the Cross etc. (group 6) is not prescribed by the formulary; freedom could lead to disorder and in the time of Timothy ii it seems to have been fixed.[1]

These Q.Q. reflect this situation: the liturgical book did not contain provisions for all matters; and even if there was a rubric about a certain case, it was rather young or caused differences and other people followed another, often diametrically opposite, line.[2]

In cases of doubt people used to go to some teacher, priest or bishop (cf. p. 104–105). The answer did not always satisfy the questioner. Therefore he wants "clear" or "exact indications", appealing to "the witness of the very old men, ancient of days" who do not live in his own time (cf. ch. iv and p. 140), but he asks his teacher who has seen and heard them (Introduction; various other places speak of this way of transmission). The teacher himself has asked, he says, many people and everyone gave his own answer (Q. 110 and ii 14, 17: "some people say"). This can be easily understood as some problems are rather difficult to solve (Q. 17, ii V. 5).[3] They need a careful examination (ii V.3) and the bad priests of his time neglected this (Introduction). Various practices are corroborated by a "proof" (Q. 89, 109, 116, 117, 123; ii 19; M. fol. $48^b$ though the author considers it in some cases nothing but a pretext (ii 34). The author's style is rather succinct and he gives hardly any argument himself. In this respect he is a striking contrast with the answer of Isho'Barnun to Isaac of Beth Qatraye who gives many references to Scripture (p. 131). In some cases the author confesses that he does not know it himself, because he has neither seen it nor heard of it;[4] he solves the difficulties by saying "according to my knowledge" (Q. 17; ii 20, 36, 38, 39 V.3 en 22). Of course, he uses this term in a way different from that in the Introduction where it indicates ill-instruction or laziness. He has investigated everything, but it was impossible to find the opinion of the old men. In some instances he leaves the decision to the questioner

(1) Particulars about these facts in the Commentary. (2) ii 16 quoted ad Q. 78; variety of opinion: Q 29, 65, 89, 101 and elsewhere. (3) ii V. 5 = addition of V. to ii 5 (see p. 69). (4) Cf. ii 36: something which that has not been done in our days but which the teacher has read in the Synodical Canons.

(Q. 116) or says that if somebody wants to act in another way, he may do so and our author is not inclined to quarrel with him about it (Q. 5, 16; ii 24, 39).[1] Yet by far the greater part shows no traces of hesitation; the author knows exactly what is required.

Where did our teacher get his knowledge from? He has heard or seen it, he assures at numerous places. He himself refuses to be called one "versed in knowledge", but he is "like one who has tried and seen things from the old men, ancient of days". He bases his knowledge not upon a written tradition, but upon an oral one. The authority was a number of initiated persons, since not every man of old age serving in the church belonged to them, for the questioner remarks that his time is deprived of such men, a statement which would be somewhat strange if it should be taken in the literal sense. Several times their witness is called upon (Q. 37, 89, 110, 118, 123). Once they are called "Fathers" or "Ancients" (Q. 116). He speaks of tradition (Q. 36, 94; ii 34 in a disapproving manner). If these statements will yield the answer to the question put at the beginning of this chapter, the contents of the following points must be defined: how where these liturgical matters transmitted, orally or by writing?–who are meant by the "old men"; do they form a warrant for an old tradition?–what was the part played by the schools because the author is a schoolmaster?–These terms suggest tradition. Is that true?

ii. Our Questions point to oral tradition. As a matter of fact it was found side by side with written regulations. In the 9th century the Patriarch Isho'Barnun answered to the question in what books it was written that the Purshana in the church is the Body of the Holy Virgin, that not everything that is traditional is written in books.[2] Although this statement does not strictly belong to the field that is explored here (it is more or less mystagogical), it is so explicit that it forms a suitable starting-point. The books are depositories

(1) It is interesting to note similar expressions in the answers of John of Tella: "I think" (*Can.* 9, Lamy, p. 70; 23, p. 78; 26, p. 82); "one should not doubt" (*Can.* 8, p. 68–70: ܡܬܦܠܓܝܢ ܐܬܪܥܝܬܐ; 9, p. 70: ܠܐ ܐܬܪܥܝܬܐ ܢܦܠܓ); he prefers 3 what is better (ܦܩܚ *Can.* 8).–*Expos.* uses the same words and offers many different opinions, but since the subject-matter is quite different, they do not form a clear parallel. (2) Isho' Barnun, *ad Macarium*, Q. 65, in: Mingana Syr. 586, fol. 440b (Purshana = Eulogia in other churches; for the connection with Mary cf. *L.E.W.*, p. 304: Prayer of Mary).

of Canon-Law[1]. If it had not been written down it was called "custom" which had the same validity unless a canon made it impossible. The same Isho'Barnun ordered that it was allowed to go on fasting after using the Mysteries, except on Sundays[2] because there was no canon forbidding it.[3] Along with the Canons custom had a large and unlimited field. By decision of a Patriarch or of a Synod such a custom was made obligatory.[4] But oral tradition is the mother of written orders which were made if required, e.g. by variety. This is the reason why the handbooks of oriental Canon-law generally miss systematic order; they do not contain all the rules; only those that settled a point of dispute.

This usage, familiar to the reader of the preceding pages, is found at the very beginning of the codification of churchmatters. It suggests even a parallel with the Jewish practice in post-exilic times, notably strong in the days of the N.T.[5] Within the limits of the present investigation it is impossible to deal extensively with this idea of Tradition *in liturgicis*.[6] Yet it will not be superfluous to recall some facts. The first who gives a remarkable notice in this respect is Tertullian. He ranks custom with the Scripture and against those who demand written authority he points to some generally accepted facts.[7] Augustin says the same: "In his enim rebus, de quibus nihil certi statuit Scriptura Divina, mos populi Dei, vel instituta majorum pro lege tenenda sunt" and mentions: "quae non scripta, sed tradita custodimus".[8] This teaching is in accordance with that of Basil,[9] of whom it was said in the funeral oration by Gregory of Nazianza that he had made νομοθεσίαι

(1) It would be interesting to compare the development of canon-law in the (Eastern) church with that of the Law in Islam, see: I. Goldziher, *Vorlesungen über den Islam*, Heidelberg, 1910, ch. ii, *Die Entwicklung des Gesetzes*, S. 35–79, which offers striking parallels to the points discussed in the following pages. (2) This is "always reputed a crime deserving ecclesiastical censure" from the time of Tertullian onwards; cf. a number of places in: J. Bingham, *Antiquities*, xvi 15, 3. (3) Isho' Barnun, *l.l.*, Q. 28, fol. 436b. (4) Cf. the fragment quoted on p. 81. (5) *παραδόσεις τῶν πρεσβυτέρων*, cf. G. F. Moore, *Judaism in the first centuries of the Christian Era*, Cambridge (Mass.), 1932, i., p. 98–99, 251–262; H. L. Strack–P. Billerbeck, *Kommentar zum N. T. aus Talmud und Midrasch*, München, 1922, i S. 695ff. (6) Vide A. von Harnack, *Lehrbuch der Dogmengeschichte*[5], Tübingen 1932–33, Index s.v.; F. Heiler, *Urkirche und Ostkirche*, München, 1937, Index s.v.; P. Tschackert, *Tradition*, in: *P.R.E.*[3], xx, S. 8–11; N. P. Williams, *E.R.E.*, s.v. *Tradition*, vol. xii, p. 411–415 (generally treating the relations between Tradition and Dogma). (7) Tertullianus, *De Corona* 3, in: *M.S.L.* 2, col. 98–99; cf. *de Virginis Velandis* 2, in: *M.S.L.* 2, col. 938–939. (8) Augustinus, *Epist.* 86, in: *M.S.L.* 33. col. 296–297, and 54, 1 in: *M.S.L.* 33, col. 200. (9) Basilius, *De Spiritu Sancto*, 27 in: *M.S.G.* 32, col. 188.

μοναστῶν ἔγγραφοι τε καὶ ἄγραφοι.[1] These quotations show sufficiently how both were thought to be of the same validity though we observe in later times a growing tendency to quote prooftexts from Scripture. If circumstances compelled to do so, the custom was fixed in an official canon. When Can. xviii of Nicaea speaks of the rumour that deacons have given the Communion-bread to the priests it says: ὅπερ οὔτε ὁ κανὼν οὔτε ἡ συνήθεια παρεδώκε; and immediately a canon is made to check such a wrong practice lest it might become tradition.[2]

In this connection it will be useful to quote some sentences from the introduction of Isho'yabh i in his letter answering the question of James of Darai on "die priesterlichen Ordnungen und kirchlichen Kanonen des Dienstes des geistlichen Lebens". He will write because the subject had not been dealt with systematically by the Fathers. Nevertheless he writes himself according to the tradition:[3] "Indem wir entsprechend der bei uns von den Vätern vermittelten apostolischen Überlieferung schreiben, weisen wir die anderen Überlieferungen zurück, die irgendwie durch irgend jemand Eingang gefunden, an verschiedenen Orten angenommen und von unvorsichtigen Leuten, die von solchen annehmen, die ohne gelernt zu haben, lehren, festgehalten wurden, von solchen, deren Überlieferungsgeschwätz das Organ zur Verführung vieler haltloser (Leute) is."[4] We learn from this quotation that there was a double custom; the right one may be learned (in the school?–see sub iv). Unfortunately the criterium which was applied to decide what was right or wrong is not so definite as to enable us to distinguish in a certain case between old and young. He also distinguishes between his answer and Canons: the latter are short "zur Einschüchterung der Ungehorsamen mit Anathemen"; the former are extensive in teaching and exposition, reproducing the doctrine of the Fathers and giving proofs from nature and Scripture. The former are discussed by teacher and pupil: "nicht in synodaler Form auf einer Väterversammlung in autoritativer Entscheidung unter Vielen aufgestellt."[5] By the incorporation in the Synodicon they also have

(1) Gregorius Naz., *Oratio* 43, 34, in: *M.S.G.* 36, col. 544. (2) In: J. B. Pitra, *Monumenta*, i, p. 434–435. (3) Cf. the beginning of his *Canon* xx (O. Braun, *Synhados*, S. 268–269): "Mein Verstand legte mir nahe, auf diese Frage nichts zu antworten, weil die Regenten und Lehrer der Kirche darüber nicht aussprechen."–He does not answer other questions: "Da sie den Verständigen klar sind, oder weil die Vorsteher der Kirche darüber nach geltender Gewohnheit verfügen." (4) O. Braun, *Synhados*, S. 239. (5) *Ibidem*, S. 271–272.

been ranked with Canones!–At the end of the Canons of his Synod (xxxi, O. Braun, *Synhados*, S. 234) it is said that everyone of the subscribers bound themselves to read them once a year before their flock. Naturally they would always have them at hand.

So we find that Canon and Custom (or teaching of the Fathers) stood side by side (the Q.Q. of Isho'yabh i are the deposit of the latter). The Canon is a definite commandment (exceptions by "necessity", see commentary), the custom is not.[1] It happened sometimes that Canon and Custom did not agree; Isho'yabh iii mentions in one of his letters such a case: "si vero apud vos per quosdam homines contra legem ecclesiasticam nunc prolatae sunt seniorum traditiones quae decretum a tua Paternitate legetime sanctitum abolent . . ."[2] Their relation is parallel to that of Dogma and Doctrine; of which the former was only formulated to exclude wrong opinions. Only when abuses creep in, the right practice is regulated; otherwise it was handed down from generation to generation without being written down. *This prevents us from defining what exactly belongs to it or when a measure was introduced;* for it might have been customary already for a long time before it became a Canon. This is the more conclusive in case of Orientals who have such a strong sense for oral transmission. It follows that it is impossible to get knowledge of these "Customs" but by indirect references. Something which has been written down at a late date, may be very old; but it is not necessarily so, because it is called "traditional". *This "Custom" is an absolutely incalculable factor.* Yet it is important to see that the limits between Canon and Custom were vague from the outset. It remains the same through all ages, though the place of the limits may change. Another cause of complication forms the fact that some places developed peculiarities of their own (see p. 110 "Gewohnheit des Ortes", and the freedom that seems to have existed and of which these pages show many examples). We now pass on to a *survey of the contents of the written tradition* since this will give us some hold and reveal us something more about the validity.

*a.* At the time the Persian Church separated itself from the Greek Church (see p. 22), it took over the regulations that had been

(1) Yet there are even at the present moment in the Roman Catholic Church (in which these matters are regulated much better than in the Oriental Churches in the past and present) "Consuetudines contra legem", cf. J. Braun, *Lit. Handlexicon*, S. 122, s.v. *Gewohnheit*. (2) Isho'yabh iii, *Epistulae*, ed. R. Duval, p. 114.

made at several synods of the Greek Church. We must keep in mind as far as our subject is concerned, that already very soon several synods were held and made regulations about questions that occurred again and again, such as: who was to be admitted to the Communion; is it allowed to take the Eucharistic bread home? These Canons together with others were taken over by the Persians and caused them to have a common basis about these matters with the Greeks. The Synod of Yabhallaha i (419–420) decided that the following should be obligatory: the Apostolical Canons, those of the Synod of Nicaea (325), Ancyra, Neocaesarea, Gangra, Antioch and Laodicea (that of Chalcedon [451] was added by Mar Abba).[1] From the liturgical point of view one Canon of Isaac (410), viz. xiii is important; he decided: "Auch im Dienste des Abendlandes, den die BB. Isaak und Maruta uns gelehrt und in dem wir alle in der Kirche von S. sie dienen sehen, wollen wir von nun an insgesammt ebenso dienen." It contains: Caruzutha's by the Deacons;[2] reading of the Scripture, offering of the oblation on one altar in all the churches, not in private houses.[3] So all matters were brought into agreement with Seleucia and the West. The "Abendland" is the Church in the Roman Empire.

The reference found about Mar Abba viz. "ordinavit ritum ecclesiae",[4] is too vague to draw from it a definite conclusion. It may simply be a reference to his translation of 'Theod.' and 'Nest.' (cf. p. 41).

*b.* α The letter of Isho'yabh i of Arzon has already been referred to several times.[5] He wrote to his correspondent that he did not say all that could be said, but only what was asked. We may summarize those that deal with the liturgy. The first prescribes that the priests should draw near to the altar with "awe" and the priests must be blameless.[6] He gives a short survey of the service, men-

(1) O. Braun, *Synhados*, S. 38–39; Mar Abba, *ibidem*, S. 138.–About this collection, cf. G. Krüger, *Handbuch der Kirchengeschichte*[2], Tübingen, 1923, i, § 29, 8; the oriental collections mentioned in: F. Haase, *Altchr. Kirchengeschichte*, S. 234–236. (2) Cf. *E.S.D.O.*, p. 294: The litany of the Deacon. (3) O. Braun, *Synhados*, S. 21.–For the reference to Isaac and Maruta compare Gismondi i, p. 26: "Interim (during the reign of Isaac) Marûtas episcopus medicus non cessavit orientalis fideles docere instituta universa ac decreta occidentalium, quae in eorum synodo communi consensu sanxerunt. (4) Gismondi ii, p. 24; cf. A. Baumstark, *L.G.*, S. 119. (5) His life and works in: A. Baumstark, *L.G.*, S. 126. (6) Cf. Isho'yabh i, *Canon* 5, O. Braun, *Synhados*, S. 206–208.

tioning the fact that the priest comes to the altar, kneels and kisses it; he greets and blesses the people and their response; then he speaks "entsprechend der Aufeinanderfolge des kirchlichen Ritus . . (das) in allen Kirchen Gottes gebetet wird" (not specified) and the signs of the Cross are mentioned. The second orders that the celebrant must first of all receive the communion as he also needs forgiveness. The order in which this must be done is given here. The Can. 18 of Nicaea is repeated in Can. 3 here; but if there is no other priest it must be done nevertheless, though in a special way which is indicated. He forbids a priest to officiate in anger (5) and a minister may not prevent an other man with whom he is quarreling from receiving the sacraments (6). An adulterous priest must be punished by excommunication (11).[1] It will be seen that these Canons are mainly dealing with the conditions for communion.

β. In the introduction to this letter he refers to a writing of his which he had composed when he was a teacher "auf der hohen Schule", at the request of the Bishops, in which he explained "klar und distinkt": "wie der Priester zu der Taufe und der Darbringung des Opfers im furchtbaren, Gott versöhnenden und die Getauften heiligenden Priesterdienst hinzutreten soll, in dem wir jedem (Text) worte seine Erklärung in einer Menge kurzer (Bemerkungen) beifügten."[2] Nothing of such a book is spoken of in the "Catalogue" of 'Abdisho'; but this writer mentions 22 Q.Q. on the Mysteries.[3] Prof. Baumstark identified these two books and supposed that in V. fol. 93 one question of it had been preserved: whether the liturgy may be brought out of the church (the latter suggestion had been expressed before by Prof. Braun).[4] This identification of three data without having seen the part in question, is somewhat too premature. For even if the first clause of this sentence may be taken as dealing with liturgical indications, yet it seems to be about the liturgy proper and the priest, but not about accidentals such as the Question in V. does. But the second part rules out the possibility of

(1) One of his arguments is Matt. 7 : 6: "Heilig und Perlen nennt er das h. Sacrament unter dem Bilde kostbar geachteter (Dinge)". (2) O. Braun, *Synhados*, S. 239. (3) *B.O.*, iii 1, p. 110–111; but Amr ascribes them to Isho'yabh ii of Gadala (J. Labourt, *Christianisme*, passim): "de Sacramentis Ecclesiae in duas supra viginti interrogationes totidemque responsiones distributum." Of I. i he wrote only these words: "canones edidit et sacramenta exposuit", in: Gismondi ii, p. 31 and p. 28. (4) A. Baumstark, *L.G.*, S. 126 and Ak. 10 (vielleicht); O. Braun, *Synhados*, S. 239, N. 1 (the number of the MS. is omitted); R. Duval, *Littérature Syriaque*, p. 349, does not mention what is said in the Synodicon at all.

this explanation and shows that we must think of a mystagogy. It cannot be said whether this is the same as the 22 Q.Q.; but in Amr they are clearly distinguished. It is not impossible because they deal with the mysteries. On the other hand the form of the "question" points to actual difficulties in the service. This fits in very well with a subject as that of V. There are some incalculable points, especially as the expression of 'Abdisho' is far from clear. Before some of the data are rashly combined and identified, all the materials that are left should be examined.

We begin with Vat. Syr. 150. The authors referred to above started undoubtedly from the "Catalogue" of Assemani (cf. p. 65). It is not clear why they confined themselves to this one alone. If we take before us V. v we read that it is ܥܠ ܐܢܢܩ̈ܐ = "on emergencies".[1] This item does not agree exactly with the description given by Isho'yabh himself, nor does it look like that of 'Abd., for they are not in the form of questions. Their contents are:

1. the precautions for bringing the communion outside the church to a sick person (published by Assemani, *B.O.*, iii 1, p. 244);
2. baking of the eucharistic bread by a single priest;
3. the place of the font of baptism;
4. consecration of the eucharist by a single priest is forbidden (only allowed by the 318 Fathers of Nicaea to hermits).

In V. these canons had a special heading. In M. the text had become somewhat confused as the heading and the first topic were omitted; consequentely this piece is put very akwardly between the Q.Q. But with V. in hand it is quite clear (it is possible that the name of I. was crossed out in codex M., since it was the same name as that of the heading of C.).

In his collection of the ecclesiastical lawbooks of Alexandria Dr. Riedel inserted and translated "Befehle der Väter, der Vorsteher, der Gebieter."[2] According to the editor they are nothing but a compilation from the Arabic times. They offer parallels to the Syriac text mentioned before. § 20 of them contains the canon about the communion of the sick (1), in every word agreeing with the Syriac text; and § 19 that one on the consecration by a single priest (4), but this recension is much longer. A striking difference between these two forms is that they are here introduced by the entry "sie haben befohlen und gesagt . . .". Is this the work of

(1) About this idea cf. commentary. (2) W. Riedel, *Die Kirchenrechtsquellen des Patriarchats Alexandrien*, Leipzig, 1900, S. 187–193.

the Compiler? How were they brought into the Alexandrine collection and why have they another order?

Another important piece of evidence is contained in one of the MSS. of the Baptismal Service J.[1]).[1] After the prayer of T. p. 65, l. 3 a long passage follows ending with the words: "The great matters of dispute solved by Mar Isho'yabh of Arzon before intelligent people, are brought to a close." G. Diettrich thought the passage "leicht überarbeitet".

Assemani has given a report of the Arabic translation of the Synodicon by Elias Damascenus.[2] It contains the following items: "14 Jesujabi statutum de Eucharistia. 15 Mosis in idem, nec non de Baptismo". Together with no. 13 they are not found in the Syriac text. Assemani's statement was derived from Vat. Arab. 157 about which he did not furnish any other information, exception being made for his quotation of the decision of the said Moses whom he identified with Moses of Kashar mentioned by 'Abdisho':[3] as the text stands it deals with the consecration by a single priest and communion outside the church; the sequence is the same as that of Riedel's text; the former decision is very short. For the rest nobody seems to have asked who was the Isho'yabh of item 14 (that is the more striking because it might have been that it was I. iii and that his work contained something about the liturgical reformation). What is contained in this Arabic text?[4]

The parts mentioned stand after two writings of George i (680–681), long after I. i. no. 13 (Ass.) begins like this (fol. 79b): "further they said", introduction to a summary of the order of the Bishops at an official meeting. Next to it come the parts that interest us here (fol. 79b–81b). "It is handed down from Isho'yabh that he laid down as a rule and taught":

1. a canon about the provisions to be made when eucharistic bread is left;

2. about the ablutions of the chalice;

3. (introduction: likewise he said) about the consecration by a single priest, which is inconsistent with the church-law;[5] joined to it is a

(1) Published by G. Diettrich, *Nest. Taufliturgie*, S. 94–99; neither this reference nor the other materials have been incorporated by Prof. Baumstark in his note on Isho'yabh i. (2) *B.O.*, iii 1, p. 514.–About the Arabic translation cf. p. 20. (3) *B.O.*, iii 1, p. 276 (the codex has here the classmark 37); A. Baumstark, *L.G.*, S. 122–123, thinks this identification probable. (4) Thanks to the kind offices of Prof. Dr. R. R. Post I received the facsimiles. Prof. Dr. A. J. Wensinck had the extreme kindness to translate these parts. (5) Syr.: Breaks the Canon.

bit of polemics against the Greeks (Rūm);[1] it was ordered by God that everything in the natural world should be done in pairs, as it is in heaven (Is. vi). The argument is reinforced by a quotation of Mar Moses from his book "The Beauty of the Works";[2]

4. (without introduction) about the communion of the sick;[3]

5. further they(!) taught (the usual introduction to all the following canons): about baking the eucharistic bread while there is no priest to consecrate it,[4] and drinking of the chalice;

6. the bread must remain on the altar until a priest comes to consecrate it; another person must be present for the "ordering"; otherwise the priest must wait and fast till somebody comes;

7. the following persons may not communicate: mad people;[5] people who have been excommunicated; heretics and mockers;

8. the deacon is allowed to "sign" the chalice if something was left, but not to say the formula: "this chalice is consecrated etc.";[6]

9. about Baptism in a special part of the church[7] that can only be entered by certain ranks of the clergy, and about laybaptism.[8]

We have given in the notes the points of similarity between the various sources. It is clear that the divison of Assemani (two treatises of I. and Moses) is definitely wrong; the Isho'yabh that seems to be quoted was i, as we may infer from V. while nothing militates against this statement; Riedel's text is a descendant of the Synodicon with some correction; its quotation in a Jacobite context explains sufficiently that the proper name has been replaced by: "they". It seems as though in V. all canons are ascribed to I. while in M. they are anonymous; in Arab. they are the decisions of a

(1) The Greeks allow: one priest in several villages (cf. ad Q. 36); the priests entering the altar with shoes (cf. ad Q. 39); the nuns to enter the altar (cf. ad Q. 29–30) and to communicate to the people (the Jacobites only, if there was no priest, *Vetusta Doc. Liturgica*, p. 7 = 33 tr.). (2) This agrees with Riedel, § 19 ( S. 192–193); variants: Elias omits: "diejenigen, welche den Bestimmungen zuwider handeln und der Tradition widerstreiten und diejenigen, welche ihnen die Erlaubnis dazu gegeben haben, sind gebannt, ausgeschieden"; the quotation of Moses is cited, but introduced with "Einige Heiligen haben gesagt . . ."; is this tendentious? (3) Quite the same as Riedel, § 20 (S. 193) = V. The quotation of Assemani gives the impression that this Canon is also of Moses. It is clear from the context that it is not. (4) = V. and M. (5) This is a general rule in Eastern churches, *Vetusta Documenta Liturgica*, p. 6–7 = 32 tr., but cf. p. 133 n. 4. That the other categories were excluded from communion is natural. (6) Cf. ad Q. 21. (7) = V. and M. (8) The quotation by G. Diettrich, mentioned before, is a very large expansion of this Canon. It is not clear, where the words of I. i begin or whether the whole belongs to this Patriarch.

Synod that met under George i[1] or afterwards. They used the traditions of I. i; his canons were once more underlined and expanded; and they profess to be in accordance with the tradition of the church. It is remarkable that Syr. and Arab. have deviations on some minor points as regards the author's name though Isho'yabh i is mentioned every time. Yet the evidence is too confused to make us say without any doubt: these canons were derived from the book: "Questions about the Mysteries" of Isho'yabh i; nor can we say that it was identical with that one referred to in the Introduction of his letter. But it is clear that the Questions were probably not mystagogical but practical and that Isho'yabh wrote another book of interpretation.

We will stick to the Arabic text. It shows that there was in this respect a tradition that was cultivated. It dealt with cases of: preparation and ordering of the liturgy.

*c.* At this point we must record the liturgical work of the great Patriarch Isho'yabh iii. His name has been mentioned before at several occasions as he is called the great reformer of the liturgy. He lived in the beginning of the 7th century and ruled from 648 (or 650)–657.[2] This time is outwardly marked for the Nestorians by the change of government, since the Persian Sassanides must cede their reign to the Islam, inwardly by a reorganization of all forces, as the church had to face so many new problems. A monograph about this outstanding man and his work in these troublesome years is still wanting, though it would be an attractive task to write it. We cannot undertake it within the limits of the present investigation. We cannot even consider the whole of his liturgical work, but the scheme of this book imposes the questions: what was the character of his activity concerning the Eucharist; what has he bequeathed to posterity? After the paragraphs devoted by Prof. Hanssens to these points,[3] it is not superfluous to put them again, since he does not offer all the materials available nor gives an answer.

The editions of the Eucharistic Liturgy which I have consulted

(1) Cf. Vat. Arab. 157, Fol. 81*b*: "the book of the collected decisions of the Synode is brought to a close, according to the Institution of the Apostles in consecutive times and the traditions of the 318 Fathers that came together in Nicaea". Or is this the end of the whole collection? (2) For the sources cf. A. Baumstark, *L.G.*, S. 197–200, and add: W. Wigram, *Introduction to the history of the Assyrian Church*, London, 1910, passim.–*D.A.C.L.* does not contain an article about him. (3) J. M. Hanssens, *Institutiones*, ii, p. 465–467, and: iii, p. 627–628.

do not offer a single remark about Isho'yabh's activity. But it should be said once more that a critical edition (p. 110) does not exist. So we do not know what may be contained in some MS. or other; at the present moment, however, the liturgy itself does not give us a clue. Among the writings of this author are no directions for the administration of the Eucharist, such as John v has given some centuries later in his Canons (p. 133–135), nor does his Book of Letters, published by Prof. Duval,[1] offer any help, since it does not contain any letter dealing with Eucharistic problems or any reference to the liturgy or to his own activity about it. The result of the direct sources is rather disappointing; so we must see whether the indirect sources yield any result, as there must be some reason to mention his name in connection with the Liturgy.

The references of the *Nestorian Chronicles* are rather poor. Mari thought 13 lines sufficient honour to this Patriarch and did not write anything about a liturgical reform.[2] Amr gives a longer note with the following detail which is of interest: "promovendis scientiis operam° dedit, *ordinavitque officum per anni circulum, uti nunc se habet* (14th century): sermones etiam, hymnosque composuit, qui inter preces recitantur".[3] The words which I italicized, point to liturgical activity, but the Eucharist is not specially mentioned; the concluding words suggest that this office remained the same in the course of time.[4] The summary in the "Catalogue" of '*Abdisho*' (± 1300) reads like this: "and he ordered an order of the churchbook of the 'Circle of the Year' and Baptism together with the Absolution and the Consecration of a new church and Ordination-formularies of all Orders etc."[5] Besides the Hudhra, about which we will speak presently, all the rituals specified here mention the name of I. in their MSS. and confirm the notice of 'Abdisho'.[6] *Our treatises* refer twice to him: in Q. 1 in connection with the consecration of a new church; in M. fol. 34ᵃ in connection with Baptism.

(1) Isho'yabh iii, *Liber Epistularum*, ed. R. Duval, Parisiis, 1904, *C.S.C.O.*, ii, 64. (2) Gismondi i, p. 55.–It may be remarked that the reference of Hanssens, *o.c.*, iii, p. 628 to Gismondi i, p. 49 and ii, p. 28 are wrong. These pages do not deal with the third patriarch of that name. (3) Gismondi ii, p. 32; see the previous note.–About: "promovendis scientiis" cf. p. 145. (4) Yet the reformation of the High Monastery (p. 148–149) also affected it; we must understand this sentence to mean that the general scheme was Isho'yabh's. (5) *B.O.*, iii 1, p. 139–140: ܘܛܟܣ ܛܟܣܐ ܕܚܘܕܪܐ ܘܥܡܕܐ ܥܡ ܚܘܣܝܐ ܘܩܘܕܫܐ ܕܥܕܬܐ ܚܕܬܐ ܘܣܝܡܝ̈ܕܐ ܕܟܠ ܛܟ̈ܣܐ ܘܫܪܟܐ. (6) Cf. A. Baumstark, *L.G.*, S. 199–200 notes passim.

Is this coincidence with 'Abdisho' merely accidental? Neither of these writers says a word about the Eucharist. Or must we interprete the fact that the author of the "Questions" refers to his great namesake at the beginning of his treatises, in this way that all the following teaching was derived from the Churchbook of Isho'yabh? The former possibility seems to be preferable; for, if the latter supposition were right, we should have expected this reference in the Introduction and not connected with a question on a particular rite. However this may be, I believe that the author of our Q.Q. had not this reason; but that it was impossible for him to connect the name of I. iii with the Eucharistic questions as these points were not dealt with in the churchbook. The chapters in the "*Book of the Governors*" dealing with the lifetime of I. iii[1] do not contain much about the Patriarch himself, since the work is concerned with monasticism and not with the history of the church as a whole. Nothing but the Ḥudra is ascribed to him; it is called here: ܦܢܩܝܬܐ ܕܩܢܘܢܐ = churchbook of the canons (it appears from the context that the Ḥudra is intended).[2] "Ḥûd(h)rā (Kreislauf), eigentlich Penqîd(h)tā (πινακίδιον, Tafel) der Kanones des ganzen Jahreskreislaufes" heisst das grosse Choralbuch des nestorianischen Ritus, das auf die Sonn- and Festtage des Kirchenjahres und die Werktage des Ninevitenfastens[3] und der vorösterlichen vierzigtägigen Fastenzeit die älteren wechselnden Gesangstücke für das kirchliche Tagzeitengebet und die Eucharistiefeier enthält".[4] Prof. Baumstark distinguished this book from the Takhsa which contained the various formularies for the priests (its contents, see p. 109), some of which were fixed by Isho'yabh iii, but up till now we did not hear anything about the Eucharist. Thomas of Marga refers to him in another place which is generally overlooked. In describing the work of Babai (± 700) he says in the sequence of the words quoted on p. 110, n. 4: "As before the time of Mâr Ishô'yabh of Adiabene the Catholicos, the orders of the services were performed in a confused manner in every place, and by the means of this man the services of all the churches acquired connected order, so also etc."[5] This

(1) Budge, *B.G.* ii, p. 131–179. (2) Budge, *B.G.* ii, p. 176–177, quoted ad Q. 106. (3) Cf. ad Q. 11. (4) A. Baumstark, *L.G.*, S. 198. (5) Budge, *B.G.* ii, p. 293; the Syriac text reads as follows, *B.G.* i, p. 142: ܐܝܟܢܐ ܕܩܕܡ ܩܕܡ ܡܪܝ ܐܝܫܘܥܝܗܒ ܩܬܘܠܝܩܐ ܚܕܝܒܝܐ ܒܫܓܘܫܝܐ ܒܟܠ ܐܬܪ ܐܬܪ ܐܘܪܚܐ ܡܫܬܡܫܝܢ ܗܘܘ: ܬܫܡܫܬܗܘܢ ܕܝܢ ܘܬܘܩܢܗܘܢ ܡܢ ܗܢܐ ܡܬܚܬܡܐ ܒܟܠܗܝܢ ܥܕܬܐ.

text tells us that there was a great confusion in the Nestorian church with regard to the services themselves, not about the singing which was the point in the time of Babai; probably every church and country had developed his own liturgy and the unity was broken. It was the great merit of Isho'yabh iii to have unified all the local varieties. The particular word "takhsa" which is used here can denote the order of every service, either Baptism, Eucharist etc. or Daily Office, but preferably the former (T. is the name of the Nestorian Euchologium). Though this text does not specially mention the Eucharist, it seems to be included and in general this notice is of great value. With it one sentence of the *Chronicle of Seert* fits in very well. It is told in the history of Ephraim: "Il (Ephraim) composa une messe dont se servent encore les Melchites. Les Nestoriens célébraient aussi cette messe à Nisibe jusqu'aux jours du métropolite Jésuyab qui, lorsqu'il régla les prières, choisit trois messes et prohiba les autres."[1] This fact can easily explain why the Eucharist is not mentioned in other places which tell something of the liturgical activity of I.: while he himself took a part in the conception of the formularies catalogued by 'Abdisho', he confined himself with regard to the Eucharist to stopping the local varieties and selecting three existing formularies. But there are two other notices found in the literature which point into another direction. The Nestorian canonist *Ibn-at-Tayyib* († 1043, in the time of our treatises) observes in his Arabic Nomocanon: "La messe des apôtres a été composée par Addaî et Mari, et le catholicos Jesus-iab l'a abrégée";[2] the same seems to be intended in the Chronicle of the Jacobite patriarch *Michael* (± 1150): "and he abridged the liturgy of Nestor, since it was very prolix."[3] As far as I know it has been impossible to detect rests of the unabridged liturgy ('Fragment' and the text of Abraham b. Lipheh, cf. p. 55, n. 5??) and these texts do not help us to determine the character of the curtailment. The MSS. do not help us either.[4]

(1) *Chronique de Séert*, ed. A. Scher Paris 1908, *P.O.* iv, p. 295–The three masses p. 29. n. 3.–Does this reveal something about the origin of 'Addai'? Dom. Engberding (cf. p. 54) has overlooked this text, though it confirms his view. (2) This Synodicon has not yet been published. The quotation in: *L.O.O.*, p. 338 and n. 1. (3) Michael i, *Chronicum*, ed. J. B. Chabot, Parisiis, 1898, iv, p. 776a (tr. iii, p. 521)–Prof. A. Baumstark, *L.G.*, S. 199 suggested that "dies angesichts der breiten Ausführlichkeit gerade dieses Formulars ('Nest.') nur auf einem Missverständnis beruhen (kann) und es muss vielmehr an die Apostelanaphora gedacht werden, deren überlieferter Text in der Tat den Eindruck starker Kürzung macht". Such a mistake would be easy for a Jacobite. (4) A monograph

Last of all we must pay attention to those places where I. is named in the "*Expositio*"[1]. At the very beginning in his apology (*Expos*. i, p. 16–18) the author declares that he wants to be in everything in accordance with I. He has been asked about the reasons of the offices of the church. There are different interpretations (*Expos*. i mentions a good many of them; it is striking that they are not found in such a large number in the explanation of the Eucharist).[2] To find the right path he wants "normam a sanctis patribus statutam tenere et exsequi, qui suis interpretationibus restrictis nonnulla tacuerunt ut aliorum laboribus aliquid relinquerent: id quod et beati Išō'yabh patriarchae consilium fuit, qui Codicem illum insignem canonum instruxit."[3] By this I. gained the victory over the heretics "qui in ignorantia haeresim suam tenent, et officia negligenter *persolvunt*. In ritibus ergo atque canonibus explicandis qui in Codice descripti et innexi sunt" our author has followed his great forerunner.[4] He describes the plan of his work in the following words: "a re chronologica incipiemus; deinde orationum nostrarum commentaria aggrediemur".[5] In executing this plan he discusses the chronological questions in liber i; ii and iii deal with the Daily Offices; iv with the Eucharist; v with Baptism; vi with the Consecration of a new Church and vii with the Funeral and Marriage-services. In comparing the plan and its execution we must conclude that the contents of liber ii–vii are summarized under the head: orationes. The consecration-formulary was at the end of the Churchbook (l. vi, c. i). We can be sure that the Eucharist as commented upon by this anonymous author was contained in it, because he says at the beginning of book vi: "Dei adiutorio absolutae sunt omnes expositiones officiorum quae in cyclo (Ḥudhrā) anni positae sunt."[6]

on the work of Isho'yabh iii must fix the relation between 'Addai' and Narsai, *Hom.* xvii (if genuine); and the investigation has to be extended over the other formularies as well.

(1) Timothy ii does not mention him a single time; the Isho'yabh being quoted was i. (2) Sometimes he combats his predecessors, cf. e.g. *Expos*. ii, p. 34: "Abraham bar Lipheh in dementia sua". (3) *Expos*. i, p. 17: ܦܘܫܩܬܐ ܗܕܐ ܕܦܘܫ̈ܩܐ ܟܠܗ; the same words as in Budge, *B.G.* ii, p. 177, see p. 125. (4) *Expos*. i, p. 18: ܠܡܫܡܠܝܘ ܠܟܬܒܐ ܦܘܫ̈ܩܐ ܡܬܟܬ̈ܒܢܐ ܕܥܘܢܝܬܐ ܡܣܟܠܢܐ ܡܢܝܢܐ (5) The prayers are defined in the next sentence: "primum mensium, hebdomadarum ac dierum, expositionem instituemus; deinde medio loco ponemus cantiones, et mystica praeteriti, praesentis et futuri temporis cantica, donec in portu quiescamus illo, ubi tempus nullum est etc." (6) *Expos*.

Our author wants to follow closely the book of Isho'yabh, of which the prayers seem to be the most important part. Did the book of I. contain very specified indications of the actions of the priests? The following sentences can give us an answer: "beatus Išo'yabh de eis rebus sollicitus fuit, atque praescripsit, quae mysteria exprimerent, neque de factis ipsis adeo curabat"[1] and when he speaks about the "Pax" (*L.E.W.*, p. 283) given by the deacon "qui proclamavit" (which is sometimes done, but had not been prescribed by I.) he says: "et ecce, quamvis apud nos ille diaconus hanc pacem annuntiet qui et proclamationem fecit, tamen, uti superius dixi, beatus *Išō'yabh* ea omnia praescripsit, quae typum aliquem regni exprimerent, neque curae fuit ei ut omnia quae scripsit plene perficerentur, ita ut nihil aut adderetur aut demeretur."[2] That everything which had been ordered by I. had a typological meaning, is the favorite dogma of our author which guides his own interpretation (cf. e.g. n. 5 of p. 127 and Expos. i, p. 126; ii, p. 75, 88, 91 etc.). These words combined with the fact that he calls the rituals "prayers" can only mean that the servicebook of I. contained the prayers together with the directions which were most needed, but that it left a great freedom to the officiating priests with regard to the rubrics, a fact which agrees with the supposition of p. 110. There are strong reasons to believe that *the text which can be reconstructed from this Commentary offers the text of I. himself* and not that of the author's time. For he says that it is not wise to transgress the rules laid down by I. ("Sine ergo res debito more procedant, et quo modo docuit beatus *Išō'yabh* . . . Quidquid ergo nobis non praecipitur, hoc facere non debemus.")[3] The evidence of the following sentence seems to me conclusive: "Officium mysteriorum scrutare, et haec *omnia* ante oculorum tuorum aciem finge, dum ritus perlegis quos praescripsit beatus Išō'yabh, etiamsi non peraguntur."[4] There are some places where the practice of his time has more than that of I. and they are duly marked[5]: ii, p. 36 I. has not given an order for the preparation of the elements; ii, p. 53 (quoted before); ii, p. 82–83 on the addition of the Lord's Prayer by Timothy i (see commentary ad Q. 105 sqq.). Once only he records an

ii, p. 106 and ii, p. 66, quoted on p. 129, n. 1.

(1) *Expos.* ii, p. 32. (2) *Expos.* ii, p. 53; about the end of the sentence cf. the commentary ad Q. 1. (3) *Expos.* ii, p. 102. (4) *Expos.* ii, p. 74. (5) Perhaps it is not out of place to stress the fact, that *Expos.* contains only very few historical particulars.

addition which I. himself has made to the older liturgy and he tells us that there were many people who opposed to it and churches where it was not said even in his own time, because they wanted to preserve the tradition.[1] The same fate occurred to the addition of Timothy i. Why are these additions and changes of the tradition allowed while others are not? Because they have been made by men guided in a special way by the Holy Spirit. The author appeals to Paul's dictum in Rom. xiii 1 and continues: "si ergo omnibus potestatibus subditi esse iubemur, cur non huic se subiciunt, qui a Spiritu constitutus fuit ut nos regeret? Cum enim Timotheum repudiarint, repudiarunt et Išō'yabh: etenim ambo pariter patriarchae fuerunt."[2] But changes made by the priests on their own authority are wrong. It must be noticed that *Expos.* does not say anything about a reformation of the Eucharistic liturgy by I., while he mentions an older practice.[3]

These are the facts that can be derived from the study of the "Expositio". They are, I think, sufficiently interesting to pay some attention to them. As a matter of fact this book gives the fullest information and it is somewhat strange that it had generally been ignored. Summarizing the results we find the following data: the author has closely followed the ritual of I. iii; it was contained in a book which comprised both Ḥudhra and Takhsa (according to the terminology of Prof. Baumstark) and which is generally called Penqitha;[4] the number of the rubrics was comparatively small; additions to these actions may be made, though it is better to stick to the prescripts of I.; additions to the prayers may only be made by the Patriarch.

Reviewing the evidence of the preceding pages we get this

(1) *Expos.* ii, p. 66: "Sciendum tibi est, frater noster, quod haec proclamatio (caruzutha, *L.E.W.*, p. 294–295) non est ex praescriptione antiquorum et apostolorum, sed beatus ipse Išō'yabh eam praescripsit et instituit per Codicem suum, ita ut vix ac molestia accepta sit ab iis qui veritati resistunt et doctoribus. Sed et multi diu manebant ecclesiae nec eam dicebant; et ferunt etiam, esse usque ad hodiernum diem ecclesias quae non eam proclamant." (2) *Expos.* i, p. 122–123. (3) It will be remarked that he does not say anything of Baptism either. But his activity concerning Baptism did not consist in a partial change, but: "dieser allein hat das unsterbliche Verdienst, an Stelle des alten nestorianischen Katechumenentaufrituals das jetzt noch gebräuchliche Kindertaufritual eingeführt zu haben" (G. Diettrich, *Taufliturgie*, S. xvii). In explaining the ritual there was no reason for *Expos.* to mention the older one; I. iii had made a new beginning. (4) It may be that the use of Ḥudhra etc., which we found before, must be explained from this point of view and not in that strict sense as Prof. Baumstark did.

rough picture of Isho'yabh's activity: when he got his highly responsible office, there existed a great confusion among the Nestorians; he put in order a churchbook which contained the Daily Offices and rituals, some of which were new, while the three Eucharistic formularies were selected from a vaster number (and abridged?)[1] Because they were real liturgies, they were called „prayers", for the liturgy is always the work of the "Ecclesia Orans." He did not decide the questions of admission to the communion and so many practical questions which might arise during the service. His few rubrics left a fairly large field uncovered (take e.g. the preparation of the elements) the custom filled the gap. But this undefined custom might be the source of much trouble; and Isho' yabh's successors fixed afterwards several rules (see below), and as they never appeal to the great Patriarch, while the Eastern people are so traditional we may find here an affirmation of our view that he had not given rules about it. The time of our Q.Q. again showed confusion, because these matters had not been fixed in writing.

*d.* The following churchman of whom something of this kind is preserved was Timothy i (780–823).[2] In connection with other decrees about ecclesiastical orders he prescribed what should be done when a layman was angry and refused to accept the communion from a priest (14) and that it is forbidden to preserve the eucharist to the next day, in proof he refers to the paschal Lamb and Manna.[3]

*e.* Several of the writings of the successor and former opponent of Timothy, Isho'Barnun (823–828).[4] They are not found among those published already by Prof. Sachau;[5] we consulted them in codex Mingana Syr. 586 and 587 (these MSS. contain the same matter, I believe, as Vat. Borgia 81 (K. VI 3).

(1) The same is said among the Byzantines about the work of Basil and Chrysostom with regard to the Liturgy of James (Pseudo-Proclus, in: *M.S.G.* 65, col. 849–852, whose verdict is generally rejected at present, see: Pl. de Meester, *D.A.C.L.*, s.v. *Grecques* [*liturgies*], t. vi, col. 1597). Is Dom. Engberding (cf. p. 54) right in his inference from this similarity, that the statement of Ibn-at-Tayyib is without any value?–The question whether I. iii has been influenced from Byzance (p. 41) does not affect the theme of our investigation.
(2) Cf. A. Baumstark, *L.G.*, S. 217-218 and the Commentary ad Q 105 sqq.
(3) E. Sachau, *Syrische Rechtsbücher*, Berlin, 1908, ii, S. 68(69) and 70(71).
(4) Cf. A. Baumstark, *L.G.*, S. 219–220. (5) E. Sachau, *a.a.O.*, ii, S. 119–147.

α. Letter to Isaac, visitor of Beth Ḳatraye (587, fol. 360a–367b). After a long introduction the Q.Q. follow, all about liturgical matters, though not exclusively on the Eucharist. They are treated very fully, stating several mystagogical reasons. It is sufficient for our purpose to summarize those on the eucharist. Q. 1: whether the "Treasury" (cf. ad Q. 16) may remain on the altar for several days; the answer is in the negative; he refers to the paschal Lamb as a symbol (Ex. xii 10); it is a King that cannot be despised and another symbol is found in the Manna (Ex. xvi 19).[1] But in any case it is better to keep it for one night than to take it unlawfully, since nobody may take more than 5 Gemurta's; then he gives the acts of penitence for those who have trespassed. The remaining particle must be given to the communicants or be buried in uncultivated soil or in the wall of the sacristy. The chalice must be "ordered" (cf. ad Q. 18) by the priests and deacons, and prayers must be offered, the punishment must be the same. The last argument is drawn from the scapegoat (but this reference is not very clear). Q. 2: what must be done if a believer or foreigner touches the altar? Answer: If an outsider enters forcibly the memory of it must be blotted out by prayers (with reference to Nicodemus and Joseph, John xix 38–39); oil is not needed. If it was a layman who touched it nothing had to be done, since it did not happen from disrespect. Q. 4: If the Qudasha is consecrated twice on the same altar, not from necessity, it must be corrected by fasting, as it was done from greed. The Q. 6 of the MS. contains two questions; the latter gives several mystical reasons why the Qudasha may not be said on the Saturday following Good Friday. Q. 8: If an altar is left without mass for 7 weeks, it need not be reconsecrated, only some hymns should be said. Q. 9: The portable altar must be kept with the same honour as the ordinary altar, though it is not quite its equal as it may be removed from its place.

β. Letter to the deacon Macarius (586, fol. 431b–441b). It contains 74 Q.Q. on various points. The answer is usually very short, nothing but a direction as to what has to be done. The following items are important for the liturgy: (Q. [?]: The Euch. Br. should not be left on the altar; in case of necessity for 3 days

(1) It may be seen already from the foregoing quotation of Timothy i, that paschal Lamb and Manna are favourite prototypes of the eucharist. They are found over and over again in Patristic literature. Of course they originate from John vi and John i 29, xix 34–35.

([quoted in: *B.O.*, iii 1, p. 244]).[1] Q. 17: Everything may be done after the communion because it is only given to blot out sin. Q. 21: On Saturday of the Holy Week mass is not said: but after communicating in the night of Sunday the fast may be broken. Q. 23: When a drop of the Wine is spilled the place must be washed and this water must be smeered on the altar or given as a "grace"[2] to communicants. Q. 25: It is allowed to cut one's hair and to enter a building before and after the communion. Q. 26: It is not strictly forbidden to talk with pagans. Q. 27: It is not allowed to eat anything in the church. Q. 28: It is possible to fast after the communion except on Sundays. Q. 29: If somebody cannot digest food he may not communicate lest he should vomit. Q. 31: No one may communicate unless he is sinless, or confesses his sins. Q. 34: No priest may leave a host on the altar after the service, or take it alone. Q. 35: If much consecrated bread is left several priests must "order" it, everybody taking no more than 5 Gemurta's. Q. 36: During the "ordering" it is not allowed to go out and speak with anybody. Q. 42: The communion may be brought to a sick man or to a prisoner only if he is a believer. Q. 45: If somebody cannot break the fast by communion he must fast some days longer and wash his cross and drink the water with prayers. Q. 47: Such a believer may not go to the churches of the heretics. Q. 55: It is not allowed to leave the Qudasha on the altar for three days. Q. 56: It is allowed to take medicine after communion. Q. 57: If one knows his sin but not the reconciliation while communicating, he must be without doubt. Q. 58: If somebody does not want to be reconciled with his brothers, one may take the communion though there exists some quarrel. Q. 62: The Lords Prayer must be said at the beginning and end of every service. Q. 65: The Purshana is the body of Mary. Q. 66: If somebody is not able to communicate he must fast till the evening; then take a Ḥenana and eat bread; the service should be said at the ordinary time, though some say only the first part of it, until: "Let us all stand up as is right" (*L.E.W.*, p. 262). Q. 67: It is not allowed for a priest to perform the service unless he has served

(1) It is not found in the form of *B.O.* in the letter I read, see Q. 55. Did I. write two letters to Macarius? (cf. p. 102, n. 4). (2) Henana "was composed of the dust of some martyr and oil and water", cf. Budge, *B.G.* ii, p. 600, n. 1–p. 601; it was also known among the Jacobites and already mentioned in the Canones of Rabbula († 435), see C. Kayser, S. 108.

at night. Q. 68: Priests or deacons are not allowed to abstain from the service for one year unless they are old. Q. 69: Fasting on Friday and Wednesday for priests is not prescribed by canon but is a tradition[1]. Q. 70: One may receive the communion daily if one is pure. Q. 71: Nightly pollution does not prevent from communion, if it does not arise from dirty thoughts. Q. 72: The menstruation does not prevent from communion.[2]

If we survey these questions it will be seen that they are dealing mostly with the conditions for communion, while some are directions about the service of the priests. It will be noticed that some points occur in both letters, though the former gives more reasons for its decision. The same will be seen in comparing Q. 45 and 47 with the regulation (§ 126) of the same Patriarch, published by Sachau.[3] Some of these Questions offer parallels to the book of Isho'yabh iv and will be printed at the proper places of the commentary.

*f.* In connection with the foregoing questions we find some others about whose author it is only said that he was not Isho'-Barnun: codex Ming. Syr. 586, fol. 444a, Q. 13: Somebody possessed by the devil may receive the communion if he does not blaspheme, but if he praises and prays and fasts. He may not drink liquors.[4]

*g α.* The Admonitions or Canons of John v Bar Abgare[5] have systematized, so it seems, the work of former generations. We saw before that he bound himself to raise the standard of the church by examination of the future priests (cf. about his life, p. 84–85). Nothing is said about the time and reasons when these canons were divulgated. Prof. Baumstark surmised that they originated from a Synod that was held during his life. This statement may find some support in Canon i, iii and xix[6]. If we compare them

(1) Did he not know *Can. Apost.* 69, ed *F. X. Funk*, i, p. 584? (2) This subject is discussed over and over again, cf. Timotheus Alex., *Resp.* 7. ed. Pitra, *Monumenta*, i, p. 631, and Jac. Edes., *Canon* 5 (cf. Kayser, S. 88–89) who hold an opposite view; it is connected with the idea of women and their place in religion; it cannot be denied that the answers of the latter are derived from the O.T. (3) *A.a.O.*, ii, S. 174(–175). (4) Cf. Tim. Alex., *Resp.* 3, ed. Pitra, *l.l.*, i, p. 630, and p. 122, n. 5; cf. the interesting discussion of Moses bar Cepha, *o.c.*, p. 33. (5) These Canons are called: "Cautelae Missae" by Browne-Maclean, p. 261 sqq, and mentioned as such by F. Heiler, *Urkirche und Ostkirche*, S. 450. (6) "It seemed good to the Holy Spirit to order through the Holy Fathers". can. iii–The same introductory clause, as found in all these canons, is

with the letter of Isho'Barnun to Macarius we find that several topics are similar (xvii = Q. 36; xviii = Q. 42; xix = Q. 55 and to Isaac Q. 1; xx = Q. 34 and Q. 35; xxiii = ad Isaac Q. 1; xxvii = Q. 67). The difference is that the Canons are more extensive and have more particulars, as may be expected from a lawbook. But the similarity of topics and the direction in which the answers are given is quite clear. From this fact we may infer that he canonized in the same way other traditions which are now found in the Canons. They are very easily accessible in the "Bibliotheca Orientalis", so we need not give a detailed analysis though they are of extreme importance for the history of the liturgy. There is another edition in the Takhsa with a different numbering (Assemani inserted a translation of an Arabic canon which is wanting in the Syriac texts v; the following numbers differ accordingly;– Ass. xii = not T. xiii, but T. xv; consequently A. xiii = T. xi etc. till Ass. xvii = T. xvi etc.); we follow T. since it is the official edition.[1] *B.O.* and some MSS. have the author's name; T. and other MSS. are anonymous. But the latter fact cannot make us believe that the name of the Patriarch is spurious. The fact mentioned in p. 133, n. 6 points to the same author and it is easier to assume that his name was left out in the service-books than that it was invented afterwards.

Canon i–ii deal with the altar that must be fixed and should not be of wood; may not be laid bare nor washed. Canon iii–iv prescribe who must mix the Euch. Br., sum up the ingredients. Canon v–vii: about the state and number of the bread that had to be brought on the altar. Canon viii–ix: on the kind of wheatflour used for the bread. Canon x: the sacristy must be swept once a week. Canon xi: an Eulogia may not be given to a pagan. Canon xii: a lamp must burn before every altar. Canon xiii: reserving of something of the Euch. Br. Canon xiv: the Euch. Br. may not be baked for two days or pass over the night. Canon xv: some leaven must be reserved in kneading. Canon xvi: 3 hosts must be on the altar, or at least 2. Canon xvii: a priest may not leave his service.

also seen in other non-Eucharistic decisions inserted in the *Nomocanon* of 'Abdisho', iv 1, v 6–7, 10 etc. I believe that they were of the same Synod and that those of the Eucharist were brought together and transmitted as a separate body, because they had a special interest for the priests.

(1) The edition of T. is not mentioned by Prof. Baumstark, *L.G.*, S. 235, Ak. 7 where he also enumerates the MSS.; Mingana Syr. 121 should be added (it has a numbering of the canons which differs from the editions; it is anonymous).

Canon xviii: communion may not be brought outside the church except for some reasons. Canon xix: the Eucharist may not be left on the altar for two days. Canon xx: the ordering of Bread and Chalice without greed. Canon xxi: a priest may not "order" alone. Canon xxii: if Euch. Br. must necessarily be left the priest must "order" with a believer or leave it on the altar during the night with great care. Canon xxiii: how the particles must be received. Canon xxiv–xxv: on the mixture of the chalice. Canon xxvi–xxvii: the conditions which the priests must fulfill before doing service. Canon v Arab. deals with the instruments and vestments of the priests during the preparation of the Euch. Br.

It should be noticed that the introductory formulas are extremely severe: the canons are ordered by the Holy Spirit and are in (according to) the word of the Lord. The highest authority in the church is invoked to protect the contents (cf. p. 137).

β. In his Arabic letter: "Quaestiones Ecclesiasticae" he has several Eucharistic points.[1] Q. 2: A priest goes to the altar while quarreling with another (heading). Q. 3: Communion of boy or girl after baptism. Q. 6: The altar must be fixed and of stone. Q. 10: The deacon may bring the elements to the altar, if no priest is present. Q. 11: The deacon may not give the communion. Q. 12: The priest must enter the altar with special sandals. Q. 13: If only two priests are present and give the communion to each other it may not be given to anybody else who comes in. Q. 14: The sacrament may not be consecrated in the hands of the deacon except by special permission. Q. 15: The Archdeacon may be permitted to consecrate the altar. Q. 19: On the communion of children who are not fasting (after baptism only). Q. 20: The treatment of the altar that had been desecrated by enemies. Q. 25: Deacons and priests may not serve unless with sandals. Q. 26: The elder priests must precede the younger. Q. 27: The liturgy is more than a mere rite. Q. 28: The Euch. Br. must be baked in a special place in the church.

γ. Some other canons of the same Bishop have been preserved by the *Nomocanon* of 'Abdisho', viz. on the communion of a woman and of one possessed.[2]

(1) Ed. *B.O.*, iii 1, p. 249–254 (28 QQ., not everyone of them has been translated; of several the heading alone is given). (2) 'Abdisho', *Nomocanon*, v 16, Mai, p. 252.

*h.* Here we must commemorate the work of George of Arbela. We have seen before that much of what was once ascribed to him is not his (see p. 75). But in V. = M. some answers of his are found: 1. The fast of Lent may not be broken before a fortnight after Easterday, if somebody communicated on Maundy Thursday, but not on Easterday. If he did not take it on either day he must be abstinent till Ascension-day though he needs not fast. 2. The Gemurta immersed in the chalice may be taken to a sick man on Easterday under great precaution (refers to Canon xviii). 3. On the case when there is dearth of bread and vegetables in the fast.

It is not necessary to speak anymore about the collection of traditions found in our Q.Q.; we may refer to the commentary and to what has been said about them in this introduction. Much of the material found in the rest of the codices V.=M. has been published in the commentary (we hope to be able to publish the remaining sections of the book of Isho'yabh iv in the near future). The commentary shows the degree of dependence upon older traditions.

We have made the above summaries of the various writings because it seemed not to be out of place to have the whole body of Nestorian tradition about these points in a short form. For it is remarkable that the *Nomocanon* of 'Abdisho' does not contain any special section on the Eucharist, whereas a section on this subject is found in the word of his competitor in the Jacobite Church Bar Hebraeus, *Nomocanon* iv.[1] The only remark of Timothy ii in this direction is about reservation the Eucharist, for which he refers to the Canons.[2]

Is this defect in 'Abdisho' for some purpose? For his book contains many remarks about the priests in Section vi. It might have been either because it was sufficiently regulated elsewhere or because it was not thought worth while. The latter possibility can safely be ruled out as it is opposed to the whole spirit of Eastern Christendom. Probably he thought the directions of the rubrics of the liturgy and the canons, supplemented by the answers found in the letters mentioned before which were inserted in the canonical books of the Synodicon, were quite sufficient.

(1) Among the Jacobites the tradition is very strong and easy to establish, cf.: Johannes of Tella, who quotes others, James of Edessa, Bar Hebraeus who marks the author's name in every entry. (2) Quoted ad Q. 16.

In reviewing the tradition about these points we saw that the canons probably used writings or traditions of some predecessors. But on the other hand *it is remarkable that we find so very few cases of overlapping*. This is the more striking as in other instances we find the same orders given over and over again, as may be seen from reading the various books of Canon-Law. It cannot be proved that the treatises to which our study is devoted were composed from extracts of older books. The few cases of repetition can easily be explained from the particular situation.

The question arises in what respect these Canons and prescriptions of the Bishops were thought to be valid. There are reasons to believe that many of them were not so well known or obeyed as one is inclined to suppose. We have already referred to two interesting cases of addition;[1] especially the history of the time of Timothy i is striking and the answer of the writer of *Expos.* is highly instructive. His idea is that the authority of all the Bishops is the same viz. inspired by the Holy Spirit, and that there can be an evolution of these matters while the other groups did not acknowledge any progress or expansion of what had been fixed centuries before. Our Q.Q. too show in many places that people did not care about the Canons. It is easy to understand that this happened to private letters as those of Isho'Barnun as these were personal before they were incorporated in the Law Books. But here we have another case. We pointed out already that the form in which they were made obligatory is very severe. Generally those decrees are introduced by the ancient church as regulations of the Apostles. But for the Nestorians the regulations of the Apostles can be expanded by a decree of a Patriarch.[2] The Patriarch himself is inspired; therefore John v appeals to the Holy Ghost and Jesus Christ Himself (cf. Act. xv 28). Probably these strong words were necessary too. I do not consider Q. 49 as evidence of neglect, where it is said that the Canon holds only good in the Monasteries, but not in the other Churches, since this is a clear example of "force majeure" (see commentary). But when in Q. 48 it is asked what should be the quantities of wine and water in the chalice, it can only be understood when Canon xxiv was unknown. Several other cases may be found where the teacher simply reproduces the con-

(1) See p. 128–129. (2) *Expos.* ii, p. 66, quoted p. 129, n. 1.–Or by a synod of bishops who declaired a certain custom valid and obligatory, see p. 122, "they" and the quotation on p. 115.

tents of various Canons (ii 26–27 and cf. Commentary passim). It shows that these Canons had authority for our teacher but the fact that he has to repeat them, shows that they were not generally known a century after their divulgation. Of course this is connected with the lax ideas and stupidity of the priests of that time. But on the other hand that would not have existed if these Canons had been known and enforced.

It is clear that the subject-matter of our questions is somewhat different from that of the Canons. The latter deal with the ordinary services and acts, while the former treat difficulties that arise where the ordinary service is disturbed. What is the origin of these directions? In some places the "proof" is given from analogy. But most times no such proof is given and we must assume that it is "custom" (cf. p. 115) or "according to the old men".

iii. What is meant by this category of old men or of the Fathers? In other words how far does this go back and can it serve as a principle to fix that the subject matter of these Q.Q. really belongs to former ages?

There is some reason to put this question. It seems easy to find the explanation; it is only necessary to reproduce the general opinion about the traditional character of Eastern Christendom. Within the limits of this tradition the Fathers hold a predominant place.[1] Among the sources of knowledge and witnesses of the truth they are numbered since the end of the 4th century along with the Councils. At first the word denotes only those who followed the Apostles; later (5th century) especially the teachers of the 4th were considered as such and after the 7th Council all the previous centuries and their teachers were "antiquity" and adorned with the crown of Authority. These teachers were inspired by God (θεόπνευστοι).[2] Actually it remained a rather uncertain and undefined category. Yet that teaching was orthodox, "für die man sich auf die Väter von Athanasius bis Cyrill berufen konnte".[3] At the Councils the statements of the Fathers were simply counted. This habit is one of the reasons to compile the

(1) A. von Harnack, *Lehrbuch der Dogmengeschichte*[5], Tübingen, 1931, ii, S. 96–99. (2) Cf. in the *Expos.* where the teachers are called: ܐܢܫܐ ܕܠܒܝܫܝܢ ܡܢ ܪܘܚܐ (text i, p. 87) or: ܐܢܫܐ ܠܒܝܫܝ ܐܠܗܐ (i passim) = θεοφόροι (on this word see J. B. Lightfoot, *The Apostolic Fathers*, Part ii. *S. Ignatius, S. Polycarp*,[2] London, 1889, ii, p. 21–22. (3) A. von Harnack, *a.a.O.*, S. 97.

collections of excerpts, that favourite form of Theology in after times. One will have to reckon with fraud. But it will be seen that as far as dogmatics are concerned the Fathers are men who possessed the truth once for all. We find the same opinion among the Nestorians (Babai).[1]

Something similar (which forms a transition to the way in which they are introduced in our treatises) is found in Mysticism. Prof. Wensinck quotes a saying of Isaac of Nineveh to the effect that Isaac writes what he has learned from contemplation of the Scriptures and the Instruction of the Fathers, while he himself had experienced only a very small part of it. Prof. W. points out that this is a general characteristic: "Nearly all of them confess, that *their own time is void* of the highest mystic experience and that they themselves are longing to reach what their predecessors seem to have reached".[2] The way in which these Fathers are spoken of in this book and by Dadisho'[3] shows that the writer has specially in view the Monk-Fathers as Euagrius and others. It will be known that "Father" is an ordinary name in the fellowships of the Monks for the older members and so the language is somewhat ambiguous. Authority is dependent on age and the dead Fathers have the greatest authority. In this case Father generally points back to the origin of the ascetic (and mystic) movement.[4]

As a matter of fact whatever field is considered, everywhere this reverence for the forefathers in contrast with the time of the writer is found. It goes so far that Leontius of Neapolis in the Introduction to his "Life of John the Almsgiver" protests forcibly against it. He says, he wrote his book to show that in his own lifetime (6th century) there were also people of very great godliness.[5] "Dogma und Recht sind geschaffen durch die alten Konzilien"; thus the opinion of the East towards these questions was summarized by Prof. Baumstark.[6] It is this tradition that gives Eastern Christendom such an oldish aspect. Can the same rule be applied to the liturgy and its accidentals? This seems to be pre-eminently a matter of

(1) Babai, *Liber de Unione*, ed. A. Vaschalde, *C.S.C.O.* ii 61, p. 3, cf. p. 305, 306 etc. (2) A. J. Wensinck, *Mystic treatises of Isaac of Nineveh*, p. xxii. (3) Cf. *W.S.* vii 2, p. 70–143 passim; we give only these examples that can easily be augmented by others from all sources related to ascetism and mysticism in every branch of the Church. (4) Compare the Jewish: אבות (5) Leontios' von Neapolis, *Leben des heiligen Johannes des Barmherzigen*, ed. H. Gelzer, Leipzig, 1893, S. 1–2. (6) A. Baumstark, *Grundgegensätze morgenländischen und abendländischen Christentums*, Rheine, 1932 S. 41.

tradition. Is it necessary to give examples? Firmilian speaks of cases "which are handed down from the beginning".[1] The great teacher Theodore speaks in several places of the regulations found in the church from the beginning.[2] Isho'yabh i answering James of Darai says that he wants to write "entsprechend der bei uns von den Vätern vermittelten apostolischen Überlieferung" und that these Fathers were not his immediate predecessors is shown by the sequence.[3] On the same line lies the statement of the author of the "Expositio";[4] it is clear that there the "maiores" and "patres" lived many years, even centuries before (Isho'yabh iii; Bar Lipheh).

All conditions of analogy of several departments are there to justify the conclusion: these "ancients" are a traditional category covering either real tradition or pseudepigraphical contents. This is the traditional opinion. Yet in this case it is wrong. *Behind this name stands immediate oral tradition*. The "Fathers" lived in the same time as our author.

This is shown by the way in which is spoken of the Elders in the "Historia Monastica" of Thomas of Marga: "I will set down in consecutive order what I have learned from the Elders whom I have met, and from these things which are already written down".[5] Here we find the two sources of tradition together. The same can be applied to its use in our QQ. It is not sufficiently clear from the wording of Q. 116.[6] But it is proved by the usage of "hear" and "see". If the solution of a difficulty was doubtful, one went to bishops or teachers (p. 104–105). The evidence of the quotation from M. fol. 47–48 (see p. 80–81) is conclusive: The teacher is asked how the "ancients" signed, the synonym of this word is "heads of the church from the day on which I entered etc."; he states that George asked the old men about his immediate predecessors; the Fathers who are mentioned later on are the Bishops who lived in the time of Mar Mari and George.[7] The same result is produced by a close

(1) Cyprianus, *Epistula* 75, 6, ed. Hartel, p. 813–814. (2) Theodorus Mops., *Liber ad Baptizandos* ii, *W.S.* vi, p. 35, 90–92, 120. (3) O. Braun, *Synhados*, S. 239. (4) *Expos.* i, p. 17, 127 and passim; cf. the wording of Timothy ii, quoted ad Q. 89. (5) Budge, *B.G.* ii p. 288; in every place in which Thomas speaks of "Elders", he means people he has met. (6) When Isho'Barnun, *ad Isaac* Q. 9 writes that the "ancients" had no tabula, it is not intended to be a category of authority; it is merely a historical reference to the times in which persecutions were unknown. (7) This is on the same line as the use of "Fathers" in the synodical Canons; a common word for the Bishops and other High Officers of the Church.

interpretation of Q. 87–89 (see the commentary) and ii 23–24 (ad Q. 11); the practice followed by our author is that of the teachers of the 10th century while the other manner was supported by older churchmen! (on the teachers of the 10th cent. see p. 84–88 especially p. 85).

From this we must conclude that there is no reason whatever to trace the decisions given here (of course not their suppositions!) further back than one or two generations. *In this way we come to* ± 920–940. *We do not possess any guarantee that older decisions are underlying them.* For when we use the argument that the "old men" of our author had been instructed in the same way by their spiritual Fathers, it is not based upon facts but merely hypothetical. We cannot say about it: this was the traditional treatment of the Nestorian Church, as long as we have no more facts at our disposal; but only: this was a certain liturgical tradition in that church, which is often young. Along side with it there existed others that are disputed. We find a strict and lax practice and this writing seems to be an exponent of the former. A further question we must put in this connection, is: What was the place of the school?

iv. Our treatises originate from the school. It appears that the discharge of the priest's functions required a great amount of knowledge. The people deviating from the usages as reproduced by our teacher, act from ignorance; the new priests are not well instructed (see Introduction).[1] This word is explained by a peculiar addition in V.; it says they were not instructed "in the sanctuaries". It shows that the future priests got their lessons in that part of the church, viz. during the service. The same observation can be made in our treatise when our author says that he has seen it or heard from the ancients before whom he served in the church. On the other hand we saw (p. 140) that people asked advice from the clergy and from the teachers. We shall go somewhat further into this matter about the Instruction of the clergy.

Hardly anything is known about the way in which it was given in the times of Christian antiquity.[2] From the beginning of the

(1) The remarks by the Chronists on the Patriarchs quoted before p. 19 should be compared. About 'Abdisho' ii it is told that he changed the recital of the Lord's Prayer "ignarus cum esset canonum ecclesiae" (Gismondi i, p. 121); many remarks are to the same effect. (2) At any rate I did not find any help in the ordinary handbooks nor in *D.C.A.* ii, s.v. *School,* and: *D.A.C.L.*, s.v. Ecole, t. iv, col. 1730–1783–Bingham, vi 3, 3 quotes something of Jerome and of the 4th

Jacobite church we have a precept of John of Tella to his Monks, which may give us an idea of this matter, canon 13: "we have heard that some priests who do not know exactly the liturgy transgress audaciously; they draw near in the awe-inspiring time to offer and they become confused in their prayers and are a source of mockery and scandal at that moment for those who meet for prayer. Therefore nobody shall dare to do so before having learned the whole Mass accurately and having repeated it before somebody who knows it well."[1] Of course this canon does not deal with the same matters as our Q.Q.; but it offers a case of the ignorance of priests and the way to stop it by requiring an examination. The way in which it was taught (the Bishop has the prayers specially in view) is not indicated. The editor Kuberczyk referred to Nestorian parallels from the Canons of Timothy ii (13th century).[2] But it should be observed that there is rather a great difference of time between them. Do we hear anything more about the liturgical activities of the schools and the Instruction of the clergy among the Nestorians? The question is not difficult to answer.

Fairly much is known about these points. Assemani already devoted a chapter to them.[3] He gave a long list of names of places where a school had flourished for some longer or shorter time with the names of teachers or of students; among them those of Nisibis, Seleucia, and of Mar Mari at Dorkoni are specially noteworthy. From his collection it appears that many such institutes were scattered over the country. He has also collected statements and regulations about their teaching. Of course this is done without much historical insight. Most of these schools are known by name; they were in the cities and villages, in the houses of the Bishops and priests and in the monasteries; both clerics and laymen were instructed there. Of course it surpasses the limits of our investigation

Council of Toledo (633) can. 25: "Sciant sacerdotes Scripturas Sanctas, et canones meditentur." But this does not say anything about liturgical study, and is rather late.–I know the thesis of H. R. Nelz, *Die theologischen Schulen der morgenländischen Kirchen während der sieben ersten Jahrhunderte in ihrer Bedeutung für die Ausbildung der Klerus*, Diss. Bonn, 1916, only by name. The famous school of Alexandria did not produce liturgical books.–E. R. Hayes, *l'Ecole d'Edesse*, Paris, 1930, derives all facts concerning the inner history from the sources about the daughter of Edessa, Nisibis and has nothing of its own. It shows sufficiently that we do know about this subject next to nothing, except the information of Nisibis.

(1) Johannes bar Cursus Tellensis, *Canones*, ed. C. Kuberczyk, Leipzig, 1901, p. 29–30 (cf. Moses b. Kepha p. 108). (2) *Ibidem*, p. 16; the references are to 'Abdisho', *Nomocanon*, ed. Mai, p. 265–266. (3) *B.O.*, iii 2, p. cmxxiv–cmxlviii.

to deal with their outward history. This is not even possible as from most of them only the name or a single fact are known. Many of them existed only for a certain time, and were not of great significance.

The most famous among them was the *school of the Persians in Nisibis*. During the last 40 years a good number of documents with important data have been published about its origin and organization. It is not necessary for our subject to enter into the questions connected with it; we may refer the reader to the latest discussion of these points by Liz. Th. Hermann, who mentions all the sources and literature about this institution. After a careful examination of the first years of its existence Mr Hermann says: "Mit der gleichen Eindeutigkeit, mit der die Quellen die Entstehung der Schule von Nisibis erzählen, werden wir leider nicht über die sog. Akademie der Perser unterrichtet und nicht nur das, auch über die an ihr entfaltete Unterrichtstätigkeit vermögen wir uns kein rechtes Bild zu machen."[1] Several titles of functionaries are mentioned in the Canones published by Prof. Guidi and return in the "Book of the Foundation of the School"[2]. It seems as though exegesis[3] of the Bible and philosophy were the main studies. As far as the liturgy is concerned, one officer is called the ܡܩܪܝܢܐ = teacher of reading. Prof. Baumstark summarizing the general opinion, says: he was the man "dem die Einübung der liturgischen Textesrezitation einschliesslich des Gesanges und des gesammten Chordienstes oblag".[4] It may be, however, that the ܡܗܓܝܢܐ = teacher of Meditation, had also something to do with this department. The explanation of this name is very obscure and several opinions have been uttered without success.[5] ܗܓܐ means: to meditate, to read syllable by syllable, to study and to take in something by murmuring (this Eastern way of learning is well known). But this meditation was somewhat different from our idea. In the Canon x of Seleucia under Isaac (410) it was pre-

(1) Th. Hermann, *Die Schule von Nisibis vom 5. bis 7. Jahrhundert*, in: *Zeitschrift f. d. neutest. Wissenschaft*, 1926, S. 89–122.–The summary in: *D.A.C.L.*, s.v. *Nisibis (Ecole de)*, t. xii, col. 1377–1386, is insufficient. (2) Ed. A. Scher, in: *Patrologia Orientalis*, iv and ix.–The Canons ed. I. Guidi, *Gli Statuti della scuola di Nisibi*, in: *Giornale della Societa Asiatica Italiana*, 1890, p. 165–195. (3) In this respect the school was very famous, see the Introduction of Junilius Africanus, *de Institutione divinarum lectionum*, in: *M.S.L.* 70, col. 105. Many of the writings and names of teachers show its predominant place. (4) A. Baumstark, *L.G.*, S. 114. (5) Cf. J. P. Margoliouth-Payne Smith, *Supplement to the Thesaurus Syriacus of R. Payne-Smith*, Oxford, 1927, p. 96.

scribed: "Dass jeder ein Exemplar dieser Kanonen besitzen soll, *dieselben zu meditiren und aus ihnen die Rechte festzustellen* etc.";[1] this connection cannot mean anything but: to consider how the older Canons might be used in the practice of the present day. In other regulations we find it used for "reading" (cf. p. 147, n. 1). It may be that it has something to do with the explanation of the liturgy in the mystagogy and with practical theology.

Of the liturgical activities in this school we hear that Narsai wrote some poems spoken of before (p. 42), but they are different in character from the subjects we are looking for here. On the same line, though with a slightly different nature are the kind of writings known as: "de Causis Festorum" which were fully discussed by Prof. Baumstark. They seem to have been lectures dealing not with the festivals themselves, but with their connection with the Economy of Christ. The first who delivered them was Mar Abba the Exegete and after him Thomas of Edessa at the instance of the "reading-master" Moses. They produce hardly anything of interest for liturgical practices, only on the receiving of the communion in hand, and on the serving of the priest while fasting. Their main interest is found on the side of dogmatics. In passing we may note, that the first book of the "Expositio" of several centuries later seems once more to take up the same theme.[2]

The two names of Abba and Thomas have been mentioned before (and this is important to notice) as the translators of the Greek liturgies into Syriac (see p. 41).

It is worth while to mention in this connection also Isho'yabh i. He had been a teacher in Nisibis himself. In the Introduction of his letter to James of Darai, that has been quoted several times, he says that he will write about points that had not been made sufficiently clear by the Fathers and Brothers. Then he goes on: "Auch sollst du wissen, dass, als wir auf der hohen Schule waren, der ἀκμή der Forschung, wir auf die Bitte . . . . . geschrieben". The contents of his writing were quoted on p. 119 where it was pointed out, that it was probably a mystagogy. But on the other hand we may consider this letter, with its "reasons", as a specimen of the way in which these matters were treated at the schools.

(1) O. Braun, *Synhados*, S. 20 (italics are mine). (2) A. Baumstark, *Die nestorianischen Schriften "de causis festorum"*, in: *O.C.*, 1901, S. 320–342, an extremely important article on Nestorian theology. For the liturgical practices cf. S. 337, n. 3–4.

Isho'yabh writes to his correspondent as a teacher to his pupil, as he confesses himself, and the teacher himself had learned the traditions very well.[1] Whether there is a connection of his canons mentioned before, with the school is not possible to decide, but it is not probable. They seem to be decisions of a Bishop rather than of a teacher.

It lies outside the scope of the present investigation to deal with the history of the growth and decline of these institutes nor with the founders and teachers of some of them. The Chronicles, published by Gismondi, and the "Book of the Governors" are full of passing references. They had all their times of growth and decline. It is noteworthy to see how many times the laxity of discipline is spoken of. The successive Patriarchs tried to keep up or to restore the high standard of study and life; but without much success. At present we look only for liturgical activities.

A remarkable story is told us from the time of Isho'yabh iii. Immediately after his accession this Catholicos enlarged the monasteries and after that "wished to build a school near his cell, and to provide it with all that was necessary and to bring to it teachers and masters and expositors, and to gather many scholars", in order that the pupils of the school might enter the monastery. But the monks did not like it and they prayed him not to put this plan into execution. Their argument was: "It is not good for us monks, while dwelling in our cells, to be disturbed by the sound of the chanting of the psalms and the singing of the hymns and the offices, and by the noise of the voices of the schoolboys . . . We are destined for weeping and mourning, while we dwell in our cells . . . Mar Jacob, our Father . . . did not command us that one should teach the other to sing and to read the offices from books."[2] Of course this is only the audible part of the school. At any rate it is important to hear that the singing of the various services was actually taught at these Institutes. By their appeal to their own Father it is shown that this teaching was not quite incompatible with the monastic order in general. The activities of Mar Babai (beginning 8th century)[3] may be recorded here. It is told: "when this blessed man had come to the country of Maryâ, he first of all gathered together the scholars and founded the Ḥudra and revised and corrected the codices". He founded a number

(1) O. Braun, *Synhados*, S. 239 and 271 (cf. p. 116). (2) Budge, *B.G.* ii, p. 131 sqq., p. 148. (3) Cf. A. Baumstark, *L.G.*, S. 212–213.

of new schools and corrected the older ones; he raised funds to run them properly. "Twice a year he visited all the schools, in order that laxity of discipline might not enter into them, and that the musical training and canons and orders of services which he had made his disciples acquire might not be destroyed."[1] The interpretation of this last sentence is somewhat doubtful. Are "Canons" the appointed hymns, or: the rules of the Church;[2] are the ܛܟܣܐ orders (in general) or those services, collected in T.? After the words just quoted follows: "and thus this manner of singing was called the 'musical system of Rabban Bâbhai' ". Does this imply that "Canon" and "Orders" had also a musical meaning? On the other hand the logical order in Syriac is generally not very strict; so it is not improbable that it is only an explanation of the "musical training" before, and that Canons and orders have the latter meaning of those offered before. Regarding the discussions on liturgical matters we do not hear anything about them. This quotation shows that this study of the liturgy formed an integral part of the course. We may infer that the future priests were not only taught the prayers, but also the actions that had to be made during the service. The danger of slackening is imminent and the Patriarch does his utmost to stop it. But it does not become clear, how the liturgy was taught.

We must now look at some regulations that are for the greater part found in 'Abdisho', *Nomocanon*, vi 3 and which were copied by Assemani. The first is of uncertain date; it gives the subject matter divided over three years. The time-table contained writing of the Mauteba's[3] and from the Scriptures of Paul and the Pentateuch; together with choirsinging and reading of the Lections they must learn the funeral (hymns). In the second year the pupils go on with the Mauteba's and from the Scriptures Psalter and Prophets; along with the Lections they must learn the Anthems of the Mysteries. The last year comprises the third part of the Mauteba's and the New Testament; together with the Lections they are taught the Antiphons.[4]

(1) Budge, *B.G.* ii, p. 296–297. (2) Cf. ad Q. 4–5. (3) Cf. ad Q. 114. (4) That the priests learned the services by heart may be illustrated by the story of the pasturer of camels who had been taken captive by the Arabs and lived in the desert, who recited every day the service of one festival of the Lord, Budge, *B.G.* ii, p. 274–277.–The powers of the Syrians are prodigious in this respect, cf. Browne-Maclean, p. 209 and p. 165.–The minimum of the requirements for the clergy in town and in the country, see: *Canon* 3 of Synod . . . ., in: 'Abdisho', *Nomocanon*, vi 4.

The date of the following regulation is quite fixed. After the death of Isho'Barnun the affairs had gone the wrong way and when in 834 Sabarisho' ii had paid a visit to the schools he found that they were almost ruined: only very few old doctors had remained: the young students were ignorant and did not serve the daily offices. The Patriarch saw that the people did not want to obey his commandments to improve this abuse. So he gave again an order: he made a table of the hymns that should be sung on the Sundays of the year and which had to be copied at the schools and sent to the priests. He repeated the preceding programme and impressed it once again upon them. Twenty years afterwards Theodosius (853–858) refers to these regulations and gives some more prescripts: the writers and surgeons must read the exposition of the New Testament and the "Book of the Mysteries" of Theodore; those who stand for the priesthood must read the Homilies of the whole year by several writers of former times. This is substantially the same as the requirements put down in the *Nomocanon* of Ibn at Tayyib. From the declaration given by John v (see p. 85) we see that his standard was somewhat lower as he asked only the reading of the Bible what was "secundum canones". If we survey this evidence and ask what is its result for the question we put at the beginning we must come to the conclusion that it is very scarce. We are informed that the future priests wrote, read and learned the books required for the Offices; but nothing is told of their study of the matter found in the rubrics nor of discussion of liturgical questions (though it will be remembered that the texts of the prayers occupy a far greater place than the actions and required more study). To speak in the terms of the Statutes of Nisibis, it is all about the work of the reading master (M^eqarjana) perhaps of the meditation master (M^ehagjana).[1]

Yet it seems that the description of this evidence is not quite complete. In the letter of Isho'Barnun to Macarius it is said that "some teachers say . . ."[2] It is not sufficiently clear to what class of teachers he is referring, anyhow we shall keep it in mind. It may be that it is a witness of the liturgical activity in the school. The "Expositio" shows also that the schools had their different opinions. The author speaks about the division of the ecclesiastical

(1) In the regulation of Theodosius ܗܓܐ is used for the work that had to be done by the pupils.–About Sabarisho' and Theodosius, see: A. Baumstark, *L.G.*, S. 233. (2) Quoted in: *B.O.*, iii 1, p. 244.

year (Ḥudhrā) and the anthems and points out that they differ in respect of the "week of Dedication"[1] for which every school had its own order, but it seems that we must infer from the words of the author that these differences existed only in matters that were not regulated by Isho'yabh iii.[2] Another instance to the same effect is found in his discussion of the order of the Night Office.[3] This statement of his about the field in which liturgical discussions were held is important; as always the authority of I. iii is unassailable. It is important to notice that we do not find such differences in the Eucharistic part of *Expos.* Whatever is not decided by his regulations is free (see Q. 1).

Another important piece of evidence may be found in the quotation from M. fol. 46b sqq. (before p. 80). There the writer tells us that he was once in the High Monastery and in that time some people were consecrated "according to the precepts of the scholars". The ritual of consecration was the same as that of George of Arbela. In this case the author reproduces the opinion of those scholars. In Q. 7 he refers to an addition made by the Patriarch 'Abdisho' i with great approval; this 'A. had been a pupil of the same High Monastery. These two facts make me think that the author of our work had some connection with (was once a pupil of) this Institute.

What was this *High Monastery?* All that can be known about this place which had a great influence upon the fixation of liturgical matters was collected some years ago by Prof. A. Rücker.[4] It is not out of place to summarize here his article. He starts with the remark that many East Syrian MSS. show the Colophon: "According to the rite of the High Monastery or the Cloister of Mar Gabriel and Mar Abraham near Mosul." It occurs specially in the Ḥudhrā, Gazza and Kashkul (never in "Before and after")[5], lectionaries and the ritual of Marriage and Funeral. About the Psalter and the Takhsa Prof. Rücker says that it is not found there "in

(1) One of the seven "Weeks" of seven Weeks in which the Nestorian year is devided, see ad Q. 37. (2) *Expos.* i, p. 29, cf. p. 128. (3) *Expos.* i, p. 160. (4) A. Rücker, *Das 'Obere Kloster' bei Mossul und seine Bedeutung für die Geschichte der ostsyrischen Liturgie*, in: *O.C.*, 1932, S. 180–187.–Something, but of course without the scientific apparatus, is given by G. P. Badger ii, p. 17, N. *; he says: "it is still a common practice among the Chaldeans who seek a special blessing to resort to these ruins, where after lighting a taper near where the altar is supposed to have stood, they offer up their prayers to Almighty God." (5) For these names see the Introduction to *E.S.D.O.*, p. xi.

welchen wohl höchstens noch die Rubriken und die in den Brevierhandschriften stehenden Gesangstexte der Messe Anlass zu Neuregelungen boten; wenn einmal sogar in einer Handschrift (Cambr. Add. 2045) dieses Sacerdotales die Bemerkung steht dass dieser Taksa d$^e$qûrbanê nach dem Brauch des Oberen Klosters niedergeschrieben sei, so kann das nur auf die sonstigen Beigaben des Buchs beziehen, oder die Notiz ist von einem gedankenlosen Schreiber aus andern liturgischen Buchtypen auch auf dieses übertragen worden" (S. 182–183). He sketches the history of this Monastery and mentions several names of teachers. Under and after Yabhallaha ii (± 1200 A.D.) it is mentioned no more. It was situated in the North East of Mosul (for the exact place see the article). In the end Prof. Rücker points out that nothing is found about it in the "Expositio" and asks whether Timothy ii furnishes some data.

These are the results of the material collected by Prof. Rücker. In connection with our subject we may be allowed to add some remarks. The question about Timothy must be answered in the negative. Assemani's account is fairly reliable and for so far we compared the book we did not meet with anything of the kind. Regarding the "Expositio" i, I am not so sure; it is certain that the Monastery is not mentioned by name, but it is possible that a careful investigation of its former part about the Daily Offices would furnish some data (it goes beyond the limits of this book to do so here). Prof. Rücker thinks it disputable "ob wir überhaupt einen bestimmten Zeitabschnitt nahmhaft machen können, indem die Reform vollendet wurde." (S. 187). This is as a matter of fact all that can be said at present about its liturgical reformation. At any rate it is clear even from this poor information that its influence was considerable. It seems to have been a sort of standard for the rest of the church and so it is looked upon in our treatise too. I believe we may assume that our author also gives instruction that runs parallel with that of this Monastery.

We must not forget that it appears from the "Introduction" that the Liturgy was learned by seeing the performance of the service by older priests, along with oral instruction (hearing) which refers with all probability to the work of the schools.

*From these data our knowledge of the schools of the Nestorians is greatly enlarged, although it belongs only to the 10th century.* For while the texts given by Assemani only show the learning or reciting of liturgical books, the others we cited indicate that what was left undecided by Isho'yabh iii, and not formulated was the subject of discussions in the schools. The school served practical life and was not merely instructing the students in antiquated matters. For once this type of religion being accepted it was an imperative necessity to perform the service with the utmost care. From the way in which Isho'yabh i wrote to his correspondent we can safely deduce that this kind of teaching had been given already centuries before our author lived, though everything was not so well defined as seems to have been the case after I. iii. But this fact does not imply anything about the antiquity of our Q.Q. For it is sure that even in the 10th century older traditions were abandoned (cf. the case referred to by Timothy ii, ad Q. 87–89). But in view of the poor state of the tradition (mainly oral instruction–perishing of writings) it is almost impossible to give a definite answer to the question when these matters have been fixed for the first time. Even if parallels in other churches can be found it is not strictly necessary that both go back to the same origin. It may be that one fact is derived from one other and why should it be out of the question that the same things arose independently of each other.

It was pointed out before (p. 111) that these Q.Q. are closely connected with the state of affairs in the Nestorian Church ± 950–1000 A.D. From the evidence exhibited on the preceding pages and in the commentary it appears that *these matters were not fixed, but circulated in oral tradition. The latter does not go back a long time. This much we can see from the historical, not hypothetical evidence* (cf. § ii and iii). It cannot be settled what points were handed down from generation to generation and what was freshly formulated. The question put at the beginning of this chapter must receive a negative answer. It is only in some cases that one is allowed to vindicate an old tradition, merely if *facts* can be adduced which prove its existence in former times. It is necessary to stress this point, since often a rule is applied in liturgical study to derive practices of the 13th or 19th century simply from the 4th or 5th century appealing to the tenacity of Eastern traditionalism and pointing to the similarities of life in the O.T. and in the 19th or 20th century in the East. But because the rules of the present-day Nestorian Church agree with those of the 10th century, it is not proved that the standards of the 10th and of the 5th century were the same. On the contrary facts show that some very important changes have taken place, first of all the fixation of the formularies by Isho'yabh iii which got a binding authority and were expanded during later ages (see ch. vi, i). To make "Rückschlüsse" is safe only in cases of well-known compilors such as Bar Hebraeus and Dionysius Barsalibi who faithfully mention their authorities. *Our treatises cannot be claimed to be from some centuries before its publication*, though some prayers and cult-objects which are spoken of were used already in the 5th or 7th cent. They warn us for hasty appeals to Eastern tradition. The book pretends to stand on the line of (incalculable) tradition and combats slackening. Everything must be maintained as strictly as possible, in honour of the holiness of the Sacrament. But there are indications that another tradition stands behind the practices of the "opponents" (cf. ad Q. 89). The standard of distinction between right and wrong tradition is not made apparent.

Now it becomes also plain why these discussions are held about the "framework" of the liturgies and not about the anaphora-part of liturgy. The latter had been definitely settled since Isho'yabh iii; it was recited by every priest. Nothing more could be said about it. It was the norm of every one. But the framework could be performed in a lax or in a strict way. It could not be learned from the books, but had to be seen or heard in the church or school. Everyone who did not learn it was "ignorant" and in fact a heretic.[1]

If we rightly assumed that these treatises had some connection with the High Monastery (and there are sufficient reasons to do so), *we do get in this way an insight into the activity exercised by this institution concerning the Eucharist.* This reformation could not be very radical, as it was bound by the limits of I. iii, it could only lay down rules

(1) Cf. this remark of *Expos.* ii, p. 102 (against people who tresspass against the Baptismal rules of Isho'yabh): "Sed dic mihi, tu, quisquis canones Išōʿyabhi transgrederis, num virtutem intelligis *eorum* quae in canonibus praescribuntur? Quod si intelligis, et si sapienter sunt constituta, noli eadem transgredi; sin vero minus sapientia, noli omnino in illius canonibus ambulare, sed in tuis ipsis . . . Si autem intelligis, commentarios prius scrutare, deinde innova; et noli in ignorantia manere."–It appears that ignorance has various aspects: of the facts which had been prescribed, of the written tradition and of the mystagogical meaning. Heresy and ignorance belong together, *Expos.* i, p. 18 (quoted at p. 127), just as heresy and pride (see ad *Introduction*).

for the accidentals although they seem to be inserted into the body of our present MSS. of the liturgy.[1] It should not be forgotten that the Eastern Church did not and does not know what the Western Church got in the "Congregatio ss. rituum" (since 1588). Yet a part that can in some respects be compared with it, seems to have been played by the High Monastery and other schools such as that of S. Mari where Isho'yabh iv taught. Then we see that *the supposition of Prof. Rücker quoted before, to the effect that it was merely rubricistic, was quite to the point.* It is of great importance in view of the young date of the MSS. that it can also be concluded *from the sources* that the liturgy itself was not a subject of discussion[2], and that *the only great liturgical reformation of which we hear in the Nestorian church did not affect it!* This statement remains true, though Prof. Baumstark says: "Freilich lässt sich auch dieser (der Text der Apostelanaphora) nicht uneingeschränkt für Ī. in Anspruch nehmen, da seiner nicht über das 15. Jh. zurückzuverfolgenden Vulgärgestalt eine noch im 13. und 14. gebräuchlich gewesene altertümlichere Form gegenübersteht."[3] The latter statement requires an exact collation of those different texts; the former is a (negative) conclusion from the study of the treatises. The result of both can only be made out in a critical history of the text of the Nestorian liturgy. For the moment we keep to the above, since we try to fix the importance of our treatises for the history of the liturgy.

*Additional Note:* Based upon the above facts, we may venture to offer an explanation of some very peculiar places in T. It must strike every one reading this text (or that of Brightman) that at several occasions it seems as though it polemizes. Nothing of that kind is found, as far as I am aware in any other Missal, nor that somebody seems to be addressed in the second person singular. The following cases I have in view: T. p. 9 = Br. p. 272: "Here I inform thy love, o my lord . . ." = Berl. fol. 83a; not in Ren. p. 581.[4] T. p. 10 = Br. p. 274: "And know that . . ." = Berl. fol. 83a–b; not in Ren. p. 582. T. p 22 = Br. p. 289: the priest must draw near to the signing "with his hands outstretched and

(1) It did not give rise to different "schools" of permanent influence nor to a divergent practice or schism. (2) In this respect there is a difference between the Nestorian and the Jacobite liturgical difficulties (cf. p. 101, n. 3). (3) A. Baumstark, *L.G.*, S. 199–200. (4) T. = Takhsa; Br. = Brightman, *L.E.W.;* Berl. = Cod. Berolin. Syr. 38; Ren. = Renaudot, *L.O.C.*, ii.

not folded as illiterate men do" = Berl. fol. 92a (the text is somewhat effaced, but it was in it); not in Ren. p. 587. T. p. 23 = Br. p. 291: "And some here sign the peristа with their thumb at the time of the breaking: but do thou beware of such an audacity etc.; . . . as others are wont to do . . ." = Berl. fol. 93a;[1] not in Ren. p. 588. (We may also compare the Ritual of Ordination, in Badger ii, p. 322: "Be it known unto thee, our brother, etc."; T. p. 75 = Diettrich, *Taufit.*, S. 52: "Und wisse, dass ohne Konsekration überhaupt keine Taufe volzogen wird"; and the additions to the Liturgy of Baptism of the MS. J[2], in: Diettrich, *a.a.O.*, S. 63, 74, 81, 101 and J Jahb, *a.a.O.*, S. 69; the former MS. has the heading: "Ferner die Ordnung der heil. Taufe, die von dem Katholikos Mâr Išô'yâbh . . . verfasst und darnach von dem Katholikos [Patriarchen] Mâr 'Eliyâ ausgelegt wurde." [S. xii; ܦܫܩ = to explain, not of mystagogical exegesis, but of specification of rubrics] This clearly shows the origin of the additions, viz. made by a particular Patriarch. This Elias might have been not the third of that name, as Mr. Diettrich assures without any proof, but the first one 1028–1049[2], who is said to have made some liturgical regulations. That would bring us into the time of our treatises!) It is obvious that the text of these passages was not fixed, as appears from other rubrics too. It is not possible to say whether the text of Ren. is the original one or merely an abridgement of the others. At any rate these places cannot be explained, unless by assuming that they originate from a liturgical school in which some often occurring faults are indicated (cf.: Illiterate men!) This point cannot be illustrated from other sources. But its tone is very much akin to that of the people speaking in our treatises, so that we seem to be justified in concluding that they arose from the same environment.

(1) Cf. the commentary ad Q. 96. (2) A. Baumstark, *L.G.*, S. 286–287; on S. 289 he expresses his doubt concerning D's identification.

# vii TRANSLATION OF THE TEXT

(V. M. 1b). *By the power of our Lord Jesus Christ we begin to write the questions and the admonitions of the service of the Altar in all its orders. Our Lord help me to its completion. Amen.*

*Request of the questioner:* Your Brotherhood, o modest[1] old man, knows that in this our time which is deprived of men, old and ancient of days, all the priests, our colleagues took recently[2] possession of the churches and were not instructed[3], and (so) did not follow the "Canons and Orders of the service of the Altar"; and about all the events that took place and[4] occurred to them, now and then, in their own churches and outside, everyone of them speaks according to his own knowledge of the events that took place. And sometimes they neglect them from carelessness and do not accurately investigate them nor do they show themselves to be experienced leaders and heads and do not set right the injuries and events which take place. (V. 2a) And if someone blames, rebukes (M. 2a) and admonishes them, they pout and speak derisively.[5] Or otherwise they say: "Who has made thee a head, master and judge over us?" And (thus) he becomes, instead of an admonisher, a culprit among them, and lacking in knowledge and without experience in this. I wish to appeal to the witness[6] of the very old men, ancient of days, in order that I may speak with confidence and without hesitation, in accordance with the testimony of our Saviour, that the witness of two men is true. Therefore answer me wisely about all the questions which I shall put to you on every subject, in the measure (V. 2b) in which the Holy Spirit grants you wisdom and confirms your words, according to the grace of the love of God.

*Further an apology of the old man to the student.* Great is the heavy burden which you imposed on me, o esteemed[7] brother. May our Lord enrich you in all scriptural and natural sorts of wisdom! I am not able to bear (that burden) (M. 2b) and I am loathe to refuse the request of[8] your love, and ashamed not to heed your high command. And lo, I am standing in the middle of the sea and a tempest is tossing me from every side and I who am not an accomplished swimmer fear that in executing swimming-movements I should

(1) V. om. (2) V.: "foolishly". (3) Or: "trained"; V. adds: "in the Sanctuaries". (4) V. om. (5) V. adds: "Where did this one pick up this perfect knowledge?" (6) V. plural. (7) V. om. (8) Following V.; M. has: "your request and your love".

fail and sink, and by refraining from the swimming-movements I should sink in the depth as lead in deep waters. And I implore the (V. 3a) Lord to hold my hands and to draw me out of the tempestuous sea and bring me into a peaceful harbour, in order that I may be enabled to answer the request of your love and that your trust in me may not be in vain; not as though I am versed in knowledge, nor did I serve in the service of the church, but like one who has tried and seen things from the old men, ancient of days – ⌜blessed be their memory![1] – before whom I laboured and performed the service of the Sanctuary and of the Church, those of whose churches I did not even dare (M. 3a) to call myself a doorkeeper in their days, I answer ⌜your question[2], in the measure vouchsafed by (divine) Grace and allowed me by the Spirit. Not that the greatness of your knowledge and training needs the[3] demonstrations of my ignorance (V. 3b) and wretchedness,[4] but that your greatness may be extolled and your humility may be exalted and your wisdom may be revealed before the eye of every man. But I ⌜will act as a man[5] under command and order, and as a disciple serving your Brotherhood which is dear to me. To everything about which you ask me, I will give an answer, not from myself nor from my own knowledge, but from the old men[6] whom I saw and questioned with accuracy.[7]

*Questioner:* I ask you to describe to me with accuracy the consecration of the altar and all its signings in good order, as you have seen the deceased Metropolitans and Bishops[8] consecrating. (V. 4a). *Answer:* Go to the Churchbook and examine the Order of Mar Isho'yabh (M. 3b) the Catholicos. You shall not add anything to it nor shall you diminish anything from it and it may be sufficient to you to see and to learn it.

2 *Question:* I have seen many people who were consecrating the altar in another way, and one added to and another took away from its consecration and signings. *Solution:* Everyone performs a certain act according to his knowledge and in the measure of his capacity, power and ability. In short, consecration is performed by those who participate in it; and if only the sign of the cross were made over the altar, it would be consecrated. In the same way when saying orally: "The altar is desecrated", it becomes desecrated. Through

(1) V. om. (2) V. om. (3) V. adds: "poor". (4) V.: "meanness". (5) V.: "I shall be as a slave". (6) V. adds: "ancient of days". (7) V. adds: "(with) great (accuracy). But if it pleases you, the Spirit will investigate the matter; but if otherwise, leave . . .(?)". (8) V. adds: "(who left) this world".

his word[1], when the altar is defiled, it becomes bound and reconsecrated. (V. $4^{b}$).

*Question:* How many times is the oil which the Bishop[2] consecrates to be oil of the altar, signed and on how many occasions? *Answer:* Every consecration, either of oil of the altar, or of the Paghra and Dema, or of Baptism, or of the Ordination, or of the Betrothal (M. $4^{a}$) and Marriage-service, needs three signings and three times they use to sign over it.

*Question:* I have seen many people consecrating oil and reciting only one prayer of inclination over it. How do they sign three times? *Answer:* Those who recite one prayer of inclination, say first: "The grace of the Lord", and sign it once and recite: "Celestial Treasury".[3] And at the end of its canon the second sign is made. (V. $5^{a}$). Then the third sign is made with the three fingers which are near his thumb, while saying: "This holy oil is signed and sanctified by the sign of the living and lifegiving Cross that it may be used for the signing of the consecration of this altar; in the name of the Father and of the Son and of the Holy Ghost". Then the three signings are (in this way) completed.

5 *Question:* Those who consecrate the oil by reciting three prayers of inclination, how do they sign, and on how many occasions? *Answer:* In the case of those who recite (M. $4^{b}$) three prayers of inclination, the first (prayer) is: "O Lord, omnipotent God, help Thou ⌜my infirmity",[4] a prayer which is said before the altar and during which the Consecrator makes a sign over himself. When they place (V. $5^{b}$) the vessel of oil on the altar, they cover it with a napkin. At the first prayer he makes a sign over himself and after that the Archdeacon intones the "Peace be with us" and (the Consecrator) says: "The grace of..." and makes a sign over the oil. Further he recites: "Our Lord Jesus is the Treasury"; and at the end of it he makes a second sign. He recites: "Celestial Treasury" and at the end of its canon he makes a third sign. Next he signs again a fourth sign with his three fingers. In support (of their view about) this fourth sign they refer to the Paghra and Dema. After having signed them three times they sign the Dema with the Paghra and the Paghra with the Dema.[5] About this question we have no quarrel with them. Accept what seems ( M.$5^{a}$) good to you.

(1) V. takes these words to the preceding sentence. (2) V. om. (3) V.: "Treasury which enriches its receivers". (4) V. om. (5) V. has the acts in a reversed order.

6 *Question:* Indicate clearly, how he signs the Altar, the Sanctuary, (V. 6a) the walls, the Temple[1] and the doors, naming each one separately.[2] *Answer:* He dips his three middle fingers in the oil, found in the vessel, and signs the top of the altar from East to West and from North to South, and says: "This altar is signed and consecrated to the service of the Mysteries etc."[3] He signs the Eastern wall[4] with his first finger from top to bottom and from right to left, and says: "This Holy of Holies is signed and consecrated etc".[5] He signs the small altar as he has signed the large one; (V. 6b) and signs the northern wall with one finger, and in the same way the southern wall. Thus he signs over the altar (which is) outside in the Temple, and says: "This Temple is signed . . .". Some people sign the western (side) of the altar(place), (while they themselves are) in (M. 5b) side and not outside. Then he returns to the altar under the candle which is in the middle of the altar(place), turns his face to the West, lifts his hand in the air, and says: "It is set apart etc.".

7 *Question:* I have seen some people who add to the prayer of inclination: "Celestial treasury", "O[6] Lord, mighty God".[7] What is this addition, by whom was it made, and is it correct to say it or not? *Solution:* Of every consecration, whether of the Paghra and Dema, or of Baptism or of Ordination, the opening words at the beginning of the prayers of inclination are: "God and Lord".[8] But in the prayer of inclination: (V. 7a) "Celestial Treasury" there is not the name of God and[9] Lord. Well did Mar 'Abdisho', the Catholicos,[10] order this addition: "O Lord, mighty God,[11] Celestial Treasury", and command under pain of excommunication that it should be said in this way, in order that it may not be without the name of God and Lord.

8 *Question:* If it happens that the sacristan in ordering the Qudasha,[12] forgets to draw the curtains of (M. 6a) the Sanctuary, and he has abluted the chalice outside the altar(place)[13] or in the Sacristy, is

(1) V. adds: "and the doorposts". (2) V. adds: "by its designation". (3) V.: "holy (Mysteries) of the omnipotent Lord, in the Name of the Father and of the Son, etc." (4) V. adds: "beyond the altar". (5) V. adds in stead of: "etc.": "to the service of the holy Mysteries of the omnipotent Lord, in the Name of the Father and of the Son etc." (6) V. om. (7) V. adds: "omnipotent, fill it . . ." (8) V.: "Lord and God". (9) V. om. (10) V. adds: "who added it to it". (11) V. inserts: "to" (reading: "O Lord, mighty God" to: "C.T."). (12) V. adds: "and ablutes the Chalice". (13) V. adds: "or inside the altar (place)".

he allowed to enter the altar(place) and draw the curtains of the Sanctuary?[1] *Answer:* He is not allowed to return to the altar at all, but if there be anyone who is fasting, the latter must enter and draw the curtains of the Sanctuary.

9 *Question:* But if there is nobody who is fasting, and it is (therefore) urgent for the sacristan to enter the Apse, is he allowed to enter or not, in case he carries a spear (V. 7b) or a cane to draw the curtains of the Sanctuary? *Answer:* If he stands outside the door of the apse, and with the cane or the spear which is in his hand, he draws[2] the curtains of the Sanctuary, he is allowed to do so. But he is not allowed to enter inside the threshold. Let him be careful that the spear should not touch the altar and cause any injury!

*Question:* I have seen a sacristan who mixed two chalices, one with wine and water and the other with water only. At the moment of the Qudasha the deacon[3] made a mistake and offered (M. 6b) the chalice in which the water was. What should be done with the altar; ⌈and what should be done with[4] the Paghra he offered thereon? *Answer:* The altar is to be consecrated with oil,[5] and that Paghra must be distributed among the faithful as an Eulogia (blessing). ⌈They must provide another Qetsatha and renew its Leaven.[6]

11 *Question:* If it happens, that, in offering the Paghra and Dema on the altar, the chalice is spilled over the altar before the consecration, is the altar injured? *Answer:* If they are careful, that what is spilled does not touch the altar, (V. 8a) but is poured out on the altarvestments and[7] the vessels, since no damp has affected the altar, it is not injured. But if damp has affected the altar, it needs consecration with oil.

12 *Question:* If it happens, that a chalice is spilled and a drop falls round about the altar and they wish to throw water on it, and it happens, that water (M. 7a) sprays fall on the altar, what should be done with it? *Solution:* They shall not throw water on it, but dip the sponge in water and wipe the place (V. 8b) carefully and not touch the base of the altar.

13 *Question:* What if a Gemurta falls round about the altar? *Solution:* They shall carefully wipe that place with the sponge.

14 *Question:* If the Dema is spilled out of the chalice, when the chalice

(1) V. adds· "or not". (2) V.: "shuts". (3) V. om. (4) V.: "together with". (5) V. adds: "in perfection". (6) V.: "they must bring a Leaven from another place. The water in the Chalice must be sprinkled over leathern bottles which have not been touched by anybody". (7) V.: "or".

is consecrated, is the altar injured? *Solution:* The altar is not injured by what is consecrated, but they shall wipe the place with the sponge.

15 *Question:* It happened once to a sacristan that he mixed wine and water in the chalice, but by mistake he mixed olive-oil instead of wine. The sacristan placed it on the altar as such, ⌜and it was consecrated[1] and the Epiclesis was said over it. In the moment of the[2] signing he noticed (it) or[3] before the administration.[4] Show me[5] clearly with exactness: if (the chalice) has not been consecrated, what must be done with the Paghra and with the chalice containing oil and water?[6] But if (M. 7b) it has been consecrated and the Spirit has been invoked over it, what must be done (V. 9a) with the Paghra and also with the chalice? *Solution:* If the Spirit has not been invoked over it, the Paghra must be distributed as an Eulogia for the faithful, and the water and the oil of the chalice must be kept to be mixed with the flour which is kneaded for the Qetsatha. The altar should be consecrated with oil. But if the Spirit has been invoked over it, and they[7] notice it at the moment of the signing, they must bring another chalice with the mixture of wine and water, and the priest who has consecrated must take the Qetsaja deBukhra, and sign that chalice, far from the altar, and speak in this way: "This chalice is signed with the precious Paghra, in the name of the Father and of the Son",[8] and he must place the chalice on the altar and complete the Mysteries and distribute to the people as usual. And the former chalice[9] should be kept so that it may be kneaded with the Qetsatha. Or they must light (V. 9b) the lamps[10] with it. But on the morning of the next day they must consecrate (M. 8a) the altar with oil.

16 *Question:* If the Gazza is left over to (the charge of) the sacristan and he guards it with care ⌜till the next morning[11], and it happens that on the morning of that day there is in that church a commemoration of a saint or a service of "Consolation", and a priest comes and consecrates the Mysteries, not knowing that Paghra is in the House of the Treasury from the previous day; show me: is the altar injured or not; does it need consecration? *Answer:* This accident is not reprehensible, but is an oversight and forgetfulness, because

(1) V. om. (2) V. adds: "last". (3) V.: "and". (4) V.: "the consecration". (5) V. adds: "this". (6) V.: "water and olive-oil". (7) V.: "he". (8) V. adds: "and of the Spirit". (9) V. adds: "of oil should be desecrated with a small quantity of water and". (10) V.: "lamp of the altar". (11) V. om.

it is not right that two Kings should sit on one Throne;[1] but those who perform the service of the altar must be careful of this.[1] The altar needs no consecration, because (the Paghra) is not something foreign to it. If however anyone says that the altar needs to be signed,[2] we will not quarrel with him, in order that there may be greater (V. 10a) care.

17 *Question:* If by accident a Gemurta or a Qetsaja or a complete Bukhra falls from the paten on the altar, and if it happens that it falls under the vestments of the altar (M. 8b) and among the Books that are on the altar, and the sacristan does not know it, and the Gemurta remains on the altar, one, two, three or more days,[3] what is to be done with the Gemurta or with the Bukhra, if he finds it? How must he put it in order: should he mix it with a new Paghra[4] or give it (without an addition) to one of the people? *Answer:* The solution of this case is very difficult and I have never seen nor heard from those who have preceded me anything like it. But I shall speak according to my knowledge. If he finds it after one day and it is his turn to consecrate, and he finds it before the consecration, let him transfer it to another altar and consecrate (V. 10b) the Mysteries, and let him afterwards return it to the paten. He must join with it a portion of what he has consecrated,[5] and give it to one of the faithful and give him the chalice at the end. But if (it remains there) two or three or more days–it is really a grave accident–he shall give it (M. 9a) to the believers, adding to it another portion from what he has consecrated on that day. But if he finds it at the moment of the Ordering, while he shakes and cleans the altar, and does not find anybody to whom he might give it,[6] he should throw it in the chalice and it should be counted as crumbs (of the Eucharistic Bread) which remain on the altar and in the chalice by accident (unwillingly). He must strive to drink[7] it at the ablutions of the chalice. (V. 11a).

18 *Question:* If it happens that while priests and Levites are ordering the Qudasha in summer or in a time of drought, and in the hand

(1) V.: "This fact is a transgression of the commandment. But they must try to be careful that it will not befall them again". (2) V.: "consecrated". (3) V. adds: "and afterwards finds it". (4) V. adds: "Qetsatha". (5) V. om. (6) V. adds: "it is not right to order it; because they have not given it to him. But if there is a deacon with him, he may order it, because nobody is allowed to receive Qudasha twice nor is it allowed to leave it till the next day. He shall not desecrate it, but clean it". (7) V.: "to receive".

of them are three or more Gemurta's, a Gemurta remains in the throat of one of them and he cannot swallow it and is about to die, what must they do to make (him)[1] swallow the Gemurta? What must be done with the part of the Paghra remaining in his hand? *Answer:* If his fellow sees that he is about to die, he must throw the Paghra which is in his hand into a chalice and give him the chalice that he may drink until his trouble (M. 9b) has passed and the portion in his throat has gone down; then he shall return the chalice to his fellow and they shall desecrate the chalice with water and take the water (that served) to take away (the trouble of) his throat.

19 *Question:* If it happens that a priest has consecrated (V. 11b) the Qudasha, and before making the last sign, (viz.) of the Paghra over the Dema and of the Dema over the Paghra, the sacristan comes in a state of agitation carrying a paten and he takes Bukhra from the paten on the altar and breaks it on that other paten in his hand. The priest who has consecrated, says to him: "I have not yet signed it", and (the sacristan) returns the Qetsaja's to the paten on which is the Paghra, and he signs the Paghra, and then the sacristan takes again the Qetsaja's and gives them to the people.[2] Tell me: is the altar injured[3] or not? *Answer:* If they take the Bukhra before the Epiclesis and break it on another paten, they cause a great injury. But if they break it after (M. 10a) the Epiclesis and return the Qetsaja's to their rightful place and if they have been signed (V. 12a) together with all the Paghra, (they do not cause) a great injury, but a small one, and the altar does not need signing.

20 *Question:* A priest takes the paten to distribute to the people, and one of the faithful comes and throws a Zuza on the paten and his hand touches the Paghra which is on the paten. Because of his joy about the Zuza the priest neglects the fact and returns the paten to the altar. Show me the kind of injury inflicted on the Paghra and that on the altar. What must he do with the paten and the altar? *Answer:* These things happen to many priests, and because of their joy about the gift they become careless about the[4] accident and the injury that proceeds from the gift; but a priest must be careful and examine exactly the person who threw it on the paten. If he threw it from a dis-

(1) In V. (2) M. has: "to the world"; V. rightly: "to the people". (3) V. adds: "by his deed". (4) V. adds: "great".

tance (V. 12b) there is no harm in it; but if he threw if from close by (M. 10b) and his hand touched the paten or the Paghra, he shall not return the paten to the altar, but it must remain in its place,[1] until he has completely distributed it to the people.[2] He must clean it with another[3] chalice and give[4] the contents of that chalice to one of the deacons outside the altarplace.

21 *Question:* When they give the chalice to the women, they (the women) are veiled, lest they should be seen; and they hold the chalice with both hands and (in this way) they communicate. Show me: is the chalice injured and should the priest return it to the altar? *Answer:* When the chalice is touched by a profane hand, a great⌝ injury affects it without any doubt. And when this happens the priest must (V. 13a) take a Qetsaja ⌜to sign with⌝ from the paten before returning the chalice to the altar and sign the chalice in the presence of the deacons and say: "This chalice is signed with the holy Paghra, in the name of the Father ⌜and of the Son etc."⌝ If no priest is near, the deacon (M. 11a) must of necessity sign it alone, ⌜and reprimand the women who have done this.⌝

*Question:* I have seen faithful who kissed the paten, when they received the Qudasha, and their hand touched the paten, and the priests by negligence did not admonish them, and they did not know what they had done with the paten of the Mysteries. *Answer:* The faithful are not allowed to touch the paten ⌜at all.⌝ The priest who carries the paten must be careful to hedge the paten well⌝ with a veil on all sides, so that nothing uncovered is seen on it. They should kiss the veil and not the paten. But if the priest does not take care (V. 13b) of the paten and the faithful touch it, the sin redounds on the priest and the faithful are set free from the blame.

*Question:* If it happens that, when a priest or a deacon carries the paten to distribute to the people, his girdle is loosed ⌜from his loins,⌝ since he cannot (M. 11b) bind it with one hand, and it is not admissible for him to put the paten[6] on the ground, and it is impossible for him to bring it back to the altar going without girdle, ⌜because the Paghra is injured, and if he brings it back[8]

(1) V.: "in his hand". (2) V.: "(to) all (the people) of the Lord". (3) V. om. (4) M. litt.: "desecrate"; V.: "drink". (5) V. om. (6) V.: "it". (7) V. om. (8) V.: "goes".

to the altar, the altar too[1] should be injured, what must be done with the Paghra and the altar? How is it to be safe-guarded? *Answer:* When the girdle of the one who carries the paten is loosed and falls,[2] he must summon a priest or a deacon, if such a one is present, and he must give him the chalice, and then put on his girdle and carry the paten in his hands and they must distribute it to the people.[3] (V. 14a) Because the Paghra is injured, he should not bring it back to the altar, lest the altar might be injured. And he must order it outside the altarplace in the Baptistery or in the Temple, but only after having ordered the altar and having drawn the curtains of the Sanctuary, lest any injury might affect the altar.

24 *Question:* I have seen some faithful who, in receiving the Qurbana, did not kiss the feet of the priests (M. 12a) of Christ neither did they ask forgiveness of their sins from them. *Solution:* I think, there is for them loss and not gain, and they do not receive anything from the hands of the priests neither Paghra nor help.

25 *Question:* When the girdle of a priest or deacon who carries the chalice falls in the Temple or in the Baptistery or in the altarplace, and he is unable to put on his girdle in the altarplace ⌈with one hand,[4] nor to return the chalice to the altar, what must he who carries the chalice do and how must he extricate himself from this situation? *Answer:* If the girdle of him who carries the chalice falls in the Temple or in the Baptistery, (and) if a priest or deacon is present, he must give (V. 14b) the chalice in his hand, remain in his place, bind his girdle and bring the chalice close to the altar and sign it with a Qetsaja and say thus:[4] "This chalice is signed (M. 12b) with the holy Paghra, in the name of the Father ⌈and of the Son etc."[4] But if there is nobody present, he must leave the chalice inside the threshold of the altarplace and then bind his girdle and take the chalice in his hand, bring it before the altar and sign it with a Qetsaja of Paghra and return it to the altar.

26 *Question:* What do you say? If[4] the priest brings the Paghra and places it on the altar, the altar is injured together with the Paghra. But in the case of the chalice you say that he must sign it with a Qetsaja and return it to the altar, while (thereby) neither the

(1) V. om. (2) V. adds: "from him". (3) V. adds: "that they may order it". (4) V. om.

chalice nor the altar is injured? *Answer:* When the chalice is injured, (V. 15ª) it must be signed with the Paghra, and then it returns to its holiness. But when the Paghra is injured, it must not be signed with the Dema; and if it comes, when injured, near to the altar, then the altar is injured as well.

*Question:* If it happens that a priest or deacon burning incense in the time of (M. 13ª) the service by negligence goes to the altar, when he is not fasting, what must be done with the altar? *Solution:* If he has reached the lamp which is in the middle of the altar there is no injury. But if he goes beyond the lamp, the altar needs the consecration with oil.[1]

28 *Question:* If a priest or deacon comes to the altar and by negligence he has not his girdle on him, and other people see him and rebuke him, what must he do? And what[2] must be done with the altar? *Solution:* If he has forgotten to gird his loins and enters accidently, (V. 15ᵇ) one step or two, immediately after remembering this he must take his napkin from his shoulder or his stole, and gird his loins; he must return backwards outside the altarplace and gird his loins ⌜with his girdle,[2] and go to the altar as usual. But if he has reached the lamp which is in the middle of the altar, the latter needs consecration with oil. But if he willfully commits ⌜this insolence (M. 13ᵇ) and contumely,[3] he must be reproved for his impertinence[3] by the head ⌜of the Church.[4]

29 *Question:* If a pagan ⌜has gone[5] to the altar, some three steps, is the altar injured? *Solution:* Some people say that the altar is not profaned by a pagan. But in order that ⌜we may not treat the matter[6] lightly, let the one who signs the altar stand in the middle of the altarplace under the middle-lamp, when the curtains of the Sanctuary (V. 16ª) are drawn, and say: "This altar is signed[7] and consecrated, in the name of the Father ⌜and of the Son etc."[8]

30 *Question:* What if he goes beyond the curtains of the Sanctuary and touched the altar? *Answer:* The altar must be consecrated[9] with oil.

(1) V.: "the Consecration of the Altar". (2) V. om. (3) V.: "insolence". (4) V. om.; but adds: "and they must consecrate the altar". (5) V.: "goes". (6) V.: "the matter may not be treated". (7) V. adds: "and is rejoiced" (sic!) – it should be read: "ܘܡܬܚܕܬ" = "is renewed". (8) V. om. (9) V.: "signed".

31 *Question:* What if one of the children of the Christians, a child under the age of discretion, comes and reached[1] only the threshold? *Solution:* There is no blame attached to him, because he is under the age of discretion and reached[1] only the threshold.

32 *Question:* I saw a sacristan who, in giving the Qudasha to one of the faithful, rebuked (M. 14a) him because of his carelessness in the communion; and the faithful became angry and returned the Gemurta and threw it on the paten and said: "Let your Qudasha be a curse to you!" What must the sacristan do with the paten[2] (V. 16b) and with the Paghra which is on it?[3] *Solution:* The Gemurta which that[4] foolish person returned, must be given to another person, and the sacristan must give another ⌈from the paten[5] together with it, and the paten must be carried with his hands, until nothing from the Paghra which is on it is left. He must clean it with another chalice and desecrate it, that is to say: he must order it with a deacon.

33 *Question:* What if a sacristan takes a paten on which the Paghra is placed, and puts cooked food on it? *Solution:* That paten must not go[6] to the altar, and the sacristan must be rebuked for his insolence.

34 *Question:* I have seen sacristans drinking in the altarplace (the water used for) the desecration of the chalice. *Solution:* They are not allowed to drink the water, used to desecrate the chalice, in the altarplace, but in the Baptistery or in (M. 14b) the Sacristy or in the Temple.

35 *Question:* I have seen altars (V. 17a) on which was a Gospel, but no Cross, and the Qudasha was consecrated on them. *Solution:* The Cross and the Gospel must not be removed from the altar, and ⌈the Qudasha may not be consecrated,[7] when there is no Cross and no Gospel.

36 *Question:* Many priests found in the church, (act in this way): when they consecrate the Qudasha, the one who consecrates with them gives them the Paghra at the Morning Service, and they distribute from it till the end; and then the priest orders alone. *Solution:* This is a reprehensible tradition from the beginning. The Fathers have allowed it in the villages in which there is only a single priest who consecrates in two or three villages for lack of

(1) V.: "passed". (2) V. adds: "in his hand". (3) V.: "on the paten". (4) V.: "the". (5) V. om. (6) V.: "ascend". (7) V.: "there may not be consecrated nor (be anyother) Qudasha".

priests. But when there is a deacon (V. 17b) in the village, the priest must consecrate with him and deliver the paten and the chalice to him, and then return to his own village to complete (M. 15a) his Mysteries. This[1] (is only allowed) in case of necessity, poverty of the church and absence of priests.[2]

37 *Question:* I saw very old priests of a very high age who consecrated in the Morning Service of Friday and Wednesday in the Hebdomada of the Apostles and of Elijah, and they entrusted the Mysteries, according to their careless habit, to a sacristan who gave them to the people the whole day; and at bedtime the sacristan took from the paten what appeared to him (to be a sufficient quantity), and he ordered the chalice and desecrated it. He kept till the next day what was left on the paten. In the Morning Service of that day he signed the chalice with the Paghra and distributed it to the people. *Answer:* ⸢Fy, this is⸣ a doubly reprehensible thing. ⸢The foolish sacristan⸣ had to distribute the Paghra which was on the paten ⸢at the end of the day⸣, and to order ⸢what was left.⸣ But he is not allowed (V. 18a) to leave anything for the next day. I saw a man who received the Qudasha one day and left something of it for the next (M. 15b). This is also greatly reprehensible.

38 *Question:* I saw a priest who made Qudasha and distributed to the people the whole day, and at the end he ordered the Qudasha alone, while there was no deacon with him to whom it could have been given. When they rebuked him for what he had done, he said: "I did it by an oversight". *Solution:* The altar must be signed and the priest must be rebuked for his[4] insolence.

39 *Question:* When a priest or deacon by an oversight goes to the altar barefoot ⸢or with pierced sandals,⸣ what must be done with the altar? *Solution:* The altar must be signed.

40 *Question:* A sacristan took a chalice to pour the mixture into it; and by an oversight he placed it on the ground. How must he bring it back to the altar, (V. 18b) after he had placed it on the ground? *Solution:* It is never right to place it on the ground; but it is sufficient to place the chalice on the ledges.

41 *Question:* What must be done with the Gemurta that falls from the paten which is upon the altar? *Solution:* They must take it (M. 16a) with care and give it to one of the people and add another one to it. But it should not be returned to the paten.

(1) V. om. (2) V.: "a priest". (3) V. om. (4) V. adds: "despising". (5) V. om.

42 *Question:* If a pagan takes the Qurbana[1] from the hands of the priest who does not know his identity; but afterwards he becomes aware (of the fact)[2] that he who received and ⌜took the Gᵉmurta[3] from him was a pagan, what must ⌜he do with it (the rest of the Eucharistic Bread)?[4] *Solution:* The priest must add another Gᵉmurta to it and give it to one of the people.

43 *Question:* If[5] one of the faithful comes to receive the Qudasha and he finds that the sacristan has ordered the Paghra; (V. 19a) and the Dᵉma in the chalice remained ⌜without the Paghra[6]; may the sacristan give the Dᵉma in the chalice without Paghra? *Solution:* If he has cleansed the paten with the chalice, and crumbs have fallen into the chalice, they must give them to the communicant. But they must not give[7] the chalice alone without crumbs.

44 *Question:* In case there is much rain from which a large flood arises which[8] goes into the Temple and the Sacristy (M. 16b) is ⌜the altar[9] injured? *Solution:* If it does not reach the altarplace there is no injury to it.

45 *Question:* What if the water has penetrated one foot[10] or two into the altarplace. *Solution:* ⌜The altar needs signing.[11]

46 *Question:* If there is no wine found for the mixture (of the Eucharistic Wine), may they take raisins and soak them in water which they would offer on the altar? *Solution:* In the case of lack of wine they must soak raisins on the same day and in case of great necessity they may offer the juice on the altar.

47 *Question:* (What) if the sacristan is obliged (V. 19b) to consecrate at Morning Service, and the water has no time to get the strength of the raisins, unless they are soaked a day or two beforehand, in order to impart strength and colour to the water? *Solution:* They must break them to pieces in a mortar, pour water over them and purify them in a vessel, and then offer their juice on the altar in case of great necessity.

48 *Question:* How must the mixture in the chalice of wine and water be composed? How many portions of (M. 17a) wine and how many of water? *Solution:* According to the "Canons" (Law) equal parts of each. But if there is not enough wine, a third part of it

(1) V.: "Gᵉmurta". (2) V.: "the case becomes known". (3) V. has the passive construction. (4) V.: "be done". (5) V. om. (6) V. om. (7) V. om. (allowed by the Syriac syntax). (8) V. repeats: "flood". (9) V. om. (10) V.: "step". (11) V. takes this to the preceding sentence, as a question. The *Solution* follows: "Yes".

(must be wine), and if there is not enough for a third part a fourth: five parts of water and one of wine. If there is not enough for a fifth, then ten of water and one of wine.

49 *Question:* It is written in the "Admonitions" that a priest is not allowed to take more than five Gemurta's, and a deacon (no more than) three. But lo, we see sacristans giving two and three to the people, and more than three to the deacons and more than five to the priests. *Solution:* This Canon holds good in the monasteries where the sacristan knows the number of the communicants[1] more or less exactly. But (V. 20a) in the churches of the laymen[2] there is no fixed number, as sometimes a hundred draw near and some other time two hundred ˹and more.˺[3] Because the priests cannot know the quantity of the Gazza which might remain for them, they distribute it to the people ˹as without their will.˺[5]

50 *Question:* I saw on Maundy Thursday that the sacristans (M. 17b) gave more of the Paghra than is due to the deacons and the clerics. *Solution:* Because of the carefulness ˹of the sacristan[4] that nothing of it should remain till the next day he distributes it because (it is) the Passion (of our Lord), I mean.

51 *Question:* Is it allowed to bring the Qudasha outside the church to the sick ˹and the invalid,˺[5] and to take it to the houses of the faithful? *Answer:* The Qudasha should not be brought outside the church and be taken over unclean places, except in case of necessity till the outer-door of the church with lights and incense.[6] But it ˹should never be taken[7] outside the outer-door of the church.

52 *Question:* I saw sacristans who kneaded a Qetsatha with ordinary leaven, in the time of the Evening-service, and at the time of the Night-service they took half of the dough and baked therewith Purshana's in the ordinary way; they signed the other half with the holy Leaven and baked this dough ˹and offered it[8] on (V. 20b) the altar under the pretext that they would give from those Purshana's (M. 18a) to the pagans and children who are not careful with them and with the crumbs that fall from them, because sometimes they eat them after their food and drink. *Answer:* The Qetsatha must be kneaded in the middle of the night, when the

(1) M. and V. use different words to express the same thought. M. litt.: "receivers".–V. litt.: "those who draw near". (2) V.: "of the towns". (3) V. om. (4) V. om.; reads: "of his carefulness". (5) V. om. (6) V. has plural: "censers" (the Syriac has both meanings). (7) V.: "is not allowed". (8) V. om.; consequently its text is without meaning.

cock cries; this is fit and right. ˹But those who desire to sleep knead it in the evening, under a pretext which is not valid. If they want the truth, they must knead the dough of the Purshana's in the time of the Evening-service and bake both parts in the Morning-service after having impressed a stamp in that profane part, that it may be distinguished from that dough that is kneaded when the cock cries; thus he shall make a Qetsatha with the holy Leaven intended for the altar, and that ordinary one for distribution.[1]

53 *Question:* If a sacristan by mistake puts oil of the lamps in the Qetsatha in stead of olive-oil and he notices ˹his mistake[2] soon after while kneading the Qetsatha, what must he do?[2] *Solution:* He must leave that dough to make Purshana's (from it) and prepare another dough (M. 18b) ˹with another leaven.[2]

54 *Question:* If a sacristan brings oil from the grocer and makes a dough with it, and the smell of the oil is (V. 21a) different from that of olive-oil, what must he do? *Answer:* He must make from it Purshana's, and prepare another dough with other olive-oil ˹and leaven to make a Qetsatha.[2]

55 *Question:* If impure olive-oil bought in the market is brought into the church and the sacristan does not notice it and makes a Qetsatha with it, is the Qetsatha profaned and the altar injured? *Answer:* If the sacristan does not notice it, he is set free from blame and the sin is on the one who adulterated the oil because of a higher price.

56 *Question:* If a piece of dough falls from the hands of the sacristan to the ground, ˹after he has signed the Qetsatha,[2] and it is covered with dust, what should be done with it? *Solution:* The sacristan must make a mark on it, in order that when it has been baked he should not bring it on (M. 19a) the altar.

57 *Question:* I saw sacristans who in baking the Qetsatha rubbed water on their hands and under (V. 21b) the Perishta, and baked it in the oven. *Solution:* The Qetsatha after having been kneaded with olive-oil[3] and signed by the holy Leaven and stamped with the sign of the Cross should not have any water on it.

58 *Question:* What if a layman touches a piece of dough or the Perishta, after its being taken from the oven, or a Bukhra from it? *Solution:* The Qetsatha is desecrated, and they needs must fetch Leaven

(1) V.: "but in this our time since they desire to serve in the Morning-service, they knead it in the Evening-service and take it in the Night-service". (2) V. om. (3) V.: "oil".

from another church, ⌈if they have no other Leaven preserved besides the one by which to sign,[1] and prepare another Qetsatha.

59 *Question:* What if water[1] falls on the Qetsatha after it has been baked? *Solution:* The Qetsatha has lost ⌈its holiness[2] and they must prepare another one ⌈in its place.[1]

60 *Question:* If a drop of water falls on a Perishta or on a Bukhra and the sacristan takes it (M. 19b) and places it on one side,[3] can he perform the Mysteries with (V. 22a) that Qetsatha? *Solution:* If a layman[4] touches a piece of dough or a Bukhra,[5] all the dough is injured. In the same way when a drop of water falls on a Bukhra, all the Qetsatha is injured. ⌈St. Paul bears witness to this: "And whether one member suffers, all the members suffer with it".[6]

61 *Question:* If a Bukhra falls to the ground from the basket which is in the hands of the sacristan, what must be done with it? *Solution:* The sacristan must put it aside so that they may not bring it by mistake (on the altar).[7]

62 *Question:* What if it happens that a deacon in helping the sacristan to prepare a Qetsatha forgets to gird his loins ⌈or steals something from the Qetsatha or from the altar?[8] *Solution:* That Qetsatha is desecrated and if[8] they bring (something) from it on the altar, ⌈the altar[8] is desecrated ⌈as well.[8]

63 *Question:* What if he prepares the Qetsatha without sandals? *Solution:* ⌈It is desecrated (M. 20a) as mentioned before.[9]

64 *Question:* (V. 22b) When the sacristan consecrates in the Morning-service of Sunday ⌈and brings[10] sufficient Paghra for his need and he is about to bring other Bukhra's in the Mysteries, and the sacristan wishes to distribute to the people Purshana's, what must he do? *Answer:* He[11] must single out more than he needs and set it aside for the communion of the Mysteries, and distribute what is left in the basket as he likes it.

65 *Question:* Some people say that it is not right to bring Bukhra's in pairs on the altar; is this true or not? *Solution:* After having reached the number of three you may bring them in the way you wish.

66 *Question:* In case there are only a few communicants, how many

(1) V. om. (2) V. om.; consequently the meaning of the preceding words changes into: "profaned". (3) V. adds: "because he may not offer it on the altar". (4) V. om.: "lay". (5) V. adds: "being baked". (6) V. om. (7) Added in V. (8) V. om. (9) V.: "It is desecrated in the same way". (10) V.: "bringing". (11) V. adds: "the sacristan".

of them (viz. the Bukhra's) must they bring on the altar? *Solution:* Less than three is not allowed.

67 *Question:* If there are no communicants at all, apart (V. 23a) from the priests and deacons, ⌜how many of them[1] must they bring? *Solution:* One to sign with and another to be signed; it is not[2] allowed ⌜under any circumstance[2] ⌜to bring[3] less than two.

68 *Question:* (M. 20b) And if they bring only one Bukhra, what must be done to them? *Answer:* Those who bring one Bukhra must be deprived of their office that they may not serve the order of the Priesthood, because they have insulted the holy Mysteries.

69 *Question:* If the priests who have been insolent have been rebuked, should they be admitted again to their office? *Solution:* After their rebuke they should stand in sackcloth and ashes in order that all who see them may know[4] their transgressions and admonish them not to repeat their wrongdoing.[5]

70 *Question:* Are they allowed to bring on the altar a Perishta that is slit (V. 23b) or torn in the oven, or a Bukhra which is defective? *Answer:* It is not allowed to bring on the altar anything defective and the sacristan must be careful in this (respect) with might and main.

71 *Question:* If they bring them on the altar by mistake, is the altar injured? *Answer:* If the thing is done by mistake, they must show condescension to the sacristan; and the altar is safeguarded. But if this was done (M. 21a) by purpose, the sacristan must be rebuked and the altar signed.

72 *Question:* If a priest comes to pour the mixture into the chalice and by mistake he pours in wine which has not been mixed? *Answer:* The chalice is desecrated and if they bring it on the altar, the altar becomes desecrated as well.

73 *Question:* What should be done with it, if he does not bring it on the altar? *Solution:* He must take a Qetsaja from the paten and sign it, as we have shown above, ⌜and say: "This chalice is signed with the lifegiving Paghra, in the name of the Father and of the Son etc.".[6]

74 *Question:* (V. 24a) And what must be done with it, if he brings it on the altar? *Solution:* He must distribute it together with a chalice that is desecrated to the people, and the next day they must consecrate the altar with oil.

(1) V. om.; but meaningless. (2) V. om. (3) Not in M., but in V. (4) V. has the passive. (5) V. adds: "blameworthy". (6) V. om.

75 *Question:* And if by mistake he pours water (alone) into the chalice in stead of the mixture? *Solution:* The same thing must be done as in the case of wine alone.

76 *Question:* If the sacristan brings Paghra on the altar in (the time of) the Mysteries and afterwards it is seen that there is not a sufficient quantity on the paten, can he (M. 21b) add something to it before consecrating? *Solution:* They bring the paten of the Mysteries with the Anthem of the Mysteries, and the sacristan may add to it as much as he desires, until they lift the veil from the paten. But after the Officiant has signed it ⌜at the first[1] "The grace of . . ." he should never[2] add anything.

77 *Question:* If the sacristan bakes a Qetsatha and together with it other ordinary (V. 24b) Bukhra's and by mistake he brings one or two of such Bukhra's in the time of the Offertory and if this error is noticed by him at the time of the breaking of the Bread, what must he do with that ordinary part and with the altar? *Answer:* (In a case like this) he must distribute the ordinary part to the communicants, because the Spirit has been invoked over it,[3] and the next day he must consecrate the altar with oil.[4]

78 *Question:* When the sacristan cleans the altar, what should be done with the dust? *Solution:* (The altar) must be carefully cleaned, and they must throw (the dust) in the river Tigris or any other river or in a place that is not (M. 22a) trodden by feet, because nothing must remain of the crumbs which are cleaned from the altar.

79 *Question:* And ⌜what about[4] the ashes that are found in the censer? *Answer:* They must throw them in the river Tigris, because prayers have been recited over them, and their perfumes have been incensed before (V. 25a) the Ark of the Lord.

80 *Question:* I saw deacons who received the Qudasha in the Mysteries at the time of the hymn: "Our Lord Jesus, the adorable King", and the sacristans then gave them Purshana's which they put in their pockets, and they returned at the last Lord's Prayer and kissed the altar and the priests while the Purshana's were with them. I think that this is reprehensible. *Solution:* Bukhra's[5] should not be brought to the inner side of the candles which are in the middle of the altarplace, and those who bring them are reprehensible. The sacristan ⌜who has to keep order and not disorder[6] must

(1) V. om. (2) V.: "not". (3) V. adds: "and it has been consecrated". (4) V. om. (5) V.: "Purshana's". (6) V. om.

distribute the Purshana's after the Lord's Prayer while standing at the entrance of the altarplace and give to everyone who goes away ⌜his portion[1] in his hand. (M. $22^{b}$) The latter must ⌜kiss it and go.[2] In case he has taken anything before the aforesaid time, he may not enter the altarplace, (V. $25^{b}$) but must leave the Purshana's on the outer side of the lamp, and enter, kiss and afterwards go away. In the same way the sacristan should not bring the Qetsatha, when it is baked, to the inner side of the lamp, but he must put it on its outer side, and there he must single out for the altar what is to be consecrated. ⌜He must be careful in the preservation of the altar, in order that the younger deacons may not cause great injury.[3]

81 *Question:* What must be done, when a Qetsatha is baked and they consecrate a part of it in the Morning-service, and they have need of consecrating another part of it in the Mysteries and the sacristan wants to distribute Purshana's from it to the children and the faithful? *Answer:* When the sacristan is consecrating in the Morning-service, he must single out what is necessary for the Mysteries on one side, and then distribute the rest.

82 *Question:* If a priest of the church sits down to make the Qetsatha, and in putting olive-oil and flour into it and kneading them together forgets (M. $23^{a}$) to put (V. $26^{a}$) salt into it, and remembers somewhat later that he did not put salt (into it); and afterwards,[3] being perplexed in his mind and wishing to ascertain whether he had put salt (into it) or not, he takes a little of the Qetsatha and puts it in his mouth to taste it. Having observed that it is without salt, he returns the small portion of dough which he had put in his mouth to the Qetsatha and spits what he had masticated out of his mouth on the ground, and throws salt on the Qetsatha and finishes his work of baking, and consecrates (a part) of that Qetsatha and distributes it to the people. What do you say about this?[4] *Answer:* It is a Jewish practice and not that of true[5] Christians. That wretched man committed many irregularities in his diabolical deed.

83 *Question:* Show me clearly the nature of his irregularities. (*Answer:*) The first irregularity is that he tasted the Qetsatha and desecrated the Leaven; the second that he broke (V. $26^{b}$) his fast; the third that he brought back to the Qetsatha what he had masticated

(1) V. om. (2) V.: "go away". (3) V. om. (4) V. adds: "tell me". (5) V. om.

and made it dirty (M. 23b) with his saliva; the fourth that he desecrated the altar by bringing a Qetsatha that was profane and dirty, and consecrated it. All this is unlawful.

84 (*Question:*) What if someone asks: "How can this wound be healed, and what must be done with his[1] Qetsatha and with the altar to return its holiness[2] unto it? *Answer:* Leaven must be brought from another church, the sacristan of which is of an established reputation in virtue and carefulness and well known[3] in the service of the alter. They must consecrate the altar, and the priest should henceforth never be trusted with the service of the church. He who admits him again to serve the altar is reprehensible in the same way.

85 *Question:* A (V. 27a) sacristan baked a Qetsatha in the oven, and because the oven was not heated as it ought to have been, the Qetsatha stuck to the oven and he could not take it out, because it was not yet baked. He brought dry vineshoots and threw them in the oven and set fire to them and heated the Qetsatha which became baked; and he took it out as he wished. What would you (M. 24a) say about this? ⌜Is the Qetsatha injured or has it been saved?[4] *Answer:* I have never heard of such a thing. But I think that the Qetsatha is not injured.

86 *Question:* What if after the sacristans have baked and taken the Qetsatha out of the oven, they bring[5] some straw and throw it in the oven ⌜that it may loose its holiness,[6] and a sacristan takes pieces of wood to which he sets fire; is the Qetsatha not injured? *Solution:* When the Qetsatha has been taken out of the oven, we throw some (V. 27b) wheat[6]-straw and desecrate the oven, in order that no layman may touch it; then we throw pieces of wood into it and set fire to them. As long as the Qetsatha is in the oven, the latter is not desecrated.

87 *Question:* How many times do we sign over the Paghra and Dema? *Answer:* Three times; apart from the signing of the Paghra with the Dema and of the Dema with the Paghra.

88 *Question:* Which are these signs and in which places (of the Liturgy) should they be made? *Solution:* The first at: "The grace of . . ."; the second at: "And for all . . ." (M. 24b) and the third at: ". . lifting up . . .".

89 *Question:* I saw some of the old men who did not sign at the

(1) V.: "the". (2) V.: "to his saints" (?). (3) V.: "knowledge". (4) V.: "is it injured?" (5) V.: "they throw". (6) V. om.

first "The grace of..." while the rest signed (there) and (do so) up till now. *Solution:* Those who do not sign at the first "The grace of.." say this: "Three signs only should be made and not four; one at: "And for all..." (V. 28a), the second at: "... lifting up..", and the third with the Paghra over the Dema and with the Dema over the Paghra. But the rest sign at the three Canons, and say that the fourth sign is separated from these three, because it is the union of the Paghra with the Dema and of the Dema with the Paghra. (They take) their argument from the Ordination-service, when the Ordainer signs three times over the Ordinand, the fourth time being when he says: "N.N. is set apart, consecrated and perfected for the work of priesthood, in the name of the Father". The same is the case with the fourth sign over the Qurbana which is (that of) the (above) union.

90 *Question:* How many are the signs which the priest makes in the time of (M. 25a) the Qudasha? *Solution:* Nine.

91 *Question:* Which are they? *Solution:* Three over himself; three over the Paghra and Dema; and three over the people.

92 *Question:* Mark them clearly for me. *Solution:* ⌜Over himself:[1] (V. 28b) the first at: "... and that we may raise..."; the second, when he signs the Bukhra; and the third, when saying "One holy Father, one holy Son, ...".

93 *Question:* Those[2] over the Qurbana are known as they have been spoken of above; (but) those over the people which are they? *Answer:* The first is at the second: "The grace of...", when the priest raises his voice, and although he signs over his own person, he lifts his hands upwards, in order that he may sign the Cross over the people; and then the people bow and adore, because the Mysteries were finished at the "The grace of...", and kiss the Cross with the symbol of which they have been signed. The second is at: "The gift of the grace of..."; and the third at: "He who has blessed us ...".

94 *Question:* I saw deacons who said in receiving the chalice to bring it out to the people: "Bless, o my Lord", and took the veil from the chalice and (M. 25b) immediately they returned it (V. 29a) and so went out. What symbol does this represent (lit. is this mystery)? *Answer:* The deacons are following unknowingly a tradition which they see from one another.

(1) V.: "his". (2) V. om.

95 *Question:* Show me clearly what symbol is therein? *Solution:* The deacon says: "Bless, o my Lord" and he bows his head, because he expects to participate in the signing which the priest makes over the people, ⌈together with them.[1]

96 *Question:* I saw some priests who in taking the Bukhra said in the moment of the last signing: "We draw nigh, o my Lord, in the true faith" and signed the symbol of the cross over the Bukhra which was in their hands, with their thumb. *Answer:* This is blameworthy and practised only by men of the villages and of the mountains. But you, ⌈o Brother,[2] be careful never[3] to let a man practise this!

97 *Question:* When the deacons come (V. 29b) from the Bema carrying the Cross and the Gospel, on which side must he who carries the Cross stand, and on which side the one who carries the Gospel? *Solution:* He (M. 26a) who carries the Cross must stand on the righthand side, ⌈with his face turned towards the people,[4] because coming out first[4] he enters first, and they go to meet him and kiss him.

98 *Question:* Why must the censer in the time of the Qudasha stand on the lefthand side and not on the righthand side? *Solution:* Because the censer must be at the righthand side of the priest, as he is the consecrator of the Paghra and (also because they burn perfume) in honour of the Qurbana and of the priest and of the holy words that come forth from his mouth.

99 *Question:* Why must the Paghra, when placed (on the altar) be placed on the lefthand side and the chalice on the righthand side? *Solution:* Because when the priest turns his face (V. 30a) towards the altar and the East, his (right) hand consecrates the Paghra and absolves the people.

100 *Question:* What symbol is there in the two fans which are in the hands of the two deacons which stand round about the altar, ⌈on the righthand side of the priest and at his left,[4] when he[5] consecrates? *Solution:* Because[6] they fill the place (M. 26b) of Gabriel and Michael who were at the sepulchre of our Lord. Although there are many angels[7] these two only have charge of the service of the altar and of the priest who consecrates.

(1) V. om. (2) V. om. (3) V. om. the negative; but the meaning is the same: "beware of letting a man practise this". (4) V. om. (5) V.: "the priest". (6) V. om. (7) V.: "(although there) were (many angels) there. So also there are many deacons present,".

101 *Question:* There was once a dispute as to which was greater the Cross or the Gospel. *Answer:* Some people say that the Cross is not greater than the Gospel, nor the Gospel greater than the Cross. These two are one. The Cross fills the place of Christ, while the Gospel is His message,[1] His word and His commandments.[2] (V. 30b)

102 *Question:* How many times does the priest say in the Mysteries: "Peace be with you"? *Solution:* Three times; once before the Gospel; the second time ⌈after the Canon:[3] "... and that we may raise ..."; and the third time before: "One holy Father". Their meaning is the peace which our Lord gave unto His disciples after His resurrection: once on the Sunday of the Resurrection, another time on the New Sunday, and the third time at the Sea of Tiberias when John said: "It is the Lord."

103 *Question:* (M. 27a) If a Metropolitan or a Bishop be present at the beginning of the Mysteries, and the priest takes the Cross, when (the procession) comes out for the Bema, where must the priest who carries the Cross stand, on the righthand or on the lefthand side? *Solution:* The Bishop stands before the altar, his face (looking) to the West, and the Cross on the righthand side on the righthand (V. 31a) of the Bishop. The Cross comes out first and they kiss first the Cross and then the hand of the Bishop. Those who make the Cross stand at the lefthand side, do it for one of the two following reasons: either from ignorance or pride, as they consider themselves higher than the Cross.

104 *Question:* Show me the meaning of the Throne in the Temple or in the House of Prayer, and of its decorative work and its coverings. *Answer:* The Throne in the church is like Golgotha on which it is believed that the Cross of our Saviour was fixed. The big cross at its head (represents) the wood on which (M. 27b) our Lord was crucified. The Cross on the Throne which is at the top of Golgotha is the image of Christ on the Cross. The Gospel which is at the side of the Cross (V. 31b) represents the word ⌈of Christ our Lord[4] with His Gospel and commandments, in the likeness of a king holding in his hands the scepter of the reign. The purple-coloured covering which is over the Cross[5] is the ⌈likeness of[6] (the purple with) which the priests covered our Saviour[7] when they brought Him out to be crucified. The two fans at the two

(1) V.: "hope". (2) V. singular. (3) V.: "before". (4) V. om.; the preceding words: "His word". (5) V. adds: "and the Gospel". (6) V. om. (7) V.: "our Lord".

sides are the two robbers at the right and at the left (of Christ).

105 *Question:* Why do all the services begin with the Lord's Prayer, while in the services of Betrothal and Marriage and in the Funeral-service they never say the Lord's Prayer, neither at the beginning nor at the end? *Answer:* You must know that in former times they never said the Lord's Prayer, neither[1] at the beginning nor at the end. There was once a Jacobite monk who began to dispute with a Catholicos of ours in the East, and that (M. 28a) monk wrote in one of his books (V. 32a) words of insult against us, saying: "You Nestorians do not recite in your services the prayer which our Lord has taught His disciples, as we recite it at the end of our services". And when the Patriarch heard the insult of the heretic,[2] the Catholicos ordered that this[3] prayer: "Our Father which art in heaven . . ." should be recited at the beginning and at the end of our services: a thing which is more than the Jacobites do, because they recite it only at the end of their services.

106 *Question:* How did formerly the service begin in the Evening, at Night ⌜and in the Morning?[4] *Solution:* The deacon intoned: "Peace be with us", and the priest recited in the Evening-service: "Let us confess, O my Lord, thy Godhead . . ." and began the Marmitha. In the Night-service the deacon said: "Let us arise to prayer. Let us pray. Peace be with us"; and the priest prayed: "Let us arise, o my Lord, in thy power" and began (V. 32b) the Hulala's.

107 *Question:* Who wrote the addition to (M. 28b) the Lord's Prayer? *Solution:* Formerly this prayer was recited without the addition as the Jacobites recite it. But when the Patriarch Mar Timothy was ordained, he added this Canon: "Holy, holy, holy art Thou, our Father which art in heaven, full are . . ." in it. He took two words from its beginning which he joined to the Canon and added at the end of the prayer: "Glory be to the Father . . . From everlasting . . ." He then returned to the first two words which he made to follow the Canon: "Holy, holy", as they farce the Marmitha's with the canons. This Canon (rule) was handed down in all the churches of the Nestorians.

108 *Question:* It is good that this prayer is said in all (V. 33a) the services and there is a great advantage in it. But why do they not recite the Lord's Prayer in the Rituals of Bethrothal and Marriage,

(1) V. om. (2) V.: "monk". (3) V.: "the". (4) V. om.

Baptism and Burial?[1] *Solution:* We have spoken at some length about Baptism and shown that it is necessary that the Lord's Prayer (M. 29a) should be recited in that service at the beginning, in the middle and at the end as it is recited (also) three times in the Mysteries.

109 *Question:* Name clearly these three times to me, because it seems that it is only recited twice. *Solution:* The first time at the beginning of the service; the second time after the consecration of the oil, because he signs it with holy (previously consecrated) oil and says: "Fit us ever, o our Lord and our God, . . ." and they respond with the Lord's Prayer. The third time when they desecrate the water of Baptism, (V. 33b) they recite in responses[2] the[3] Lord's Prayer and the rest and they sing in praise: "One is the Lord etc.". They describe the power of the Lord's Prayer fully in those two antiphons. A clear demonstration and confirmation of these (prayers) is the prayer that accompanies it: they pray after these: "O Compassionate One whose name is holy" and its alternative prayer, and the Priest seals.

110 *Question:* What is the reason that this prayer is not used in the Ritual of Betrothal and Marriage? *Solution:* We have (M. 29b) asked many people about this, and everyone gave his own explanation.

111 *Question:* Mention them to me. *Solution:* Some say that the Lord's Prayer comes ⌜from the mouth of the Saviour and[4] must be recited by the mouth of the whole congregation, when they are calling for help, hallowing His name, magnifying His heavenly[4] kingdom and asking for (V. 34a) food for the sustenance of their lives and deliverance from evil. But in the Betrothal- and Marriage-services every prayer and supplication is for two persons, that their doing may be successful and their consent ⌜and betrothal[4] may be blessed and their drinking-cup may be consecrated; and at a Marriage that their wedding may be blessed and their bed consecrated and their conjugal intercourse perfected. They do not ask at that time for the forgiveness of sins nor for the abundance of food. But others say that they do not recite the Lord's Prayer because of the laziness of the priests.

112 *Question:* ⌜But you, (M. 30a) what do you say about this? *Solution:*[4] I say that all things that happened to the faithful in ancient

(1) V.: "Burial of the Dead". (2) V. singular. (3) V.: "this". (4) V. om.

times were performed in the church and accomplished in the middle of the congregation of the faithful. (V. 34b) Usually they performed the betrothal in a Sunday-service, so that there would be a great congregation in the church; and after the morning-psalms they recited the Lord's Prayer and immediately after this they performed the Ritual of Betrothal while the Lord's Prayer had already been recited.

113 *Question:* But if they do not marry in the church, but go into the house[1] of the bride to marry, how can they share[2] in the Lord's Prayer? *Solution:* First they begin with the Lord's Prayer to which they join the Ritual of Betrothal.

114 *Question:* But if their wedding takes place after days or months, will they be without participation in the Lord's Prayer? *Solution:* The Betrothal and Wedding is one act. (M. 30b) As the clergy recite one (V. 35a) Mautebha at night, in the time of the Evening-service, and sleep the rest of the night, and arise at the end of the night and finish their service without the recitation of the Lord's Prayer having been said, but praying[3] and intoning the Hulala, so also at the Wedding-service. Because the Lord's Prayer, once said, does not need to be repeated.

115 *Question:* What is the reason that they do not recite the Lord's Prayer in the Funeral-service? *Answer:* A dead man who passes away returns to the earth whence he was formed. He does not recite prayers nor does he hallow the name of his God nor can[4] he praise his Lord and magnify His kingdom. God's will has been fulfilled for him, because he returned to his dust, and he does not need any sustenance or food. He is delivered from the harms of evil (V. 35b) and those who pray for him ask that he may be accepted by his Lord and acquire confidence before Him and his sins may be forgiven. As from the mouth of the dead man (M. 31a) they make supplications, such as this: "O Lord, Thou God of my salvation", and: "Behold the dead", and "You shall not forget my soul", and: "O Lord, (rebuke me) not in Thine anger" ⌜etc., together with Antiphons and hymns etc.[5]

116 *Question:* But what is the second method? *Solution:* If a man

(1) V.: "church" (meaningless). (2) V.: "add". (3) V. adds: "a prayer". (4) V.: "does" (omitting: "can"). (5) V.: "and: 'Till when', and: 'A man as inhabiting', and: 'O Lord, my hope', and the Antiphons of the same kind; and the hymns: 'Have mercy on me, o Lord', and: 'Who is upright', and: 'Have mercy on me in His mercy', and the rest of the 'Antiphons of the Way' ".

dies at the end of the day, after the Evening-service, the priests[1] must go to the house of the dead man and recite the Mautebha over him, and in this way the Lord's Prayer is recited, (V. 36a) and during the Morning-service after the morning-psalms they begin the Mautebha's of the Funeral-ritual and all their service over him, and in this way the Lord's Prayer has been recited: a clear argument that we must recite the Lord's Prayer over the departed. I have buried many dead in the village Nineveh, ⌜the house⌝[1] of the ignorant, and I saw their priests who after[2] the dead man had been buried and they had sealed the prayer over the grave, returned to the church with the whole congregation of the faithful and recited the Lord's Prayer; they kissed the Cross (M. 31b) and gave peace to one another and recited two prayers and sealed. Then they went to the house of the dead man and ate. Then the Lord's Prayer is properly recited in the Funeral-service. I have heard that also in the country of Ḥazza (V. 36b) they recite the Lord's Prayer at the Funeral-service. We are not able to find the custom of the Ancients about this question. Do what may please you!

117 *Question:* I saw many priests who when reciting the Mautebha of the Evening-service over the dead recited two prayers only. They did not recite the Seal of the prayer nor did they sign over the assembly or over the dead man. Some of them, however, did recite the Seal and made the sign over the assembly and also over the dead man. What is the reason of this difference and what is the reason of those who sign and the argument of those who do not sign? *Answer:* The argument of those who do not sign is as follows: the Service and the Burial (M. 32a) of the Departed has no regular beginning and end; they simply join in it one Mautebha with another, followed (V. 37a) by the "Antiphons of the Way". After having buried the dead man and finished their whole service, then they seal. They reckon in this way that Mautebha of the Evening-service as the beginning of the Mautebha's of the Morning. This is the argument of those who seal after the end of the Burial-service. As to those who seal in the Evening-service, they argue as follows: This day we recite one Mautebha, and it is not necessarily joined with the Mautebha's of the Morning-service, sealing the Evening-service, because (the service) is ended. The

(1) V. om. (2) V. om: "after"; consequently the translation should be changed a little.

next day we begin with the Service of the Departed. In this way the Mautebha of this day is not reckoned with that of to-morrow. Therefore we sign and seal the people that is assembled, in order that it may not be sent away without blessings and the sign of the Cross ⌈of the Lord.[1] He (the priest) makes also the dead man a partaker of his signing as though he was still with us in his body and needing the signing ⌈of the Cross.[1] (V. 37b).

118 *Question:* When[2] a Bishop or a Metropolitan (M. 32b) begins the Mysteries and they (the procession of priests) go out while (reciting) the Anthem of the Sanctuary,[3] where must the Cross stand, on the righthand side of the Bishop or on his lefthand side? *Solution:* The Bishop takes the place of Christ, as is written: "The priest like Jesus Himself etc.",[4] and the Cross is the symbol of the victory, as we sing in the Antiphon: "The head of the Angels Gabriel extolls the symbol of the Cross". Therefore the Cross must stand and be on the righthand side of the Bishop. The assembly kisses (first) the Cross and then the Bishop. The Ancients did so.

119 *Question:* We see now in our days that they do the contrary: the Cross stands at the lefthand side of the Bishop and the faithful (lit. men) kiss first his hand[5] (V. 38a) and then the Cross. The same thing is done on Palmsunday: when they recite the Antiphons and celebrate the feast with a procession, the Cross is on the lefthand side of the Bishop and the Gospel on his righthand.[6] *Solution:* The ecclesiastical chiefs of our time do this for one of the two (M. 33a) following reasons: either from pride or ignorance.

120 *Question:* How is this (to be understood)? *Solution:* Because they have the presumption that they are the Church and the Altar, having power over all and being higher than the Cross and the Gospel. O ignorant Bishops, who do not know how to stand! Those who kiss the hand of the Bishop before the Cross do this from ignorance as well.

121 *Question:* There are also some priests who when they begin the Mysteries place the Cross on the platform in front of (V. 38b) the altar, the Cross facing the altar, and when they carry the Cross while reciting the Anthems of the Sanctuary[7] they turn its front to the West and go in this way to the Temple. *Solution:* Every Cross when it is set down must face the West and be

(1) V. om. (2) V. adds: "either". (3) V.: "of the sacristans" (cf. n. 7). (4) V. om. (5) V. adds: "of the Bishop". (6) V. om. (7) cf. n. 3.

placed in the East, and the priest who carries it and goes out to the Temple is bound to bow and adore first before the Cross; then take it and go out. But those (M. 33b) who let the Cross face the altar,[1] argue that they carry it in the same way as they come; they need not to turn the front of the Cross from East to West. They act in this way either from laziness or ignorance.

122 *Question:* There are some who in bringing out the Cross place it (V. 39a) on the Bema facing the altar while the Gospel which is at the side of it faces also the altar. *Solution:* I have never seen this nor have I heard it from the Ancients. Wherever[2] the Cross and the Gospel are placed they must be placed in the East, in order that they may be adored by the faithful (lit. men). He who does something else strays from the truth of the Church.

123 *Question:* To say more of what I asked you concerning the Palm-sunday, to the effect that we see that the Cross stands at the left-hand side of the Bishop and the Gospel at his righthand side: you have not given me an argument for this. *Solution:* Those who do this argue (M. 34a) that the Gospel is higher than the Cross and do not know that without the Cross the Gospel would not have been known nor that the Cross taking the place of Christ comes first. Let these things (V. 39b) be known to you! ⌜*Here end the various (questions) concerning the ecclesiastical orders and*

*PRAISE BE TO GOD.*⌝[3]

(1) V.: "the East". (2) V.: "however". (3) V. om.

# COMMENTARY

## General Observations

The Commentary which follows must explain the contents of the preceding questions and answers. But before we do so, it is not superfluous to say a word about the translation and the manner in which the Commentary has been compiled, as it often happens that such explanations give either too much or too little.

Our *translation* has followed the original as far as possible. In cases insertions were made to get a text that was well to read for us, it has been done silently as the words were generally of small importance. The difference between the syriac and english idiom is so great that an absolutely literal translation (even if it were possible) would be practically unreadable. Yet we tried to translate the same syriac words by the same english equivalents. A number of technical terms in syriac denoting the eucharist have been simply transliterated. Often they are hard to reproduce in a western language, as the original has got a certain shade that has no identical word in another tongue. It seemed to us that those who use the translation alone can see here in what connections various words have been applied; a translation of these terms will be found here after.

As to the *explanation* the danger of too great fullness of detail was not imaginary in connection with the comparative methode. It could be avoided for a good deal by continual references to the standard collection of parallels brought together by Prof. Hanssens in his "Institutiones etc." ii and iii. Undoubtedly everyone interested in our writing will have this indispensable book at hand, along with *L.O.C.* and *L.E.W.* which have been worked up in that book though they are not superseded by it.

The contents of this book are, as we pointed out (ch. iv and vi), closely linked up with the whole state of affairs of the nestorian church in the 10th century. Therefore it is often impossible and needless to look for parallels as they will fail owing to the fact that the Nestorian liturgy was different from those in other countries. The aim is only to adapt this writing when it is used in studying the Nestorian and Eastern churchlife.

The first thing that is needed is to compare it with the various other Nestorian sources we met before. As several of them are still unpublished, these texts had to be quoted in full. *Because of their incidental character our Q.Q. are ill adapted to serve as a basis of extensive liturgiological dissertations concerning the Eucharist as a whole.* And we had to comment upon *this* book. So the present writer is quite aware of the fact that much had to be left open. Nevertheless I have tried to show on places that permitted it, how the responses and the suppositions of these Q.Q. throw light upon several problems of wider interest than can be examined here.

Much interest has been paid to Syriac and Coptic Jacobite parallels, a consequence of the fact that the Nestorians seem to have had a fairly regular intercourse with these churches, (at least we find that they have read the books of the others, cf. e.g. p. 21, n. 1 and the list of Elias Nisib., *Opus Chronologicum*, ed. E. W. Brooks, Parisiis, 1910, in: *C.S.C.O.*, iii 7–8 (7, p. i–iv Praefatio), a fact that is often neglected). In this way it may be possible to find relations of which we have no direct witnesses. For these parallels we used only printed texts, not Mss. Such a connection did not consist with the other churches and the parallels we find in those cases must be explained, if they are real parallels, in another way. If it was possible to compare these advices with writings from the "Ancient Church" we have noted them. For this is the only way to fix in what respect these Eastern churches have been traditional. But this principle is not carried through too far. When the word "Lamp" is met a big volume could be written on the liturgical and archaeological material about this usefull article. It would hardly have anything to do with our Q.Q. Therefore such subjects were only investigated so far as a certain peculiarity was stated and this one was compared. Otherwise it seemed to be sufficient to refer to some encyclopaedias though they are not very complete on the Eastern side. On the other hand when somebody wants to deal with such an object in a monograph, he will be obliged to use these questions. In the same way words used for "Eucharist" (mysteries etc.) are used without the slightest reference to the "original" sense. Therefore it is needless to compare these words with terms of other churches in explaining our writing. Such a lexicographical research is wanted, but lies outside the scope of this book.

For the same reasons we did not look for parallels from other religions. Of course they can be found and may illustrate some points (e.g. burying in uncultivated soil). But such an investigation must be based upon more data than we were able to collect for the explanation of our book. The purpose of such an investigation must be: to fix the relation between Christianity and heathen religions. Moreover it is questionable whether we can speak here of pagan influences making themselves felt after a long time or of a usual form of thought that is neutral from the religious point of view. It should not be forgotten that several ages of Christian thinking and feeling had preceeded our writing and that such a borrowing belongs to an earlier stage. The influence of the O.T. might have been considerable though it has never been properly traced. I am sure that the Law has deeply influenced certain parts of christian living. This inquiry will, even if it is concerned only with a special point, never be limited to liturgical sources and one must be conscious of the historical connection and of the differences.

We have pointed out in ch. v that this book of Questions and Answers misses systematic order. But on the other hand, in perusing this writing of Isho'yabh iv one will find the same words and ideas over and again. The points of several questions show a certain similarity. It will be useful to explain them before we start upon an examination of the separate Q.Q.

But before we do so, one point must be mentioned. Von Harnack wrote in 1909: "Die Entwickelung des Mysterienwesens und Cultus von Origenes bis zum 9. Jahrhundert gehört nicht in die Dogmengeschichte. Sie ist sammt den Auffassungen von Taufe, Abendmahl, Sacramenten und Bildern eine – noch niemals geschriebene – Geschichte für sich, die der Dogmengeschichte parallel läuft" (*Lehrbuch der Dogmengeschichte* [4], ii, Tübingen, 1909, S. 441). It is possible to repeat these words in 1937, for this history has not yet been written. It is true for the Eastern Church in general, and the Nestorians do not form an exception. Because of this defect, it is impossible to refer to a book describing the doctrinal background and setting of our Q.Q., viz. the Nestorian conception of the central Sacrament (cf. Elias Nisib., *Beweis*, S. 101: "Bei ihnen [heretics] und bei uns bildet das Abendmahl die Grundlage"). Isho'yabh iv does not mention it explicitly either, because it was selfevident for a Nestorian. We cannot think of giving such a description within the limits of the present book (many investigations on which such a description must be based, are still to be done; we have signalized the dangers which make this task so arduous); the following sketch is only provisional; because of this we refrained from a discussion of other interpretations. We have inserted very few references; the evidence will be found in reading the books on liturgy and canon-law mentioned in the preceding pages. This sketch has been made to illustrate the present book and not the Nestorian conception as a whole (e.g. the conditions for the believers who want to receive the communion etc. are not discussed).

The fundamental distinction in these Q.Q. is that between *holy and profane* (it is not: "mysteries", the word by which many people express the idea of the Eastern cult; it is used several times to denote the Eucharist or the elements, *L.E.W.*, p. 583; in *Expos.* ii, p. 6 this definition is read: "'Mysterium' nomen est alicuius rei, quae aliquid quod abest repraesentat atque imitatur . . . Ita et mysteria ecclesiae: figuram alicuius rei praeteritae vel futurae depingunt. Quod praeteritum est, per narrationem, quod autem futurum est, per fidem praesentamus"; it is true that Isho'yabh iv knew this mystagogical interpretation, see Q. 94, 100, 104; but it cannot help to explain our treatises). Every thing or person belonging to the sphere of God is holy; and every thing which misses this character is profane.[1] It should be remembered that according to the Eastern Christian conception the universe consists of these three spheres: the unseen kingdom of God; its counterpart, the unseen kingdom of Satan and his demons; and between them the created world which is the battlefield of the spiritual powers of God and Satan. "Profane" does not imply the idea that a thing bearing this character is possessed by demons; it is neutral, simply meaning: something missing the special character of Gods kingdom, viz. holiness.[2] "In primitive Semitic religion, holiness might be regarded as the nimbus or outflow of Deity which attached itself to everything that mediates in worship, whether persons or things, between the God and the worshipper" (O. C. Whitehouse, *E.R.E.*, s.v. *Holiness*, vol. vi, p. 752). This very same definition is also the leading conception of the Nestorians of the 10th–11th cent. It was not weakened, but intensified by the authority of the Bible, mainly the legal parts of the O.T. (e.g. Lev. and Ez.; it is interesting to quote Browne-Maclean, p. 315: "The Mosaic law is looked on as almost, if not quite in force now. The book of Leviticus will be known thoroughly by those who can hardly pass an examination in Gospel history"). The Sacraments effect consecration (ܩܘܕܫܐ); they have all one end: to impart this holiness which puts men in a position to communicate with God (this is the reason

(1) ἅγιος-κοινός, cf. G. Kittel, *Theologisches Wörterbuch zum N.T.*, Stuttgart, i, 1933; iii, 1937, s.v.v.; Syriac: ܩܕܝܫ and ܚܘܠܢ. (2) It is interesting to notice that the distinction made in our treatises is not that between "pure" and "impure" (see: G. Kittel, *a.a.O.*, Stuttgart, iii, 1936, s.v. καθαρός). "Pure" is sometimes used for the state of persons going to communion, but it is not predominant.

why the various formularies are used as a proof, see ad Q. 3, 92, 114). The fundamental conception may be formulated with these words of Gregory of Nyssa (*De Baptismo Christi*, quoted by Bingham, xi 10, 4): "Do not contemn the Divine laver, nor despise it as a common thing, because of the use of water. For great and wonderful things are wrought by it. This altar before which we stand, is but a common stone in its own nature, differing nothing from other stones, wherewith our walls are built; but after it is consecrated to the service of God and has received a benediction, it is a holy table, an immaculate altar, not to be touched by any but the priests and that with the greatest reverence. The bread also is at first but common bread, but when once it is sanctified by the holy Mystery, it is made and called the Body of Christ. So the mystical oil, and so the wine, though they be things of little value before the benediction, yet, after their sanctification by the Spirit, they both of them work wonders. The same power of the word makes a priest become honourable and venerable, when he is separated from the community of the vulgar by a new benediction" (cf. *Expos.* i, p. 28). It is interesting to see this sequence; bread and wine do not form an exception. It is a well-known fact that the Eastern Church did not fix the number of the Sacraments, and that the distinction between Sacraments and Sacramentalia is not clear. The only point that matters is: the Holy Spirit has taken them as vessels to impart what is hoped for (cf. in the Epiclesis, ad Q. 15). By the benediction a certain person or thing has got a new quality. The holiness is like a veil which qualifies a thing as belonging to God.

We should observe that there is an apparent difference between persons and things. Persons, once imparted with this holiness (priesthood) do not loose it, except by very grave sins by which they become impure (sexual sins; heresy). But things loose it every time when they are touched by something profane (the oven is desecrated, see Q. 86; the altar is often desecrated or reconsecrated, passim; the consecration is taken away by water, ad Q. 78; see below).

Holiness is not transmitted mechanically; if something profane is touched by something holy it does not become holy; on the contrary, the holiness is broken (cf. Haggai ii 12–13; ad Q. 10). It is not mana, as in the conception of the Mass among the Melanesians, see: G. van der Leeuw, *Phaenomenologie der Religion*, Tübingen, 1933, S. 6); it does not extend itself as an oil-staint. The situation is like this: God, the Holy One, has given unto this world of men who are separated from Him by their sins, canals of grace which restore the broken connection. Jesus Christ in His work of Death and Resurrection is the Restauration Himself. He has instituted the Sacraments which distribute the grace after His ascension (cf. Isho'Barnun, *ad Isaac*, Q. 9: consecration imparts grace ܛܝܒܘܬܐ). On purpose I used the word "canal". Grace is not a river "flowing free", but bound within the borders revealed by God according to His plan. Certain elements, acts and prayers have been choosen and form these borders. Everything which does not belong to this group prescribed by the Bible or Canon law (Patriarchs guided by the Holy Spirit, p. 137) is wrong (see ch. vi, ii), especially when it does not fit in with the leading dogmatical interpretation (e.g. *Expos.*), seems to be an expression of heresy or betrays disrespect. It interrupts the stream. To eliminate even the slightest interruption everything had to be regulated (see ad Q. 52 sqq). For it is a current idea that those objects which had to serve as a vehicle of the Spirit, had a "proleptic" holiness. What are the requirements for a valid Sacrament or with the words of 'Abdisho', *Pearl*, iv 1: the holiness and sacramental nature of the Sacrament? "First: a true priest who has attained the priesthood rightly, according to the requirements of the Church. *Secondly*, the word and command of the Lord of the Sacraments whereby He ordained each of them. *Thirdly*, right intention and confirmed faith on the part of those who partake of them, believing that the effect of the Sacraments takes place by a heavenly power".[1] The Eucharistic Sacrament is more frequently used than the others; it shows most clearly this general conception. God acts in the Eucharist in the way of a certain order; a deacon is not allowed to do the work of a priest. But it is wrong to think that the Sacrament is merely a rite, cf. John bar Abgare, *Quaest. Eccl.*, Q. xxvii: "Christianus quidam de Oblatione minus recte sentiens dicit eam esse meram legem, seu ritum quendam. Respondetur, communione privandam esse, donec a peccato suo resipiscat, et poenitentiam ostendat, atque confiteatur Oblationis excellentiam, et convenientem eidem honorem, illamque esse Corpus, et Sanguinem Christi, quo peccata delentur, et debita remittuntur." This statement of a Patriarch who was considered by our author as one of the leading authorities in ritual matters, is interesting from various points of view. It shows most clearly, a) that the Liturgy is more than a simple venerable rite, performed without the faintest notion; b) that the Eucharist is looked upon as the "Body of Christ", and c) the aim of the Eucharist.

Some words must be said on b) and c). Does b) mean that the Nestorians confessed the Transsubstantiation? No! This is excluded by the doctrine of the Sacrament as expressed by Gregory. *Expos.* ii, p. 61–62 is quite conclusive: "quidam theophori viri dixerunt haec mysteria esse proprio sensu corpus et sanguinem Christi, non corporis et sanguinis eius mysterium . . . Quae cum ita sint (the author has drawn the usual parallel with the Nestorian Christology), etiam panis hic et vinum facta sunt corpus et sanguis, non natura, sed unione". This idea was generally accepted, see: Babai, *de Unione*, ed. A. Vaschalde, p. 223: "In its nature the bread which is placed upon the altar and is broken, consists of wheat; but through the prayer of the priest and the brooding of the Holy Spirit, it receives power (ܚܝܠܐ) and it is the Flesh of the Lord in power and remision and forgiveness of sins; together with the Flesh of the Lord in heaven one Flesh in unity.[2] c) The Eucharist[3] imparts forgiveness. This is not only a particularity of John, but it is also found in the quotation of Babai and in a saying of some monks under Sabarisho' (O. Braun, *Synhados*, S. 289–290): "Nachlassung unsrer Schulden und Verzeihung unsrer Sünden gemäss der Verheissung unsres Erlösers" (according to *Expos.* ii, p. 73–74: the communion is a symbol of the last Judgment). Narsai, *Hom.* xxi, Conolly, p. 60, and: Elias Nisib., *Beweis*, S. 93 add to it: the resurrection of the dead. It is typical to see

(1) Elias Nisib., *Beweis*, S. 101: "Was für einen Nutzen könnten wir von dem Genuss eines Abendmahls haben, von dem wir wissen, dass derjenige welcher es auf den Altar bringt, unreinen Glaubens und Priesterthums ist, sich in Sünde und Unwahrheit befindet, die rechten canonischen Regeln nicht beobachtet, noch nach den wahren Kirchengesetzen handelt." (2) To explain "nature" and "power", cf. Narsai, *Hom.* xxi, Connolly, p. 58: "not in (His) nature does the Spirit, who does not move about, come down: it is the power from Him that comes down and works und accomplishes all." (3) The Eucharist is considered in our treatises only as an act of God or the Church. Its character of "sacrifice" on the part of men is not mentioned. A complete history of the Nest. doctrine could not neglect the latter aspect. It may be said, however, that it is not preed ominant. It is: oblation, before the consecration. The Roman theory of sacrifice differs in many respects!

that in after times this idea has partly disappeared, while it is a leading idea of the exposition of Theodore Mops. We must stress this point, as the opinion is widely-spread that the Eastern Church had its doctrine formulated once for all by Ignatius, *ad Ephes.* 20, 2: φάρμακον ἀθανασίας, ἀντίδοτος τοῦ μὴ ἀποθανεῖν. It may be that this phrase expresses the opinion of the greater part of the Eastern Church; it cannot be called a definition of the Nestorian idea.

This consecration comes into being by the prayers and actions of the priest, the prayers being of greater importance (cf. p. 127, n. 5). [1] Here we touch upon another generally accepted judgment, viz. that the Eucharist is a magical ceremony; if some special formula's are said, the effect is guaranteed. It will be observed in reading the Nestorian books, that people felt a great difference between the Sacrament and magic (against which many severe canons were made, see: O. Braun, *Synhados*, Index, s.v. Aberglaube and other law books); it is remarkable that wonders with the Eucharistic elements, of which the Middle Ages have so much to say are hardly found, if any, among the Nestorians). Q. 2 describes the means of consecration in this way: "by the word of the priest it is bound or loosened". But we must make a clear distinction. It is not said, that it happens by the word of any person; the word itself is not a charm; but it is the *priest* who acts and speaks "vice Christi" (cf. ad Q. 118), see: Narsai, *Hom.* xxi, Connolly, p. 48–49. "To bind or loosen" is to act with Gods authority (see: G. Kittel, *a.a.O.*, ii, 1935, s.v. δέω, and: I. Goldziher, *Vorlesungen*, S. 56). Secondly: the Nestorians have always known that these prayers instituted by the Holy Spirit Himself had a meaning which they understood (e.g. ad Q. 110 sqq.). The effect is the answer of the Holy Spirit who "listens (to their invocation)", even when wicked priests are praying. The personal virtue of the priest does not matter (cf. ad Q. 84). "For as the righteous do not bring down the Spirit through their righteousness, neither can sinners prevent His descent by their sins. This is a gift of grace given for the pardon of mankind . . . He does not regard the actions of him who invokes, but the supplications of those who stand behind the priest" (Badger ii, p. 164, n. from the book, mentioned p. 95, n. 1). The Holy Spirit answers by coming down. Every thing depends on His good pleasure. The priest is mediator. He can prevent it in one way, viz. by being disobedient to the rules of the Spirit.

Because of their holiness before (Q. 52 sqq.; proleptic) and after the Epiclesis the Elements of Body and Blood which are precious (*Can.* xxiii) must be honoured (it is the [type of the] Lord or King = Malkha, ad Q. 16), and must be handled with *care*. This is one of the most striking words in these treatises. It can be excellently explained by a quotation from Hieronymus, *Epist.* 60, in: *M.S.L.* 22, col. 596: "in omnes caeremonias pia *sollicitudo* disposita non minus, non maius negligebat officium". On the other hand the element of "awe" or "fear" is missing. We stress this point because here we notice a difference between the older and younger Nestorian feeling towards the Sacrament (cf. E. Bishop, in:

(1) Of the actions the ܪܘܫܡܐ signing is of extreme importance; see ad Q. 15, 87–89 and ii 9 ad Q. 41. In Q 16 there is a variant reading: ܪܫܡ. It is the making of the sign of the Cross (cf. *D.C.A.* s. v.), a very common action among the Christians and applied to all sorts of benedictions. Cf. 'Abdisho', *Pearl*, iv 1 calls it a sacrament: "the sign of the life-giving (a standing adjective!) Cross is that by which Christians are ever kept, and by it all the other Sacraments are sealed and perfected."

Connolly, *Narsai*, p. 92–97 who points out that this feeling of "awe" is particular for the Antiochene preachers; among the Nest. we find it in Narsai and Isho'yabh i). If anybody does not handle the elements with care, if he despises them by his greed (*Can.* vii) and insolence, he runs the risk that the holiness is *injured* (ܚܒܠ), he makes a wound (Q. 84). These acts of carelessness[1] consist in doing the wrong act at the wrong moment, in touching or using wrong elements. If something is holy, it becomes profane; if it is not holy, it cannot be consecrated. Negligence is the counterpart of this care. It was the habit of those priests who did not know the liturgy and were not real Christians. The blame or sin of such a mistake redounds upon the man who made it or made no effect to stave it off. But always upon him who was the "prima causa", not upon the actual sinner. Some of these mistakes are made from audacity (sometimes a deviation from the order of the Formulary) because the officiants did not think of the greatness of their work or because they dispised the things sanctified by the Spirit (which is the same as blasphemy). But however grave the mistake may be, a difference is always made between those who do it willingly or repeatedly, and others who do it by forgetfulness or against their will. The latter are always free; the former are rebuked and punished (see ad Q. 68–69). Again we see here that the Sacrament does not operate mechanically; but that an ethical factor on the priests side must be taken into account.

In our treatises we must say: *Cult is "religio"*, it is: "service" (ܬܫܡܫܬܐ). The liturgy must punctly be done to effect the consecration, to prevent injury, to obey the commandments of the word of the Lord (written and unwritten tradition). We find that practices done by the priests on their own hand are not allowed (Q. 1), because every act and prayer has its particular place and meaning. Nevertheless we hear of many additions and changes; we observe an evolution of the liturgical practices (and it has not caused a great schism as in Russia, cf. N. Bonwetsch, *Nikon*, in: *P.R.E.*[3], xiv, S. 187). But these changes are made by Patriarchs and bishops (*Expos.* i, p. 115). If they are made to enhance the honour, due to the Sacrament, they are permitted. The same holds good for many practices which had not been regulated by law or tradition.

In this connection we must discuss the meaning of ܘܠܝܐ and ܙܕܩ, two words which are used so many times, not only among the Nestorians but also in Jacobite books. Lamy (p. 64, n. 1) said that they are used promiscuously (along with ܡܦܣ that is not found in our books); he translated ܙܕܩ by "justum est, fas est, oportet, decet, convenit", its meaning varying between "res praecepta" and "res conveniens". Kayser (S. 86, on account of James Edess., Q. 4 where both words occur next to each other) defines the former by: "durch kirchliches Gesetz und Sitte erlaubt", the latter by: "der sittlichen Norm, dem göttlichen Gesetz entsprechend" (the equalization of the two halves is somewhat strange!). These two expositors did not adduce the Greek equivalents found in the Questions of Timotheus Alex. (ed. Pitra, *Monumenta*, i, p. 630–645, passim), viz. ὀφείλει — δεῖ = ܙܕܩ; ἔξεστι — δύναται — προσήκει = ܘܠܝܐ. These equivalents

(1) Carelessness of the communicants enlargens their sins (loss) and deprives them of the benefits of the Sacrament (see before).

show that these words are not quite interchangeable and bring out their meaning. The former is stricter than the latter.

In some cases the requirements for a proper performance cannot possibly be or are not fulfilled. This is called: ܐܢܢܩܐ = *necessity*. It is generally distinguished from sickness. It happens in spite of the activity and vigilance of the priest; and comes from outward circumstances. Isho'Barnun, *ad Isaac*, Q. 4 admits that: "necessity knows no law." Isho'yabh i wrote a book about such cases (p. 120). They were the cause of several letters (see ch. iii). It is not surprising that this word belongs to the "eisernen Bestand" of canonical literature. But its contents is unlimited and variable as Life itself.

These few words must suffice to sketch the background of our treatises. But there is one more point to which we must draw the attention of the readers. It is a matter of fact that the very same ideas as found among the Nestorians occur in the books of the other churches too (cf. Timotheus Alex.; John Tell.; James Edess.; and others quoted in the commentary). It is true, the whole Eastern Church, however divided, held the same conception of the Eucharist. And it does not surprise us to find that the liturgical part in polemical literature is very small. This fact would astonish us, observing the liturgical differences, if the *wording* of prayers, sequence of actions etc. were exclusively valued. But if such differences are mentioned, it has some *dogmatical* reason (cf. Elias Nisib., *Beweis*, S. 98–Moses b. Cepha, *Commentary*, p. 69, ed. Codrington-Conolly) or the opponents are accused of disrespect.

Our treatises use a good many words to denote the Eucharist. Some of them which are somewhat particular are discussed in the commentary. But most of them are very common in the Eastern Church; so we may refer the readers to the excellent "Glossary" of Dr. Brightman in quoting what is necessary for our purpose (see the desideratum p. 188).

*Paghra* (Body-Flesh)–*D'ma* (Blood), see before–from the Gospels. (Mt. xxvi 26–28.)

*Bukhra*, 'firstbegotten', Hebr. i 6 (it is interesting that Babai, *De Unione*, who speaks frequently about Christ as the firstbegotten, p. 135, 139, 201, 210, never alludes to the liturgy) name of the Eucharistic host., *L.E.W.*, p. 572.

*G'murta*, coal, *L.E.W.*, p. 573 "a formal title of the consecrated particle" (cf. *L.E.W.* p. 584; four of them form a complete host.). *Pearl:* Margarita is never used among the Nest.

*P'rishta:* Euch. bread.

*Qurbana: L.E.W.*, p. 579: "oblation, offering: (2) the concrete eucharistic oblation" (the first meaning viz. sacrifice is not found here).

*Q'tsaja*, act of fraction.

*Q'satha*, "broken portion", name of the Euch. bread.

The Bread of the Nestorians is " round, leavened, cake, 2 × ½ in., stamped with a cross-crosslet and four small crosses" (*L.E.W.*, p. 572).

# COMMENTARY

*Introduction:* In the previous discussions of ch. iv and vi most of the points that are raised in these sentences have been investigated, and we may refer the readers to them for the explanation of most of the expressions. Some points however remained. Canons and orders are put between quotation-marks since it is indisputable that the canons are those of John Bar Abgare (p. 133–135) and the "orders" is the same word as used for the formularies in T. It is striking to notice that they are quoted anonymously. Does this happen because the respondent does know that the matters discussed here could not possibly be found in those books drawn up in order of I. iii (cf. ch. vi, iic). The answer given by those neglectful priests who mock at the sacred things and the commands of the elders looks very much like that of Exodus ii 14. „The word of the Lord", cf. Matthew xviii 16 and John viii 17 (a quotation from Deut. xix 15): the questioner means to strengthen his point against his opponents by referring to this teacher. The good wishes at the end may express that it was thought that this theological knowledge was given by inspiration and could claim the prerogative of inspiration. Nevertheless this explanation is not very probable in view of what we found in ch. vi about tradition. Therefore it is simply an ordinary Eastern wish that is always uttered in somewhat excessive words and with a kind of repetition, especially in matters of high importance. "Your brotherhood" and "your love" (in the apology) are ordinary Eastern expressions to address somebody (cf. our: "Your Majesty"). The author describes in a vivid manner how troublesome he thinks his task. "Sea" may also be translated with "lake". The translation "peaceful" was adopted for the sake of giving a close translation. In spite of industrious searching I have not found any proof that this comparison is traditional. Yet swimming is not a common sport in the East and travelling by sea not an ordinary occupation of those teachers. These observations make the invention by the author himself somewhat suspect. On the other hand it is not uncommon that people take their examples from places far away. "May their memory be a blessing" is a common addition to the names of the departed, cf. Budge, *B.G.* ii, p. 303, 458, 495, and: Proverbs x 7. "Doorkeeper" seems to be reminescent to Psalm lxxxiv 11, for here it is a sign of humbleness though this order ranked among the (inferior) ecclesiastical orders in ancient times (cf. *D.C.A.*, s.v. *Doorkeepers*).

A striking feature of this introduction that is also found elsewhere in our treatise Q. 120 (cf. also ii 10) is the note of humility and personal ignorance opposite to the greatness of him who is asking on one hand and on the other hand the haughtiness and conceitedness (which is mere stupidity) of those people who do not care for the traditions of the Ancients (cf. Isho'yabh iii, *Epistulae*, ed. R. Duval, p. 202–203 (tr.) who accuses some people of heresy because they are ignorant of the laws of God and "insane" [nevertheless they are Nestorians]; before p. 151 n. 1). These characteristics together are often found in other places in Eastern literature. They may be called the usual adjectives for people who are not in accordance with the speaker. Humility is the great virtue in Judaism, both in the O.T. and afterwards, cf. G. F. Moore, *Judaism*, ii, p. 245–246; 273–275 who refers to several places of the O.T. and the Apocrypha. The first Epistle

of Clemens with its stress upon humility is another instance, at the ver·· beginning of Christianity. Time and again it is to be read in the Refutation of heretics, e.g. Irenaeus, *Adv. Haer.* iv 26, 2 (ed. Stieren, i, p. 645), who are lacking it, because they oppose in every part the truth of the Church. Dom. Leclercq calls this repeated stress upon humility a mere "clause de style", *D.A.C.L.*, s.v. *Humilis*, t. vi, col. 2791. It is hardly necessary to give here a great array of examples, showing how this humbleness is thought to be the right Christian attitude, because it is found so often; some from the Nestorian Church will suffice. It is clearly expressed in this sentence: "It is evident that meekness and humility are the most excellent of all virtues which are cultivated and perfected by the body and soul . . . there is nothing worse than pride and arrogance" (Budge, *B.G.* ii, p. 60). A bishop governs his diocese "with all the humility which befits the governors of the flocks of Christ" (Budge, *B.G.* ii, p. 282) cf. also *B.G.* ii, p. 436 and the introductions to every seperate Life; O. Braun, *Synhados*, S. 40 ff; 88–89; 182. It is evident that though the Eastern mind tends to meekness and the Christians had learned it from their Lord (Mt. xi 29), its use had become highly traditional and lost a good deal of its power. Such an "apology" of a "modest old man", full of the expressions of humility was usual; cf. e.g. Dadisho', in: *W.S.*, vii, p. 76–77, and *Expos.* i, p. 16–18.
The text of the addition in V. (p. 158, n. 7) is not easy to read; I do not see quite what is meant here.

Q. 1. The point of this question is shown in the differences of practice discussed in the next Q.Q. "Metropolitans and Bishops" see besides the Handbooks Labourt, *Christianisme*, p. 326–329. About Isho'yabh iii and his churchbook see the references in: ch. vi, iic. In the present (N.B.! p. 109–110) form of T. there are two formularies of altar-consecration, one with and the other without oil, the former being ascribed to I. iii. The former consists of hymns, prayers after which the oil is put upon the altar and signed several times (Q. 3), followed by anointing of the altar with the oil (Q. 6) and ending with prayers and hymns. The latter uses other words and misses of course the anointing, the altar being simply signed (cf. Badger ii, p. 349). "The former is only for new churches, or for churches rebuilt, or when for some grave cause the church has to be rededicated. The latter, which may be performed by priests commissioned by a bishop, is for more ordinary occasions. Consecration with the Syrians is not looked on by the Syrians so much as a 'baptism of the church', a formal dedication once for all to God which may not be repeated, but rather as a blessing of the building" (Browne-Maclean, p. 303) –Similar rites of consecration with oil are found in other departments of the Church, cf. P. de Puniet, *D.A.C.L.*, s.v. *Dédicace des Eglises*, t. iv, col. 397–398; but for the present purpose it is superfluous to compare them, since the distinction made here is typically Nestorian.–Because it is of some importance for the understanding of the Q.Q., which follow in the course of this treatise, we may translate here the rubric of T., p. 119: "if one of the Bukhra's should be left in the oven, or a Gemurtha falls from the hands of the priests in the altar or a beetle or any other insect falls into the mixture, or they bring a mixture without water or water without wine, or the foot of a child comes into the altarplace or the girdle is loosened in the altarplace, all these do not need the consecration with oil. Further if water is spilled in the altar-place or the chalice is spilled over the altar or a dead mouse is found in the chalice or a beetle or mouse eats from the Paghra or the chalice is broken in the altar or a thief enters the altarplace or an altar-cloth is stolen or a Bukhra or vessels, these (accidents) need consecration with oil." There exists a monograph of J. F. Irving, *The ceremonial use of oil among the Nestorians*, London, 1903 which I was unable to consult, but found quoted in: *D.A.C.L.*, t. vi, col. 2791. "Not adding to or taking away from" is a typical feature of orthodoxy, cf. Deut. iv 2, xii 32 where the law of God is sanctioned by this command, and Revelation xxii 18–19 with its grave penalties for those who dare touch the book of the Seer. The same is said by Polycrates (2nd cent.) ap. Eusebius, *Hist. Eccles.* iv 24, 2 ed. Schwarz, i, p. 490. It is perfect, exactly like the Trinity to which nothing can be added or from which nothing can be taken (Babai, *De Unione*, ed. A. Vaschalde, p. 295). In *Canon* 12 of Athanasius, ed. Riedel-Crum, p. 24 the text Deut. xii 32 is quoted in view of the singing of Psalms (the editors refer in a footnote to Athanasius, in: *M.S.G.* 26, col. 1437 on the canonical Scriptures, Can. Laod. 59 and Can. Basil. 97). Cf. the statement of the Byzantine Patriarch Photius, *Epist.* 13, in: *M.S.G.* 102, col. 754 D., that even the slightest deviation from the liturgical practice leads to contempt of the dogma. For the Nestorians we may refer to the following writers: about dogmatics, Elias of Nisibis, *Beweis*, S. 22, 98 and John Bar Abgarè's Promise: "si quid in fide ecclesiae mutavero aut addidero aut dempsero, futurum hoc mihi esse in opprobrium" (Gismondi ii, p. 47–48); for the liturgy: 'Abdisho', *Nomocanon*, v 2 (cf. ad Q. 106) about the Horae and cf. Q. 122. The sentence quoted on p. 128 is in flat defiance of the general rule which is reflected in its wording. But the author of *Expos.* has clearly written it to save his own theory of explanation (viz. that I. iii expressed a type of the Kingdom of Heaven in the liturgy). Extremely important is the rule laid down by John Bar Abgare, in: 'Abdisho', *Nomocanon*, v 6: "Placuit spiritui sancto, et praecepit, ut nemo fidelis, quicumque fuerit, diaconis, aut presbyteris in ecclesia, et in tempore ministerii, et in eius ordinationibus, ac temporibus (*divino cultui adsignatis*) ullo pacto praecipiat, aut loquatur, aut dicat, neque *scilicet addendo negere diminuendo in his qui divine perficiuntur*." Our author reflects these words. In spite of these strong rules it seems as though the whole of this ritual was not essential, for Q. 2 shows that some people performed it in an other way and our author does not rebuke them. He acknowledges that it depends on one's knowledge and on those who perform it. Essential is to make the sign of the cross or to say the words. See p. 189 sqq. about the consecration.

Q. 3. According to T. it is really done three times. The oil is brought upon the altar, p. 131, and the signings are found in the rubrics on p. 132, 133, 134. We find here that all formularies must be treated in the same way and that they are to a certain extent parallel (see p. 190). The point that matters is the number: t h r e e. The same insisting upon this number is found in Q. 5, 67, 90. In commenting upon the last place a reference to the Jacobite commentaries will be included showing that they too wanted a multiple of three. The commentators always hint to the Trinity. This reference forms I think a sufficient explanation of this insistence of Eastern people and Eastern rituals on the number three. Once the mystagogical explanation being adopted in one sense or another, it is quite natural that it should influence the rite itself to make it more impressive and in accordance with its explanation whenever it did not fit properly. The symbol of the Trinity was of course directly at hand showing forth the essence of Christianity. Whenever the number of acts is about the same as has been discussed and when there are differences between churches it is always for dogmatical reasons that they combat one another. This is the primary reason. It seems to me to be quite superfluous to surmise here influence of ideas connected with the number three in other religions (cf. about the symbolical meaning of the numbers, three included: F. Cabrol, *D.A.C.L.*, s.v. *Nombres*, t. vii, col. 1464–1469, and: W. Cruickshank, in: *E.R.E.*, s.v. *Numbers*, ix, p. 416–417; O. Rühle, *Zahlen*, in *R.G.G.*², Tübingen, v, 1932, Sp. 2063–2068).

Q. 4–5. The turning point of these questions lies in the number of the signings which should be three. It seems to be supposed by the author that the signing is bound up with the "prayer of inclination". This is called in Syriac a Gehanta = a prayer said in a low voice (as is always said in the rubrics). "Canon" is the end of those Gehanta's which is said aloud; the various meanings of "Canon", see in: *E.S.D.O.*, p. 292 (rule; prayer; antiphonal chant), and: F. Cabrol, *D.A.C.L.*, s.v. *Canon*, t. ii, col. 1847.

In T. the manner of signing is according to Q. 5. The sequence of the prayers given in 5 corresponds to T. resp. p. 141, l. 14 (prayer ascribed to Narsai), the sign over himself being found p. 142, l. 4 (mentioned twice in Q. 5); the placing of the vessel etc., p. 142, l. 5; the cry of the arch-deacon, p. 142, l. 12; but in T. it is found after the benediction of the priest and the sign over the oil, p. 142, l. 7–8; 2nd sign, p. 142, l. 26 (prayer)–p. 143, l. 18; the 3rd one, p. 143, l. 21 (prayer)–p. 144, l. 17; the 4th sign is p. 144, l. 18–19. The places mentioned in Q. 4 are: p. 142, l. 7; 2nd: p. 143, l. 21–p. 144, l. 17 (this being the only one Gehanta, while the prayers mentioned in Q. 5 and T. are all such prayers); the 3rd: p. 144, l. 18–20 (though the rubric in T. indicates that it should be said softly).

The difference is of no great importance to our author; see p. 193. *This observation is of some moment with regard to the so called magical practices of the liturgy* where everything must be done according to a fixed number and where the validity was dependent on it. The end of Q. 5 may be compared with the question in Q. 89 sqq. That it could be used as a proof see p. 190.

The addition in V. (p. 159, n. 3) not in T. That the Nestorians signed with three fingers is also expressly stated in the rubric p. 145 and introduced by the formula: "and be it known to you, o Brother that all signings of the rest must be signed with three fingers". (p. 000) It is well known that the number of the fingers was thought to express a kind of confession. The Jacobites used only one finger because of the one nature, and the Melchites or Byzantines used two fingers, cf. Elias Nisib., *Beweis*, S. 39; he goes on: "unsere Genossen, die Orientalen, fuhren fort sich wie in alter Zeit mit der ganzen Hand zu bekreuzen, was mit den Erfordernissen des Christentums, welches von keiner Veränderung getroffen und unter keinen Widerspruch gelitten, übereinstimmt." Cf. on the different manners of signing E. Fehrenbach, *D.A.C.L.*, s.v. *Bénir (manière de)*, t. ii, col. 746–758. Three fingers is always an expression of the Trinity. (The reversion of V. p. 159, n. 5 is clearly mistaken, cf. *L.E.W.*, p. 291.)

Q. 6. The answer is the same as the contents of T., p. 144–146, respect. p. 144, l. 25 sqq. (cf. l. 22 sqq.); p. 145, l. 6 sqq. (though it is said here and in the next case that he should sign with *three* fingers); northern wall, l. 12 sqq; southern wall, l. 15 sqq; the door-post (only in V.) l. 18–sqq.; small altar, l. 22 sqq. (it is also mentioned in: Gismondi i, p. 89; "fidelibus ex ara minori eucharistiam sumentibus"; but it is not clear what was its place in the sketch of Dom. Connolly, *Expos.* i, p. 196). Only the signing of the temple is not mentioned separately but in the concluding formula, p. 146, l. 22. T. supposes signing of the Western side, inside the altarplace. It is not said in the rubric that the consecrator goes under the candle, but he stands "on the platform" (see Q. 121) p. 146, l. 20, quite in accordance with the description here.–This question can only be explained, I think, by assuming that there existed some differences about it though they are not specified. The additions in V. are merely fuller quotations.

Q. 7. The prayer discussed here is T., p. 143, ascribed to Bar Sauma of Nisibis; see: A. Baumstark, *L.G.*, S. 108–109, and add: Wigram, *Introduction*, p. 142–171. In T. it begins with the opening words that are discussed here. Here again we find the parallellism in the formularies (p. 190). About 'Abdisho' see p. 86. We do not know anything about this addition (which was, it is readily admitted, of no great importance from the liturgical point of view) from other sources. It seems, however, that 'A. attached some great weight to it since disobedience is punished by excommunication (cf. *D.C.A.*, s.v; for the Nestorian Church, see J. Labourt, *Christianisme*, p. 344; it "is still a very serious punishment . . . It can, however, always be revoked in as much as it is a command to the offender to repent' ", Browne–Maclean, p. 191–192. 'A. was very ready in distributing this punishment', Gismondi i, p. 90: "Excommunicationis poenam saepissime infligebat"; what is done often, looses its force.

Q. 8–9. The ܩܢܟܝܐ translated always by "sacristan" is somebody who has to do with the ܩܢܟܐ, a word borrowed from the Greek, meaning: shell; it is typically Nest. to denote the Apse or Sanctuary (cf. *Expos.* i, p. 90–93; for the archaeological material see: *D.A.C.L.*, s.v. *Abside*, t. i, col. 183–197), though it is sometimes found in Greek (Bingham, viii 6, 9, who refers to Dufresne) because it has the form of a shell. (T., p., 7, l. 21 = *L.W.E.* p. 270 it is explained by "altar": ܩܢܟܐ ܕܗܘܝܘ ܡܕܒܚܐ; this quotation shows once for all that "altar" has a wider meaning than of table alone; cf. θυσιαστήριον. Ignatius, *Eph.* 5, 2, *Trall.* 7, 2; hence we often translated it by: "altarplace"). His task is the same as that of the Skeuophulax among the Greeks (*D.C.A.*, s.v.). He had to take care of all matters required for the right preformance of the service and had to order the vessels at the end. The office could only be held by priests and deacons since only they were allowed to come everywhere in the church (*E.S.D.O.*, p. 298 adds: "according to the books" without a further reference). It is not always certain what functionnary is meant. But from Q. 81 it seems to be sure that he was generally a priest; a variant of ii 12 might be compared where M. has ܩܫܝܫܐ and V. ܩܢܟܝܐ of whom is spoken before in the same Q. and who distributes the communion which was only allowed to a priest.

"Sacristy", lit.: "Deacon's house", see Q. 34, 44 and p. 226; *L.E.W.*, p. 587 (to distinguish between Nest. and Chald. as is done by Brightman is wrong): "the chamber attached to the church in which the sacred vessels etc. are kept under the charge of the deacon"; in the Sketch of Dom. Connolly, *Expos.* i, p. 196:E.

At the end of the service the veils are drawn, cf. *L.E.W.*, p. 302 (T. uses slightly different words). When there is no service the altarplace may not be entered. A young priest was once rebuked "quod altare inierit . . . quo tempore minime id fert consuetudo", viz. at night (Gismondi i, p. 107). The places of the laymen in the church were separated from the Sanctuary by an elevation (ܩܢܩܠܐ) with openings that were closed by veils "utque ab oculis mortalium abscondantur ea quae ibi observantur" says *Expos.* ii, p. 114 cf. i, p. 90–93 (*D.C.A.*, s.v. *Cancelli* and *Veils; L.E.W.*, p. 590; *D.A.C.L.*, s.v. *Cancel*, t. ii, col. 1821–1831 about its aim and shape; it is the usual scheme found in the Eastern church since the 4th century. Pictures of such veils in C. M. Kaufmann, *Handbuch*, S. 569–571). At certain moments of the liturgy they were opened and closed (see e.g. T., p. 7; there are slight variations between rubrics and practice). This was specially done during the communion. Then the firmament is put aside and the unity of Heaven = Sanctuary and earth = church that is aimed at in the liturgy is realised (*Expos.* ii, p. 37, a usual symbolism, see e.g. Chrysostomus, *in Eph.* iii 5 in: *L.E.W.*, p. 480). When the liturgy is finished this connection is broken and the altar protected against defilement. This seems to be the obvious explanation. (See also: E. Bishop, in: Connolly, *Narsai*, p. 90–91). Yet it is highly probable that we are here on the wrong track. I believe that the writer has in mind altarveils proper viz. those close around the altar, *L.E.W.*, p. 590–591. For in ii 39 sqq. (quoted ad Q. 39) a sacristan is spoken of who stands on a ladder in the altarplace to fasten the veil and the evidence of Q. 29–30 is conclusive by its climax. In our Q. the sacristan may not enter the Sanctuary, yet to put it right again he has to reach over a long distance, therefore using a cane which would not be necessary if the veils of the Cancelli were meant; and he risks to touch the altar.

At the end of the service follow the ablutions, cf. Q. 18. By doing this the priest breaks his fast after which he was not permitted to enter the altar (*Can.* xxvi and ad Q. 27). It is a clear case of collision of two precepts and of course that of the guarding of the altar prevailed. About touching the altar see ad Q. 10.

Q. 10. The chalice is in all christian liturgies composed of wine and water (see ad Q. 46 and 72–75). It is mixed before the service (*L.E.W.*, p. 251). One of the two chalices which are mixed here (in view of the 2nd one: fill, would be a better translation) was reserved for the Eucharist. It is not clear for what purpose the other one was made; possibly for the ablutions (see ad Q. 18). The deacon was permitted to bring the elements on the altar, at any rate the chalice and if there was no priest present also the bread (John Bar Abgare, *Quaestio Eccl.* x, cf. Isho' Barnun, Q. 23 and ii 23–24 ad Q. 11). V. omits "deacon"; it may imply that sacristan and deacon were thought to be equivalents. It is not certain if it must be inferred from M. that the sacristan and deacon were separate persons. ܐܣܩ] Aphel of ܣܠܩ = to bring on high. In itself this does not express the thought of offering, though it is also found in that meaning (*Thesaurus Syriacus* s.v.) and that a certain shade of it was found in the word is proved by ii 17 quoted ad Q. 15 (the same is the case with the latin "offerre", see: Lietzmann, *Messe*, S. 182). We may compare John Tell., *Canon* 12 (Lamy p. 72): Is something that was put on the altar by mistake, holy or can it serve a common end (ܦܫܝܛܐ)? Answer: Yes, if the mysteries are performed over it; otherwise it may be taken away. A reference to Exod. xxix 37 may be useful: "it shall be an altar most holy: whatsoever toucheth the altar shall be holy"; the same in: Exod. xxx 29. Cf. ii 1: a chalice with insects must be thrown away (cf. ad Q. 78) "because it has been placed on the sacred altar". Yet it seems to be better to take the neutral sense, cf. ad Q. 15. The mixing was done after the example of Christ; bringing an unmixed chalice causes a great injury. Therefore the altar should be consecrated with oil; that differs from the rubric of T., p. 119, where it is mentioned among the cases that need consecration without oil. Of course the Paghra is also affected and cannot be used any more for consecration and communion. It is distributed as a ܒܘܪܟܬܐ = blessing. For since it was separated and set upon the altar it had got something of consecration that should have been completed in the liturgy. That is the reason of the often occuring "distribution", a word used without addition as a terminus technicus, not to be confused with communion. ܒܘܪܟܬܐ = eulogia. The latter word has many shades in the ecclesiastical language, (*D.C.A.* s.v. and: *D.A.C.L.*, s.v. *Eulogie*, t. v, col. 733–734; *L.E.W.*, p. 579). At the end of the early christian times it means preferably: a particle of the bread from which the host is taken; but which was not consecrated, and which was given to some people instead of the communion. The Nestorians do not use this name, but Purshana, cf. p. 114, n. 2; ad Q 80. Brightman gives the word M<sup>e</sup>caprāna and says that our word is specially Jacobite. It may be that it has not such a specialized meaning; it was given together with the host (Q. 32) as an extra-gift. (We should notice that there does not exist a transliteration of the Greek Eulogia as in Coptic; does this show that the technical meaning of this word is from a date after the separation?)

We may compare with this question a piece that is only preserved in V. (fol. 83b–84b); it may be that it was omitted in M. because the writer (or copyist) thought that it was sufficiently dealt with in this Q, cf. p. 69. It reads as follows: "*Question:* A priest of the church throws water into the chalice and by mistake he forgets to mix wine with it, and he brings the paten and the chalice upon the altar and completes the Qudasha. At the end of the Qudasha the deacon draws near and receives the Qudasha. Having tasted it (communion, *L.E.W.*, p. 298), he says to the priest: 'this is water without wine', and (then) the wretched priest remembers that he did not mix wine with it. After that the sacristan comes and throws pure (lit.: living = not mixed with water) wine into the chalice, takes a Q<sup>e</sup>tsaja from the paten, signs the chalice and offers it on the altar. *Solution:* The altar has been profaned since they brought profane water upon it. *Question:* What must be done with the Q<sup>e</sup>tsaja that has been consecrated together with the profane water, and with that chalice in which new wine was thrown in the end? *Solution:* It must be distributed among the people, and the altar must be consecrated with oil. Thus that stupid sacristan should have acted, instead of throwing pure wine into the chalice by which act profanation was added to profanation. His behaviour was stupid in all respects.

But he must mix equal parts of wine and water and throw the mixture into the chalic and give it to the people; and on the morning of the next day the bishop must efface the profanation of the altar". This seems practically the same question; and the solution is similar. There is only one difference viz. that in this case consecration has taken place while in our Q. it had not yet been consecrated. Yet it does not remove the profanation: if the elements are not made according to the law, they do not become consecrated. The sacristan thought he could put it right by pouring wine into it at random, instead of the usual half and the ordinary signing by which the consecration was always brought about. But everything is wrong from the very beginning. Only the consecration of the altar can bring relief. That makes the lawful state in which the consecration of the Eucharist may become effective. This case is mentioned in the rubric of T., p. 119 (cf. p. 196).

These questions are important to supplement Q. 10, since nothing was said there about the chalice. We may conclude from the parallel that the matter could not be put right by simply substituting the right elements. The whole affair should be built up from the beginning. In M. it is said that new Euch. Br. must be provided and the Leaven renewed (see Q. 58 and 84), but not how it should be done. According to V. it must be brought from another place, (see the same Q.Q.). The treatment of the water which is prescribed here differs from that of Q. 75 where the same matter of bringing a chalice with water alone is discussed and where the connection of the sentence suggests that the chalice with water must be distributed together with the Eulogia. Here it must be preserved, though it is not said for what purpose (ablution?).

Among the Copts. the deacon was ordered to smell whether the mixture was all right (Villecourt, *Observances*, p. 249); probably this was prescribed for the deacon to notice whether the mixture was not yet corrupted; but it had also the effect that he could see whether it was water alone or mixture.

Q. 11, 12, 14. They must be treated together since they deal with the same matter, viz. the dropping of one of the Eucharistic elements, the wine. The bread is spoken of in Q. 13, 41, 56 and 61. Both during the preparation and the communion something might easily be dropped and admonitions to make the administrance careful are very old. See p. 234 Generally the point is there that the elements are injured in some way while here the effect upon the altar is considered. Therefore no difference is made between "consecrated" and "unconsecrated". First the unconsecrated wine is dealt with. In various places this spilling of the wine is treated. In *Canon* 100 of Basilius (Riedel, S. 278) the priest is advised not to fill the chalice "bis zum Rande . . . damit nichts auf den Boden verschütet wird". Gabriel Ibn Tarikh, *Can.* ii (ed. O. H. E. Burmester, in: *Le Muséon*, 1933, p. 52) says: "he who has not reached his majority shall not carry the chalice, lest some of it be spilled, and this is a great sin; but he shall carry it who has the ability to take care of it". The point in question is not: what must be done with the wine, as in John Tell., *Can.* vi (Lamy, p. 66) and James Edess., *Can.* 32 (Kayser, S. 21–22; text, S. 1), but with the altar. Isho'Barnun, *ad Macarium* speaks about spilling in every place in general terms: Q. 23: What must be done if it occurs to a deacon carrying the chalice that something of the blood is shed on the earth? *Solution:* The place must be washed with water. This water must be used to cover the wall of the altar or to be a Ḥenana for the true believers who must necessarily receive the communion together with it in the church." (It must be concluded that it was wine from the chalice which the deacon carried to communicate; otherwise it was forbidden that water should touch the altar; for covering the walls see ii 1 ad Q. 78; Ḥenana see p. 132, n. 2). Here the matter is pursued with the unconsecrated wine. Q. 11 is referred to in ii 19 (ad Q. 59). The meaning is perfectly clear. It is spilled in the prothesis. According to Q. 15 the consecration takes place at the Epiclesis. The altar was covered with a number of vestments and various vessels used during the service, specially the paten was placed upon it (cf. *L.O.O.*, p. 51–62 and T., p. 146). These objects prevented the altar itself of becoming touched and thereby desecrated. If the stones of the altar are reached, consecration with oil is necessary, see also the rubric T., p. 119.

In ii 23–24 the same question is put in a different form. There the author does not seem to be so sure. He gives an other solution and finishes by expressing his doubt. The text reads as follows: "*Question:* A deacon of very good reputation[1] in our country who was in a town in the neighbourhood said to me: 'I saw a priest and a deacon bringing the paten and the chalice on the altar at the time of the mass[2] and the contents of the chalice were spilled over the altar and the altar with all its vessels and vestments was drowned by the mixture of the chalice. They went to tell the bishop about it.[3] He answered them that the altar was not injured by it. What is your opinion about this fact? *Answer:* The priest must judge as his eyes saw it.[4] By the word of his mouth the altar becomes consecrated and by his words it loses its consecration.[5] *Question:* The bishop has authority over his diocese, cathedral and residence.[6] But if to us happens something like this, what ought we to do?[7] *Answer:* I do not know it from a bishop, but I only tell what I have seen. It was in the days of Mar George, Metropolitan of Mosul,[8] while I was a deacon, on the Wednesday of the Fast of the Ninevites[9] and at the moment of the Offertory I took the chalice and the priest took the paten. After I had taken it, the contents of the chalice were poured from my hands over the altar. The altar with all its vessels and vestments was drowned by that mixture. The parish-priest went out to tell it to His Holiness (the bishop) and he ordered to carry out the altar and its vessels. They brought in other vessels and vestments and endued that altar and they brought a consecrated wooden altar[10] and placed it on the large altar. The bishop celebrated the Eucharist according to the liturgy of the Holy Mar Nestorius[11] and distributed the Euch. bread to the believers. In the morning of the next day[12] the bishop came back and consecrated the altar. So we have seen it with our eyes. But if somebody says something else, we shall not quarrel with him." We find here a supplement of what is discussed in Q. 11. From

(1) See ad Q. 84. (2) *L.E.W.*, p. 267; cf. ad Q. 10. (3) It seems as if it did not occur very often. (4) The answer of the bishop suggests that nothing had happened to the altar. Yet the point is uncertain, as it is written that everything was drowned. It would be quite probable that the altar was actually profaned. It can only be decided by the priest who assisted. (5) Cf. ad Q. 2. (6) Lit.: "Country, church, town" (V. reads instead of the last word: "Altar"). (7) Does this clause imply that the questioner was a monk who did not live under the jurisdiction of a bishop? (8) See p. 74-75. (9) The date of this Fast was not fixed since it was held 70 days before Eastern, *E.S.D.O.*, p. 268 and note, and A. Baumstark, *Festbrevier*, S. 191–194; it seems to be a Mesopo tamian speciality, but it is also found in the Ethiopic church. (10) Cf. *Canon* i and Isho'Barnun, *ad Isaac* Q. 9 (quoted ad Q 29–30). (11) See p. 29, n. 3 for the dates on which it should be said. (12) The conseoration takes always place at this time; probably because it was a new day and a fresh situation (cf. Q. 74).

this quotation we can induce that our author starts from the method in which George of Arbela had solved this difficulty though he did not consider it obligatory.

Q. 12 does not state clearly at what moment the chalice was shed and therefore it is not known whether it was consecrated or unconsecrated wine. No similar questions besides that of Isho'Barnun are known to me from the Nestorian church. Among the Jacobites Bar Hebraeus, *Nomocanon*, vi 4 brings several Canons prescribing the treatment if consecrated wine was spilled (at any rate this interpretation is suggested by its connection and by the similar decision, of John Tell., *Can.* 6 (Lamy, p. 66) who orders that coals of fire should be laid in that place). Very interesting in this respect is the response of James Edess. who tells us that there was a double practice about this point: some people throw water in that place while others lay glowing coals on it; the former do it to cover the place, the latter to purify it; "jedoch weder diese noch jene können jenen heiligen Tropfen von dem Orte entfernen. Denn ihre Absicht ist die, dass er nicht mit Füssen getreten wird." Therefore James advises to scrape off that place with a knife and to throw away or to burn these scrapings. If that cannot be done, the practices mentioned before are allowed. He does not think it to be of great importance since the power of the consecrated elements is not attached to the earth but to the hearts of the faithful (*Can.* 32, Kayser, text S. 1, tr., S. 21–22; it is not found in Lamy's text as it fails in the Paris Ms.). Rabbula ordered what was rejected by James whose directions are taken over by Bar Hebraeus. It is not superfluous to notice that burning holy things was an atrocity to our author ii 15, ad Q. 78). The Nestorians seem to have followed the first practice. They run the risk that the altar will be affected, e.g. by the flowing away of water. This can be prevented by using a sponge. This article is found in all Eastern rites and is used to wash the chalice and the paten (*D.C.A.* s.v. *sponge*, *D.A.C.L.*, s.v. *Eponge*, t. v, col. 344 and *L.O.O.*, p. 58. Of course it was also holy. John Tell., *Can.* 15 [Lamy, p. 74] ordered that if a sponge could not be used any more it should be burnt lest it may be despised.) Even in this case one should be careful not to transgress the Canon. For it was prescribed that the altar should never be washed when it had once been established (*Canon* ii).

Q. 14. Belongs to Q. 11 dealing with the other possibility. Its principle is a logical one, but *is never expressed so plainly*. Some people however thought that in such a case the altar did need signing. The author did not want to quarrel with them but he did not think it necessary, if only care was displayed (ii V. 25, quoted ad Q. 16).

Q. 13. For the Eucharistic bread the same measures are applied as for the wine in Q. 12. Basilius, *Can.* 99 (Riedel, S. 277) impresses on the priest to take care that nothing should fall upon the earth during the fraction (Copt.). Cf. below Q. 40–41, 61.

Q. 15. This is analogous to Q. 10. Olive-oil was necessary for preparing the dough (cf. ad Q. 53) and for the lamps (*Can.* xii). It is not easy to see why the sacristan could make this mistake since the smell and the nature of these two liquids were so different. At any rate there was a mistake. The literal translation was: "and the Descent was called" and in Q. 19 it is styled: "the calling of the Spirit", a common name for the Epiclesis among Jac. and Nest. In *Expos.* ii, p. 60 (text) ܡܚܬܬܐ is also used absolutely. Another name was ܘܬܐܬܐ ܡܪܝ from the first words of the prayer: "and may there come, o my Lord" (*L.E.W.*, p. 287) in which the Descent of the Spirit is prayed for. "The moment of signing" is that part of the liturgy in which the priest breaks the host and signs the chalice with it reciting several prayers, and then he signs the bread with the chalice in saying a special formula (*L.E.W.*, p. 289–293; *L.O.C.*, ii, p. 587–589 is much shorter). The "administration" seems to be another name for the communion. Some attention must be paid to the variant in V, though it seems to me that this text does not fit in with the following sentences. The answer does not agree quite with the Q. so far as the former part is concerned. It is a habit of the teacher to give an answer which contains more than a simple answer of the question.

It is here the place to enter into a discussion: what is the moment of consecration? In our Q. the Epiclesis forms a clear division between one state of the Elements (viz. unconsecrated) and another (viz. consecrated). This prayer is one of the most central points of liturgical investigation. It turns about the points: at what date this prayer was introduced (historical); why it does not take such a prominent place in the Western formulary (when it is found there) as in the Eastern liturgies (liturgical) and what was its effect (dogmatical). The debate has been very sharp since it was one of the points of difference between Eastern and Western Christianity; see: F. Cabrol, *D.A.C.L.*, s.v. *Epiclèse*, t. v, col. 142–184 (very important); F. Heiler, *Urkirche und Ostkirche*, S. 256–262; Hanssens ii, p. 454–463. What consecrates the elements: the words of the Institution or the Epiclesis? It is well-known that the former answer was given by the Western church while the Eastern church ascribed the effect to both while stressing the latter (cf. the fact that in most liturgies they are found both together; it is clearly expressed by 'Abdisho', *Pearl* iv 5: "The form He conveys through His life-giving word, and by the descent of the Holy Ghost".) But from the expositions of the liturgy it is obvious that they ascribed this power to the Epiclesis since they pass over the words of the Institution while they have much to say about the E. The questions referred to above are very complicated, but need not be answered here (cf. E. Bishop, *The Moment of Consecration*, in: Connolly, *Narsai*, p. 126–163; and: Lietzmann, *Messe*, S. 68–81). The Nest. church shared the general conception of the completion of the consecration by the Epiclesis, cf. M. Jugie, *Theol. dogm.*, v. p. 308–316 (who tries to weaken this statement as far as possible, and to bring it into agreement with that of the Roman Catholic Church.) They even omitted the words of Institution in the Mss. of 'Addai' (p. 56) though it is said there in practice; at any rate they are found in the 2 others). All the Mystagogies pass over these words while it is emphasized that the Spirit brings about the change (Theodore Mops., *W.S.*, vi, p. 111, 113, cf. p. 103–104; Narsai, tr. Connolly, p. 20–21; *Expos.* ii, p. 56; Timotheus ii, Ming. Syr. 13, fol. 129*a*).

Yet there existed at the time of our treatise another point of difference with regard to the consecration. ii 17 discussed the question whether it is right to bring back the wine into the chalice, if the contents of the chalice had been shed over the Paten with the Bukhra, as some very learned teachers permitted. The answer is as follows: "some people think that when the Paten and Chalice are brought upon the altar, they are immediately consecrated from the mere fact that they have been placed on the altar and become Paghra and Dᵉma. But others say that only at the moment when the power of the Spirit comes down on the elements, and the Dᵉma has been signed with the Paghra and the Paghra with the Dᵉma they are signed and completed and have become Paghra and Dᵉma." Parallel points are mentioned ad Q. 10. The latter view is the only right one according to our author who sticks to the traditional opinion. Yet it is interesting to find this former view. Already at the Prothesis and *L.E.W.*, p. 267 the elements are styled: Body and Blood. It is not particularly Nest., but is also found elsewhere (see: Lietzmann, *Messe*, S. 190 ff; and: *L.O.C.*, i, p. 171). It shows once more that the words of Institution were not thought of in this connection, and that the exact dogmatical definition of this point was not yet given. We may insert here also a piece that has been preserved only by V. (fol. 81). It mentions once more the case that bread and wine are mixed by accident, and it is asked whether anything is injured if it happens before the signing of the elements. The answer is sufficiently clear: "no consecration is completed before the Epiclesis, but through the Epiclesis it is consecrated. If the chalice is shed after the Epiclesis the altar is not injured. and the signing after the Epiclesis is only a supplement of the consecration" (cf. *B.O.*, iii 1, p. 246 and Q. 19, Q. 89). Here another possibility is offered viz. that only at the signing (*L.E.W.*, p. 291) the effect which is required is brought about. But our writer considers it only as an addition; his view of the moment of consecration is very definite. It is also shown here. If it is noticed before the Epiclesis the same must be done as in Q. 10; what is said there about the renewal of the bread is undoubtedly supposed here though it is not expressed; after that the service can go on. About the ingredients of the bread see ad Q. 53. The treatment is different if the Epiclesis has been said, for then something has happened. A single formula is said over the renewed chalice, which is not the same as the ordinary one: "the precious Blood is signed with the lifegiving Body of our Lord Jesus Christ etc." (*L.E.W.*, p. 291). Of course, the normal form cannot be used. But to this word of consecration applies what is said Q. ii 23: "by the word of the priest it is consecrated", cf. Q. 2. After that the mysteries are ended by communion. The wrong chalice that came in touch with the Holy must be reserved for the holy use. It seems as though it was a valid Eucharist. Yet the altar is injured and needs consecration.

Q. 16. The word "Treasury" is rarely met with; in our treatise cf. Q. 49 and ii 4: dealing with the signing of chalices where it is allowed by lack of a consecrated chalice to sign "the chalice with the particle of the Paghra, the Treasury" (the last words are omitted in V.). It seems as though this name is only found among the Nestorians (it is not found in the index of *L.E.W.*, nor anywhere else; the example given by Payne Smith, *Dictionary*, s.v. is a Nestorian quotation that will be cited afterwards. The first place where it occurs as far as I know, is in the letter of Isho'yabh i to James of Darai, *Canon* 3, in: O. Braun, *Synhados*, S. 243: he describes the way in which a priest should receive the communion, if only a deacon is present. He must act in the same way, if no deacon is present, but "wenn der Schatz der Eucharistie vorhanden ist". This word is used without any further explanation; this fact shows that it was not an invention of I., but already existing (it may be that the hymns of Ephraem contain some help to detect the origin of this word). In Isho'Barnun, *ad Isaac* Q. 1 it is asked whether the treasury may remain on the altar overnight. The answer is to the negative for various reasons (parallel with the Paschal Lamb Ex. xii, and the Manna Ex. xvi); only one exception is made, viz. if there is left more than may be taken at the Ablutions (cf. ad Q. 18); this is on account of the weakness of our nature. If neglectful people leave it for many days they must be punished. A similar, though shorter Q. is found in the same author's *ad Macarium*. But there the word "Treasury" is not found; he uses "Holy Paghra of Christ". The same regulation about the Treasury is given in *Can.* xiv in slightly different words. It is said there that it was prohibited in the law of Moses (Ex. xii 10, Lev. vii 15; the parallel with the Paschal Lamb is a very favourite one among the Eastern Christians, cf. for the Copts, Riedel, S. 276, Villecourt, *Observances*, p. 208). It is not difficult to decide what Treasury means here. Isho'Barnun uses as a synonym: Qudasha and Mysteries, and he and *Can.*: Paghra. It should be observed that it is always used of the Paghra that was left. This may also account for its special name (we should also compare the addressing of the Lord as "Celestial Treasury", in the hymns Q. 7). These regulations repeated on various occasions, cf. very severely Q. 37, are directed against the old Christian use of the reservation of the Sacrament (*D.C.A.*, s.v. *Reservation;* W. H. Freestone, *The Sacrament reserved,* Alcuin Club Collections xxi, 1917, (which I did not consult). Originally the laymen had taken the communion home and preserved it for private communion (see ad Q. 51, which was strictly forbidden, because it gave rise to various abuses, e.g. as a charm Jac. Edess., *Can.* 9 and Kayser, S. 94–95). At an early date it was already condemned by Origenes, *in Lev.* v in: *M.S.G.*, xii, col. 459 saying that Christ did not allow the Euch. Bread to be left till the next day. Later on this preservation was definitely forbidden, but practised still by the clerks and monks. In the churches it was preserved for the communion of the Missa Praesanctificatorum (cf. *D.C.A.*, s.v. *Presanctified,* and: Hanssens, ii, p. 86–110, xix and iii, p. 546-556), consecration of altars, communion of the sick. But those practices do not seem to have occurred in the Nestorian church; for the communion of the sick see ad Q. 51; *Expos.* i, p. 52: "Mysteria plena, *id est* cum consecratione non conficiuntur", cf. also ii, p. 67, do not deal with a "missa Praesanctificatorum"; "mysteria" means here: "liturgy" and not: "the sacrament"; for the consecration of the altar see before. The Nestorian Canonlaw prescribed to "order" the elements directly after the service (Q. 18). If this were impossible, the Bread might be left upon the altar under the light of a candle and should be carefully guarded; the guarding priest was not allowed to eat, to drink or to sleep (*Synodicon Arab.*, fol 80b). In plain words it was interdicted by Timothy i (E. Sachau, *Syrische Rechtsbücher*, ii, S. 70–71): "Q. xvii: Is it right to leave the Qudasha on the altar till the next day? *Solution:* It is in no wise right to leave it. It must be taken on the day itself. For it was not allowed to leave anything from the Manna or from the Paschal Lamb which were types of the Body of our Lord. The fact that the Manna was reserved for the Sabbath, is a Mystery in a type like this: that we cannot draw near to God, neither in this world the type of which is the Sabbath eve, nor in the world to come, the type of which is the Sabbath, except by the manhood of Christ who is the Mediator between God and men." I do not know whether this was formulated by him for the first time. At any rate it is sure that it was repeated at several occasions by his successor Isho'Barnun (see before; in the letter *ad Macarium* he states that many teachers do not allow it at all, but that some permit it in emergencies up till three days; he himself adhered to the former point of view, cf. Ming. Syr. 586, fol. 439b, Q. 55: "Is it allowed to leave the Qudasha on the altar for three days? *Solution:* That is absolutely not permitted"). The arguments given by Timothy ii are very curious. He says that it was ordered by the Fathers that the priest must do his service standing before the altar as long as Eucharist was upon it (cf. the *Arabic Synodicon* before and *Can.* xxii afterwards); but they understood that the priest could not do so night and day and therefore they ordered that nothing should remain (this is exactely the opposite view of that given in *Can.* xxii and ii 29). His other explanation is that it is a type of Christ depicted in the O.T., referring again to Paschal Lamb and Manna that became spoilt if they were left. Therefore he repeats the commandment that is only broken by some daring people (Ming. Syr. 13, fol. 135a–136a). Besides these Nestorian canons we draw attention to Pseudo-Nicaea, *Canon* xix, in: Mansi, *Conciliorum nova collectio*, ii, col. 1029–1030: "Quoties fiunt commemorationes in ecclesiis, monasteriis et martyrum aedibus et aliquid eucharistiae residuum fuerit, eo honorentur sacerdotes in sequentis diei mane, antequam communiat: si autem residuum multum fuerit, partiuntur illud inter se, et unusquisque suam sumat portionem unica tantum vice per modum unius boli, sive parva sit illa sive magna, nec iterum aut tertio id fiat."–The origin of this rule is unknown; it is not quite the same as those we have met before; but it offers a parallel since it does not allow that Euch. Bread remains during another service. Cf. Athanasius, *Canon* 78, ed. Riedel-Crum, p. 48–49: "And concerning the holy Mysteries, the body of Christ and His blood, they shall not let aught thereof remain over from evening to the morning, but shall do with it whatsoever they will. The holy altar having been prepared and so long as the holy Mysteries are thereon, ere he hath raised it up (ἀναφέρειν), the readers shall not be silent before it . . . . And because it is His body and blood, so shall they not leave praising Him until the time when the place is cleansed", and Timotheus Alex., Q. 16 (2nd series), in: Pitra, *Monumenta*, i, p. 641.

It will be seen from these examples that the later Nestorian Canonists emphasized this point and did not know anything of a permission to reserve the bread. We must reconstruct the history in the following way. It was not allowed to end the service if anything of the Eucharist was left; this was hard in practice. Then the priests were allowed to take at the Ablutions more than usual. This commandment should not be contravened although it was rather difficult, see Q. 49. The case provided for in *Can.* xxii: ". . . if by urgent circumstances or without the will of the priest the urgent case arises in which the Holy Sacrament is kept overnight on the altar, because there is nobody to order it, let him do one of the two following things with the sacrament: if a believer, male or female, is found let them order among themselves the chalice, and this must be reckoned as the two elements of the sacrament, when the priest knows that this remained from the communion of the sacrament. He should order the chalice only; for he should never order all the Eucharistic bread. Because of its abundance the Eucharistic bread may stay over night on the altar, if sufficient care is displayed towards it through the burning of the lamps and the service of the night. But if it happens that there are no persons who can order the two elements of the sacrament, the man who is in charge of them shall stand on his feet, till the moment they order it, be it night or day; and he should never leave this service without a substitute." This canon explaining what is meant by the information that he "guards it with great care" is also reproduced in ii 29.[1] In ii 33 we have a case of a priest who forgot his duty for he placed the Paghra in the House of the Treasury (see below). Those priests who broke these rules were heavily punished (see ad Q. 69) and this shows that great weight was attached to it. The reason of it was that one was anxious that the elements should become corrupted; as is apparent from the parallel with the Lamb and the Manna. It can also be seen from the rebuke of Elias Nisib. to the other Christian churches (*Beweis*, S. 99): "sie bewahren es (die Eucharistie) eine lange Zeit auf, und setzten es den Motten, den Würmern, der Fäulniss, den Mäusen and anderer Verderbnis aus; also strafen sie das Wort der Schrift Lüge, wenn sie sagt: keine Änderung und kein Verwesung soll sein Leib treffen (Act. ii 27, 31)." He is right in saying that it was not practised by the others. The Jacobites did not know it, cf. John Tell., in: Bar Hebraeus, *Nomocanon*, iv 1: "si superest ex margaritis, custodiantur caute, et aliis diebus dentur" (this being the practice allowed by the Nestorians in urgent cases!), and James Edess. (*Ibidem*) went even further in saying: "xatam, quae superest, possunt sacerdotes vendere, verum sacerdotibus sociis suis." We surmise that in this case too the Nestorian practice had become stricter in course of time and that the allowance made for urgent cases was really the more ancient practice. We suppose that this stricter rule was made sometime in the middle of the 8th century. For there we find for the first time this Canon directed against reservation. It is not improbable that one might challenge our statement that the Nestorians did not know the reservation by pointing to a sentence of P. Bedjan (*Isaac Ninevita De Perfectione Religiosa*, Leipzig, 1907, p. xvii): "Ce qui prouve l'usage de la Ste. Réserve." The emphasis with which this point is underlined by drawing attention to it in the preface, proves sufficiently that this place was also a pecularity for this connoisseur of the Nest. Literature. The place he referred to was found in what seems to him a letter of Isaac that he published in an incomplete form, but was reedited completely by Dr. Mingana as a word of Dadisho' (end of the 7th cent., cf. A. Baumstark, *L.G.*, S. 226–227). There we read (*W.S.* vii, p. 90) that a recluse was advised not to go to communion until the end of his solitude of the 7 weeks. "If, however, you converse with others, and thus do not live in complete solitude, go out of your cell on the night of Saturday, a little before the bell of the Night Service, and receive the Communion from the Sacrament that has been consecrated on Friday." It proves that in monks' circles the sacraments were reserved from Friday on which mass was said, to Saturday. But this is not so amazing since the Nestorians did not consecrate on Saturday, as is stated by Elias Nisib., *Beweis*, S. 110–111; he objects to the Greeks that they do so and

(1) Cf. Elias Nisib., *Beweis*, S. 99: "Zur Fastenzeit heiligen sie die Elemente am Sonntag für die ganze Woche, und nehmen dann jeden Tag davon, was sie brauchen; die heiligen Canones verbieten solches; das Abendmahl soll kein einziges Mal übernacht aufbewahrt werden."

continues: "Es ist aber bekannt, was das Abendmahl an diesem Tag besonders unwerth macht; zunächst das wir die jüdische Sitte verwerfen und die Juden nur am Sabbat in ihre Kirchen gehen . . . .; ferner noch das Abendmahl ist der Leib des Herrn und es ist bekannt, dass er am Samstag im Grab und bei den Todten war. Daher muss man für die Feier des Abendmahls dem ersten besten Tag in der Woche den Vorzug vor dem Samstag geben, es sei denn dass ein Festtag darauf falle, an dem das Ausbleiben des Abendmahls unstatthaft wäre"; and cf. the special case quoted ad Q. 50. It might be explained to the Nestorian mind by referring to the fact that it was expressly stated in Scripture that Manna should be taken on Friday for 2 days. And Dadisho' lived before the time of the rules against the reservation.

At this place we should also mention a formulary published by Mr. H. W. Codrington in 1904 which seems to be inconsistent with our conclusion, as it is called an East Syrian Liturgy of the Presanctified (H. W. Codrington, *The Syrian Liturgies of the Presanctified* iii, *East Syrian or Persian*, in: *J.Th.St.*, 1904, p. 535–545). It will be useful to give a summary of this article. Mr. C. found this rite which is now obsolete, in two MSS, viz. Cambridge Add. 1988 (A.D. 1559 ) in which Israel, bishop of Kashkar († A.D. 877,) is called the author, and British Museum Add. 7181 (A.D. 1570) under the name of 'Abdisho' of Elam (13th cent). The former MS. is more detailed. „The rite is constructed in the same manner as the Jacobite Presanctified, from which the idea may have been borrowed by the Nestorians of the plains, and is adapted to the normal Persian liturgy." Its use is obscure, because the Nestorians rejected the reservation (Mr. C. quotes: Elias Nisib.; our Q. 49; *Can.* xix). But Isho'Barnun allowed it to remain for three days (but see before). "The present rite would therefore seem to provide for the contingency of the Body alone remaining." He finds a difficulty in the rubric: "when the Treasure remains in the night in which the Holy Thing is baked," as it could be consumed at the celebration of the Mass which follows the baking. The text and its translation will be found on p. 538–545.–Prof. Hanssens ii, p. 91 accepted the conclusion of Mr. C. though with some hesitation (cf. iii, p. 556 and p. 627). The article summarized before seems to have escaped the attention of Prof. Baumstark. He mentions only the Cambr. MS. and dates (*L.G.*, S. 334) this Israel "spätestens in der ersten Hälfte des 16. Jhrh." and credits him with other liturgical activities. This formulary is called: "ein Formular zur Konsekration des Kelches ausserhalb der Messe" and Ak. 6 adds: "So und nicht 'der Präsanktifikaten-Liturgie' wird zu sagen sein, da eine solche im technischen Wortsinne dem nestorianischen Ritus fremd ist."

Whose opinion is the right one? Baumstark's dating is based upon the year of the MS he knows, but is rather vague. On p. 81 a liturgical authority, called Israel was mentioned (n.b. "the learned", in n. 4). I do not see any reason why we should not assign the making of the formulary under discussion, to the later half of the 10th cent. as the rubric supposes the canons given before and this time showed a great liturgical activity. It is even more important to answer the question whether it is a "Missa Praesanctificatorum"; it will be good to copy the rubrics at the beginning. "The order of the signing of the Chalice or of the Treasure, that is, when the Treasure remains in the night, in which the Qudasha is baked; ordered by Mar Israel the sharp of wit, bishop of

Kashkar. First it is not right that the Treasure should stay the night, except from necessity; and when it happens to stay the night, let there not be therein anything that is kneaded at all, except the true bukhre, or perisatha; (but let not the chalice stay the night in any way) a light not departing from before it." It appears that the Qudasha remained in a special vessel. Next follow the prayers etc.–Everything in the rubric fits in very well with the evidence we have collected ad Q. 16 and 18. This formulary was not performed as an ordinary ritual such as the Greek Praesanctified, *L.E.W.*, p. 345–352, but only in case of emergency, viz. when there were not a sufficient number of people to "order" and the quantity of Bread too large. The difficulty which Codrington found here is quite easy to solve as "it is not right that two Kings should sit on one throne". It is not a "missa praesanctificatorum" as Baumstark already observed, but the sequence of the "ordering" in the morning of the next day (why 'Abdisho' is mentioned in the other MS., I do not see. A. Baumstark, *L.G.* does not mention him).

The teaching of the Nest. about this point is clear though it is not always the same from the beginning; among the Jacobites there was none such prohibition. They order that the priests must take care that the bread grow mouldy and that the chalice must be cleaned to prevent the wine becoming sour while it is supposed that the bread is always left (James Edess., *Can.* 16 and ap. Bar Hebraeus, *Nomocanon*, iv 2–8, quoted by Kayser, S. 41, cf. Lamy, p. 216–218 "De asservatione euch."). I have not found any changes mentioned. But that does not imply that they did not exist. At any rate this was the teaching of the leading Nomocanonists. And it differs from the Copts who strangely enough seem to have points of contact with the Nest. They also refer to the Paschal Lamb: "Et pareillement, nous, nous mangeons le vrai agneau Pascal, le corps et le sang de notre Signeur Jésus Christ qui a été immolé à cause de nous, et nous n'en réservons rien jusqu'au second jour." One pointed also to the example of the Lord (Villecourt, *Observances*, p. 208; an exception in the week of the Passion; what had been consecrated on Palm-Sunday might be distributed on Tuesday, see: L. Villecourt, *La Lettre de Macaire*, in: *Le Muséon*, 1923, p. 41). In the same way it was strongly impressed upon the clerks not to leave anything till the next day cf. *L.O.C.*, i, p. 273, and: "*Statutes of the Apostles*" (tr. G. Horner, London, 1904, p. 201, 277, 344–345); the Arabic text reads as follows: "And the little (pieces) which remain over let the deacons take care of, lest any should be left of the Oblation, and let the priests take great care that there should not be much left".

The Greeks do not know *this* reservation; they have a large host consecrated on Maundy Thursday from which pieces are taken during the year (Salaville, *Les liturgies Orientales*, p. 138–139; *D.C.A.*, s.v. *Dove*). Special measures are not found. We have reproduced the evidence because the Nest. have a development of their own about this point and because it shows that the statement of Mgr. Rahmani (*L.O.O.*, p. 61–62), "tous les ancients documents attestent que les syriens, les grecs, et les copts conservaient le saint sacrement", based totally upon Jacobite evidence needs some rectification.

It has already been indicated how this Treasury should be guarded (cf. also ii 34). It was laid in the Beth-Gazza. According to Payne Smith (*Dictionary*, s.v.) it means: "a recess in the north wall of the Sanctuary", an explanation given by Dean Maclean (*E.S.D.O.*, p. 294 and: *L.E.W.*, p. 590, referring to p. 262 where it is said that the priest places the Paten in the Treasury until the cārūzūtha is finished). It is not said on what evidence this explanation is based. The term is not found anywhere else. Certainly, the name Gazophylacium is found (cf. *D.C.A.*, s.v.), being a "storehouse attached to a church, for the reception of the offerings of the faithful, made either in bread and wine, or in money for the service of the altar." It is clear that in this connection it is used in a different sense. Nevertheless it may be that after the time in which the offerings of the people fell into disuse, the name was retained and attached to another place. On the other hand it may be a simple derivation from the word Treasury in its special use as has been discussed before. For the moment we must leave this matter open. I suppose that the translation given before goes back to the practice as seen by Dean Maclean among the Nest. at the end of last century. The word is also used in the rubrics of the "Consecration of the altar with oil" of I. iii: "And if there is a small altar, that is to say a Beth-Gazza etc." (T., p. 135). Unfortunately it is not clear what is the precise relation between the "big" and "small" altar. (Cf. ad Q. 6. Several altars in the church are also mentioned in *Can.* xii and Q. 17.) This gives a meaning somewhat different from that of Maclean. I do not know what must be chosen here.

The Eucharist was held "on festivals and memorials and Sundays and Fridays, except Good Friday", T., p. 150. (Cf. also *Expos.* i, p. 107). The practice in the ancient church varied in different countries; many people held daily communion which is also implied in: Babai, *De Unione* (ed. Vaschalde, p. 284), see: *D.C.A.*, s.v. *Communion*, and: *D.A.C.L.*, s.v. *Communion quotidienne*, t. iii, col. 2457–2462. On the memorials some prayers were different from those that were usually said, see notes in *L.E.W.* ܕܘܟܪܢܐ is the yearly memorial service for the saints ('Abdisho', *Nomocanon*, v. 12). For the service of "consolation", cf. Browne–Maclean, p. 287: "For the second and third day (after the funeral) services of 'consolation' for the mourners are appointed; and on other days also 'memorials' are very commonly made of the dead. The Holy Communion is celebrated, alms are offered by the relatives"; formerly it was held on other days. As "memorial" and "consolation" are distinguished here, I have adopted this interpretation. But in *Expos.* ii, p. 137 (text: p. 152) ܕܘܟܪܢܐ is used of the "consolation" too (cf. the question: "Quare tertia die, non secunda, commemorationem faciunt? et quare iterum *die* septima, nec non quinta decima, et in fine mensis?").

"King" cf. the quotation from *Can.* ix ad Q. 52; it proves that it was specially used in connection with the Holy Leaven. The simile of Abraham b. Lipheh, *Expos.* ii, p. 162 shows that it laid at hand to use it in connection with the host. Later on it got a pregnant meaning (cf. ad Q. 52–but not here.) "Throne" as a name for the altar is also found in the Byzantine writings (*L.E.W.*, p. 569 and cf. ad Q. 100) but Suicerus, *Thesaurus Ecclesiasticus*, and: Sophocles, *Greek Lexicon of the Roman and Byzantine Periods*, Cambridge (Mass), 1914, s.v. do not mention it. The Syriac Jacobites and Nestorians have it both (see also: *L.O.C.*, ii, p. 52. It is a common Nestorian name–Diettrich, *Tauflit.*, S. 31, 77). In our treatise it is found Q. 104: ܟܘܪܣܝܐ; T. uses the word ܬܪܘܢܘܣ. Brightman thought the name had been derived from Isa. vi which had a considerable influence upon

Mystagogy; Renaudot pointed out that it was called so because Body and Blood were placed upon it. It is not clear at what time the name arose nor from what place it was borrowed. The agreement between the great Christian communities points to a time before the separation and from Antioch(?). In: *Expos.* ii, p. 62 the altar is called the mystery of the "throne" of Christ; and altar is here clearly distinguished from the Apse (not: = "altarplace"). This makes Dean Maclean's explanation of the word: Beth-Gazza less probable for our Q. As far as I know it was not specially commented upon in the Mystagogies though one would expect it. Is it lawful to infer from this fact that the name came into existence outside the sphere of the explanation of Eucharist (in contrast with "grave", Q. 100)? In that case Brightman's derivation was wrong. I should like to point to the possibility that the identification of altar and throne is a very old one, though it is only found at a late date in Christian Literature; see the word in Apoc. ii 13, the throne of Satan in Pergamus = the altar of Zeus (E. Lohmeyer, *Die Offenbarung Johannis*, Tübingen, 1926, z. St.; and others).

"Foreign" = hostile to God; cf. Lev. x 1, where it is said that the sons of Aaron "offered strange fire before the Lord, which he commanded them not". The place is of a somewhat doubtful interpretation as to what kind of fire is meant; but the meaning of "strange" is clear; see also Exod. xxx 33; *Ode of Solomon* vi 3 (ed. Harris–Mingana, Manchester, 1920, ii, p. 232): "for he destroys what is foreign, And everything is of the Lord"; so-called *Churchorder of Hippolytus* c. 60 (ed. Hauler, p. 117); "nolito effundere (calicem quasi antitypum sanguinis Christi), ut non spiritus alienus velut te contemnente illud delingat." *Canon* xx speaks of a priest who is insolent in regard to the Eucharistic element that "he is a stranger to the holy Sacrament" and must be deprived of his office. All these places point to the same meaning.

Q. 17. This Q. does not treat of the same matter as Q. 11. The latter deals with "falling" upon the altar; the former with remaining upon it. The present Q. is a counterpart to Q. 16. In the previous Q. the *consecrated* elements remained there without it being known; here something *unconsecrated* is lying there.

Books upon the altar: either liturgical books summed up in: *E.S.D.O.*, p. xxv–xxx, or simply the Gospel. For the form of the answer see p. 113.

The answer distinguishes between 3 possibilities: a) before the consecration after one day = after one consecration[1]; it is set apart upon another altar (Q. 16) during the next mass to prevent a second consecration. Though the matter is not quite right it is given as a communion with the chalice while another host is added. The last clause is omitted in V, thereby considering it as an ordinary host. b) Discovered after several days = after several consecrations; given as an Eulogia (see ad Q. 10). c) If it is not possible to distribute this blessing from lack of people present, the altar must be shaken (see ad Q. 78); the particles must be put in the chalice as the crumbs and be drunk, as in the Ordering Q. 18. V. adds that it was not allowed to take twice the Eucharist, of course because one was not fasting any longer after the first time. "Not leave anything" see Q. 16.

(1) It was forbidden to consecrate twice a day upon the same altar, cf. Isho'Barnun, *ad Isaac*, Q. 4..

Q. 18. The climate of the country round Mosul (Irac, Kurdistan, Persia) is well known. Water is scarce. In summer and time of drought it is difficult to get. Dr. Budge has collected (*B.G.* ii, p. 336, n. 1) many instances of droughts which are recorded in history. Several prayers for rain and against drought are found in: *E.S.D.O.*, p. 231, 249.

The "Ordering" of the Mysteries takes place at the end of the service. After the communion and thanksgiving the deacon draws the curtains of the Sanctuary (see Q. 8) *L.E.W.*, p. 302. Next follows the dismissal and the distribution of the Purshana's. (Q. 80). *L.E.W.*, p. 304–305 gives some prayers to be said "when they order the mysteries". But it is not indicated what should be done. Yet from other sources we find the following data.

ܛܟܣ = to order, is used *Expos.* ii, p. 36 in an other sense: to prepare. But in our treatises it is always used of this special Ordering at the end of the service, the Ablutions. In Q. 16 we saw that the Nest. did not allow that anything of the Eucharistic elements was left. Yet it was not always possible to make the number of particles exactly correspond to the number of the communicants (see Q. 49). Then something remained. The first of whom we read something about this point, was Isho'yabh (cf. p. 122): "If something of the Eucharist remains, the lamp may not be taken away from it. If many Gemurta's are left, after the communion of the people, the priests who are on the altar and have not communicated, take from them, so that every one takes a mouthful only once. For it is not allowed to communicate twice a day. If the priest who distributes the Eucharist is alone, and nobody is present to receive a portion, he is not allowed to take it himself. He can only give it to somebody who receives it from him. As to the chalice (cf. ad Q. 26), if there is no priest, one of the monks must order it, and if no monk is present, one of the faithful, a man of goodness, piety and virtue, shall order it and empty it at one draught" (*Synod. Arab.*, fol. 79b–80a). Isho'Barnun directed in: *ad Macarium* Q. 35 in answer to the question: "Are one or two priests allowed to order it when much Qudasha is left, and how much may they eat after the Qudasha, more than one Purshana? *Solution:* If much Qudasha is left, it is not right that one or two order it. But every one may take in the Ordering three or four Gemurtha's. If it is an urgent case he may go up to five. But if he eats more than five, it is audacious and careless. After the Qudasha he is allowed to eat one Purshana, and if the Perishta is large, a fourth." In his letter *ad Isaac* the same Patriarch said (Q. 1) that every one who trespassed against this commandment, did so to his own condemnation (cf. 1 Cor. xi 29). Like several others of his prescripts this one was taken over by John Bar Abgare in his *Canon* xx though with a somewhat different phrazing (cf. ad Q. 49). The same canonist decided that the chalice should not be filled too full. With emphasis it is said that one should not trespass against these regulations: "that act should not express greed and insolence as regards the Ordering of the sacraments which by grace had been given to the congregation." In *Canon* xxi it is strictly forbidden that a priest or deacon should order alone under pain of deposition. If it is impossible to do so, the Paghra must remain on the altar while it must be duly preserved (see ad Q. 16); after that it must be ordered in the usual way. First the bread must be taken and then the chalice. In our treatises the writer solved various difficulties connected with the execution of these Canons (cf. also ii 7, 11, 33–39). We find the following acts mentioned: the curtains must be drawn "lest any injury might affect the altar" (Q. 23); then the altar must be cleared, the crumbs of the paten must be swept into the chalice; the bread must be consumed by two persons in the altar, but not more than is ordered in the Canons (during this act people who wanted to communicate could come and take it (Q. 43); after that the chalice should be taken to the sacristy (deacon's house) or any other place outside the Sanctuary and be consumed there. This drinking of the chalice was done to desecrate it, therefore it could not be done in the holiest place of the church (during these ablutions the "injured" bread was also eaten). We see that these measures are quite in accordance with those of John; but the cases that made it necessary to lay down these rules, show sufficiently that the canons were not always observed in spite of their severe penalties.

Having thus summarized the Nestorian ways of treating the remains of the Eucharist we must look at the similar material in the other churches. Unfortunately I was not able to consult the monograph of W. Lockton, *Treatment of the Remains at the Eucharist after Holy Communion and the Time of the Ablutions*, Cambridge, 1920. Not much is known about it (Hanssens iii p. 527–533), and it seems as if the Nestorians were the only people who had strict rules for it, though Prof. Hanssens (*l.c.*) has little to mention about their present rite, and nothing about its history. The Byzantine church used to give the rests of the consecrated loaves to young children after some days, a practice which still existed in the 14th century (Euagrius, *Hist. Eccl.* iv 36; Nicephorus Callistus xvii 25, quoted by Bingham xv 7, 4). In the present Greek rite the priest and deacon consume the remains in the prothesis (A. Baumstark, *Messe im Morgenland*, S. 169; S. Pétridès, *D.A.C.L.*, s.v. *Ablutions*, t. i, col. 110) and purify the vessels, of course while saying certain prayers. The same is done in the Jacobite rite (*L.E.W.*, p. 106–109) where it seems to be done however in the sanctuary itself, together with the chalice. According to John Tell., in: *L.O.O.*, p. 707 and notes, this was the function of the deacon. James Edess., quoted by Kayser, S. 38–39: "Die, welche des heiligen Kelches warten, sollen wenn sie auch Wasser um ihn auszuspülen hinein thaten (und das Wasser tranken), nicht verhindert werden, wenn sie an dem Tage noch communiciren wollen, weil sie nicht gewöhnlichen Trank genossen" (cf. Kayser's comment., S. 176; interesting parallel to the quotation from Isho'yabh i). Concerning the church in Jerusalem the well-known place in Hesychius (quoted ad Q. 78) tells us that there the remains were generally burnt. The Copts, just like the Nestorians, did not allow it to be left on the altar; therefore they ordered the priests should take it whether it was much or little (Villecourt, *Observances*, p. 257, cf. ad Q. 16, 49). However these usages may vary in the different churches, all of them were used to purify and desecrate the chalice by pouring water into it (the Byzantines used hot water, a practice severely impugned by the Nestorians, Elias Nisib., *Beweis*, S. 99). In the present time it is usual among the Nestorians that the priests take their communion at this moment (*E. S. D. O.*, p. 297; already in the 10th. cent?, cf. ad. Q. 43).

The foregoing excursus explains sufficiently why one priest has several Gemurtha's in his hand and what is the meaning of: "his fellow". "Levites" is a common name for the deacons since the very beginning of the Christian church (1 Clemens 40, 5; it is not necessary to give examples of this use since the name is found in all the departments of the church; see: *D.C.A.*, s.v., and: *D.A.C.L.*, s.v. *Levita*, t. viii, col. 2992–2996 give exclusively western texts.) The clergyman has not sufficient saliva to masticate the bread because of the dryness of the atmosphere; he almost chokes in swallowing it. The Answer of our author is not immediately clear as is often the case in oriental books owing to change of subject. The fellow must throw a particle of the bread into a chalice that is not consecrated, but becomes so through this particle and is therefore similar to the chalice of the ablutions.

Q. 19. The places of the liturgy in which the priest makes the sign of the cross are specified in Q. 90 sqq. The one meant here is: *L.E.W.*, p. 291. The influence of this signing has already been spoken of on page 192, n. 1. Since this last sign has not been made, the bread is not "made perfect". The moment when the sacristan comes, is not exactly indicated. Therefore the answer is twofold and the division is again made at the Epiclesis (see ad Q. 15). In this state the sacristan is not in the least able to administer the Eucharist; of course he will be inclined to make mistakes. For one should not add to (cf. Q. 1) nor take something from the bread of the consecration during the most holy moment of the Eucharist. ܦܬܘܪܐ lit. = table = paten, cf. Budge, *B.G.* ii, p. 430, n. 3; in our QQ. it is the only word used for this article while T., p. 12, l. 22, *Can.* xxiii uses also ܦܝܢܟܐ; both words together T., p. 6, l. 10–11. It is never used to mean "altar" as among the Jacobites (cf. John Tell., *Can.* 46, Lamy, p. 94; Lamy, p. 241, quotes Dionysius B. Salibi who clearly states this identification; James Edess., Lamy p. 100). Several other words for this plate are mentioned by Rahmani, *L.O.O.*, p. 54 (cf. Kayser, S. 83–85) who however does not mention our word. Pictures of it in: *D.C.A.*, s.v., and: Kaufmann, *Handbuch*, S. 571–573. There were always several patens at the altar-place for the usual distribution. The course of events is clear if one remembers the meaning of Qetsaja and Bukhra (p. 194) and the effect of the consecration. It is clear too that in the latter case there is a slight mistake as the sacristan brought it on the paten in his hand before the time appointed in the formulary.

Q. 20. A Zuza is a coin, according to Payne Smith = a quarter of a jewish shekel = a Greek drachma worth ± 10 pence (*Dictionary*, s.v.; Budge, *B.G.* ii, p. 403 n., gives a somewhat different account: "the ܙܘܙܐ is explained by *Dirham*. The gold *dînâr* which weighs from sixtyfive to seventytwo grains was equal in value to twenty *dirhams*, or about 10½ English shillings"). In this case it had probably been given for the sustenance of the priests. This is the reason of the priest's joy! It is uncertain what was their income among the Nestorians. In the ancient church it was taken from the church-property of land and slaves, gifts from the state and occasional gifts (*D.C.A.*, s.v. *Property of the church; D.A.C.L.*, s.v. *Libéralité des Fidèles*, t. ix, col. 489–497, deals with the various sources of income, but admits that little is known about it). The Persian church has always been under non-christian rulers, therefore it was dependent on the gifts of the faithful and even if it had some property of its own there was always the danger that it might be seized by the Government.

The piety of the people expressed itself in the building of churches and monasteries, as is said by Isho'yabh i; he quotes this as an example to his contemporaries who neglect their churches because they do not want to give any money, or they spend it on other holy places than those of their own parish, because they are so unbelieving as to think that God will hear them better there (*Canon* x–xii, in: O. Braun, *Synhados*, S. 214–216, referring to John iv 23–24). But we shall not be wrong in assuming that the income of the priests was not very high. Isho'Barnun prohibited to give the Qudasha for money (E. Sachau, *Syrische Rechtsbücher*, ii, S. 122–123) cf. the same order of Rabbula in: F. C. Burkitt, *Early Eastern Christianity*, p. 149. Therefore we must think here of a voluntary gift. The answer covers more than is asked. A Zuza may be thrown from a distance, but the touching of paten and bread is forbidden. The distribution means the communion. The paten is unclean and may not be cleaned at the altar, cf. Q. 18 and Q. 78. Touching of the Pathora is also strictly prohibited by James Edess, *Can.* ii and xxiv, though in these regulations the upper part of the altar seems to be intended. Cf. p. 190 about touching. We might compare a part inserted in V. after ii 3 (M. fol. 68a–b) which is possibly omitted in M. because it agreed with what has been said here. "*Question:* If the sacristan receives the paten to order it and he has taken one or two parts, and a believer enters to receive the Qudasha (cf. Q. 43), and the sacristan gives the Paghra and the believer throws a Zuza on the paten and his hand touches the paten or the Paghra on it, is the Paghra of the paten injured or not? *Answer:* Yes. *Question:* What must be done with the paten and the Paghra on it that is injured; can he return the paten to the altar or take the Paghra standing (in the same place). What must he do with the chalice and how must he take the chalice after that defiled Paghra? Is the chalice injured together with the altar? It is a grave mistake. Tell me: how must the sacristan extricate himself and the altar that it may not be injured? *Answer:* Your question is difficult and needs a careful investigation. *Question:* Explain it carefully. *Answer:* Our Fathers appointed in their "Admonitions" that when a sacristan orders and has taken only one Gᵉmurtha, he is not allowed to give something of it to anybody. If he does something trespassing against this Canon he must expiate (where is this written? It is not found in the Canons of John B. Abgare). The fact that a believer touched the Paghra while throwing a Zuza upon it, is an injury to the Paghra and also to the paten. If he takes it standing near the altar it is not certain that the altar and the chalice thereon are not injured. As it seems to me he must place the paten on the Gospel, receive the chalice to order the altar while the curtains are drawn, next take the paten (standing) at the door of the deacon's house near the altar, clean the chalice, desecrate it with water and use the crumbs left on the paten for the ablutions" (for the answer see ad Q. 18).

Q. 21. Quoted by Assemani, *B.O.*, iii 1, p. 248, to demonstrate the care of the Nest. towards the Eucharist (Mr. H. W. Codrington, in: *J.Th.St.*, 1904, p. 237 has quoted the essence of this Q. from Denzinger, *Ritus Orientalium*, i, p. 85, whose source was Assemani, who is not mentioned by Mr. C.) It was not definitely prescribed for christian women to wear a veil, but at any rate it was decent. It is a well-known fact, that wearing of veils was common in the East and it may be that the christians specially based it upon the words of Paul 1 Cor. xi 3ff (cf. H. Lietzmann, *Die Korintherbriefe* 3, Tübingen, 1931, z. St.). It was specially worn by the "Virgins", cf. Tertullian, *De Virginibus velandis* (Bingham, vii 4, 6; C. M. Kaufmann, *Handbuch*, S. 564–565). That the women should come to the communion dressed with veils, is also ordered in the *Apost. Const.* ii, 57 (ed. F. X. Funk, i, p. 167): "Let the women approach with their heads covered, as is becoming the order of women", and the reason is: "lest they may be seen", and is perhaps depicted in the well-known "Fractio Panis" (so Kaufmann). *D.A.C.L.*, s.v. *Femme*, t. v, col. 1300–1353 does not say anything about the dressing of women in the church nor about their relation to holy things. Afterwards it was called "Dominicale" in the Western church (Concil. Auxere A.D. 587, Can. 42; it is not right to take this Dominicale to mean the veil over the hand, cf. *D.C.A.*, s.v.; J. Braun, *Lit. Handlex.*, s.v.; *D.A.C.L.*, s.v. *Dominicale*, t. iv, col. 1385 quotes a letter of Leo the Great in which it is said: "mulieres possunt sub nigro velamine sacrificium accipere ut Basilius indicat." Rahmani who generally reproduces very faithfully the Syrian (Jac.) usages, does not speak about it. From our Q. it is clear that it was generally used. A modern description is given by Browne–Maclean, p. 93: "A cap is worn on the head, covered by a muslin veil, one end of which is carried from the back of the neck to cover the mouth in the case of married women, but the rest of the face is exposed. It is considered improper to let the hair be seen. The women generally move this veil aside when they kiss the hand . . . The girls . . . do not wear veils." Something among the orders of Gabriel Ibn Tarikh in the Coptic Church may be compared with it (*L.O.C.*, i, p. 264–265): "Communio autem mulierum summam diligentiam et curam exigit: nam cum mulier velata sit, nemo quaenam illa sit agnoscere potest . . . curam adhibere vos oportet, o sacerdotes, ne detis corpus Christi et sanguinem indignae" (see the Can. in Riedel, S. 209, that women should be veiled if they were of age). Its usage is defended by pointing to the decency and is not connected with special physical qualities of women that would cause special rules for the behaviour of women in the cultus (as e.g. the Canons about communion after menstruation found in all churches)[1]. The chalice was generally given by the deacon, but it is not said that it should not be taken at hand by the communicants as was for some time done with the bread (see ad Q. 32). Again the answer generalizes. Reconsecration see Q. 15 with practically the same formula. As to the rule about the deacon we must connect ܒܐܝܕܘܗܝ grammatically with ܡܫܡܫܢܐ but it implies also that he was only allowed to make the sign and not to say the formula. Cf. the *Canon* in: *Synodicon Arab.*, fol. 81a: "If a deacon wants to sign the chalice, if something of the Eucharist is left, he must sweep the altar called the Holy of Holies and light the candle, prepare the perfume, put the vestments on the altar, bring forth the napkin or vessel in which it is and place it on the altar, adore and kiss the altar and a Gemurtha, sign with it the chalice without saying a word. *For he is not allowed to say the Canon of the priest.* As to the priest he is allowed to say: ܡܬܪܫܡ ܟܣܐ ܗܢܐ ܒܓܡܘܪܬܐ ܡܩܕܫܬܐ ܒܫܡ ܐܒܐ ܘܒܪܐ ܘܪܘܚܐ

(1) Cf. p. 133, n. 2; a woman was not allowed to enter the altar, e.g. for the communion after baptism, Johannes b. Abgare, *Quaest. Eccl.* iii; "si vero femina fuerit, nefas esto huius modi (as a man, ad Q. 39) ad altare progredi, sed pro ejus foribus consistens, communionem percipiat" (and see the note of Assemani, B.O., iii 1, p. 250).

ܕܩܘܪܒܐ ܠܟܠܟܘܡܝ (this formular of the priest is written in the Arabic text in Syriac speech; cf. H. W. Codrington, in: *J. Th. St.*, 1904, p. 236 [see before p. 210]: "According to the directions at the end of the Cambridge text, the Catholicos Isho'yabh iii [† A.D. 660] permits the deacon in cases of necessity to 'sign the chalice' in the absence of the priest [cf. *J. Th. St.* vol. iv, p. 70]. In the formula given the consignation is with 'the propitiatory coal, in the name of the Father, and of the Son, *and the rest*' differing from that in the texts," and p. 542–543: "This chalice is signed with the lifegiving Body of our Lord Jesus Christ, in the name etc."; the phrasing shows slight varieties and is almost identical with that of our Q.). But it does not matter, if he does not say it, since there is blood (sic!) in the Gemurtha as the priest has consecrated it, and this consecrates the chalice". It is clear from this quotation that the principal thing was the action while the words were only accidental. The bread had already been consecrated, by the word of the priest. Why it was impossible that the priest should be near, is not apparent; does it mean that he himself was busy in distributing the communion? If this is the case there is no punishment.

Q. 22. The kissing of the paten is no liturgical action properly speaking and is not mentioned anywhere else. It is as the kissing of the feet of the priest (Q. 24), of the Eucharist (Q. 80) and of the Cross (Q. 93) a sign of deep devotion. It should well be distinguished from the "kiss of peace". Several instances of this practice such as kissing of the altar etc. are found, see: Bingham, viii 10, 9; *D.C.A.*, s.v. *Kiss* (F. Cabrol, *D.A.C.L.*, s.v. *Baiser*, t. ii, col. 117–130 deals with the "Kiss of Peace" and the liturgical discussion of it). In the same way as the altar itself must be protected by vestments (T., p. 146, l. 18), the substitute of the altar must be covered. "Veil" = ܡܥܦܪܢܐ; this word is used elsewhere for "humeral veil, ... worn by the deacon who holds the paten at the communion of the priest" (*L.E.W.*, p. 591); this use in T. p. 25, l. 19; ii 11 (in Ordering the M. touches the paten and takes away a particle of the bread), and: Budge, *B.G.* ii, p. 485 and n. 3; Timotheus ii, Mingana Syr. 13, fol. 119b mentions it as a "humeral veil" worn by the priest who carries the Gospel, (*L.E.W.*, p. 260). But this is impossible here or it must be that this stole was used to cover the paten, a kind of corporale of the paten. The ܫܘܫܦܐ was laid over the bread; this veil was under it (see also ii 25: by mistake the chalice is poured out over the paten; "the priest took the mixture of the paten and returned it into the chalice, and placed it on the altar. He took the Bukhra's on the paten on one side, and covered the paten carefully with the M.; after that he placed other Bukhra's on the paten"). (For the words used before, see: J. Braun, *Lit. Handlex.*, s.v. *Humerale* and *Korporale*).

The end of the answer proves once more that the Eucharist is not a magical ceremony. For in that case he who made the transgression should be punished. But here the guilty person is the priest who did not take care to prevent a mistake (cf. "his sin falleth upon the bishop", in: Athanasius, *Can.* 23 and 24, ed. Riedel-Crum, p. 29 and 30).

Q. 23. ܙܘܢܪܐ = cingulum; mentioned in several rites as an indispensable part of the priest's vestments, especially necessary for the Euch.; it was also necessary during the preparation. James of Edessa, *Canon* 14 (Lamy, p. 116

and Kayser, S. 100–101) calls it: "Altar-girdle" (cf. about this vestment: *L.O.C.*, i, p. 161–162; *D.C.A.*, s.v. *girdle*; *L.E.W.*, p. 592; *L.O.O.*, p. 78). It is not said how it was made in former times; Mgr. Rahmani, who gives only the name ܐܣܪ ܚܨ̈ܐ (cf. Q. 28, 80), says that it consists at the present time of "une pièce d'étoffe de petite largeur, ayant à ces deux bouts deux agraffes en argent ou en métal pour la boucler par devant". An interesting statement about it is found in: Gismondi ii, p. 32, about Mareme, living before Isho'yabh iii: "ipse primus fuit qui mandavit sacerdotes vestem gerere cingulo palam obstrictam ut a ceteris distinguerentur" (what is meant by: "ceteris"? the laics or the priests of other churches. For the latter interpretation, cf. the fact that the Nestorian monks had another tonsure than those of the Monophysites, Budge, *B.G.* ii, p. 40–41; the former is based on the *Canon* of John v). If anybody leaves the service he loosens his girdle, see: Gismondi i, p. 102: Marcus of Tagrit apostasized to Mohammedanism and "progressus in aedes chalifae proprium cingulum scidit et Christo renuntiavit", and: i, p. 81: A certain Theodore is accused of being married; he went to the palace of the caliph "ut fidem suam eiuraret. Haec retulit Abu-l-Farağ filius Dînâr: 'aderam ipse eumque vidi, antequam ingrederetur ad vestes decoras deponendas ac cingulum scindendum'." According to John Bar Abgare ('Abdisho', *Nomocanon* vi, Mai, p. 277) there was a difference between the priests and laymen in the vestments and cloaks and the Tonsure and "especially in the girding of the loins"; they should not gird themselves as the soldiers, though it is uncertain what was exactly meant thereby. It is not superfluous to draw attention to the opposite view of *Canon of pseudo-Nicaea* lxvi (Mansi, ii, col. 1002) prohibiting "ne lumbos suos praecingant zonis tempore orationum clerici, quia ingenui, ac liberi sunt, et nemo eis dominatur nisi Dominus Christus Deus eorum". In Q. 25 and 28 something similar to this Q. is dealt with; if the girdle failed, it was a sign that there was no service, cf. *Can.* xvii: "no one who administers the altar, is allowed to leave the sacrament and sit down or loosen his loins and sandals"; for the sandals see Q. 39; and also the *Arabic Can.* v of John B. Abgare quoted ad Q. 52. We may also compare Severus of Ashmonin, *De Agno Paschali* (*L.O.C.*, i, p. 162): "Sacerdotes fideles calceos in pedibus habent, dum consecrant corpus Christi, signum externum rei internae: sicut etiam quod Zonis praecinguntur signum est praecinctionis interioris" (is this really Coptic as far as the sandals are concerned? Cf. Q. 39). In the *Pearl* of 'Abdisho' the girdle is one of the signs that praefigurate the world to come (v 6; Badger ii, p. 418–419): he points out that it is a sign of "preparedness for service, and a ready appearance before the Lord, after the manner of those who stand in the presence of Kings of the earth", but specially as a divine commandment (Ex. xxviii 4, Luc. xii 35–36); it teaches that its bearer is a worshipper and minister of the Kingdom; possesses "a wakeful mind, pure intention, and being in wait for Him"; it is a sign of death (John xxi); travellers are girded and it shows that we are pilgrims to heaven and must make a viaticum for it viz. "orthodox faith and practice of good works". It is remarkable that nothing is said here about the Eucharist. He speaks only about "girding of christians (in general) at the time of prayer". Yet it is curious to read this exposition; for this is the only vestment to which such a meaning and importance is attributed. Unfortunately it is unknown in how far 'A. reproduces here tradition (the Greeks give quite another explanation, cf. Salaville, *Les Liturgies Orientales*, p. 162; among the Copts, it is not specified but only a sign of an inner state as it is in the Canon of Pseudo-Nicaea, see the quotation given before). At any rate it shows that great importance was attached to it. Without it the priest was not in the right condition; and unable to do his service. Therefore he was not allowed to enter the altar and the Paghra was not treated in the right way. One of the charges of Elias of Nisibis against the validity of the Patriarchate of Isho'yabh iv was: "(Denket an) den Gürtel, der dem neugewählten Patriarchen losging zur Zeit, da er in der Mitte des Altares die Gewänder anlegte" (*Letter*, ed. B. Vandenhof, in: *O.C.*, 1913, S. 260); it had been a "malum omen" (as to the rules of the ancient church it is worthwile to quote Timotheus Alex., Q. 13, 2nd series, in: Pitra, *Monumenta*, i, p. 641: Εἰ ἔξεστιν ἱερέα ἐκ μοναχοῦ τάγματος καταγόμενον ζώνην ζώννυσθαι καὶ οὕτω προσφέρειν, ἢ οὔ; Α: ὁ κανὼν Ἀλεξανδρείας οὐκ ἔχει). The altar did not need consecration with oil, cf. p. 196. It is not surprising that this girdle is spoken of in several places in particular since it naturally slipped down very easily.

To put on the ground see ad Q. 13. The places of "ordering" ad Q. 18 and 34. "Chalice" as read in both codices is rather akward since it is not spoken of before and I do not know that it was taken together with the paten under the name "paten". It may be a mistake and perhaps simply ܦܬܘܪܐ should be read. It does not become clear from this Answer how it should be done if nobody is near by. It must be concluded from this sentence that a deacon too was allowed to carry the paten for the distribution. This is not found anywhere else and the Q. does not speak of an urgent case. So I suppose that this distribution is not the communion, for from: *Expos.* ii, p. 72 it is clear that it was not done. To "distribute" is also used of the Eulogia's (see Q. 80). Perhaps it should be taken in this sense.

Q. 24. Omitted in V. which goes on immediately with Q. 25 that offers the same contents of Q. 23. That the communicants were obliged or used to kiss the feet of the priest as a token of honour, see ad Q. 22, is found, as far as I know, no where else. Kissing of the hand of the priest was very common, *D.A.C.L.*, s.v. *Communion*, t. iii, col. 2437 (where Dom. Leclercq implicitly corrects the statement of Prof. Drews, *Eucharistie*, in: *P.R.E.* [3], v, S. 567, who only mentions the picture in Cod. Ross. Tab. vii and goes on: "wie weit dieser Brauch kirchlich war, ist nicht sicher"). Gabriel Ibn Tarikh of the Coptic Church commanded that "e laicis qui communionem accipiet, metanoeam sive prostrationem faciet versus altare dei", in: *L.O.C.*, i, p. 264. But no where if found this adoration of the priest. "To ask forgiveness of their sins" hints at private confession. About the connection between Eucharist and forgiveness see also the commentary of Theodorus Mops. (*W.S.*, vi, p. 118 sqq.). We cannot enter here upon an investigation of the Eastern doctrine of confessions and its development, cf. M. Jugie, *Theol. Dogmatica*, passim; the Nestorian doctrine in: v, p. 318–321, though it is worthwhile to investigate it. It is well known that confession should precede the communion (Isho'Barnun, *ad Macarium*, Q. 31, 57 and 59; 'Abdisho', *Pearl* iv 7. Loss and gain: see p. 193.

Q. 25. A parallel case to Q. 23. Two possibilities are distinguished: a)

Somebody helps and thereby the injured chalice is restored by signing; the formula see ad Q. 21. b) Nobody is able to help; the sacristan is allowed to put the chalice on the ground (that is not allowed for the paten!), but only inside the threshold of the altar as this ground has shared in the consecration of the altar.

Q. 26. It is very properly observed that the two elements are not treated in the same way. It remains obscure why the chalice can be reconsecrated by signing with the bread, but the paten not. At any rate it appears that greater holiness was ascribed to the Paghra than to the Dema. The same can be concluded from other places. *Expos.* ii, p. 72, says that they are one. Yet some difference was felt, since the question is asked why the chalice, too, should not be carried by a priest. However this may be, it is true that the chalice could be carried by the deacon (the lower officer) and the paten not, in bringing the Elements to the altar (cf. ad Q. 10). In the same line lies the remark of Timothy ii that the Blood cannot augment the Bread in the same way as the Bread does the Chalice (he explains it by pointing out that blood is soon corrupted while flesh can be preserved and that flesh is the cause of the blood, because without flesh there would not be any blood. Ming. Syr. 13, fol. 133a–b). I have not found this remark anywhere else, but one should not be surprised at that on account of the poor tradition and it is possible that nobody else has ever thought of it. It does not seem to be particularly Nest. But we must also remind the readers that they had a special doctrine about the Holy Leaven which is said to be descended from the Last Supper; and this doctrine though it is of very young tradition shows that the Paghra was estimated very highly (cf. ad Q. 52). This feeling about the bread may be a heritage of the Ancient church, cf. the remark of Prof. Drews, *P.R.E.*[3], v, S. 567: "(Kelch) der weniger als das Brot galt". Prof. Lietzmann (*Messe*, S. 248, cf. S. 238–249) pointed out that it seemed as though there existed a religious meal of the Christians alongside with the ordinary Eucharist in which bread was the sole element. This type was perhaps the base of the Serapion-Lit. and was afterwards influenced by and transformed into an ordinary Eucharist. He speaks of "relative Gleichgültigkeit gegen das zweite Element der Eucharistie". This dictum remains true, it seems to me, although the rest of his construction is still disputable. The question of the connection between the views of this early time and those of the 10th century, cannot be solved with the present material and will remain unsolved unless the links between them are found. In any case it is a remarkable coincidence that has to be explained somehow. For though our treatise feels here a difference, it states it merely and fails to give any clue for the explanation. Timothy's words do not give an answer which is historically sound.

Q. 27. Lamps in the service are mentioned in the christian church from the beginning of the 4th century, even in cases where they were not so strictly necessary, as in the Catacombs. Some opposition against them had to be overcome because of their pagan precursors. They are preserved in various forms (*D.A.C.L.*, s.v. *Lampes*, t. viii, col. 1086–1221; *D.C.A.*, s.v. *Lamps, Lights*; Kaufmann, *Handbuch*, S 581–592). It is not specially stated that they were used for the altar, and this is the point in question. *Can. Apost.* iii (ed. F. X. Funk, i, p. 564) speaks for the first time of "a holy lamp" for which oil should be given. It is uncertain how this must be understood, but the connection seems to point to an altar-lamp. According to Paulinus of Nola there were several. The places given by Brightman (*L.E.W.*, p. 580, viz. Chrysostomus, in *Matth.* xxx 6 and Joh. Damasc., *de Imaginibus* iii 33), which mention λυχνία (resp. plur.) are not very clear about this point. Though the context shows that lamps in the sanctuary, standing or hanging, are intended. In the *Canons* of the *Arabic Synodicon* (fol. 79a and 80a) it is ordered that the candle may not be removed from the altar as long as the Eucharistic bread is upon it. The interpretation is doubtful: is a lamp meant hanging over and in front of the altar or one upon the altar as the present Eastern rites show (2 among the Nest.); *L.E.W.*, p. 530 calls this however "at earliest medieval use"; cf. N. Müller, *Altar*, in: *P.R.E.*[3], i, S. 396). The former possibility must be chosen I think. At least John Bar Abgare summarizing the tradition(?) says something similar in: *Canon* xxii: The Eucharistic bread may be preserved if only care is displayed in the "keeping of the lamps". These lamps or lights must be those hanging over and in front of the altar; see: *Can.* xii: ". . . there must be a lamp before the altar, filled with pure olive-oil, burning always night and day. It should not go out under any circumstance, there may be or may not be consecrated bread. Where ever there are two fixed altars, there are also two lamps needed etc." (cf. also *E.S.D.O.*, p. 297 s.v., who adds: "this is not done in practice".–It is recorded from the time of Machicha i, 1091–1108 that one of the great outrages of a monk was that he extinguished the lamps in the sanctuary, Gismondi i, p. 120.–When Narsai, *Hom.* xvii, tr. Connolly, p. 12 says that lamps shine in the church, his statement is of no use for the present investigation since he does not describe their place). It is not easy to decide whether this Canon is of ancient date. Yet we may refer to possible influence of the O.T. Ex. xxvii 20; Lev. xxiv 2 though the author himself did not suggest it.[1] There are also lamps mentioned in: *Can.* xxvi: ". . . no priests or deacons may touch the altar after the breaking of his fast; and when the Holy Sacraments have been ordered, he is not allowed to draw near, under no circumstance, not even to the door-post of the Sanctuary (beth maqdᵉsha). But if there are no Sacraments on the altar, and it is an urgent case, as far as the outer-candle. But when he enters and passes the lamp, if he is drunk, even if the enters when there are no Sacraments prepared or ordered, and does not enter the Sanctuary nor a part of it, because of the greatness of the evil and the sin, there is no absolution for him". Whether the same lamp is spoken of is not clear. For our question *it is important that we find mentioned here a candle in the sanctuary that served as a limit.* Nothing of this kind is found in other churches; at least *D.A.C.L.*, s.v. *Choeur*, t. iii, col. 1409–1413 does not say a word about it. The *Expos.* contains several places about various kinds of lights in the service (ii, p. 9, 11, 92), but they are very well distinguished from the lamps that are spoken of in: i, p. 108–09, ii, p. 36, and that should be cleaned before the time of the services according to the rule of Isho'yabh iii. It is the row of lamps indicated in the sketch (i, p. 196) by C. Among other things it is said that the deacons are allowed to go to the throne = altar in the apse, but that the sub-deacons should not go further than "usque

(1) It is done in the somewhat confused *Canon* 13 of Athanasius, ed. Riedel-Crum, p. 24.

ad mediam absidem, sive ad lampadum locum" (i, p. 109, cf. p. 120; in agreement with this information is the statement in: Badger ii, p. 325: "sub-deacons to be admitted as far as the lamp, hung in the middle of the bema", "bema" being here the alter-place; cf. ad Q. 97). Our treatises mention candle-sticks on the altar at the time of the Sacraments (ii 10, text somewhat obscure); but along with it, as in our Q. "a candle in the middle of the altar or Sanctuary" (Q. 6, 28, 29 and 80). In Q. 28 and 80 distinction is made between the part before and beyond the lamp. Only if this limit is passed the injury proper takes place. This is the entrance of the Sanctuary in the strict sense of the word. Another parallel of this use is *Can.* 26 of an anonymous Synod in: 'Abdisho', *Nomocanon*, vi 4. It ordered that beer for the priests should not be brought "inter cancellos" during the funeral service but should be placed on the steps in the middle of the temple. Only the beer for the Patriarch may be brought "in cancellos" till the lamp if one wants to do so, in order that it is placed in his grave (in the chronicles it is often found that Patriarchs were buried in the oratorium, is this the same place?) One should be inclined to call the place beyond the lamp "holy of holies". According to: *E.S.D.O.*, s.v. (the same in: *L.E.W.*, p. 578) this is a general name for the sanctuaries (the same remark is found in: *L.O.O.*, p. 39–40, but Mgr. Rahmani has generally only Jacobite matters under consideration) and specially for "the space under the baldakyn of the altar". The latter explanation fits in very well with our Q. while the former may suit to *Can.* xxvii where it is said that a priest or deacon who has not taken part in all the services of the day, is not allowed to enter the holy of holies; although this can also apply to the place around the altar (at least if this Canon must be interpreted in accordance with this Question of Isho'Barnun, *ad Macarium*, 67: "Are a priest or deacon who have not served in the Night-service, allowed to go to the Apse to serve the Order [Takhsa] and to consecrate the Qudasha, or not? *Solution:* He is not allowed to serve the Takhsa, to go to the Apse and to consecrate the Qudasha. He is allowed to receive the Qudasha."). We should also observe that the name is used in the Formulary of Consecration of the Altar with oil for the most oriental wall of the sanctuary (T., p. 145; before Q. 6; also *D.C.A.*, s.v.). It is not certain what is the date of this statement; the formulary is ascribed to Isho'yabh iii. Must we also assume some influence of the division of the Temple in the O.T.? Incense is mentioned in several places of the Nestorian Liturgy (*L.E.W.*, p. 262, 282, 289; the various formularies do not always mention it in the same places; so Tim. ii adds it to *L.E.W.*, p. 292). It is not clear what point of the liturgy the author has in mind. His mistake is not that he brings the incense, for it is always an offering to make men pleasant for God. But it is a parallel to the case quoted in: *Canon* xxvi since he is not fasting; John b. Abgare, *Canon* iii, ap. 'Abdisho', *Nomocanon*, vi 6, Mai p. 278, forbade any priest, deacon or monk to do their service after a meal, if he was not kept by the holy fast (cf. *Can.* xxvi quoted before; for the meaning of ܠܗܛܪ see: Payne Smith, *Thesaurus*, s.v. and also Q. 8, 9, ii 2 quoted on Q. 82) and in such a state it is not allowed to come near to the altar not even if covered by the Holy incense. This case is not provided for in the rubric T. p. 119.

Q. 28. Belongs to Q. 23–25 for the essentials. Here however he is inside the sanctuary with the polluted elements. He must try to restore the fact as soon as possible even if the altar is injured. The ܡܟܒܪܝܬܐ is not mentioned by Brightman's index nor by Rahmani. It is according to the context a napkin hanging loosely over the shoulder. Another use of it is found in: John Tell., *Can.* v: ܡܟܒܪܝܬܐ ܕܡܟܝܬܐ ܠܗ ܡܢ ܦܓܪܐ, translated by Lamy: "mantille quae corpus sanctum attigit" (p. 66–67; cf. note 4, where he compares it with the latin mantille "linteolum . . . abstergendis manibus inserviens". Among the Syrians however "ad oblationem tegendam vel sustentandam, ad instar mappulae, ex quaestione praesenti conjecerim"). According to Dean Maclean it is either a white Baptismal robe or a napkin, without further comment (*E.S.D.O.*, p. 295). Prof. J. Braun styles it a medieval word for: altarveil, manipel, covering of the chalice, "Schultervelum des Patenarius" (*Lit. Handlexicon*, s.v.). The Syriac places given before are covered by this explanation. Only the view that it was medieval though it may apply to the western church, should be revised. For it appears already in the 6th century in Syria. In our Q. the last meaning given by Braun is the right one. About ܓܘܠܬܐ Dean Maclean says (*E.S.D.O.*, p. 293): "an ecclesiastical vestment now obsolete (shape unknown); an altar-cloth". The definition given by Browne–Maclean, p. 263 is rather obscure. In the *Dictionary* of Payne Smith, s.v. it is added that the latter meaning is specially East Syrian and another explanation is offered viz. "a woollen cloack worn by monks or shepherds". For our Q. only the first meaning remains. A rubric of the Pontificale prescribes at the ordination of new priests: "the consecrating Bishop takes the Gulta that lies upon his shoulder, and covers him with it". Mgr. Rahmani (*L.O.O.*, p. 81 and n. 1) who describes this vestment as belonging only to the Nest., translates: "shape"; but that cannot be applied in our case. The etymology of ܓܘܠ = to twine round, does not bring us further. Is it perhaps a Nest. name for: orarium = stole that was worn both by priests and deacons? If one passes by the lamp (see ad Q. 27), the altar is injured and must be signed with oil. The rubric T., p. 119, does not provide for this occurrence. It orders consecration with oil if the girdle is loosened in the altar. The punishment of the priest is simple rebuke cf. ad Q. 69. "Head of the church", must be taken as Bishop, as appears from Q. 119 and *Can.* xviii.

Q. 29–30. Another case of the *degrees of Holiness in the sanctuary* marked by the threshold (31) and veils (cf. ad Q. 8). Several places in this treatise speak about pagans (cf. ad Q. 42, 52). *Can.* xi specifies: pagans, Magians, priests of another religion. A useful comparison is offered by the letter of Isho' Barnun, *ad Isaac, second question:* "If it happens that one of the faithful or a foreigner [1] enters (the church) and lays his hand on the altar, how should one put this right? *Answer:* If a foreigner enters forcibly or without the knowledge of the servants of the altar, since the affair is not blameworthy, its memory will be blotted out with prayers; [2] because it was not Nicodemus who drew nigh unto the grave [3] nor was it Joseph the Councillor, the honest anointers

(1) Cf. ad Q. 17. (2) It will be seen that the injury is determined by the guilt of a christian who knew what to do or had no respect, in short that something is blameworthy; if it is forced upon somebody he is not guilty. The most remarkable thing is the memory of the misdeed. Cf. p. cf. 193. (3) Name of the altar, see Q. 104.

of the Holy Body,[1] let the priest recite in a special Hulala[2] the ode which David sang prophetically in the person of the Maccabees and it is 'O God, the gentiles have entered in Thy inheritence',[3] and with the 'Onitha[4]: 'Thy altar, omnipotent God'[4], and the hymn: 'High and Holy'. There will be no need of oil or of anything else. In case that he who entered and touched the altar was a believer if the cause of his entry was the abundance of his faith or his ignorance,[1] none of the above things are to be done because he did not do it in disrespect.[1] This is not comparable with the case of a son who touches the honourable things of his Father or a servant those of his master, because the son would then be in need of admonition and the servant of rebuke."

It is not remarkable that pagans are spoken of in this country. Christianity was surrounded on all sides by Mohammedans, adherents to the old Persian religion and people that were not Christians because they did not belong to any other of the great religions (Jews are not mentioned! It does not imply that the rule was not applied to them; but simply that they did not seem to form part of the population that counted). See: Budge, *B.G.* ii, Index s.v. *Arabs, Magians, Pagans* (and the division of Bar Hebraeus, quoted by C. Kayser, S. 112). The three groups are sharply distinguished there: at any rate, the Arabs worship one God while the pagans adore mute idols (p. 508); the Magians are those who venerate the celestial bodies (p. 307). But this makes no difference in fact. It is a matter of course that pagans were not allowed to enter into the sanctuary where even those who had the "sign of life" were prevented from doing so (Bingham, viii 6, 7; Kayser, S. 80–81. Only the higher clergy from the deacon upwards were allowed to enter. The deaconesses should be consecrated "in the deacon's house (cf p. 200), before the door that leads to the apse", because they are women, Synod . . . (?), *Can.* i, in: 'Abdisho', *Nomocanon,* vi 4, Mai, p. 275). It should be observed that James Edess., *Canon* i, calls this a particularity of "these Eastern countries" (cf. *D.C.A.*, s.v. *Laity*). Yet it was often impossible to prevent pagans from entering into it; attacks on the churches during progroms are often recorded in history (cf. in the above quotation: "Forcibly"; cf. James Edess., quoted in: *L.O.O.*, p. 169 and n. 4: it is necessary to close the doors of the churches "pour défendre l'entrée aux Hageréens [= Mohammedans], qui de nos jours dominent, d'entrer audacieusement dans les églises, troubler le peuple de Dieu et profaner les saints Mystères). About pagans at the Christian Service, cf. ad Q. 42. The measures that should be taken in that case were mentioned by John Bar Abgare, *Quaestio Eccl.* xx: "Accidit Altare consecratum in loco hostilibus (these "hostes" may be heretics as well, but that does not make any difference) incursionibus obnoxio reperiri. Quaeritur, an illud tollere et condere liceat, postea loco suo refigere, atque in eo Sacrum facere? Respondetur, id minime licere. Nam si Altare in loco, cui fixum fuit, convelli contingat, ne dicam alio transferatur, nova consecratione indiget. Quodsi accidat fidei nostrae hostes Sanctuarium intrare, nec Altaris arcam convellere, communes Ecclesiae preces inibi celebrari

(1) Joh. xix 38–39. (2) Cf. ad Q. 106. (3) Ps. lxxix 1; cf. T., p. 134. Quotation from Theodorus Mops. Ταῦτα οὖν ὁ μακάριος Δαβὶδ ἐκ προσώπου τῶν Μακκαβαίων φησὶν κτλ., in: F. Baethgen, *Siebenzehn makkabäische Psalmen nach Theodor von Mopsuestia*, in: *Zeitschrift f.d. alttest. Wissenschaft*, 1887, S. 49 (similar views on S. 48). *Expos.* i, p. 125 refers it to the time of Nebucadnesar. (4) T.: Consecration of the altar without oil, p. 120; with oil, p. 135. The differences between the facts and the treatment should be observed.

hoc minime obstante licebit, modo sanctuarii pars orientalis cruce signetur manu, non autem chrismate, citra Arcam . . . Si vero Arca e loco, in quo fixa est moveatur, aut alio asportetur, iterum eam consecrari oportet." We may compare James Edess., *Can.* xxv–xxvi (Lamy, p. 126–128. Or is in xxv special stress laid upon the eating = contact with the demons?), who ordered that the Tablitha = the altar-table that was not fixed must be washed carefully and be counted as profane or that it must be broken, as would be the case with the altar, and buried carefully (for the difference between the two cf. Isho'Barnun, *ad Isaac* Q. 9 who says: that this Tabula is "not equal in honour to the altar is known by the fact that if the altar is shaken it becomes desecrated, as to the portable altar although it is carried to many places, the grace is kept in it." He says also that the Tabula was an invention of the time of tribulation. Cf. also John b. Abgare, *Canon* i; ii 24, ad Q. 11; *L.O.O.*, p. 49; on "autels portatifs" see: *D.A.C.L.*, s.v. *Autel*, t. i, col. 3187.–It is the Greek "antimension", not used before the Iconoclastic War, S. Pétridès, *D.A.C.L.*, s.v. *Antimension*, t. i, col. 2319–2326). The remark of Kayser was very much to the point saying that not all the canonists were so strict, referring to "Prières du rite de réconciliation d'un autel ou d'une église qui avaient été profanés par des hérétiques ou des païens" in Dr. Zotenberg's Catalogue of the Syriac MSS. of the Bibliothèque Nationale (Kayser, S. 113; cf. his comments, S. 112–113. As to the Coptic church he might have referred to: *L.O.C.*, i, p. 55–56 and 312: washing with water, reciting of prayers, incense, crossing of the altar, after the ritual of Gabriel of Alexandria). The burying that is also found elsewhere (cf. ad Q. 78) was a usual manner to dispose of sacred objects. Yet I have not found that it was practised by the Nestorians in cases of injury of the altar by pagans. Isho'Barnun gave restoration without oil. John Bar Abgare distinguished between being shaken or not; if it was simply touched, signing and prayers = consecration without oil, as ordered by Isho'Barnun was sufficient. If it was shaken it should be consecrated with oil for then it had lost its "grace". It is exactly in the line of our QQ. that have only introduced the limit of the veil. The rubric T., p. 119 does not mention these cases. The quotation Q. 29 = T., p. 128. A view that the altar would not be profaned by the entering of pagans is not found anywhere. It seems to me to run counter to the whole Eastern tradition and only proves lax views. Or did they think that it was only profaned by actual touching?

Q. 31. Children of the Christians (naturally baptised) see Q. 52, 81. *Can.* vii and xi. The question is: what is the age of discretion? According to Payne Smith, *Dictionary*, s.v., ܫܒܪܐ means a child under the age of 5 years. It will be instructive to quote an answer of Timotheus Alex. Q. 18 (1st series), in: Pitra, *Monumenta*, i, p. 634): "From what age onwards are the sins judged by God? *Answer:* (It is done) according to knowledge and intelligence of everyone, some from being 10 years of age and some even older" (Pitra, *l.l.*, p. 644, remarks that something similar is asked by Nicephorus about the ordination of the clergy, and thinks that it might be here the same case. Yet this seems to be wholly improbable). "Threshold" see Q. 9 and 25. It is always a holy limit. It is not indicated in the sketch of Dom. Connolly (*Expos.* i, p. 196), and I did not find it referred to elsewhere. It seems to be the place indicated in this sketch by *d.d.*, the small wall between apse and katastroma (Cancelli).

Once more this whole question is a clear proof against considering the Eastern idea of holiness simply as magical. It is absolutely clear that the age of the trespasser was taken into account! According to V. the boy may go further into the sanctuary than in M., but the state of affairs is the same.

Q. 32. The point is the "carelessness in communion". Care was necessary for one who received "the precious Paghra that may not be despised" (ii 3). The formulary does not indicate how the communion should take place, nor is it stated in our QQ. (for Q. 12 deals with another matter). In what did this care consist? Of course one should not drop anything (Q. 11 sqq.), to kiss the hand of the priest (Q. 24). But this was not the only care; for if the angry communicant throws back the Gemurta, this carelessness must refer to something before the communion proper. In Narsai, *Hom.* xvii (Connolly, p. 28–29) we read: "He who approaches to receive the Body stretches forth his hands, lifting up his right hand and placing it over his fellow. In the form of a cross the receiver joins his hands; and thus he receives the Body of the Lord upon a Cross . . . (Narsai gives a further explanation of this symbol in which the following words occur "on the same cross He flew and was exalted to the height above", a remark not commented upon by Dom. Connolly. Yet I do not understand what the writer had in mind) . . . He receives in his hands the adorable Body of the Lord of all; and he embraces it and kisses it with love and affection. He makes to enter, he hides the Leaven of life in the temple of his body etc." thus: receiving upon the crossed hands, kissing and eating of the Euch. This East Syrian practice agrees with the way of communicating elsewhere in the Ancient church. It is needless to give references here since no other practice is found, cf. *D.C.A.*, s.v. *Communion*, and: Bingham, xv 5, 3 and 6. Generally one communicated standing. This way of communion is also supposed in the communion-prayer: "strengthen, o our Lord etc." (*L.E.W.*, p. 300; it is ascribed to a certain Isaac, A. Baumstark, *L.G.*, S. 133, Ak. 12–134). The present practice is that it is given by the priest into the mouth of the communicant, cf. Badger ii, p. 242. But cf. E. Tisserant, *D.Th.C.*, s.v. *Nestorienne*, t. xi, col. 315: "les adultes reçoivent la parcelle dans la main droite et se communient eux-mêmes" (the learned author has confused the former with the present practice). This practice existed already, so it seems, at the time of our treatise; at least this may be inferred from the fact that a Bishop is rebuked in ii 10, who "despising the particle in the cup took it in his hand, placed it in his mouth and communicated as if it were from the hands of the priest." It can also be deduced from: *Canon* xxiii which ordains that any who orders must do so with care; the precious Paghra must be received "on a piece of leather or on the covering of the chalice or at all events on the palms of his hands; he shall not bring any particle of the Paghra with his hand to his mouth, but take it (directly) with his mouth, because it is heavenly pasture". We should realize that from the information of this Q. the conclusion may be drawn that the Gemurtha was given into the hand and thrown back, yet in fact he received it in his mouth, took it from there and threw it back. The reverse of a blessing is always the curse, cf. i Cor. xi 29. Naturally he acts "foolishly" for he despises the gift of God and causes it to become the opposite. It is not said what should be his punishment; was the fact that he did not receive the Eucharist or better that he cut himself off, a sufficient punishment? The way in which the polluted paten should be treated is the usual one. "Clean" viz. the crumbs, cf. ad Q. 18 about the Ordering.

Q. 33. I have not found any parallel of this Q. (but cf. Dionysius b. Salibi ad Q. 46–47?) It is not clear why this cooked food should be placed on the paten together with the Paghra. It is a matter of course that the paten is defiled since the cooked food was not consecrated nor fit for consecration (since it did not belong to the Euch. Elements), and only something answering this condition may be brought on it. It is a case that "holy" and "profane" are brought together, which is not allowed under any circumstance (cf. Rabbula, *Canon* 31, in: Burkitt, *Early Eastern Christianity*, p. 147: "Let not any of the Priests or Deacons or any of the Sons of the Church dare to place common vessels side by side with the Sacramental vessels in any box or chest.")

Q. 34. "Ablutions" see ad Q. 18. That this must be drunk in the places mentioned in the text, is also stated in Q. 23 to which may be referred.

Q. 35. This Q. teaches that Cross and Gospel on the altar are indispensable for a valid Eucharist (cf. T., p. 146). This agrees with, looks like a quotation from the *Expositio* of Abraham Bar Lipheh: "Crux vero et evangelium quae ponuntur super altare, et imago Domini nostri super ea, ipsum Dominum nostrum repraesentant. Quare omnino non licet consecrari mysteria sancta sine praesentia crucis et evangelii et imaginis Domini nostri" (*Expos.* ii, p. 161). This means that those two objects should be standing upon the altar during the Mass. Cf. ad Q. 118 sqq. ܠܘܬ ܡܕܒܚܐ cf. *Expos.* ii, p. 33 text: ܠܐ ܡܫܡܠܝ ܠܗܘܐ (ܙܩܝܦܐ ܘܐܘܢܓܠܝܘܢ) ܠܘܬ ܡܕܒܚܐ ܠܡܕܢܚܐ ܕܐܬܩܢܝ ܘܠܐ. This Cross and Gospel were always on the altar, see the story in: Gismondi i, p. 106–107. This is confirmed also by Narsai, *Hom.* xvii (Connolly, p. 12): "The altar stands crowned with beauty and splendour, and upon it is the Gospel of life and the adorable wood (*sc.* the Cross)". It does not matter that the authorship of this Homily is not quite sure since the Cross upon the altar is found in other places of Narsai too (cf. Connolly, p. xxx). From this oldest Nestorian statement it is not clear whether it was a simple Cross or a Crucifix as in the example quoted by Prof. Baumstark from the Biography of Bar'Itta (cf. A. Baumstark, *Altarkreuze in nestorianischen Klöstern des* vi. *Jahrhunderts*, in: *Römische Quartalschrift*, 1900, S. 70–71; also in C. M. Kaufmann, *Handbuch*, S. 575, who gives some more examples, but that of Narsai that could not be known to Baumstark seems to have escaped Prof. K.'s attention). An example of a Crucifix was known to Baumstark only from 872 A.D., but he does not say, what (on the use of the crucifix by the Nestorians, see: L. E. Browne, *Eclipse of Christianity*, p. 78, 79). Cf. also Q. 104: The Crosses the author has in view are not those on the sides of the altar nor crowning the ciborium, since they are put on the same line with the Gospel. For the western materials see the short statement by N. Müller, *Altar*, in: *P.R.E.* 3, i, S. 396, and: *D.A.C.L.*, s.v. *Croix et Crucifix*, t. iii, col. 3079; Dom. Leclerq says on account of the article of Baumstark: "le fait de la présence du symbole sur l'autel est certain, et l'Orient, sur ce point, est en avance de six siècles sur l'Occident". An image of the Lord is not mentioned here. The context of Abraham shows that it was not a Crucifix, but probably a picture. Mgr. Rahmani gives an instance from the Jacobite church of the 6th cent. viz. in the *Admonitions* of John Tell. to a deacon which he quotes in translation (*L.O.O.*, p. 52: "Si le prêtre t'ordonne de préparer l'autel pour la messe, . . . aie soin lorsque tu t'en approches . . . que la croix ne soit pas inclinée par négligence; si tu la trouve ainsi, tu dois la remettre en place d'une manière digne de la liturgy sacrée." Otherwise I did not find a statement proving that Cross and Gospel on the altar were indispensable requisites for the Jacobites (Syr. or Copt.), though it was certainly the case, as in the Byzantine rite (Salaville, *Liturgies orientales*, p. 142, 185).

Q. 36. Morning service see ad Q. 105. It seems to be supposed here that it was a High Mass in a big church where several priests were wanted for the distribution of the Eucharistic bread. The matter of discussion is that they wait until all the bread is given to somebody (cf. ii 14, a sacristan distributes from the early morning till noon) and do not return to the altar. The officiant goes on with his service, and finishes it while he "orders" alone. In: *Canon* xx and especially xxi it was strictly prohibited under pain of expulsion from the office. At least two ministers were necessary to give Bread and Chalice to each other or a priest and a deacon (Isho'yabh i, *Can.* iii, in: O. Braun, *Synhados*, S. 243–244). According to our author there is one exception, namely the villages since the necessary priests and deacons are not found there on account of the small number of the inhabitants and of the priests caused by persecutions. Nearly one thousand years later Badger's description from 1840 gives a good impression of such a state: "Very many of the Nestorian villages in these two districts are consequently left without resident clergy, and are dependent for the ordinances of religion upon the ministrations of a single priest who travels among them from place to place" (i, p. 195). For the state of Christianity in the country see also ad Q. 96. In any case it was strictly forbidden to consecrate alone, (Riedel, S. 192; cf. p. 121–122). It is supposed that a priest is travelling while a deacon is found in several of the villages that have no priests. It was forbidden by an anonymous Synod, quoted in: 'Abdisho', *Nomocanon*, vi 4, *Can.* 3–4 (Mai, p. 276; 2nd Synod of Carthago, *Can.* ix?); but it might be allowed by the Chorepiscopos; cf. George i († 680), *Canon* x, in: O. Braun, *Synhados*, S. 342: "und sie (the priests) dürfen sich nirgends hin von der Kirche und Stadt entfernen, . . . ohne Erlaubnis des B."; the priests could not decide this themselves except in urgent cases. If therefore a priest wished to consecrate on one day in several villages he was allowed to do so, and this seems to be the intention of the writer. – ܟܗܢܐ = "priest" is especially the priest as officiant; otherwise it is practically identical with ܩܫܝܫܐ = "presbyter"; cf. *Expos.* ii, p. 46: "nunc autem (*L.E.W.*, p. 282) ablatum est nomen 'presbyter' et 'episcopus', et 'sacerdos' vocatur. Cum iam sacerdos, Christus, officium hoc persolvat, sublatum est nomen 'presbyter' et 'episcopus'," referring to some verses of Ephraem. What allowance of the Fathers is meant, is not clear. We may suggest that it was an unwritten tradition of the men of the High Monastery (p. 148) or it may be that it refers to the 318 Fathers who allowed that solitaries who could not go to a church might consecrate alone (Riedel, S. 192). In that case our answer gives an expansion of that Canon. The urgent cases are twofold: a) a travelling priest (allowed by the Greeks, see p. 122, n. 1,) comes into a church without any clergy; b) he comes into a church where a deacon is found. In a) he must do all the service alone, the ordering included; in b) he must leave the rest of the service to a deacon who may take over the priest's duties in emergencies (cf. *Canon* iii of Isho'yabh to James of Darai, in: O. Braun, *Synhados*, S. 243). ܡܫܡܠܐ ܐܪ̈ܙܘܗܝ may be either: finish his mysteries, or: consecrate. The former opinion seems to be intended; but cf. *Expos.* ii, p. 145 (text): ܡܫܡܠܝܢ ܐܪ̈ܙܐ translated by Connolly with: "iam consecrata mysteria" (ii, p. 132).

Q. 37. Since the end of the 2nd cent. Wednesday and Friday (feria quarta and sexta) had already been not only days of fasting, but also of celebration of the Eucharist (Bingham, xiii 9, 2; xv 9; Drews, *P.R.E.*[3], v, S. 569–570; for the practice of the Nestorians of the last century see: Badger ii, p. 242–243: often there is no Eucharist at all, and Maclean, *E.R.E.*, s.v. *Syrian Christians*, t. xii, p. 177). – "Hebdomada" = week; we have introduced this term because otherwise some confusion might arise. For the week mentioned here is a typically Nestorian liturgical division that is, as far as I know, not found anywhere else. The year is divided into 7 periods each of which had about 7 weeks, named respectively: Moses; Annunciation and Birth; Baptism; Fast; Resurrection and Ascension; Apostles; Summer; Elija (and the Revelation of the Cross). This is the summary given by the *Expos.* i, p. 27–28. Maclean gives a somewhat different one (*E.S.D.O.* p. 265, n. 4; where p. 264–281 show the Nestorian calendar). He added to "Moses" the "Hallowing of the Church" (this is a subdivision of Moses in the *Expos.* and definitely settled, i, p. 28–29); he began with Advent. This latter fact is in agreement with the ordinary liturgical year. Therefore it is possible that the order of the *Expositio* which is of course ascribed to Isho'yabh iii must be preferred, since it stresses the point that one should begin with "Moses". From Gismondi i and ii it will be seen that these names occur in the histories of the Patriarchs after the reign of I. iii. It is not known what reasons led this Patriarch to this division nor if there were older examples. To answer these questions the data are failing. A treatise of Berikhisho' about the division of the year by Isho'yabh iii (cf. ch. vi, ii c) as an introduction to the Ḥudhra in: Cambr. Add. 1981 and published by: W. Wright-St. A. Cook, *A catalogue of the Syriac Manuscripts preserved in the library of the University of Cambridge*, Cambridge, 1901, p. 164–168.

The fasts of Apostles (middle of July, it lasted 7 weeks from Whitsuntide till the last Sunday of the Hebdomada of the Apostles; often mentioned as date, e.g. Gismondi i, p. 71, 74 etc.) and of Elija are treated in connection with the origin of the four fast terms in the Greek church by Prof. K. Holl, *Die Entstehung der vier Fastenzeiten in der griechischen Kirche*, in: *Ges. Aufsätze zur Kirchengeschichte*, ii, Tübingen, 1928, S. 177–180. It lasted 40 days (*Expos.* i, p. 52). The times of these fasts may be previous to the order of Isho'yabh.–The sacristan trespasses against: *Canon* xx, for he takes so much *as seems good to him* [in stead of following the *Canon* (this is his mistake!)] and leaves the rest for the next day, probably without precautions, a practice that was strictly forbidden. He seems to be administering a kind of "missa praesanctificatorum". See about this point the discussion ad Q. 16. The chalice was as ever cleansed the previous evening, and is simply reconsecrated by signing (cf. also ii 4: "this that they sign the chalice with the particle of the Paghra the Gazza, may be done, if they are forced by lack of a consecrated chalice; but where a consecrated chalice is found they are not allowed to sign with a particle"; cf. about the end ad Q. 72).

The end of the answer looks like a separate Q. and A.; it deals with reservation by the communicants (the beginning mentioned the priests).

Q. 38. Cf. ad Q. 36. He trespasses against: *Can.* xxi. We may also compare ii 34: "A priest consecrates in the Morning service a Qudasha, and preserves it till noon or evening. When he does not find a deacon to order with him, what must he do?" In our Q. the priest himself solves this question as is also said in the answer: "This is a blameworthy tradition; priests of our time maintain it and make a steady use of it, giving as a pretext that they cannot find anybody to order with them owing to lack of deacons. But at the end of the Qudasha the priest should deliver it up to a deacon and say: 'the precious Paghra is delivered up from the altar, pardoning the modest priest of God, that he may distribute it to the people of the Lord, and order it to life eternal'. Likewise the chalice in the same way." Here the formula that should be said is given; naturally it is not the same as that of the communion. It is a matter of course that the altar is defiled though this case is not found in the well-known rubric on p. 119 of T.–About the answer of the Priest and his punishment see Q. 69.

Q. 39. Assemani cited this Q. (*B.O.*, iii 1, p. 251) in commenting *Quaestio Eccl.* xii of John B. Abgare. When asked if a priest may serve with ordinary sandals John answered that this was allowed in urgent cases though the use of special vestments and shoes for the service of the church was advisable. In Q. xxv he forbids expressly to serve without sandals. During the Preparation (cf. ad Q. 52), too, the Priest should wear sandals. An adult man, being baptized, must come to the altar to communicate "atque calceamenta ferre et suis incedere pedibus permittatur" (John b. Abgare, *Quaest. Eccl.* iv). Our Q. is an answer to the question what should be done if somebody trespassed against it (cf. also Q. 63). This point seems rather important for the Nestorians. In the *Arabic Synodicon* fol. 80a = Riedel, S. 193, cf. p. 122, n. 1) objections were made to the Greeks that they entered the altar naked and barefoot, and the first accusation of Elias Nisib. against the Jacobites (*Beweis*, S. 98–99) was: "Ihre Priester, zu der Schändlichkeit ihres der Wahrheit wiedersprechenden Glaubens, halten es für erlaubt, barfuss und ohne Beinkleider den Altar zu betreten." I have not found any regulations about this point among the groups that are accused here. On the other hand it is remarkable that Bar Hebraeus, *Nomocanon* iv 2, quotes the decision of John Bar Abgare with the entry "Persians". At the end of the last century the Nestorians were liable to the same error of which they accused their neighbours (cf. Browne–Maclean, p. 214 who point out the difference); the people of the mountain districts (see ad Q. 96) exchanged their shoes for special slippers. Several rules about the footwear are found among the Copts and it is possible that Elias hinted at them in his book. The priests had to wear special liturgical vestments that might not be taken outside the church[1]; and: "keiner soll innerhalb des Chores Schuhe anziehen", referring to Ex. iii 5, (Basilius, *Can.* 96, Riedel, S. 273; *L.O.C.*, i, p. 160–163). Coptic fragment of uncertain origin, published by Dr. Crum, in: W. Riedel–W. E. Crum, *The Canons of Athanasius of Alexandria*, p. 144: "No priests shall put sandals upon their feet, when they go into the church", referring to Ex. iii 5, Josh. v 16. The first Canon of Christodoulos of Alexandria (11th cent.) ordered the same: "... no one shall enter the church unless bare-headed and bare-footed" (O. H. E. Burmester, *The Canons of Christodoulos, Patriarch of Alexandria A.D.* 1047–1077, in: *Le Muséon*, 1932, p. 79; Assemani, *l.l.*, referred also to it). Here the rule seems to be extended over all the faithful (about the uncovering of the head cf. *L.O.C.*, i, p. 264–265). Yet it is not quite fixed, for Renaudot quotes a book of Severus of Aschmonin, *de Agno Paschali*, of which no date is given, and that expressed the opposite: "Sacerdotes fideles calceos in pedibus habent, dum consecrant corpus Christi ..." (*l.l.*, p. 162). It is difficult to decide which is original and which derivative. It may be that the O.T. had some influence as is also suggested by some Egyptian canons (the same was found among the Jews, as appears from the Talmud Jerus., *Pessachim* 7, 11 [35b]: "our scholars put off their shoes when they entered the outer door of the mountain of the Temple", quoted by J. Klausner, *Jesus von Nazareth*[2], Berlin, 1934, S. 433). John Bar Abgare refers in other places also to the O.T.; he draws a parallel between a prince of this world before whom nobody will come unshod, and the Lord of Heaven, but he did not cite a special place (ap. 'Abdisho', *Nomocanon*, vi 6, 2, Mai, p. 277–278). It may be that in the Nestorian prescripts a certain awe inspired the Canonists viz. not to touch the holy ground, or the fact that a person was not well dressed without sandals (cf. John Bar Abgare) as we found also in regard to the girdle (Q. 23). We must also refer in this connection to the Q.Q. in ii 39–42, that suggest that the former opinion is the better. The author discusses what should be done if a sacristan standing on a ladder to fasten the veils of the altar loses his sandal that falls in the middle of the altar-place. The Solution is that "as long as he is on the ladder, he does not do anything blameworthy", he must try to pick up his sandal without touching the ground with his bare foot; if he cannot reach it he must walk on his hands and one foot "as cattle, holding his bare foot in the air" and reach it in this way. If both his sandals fall he must try to reach the nearer and so on, but if that is impossible: "he must call for the Bishop that he may consecrate the altar". One sees what capers the poor man must cut to prevent his touching the earth and thereby desecrating the altar.

The difference in practice may be old and the losing of the sandals something that was typically Egyptian (among the Nestorian it was the sign of rest and that the priest was not serving, cf. the quotation ad Q. 23). Its origin was probably to be found in monks' circles. Only a single place was quoted by Bingham (viii 10, 6), from Cassianus, *Institutiones*, i 10, which refers to it as a pecularity of the Egyptian monks: "Nequaquam tamen caligas pedibus inhaerere permittunt, cum accedunt ad celebranda vel percipienda sacrosancta mysteria, illud aestimantes etiam secundum literam custodiri debere quot dicitur ad

(1) Cf. Athanasius, *Can.* 28, ed. Riedel-Crum, p. 31: "The garments of the priests, wherein they celebrate, shall be white and washed. They shall be laid in the storechambers of the sanctuary..... even as the prophet Ezekiel hath ordained". (xliv 19, cf. *ibid.*, p. 77).

Moysen vel ad Jesum filium Nave" (see before). But for the rest Bingham observed: "We do not find it mentioned as a general custom prevailing among the primitive Christians." This statement is true. That it is found among the Abessynians, as Bingham already remarked, is of course owing to Coptic influence.

Q. 40. Mixture of the chalice etc. cf. ad Q. 72 sqq. One should be careful not to place it on the ground. The chalice was, as will be remembered, already before the consecration itself holy to a certain extent, as it contained the holy mixture and might not be polluted. Special Canons about it as among the Jacobites (Bar Hebraeus, *Nomocanon*, iv 2) are not found among the Nestorians so far as I know nor special consecration-prayers as among the Copts (*L.O.C.*, i, p. 307). It is possible that the fact that the chalice was "separated" or "set apart", or put on the altar, was already thought sufficient as seems to be supposed by John Tell., *Can.* xii (Lamy, p. 72). ܦܪܣܐ: not in the *Thesaurus* of Payne Smith and the other Dictionaries. For the meaning "shelf", see: Thomas Audo, *Dictionnaire de la langue chaldéenne*, Mosul, 1897, vol. ii, s.v.

The point is: not to place it on the ground of the Temple (ad Q. 44); for in Q. 25 it is ordered to place it beyond the threshold of the sanctuary, if it is impossible to give it into the hands of a priest, as this ground shared in the consecration of the altar. Cf. also Q. 23 where a prohibition concerning the paten is given. The "ground" always plays a desecrating part, see also Q. 56 and 61. The same regulation was made concerning the water of Baptism (in two MSS $J^1$ and $J^2$): "und es sei Vorsicht, dass man nicht Taufwasser auf die Erde fallen lasse" (G. Diettrich, *Tauflit.*, S. 79–80. Prof. Drews (quoted by F. Loofs, in: *P.R.E.* [3], xxiii, S. 3) supposed with reference to Tertullian, *De Corona* 3, in: *M.S.L.* 2, col. 98–99: "we feel pained should any wine or bread, even though our own, be cast upon the ground", that this anxiety arose from fear of the demons who were thought to have their home especially in the earth. This opinion is right, I think. We know of the great importance of the "chtonic" gods in the ancient religions, and it is a matter of course that these gods had become demons for the Christians. We may refer to Hippolytus, *Canon* 29: "Der welcher die Mysterien austeilt, und die welche sie empfangen, sollen scharf aufpassen, dass nichts auf die Erde falle, damit sich nicht ein böser Geist dessen bemächtige" (Riedel, S. 219), cf. the Latin text of the Churchorder of Hipp. (quoted ad Q. 16) and: Horner, *Statutes of the Apostles*, p. 181. The demons were specially connected with the earth; and they could not enter the altar-place because it was consecrated and exorcised.

Q. 41. This fact does not happen in the communion as in the cases that are generally quoted to show the care taken with regard to the Eucharist (Bingham, xv 5, 6), but it is a matter of the priest as in Q. 13 which says what should be done with the place and Q. 15 about the wine. Here the same rule holds good: the holy altar is not desecrated by the holy bread. But since the mistake of dropping has been made, the G. cannot be given in the ordinary way. About the "paten which is on the altar", see ad Q. 19 and: *L.E.W.*, p. 267–268 rubrics. This Q. is the one that is quoted in ii 5 when it is said "I asked you before about the Gemurtha which falls from the paten of the sacraments on the ground: is it allowed that it returns to the paten?, and you answered: No" (a wording somewhat different from our Q., but with the same meaning); and it becomes certain when it follows, though the connection is somewhat loose: "Now I want to ask you again: If the sacristan offers the paten on the altar and the Bukhra falls on the altar-vestments, is he allowed to return it to the paten or not? *Answer:* If he returns it to the paten, he does it rightfully, as in the case when we return a Gemurtha when it has fallen from the paten on the altar." Since the subsequent Q.Q. offer a good parallel to others of our treatise we may give them here in translation: *Question:* And if the Bukhra falls on the ground? *Answer:* He may in no wise return it to the altar. *Question:* What must be done if it comes on the altar? *Answer:* They (the priests) must set it apart, and take it outside the altarplace after the Ordering. *Question:* What if the priest lifts up the veil (over chalice and paten) to consecrate (*L.E.W.*, p. 282) and a Bukhra falls to the ground? *Answer:* He must deal with it in the same way. *Question:* If it happens after the first, second and third signing that a Bukhra falls, how must he deal with it? *Answer:* The priest must return it and take it into his left hand and make it partake of all the signings which he makes, and distribute it to the believers joining with it another portion" (cf. ii 11).

Q. 42. *Canon* xi impresses on the priests to take care that no host mixed with the holy leaven of the Eucharistic bread (cf. ad Q. 52) should be given to a pagan, magian or priest of any other religion (ܕܢܘܟܪܝܐ may be used for Jews and Mohammedans; while it is also a usual word for the members of Christian sects; all this is comprised in it. That the magians or priests of the Persian religion are specially mentioned must be explained from the Persian origin of the Canons; in many places in the *Book of the Governors* and the *Acts of the Persian Martyrs* it may be seen that they still exercised a considerable influence) cf. ad Q. 29 and Copt.: Hippolytus, *Can.* 28 (Riedel S. 218): "Die Kleriker sollen achtgeben und keinen an den heiligen Mysterien kommunizieren lassen als allein die Gläubigen"; and: Basilius, *Can.* 98 (Riedel, S. 276).

It is well known that the Mass was divided into the "Missa Catechumenorum" and the "Missa Fidelium", and that after the reading of the Scriptures and Prayers the deacon shouted that those who had not been baptised, those who had not received the Sign of Life, those who would not communicate should depart (*L.E.W.*, p. 267; we take the Nestorian form; but in a slightly different wording it is found in all the liturgies; cf. also *L.O.O.*, p. 164–169; Hanssens iii, p. 265–272). We confine ourselves to the Nestorian material. In the time of Narsai this usage seemed to be still in practice (*Hom.* xvii, tr. Connolly, p. 2–3). Abraham Bar Lipheh gives a very queer explanation; according to him it meant the entering of the souls into Paradise. It is impossible however to decide whether this meant a real expulsion or not (*Expos.* ii, p. 160–161). In the time of the *Expos.* it had already become obsolete; the older meaning was known; but had been replaced by another (ii, p. 30–33). Timothy ii connects it with the congregation itself (Ming. Syr. 13, fol. 121a). It seems as though this institute had lost its meaning as it happened in the other Eastern churches (cf. e.g. Moses bar Cepha, in: R. H. Connolly-H. W. Codrington, *Two Com-*

*mentaries*, p. 31: "at one time", the whole explanation is in the past tense. Practically it was out of use.) Pagans assisted at the whole service. This appears e.g. from the History told by Bar Hebraeus (*Chron. Eccl.* iii, col. 239–241) that a Mohammedan Vizier asked the Catholicos Abraham (p. 85) how the communion was distributed, and the answer was that the Mohammedans knew it very well as they had often seen it. John Bar Abgare strictly forbade Christian people to send their children under the guidance of a pagan to receive the communion as the holy Mysteries would be an object of mockery and derision for those infidels.This evidence shows sufficiently that pagans assisted at the service. Naturally the priests could not always distinguish a pagan from a christian (unless they had different dresses, p. 88).–The similar case of a heretic coming to communion is not found in our QQ., but was dealt with by Timotheus Alex., Q. 20 (2nd series), in: Pitra, *Monumenta*, i, p. 642: The answer is: *οὐκ ἔξεστιν εἰ μὴ ἄρα τις τῶν ἐν πολυοχλούσῃ ἐκκλησίᾳ λάθοι προσιών, τότε γὰρ ἀνεύθυνος ἔστω διὰ τὸν ὄχλον καὶ τὴν ἄγνοιαν ὁ ἐπιδιδούς*. At one time it was usual that a foreigner before being admitted to the communion had to show a commendatory letter of his Bishop (*D.C.A.*, s.v.; *D.A.C.L.*, s.v. *Litterae Commendatitiae et Formatae*, t. ix, col. 1571–1576); but there was a great distance between Canonlaw and practice!–The fact that the pagan had communicated, had, of course, polluted the whole Gemurtha (since a pagan stood under the influence of demons). The care for the holiness of the Sacrament went so far as to avoid speaking to a pagan after the Communion, although this intercourse could not really affect the Sacrament, and therefore if it was necessary one could talk with a pagan (Isho'Barnun, *ad Macarium*, Q. 26).

Q. 43. "Ordering" cf. ad Q. 18. It can be gathered from several other QQ. too that no communicants were present during the service; see ii 13 in which is told how the priest had to act in such a case when he had another occupation [1] (the *Solution* is: "From sheer necessity he must throw the particle of the Euch. Bread into one of the unconsecrated chalices and pour water on it and keep it till the Ordering and mix it with the rest of the chalice and take it to the deacon's house after the Ordering"; and ii 11: "after a Gemurtha had fallen that had to be given to one of the people (Q. 41) it lasted some time before there appeared somebody (V. adds: to receive the Qudasha) to give it together with another Gemurtha which had been joined to the former, and nobody was present, and the sacristan wants to order etc." It shows that the priests waited some time to see whether a communicant should appear. Cf. John Bar Abgare, *Quaestio Eccl.* xiii: "Accidit duos sacerdotes nullo alio praesente solos ad altare adesse: quare alter alteri porrigit communionem. Contigit post advenire fidelium quempiam, et communionem expetere. Quaeritur, liceat necne sacerdoti communionem petenti porrigere ex ea, quam manu tenet hostia? Respondetur, hoc minime licere: nam quod pro Sacerdote offertur, ejus oblatio est, nec ei fast est quidpiam ex eo alteri cedere, nec duorum Sacerdotum praedictorum cuivis licet communionem ex disco et calice alteri porrigere, deinde abire et relinquere, ut ex eodem percipiat communionem quisquam pro suo

(1) I do not know what is meant by "occupation". I did not find that the priests in this time had all sorts of business as in the days of the *Canons* of Athanasius, 49–50, ed. Riedel-Crum, p. 36 and passim. – Most of the priests were monks.

arbitratu", etc.). The Priests communicated at the Ablutions (cf. ad Q. 18). Our Q. makes it, nevertheless, possible. "Crumbs" and their treatment cf. ad Q. 17. This applied to the bread. Communion with the chalice only is never found. The opposite, however, occurs sometimes in urgent cases (cf. ad Q. 51 and: Lamy, p. 181) for the sick.

Q. 44–45. In Mesopotamia the chance of floods in the rainy season must be considered or the rising of Tigris and Zab in the months from February to April when the snow on the Armenian mountains is melting. This causes a rising of the water-mark of several feet. "Floods on the Tigris are often accompanied by violent south-eastwinds which literally blow craft up the river or into the banks" says Mr. Budge (*B.G.* ii, p. 553 n. 1–554). Several times large floods are recorded in history. In connection with our Q. it is worth while to give the following quotation of the time of 'Abdisho' (Gismondi i, p. 91–92): "Anno autem 367, Tigris fluvius adeo enormiter excrevit ut obrui bagdadenses periclitati sint, ni agger stetisset quem tempore alluvionis plagae orientalis Mu'izz ad-Daula excitaverat". These floods occur so often that we cannot identify this one with that mentioned in our Q., apart from the fact that this speaks of Bagdad and not of the place where our author was probably teaching p. 83. It is clear that "altar" means here the whole place round about the altar-table, the Sanctuarium. For the water enters into it several feet. The difference turns here again about consecrated and unconsecrated places cf. ad Q. 27, 40. Several steps always lead from the Temple (= nave, *L.E.W.*, p. 583) to the altar. It appears that the "deacon's house" was not on the same level as the altar, a detail that is not seen in the sketch of Dom. Connolly, *Expos.* i, p. 196. The rubric T. p. 119 does not mention this case. "Signing" seems to imply that a formulary without oil had to be used.

Q. 46–47. About mixing the chalice cf. ad Q. 72 sqq. There and in Q. 10 it is clearly stated that the chalice should never be given with water only, as was the practice of some sectarians, probably from ascetical reasons (cf. Hanssens ii, p. 223–224). But it might happen that wine was scarce (Q. 48) or failed altogether. Mesopotamia and the mountain districts did not produce much wine (especially since the Government was Mohammedan). From Q. 47 it appears that it was important that the mixture had the ܚܝܠܐ = strength and colour of wine. As to the latter point Hanssens ii, p. 230–231 gives some information, but that is of little interest. The point of the colour: red or white, was left undecided. Probably it was red, the blood (dᵉma) of Christ. (Cyprian, *Epist.* 63, 7, ed. Hartel, ii, p. 705–706, and: Chrysostom, *Hom.* 82 *in Matt.* xxvi, in: *M.S.G.*, 58, col. 738). The former quality might be defined by "taste". This word is used by James Edess., *Can.* 32 (Kayser, S. 22) and Isho'Barnun, *ad Macarium* Q. 25 in connection with the sacraments but with a different meaning, viz. "das in den Sakramenten Wirksame". There it points to the consecrated elements and must be identified with the effect of the Descent of the Spirit on them. This possibility is out of the question here and with regard to what will be said ad Q. 48 we must offer an other translation as: "essence, nature". Though in that case ܟܝܢܐ would be expected.

This scarcity or lack of wine is not rebuked, as it was no fault of the sacristan.

Why not? We should certainly expect a remark about it. The reason lies, I think, in: *Can.* xxv: "It seemed good to the Holy Spirit to order that no one who is in charge of the service of the altar may offer without necessity marred wine in which is a defect, on the holy altar when good wine is left; nor mix marred wine for the 'Chalice of the Blood of our Lord';" the trespasser profanes the divine sacraments. Wine soon gets spoilt in the eastern climate; once spoilt it is forbidden to offer it. But it is rather difficult to notice it beforehand. Therefore the sacristan is not rebuked. For that reason, too, it was impossible to soak the raisins for one or two days, as would be necessary to get the result which was required (47). These raisins were pure at any rate. "Purify" means of course: pare off the skin and remove the stones.

The same view is found in the Maronitic *Nomocanon*, quoted by Mgr. Rahmani (*L.O.O.*, p. 71; following a MS. in the Vatican Lib.; it is said to be "traduit l'an 1069 de notre ère du syriaque en arabe par le métropolite David", p. 722): "Le vin doit être l'extrait du raisin, fruit de la vigne selon la parole de notre Seigneur dans le s. évangile. Il sera de la meilleure qualité possible, ni aigre ni d'un goût désagréable. Les autres extraits de dattes, de miel, de bananes etc. . . . sont sévèrement interdits. Cependant l'usage du vin tiré du raisin sec est autorisé par quelques pères là où le jus de raisins frais fait défaut." The prohibition could not be traced among the Nest.; the view of our Q. is mentioned here as allowed by some fathers (ch. vi. iii). The whole Canon fits in very well with the spirit of our QQ. It is possible that its origin was the same as that of our treatise, this is the more probable as the Maronites have more points of the liturgy in common with the Nest. (p. 54) and the date suits very well. Yet origin and connections of the Maronites are so uncertain that it is better to leave this question to someone who will in future investigate the whole problem of this sect (cf. E. Roediger–K. Kessler, *Maroniten*, in: *P.R.E.*³, xii, S. 355–364, and: P. Dib, *D.Th.C.*, s.v. *Maronite* (*Eglise*), t. x, col. 1–142).

As to the Coptic Church it was told by Renaudot how an Egyptian prefect wanted to tease the Christians and prevented them from getting any wine, and how they used palm-wine from sheer necessity. He also cites from the *Quaestiones Ecclesiasticae* of Michael of Melicha the following decision: "Licetne Eucharistiam offerre ex picato aut resinato vino, vel eo quod maceratione exprimitur? *R.:* Picatum quidem adhiberi potest, quia medicamento quodam e genere picis praeparatur, in eoque non est aqua, verum odor tantum et fumosum aliquid; sed quod maceratione exprimitur, cum in eo aqua sit, illud omnino usurpare non licet ad Liturgiam celebrandam." The same Bishop decided quite in agreement with the Nestorian Canon that it was strictly forbidden to offer sour wine because that had lost the taste, name and use of wine and had changed its nature. The other Coptic Canons (also found in: Hanssens ii, p. 219–221; who tells exactly the same as Renaudot) agree closely with it. From the Jacobites he reproduced a decision of Dionysius Bar Salibi (not found in the Syriac *Nomocanon*) which differs a little from the foregoing because it allows to use "uvarum succus" in urgent cases, if it had not been in touch with fire or cooked food. The Etiopians, too, employed raisins (*L.O.C.*, i, p. 176–177; ii, p. 67). This is the same as found in Nest. We see that the Maronitic view is practically the same as that of the Nest. while the Jacob. and Copt. though similar in many respects, vary as to the decisions in emergencies.

Q. 48. About the proportion of wine and water in normal and abnormal cases viz. scarcity of wine (the opposite case is not spoken of). The *Canon* quoted is: xxiv (but Assemani did not illustrate this Can. by our Q.): "... the mixture of the chalice should be made of equal parts of wine and water. For it is said that blood and water came from the side of our Saviour (Joh. xix 35, this text is always referred to in this connection from the time of the commentaries of Augustin and Chrysostom.); and in the same way must the mixture of the chalice consist of equal parts of wine and water; if it is necessary owing to lack of wine, it is allowed to use one part of wine and two of water; and if there is not even enough for that, one part of wine and three of water. But less than three is not allowed under any circumstance..." In spite of this last clause our Q. allows even more water and less wine.

Nothing is found about it in the ancient church. As far as I know, the Jacobite John Tell. was the first to give a regulation similar to the first part of the Nestorian one: "et in calice dimiduum vini, et dimiduum aqua misceatur" (this place known from Bar Hebraeus, *Nomocanon*, iv 1 appears to be borrowed from John's *Admonitions to the deacon*, quoted in: *L O.O.*, p. 71; Mgr. Rahmani, *l.c.*, informs us that the Jacob. rubrics have the same rule). The Coptic Church prescribed (*Can.* 99 of Basilius) not to pour in too much water, no more than a third part; "sind viele Geräte(?) am Orte der Zubereitung, so genügt ein Zehntel." Never should the wine be taken unmixed (1 John v 6; John xix 34–35); neglect is punished by lifelong deposing off the office (Riedel, S. 277). This is the opposite of the foregoing rules; small quantity of water and diminishing of it in relation to the number of the chalices. Practically the same is found in other places. For the rest of the material cf. Hanssens ii, p. 242–250.

It is clear that there did not exist any agreement except in the fact that the chalice should be mixed. The proportion depended on local circumstances. As to the Syrians we may be sure that they kept in view this rule that not: "vini proprius sapor mutetur in saporem aquae" (rubric of the Russian Missal, quoted by Hanssens ii, p. 243, tr. appendix, p. 78). This (probably late) Canon expresses very well the thoughts of the Syriac Christians too (what has been said before about the "nature" of the wine and what has been quoted ad Q. 70 offers a very instructive parallel).

Q. 49. "Admonitions" = *Canon* xx where our Q. is quoted by Assemani. This Canon to which we have referred already ad Q. 18 (compare the commentary of that Q. to understand the present Q.) is derived from Isho'Barnun, *ad Macarium* Q. 35 and reads as follows: "... he who orders may not take more than four Gemurtas or parts which form a complete Bukhra. If a very urgent case arises, they may take five parts which is however illegal and abnormal. But if much is left, it is by no means possible to order it. Whosoever dares to trespass, the justice of the Lord shall punish him ..." (In the Coptic Church the following rule is given by the *Statutes of the Apostles*, ed. Horner, p. 205, 280–281, 349: "Concerning that which is left of the Oblations. The Eulogia which is left of the Mystery besides that which they offered, the deacons shall distribute among the priests, with the knowledge of the bishop or presbyter. Four parts shall be given to the bishop, and three shall be given to the presbyter, and to the deacon two parts, and to the others, to the subdeacon and to the reader and to the singers and to the deaconesses, one part", according to the Ethiopic text; the others have slight variations in wording, but not in facts). Here arose a collision of the law to leave nothing (ad Q. 16) and the real situation. The communicants had already gone home, and there was the danger of the perishing of the Body of the Lord. This was the decisive point. "Gazza" ad Q. 16. The condition of our sources does not allow us to say anything about the church-going among the Nestorians. Of course it has always been a rule that all the members of the church should communicate every time. But that was an ideal. Here it appears that the number was rather fluctuating and could not be ascertained beforehand (an other variation allowed by the differences in the number of communicants viz. in cases the Euch. Bread is short, is found in the direction of Bar Hebraeus, *Nomocanon*, iv 5.) This variety seems therefore to be a case of emergency.

Q. 50. This is the well-known prohibition of reserving Paghra till the next day (see ad Q. 16). ܦܨܚܐ = Passover is according to: *E.S.D.O.*, p. 297, s.v. Piṣkha; cf. *Diction.* s.v., a specially Nestorian name for Maundy Thursday. As a matter of fact I have not found it elsewhere. It is uncertain when this name arose. The *Expos.* states that on this day the Mysteries were held in the Evening (instead of at the 3rd hour) because this was the time of the true Mysteries (ii, p. 6); it formed the end of the Fast (i, p. 51–52). The *Quaestiones* of George of Arbela use also this expression (cf. ad Q. 51). The *Formulary of the Renewal of the Holy Leaven* that took place on this day (cf. Ex. xii 15; 1 Cor. v 7!), called this day ܚܡܫܒܫܒܐ ܕܦܨܚܐ = Feria quinta of the Passover. It is probable that the name was an abbreviation by omitting the first word (cf. "Hosanna" = Ṣunday of Hos. = Palmsunday). The expression is used in its technical sence by Thomas Marg. in the mouth of somebody who lived some generations before (*B.G.* ii, p. 547–548): a monk asked a certain Narses how the Quaestiones in the Paradise of Palladius had been preserved. N. answered: "Now on the holy days of the Passover, and the Passion, and the Resurrection when they (the monks) were going forth from the restraint of fasting between one service and the other," the answers were given by the Fathers to novices and written down by secretaries. This story may be true or not for the time of Palladius, at any rate it shows that the practice of the name existed already long before Thomas; the three days are the same as those mentioned by George, and for the end of the Fast see the *Expos.* i, p. 52. This reference is a "terminus ante quem". It had probably been instituted by Isho'yabh iii. It was strictly forbidden to consecrate on Good Friday according to the rubric at the end of the formulary of the *Consecration of the altar with oil* ascribed to I. iii (T., p. 150). Nor was it practised in other churches, but there existed the "Missa praesanctificatorum" (cf. *D.C.A.*, s.v. *Good Friday*), but this was not done by the Nestorians. Reasons for it are not found anywhere, but on the analogy of the fact that Isho'Barnun prohibited the Eucharist on the Sabbath, a.o. because the liturgy supposes that Christ lived while the Sabbath was the day of his death and the liturgy represents His resurrection (*ad Isaac*, Q. 7; *ad Macarium* Q. 21; cf. *Expos.* ii, passim), we may say that this day of the

"Passion" (the Nest. terminus technicus together with ܥܪܘܒܬܐ) did not permit the Euch., since all attention was concentrated upon the sufferings and not upon the Victory of the Lord. (The name Pascha is also found in ii 35, but there it must have had another meaning following from the context and probably means there the week before Good Friday).

Q. 51. A very famous question in the Oriental Church. We begin with the Nest. material. The first is the famous *Question* of Isho'yabh i, that is always quoted since Assemani published it from V. fol. 93a to illustrate *Can.* xviii; together with it he cited our Q. It reads as follows: "If somebody is ill, or in an urgent case (agony?) (the priest) must take a particle, dip it into a chalice, place it in the cloth of the chalice and go to the sick man in the early morning while it is still dark, reciting in his heart psalms as long as he carries the Gemurta, and give it; not sitting down in the meantime. Then he must return to the church, going on with his service". The text of the *Arab. Nomocanon* (cf. p. 122) is slightly different; we remind readers that Assemani's quotation of Moses Cascar. to the same effect is a mistake. Riedel's text gives the following translation: "Man darf das Opfer (Qurbana) nicht aus dem Chore (Tempel) [1] herausbringen, ausser zu einem Kranken oder wo es sonst nötig ist bei einem, der aus irgend einem Gründe nicht zur Kirche kommen kann. Zu einem solchen soll er es in einem Gefässe bringen und es in seinem Gewande geben, mit Lichten und Weihrauch und Lesern vor sich, damit der Kranke oder in Not Geratene davon kommuniziere. Keiner aber von denen, welche es tragen und vor ihm dienen, soll sich auf die Erde setzen bis sie es zum Altare zurückgebracht haben." We see that the Arab. text has an expansion about the carrying of the lights etc. Isho'Barnun (*ad Mac.*, Q. 42) brings in a new element: "Is it allowed to take the Qudasha to a sick man or a prisoner? *Sol.*: If it is necessary and the sick man or the prisoner is a *true believer* (italics are mine), it may be done, as is prescribed in many places in the Law. But if that is not the case, it is forbidden." Some further restrictions are made in: *Canon* xviii though it moves on the same lines: it is not allowed "except to a prisoner or a sick man, dangerously ill, on the day of the Feast of the Resurrection of our Saviour (by command of the Head and Leader; this clause is missing in Ming. Syr. 121 and means: allowance of the Bishop), and at night". If it is done on other occasions, one despises the divine sacraments to please the people. This "dangerously ill" is not superfluous; Budge, *B.G.* ii, p. 402; 268 tells us that a very old monk who could only come once a week to communion did so, although it was the only thing he could do; another was carried by a fellow pick-a-back. Several parts from the foregoing quotations were put together by George of Arbela when he answered the question: "If a man is so ill that it is impossible to carry him to the church on Maundy Thursday, and he asks for a Qudasha, what must be done for him?" by saying: "There is no necessity on Maundy Thursday; but on Easterday the Canon orders that the Gemurta should be carried immersed in the chalice, secretly at night, and they must not stop their prayers, and leave off from incense and lights, and they must take the

(1) This is a clear proof of Syrian origin; Temple = nave, not: "Chor" or Sanctuary, as in Egypt, cf. Riedel-Crum, *Canons of Athanasius*, p. 42, n. 9 and *L.E.W.*, p. 583, 587.

Gemurta to the sick man". He is clearly linking up *Can.* xviii with that of I. i. In contravention of these rules our Q. prefers to take the certain for the uncertain and forbids it. He does not want to take the risk that the sacrament should be defiled being put in unclean places; it is not quite clear, but it is highly probable that this unclean is meant in the ritual sense (cf. Kayser, S. 104). *All the precautions apply to the church!* The use of incense and lights, mentioned on several occasions in the *Expos.*, are necessary requirements at the celebration of the Euch., see: Rubric in T., p. 150 (they are also used in the other churches, *D.C.A.*, s.v. *light, incense*). The author was very much afraid of desecration by taking it outside the church (cf. ii 22: "A Bukhra that was defiled because wine had been poured out, may under no circumstance be taken outside the church"). *This makes the Communion of the Sick* (*D.C.A.*, s.v.; *D.A.C.L.*, s.v. *Communion*, t. iii, col. 2437–2440, where the later development is neglected) *absolutely impossible.* What is meant by "to take it to the houses of the faithful", becomes clear from the parallels in the ancient and Jacobite church. I do not know what is the practice of the present time.

Lamy, p. 180–182 has collected and discussed several points; he did it in his way to show that the practice of these churches was practically the same as the practice of the R.C. church: "Communio infirmorum sub una" (but it should not be overlooked that the Bread had been dipped into the Chalice first, as it was hard to walk with a chalice of wine to the house of the sick)[1]. The oldest Canon is that of John Tell., *Can.* 8. James Edess., *Can.* 9, 10, 17 specified some points. It was summarized by Bar Hebraeus, *Nomocanon*, iv 4. It suffices to note the essential points. John Tell. is asked whether the holy Margaritha may be sent to a sick person in a ܟܥܟܐ as the authorities did not agree about this point. Lamy translated this with: "in canistro" and explained it by "vas ecclesiasticum in quo distribuantur eulogae seu panes benedicti". But it means "cake" (*Diction.*, cf. Kayser, S. 97). Therefore the answer is that in such a case either the Margaritha or the cake can be broken. It is preferable to send it in a piece of linen or paper that can be burned afterwards (probably because it was sanctified by its contents and could not be used in another way). In emergencies it may be sent by a layman and even by a woman. *Can.* 11 refers to this matter according to Kayser ("Noch im 6. Jahrhundert gestattet Johann von Tella [Entsch. 11 bei Lamy] dem Priester den Kelch und die Hostie mit blosser Hand, wenn Eile nötig, zu dem Kranken zu tragen, S. 93). This question was quite rightly not noted by Lamy among those about the communion of the sick; for that it refers to the sick, is an addition of Kayser himself. The text has: outside the ܒܝܬ ܩܘܕܫܐ = Sanctuary. It is simply a case about the ordinary communion. James Edess. joins John, adding that he has no objection to take a leaf of a cabbage. It would be proper that if it was taken home the priest should inquire beforehand what use would be made of it; this is however impossible in most cases. Therefore they must go themselves (they may go on horseback, *Canon* 17) or entrust it to faithful laymen or women. For its does not matter that the sick should take a part of the Eucharist for cure of body and soul. But it is strictly forbidden to preserve it in beds, walls

(1) The interpretation of Lamy is absolutely impossible, cf. *Arab. Synodicon*, fol. 80b: "It is not allowed to take the Euch. Br. without chalice, as the Bread is the Body (Paghra) and the chalice the Blood (D$^e$ma) and these two may not be separated".

or as charms for magical practices (*Can.* 9 and 12, cf. Kaysers Commentary). Besides that we observe that according to James, *Can.* 11 the Eucharist may be administered in various places outside the church. Renaudot, *L.O.C.*, i, p. 270 borrowed from Bar Hebraeus as these regulations have the same authority among the Copts. The differences that occur are of no importance; "nam etiam in ipsa qualiscumque sit, dissimilitudine, eadem animadvertitur religio circa Eucharistiam, ut quam decentissime tractetur, nullusque sit profanationi, neglegentiae, imo nec superstitioni locus". Before following this track we must see the Coptic texts. For this remark of Renaudot's may be conclusive from his point of view, the historian of the rite is interested in the differences. Basilius, *Can.* 98 (Riedel, S. 276) bases itself upon the precept in Exod. xii 46: the Paschal Lamb must be eaten at home and no bone may be taken outside. "Wir aber bringen das Mysterium überhaupt nicht aus der Kirche heraus um es jemand zu geben; nur bei Todesgefahr geben wir jemand von den Mysterien". The same argument is used in the book of Abul Barakat (Villecourt, *Observances*, p. 208); he does not say anything, however, about the danger of death. Athanasius, *Can.* 36, ed. Riedel-Crum, p. 32: "No priest shall carry forth the mysteries and go with them about the streets, except for a sick man, when the end and death's hour of need draws nigh. And when they carry the mysteries (without), they shall suffer none but the sick to partake. And they shall not do according to favour and give unto one beside the sick, but unto the sick alone." We see that they hold a position between the Nestorians and the Jacobites.

Concerning the practice of the Ancient church it is well known that in the first extra-canonical account of the Eucharist the deacons take the Sacrament to the absent faithful (Justinus Martyr, *Apol.* 65, 5, ed. Goodspeed, p. 74). Many other examples from the following centuries are known that tell us that the Eucharist was not eaten in the church, but taken home by the faithful and preserved there to be used later. This "taking home by the faithful" (cf. our Q.) was the origin of several practices inconsistent with the meaning of the Sacrament as was shown already by James Edess. (it is not necessary to repeat here these instances, cf. *D.C.A.*, s.v. *Reservation* and: Bingham, xv 4). This custom was abolished afterwards and instead of that we find the Reservation of the Sacrament in the church from which the sick and the dying men got their communion. We have observed already that this practice is not found in the Nestorian and Coptic church, see ad Q. 16. It could not be treated in the same way as it was done by the Jacobite, in agreement with the Ancient church. It was only possible to take a particle by means of a priest who had to do a service, to sick people and prisoners. This limitation of the older practices was even forbidden later and confined to the highest service of the whole year at Easter. It is interesting to see the development among the Nestorians to a stricter observance. Our Q. is the strictest of all.

Q. 52ff. The following category deals with questions concerning the Preparation of the elements. The data as far as they are known at present were printed together by Hanssens ii, p. 206–211 Usus praesens; p. 211–217 Historia; iii, p. 283. The former part consists mainly of Canons of the Eastern Uniates which display a great care for the preparation. But most of them are of a recent date and nothing is said about their origin. The Nestorians and Aethiopians are the only bodies of non-Uniates mentioned. As to the history this consists mainly of Nest. and Coptic Canons. Those of the churches outside Persia prescribe mostly that the bread must be baked on the same day on which it is offered and the material is merely traditional. In reviewing this collection of Hanssens we see that it was especially the Nestorian Church that had at an early date (10th century) a Canon-law of fairly detailed regulations. They have also a special: *Formulary of kneeding and preparing of the mixture*; (T. p. 105–110; translated together with 'Addai' in: *L.E.W.*, p. 247–252). It does not seem to occur in the ordinary copies of the liturgy. Renaudot and Badger did not mention it and in T. it seems to have been published from one MS. (cf. p. 112, it should be noticed that the Prothesis of Baptism is also found apart, see: Diettrich, *Tauflit.*, S. 55 [in *J.* [2], p. 110]). At what time did it come into being? An important though negative indication concerning this question is given by the *Expos.* ii, p. 36. It asks why Isho'yabh iii prescribed (*L.E.W.*, p. 268) the priests to order the Mysteries on the altar, but did not prescribe how it should be done nor how the bread should be baked and the wine mixed while he has given regulations on so many points of minor interest. The writer gives for it a mystical reason that does not furnish any point of liturgical importance. At any rate he sticks to what was dictated by Isho'yabh, and it does not become clear whether the rite of T. or something of that kind existed already. Anyhow it is sure that it was not ordered by Isho'yabh, but was of later date. The only regulation that is known before the Canones is *Canon* 26 of the Apostle Addai (Bar Hebraeus, *Nomocanon* iv 1) that is nothing but a form of *Canon* 27 of the Apostles (Syr. rec. in: Mai, *Scr. Vet. Nova Coll.* x, 2, p. 5) to the effect that the bread of the oblation must be brought upon the altar on the same day and not afterwards. The *Canons* of John Bar Abgare are full of this matter and because we do not know whether this had been fixed before, they exhibit the first rules. As Prof. Hanssens did not translate them in full we will give them here all together, (following the text of T.): iii "It seemed good to the Holy Spirit through the Fathers (to order) that the mixers of the Holy dough should be priests and deacons. It is not allowed that anybody else than a priest or a deacon should draw near it. If a layman or an unordained monk does so, it is under pain of the Word of our Lord" (cf. Armen. Sion i, *Can.* 12, 8th cent.(?) in: Hanssens ii, p. 211). iv . . . (we omit the introductory and final formulas) "nothing else should be used to prepare the dough, but pure, fine wheat flour and clear water and pressed olive-oil" (cf. also the rubric in: *L.E.W.*, p. 247, and that for the renewal of the Holy Leaven T., p. 105. It is remarkable that nothing is said about salt though it was used, cf. Q. 81. This mixture was the same as that of the Jacobite Syrians who had at some day a controversy with their Coptic co-religionists as the latter did not mix in it salt nor oil, cf. Hanssens ii, p. 167–169 and his reference to Renaudot. Does this agreement point to the time before the separation?) v (Arabic addition of Assemani). "Presbyter aut diaconus, qui oblationis panem praeparat sui instrumenti munditiem curet, habeatque, ne a laico contingatur. Habeat praeterea lumbos succinctos et calceamenta in pedibus suis, (cf. ad Q. 23, 39; this shows that the Elements had already a "proleptic" holiness), faciem ad orientem et amictu velatam. Ministret autem cum psalmis." viii "There may not be in the Qeṣatha two forms through two kinds of wheat flour, one white and one black. But there must be one dough each day consisting of one kind of wheat flour; for in Christ's Body (Paghra) there is not black and white" (lit.: "Cush and Ionian", a play of words on Paul's Gal. iii 28, Col. iii 11). ix "No priests nor deacons serving the altar shall make purshana's of wheat flour when the 'Malkha' is of black flour. Because it is not fit that they should make 'Malkha' a black man who is a slave and not a free man, while the Roman is white" (the pun of Can. viii must be kept in mind; Malkha = King is used her in a twofold sence, viz. for the priest's loaf and the Emperor of Byzance whose ordinary Syriac title it is, cf. *E.S.D.O.* p. 295, and p. 246–247. At any rate it is a highly remarkable quibble that one should not expect among the Nestorians since they were not adherents of the Byzantine church or subjected to that sovereign, on the contrary that might be considered to be high-treason). *Canon* xi tells us that the bread must be mixed with holy leaven and xiv forbids to bake bread for two days (cf. the texts in: Hanssens ii, p. 212–215; iii, p. 283: Athanasius, *Canon* 64 ad Q. 70; add to the *Canon* of John Tell., p. 212 a reference to: *L.O.O.*, p. 69). In his *Quaestio Eccl.* 28 the answer of John to the question whether a priest who is afraid of staying the night in the church may bake the Euch. bread at home and take it to the church, is that it is not necessary to take it into the church at night, but to bake it in the church. It may be done at home in emergencies, but in a special oven and only by priests and deacons (cf. Cyril. iii Ibn Laklak, in: Hanssens ii, p. 214 and: Villecourt, *Observances*, p. 247: "ne coquatur panis extra ecclesiam. Et si non est furnus in ecclesia neque ibi confici potest (panis), sacerdos vel aedituus eum coquat in domo sua. Neve sinat feminam aut aliam quemlibet praeter semet ipsum illum tangere"). Reviewing this evidence we see that they give regulations about officiants and their habits, place, time and materials that are necessary for a right baking. The questions that follow are also concerned with these matters; they suppose that the Canons were not used or were not known as they ought to be known. They show that as much weight was attached to them as to the liturgy itself. But it is not possible to state whether the formulary mentioned above was already existant. Nor can it be fixed whether these regulations were traditional (cf. p. 150–151). At any rate it seems to be a tradition that is peculiar to the Nestorian church. We do not hear anything of it in the Ancient church (*D.C.A.*, s.v. *Elements:* "The more minute directions for the preparation of the Eucharistic bread belong to a later age"–cf. R. M. Woolley, *The bread of the Eucharist*, Alcuin Club Tracts, 1913, a book which I was not able to consult). Originally it was taken from the oblata of the faithful (cf. the rule of Christodoulus of Alexandria, in: Hanssens ii, p. 217 that mentions still the ancient practice). But afterwards it was mainly done by ordained people. The evidence collected by Prof. Hanssens is mainly concerned with this[1] (the Aethiopians baked it in a special house near a church, the Bethlehem; cf. Hanssens ii, p. 210–211, and this seems also to be found elsewhere; at least Mgr. Rahmani states: *L.O.O.*, p. 69: "On en voit encore de nos jours dans quelque églises syriennes [probably Jacobite] des villages et dans les églises du vieux Caire"). One of the points of reproach to the Jacobites who do not seem to have followed this strict practice was: "ihre Abendmahls-

(1) Hanssens, *l.c.*, did not quote the interesting *Canon* 34 of Athanasius, ed. Riedel-Crum, p. 32 "It is not permitted unto a priest to go out on account of the bread of offering, and to stand at the oven; but as he serveth the people, so shall the subdeacon serve him".

elemente werden auf den Markt gekauft, von Weibern geknetet, von Ungläubigen gebacken" (Elias Nisib., *Beweis*, S. 99; the elements must be distinguished from the ingredients, for from Q. 55 it appears that also the Nestorians bought them in the market place; the prohibition that women should knead it is also found among the Copts, Hanssens, ii, p. 214, on the other hand it seems to have been a peculiarity of the Nestorians, cf. the invective of a Greek author against the Armenians, Hanssens ii, p. 216, for the Greeks themselves allowed it as well). To praise the Eucharist of the Nestorians themselves the same author says (*a.a.O.*, S. 102): "Niemand handhabt bei uns irgend etwas beim Abendmahl, als der Priester und der Diacon, dem das Lesen des Gebets, das Kneten des Brots und dessen Verfertigung zukommt." No directions about it besides those of Addai 28 and John Tell. are found in Bar Hebraeus, *Nomocanon;* so the way to make the Elements was free and therefore such events could happen.

We have reviewed the material because it explains why it is practically out of the question that we can find parallels to the subsequent questions. They seem to be impossible in any other church but the Nestorian, at least as far we can see from the present state of our knowledge. What is mentioned by Prof. Hanssens under the "Usus praesens" is of too late a date to give any historical explanation and insight. It is well known and does not need further comment that the Nestorians as well as the other Eastern Churches except the Armenians used the Euch. bread with leaven (cf. Hanssens ii, p. 125–141).

Q. 52. About the "Horae" mentioned here see ad Q. 105. It is not clear from the *Canons* etc. when the bread must be baked. It seemed that it was allowed to do so in the morning (*Quaest. Eccl.* 28, see p. 245). As to the leaven it is distinguished in: "Ordinary" and "Holy". These words are not used as in most cases where the former means something unconsecrated and the latter something consecrated (see e.g. for the altar Timothy ii, in: Ming. Syr. 13, fol. 49b; and at the end of this answer about the dough). In Q. 58 we also see that two kinds of leaven are distinguished: one to sign with and an other that must be kneaded into the dough (is this an invention of the time after the *Canons* as it is not mentioned there in iv [that seems to be the opinion of Hanssens ii, p. 171] or does this Canon only sum up the ingredients?). The "Holy Leaven", also called Malkha, is a terminus technicus[1], cf. T., p. 106: ܚܡܝܪܐ ܩܕܝܫܐ ܗܘܝܘ ܡܠܟܐ and see p. 105, 114, 118. The *Supplement to the Thesaurus Syr.*, s.v., says: "holy leaven", made "with the leaven (ܚܡܝܪܐ) kept from the last baking and with this holy leaven handed down from age to age and renewed yearly" (its second meaning is: priests Euch. loaf, p. 245). The Nestorians have a piece of leaven that is renewed once a year with ceremonies of the formulary (mentioned ad Q. 50) on Maundy Thursday. It is said in a prayer and told in the legend that it descended by succession from the Eucharistic bread that was given by the Lord to His disciples of the East and bequeathed to the Persians (prayer: *L.E.W.*, p. 248; the legend: *B.O.*, iii 2, p. ccxcv–ccc; Hanssens ii, p. 171–174; M. Jugie, *Theol. Dogmatica*, v, p. 305–308). The writers who mention this story

(1) Malkha = King, is a typical Nestorian term.

are all of later date, after the 12th century[1] and Badger pleaded (ii, p. 161) for a late date as he had not found this special leaven in any other ritual than in that Formulary that he assigns to the 12th or 13th century, without giving however any reasons for this dating. At any rate we see that this special leaven existed already in the 10th century (though it is possible that the legend did not yet exist). At the same time Elias Nisib. boasted that only the Nestorians had Holy leaven (*Beweis*, S. 102). On the other hand the Holy leaven of the Qeṣatha of *Canon* xi (see p. 245) does not refer to it; this appears from the apposition; it is the leaven called in our Q. "ordinary" viz. that of the Eucharistic bread of the foregoing mass that was left and mixed with the dough (to indicate the continuity of the several Eucharists), cf. *L.E.W.*, p. 247, n. a.

This Holy leaven blesses the dough in the Preparation by signing (*L.E.W.*, p. 248). It is impossible to conclude with any certainty from the data what was its origin and at what time it was first used. It must remain undecided if there is really a connection as Prof. Baumstark (*L.G.*, S. 310 Ak. 9) and after him Prof. Hanssens (ii, p. 170) supposed, between this leaven and the old-roman rite of the preservation of the sancta from one papal mass to the other. We think it possible to point to another parallel viz. that the Greeks have a holy Reserve of a piece of bread that is consecrated on Maundy Thursday (cf. ad Q. 16). It was known already in the time of James Edess. who rejected it (*Canon* 7 and cf. commentary of Kayser).

According to the Formulary the priest mixes while reciting Ps. 1–30 and he kneads it with the (ordinary) leaven; next he makes a mark in the middle and on the four sides and covers it carefully "until the time of preparing" (Mixing and baking are two separate acts). If this has been done he takes a piece of dough Meaphrana, then a piece for the leaven (of the next day); and from the middle the "royal Purshana". After that the priest recites Ps. 145: 1–7a and takes a piece Malkha = Holy Leaven and blesses the dough by signing it with the Malkha. After that he signs the Qesatha; the Malkha is returned to its place on the altar and the priest goes on with kneading and baking.

Those who are spoken of in the Q. did this accurately, but with one dough. It was forbidden in *Can.* xi "to give a Purshana of what has been mixed with the Holy Leaven of the Qeṣatha to a pagan or to a Magian (priest of the Persian religion) or a priest of any other religious body, not even to a christian boy". They trespassed against this rule by giving bread that had something holy in it, because it had been in contact with something that was destined for the Eucharist, while they themselves admitted that there was a danger of defiling (about fasting before Communion, cf. ad Q. 82; crumbs were always dealt with carefully, cf. ad Q. 78; that children could be somewhat negligent is also said in *Can.* vii; "pagans" see ad Q. 42). The "stamp" ܛܒܥܐ is not a terminus technicus as among the Jacobites for: Euch. Bread (*L.E.W.*, p. 71 l. 8, cf. p. 571).

Our teacher specifies some points for it was not clear from the formulary, at what time of the day the dough should be made; it was, as has been shown here, at night. "Crying of the cock" is also found among the indications of the

(1) The opinion of M. Jugie. *Theol. Dogm.*, v, p. 305, n. 3 is: "ad hanc traditionem jam alludit Joannes v bar Abgar" – but this rests upon a wrong interpretation of *Can.* xi (quoted in the text); and John does not say a word about nor alludes to the apocryphal story.

"Horae" in: 'Abdisho', *Nomocanon*, v 3 (Mai, p. 246), see also: *Can. Hipp.* 29 (Riedel, S. 219). From the Gospels it is well known as the Roman name for the third vigil, 12–3, see: *D.A.C.L.*, s.v., *Gallicinium*, t. vi, col. 593–596. Instead of this they did it in the evening, went to sleep instead of serving the whole night (this was prescribed by Isho'barnun, *ad Macarium*, Q. 67: "Is it lawful that a priest or deacon who did not serve in the night-service, should go to the apse to serve his order and to consecrate the Qudasha, or not? *Solution:* It is not lawful that he should do so. But he is allowed to receive the Qudasha"; and *Can.* xxvii repeats it and says that the priests must serve in the evening, night and early morning. Or is it a counterpart of the service of *Can.* xxii ad Q. 16, because this bread was already "holy", cf. p. 190.) Sufficient proof of their laziness! If they want to give something to children or pagans they may do so if they make dough in the evening and mark it; but at the aforesaid time they must prepare the real Euch. dough with the leaven; and bake them together.

Q. 53-55. Among the ingredients is mentioned olive-oil, p. 244. *Canon* xii ordered that pure olive-oil should be burnt in the lamps of the altar, and if "there is no olive-oil available, they must take pure oil for the lamp in its stead (in passing I note that Dionysius B. Salibi objects to the Armenians, that they use Sesam-oil for the chrism instead of the *Biblical* olive-oil, *W.S.* iv, p. 37–38, 57); olive-oil for the lamps: Ex. xxvii, 20. But the Qetsatha may not be prepared with other oil under any circumstance" (the oil of Anointing at Baptism should also be olive-oil, cf. Diettrich, *Tauflit.* S. 31, A. 1). The liberty granted here seems to have allowed the practice of distinguishing the oil of the lamps and the olive-oil. The latter was not only biblical, but also more refined and pure, while the former might be of somewhat inferior quality. Only at the second act when the leaven (of the previous day) had already been mixed, the mistake was observed. Everything had to be done again otherwise it would be wrong from the very beginning. About Purshana and double leaven cf. ad Q. 52. In Q. 54 a similar case with a similar solution; he notices it from the smell. Q. 55: the "purity" of the oil does not depend on the fact that there is dust in it, but that it is unmixed and is not what it is called. Of course this case stands upon the same line with bringing bad wine upon the altar, cf. ad Q. 46 (in this connection cf. Villecourt, *Observances*, p. 249, where it is prescribed that the sacristan must smell to see if the wine has not undergone an "alteration"). This Q. is very important for the meaning of injury.

Q. 56. The dough must be broken to pieces, see p. 247; about the falling on the ground see ad Q. 40. The signing mentioned here is the one that is made with the holy leaven. It was baked in any case. The writer does not say that it must be given as a Purshana, but this was probably the case. From this and the preceding questions it is clear that according to our author the priests should take care during the baking etc. that everything was done according to the prescripts. It seems that this was of the same importance as the later parts of the liturgy though they are generally neglected. A mistake here spoils everything.

Q. 57. It is not said what use was made of the water. Possibly it was used lest the bread should stick to the hands of the priests and so get a wrong shape. At any rate this was not ordained in one of the Canons and therefore it was wrong to use it, since it had nothing to do with the holy act. The olive-oil is not the oil used in the mixture, but that used for the special loaf of the priest (T., p. 105, l. 12; *L.E.W.*, p. 247, l. 20). That it must be made in or with the form of a cross is not definitely stated in the formulary (ܨܪ = to paint, to model, to adorn). The form of the bread is not given officially in the Canons. Prof. Brightman says that it is "a round leavened cake, $2 \times \frac{1}{2}$ in., stamped with a cross-crosslet and four small crosses" (*L.E.W.*, p. 571–572; the forms in the other churches, cf. also: *L.O.O.*, p. 68 and figure at the end of that book). The oven should be somewhere in or near the church, see the *Q. Eccl.* 28 of John B. Abgare, p. 245, as in the other churches, (it is not mentioned in the *Expos.*, therefore not indicated in Dom. Connolly's sketch i, p. 196). It is not indicated in any regulation where it should be. In any case, it stood in a place where every one could enter (see Q. 86). The formulary of baking provides a little consecration for every time the oven is used (*L.E.W.*, p. 248), so it should not be used for anything else (John b. Abgare: "nihil aliud in illum immissum fuerit"; after the baking it was desecrated. Brightman came to the conclusion from the use of Ps. xl 2, that it had the usual form of an eastern oven: "a clay-lined cavety in the floor" (*L.E.W.*, p. 584; cf. the various forms of ovens in the East in: P. Volz, *Biblische Altertümer* [2], Stuttgart, 1925, S. 317–318. See ad Q. 85).

Q. 58. Originally (up till the 5th cent.) the laymen were allowed to bring personally the offerings to the altar; after having done this they should retire to the nave (cf. *D.C.A.*, s.v. *Laity*). We observe a growing tendency of excluding laymen from the service. Among the Nestorians the preparation was, as we saw, exclusively the work of priests and deacons and no laymen should touch it, and certainly not after that it had been signed by the holy leaven and addressed as "King of Kings" (*L.E.W.*, p. 248). If only one piece was touched all the dough was desecrated. In such a case one should begin anew from the very beginning, with a part of leaven from another church (see Q. 84).

Q. 59–60. Water has the same desecrating effect as a layman (cf. also Q. 57). This Q. is referred to in ii 19: the author gives a "proof" that his answer in ii 17 (see ad Q. 15) is the right one, and says: "When they offer a chalice on the altar and its contents are shed over the altar do you not know that the altar is injured from that mixture? (= Q. 11) Again if a drop of water falls on one of the Perishta's in the basket before some particle of it has been consecrated, the whole of the Euch. Br. is desecrated," etc. The Nestorians are stricter in this respect than the Jacobites, cf. James Edess., ap. Bar Hebraeus, *Nomocanon*, iv 1: the Body of the Lord is not injured if touched upon with water, Among the Copts on the other hand it was ordered that after the sacristan had brought the bread on the altar, "il essuie (lave) chaque (pain d') offrande de face et de dos" (Villecourt, *Observances*, p. 249). It is strange that suddenly a biblical text is used as an argument (but only in M.!). It is: 1 Cor. xii 26a; the quotation is not quite according to the Peshita (*The N.T. in Syriac*, ed. British & Foreign Bible Society, London, 1905–1920), but the variations are practically of no importance.

Q. 61. "Falling", see ad Q. 41. It happens during the transfer of the bread to the altar. After the preceding QQ. it is clear that it should not be used. It is not said what should be done with it; probably used for distribution.

Q. 62–63. About the girdle see ad Q. 23 and the sandals ad Q. 39. Ad Q. 52 we quoted already the *Canon* of John b. Abgare (Arabic, Assemani v) to the effect that nobody could prepare the bread unless he had them on. In Q. 23 and 39 we saw that no priest could do the service of the altar without them. It appears here once more that this preparation was considered as a close parallel to the Eucharist proper. The same is true as regards of the theft of a particle. For the rubric (T., p. 119) ordered to consecrate the altar with oil: "if an altar-cloth is stolen, or a Bukhra or vessels". In that case the bread was not complete any longer as it ought to be; no more was the Q<sup>e</sup>tsatha (Q. 60), and unconsecrated things defile that what has been consecrated, viz. the altar.

Q. 64. The same point in a somewhat different wording is treated in Q. 81. I cannot guess why it is dealt with twice, because there is no reference in the latter Q. (there is no indication whatever that this book should have been compiled from two sources). About the services of Morning and Mysteries it will be dealt ad Q. 105 (mysteries do not mean here "Eucharist" or "Sacrament", but the service at the third hour on Sunday-morning). It is quite clear from both questions what should be done. It is in accordance with: *Canon* xiii: ". . . any one who is in charge of the service of the altar, after having brought the Q<sup>e</sup>tsatha to the altar, must before one Purshana of the Bukhra's or P<sup>e</sup>rishta's is distributed single out from what remains and carefully preserve it. If he is forced to consecrate at the end of the day, he must consecrate from what he has singled out, a token to supply his need." The bread was only baked once a day (the time see ad Q. 52). If it was distributed without these precautions it was possible that nothing of it should be left (the lowest limit was two, Q. 67). The different words for the bread see p. 194. Purshana's for children ad Q. 52.

Q. 65–67. These three QQ. were quoted by Assemani (*B.O.*, iii 1, p. 243, and after him by Hanssens ii, p. 199–200) ad *Canon* xvi. It says that: "there should not be consecrated on the altar fewer than three Bukhra's; if there are very few people only two: one with which the priest must make the sign of the cross and an other to be signed. But it is not allowed to consecrate one Bukhra". The rubric (T., p. 5, l. 13 = *L.E.W.*, p. 262) only said that the priest must place them "according to his discretion". Probably to give a more definite number in stead of this vague indication, the *Canon* was given by the Patriarch John. Yet our questions do not quite agree with it, though the difference is only very slight, since Q. 67 admits two only in cases when there are hardly any communicants. In other cases they keep the number three. Undoubtedly this number was suggested by the thought of the Trinity. This is shown by the parallels that are found in the other Eastern churches, printed together by Hanssens ii, p. 182–200. Very interesting and instructive for a comparative study of the liturgy is the similar practice adduced from the Russian church by Hanssens ii, p. 193, which also denotes that it is unlawful to celebrate the

Eucharist with one loaf only. For it is rather unconceivable that here the influence of the Nestorians was felt. Neither do they both go back to a regulation of the ancient church. For in reviewing the various Canons given by Hanssens, we see that there existed a difference as to the number of the loaves. Generally it was an odd number (among the Greeks 5 or 7; the Jacobites generally 3, cf. *L.O.O.*, p. 277, n. 1 [Basilius, *Can.* 99: "in case there are few communicants only one!"]). It is not out of place here to draw attention to the remark of the traditional canonist Bar Hebraeus, *Nomocanon*, iv 1, to the effect that there was no apostolic Canon about this matter. In mentioning the number 3 the Trinity is generally referred to. Why was this asked as the answer could be found in the Canons? Again we must answer by pointing to the lax disciple of the time. In the rubric: *L.E.W.*, p. 291 is mentioned the signing with half a Bukhra. In reference to what has been quoted before, this sounds somewhat strange, as it seems to suppose that there was only one Bukhra on the altar. I do not know how this contradiction should be solved unless by assuming once more that this rubric is of a later date.

Q. 68–69. Deal with the question that was left unanswered by *Can.* xvi. "Insult" see p. 192–193. The question must be seen in connection with the previous ones: Two is the minimum because of the signing. This cannot take place with one Bukhra; if it should be done with one it would be a deviation from the formulary. Then it speaks about the punishment of the priest (see also Q. 38). The way in which the priest should be corrected etc. is not often mentioned, nor is the kind of his punishment. The nature of his penance is dependent on the degree of the mistake, viz. whether it is of great importance or not, and whether it was done on purpose, and whether it is a recidivism. Isho'Barnun (*ad Isaac*, Q. 1) says that one should not leave the bread during the night upon the altar; those neglectful people who do so, must be punished by the ecclesiastical dignitary, but he must "make use of the usual long-animity of Christ, His prototype, and order that those who dare leave it, should stand in sackcloth and ashes while fasting and reciting prayers of penitence during as many days as the number of the days in which they have left it." The canons say in several places that one who trespasses against the Canon given "according to the word of the Lord" should be deprived of his office (xv, xx, adding: he is a stranger to the Holy Sacrament and is anathematised by the Holy Spirit; xxi, xxv which adds "and becomes a layman, because he has profaned the divine Sacrament). Here we find some very grave penalties (lay-communion is one of the most severe punishments; "they [the priests] were reduced to the condition of laymen, deprived of office, and forbidden to exercise their clerical functions"; it is not specially connected with the Eucharist, cf. *D.C.A.*, s.v.; about "anathema" cf. ad Q. 7; the same climax, first an admonition and after repeating the mistake a penalty by the bishop is found in: *Resolutio* xxvi of the *Letter to the Eastern Jacobites*, in: I. E. Rahmani, *Vetusta Documenta Liturgica*, p. 11–12 [text]). Very instructive is the case in ii 30–32 as it exhibits the various degrees. They speak about ordering by the priest alone without anybody else being present. The answer is given according to *Canon* xxii and the questioner Q. 30 goes on saying: "But if a priest by mistake thinks that it is entrusted to him as is the custom of the rulers, and received it for himself and takes the cup, in what respect is the altar injured? *Solution:* The altar must be signed, and the priest must be *rebuked* for his insolence, if it has happened *without his knowledge*. *Question:* But if he has done this *wilfully without any outward reason*, what must be done with the altar and in what respect must the priest be corrected? *Answer:* The altar must be consecrated with oil and the priest must be *suspended for two weeks*. If mercy is shown to him, he must stand in *sack-cloth and ashes* and *confess* his stupidity before (the eye of) everybody, lest he should do again something like this. *Question:* But if there is evidence against him that he has done it once or twice, what must be his punishment? *Answer:* He must be *dismissed from his rank for one year*, and after that he must stand in sackcloth and ashes. Next he must do the service of his rank, but the service of the altar shall never more be entrusted to him, because of his insolence against the Sacraments" (italics are mine). All these measures correspond exactly with the rules of the ancient church about the punishment of the church. The best summary of it will be found in: Bingham, xvii to which we may refer; for the Persian Church cf. J. Labourt, *Christianisme*, p. 340, 343–346. It seems as though the Eastern church did not go beyond the development of these rules of the 4th and 5th century (sackcloth and ashes are the ancient symbols of deep mourning known already in the O.T., cf. P. Volz, *Altertümer*, S. 325; for the Christian use see *D.C.A.* s.v. *Sackcloth*, and: F. Cabrol, *D.A.C.L.*, s.v. *Cendres*, t. ii, col. 3037–3040). The teaching of the different oriental churches about these points seems to have been the same, see e.g. J. Pargoire, *L'Eglise Byzantine*[3], Paris, 1923, p. 304–305: "les clercs fautifs, à qui leur repentir vaut d'être réintégrés dans leurs emplois, n'en méritent pas toujours pour cela d'être réadmis à l'autel"; John Tell., *Can.* 6 (Lamy, p. 66): if the mistake in mixing the wine (ad Q. 13) is made from negligence, "he must receive the canonical punishment" which is not defined; and Basilius, *Can.* 99 (Riedel, S. 277: "Wenn einer die Bestimmung betrügt und thut, was unerlaubt ist, so soll er seiner Würde für immer entkleidet und ihm niemals etwas überlassen werden, womit er seinen Scherz treibt.") This is not surprising since all these churches maintained the tradition of the ancient church.

Q. 70–71. The decision reproduces the precept of *Can.* vi: "... there may not be any defect in what is singled out from the Qesatha for the sacrament. It was not allowed under the old Convenant to offer anything which was cripple, blind, weak or in which a defect was found; howmuch more caution must be taken with regard to the divine sacraments." This is a reference to Deut. xv 21, cf. Lev. xxii 20, Deut. xvii 1. The same is found in: Athanasius, *Can.* 64, ed. Riedel-Crum, p. 42: "An offering that remaineth over from yesterday they shall not offer, neither that which hath been divided in pieces in any church, but bread warm, fresh and whole." Basilius, *Can.* 98 (Riedel, S. 275): The deacon must take care that the bread should not be burned or that a "Fehler daran ist, damit sie keine Sünde begehen". A somewhat different answer was given by the Coptic Bishop Michael in his: *Responsa Ecclesiastica* 31 (quoted in: *L.O.C.*, i, p. 177); *Q.*: "Panis Eucharisticus fissus est aut ruptus: potestne offeri ex eo? *R.*: Eligendus est melior et integer: tamen ob earum rerum defectum quae ad melius conducunt, non est abstinendum ab Eucharistia celebranda." This is in contra-distinction with the wine; for he says that if anything of this liquid is failing, it is not wine any more, while the nature of bread remains the same. In the Scriptures bread and wine have been prescribed, but nothing was said about their condition. The same judgment is given by other Coptic canonists, and among the Syriac Jacobites by Dionysius B. Salibi who allows a defect Euch. bread in urgent cases, as is stated in: *L.O.C.*, i, p. 177. The decisive point is thus the nature of the element. It is remarkable that we notice that the O.T. has influenced the Nestorian Canon. On the other hand the result was practically the same, for it becomes clear in Q. 71 that it was not a mistake such as would make the liturgy impossible. It is exclusively a matter that concerns the sacristan.

Q. 72–75. Something must be said here on the mixing of the chalice. Among the foregoing Q.Q. 10 and 46 sqq. gave an opportunity to say something about it. It goes without saying that Hanssens ii, p. 217–271 has collected most of the material that would be necessary for a comparative study. Apart from some obscure sects that are always mentioned in this connection (the Aquarians, cf. *D.C.A.*, s.v. *Elements*, i, p. 604–605; P. Battifol, *D.A.C.L.*, s.v. *Aquariens*, t. i, col. 2648–2654.) Dionysius B. Salibi says, *W.S.* iv, p. 30: "when he [John Chrysost.] noticed that the Manicheans, the dirty Messalians, and Severus the heretic were offering the Eucharistic sacrifice with water only etc."; in: *M.S.G.* 58, col. 740, Chrysostomus speaks of Marcion, Valentinus and Mani; about Severus cf. Eusebius, *Hist. Eccl.* iv, 29, 4–5, ed. Schwarz, i, S. 390, and: Epiphanius, *Haer.* 45, ed. Holl, ii, p. 199–202) the whole church always used in the chalice a mixture of wine and water[1]. The only important exception are the Armenians who poured in wine only. They were severely attacked for this practice by the Greeks at the Council of Trullo (692) and otherwise in controversial writings and by the Jacobites who had close relations with them (particulars in: Hanssens ii, p. 265–271; at p. 268–269, the "adversus Armenos" of Dionysius, *W.S.* iv, must be added). At the mixing (*L.E.W.*, p. 251–252) the priest took wine and water and poured it crosswise into the chalice reciting texts that had some connection with it, ending with John xix 34–35 which always forms the keystone. In ii 26–27 some more questions are put on this point: "When the sacristan mixes the chalice, what must he pour in first, water or wine? *Answer:* First they must pour in the wine and next the water, for about the water it is said: From His side came out wine and water (John xix 35)–*Question:* When they have consecrated the Euch. bread and wine and there is not enough mixture in the chalice, what must they do? *Solution:* They must mix another chalice, sign it with the consecrated one, place it on the altar and distribute it to the believers" (H. W. Codrington, in: *J.Th.St.*, 1904, p. 544–545, published a formulary of "the Signing upon the Chalice on a day of want, before it goes up to the alter" from 2 MSS., see ad Q. 16.–It is a clear proof that the communion was not given sub una; only in the communion it became apparent that the wine became deficient).

This series of questions is to a certain extent a complement to Q. 10. The situation is the same though the motive is different. There it was already stated that the altar becomes desecrated by it, as is the case here. There it was asked

(1) Athanasius, *Can.* 9, ed. Riedel-Crum, p. 21 referred to Prov. ix 5.

what was the effect on the Paghra. Here it is discussed how this matter can be solved. That the chalice is desecrated is obvious for it has been treated in the wrong way and is not fit for ordinary use. Signing is necessary. "As we have shown above" refers probably to Q. 15 (see *in loco*).

In Q. 74 it has got something of the consecration, consequently it must be distributed as an Eulogia. Consecration on the next day see p. 203, n. 12.

The elements are treated in the same way Q. 75; none ranks prior to the other.

Q. 76. The counterpart of what was quoted from ii 27 ad Q. 72. The case occurs while the number of the people present changed (Q. 49). "Anthem of the Mysteries" after the Offertory (*L.E.W.*, p. 268–269). The elements when lying upon the altar are covered with a veil. It was lifted up at the beginning of the Anaphora proper (*L.E.W.*, p. 282); almost immediately it was followed by the first blessing (*L.E.W.*, p. 283). For the signing see p. 192, n. 1.–Compare with this Q. the remark of Dionysius b. Salibi, *Expositio Liturgiae*, c. 6 (Labourt, *C.S.C.O.*, ii 92, p. 24–25: "Si vero adhuc expanditur anaphora (= veil), et necessarium est additamentum, [alios panes] offerre licet, modo sint ordine impares, ut diximus, et numero impari, non vero pari seu equali, nisi tamen sint duo . . . Quamdiu expanditur [super vasa] anaphora . . . hostiae convenienter adduntur; at postquam anaphora amota est, [panes] signatos addere non decet."

Q. 77. This is the analogy for the bread of Q. 15, 2, where a mistake concerning the chalice was dealt with. "Time of the Offertory," (*L.E.W.*, p. 267ff; "time of the Breaking" *L.E.W.*, p. 289. That chalice of Q. 15 could not be distributed; but this bread could. Otherwise the situation is the same.

Q. 78. Assemani referred to this and the next Q. without quoting them literally in his Comments upon: *Can.* x. This Canon reads as follows: ". . . the minister of the altar must clean and sweep the sacristy every day on which he has said the Qudasha. Before giving the Holy Mysteries he is obliged to sweep the whole sacristy and its walls once a week." So we find here two ways of cleaning. In our Q. the first one is spoken of, as in Q. 17b (the Jacobites allowed this to be done by a deaconess, James Edess., *Can.* xxiv. The second manner of sweeping e.g. in the *Arabic Nomocanon*, fol. 81a (cf. ad Q. 21). But this Canon does not say what must be done with the dust that was swept together. Therefore this question. For as appears from the text it was not the dust itself that caused the Q., but the crumbs in it. The same rule applied to these remnants of the Euch. bread as well as to the more voluminous quantities (cf. ad Q. 16). In breaking the bread some crumbs would naturally fall on the paten and on the altar itself. Those should be carefully collected into the chalice (Q. 17 and 43) and in this way be taken by the sacristan during the ablutions, (cf. ii 14 about crumbs that are found together as debris of a Bukhra in the altarplace). The same is found in ii 15 and 16: "I have seen a sacristan of a church who while he was cleaning the altar, found many crumbs underneath the altarvestments. He went to the priest of that church and asked him: What must I do with them? The priest answered: Gather them and throw them into the oven to be burnt. This act is altogether wrong I think. What is your opinion about it? *Answer:* Oh, this is a great insolence: to burn the 'Body' of our Lord with fire. This is not right." We observe that in any case it was allowed by some people who probably did not consider it to be the body of the Lord. We can illustrate it by an historical witness, though from another part of the church, viz. the well-known place from Hesychius of Jerusalem, *in Lev.* ii, in: *M.S.G.*, 93, col. 886d, also in: *L.E.W.*, p. 487 and elsewhere, although he dealt with everything that remained: "sed hoc quod reliquum est de carnibus et panibus in igne incendi praecepit (Lev. xiii 32, cf. also Ex. xii, 10 about the remains of the Paschal Lamb). Quod nunc videmus etiam sensibiliter in ecclesia fieri ignique tradi quaecumque remanere contigerit inconsumpta, non omnino ea quae una die vel duabus aut multis servata sunt; sicut enim apparet non hoc legislator praecepit sed quod reliquum est incendi jubet." This shows that such a practice based upon the O.T., existed, but it was severely condemned by our writer. He prescribes what should be done in 16: "He must gather them in one of the unconsecrated chalices and pour water on them and desecrate them. After receiving the sacraments, the sacristan must after the ablution of the chalice take them in the sacristy." This agrees perfectly with the precept of John Tell. to the deacon, commanding him to be on his guard that any crumb should remain on the altar or on the vessels after the service and to drink them together with the chalice (text in: *L.O.O.*, p. 707, n. 2-3).

In contrast with this our question is concerned with the crumbs that have fallen round the altar in the dust and can not be distinguished any more. Since it seems as though the Canonist was somewhat afraid of applying the same rules to this case which might have some bad influence upon the health of those who take them he indicates two ways of removing them viz. either throw them into running water or buy them in the uncultivated soil. Both these forms are also found together in ii 1 to remove mixture that has been defiled by insects (besides those mentioned before it offers the possibilities of throwing it into a fountain or sprinkling it on the walls of the church); and in ii 34 about the reservation of Paghra: it may be done according to *Can.* xxii "or they must bury it in uncultivated and untrodden ground and conceal it there, or it must be thrown into the Tigris viz. that it may lose its consecration and may be defiled by the water and the fishes may eat it." The last sentence reveils unmistakably what was the meaning of this act.-The same rules were applied to the water of Baptism, cf. G. Diettrich, *Taufliturgie*, S. 103: T., p. 75 orders that the water should be shed in a pure, untrodden place; MS. J.[2] adds: "or he (the priest) must give it to the faithful as a blessing or it must be thrown into a river".

Both manners are also found among the Jacobites[1]: John Tell. dictates that the water in which the holy vessels had been washed should be thrown into

(1) On the various ways of removing holy things, cf. Timotheus Alex., *Q.* 17 (2nd Series), in Pitra, *Monumenta*, i, p. 641: Ἐὰν συμβῇ τίμια δῶρα σφαλισθῆναι, καὶ μὴ δύνανται εἰς μετάληψιν ἀναλώσεσθαι, εἰ καίειν αὐτὰ δεῖ σὺν τῷ ἀρτοφορίῳ ἢ οὕτω λιτά, ἢ ῥίπτειν ἁπλῶς ἐν ποταμῷ ὕδατι, ἢ πῶς ἔτι χρηστέον αὐτοῖς; Α: πρῶτον μὲν προσήκει πολλὴν πρόνοιαν ποιεῖσθαι τοῦ μὴ ἐᾶν ἵνα σφαλισθῶσιν. Εἰ δὲ συμβῇ ἐξ ἀμελείας τοῦτο γενέσθαι, οὔτε καίεσθαι δεῖ, οὔτε μὴν ῥίπτεσθαι, ἀλλὰ μετὰ γλυκέος οἴνου σκευάζειν τὸ ποτήριον, καὶ ἀναλίσκειν αὐτά. — James Edess, *Can.* 32, ad Q. 12.

a deep hole in an honourable place, and the same must be done with the fragments of the holy vessels (Lamy, p. 64, *Can.* 3, cf. 2). This is slightly different, but James Edess. forbids to throw the dust of the sanctuary into a fountain, because one risks that animals shall drink from it; if no risk is run it is allowed to do so; but it should be buried in a pure place in a field (*Can.* xv). To explain this word "pure" Kayser, S. 101 refers to places such as Lev. xviii 28, Num. xix 9, Deut. xxi 23, Ez. xliii 7–9, viz. a place that is not polluted by idol-worship, cadavers etc. Among the Copts it was prescribed to throw it into a swollen river (Hippolytus, *Can.* 29, Riedel, S. 219, and: Basilius, *Can.* 96, Riedel, S. 272). This change probably depended on the geographical conditions. The Tigris is mentioned specially (in V. even alone) because it was the most important river in the Nestorian country, flowing along the place where our author was teaching (p. 83).

We are unable to enter into the interesting "religionsgeschichtliche" parallels that show that these points are not specially Christian. It suffices to state that the uncultivated soil was "virgin" and if it was trodden upon it was defiled cf. Kayser, S. 91, and: Deut. xxi 4. Running water is generally a purifying element; but here it serves to take away the "holiness" before it is touched by the unholy, p. 190 (cf. G. v. d. Leeuw, *Phaenomenologie der Religion*, Tübingen, 1933, S. 320ff.–*D.A.C.L.*, s.v. *Eau* and *Fleuve* does not contain anything of importance for our Q.).

Q. 79. "Prayer of the Incense": *L.E.W.*, p. 282. "Ark of the Lord" is not a usual name for the altar in the Nestorian church. Neither is it a common expression in other churches except the Aethiopian, though here they do not speak of Aron, but of Tabot. For the rest of the question cf. ad Q. 78. In the Coptic church the following was ordered: "s'il y on avait (viz. of the incense) de reste, qu'il soit brûlé entièrement et sa cendre conservée et jetée dans le fleuve" (Villecourt, *Observances*, p. 260). This "fleuve" is undoubtedly the Nile, as is conclusively shown by the parallels of the foregoing question, and not "la piscine, la θάλασσα" as it was explained by M. Villecourt (*l.l.*, n. 1), an equalization that is not clear without any further comment.

Q. 80. The Teshbuḥta or Hymn: "Oh our Lord Jesus,": *L.E.W.*, p. 299 n. a (is only said on Sundays) during the communion, instead of: "strengthen oh our Lord." It seems as though *Expos.* ii, p. 80 knows a practice that uses them together. It was followed by Thanksgivings and Dismissal. After that the Purshana's were distributed; therefore in this case this distribution was made in the wrong place, too soon. The deacons were allowed to distribute (of course not the Euch. bread!) as is also stated in the rubric: *L.E.W.*, p. 304. The "last Lord's Prayer" (cf. ad Q. 105 sqq.) is found: *L.E.W.*, p. 303. The sequence of events is not quite clear in the short rubrics of T.; a somewhat clearer picture is shown by the *Expos.* ii, p. 70–80, which gives an extensive explanation of all the facts that took place at communion. For our purpose it is sufficient to know that the deacons communicated at the altar (p. 71). About ܗܘܐ + another verb, denoting a modification, see: Nöldeke, *Syrische Grammatik*, S. 264. The fact of "kissing the altar and the priests" is not found elsewhere. *L.E.W.*, p. 302, states that "the priests are giving the kiss of peace to each other"; but *Expos.*

ii, p. 82 has a somewhat different remark, viz.: "Diaconus pacem secretò instituit; et qui in abside sunt pacem invicem secreto dant." Yet it is known that kissing is a common form of adoration which is not always laid down in the formularies (cf. Q. 24). In the answer several points should be distinguished. 1) The lamp in the middle of the altar is again the limit, cf. ad Q. 27. That the Purshana's may not pass this mark is clear since they are not consecrated nor destined to be so. Therefore the mistake was not only that they were given at the wrong moment, but also, and this is the main point, that they were taken to the wrong place. The inaccuracy of the reading of M. is shown e.g. by *L.E.W.*, p. 290 l. 2 where a Bukhra on the altar is mentioned. "After" opp. to "during"; it does not include that it took place before the Dismissal. The rubric *L.E.W.*, p. 304 says that: "The people kiss the cross in the priest's hands and the Eulogia which was baked along with the buchri, is distributed by one of the priests or deacons standing at the nave entrance of the baptistry" (this seems also to be meant in our answer. This is the ordinary course). 2) If this is not followed exactly, as in our Q., because the P. is given too soon, he must act as is said in the clause: "In case . . . go out"; consequently not making them pass the limit. (3) About the "singling out" of the Qeṣatha, this belongs to the preparation. It is possible that it was added because of the "Stichwort" ܦܪܫ. It may account for the origin of the word Purshana: the part that was separated for distribution. *Canon* xiii, quoted ad Q. 64, is followed in our Q. The Canons know the "lamp" (xxvi); therefore it is clear that ܐܣܩ is not: "to offer on the altar" but "to take into the altarplace." See also ad Q. 10.

Q. 81. This Q. agrees perfectly with Q. 64 (see *in loco*).

Q. 82–84. For the ingredients of the dough cf. ad Q. 53. Salt is prescribed in either of the Syriac churches as well as among the Greeks and Armenians (*D.C.A.*, s.v. *Salt*); but not by the Copts (*L.O.C.*, i, p. 174). What takes place does not need any comment. "Jewish" must be taken here metaphorically, as: "scandalous, impious." We can compare an exclamation of Chrysostomus that those who take the treasury of the souls of men and (at the same time) gave alms from their murders to the church, gave *Jewish, indeed diabolical alms* (*Hom.* 85 *in Mt.*, in: *M.S.G.*, 58, col. 761). For I cannot guess what the author is hinting at if it should be taken literally. Leaven, see ad Q. 52; this was left from the previous day and was holy, because it had been consecrated then. The Eucharist must be received fasting; this is a Canon definitely adopted in the church since the 4th cent. and strongly maintained since that date (*D.C.A.*, s.v. *Communion*, p. 417–418; *D.A.C.L.*, s.v. *Jeûnes*, t. vii, col. 2486; for the Syriac church see: P. de Lagarde, *Reliquiae juris ecclesiastici antiquissimae, syriace*, Lipsiae, 1856, p. 18). *L.O.C.*, i, p. 266–267 collected the material from the Jacobites, (cf. John Tell., *Can*, 17, Lamy p. 74; Bar Hebraeus, *Nomocanon*, iv 2 and: Lamy, p. 182–184). Nevertheless it was one of the objections of Elias Nisib., against them that they communicated without fasting (*Beweis*, S. 99; he probably generalizes from one or two instances. The same objection could be made against the Nest. according to our Q.Q. Elias is a polemist!) Cf. ad Q. 27. In Q. 52 we saw that the children were allowed to receive the Eulogia only a.o. because they use it sometimes after other food.[1] In the main the Jac. and Nest. laws agreed on this point, though they varied in particulars. E.g. John Tell., *Can.* 9 (Lamy, p. 70) answered a question: "whether anybody who had drunk anything before sunrise was allowed to communicate on that day?" with: that he might do so, if he only fasted the rest of the day without having any doubt[2]. The Nestorians did not allow it to a priest:[3] cf. ii 2: "If a deacon or a monk or a priest drinks water, while it is still dark and makes a mistake and tastes something and by mistake has taken a draught and comes to receive the oblation; and while the oblation is still in his hands, he remembers that he is not fasting, what must he do with the Gemurta?" The answer does not matter here, but we must notice that the Gemurta is called "an injured Paghra" (ii 3). Has saliva a specially polluting quality that it is mentioned here? cf. spitting as an expression of strong aversion. It is not remarkable after what we found at the beginning of our treatise that the altar is defiled. Since the leaven is desecrated, another must be fetched from another church as in Q. 58. It is well known that the moral qualities of the priests have no influence on the efficacy of the sacrament (for the Nestorians it is clearly expressed in: Narsai, *Hom.* xvii, Connolly, p. 21–22: "The Mysteries of the Church are not celebrated without a priest, for the Holy Spirit has not permitted (any other) to celebrate them . . . These things the Holy Spirit celebrates by the hands of the priest, even though he be altogether in sins and offences"; cf. Badger ii, p. 163–164 with an interesting quotation which is, unfortunately, of uncertain date). But on the other hand it was inculcated upon the priests that their high office implied great obligations to preserve themselves pure, and priests who failed to do so were suspended (some instances from a great array: Isho'yabh i, *Canon* v, in: O. Braun, *Synhados*, S. 206–208; John B. Abgare, *Canon* iv, ap. 'Abdisho', *Nomocanon*, vi 6, Mai, p. 278; Kayser, S. 158 and N.). But this is not intended here. Our writer only wants to be sure that the Leaven that is brought, is absolutely pure, that no mistakes have been made in preparing it, that the priest has acted as he should do. ܡܟܫܪܘܬܐ in itself is no moral faculty; it denotes the qualities of its possessor in one field or another. All the qualifications, as in ii 23: "A deacon of the best reputation of our country" are exclusively concerned with the knowledge of liturgical usages (opposite to those priests mentioned in the Introduction). The first sacristan was unreliable and had to be deposed (for the penalty cf. ad Q. 69).

Q. 85. Something about the oven is said ad Q. 57. The bread was baked by heating the surrounding stones. The sacristan raises the heat by adding

(1) There is one exception allowed, viz. immediately after their baptism, according to Johannes bar Abgare, *Quaest. Eccl.* xix (communion was attached to baptism, G. Diettrich, *Tauflit.*, S. 92, and: *Expos.* ii, p. 105).–Priests serving the altar had to fast till nine o' clock, Joh. B. Abgare, *Can.* 5, ap 'Abdisho', *Nomocanon*, vi 6, Mai, p. 278 (times of the "Nupteries").
(2) Timotheus Alex., Q. 16 (1st series), in: Pitra, *Monumenta*, i, p. 634: Ἐὰν νηστεύων τις ἐπὶ τῷ κοινωνῆσαι νιπτόμενος τὸ στόμα ἢ ἐν τῷ βαλανείῳ κατέπιεν ὕδωρ μὴ θέλων, εἰ ὀφείλει κοινωνῆσαι; — Α: ναί, ἐπεὶ εὑρὼν ὁ Σατανᾶς ἀφορμὴν τοῦ κωλύειν αὐτὸν τῆς κοινωνίας συχνότερον τοῦτο ποιήσει. — Drinking at the Ablutions was allowed, cf. ad Q. 18.
(3) This fact was used by some priests as a pretext to get free from service, cf. Gismondi i, p. 38: "(presbyteros) vituperabat, quod causantes, quum ad ecclesiam accedebant, se aquam bibisse sanctuarium minime ingrediebantur".

new fuel to prevent the Qeṣatha of becoming unbaked or defect (Q. 70). It is worth while to quote here some words of the description given by Browne-Maclean, p. 40–41 about the baking of ordinary bread. They are highly instructive. "On the floor enclosed by this truncated hollow cone of solid clay a fire is made ... The fire is swept away, and a broom dipped in water is used to clean the interior of the oven of all dust and smoke. Then the dough cakes are forcibly slapped against the side of the oven to which they adhere until they are baked. Sometimes it is necessary to put the embers back into the oven to bake the bread thoroughly." The questioner thinks probably that there is a possibility of injury, because it was not provided for in the formulary, or that it was not allowed to add something afterwards, (parallel to Q. 76). Dry vineshoots are very common fuel in the East, Ez. xv 4.

Q. 86. The oven is reconsecrated every time when it has been used (*L.E.W.*, p. 248, cf. ad Q. 57); the consecration is removed after the baking, but not as is said here by means of some wheatstraw, but by incense, while these words are recited: "This earthen vessel is loosed and let it return to its former nature; in the name etc." (*L.E.W.*, p. 251). It is not said what is the purpose of the throwing and kindling of the wood. A statement to explain it has not been found anywhere. Must there always be some glowing coals near, without the priest being obliged to make fire by burning wood?

Q. 87–89. Something has already been said about the meaning of these QQ. on p. 111–112, 150–151. Though we observed that the formularies in: *L.O.C.*, T. = *L.E.W.*, and Berol. Syr. 38 vary, especially in the rubrics (p. 00), yet they have all these 3 signings in the same places; respectively: 1) *L.E.W.*, p. 283 = *L.O.C.*, ii, p. 583 = Berol., fol. 88a; 2) *L.E.W.*, p. 285 = *L.O.C.*, ii, p. 584 = Berol., fol. 90a; 3) *L.E.W.*, p. 288 = *L.O.C.*, ii, p. 586 = Berol., fol. 91b. It is difficult to draw conclusions from the formularies underlying the Expositions since they do not comment on every act. "Canon" always means here the end of a prayer said in an audible voice (contrast: Gehanta), see the word in Q. 89, and cf. ad Q. 4. This order of signings applies only to 'Addai', for in the other two occur also 3 signings, but in different places ('Theod.': 1) T., p. 33; 2) T., p. 36; 3) T., p. 39.–'Nest.': 1) T., p. 41; 2) T., p. 46; 3) T., p. 52). We have here a similar question as in Q. 5. From Q. 89 it becomes clear what is its bearing. One insisted on the making of 3 signings in the whole liturgy. The point of controversy is clearly stated here. The first group is that of our writer and the liturgical practice of the present day. The second one omits the first blessing and counts as the third one that signing that is made during the Consignation (*L.E.W.*, p. 291), while the former considered it as of a different order. This opinion seems in fact to have been the most usual one. For in perusing the explanations of the liturgy we see that none of them mentions the signings, though they quote the prayers at which they are made. Of course it might seem to be possible that these signings were not made in the time of those expositors; but this observation misses the point as we see that it also applies to Timothy ii and we know that they were performed in his time (see below). But the signing of Paghra and Dema in the Consignation is known to all. And they agree in their explanation of it, following Theodore Mops. who explained it by the "Union" though their exposition is different (Theodore Mops., *W.S.* vi, p. 105; Abraham B. Lipheh, *Expos.* ii, p. 164; Narsai, Connolly p. 23; *Expos.* ii, p. 61; Timothy ii, Mingana Syr. 13, fol. 129b–130a. This thought of the Union is also found among the Jacobites, cf. Moses B. Cepha (tr. Codrington–Connolly, *Two Commentaries*, p. 67). From these facts it appears that the one mentioned last was thought to be higher, at any rate different from the other, and deserving a special treatment. "After the Descent of the Spirit that is thought to be completed by this, the priest makes no sign any more over the Mysteries for they have been brought to an end" says Bar Lipheh, an explanation adopted afterwards by Timothy ii. We may also refer to ii 17, quoted ad Q. 15 and to V. ad ii 25 which also makes a difference between signing before and after the Epiclesis. The argument of the Ordination: in the formularly "The Ordering of the Clergy," translated by Badger ii, p. 322–350, is only found the signing that is also mentioned here viz. that at the Consecration proper; nothing is said about the other three. That arguments were drawn from other formularies appears also in: M. fol. 48b–49a (cf. p. 190). There some people make an analogy between the Ordination and the Consecration of the Church; pointing out that all signings must be executed in the same way. This shows that the Consecration and the manner in which it was performed, was conceived as a unit; and that every consecration of whatever formulary was thought to have the same effect. It was considered unlawful that one should differ from another, cf. Q. 3.

We return to the point under discussion. The Exposition of Timothy ii contains an echo. His information comprised some historical particulars, which are the more interesting since they are so scarce in this book (we translate this part in full, in spite of the fact that the sequence of this question does not belong to the present Q., but to Q. 92). He writes iv 16 (Ming. Syr. 13, fol. 137a f.): "*Concerning the signings:* For it is right to know that the (number of the) signings that are performed in the Mysteries of Body and Blood, is three. In this way every Mystery is completed (!), because they are performed in the name (MS.: "In the heaven", sic!) of the Holy Trinity, even though those over the Mystery of Baptism are called nine: the question is that besides those over the Mysteries three others are given to the people and three to the priest (himself); in the same way it happens in Baptism: three over the oil, three over the Baptizand and three over the Font. (They are specified on fol. 139a). They are distinguished in this way: first of all the signing of the Mysteries: at the first 'the Grace of...', and at: 'and for all...', and the last at: '... lifting up'. There exists an uncertainty about this signing on the part of some people. For they say that it is not right to sign after the Epiclesis (lit.: descent of the Spirit, see ad Q. 15), as the Mysteries have got a sufficient completion by the Epiclesis. But we practice according to the ruling Law, and a given commandment. This is according to the opinion of the Catholici and Patriarchs Mar Abraham and Mar Emanuel (cf. p. 85) But according to the opinion of the Catholici and Patriarchs Isho'yabh, Ṣeliba Zakha and Isho'Barnun (Isho'yabh i 581–596; S.Z. 714–728; I.B. 820–824) the first signing takes place at: 'and for all...', the second at: '... lifting up..." the last at: '... have been set apart and consecrated...' (*L.E.W.*, p. 292).– But the signings which are used to-day by the ministers of the church are those of Abraham and Emanuel the Catholici. For they say: 'The signing of the

Blood by the Body and of the Body by the Blood is the Mystery of the Unity and the return of the Soul to the Body we depict in the Fraction and the Unity (compare Abraham Bar Lipheh, *Expos.* ii, p. 164 who has the same explanation); they are performed in the signing with the adorable names of the Trinity. They do not necessarily need signing. The signing over the priest: according to the opinion of the holy doctors (lit.: men) the first takes place at: '. . . and that we may raise . . .'. They give as an argument for this that every one who draws nigh unto a matter he wishes to complete, first of all beseeches help from God that this matter may be completed by means of him. In the same way the priest who consecrates must first pray for himself and show his wretchedness and weakness, and that he is not worthy. He signs over himself that he may be accounted worthy by the strength of the Cross to complete it. The second signing at the second 'the grace of . . .'; the third at: 'Yea, o our Lord and our God . . .' (*L.E.W.*, p. 296). But according to the opinion of others the first at: '. . . and that we may raise . . .'; the second at: '. . . it is set apart . . .', that the priest agrees with it and shows herewith that up till now he has blessed and consecrated the Mysteries, so that they are completed; but that now he needs to be signed himself with the Mysteries; the third at: 'Yea, o our Lord and our God . . .'.–Those over the people are in the same way three: the first at the first: 'Peace be with you'; the second at the last: 'The Grace of . . .'; the third at the last: 'Peace be with you.'–According to the opinion of others: the first one at the last: 'The Grace of . . .'; the second one at: 'The Gift of his Grace . . .'; for the third one is at the end of the Mystery: 'He who has blessed us with all blessings . . .' of the Ḥutama's (see ad Q. 109)." After this follow the signings at Baptism that are of no importance for the present moment.

The end of this quotation will be verified with our Q Q. in its proper place. Here it is worth while to observe that our question deals with a point that was of actuality and importance in the time of the writer, since the men who replaced the older practice by a new one, lived some decades before his time and the signings were a part that could not be neglected in the liturgy. That older practice was covered by the name of Isho'yabh i, it is most probable that Timothy refers to the answer of I. i to James of Darai, *Canon* i (in: O. Braun, *Synhados*, S. 240–242). It informs us that the manner that was prescribed by our writer and inserted in the liturgy is a later one. For the two points of view of Timothy agree closely with that of our Q.; for the apparent difference of the last signs is not one in the mind of the Nestorians, as it happens during the same act.

Q. 90–91. "Nine signings": the Nestorian expositors do not say anything about it; but their Jacobite colleagues often speak about it though there are differences as the Jacobites signed every time 3× and separately over chalice and bread etc. while of course the frame work of the liturgy was also different. But at any rate we find that the exposition of James Edess. (in: *L.E.W.*, p. 493), Moses B. Cepha (tr. Connolly p. 70–71) and their plagiarist Dionysius B. Salibi (tr. Labourt, p. 89–90) speak extensively of the number of signings and they always have the string 3–9–18, as characteristic. Cf. ad Q. 3 on "three".

Q. 92. The quotations are again following 'Addai', since 'Nest.' and 'Theod.'

have them in other places. They are found: *L.E.W.*, p. 274 = Berol. fol. 86b (has a very extensive rubric on the making of the sign); *L.E.W.*, p. 293 = Berol. fol. 94b; *L.E.W.*, p. 296 = Berol. fol. 95b. As to the last one we observe that this signing does not occur in T. at this place, but somewhat earlier viz. at: 'Yea, o our Lord and our God' on the same page. This agrees with Timothy ii (see ad Q. 87–89). In the meantime this last sign seems to have changed its place.–The difference of the second opinion in Timothy ii consists in the second signing; this one is also found in: *L.E.W.*, p. 292.

Q. 93. The reference is to Q. 87–89. The first *L.E.W.*, p. 293, where the rubric has the same remark: "And he signs himself lifting his hands a little upwards on either side, because this signing is received on behalf of the people although he makes it on his own person" (the same in: *L.O.C.*, ii, p. 589), but not in: Berol. fol. 94b that says simply: "And he signs himself"). It is not stated in the formularies that the faithful must kneel down at this moment nor that they must kiss the Cross. The latter usage is not found anywhere as a prescript. It is not necessary that it had become a fixed liturgical practice, but it might have been a sign of deep veneration as all other kisses (cf. ad Q. 22). The thought that the mysteries are completed at this moment is found everywhere in the Expositions.–2nd signing *L.E.W.*, p. 298 = Berol. fol. 97b (adding: the priest stands at the door of the apse)–3rd *L.E.W.*, p. 303 = Berol. fol. 97b (the prayer that is also occurring fol. 99a–100b is ascribed to Elias of Nisibis, cf. A. Baumstark, *L.G.*, S. 288 and Ak. 11). In comparing this with the statements of Timothy ii, cited before, we see that this is the second opinion mentioned by him that is also incorporated in the usual formulary. In the manner indicated by Timothy it takes place: *L.E.W.*, p. 260 (or does "the first" mean: in the Missa Fidelium, p. 275?–(p. 293 = the first (one) in the other manner)–p. 296. It will be seen that this offers considerable variety. Yet I fail to see what might have been the reason of it, and the sources are silent about this preference of one way to the other.

Q. 94–95. "Bless oh my Lord," in: *L.E.W.*, p. 298 = *L.O.C.*, ii, p. 590 = Berol. fol. 96a (l. 21; we mention this line because this MS. has the same exclamation on that page l. 11, before: "Let us pray," *L.E.W.*, p. 298 l.3; see below). Dr. Brightman pointed out concerning the Greek equivalent, that it was addressed to the celebrant by the deacon "often only as a signal for a prayer or blessing"; but that the Nest. thought that it had to be said to God, hence this translation (*L.E.W.*, p. 597; the same opinion has been quoted from the English translation of T., London, 1893, by Diettrich, *Taufliturgie*, S. 25, A. 6). As a matter of fact it is found to have been used in this way, cf. e.g. *L.E.W.*, p. 272, 274, 284, 286, 289, (*L.O.C.*, and: Berol. do not always offer here the same text; this shows that it was not an indispensable element, but a free interjection; the Jacobitic opinion is expressed by Moses b. Cepha, tr. Codrington–Connolly, p. 36: "the deacon, by saying *Bless, my Lord*, really asks the priest to bless and pray"). But this case does not occur here and the person addressed to is certainly the priest as is shown by the sequence of the sentence. So it was understood by Timothy ii who appends to it: "And the priest blesses the gift with his blessing etc." (in: Ming. Syr. 13, fol. 133b). It is also clear from the statement in Berol. (fol. 96a–b): "at the end of the antiphon the deacon exclaims and says: 'Bless oh Lord!', and being asked to bless the people in the Temple the priest leaves the deacon who carries the paten at the word: 'The gift of . . .', in the middle of the altar, goes to the door of the apse and blesses the people." ܟܘܦܪܐ is the small veil that covers the elements; the same word is found in V. fol. 93a. The word generally found in the liturgy is: ܦܘܫܟܐ T. p. 12, 24, *Expos.*, p. ii 38, The fact in itself is not quite clear; the last time but one that something about the chalice was said, was exactly the opposite, as found in the rubric: *L.E.W.*, p. 292: "Let him unwrap the veil which is folded round about the paten and the chalice" (this is missing in: *L.O.C.*); a special veil over the chalice is not mentioned, except *Canon* xxiii, ad Q. 32: "covering" (of: ܟܦܪ). None of the actions stated here are found anywhere. It seems to be a peculiarity of some deacons. Nothing about it is found in the expositions, although they deal with everything that expresses a "symbol" or "type" (this word can mean, as in the Greek, several things; here, cf. Q. 100 and *Expos.* passim, it is the prototype that is expressed by the image; "mystery" is taken here in a very broad sense, as often, viz. a liturgical act. This mystagogical explanation seems to be wanted. But in Q. 95 the questioner is not satisfied and repeats his question. The answer however is no explanation of something that is hidden, but states exclusively the reasons of the deacon's acts. Some difficulties remain. For it is clear that the deacons follow a certain tradition. But what means: ܕܚܙܝܢ ܠܚܕ̈ܕܐ and: ܟܕ ܠܐ ܡܝܕܥܝܢ? Should we take the translation adopted in our text or must the latter number of words be taken in the second part of the sentence and mean: when they do not know (one another); that it formed a kind of sign of recognition. Or does the former part mean: which they see from one another: and learn by seeing though in that case ܡܢ should be expected. The text is found in both MSS. But where does that "one another" come from; nothing has been said about another group. One would expect that Q. 95 would give an explanation for the lifting of the veil. Instead of that it is said that the deacon bows his head to share in the signing over the people (*L.E.W.*, p. 298 and cf. ad Q. 93.) This bowing does not occur in the rubrics and is not at all mentioned in the foregoing Q. which has not been answered. The 2 MSS. agree. It seems as though there is no other solution than assuming that the matter was already confused at an early date and that the words *Q.* and *S.* have disappeared in Q. 95.

Q. 96. Again something exclusively Nest. About the last signing is spoken in Q. 89; it is the one of the elements (4) *L.E.W.*, p. 290–291 etc. There is also found the prayer "we draw nigh etc." T. has here the following rubric: "While naming the Trinity he breaks the Būchra that is in his hands attentively into two halves. *And some here sign the P*'*rista with their thumb at the time of breaking: but do thou beware of such an audacity, for it is not necessary here to sign, but only to break in the name of the Trinity, holding them in both hands*" (see about this place p. 153). This is exactly the mistake that is blamed in our Q. The italicized words fail in: *L.O.C.* and in: Berol. fol. 93a. The latter has before this rubric the following remarkable addition: "You must know that those signs according to the mind of Mar Elias of Nisibis save us from introducing a quaternity in the breaking (E. of N., 975–± 1050, writer of a good many books on various topics in Syriac and Arabic; his liturgical interest is shown by his composition of prayers and hymns; cf. A. Baumstark, *L.G.*, S. 287–288, and: G. Graf, *Die christlich-arabische Literatur*, Strassburg, 1908, S. 59–67. We can infer from this note that he had decided this point; therefore it shows once more that our author dealt with QQ. that were being debated then). We can assume that the shorter text is the original one and that the interpolation is made perhaps not under the influence of the present Q., but at any rate on account of the same combated practice, the more so because the audacity in both is the point attacked. Yet it is nowhere told what were their contents; anyhow it is not found in the making of the sign of the cross with the thumb, but in the fact that it should only be broken and not signed. This last act had to follow later. Probably the trespassers did so here because it is mentioned in the prayer. It is once more seen here that deviation from the sequence laid down in the formulary is severely forbidden. Q. 36 revealed already that the state of affairs of the village churches was not as it was desired by the High Church. The *Book of the Governors* of Thomas of Marga, so important from the point of view of the history of Culture, informs its readers over and over again that in rural districts even of Christian countries paganism was still prevalent and this had of course an influence upon Christianity. The people living on the mountains were always rough, uncultivated and retained practices which had been condemned by the leading churchmen; so it is told that at the time of Mari 12th century they still held Agapae which had elsewhere fallen into disuse (Gismondi i, p. 4). This backwardness of those far-off places is not particulary Nestorian, but is also found at other times, even in the great ages of Antiquity, cf. K. Holl, *das Fortleben der Volkssprachen in Kleinasien in nachchristlicher Zeit*, in: *Ges. Aufsätze*, ii, S. 246–248 and: John of Ephesus, *Lifes of Eastern Saints*, ed. Brooks, *P.O.* xviii, p. 231–233. It should not be overlooked that a rigorous jealousy between the people of the plains and of the mountains existed through all ages (Browne–Maclean, p. 168). We must also take into account the bad means of communication that prevented the priests of the villages to have regular contact with the rest and brought about a relaxation. We must also remember that the instruction of the clergy was often very bad; a priest that was not well instructed could naturally not give good instruction himself (ch. vi).

Q. 97. Cf. ad Q. 118 sqq.

Q. 98. The ordinary liturgical books do not say where the censer had to stand though both the liturgy and the *Expos.* (index, s.v. Thuribulum) mention the censing in several places (cf. *D.A.C.*, s.v. *Censer* and *Incense*; E. Fehrenbach, *D.A.C.L.*, s.v. *Encense* and *Encensoir*, t. v, col. 2–21, 21–33.) Neither do other rites give any information. Mgr. Rahmani says only (*L.O.O.*, p. 60) that "l'auteur anonyme de l'Explication de la messe (with the vague reference: "dans le manuscript de notre bibliothèque" n. 2 about which the notice bibliografique does give any explanation) dit que l'encensoir se place sur l'autel; mais cet usage a disparu depuis longtemps." Yet he does not say where nor how it is done at present. In spite of difference in space and time we must quote here *Can.* 106 of Athanasius, ed. Riedel-Crum, p. 68, because it contains an indication: "At all incense(-offering) that is offered up in the holy place, morning and evening, especially at the divine *anaphora*, before the Gospel (lesson), the archdeacon shall take in his hand a censer and fill it with coals and shall stand before the altar *over against the Gospel* (*book*) and into it shall be put for him the incense and he shall cause it to rise up until the Gospel is read. Then he shall go with the censer before the Gospel into the inner part of the holy place. It is not that the Lord hath need at all of incense. Nay, but man shall remember the incense of the ages of light where is no hateful smell before the Lord, the God of the living, where (are) hymns of praise." The big question here is what means: left and right? Is it said looking from the church or from the east (cf. ad Q. 121)? In combining the data of the Q Q 97–99, 103 and 118 sqq. we come to the following sketch of the situation.[1] In the prayers of the incense

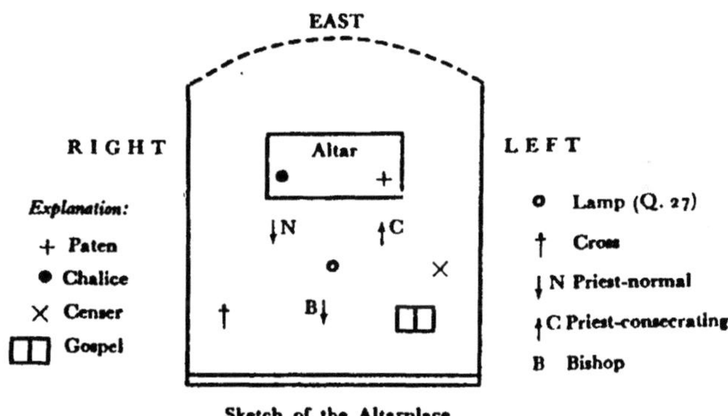

Sketch of the Altarplace.

(*L.E.W.*, p. 282 and 289, cf. the comparative study by Prof. Lietzmann, *Messe*, S. 86–93), it expresses the pleasant savour that makes the gifts agreable in the eyes of God; according to Timothy ii (Ming. Syr. 13, fol. 117a–b) it expresses the pleasant smell etc. that will be the share of the elect. But nowhere the thoughts expressed here are uttered. Yet they were certainly connected with it, cf. J. Braun, *Lit. Handlex.*, S. 369: "Ausdruck entweder der Anbetung od. blosser Ehrung".

Q. 99. The rubric: *L.E.W.*, p. 267 = Berol. fol. 81a, prescribes in the Offertory that the priest and the deacon must bring the paten and chalice on the altar and then: "The priest takes the paten in his left hand and the chalice in his right putting his hands in the form of a cross" (*L.O.C.*, ii, p. 580 mentions this crosswise, but does not say how; cf. Gismondi i, p. 16: "narratum est sacrum fecisse Simeonem [bar Saba'i, martyred in the great persecution of Sapor, Labourt, *Christianisme*, index, s.v.; *Martyrium* and *Narratio*, ed. M. Kmosko, in: R. Graffin, *Patrologia Syriaca*, i, 2, Parisiis, 1907, which do not contain this story] feria quinta paschatis in carcere, constituisseque loco altaris unum e suis pres-

(1) When Isho'yabh i writing to James of Darai, *Canon* ii, in: O. Braun, *Synhados*, S. 243, says: "und steht zur Rechten gegen Süden", his point of view is that of the congregation.–On this confusion of right and left, cf. *D.A.C.L.*, s.v. *Orientation*, t. xii, col. 2666.

byteris stantem deposito in eius dextera patena et in leava calice"; exactly the same words in *Chronique de Seért*, ed. A. Scher, *P.O.*, iv, p. 305. But this piece of evidence is from a time before the exact rules.) The expositors do not comment on it. Only Timothy ii (Ming. Syr. 13, fol. 121b) says that the paten must be on left and the chalice on the right, comparing in a very queer way the chalice with the liver which changes all food into blood and feeds the body. This remark is the same as that suggested in our Q. The difference between the rubric and this decision is merely the way of approaching the altar viz. in the former case from the west, in the latter from the east (see sketch). The Syriac St. James (*L.E.W.*, p. 70–74) has something of the same kind. The text has merely: "Hand", but the whole connection shows that it must be the right one. Nevertheless nothing is found about that in the formulary.

Q. 100. ܛܘܦܣܐ, 'symbol" see ad Q. 94. M. has here ܡܟܢܫܐ, V. ܡܟܢܫܢܐ; the first word is missing in Payne Smith, *Thesaurus Syriacus*. In their present form both words are derived from ܟܢܫ "to collect, to wipe together" (the ending ܢܐ, cf. Nöldeke, *Syr. Gramm.*, S. 104) one who gathers together. This is impossible here. It must be an object in the hand of the deacons. Therefore I suppose that it should be read ܡܢܦܢܐ of ܢܦ = "to drive, flap away"; the word is not found in the *Thesaurus* in this form; it gives the forms ܡܢܦܢܝܬܐ and ܡܢܦܬܐ (this in: Narsai, *Hom.* xvii, ed. Mingana, i, p. 281, cf. tr. Connolly, p. 4, n. 1). But in the *Expos.* ii, p. 78 (text) this form occurs and was rightly translated by Dom. Connolly into "flabellum". All Eastern rites know these fans in the hands of the deacons; see: *D.C.A.*, s.v. *Flabellum*; *D.A.C.L.*, s.v. *Flabellum*, t. v., col. 1610–1625 (Dom. Leclercq gives reasons for its falling into disuse in the West); both articles with pictures, and: *L.O.O.*, p. 52–53 and fig. i. The first time it is mentioned is in: *Const. Apost.* viii 12, 3, Funk i, p. 496; here it is said that they were used to drive away the flies from the elements. This forms a sufficient explanation of its origin since so many little insects were found in these countries (ii 1 deals, e.g. with the question of the desecration in case some of these insects should be found in the chalice). This view was expressly combated in the explanation of Bar Cepha (Connolly–Codrington, p. 36 tr.) where he says that they were used lest anything unlawful might come near. He compares these deacons with the angels viz. the Cherubim and Seraphim. This is a very common explanation of the Eastern Fathers. It is met with already in Theodore Mops. He combines both views. He compares these deacons with the angels spreading linen over the grave of the Lord. After that: "They stand up on both sides and agitate all the air above the holy body with fans, thus keeping it from any defiling object." This thought is then expanded further (*ad Baptizandos*, *W.S.* vi, p. 86–87). The first part is borrowed by Narsai; he omits the object of the "fanning", but his symbolism is the same (tr. Connolly, p. 4 and 12). Neither Abraham B. Lipheh nor Timothy ii (the latter speaks of deacons on both sides of the altar, but not about the fans) mention it neither does the Formulary. The *Expos.* mentions them only in passing. The symbolism of the angels near the grave has been abandoned: "neque illi diaconi, qui ad altare stant, ad negotium flabellorum accedere audent, donec sacerdos permiserit eis." They are well distinguished from Gabriel who is also represented by a deacon, in this connection (ii, p. 71). The fans are mentioned once more at Baptism; those who carry them are compared directly with the Cherubim in reference to the vision of Isaiah vi (*Expos.* ii, p. 92). Regarding this evidence we observe 1) that the doubt uttered by Renaudot, whether the Syrians knew fans in their liturgy (*L.O.C.*, ii, p. 80) as the Greeks did, is gratuitous; 2) the judgement of Dr. Brightman concerning the fan: "Not used apparently by Nest. and Abyssin.", *L.E.W.*, p. 577 must be modified as far as the former group is concerned (about the latter I must abstain from judgement, though I think it highly improbable that it would not be found there). At any rate the word used by the Jacobites is different from that of the Nestorians. It becomes clear too why this question was put. For in the older explanations (as far as they are preserved) it held a real place, while we see that it is almost wholly neglected in the later ones. This gap had to be filled and it was the aim of the questioner to do so.

Gabriel and Michael are prominent figures in the Nest. mystagogy as far as we know it from the *Expos.* They are not specially mentioned by Theodore and other older expositors. Neither do they play a predominant part in Jacobite liturgical literature (the highly traditional Dionysius B. Salibi mentions twice Gabriel but only in connection with the Annunciation and he does not mention Michael at all; Labourt, p. 34 and 81). Narsai is the only one among the Nestorians who mentions them separately among the choirs of the angels (Connolly, p. 48); the others do not refer to them, except the *Expos.* There they officiate as watchers; their "picture" in the liturgy are two deacons who address the people, read the Scriptures, recite the litanies etc.: Gabriel is the functionary of the New Testament and Michael of the Old (ii, p. 9, 14 etc.). This division of functions will be explained by the fact that Gabriel announced the birth of Christ (Luke i 26) and Michael who was highly venerated in the East, (cf. W. Lueken, *Der Erzengel Michael,* Göttingen, 1898) was thougt to be the guardian angel of Israel (cf. Dan. x 13, 21; xii 1). They are, as Dom Connolly aptly remarks the "Diaconiae officiales" (*Expos.* ii, p. 9, n. 2). They play here the same part as at the end of our Q. V adds to the last clause: "In the same way there are many deacons." It is difficult to decide whether this is the original text. At any rate it is the right "tertium comparationis." Their service at the grave implies the identification of them with the two men "in shining garments" of Luke xxiv 4, an identification that is not far out of the way, but that I do not remember having found somewhere else. Though the names are not found, the explanation seems to be traditional; Narsai sings in one of his hymns (*Hom.* xxi, Connolly p. 56): "Two angels the disciples saw in the tomb of our Lord who were attending the place of His body as though it were the body (itself). In that apparel of the two watchers the two deacons are standing to hover over the Mysteries." The equalization: altar = grave of Christ is a term of the Mystagogy that seems derived from Antiochene theology. Theodore Mops. expresses himself clearly in connection with what has been quoted before: "when we see the oblation on the communion-table–something which denotes that it is being placed in a kind of sepulchre after its death . . ." (*W.S.* vi, p. 86–88). This agrees with his fellow countryman and contemporary John Chrysostomus; for in the Explanation of Bar Cepha (p.34) a word of his (not traced in his works by Dom. Connolly) is quoted with approval, while other opinions, a.o.

that of Dionysius Areopagita(!), *De Eccles. Hier.* iv, in: *M.S.G.* 3, col. 484 D are rejected. This was copied out by Bar Salibi (p. 50). The same thought is found among the Byzantines; but in view of the present state of research it cannot be decided if it is a traditional feature there. At any rate the altar is styled by Symeon of Thessalonica † 1429(?), *De Sacra Liturgia*, cap. 98, in: *M.S.G.*, 155: "Throne" and "grave". The former name, see Q. 16 and 104; the second here. They are also found both in Narsai, *Hom.* xvii: "The altar is a symbol of our Lord's tomb, without doubt (Connolly, p. 4, cf. 7, 11 and 56) and it is followed by: "In another order . . . the adorable altar . . . is a symbol of that throne of the Great and Glorious, upon which He will be seen of watchers and men in the day of His revelation" (p. 4–5). We see, the name „grave", meaning "altar" is very current in Narsai. The same holds good for the other exegetes (Bar Lipheh, *Expos.* ii, p. 161; Timothy ii, Ming. Syr. 13, fol. 122a) and in the letter of Isho'Barnun, *ad Isaac* Q. 2, and in *Canon* ii, the parallel between the altar and gra· of the Lord is used as a conclusive argument, in the case of people drawing near to it; they can only do so if they come as respectively Nicodemus and Joseph or the women. These facts form a sufficient refutation of the remark of Prof. F. Kattenbusch, *Lehrbuch der vergleichenden Confessionskunde*, Freiburg i. Br., 1892, i, S. 496, Anm. 1: "Diese Specialitäten (viz. the symbolical burial of the Lord) haben sich . . . erst zwischen dem elften und sechszehnten Jahrhundert ausgebildet." In reading the expositions it becomes clear that this name fits in originally with the whole course of thoughts. Their view of the liturgy is, whatever may be the differences in regard to particulars, that it represents the incarnation, life, death and resurrection of Jesus Christ. This principal train of thought is crossed by another; therefore Narsai can say: "In another order." But the motive out of which the name "grave" arose is the principal one. It accounts wholly for its use. And its meaning does not go further. It is simply a mystagogical name and it is rightly missing in the collection of names, made by Dr. Brightman, (*L.E.W.*, p. 596). We point this out because it is a well-known religious idea that the altar is a grave, as Prof. G. v. d. Leeuw remarked (*Phänomenologie*, S. 375, Anm. 1); this latter designation seems to originate from the fact that the dead members of the family were originally buried near the altar of the house. It is obvious that here exists only a similarity of name and that the thought is not the same. That relics were preserved on the altar of the Christian Church, that even the name "Sepulchrum" occurs in the Roman Catholic Church, may lie in the same line as Prof. v. d. Leeuw observes. But this was never the cause of special speculations in the liturgy.

Q. 101. ܐܘ as comparative instead of the usual ܡܢ as in the answer cf. Nöldeke, *Syr. Gramm.*, S. 187, Ak. 1; it is generally found in translations of the Bible under Greek influence and only very few times in original Syriac works. A discussion as is mentioned here and meant in Q. 123 has not left any traces in literature as far as I know. Unless one would like to refer to a story in: Budge, *B.G.* ii, p. 506, 516, that a saint wore on his breast a complete evangelium instead of a simple cross. But this is not liturgical as in our Q. The use of "other people say" is rather peculiar as another opinion would be expected. The same division as is found here is given by Timothy ii, cf. ad Q. 35;

it is possible that he had borrowed it from our Q. The *Expos.* does not mention this debate; it declares merely that the Cross is the "sign" of this conquering King and the Gospel the series of His commandments (*Expos.* ii, p. 10; i, p. 135: Cross instead of Christ). Abraham Bar Lipheh says that they are one, viz. the corporal being of Jesus (*Expos.* ii, p. 159). That the Gospel was thought to be representing Christ is shown by the fact that at the Council of Ephesus (431) a Gospel was laid in the middle of the "Church of the Virgin" on a throne to show that Christ Himself was present (J. D. Mansi, *Sacrorum conciliorum nova et amplissima collectio*, t. iv, col. 1237).

Q. 102. The quotations from the liturgy are found in T., p. 5 = *L.E.W.*, p. 260; p. 11 = p. 275; p. 26 = p. 296 (the first and the last are the same in 'Theod.' and 'Nest.'; the second T., p. 33 and p. 40 respectively stand in another connection as that given in this Q.; this confirms the result of p. 259). In Berol. Syr. 38 and: *L.O.C.*, ii the first fails (the two others are found: Berol. 87a = *L.O.C.*, ii, 582; and: Berol. 96a = *L.O.C.*, ii, 590); this fact is probably the cause of putting the Q. The witness of the Expositions is not very certain in this respect: the first one is not found in Narsai who does not deal with the beginning of the Mass, Abraham B. Lipheh and Timothy ii (this omission is very remarkable); but in Isho'yabh i, cf. O. Braun, *Synhados*, p. 240, and: *Expos.*, ii, p. 21–22;–the second in all: Narsai, *Hom.* xvii, p. 8 Conn.; Abraham, *Expos.* ii, p. 162–163; *Expos.* ii, p. 42; V. has the variant "before", but this does not correspond with any textform; Timothy, fol. 125b, has it in a somewhat different place;–the third in all: Narsai, *Hom.* xvii, p. 26 Conn.; Abraham, *Expos.* ii, p. 69; Timothy ii, fol. 131b. (Hanssens iii, p. 206 finds three salutations in: Narsai, *Hom.* xvii, viz. on p. 8, 23 and 26 Conn. This second greeting is missing in my list, since on p. 23 the Priest gives a "blessing" = *L.E.W.*, p. 293, and there is no reason whatever to suppose with Dom. Connolly, p. 23 n. 4 that "it would seem, 'Peace be with you'" or to replace the present formula with Prof. Hanssens.) "New Sunday"–name of the first Sunday after Easter, typical Nestorian name, about the origin of which nothing is known. The Bible-texts alluded to are: John xx 19, 26 and xxi 7, though it may be observed with respect to the last text that it is not said that Jesus gave peace, as is suggested here; it may be an expansion of some Homilist. The explanation of these texts is quite different from that given by other expositors. Their explanations show a great variety; the single point of agreement is that the last blessing is always connected with the events after the Resurrection. Probably the explanation given here is quite incidental; for it does not fit in with any other one. For whatever may be their differences all exegesis correspond in finding the Resurrection after the Consecration. This cannot possibly be connected with the remark made in this answer. The number of greetings varies very much in the different rites; see the complete materials in: Hanssens iii, p. 194–198 (usus praesens), p. 198–209 (historia). The quotation from John xxi 7 is in accordance with the Peshita-text that reads: our Lord, and not: the Lord, as the Greek text (but cf. codex D.).

Q. 103, will be treated together with Q. 118 sqq. since it treats of the same subjects.

Q. 104. What is meant here by the "Throne"? The first thing that will be thought of is the Bishop's seat that was not only found in the apse, but also on the Bema (cf. *Expos.*, i, p. 91 and the plan of the church drawn up by Conn. p. 196–197 indicated by P.). But when one tries this exegesis it appears that the explanation of the rest is impossible; for in reading what is said about the Cathedra in the handbooks (cf. C. M. Kaufmann, *Handbuch*, S. 164–165 and 525ff) we find there all kind of information, but nothing that shows any connection with the answer. The page of the *Expos.* mentioned before shows the right way. In his Mystagogical explanation of the whole church he also deals with the Bema, the platform in the middle of the nave. It represents for him as for others as Bar Lipheh and Timothy ii, Jerusalem. "Altare autem, quod in medio Bemate est, locum Golgothae implet." This is the same view as that of our question, for we have found already in Q. 16 that the altar was styled "Throne", though in that case it was not quite sure whether it was a metaphorical phrase or not. There are two other places in which the present writer found the name "Golgotha" in connection with the liturgy. Mgr. Rahmani, *L.O.O.*, p. 42 and n. 4 states in summing up the parts of the church that: "à l'entrée du chœur on dresse un pupitre, où est exposé le livre des ss. évangiles," and indicates that this was called Golgotha. Unfortunately he does not say whether this name is generally found among all the Syrians or only among the Jacobites or Nestorians. He does not add any reference so that his information is for the greater part useless since we do not know at what time it was found first. At any rate it cannot be the same as that of our Q. as is clear from the place in which it was erected. It is possible that the Eastern Scholar had in mind the same practice as found in the information of Mr. Badger ii, p. 20 and n. He informs us that in this time (1840–1850) the Apostolos was read near the altar, but formely on the Gagolta, "the name given to an ambon at the western end of the church, consisting of two raised stone platforms, placed opposite to each other, and reached by several steps or stairs". A picture of it is given, facing p. 21. He adds that the only one he has met with was that in Tahara, a church dedicated to the Blessed Virgin in Mosul; for this object has fallen into disuse, and B. supposes that it has never existed in many small village-churches. He does not give the data on which this opinion is based. Comparing these facts with our question it is clear that they do not agree. It stood in the Temple = nave and in the "House of Prayer". The latter name is not found in the list of: *E.S.D.O.*, p. 294 nor in the *Dictionary*, and is failing in the description of the *Expos.* Without any doubt it is the same as the Greek εὐκτήριον, an oratorium, cf. *D.C.A.*, s.v. *Oratorium.*–*D.A.C.L.*, s.v. *Oratoire*, t. xii, col. 2346–2372 does not contain any help for the explanation. A word with various meanings, among others: a part of the church, distinguished from Bema and Narthex, but not the choir. It is mentioned in several places of Amr and Mari as a place where Bishops were buried (Gismondi i, p. 126; ii, p. 60, 64, 68). In another place (Gismondi i, p. 91) it is said: "Oratorium etiam condidit ('Abdisho') in atrio majori, cuius altaris faciem Moyses . . . velamine auro texto obtexit"; here we have together the place of the House of Prayer and the altar in it. Yet it is not clear where it should be placed in the sketch of Dom. Connolly.

Two crosses are spoken of, a big one that is supposed to have stood on the

Bema on the east side (head) and next cross and gospel that are explained as in Q. 101. I did not find purple-coloured coverings over the Cross mentioned elsewhere. The writer is not very exact as regards the biblical data. For the priests and not the soldiers are mentioned here as mocking Jesus, against the testimony of the Gospels, cf. Mat. xxvii 28 par., who also say (Mat. xxvii 31 par.) that Jesus was put on the Cross in his own clothes. Two fans see Q. 100. Here we have a different connection as this is in the Missa Catechumenorum. The *Expos.* also says that it is an indication of the Cross. In: *L.E.W.*, p. 249, the robbers are mentioned for the Buchra's viz. Titus and Dumachus (cf. C. Tischendorf, *Evangelia Apocrypha*, Lipsiae, 1853, p. 184); some other names are found elsewhere, cf. A. Meyer, in: E. Hennecke, *Neutestamentliche Apokryphen* [2], Tübingen, 1924, S. 79.

The questions 105–116 deal with the Lord's Prayer in the various services (Q. 117 is an addendum suggested by the preceding question). For while it was said in most rituals at the beginning and end, it was not done in the ritual of Marriage and Funeral service, as is observed by Q. 105.

It is known from various other sources that it was discussed on different occasions. The subject of debate is the number of times the Lord's Prayer had to be recited in the Eucharist (we may take this one for example, since it is used most of all): T., p. 1 and 30 = *L.E.W.*, p. 252 and 303 (in: *L.O.C.*, ii, p. 589 only the latter is found; it is missing at the beginning, the text of which varies largely from that of T.–Berol. Syr. 38 has it in neither place!). The Lord's Prayer of T., p. 25–26 = *L.E.W.*, p. 295–296 is out of discussion. It is old and was fixed by Isho'yabh iii; cf *Expos.* i, p. 191 [1]. This latter finds its counterpart in nearly all the other liturgies between Consecration and Communion (it is not found in: Test. Dom.; Const. Apost., East Syrian fragment, cf. *L.O.O.*, p. 240–241, and: *D.A.C.*, s.v. *Lord's Prayer.* It is mentioned already by Cyril of Jerusalem. That it is not quoted by Theodore Mops., is hardly of any weight. The wording of James of Edessa quoted in: *L.O.O.*, p. 240, N. 2 seems to suggest that it did not belong to the ancient form of 'James'.) But our topic is not found in any of them. It is a typical Nestorian controversy; *D.A.C.L.*, s.v. *Oraison Dominicale*, t. xii, col. 2244–2255 has nothing about it. The point must be cleared from information of the Nestorians only. The oldest witness about a question of the use of this prayer is from the time of Isho'Barnun (820–824). In his letter *ad Macarium* he answers the question (Q. 62): "Should the Lord's Prayer be said at the beginning and at the end of the service? *Solution:* Officially it must be said. In this way one sticks to that Chrysostomus or Mouth of Gold, the blessed John and the blessed Nestorius. For they wrote as follows: "Every service of the church which does not begin or end with the Lord's Prayer that the Saviour delivered to the church, is sinful and mutilated, and not perfect." I do not know what places the author has in mind; it is not surprising since the tradition of the writings of Nestorius is so incomplete; but the quotation of Chrysostomus is somewhat suspect, the more so since we find that this point was debated, but never do we find this quotation of the famous Father cited.

(1) Cf. *Expos.* i, p. 153: those who followed the ancient practice, as against the innovation of Timothy i, say it once: "tempore mysteriorum cum consecratione".

This question was raised by Timothy i (780–820; see about his life and times the sources mentioned by A. Baumstark, *L.G.*, S. 217–218). This Patriarch ordered at a Synod "ut Canonicae preces oratione Dominica et incoharentur et terminarentur" (Auctor, *Collectionis Canonum Ecclesiae Syro-Nestorianae*, Cod. Arab. 36, t. 2, p. 507, quoted in: *B.O.*, iii 1, p. 100–101). Here we find only the Daily Offices mentioned but not the other liturgies. The *Expos.* has more particulars. The case is discussed there three times. In: *Expos.* i, p. 121–123 two questions are put on account of the Evening service, viz. *a*) why some people pray the Lord's prayer at the beginning, while others do not? and *b*) why in some places the priest prays before the Lord's Prayer and elsewhere after it? The Mystagogical reasons of the author need not to detain us. Within the whole of his work the reasons are clearly those of the author himself (i, p. 125 end) and are not historical. Concerning the matter itself he says that Isho'yabh iii did not order anything about it. It was introduced by Timothy i to be said at the beginning. Some people stuck to the older tradition while others obeyed the Patriarch. The author judges that this is right and that first the Lord's Prayer and then the Office should be prayed. These statements are completed by i, p. 153: why some people do not recite it at the end. The answer is practically of the same tenor. He leaves it undecided whether it must be said with or without Canon (cf. ad Q. 4). In explaining the Eucharist ii, p. 81–83 he states once more that this Prayer (*L.E.W.*, p. 303; the former is not mentioned; the beginning of T. does not quite agree with the *Expos.*) is an addition of Timothy i, and is said by those within and outside (the altar). ('Abdisho' i has changed this; up to his time it was said by two choirs in the altar and in the nave; since his time it had to be said by all together, cf. Bar Hebraeus, *Chr. Eccl.* iii, col. 253. This is at any rate a "tempus ad quem" for dating the *Expos.*–The other question about the Lord's Prayer at the end of the 11th century of 'Abdisho' ii and Machicha i [cf. Gismondi i, p. 121–122] is a totally different matter).

Nothing about this question is found in the letters of Timothy i, published by O. Braun, *Timothei Patriarchae i Epistulae*, in: *C.S.C.O.*, ii 67, Parisiis, 1915 nor in the short biography by H. Labourt, *De Timotheo i Patriarcha*, Parisiis, 1903. But there is no reason whatever to doubt the information given before. It also explains the question of his successor. They fit in very well with our Q.Q. which deal with points that are not cleared up in other places. The anonymous Patriarch or Catholicos of the East is Timothy i who is mentioned expressly in Q. 107 (in passing it may be remarked that Q. 105 and 107 do not treat the same subject. First Timothy ordered the recitation with "farcings" ("farcing", see ad Q. 107) after his ordination, after that at the beginning and end of every service). It is corroborated by the fact that we hear that it was ordered after a dispute with a Jacobite in "books" and we know that Timothy i debated with a Jacobite. Bar Hebraeus, *Chr. Eccl.* iii, col. 181 sq. tells us that Timothy had a dispute with the Jacobite Patriarch George of Be'eltan (it is nowhere said by 'Abdisho', *Catalogus*, § 86 that the (answers of) Questions, contained confessional polemics as was supposed by A. Baumstark, *L.G.*, S. 217. -That a Nestorian speaks in a way as is done in our Q. of a Patriarch of the Jacobites is not so remarkable; on the contrary its tone is rather gentle).

It is important to hear what was the exact reason of this new practice. For though it is in itself of minor interest, yet it is an example how one rite influenced the other; it should be observed that it is stated here that the Nestorians did so to overtrump the Jacobites! Very often such influences are suggested by the similarity between two liturgies, but hardly any direct testimony can be found about it. Though it is very sad, yet it is true that liturgical changes have been brought about silently (cf. p. 14); so it can seldom be historically fixed and even if that is possible we do not know the circumstances which led to it. Another remarkable thing is that here it is not only similarity which is the result in the formularies, but a disagreement which nobody however would suppose to be dependency. This point is useful to show how difficult it is to prove this borrowing. In view of this question Mgr. Rahmani said simply that Timothy "a fait cet emprunt au rite byzantin", *L.O.O.*, p. 350 (this fact makes the other references to the Byzantine Liturgy on the same page rather questionable. It is an important point for the question of the genuinity of *Homily* xvii of Narsai, cf. p. 48–49,) referring to the places in 'Chrysostom' *L.E.W.*, p. 353 and 393. But these prayers do not stand in the same place as in the Nestorian Liturgy; hence there is no parallel between the two rites in this respect. Here we are informed that is was not derived from a Byzantine source, but sprang up among the Nestorians themselves in contradistinction to the Jacobites. The last Lord's Prayer is also commented upon by Narsai, *Hom.* xvii (Connolly, p. 30), but the translator rejected it (p. 82) as an interpolation.

We will examine now the details of the Q.Q.

Q. 105. Puts the question; the answer is an historical reminiscence stating the original form. The Jacobite 'James' has a Lord's Prayer in the prothesis *L.E.W.*, p. 72 and at the ablutions p. 109, but this does not exactly agree with the Nestorian facts, it looks like a parallel with the Byzantine Lit. On the liturgy and its place in the intercourse between the various Eastern Churches something was said already on p. 194. Though the matter is worth while a closer examination it cannot be studied here. Many works of polemics are mentioned (about the polemics between Jacobites and Nestorians cf. the "Register" in: A. Baumstark, *L.G.*, S. 363, s.v. *Antihäretische und konfessionell polemische Literatur*) and in other places too we hear that there were relations between the two bodies and their nature was not simply that of "Todfeindschaft" (A. Baumstark, *Messe im Morgenland*, S. 48). The Answer was not a response to the question. But first of all the questioner goes into what was answered.

Q. 106. What was the state before Timothy?–V. misses: "And in the morning". It may be that it was done on purpose because this service is not dealt with in the answer! The three services mentioned here are the principal ones of the Daily Office. It is known that fixed hours of Prayer go back to the oldest times of Christian worship though there were differences in the times at which they should be said, cf. *D.C.A.*, s.v. *Hours of Prayer*, and: F. Cabrol, *D.A.C.L.*, s.v. *Office Divin*, t. xii, col. 1962–2017 (mainly Western). It is not known in how far this was taken over by the Nestorians. In any case Isho'yabh iii has regulated it. He had a book composed by 'Ananisho' indicating the prayers for a whole year. (Budge, *B.G.* ii, p. 177, cf. p. 189.–This book was the Ḥudra, cf. p. 125 On the way in which it was done Thomas says: "He alone possessed in a sufficient measure a clear mind, and a natural talent for the art of music, and a knowledge how to arrange words." It is uncertain whether he has also fixed the hours of the day. The *Expos.* i, p. 106–108 has the answer to the question why the *Fathers* fixed three Daily Offices, viz. Evening, Night and Morning; why they ordered that on Sundays and Festivals the service of the Mysteries should be held and in Lent the Completes after the Evening-service and the Tertia, Sexta and Nona. The answer informs us that Evening and Morning-service were obligatory for everybody, but the Night only for priests and ascetes. This wording suggests that this does not go back to a regulation of Isho'yabh. In *Expos.* ii, p. 1 it is asked why Isho'yabh ordered to hold the service of the Mysteries at the third hour and it seems as though he had some connection with it. At any rate the present state of tradition is not very clear. The *Expos.* cannot exactly be dated, but gives the reflex of the situation probably in the 10th century. George i († 680 or 681) decided that the laymen should assist the services in the congregation in the evening and morning, *Canon* xv, in: O. Braun, *Synhados*, S. 344–345. According to Elias of Nisibis the following services are obligatory for all the faithful: Morning, Evening and "Sacramentsgebet zur 3ten Stunde"; the priests, deacons and monks have beside them: Sexta, Nona, Completes and Night, *Beweis*, S. 91f, quoted also in: *B.O.*, iii 1, p. 304–305. (We pass over the witness of the Exposition of Abraham Bar Lipheh who mentioned only Night and Morning as it is not quite sure if this part is complete and not mutilated as are some others). Assemani did not trust this information; I think, wrongly for as to the former part it agrees completely with the Canon of George taking into account that the prayer of the Sacrament is only on Sundays. His objection is that "ex ipsis Nestorianorum Officiis constet, eos praeter Vesperas, Nocturnum, et Matutinum, nullas alias horas celebrare ." But this is merely based on the *Expos.* and, though we cannot investigate it here, it is probable that it gives us the practice of the High Monastery (p. 148–149), while in other places the old practise was maintained. According to the *Nomocanon* of 'Abdisho' v 1 and 2, Mai p. 245–246, one gets the following state of affairs (from this place is derived the information of: *B.O.*, iii 2, p. cccxxxvii–cccxli, and: *E.S.D.O.*, p. xii, cf. Badger ii, p. 16–17): seven times of prayer are instituted by Jesus Christ; the Oecumenical Fathers have prescribed these seven hours to the monks, pure priests and steadfast laymen. The Fathers of later times ordered that, because it was impossible to do so for many people, that four would be sufficient, viz. Evening, Completes, Night and Morning. The first and the last are the principal and "can neither be added to nor abridged" (cf. the note ad Q. 1); the other two are facultative for laymen. Badger and Maclean observe that the Completes have practically fallen into disuse (except for some days); this was already the case in the time of the *Expos.* and of our treatise. 'Abdisho' says about the Completes and Night that they must be performed according to the rules of the (High) Monastery (the word "High" is not found in the edition of Mai, nor in: *E.S.D.O.*, but in the text used by Badger, and probably right, because otherwise the statement is somewhat obscure). It may be that the Fathers mentioned by him in the last place are the same and it fits in very well with what we found above. In v 3 he gives the names of the various services It is not known how old these rules laid down in this book are. Timothy ii repeats a Canon that agrees closely with the description of Elijah, *Canon* 3, in: 'Abdisho',

*Nomocanon*, before Tomus ii, Mai, p. 263. We have summarized once more these places though they are also given in other books (cf. O. Braun, *Synhados*, S. 344, N. 2–345) because it seems to the present writer that they have not always be looked at in the exact historical sequence. It was asked how the Nestorian church divided its Horae without taking into account the historical connections and in this way the statements were somewhat contradictory. From these statements we can make the following reconstruction: the Nestorians took over at their separation the seven Horae as they had been developed in the cloisters and after that in the church; Isho'yabh iii reserved the 3rd hour for the Eucharist and laid down a rule for the Lessons and Prayers that had to be used. It is easy to understand that it proved to be impossible for laymen to share in all services; the result was that they had only to assist at the Evening, Morning and Eucharist-service. Clerics and Monks had also the Night-service (and Completes), a rule probably going back to the High Monastery, of which it is known that it revised the Offices (p. 148–149); the others were not used any more. In this way a good explanation is found for the sequence given by 'Abdisho'.

An excellent survey of the three services may be found in the *East Syrian Daily Offices* of Bishop Maclean (p. xiii–xvi), whose introduction and translations must be used to get an insight into these services of the Nestorian Breviary (it is well known that the edition of P. Bedjan in his: *Breviarium Chaldaicum*, Parisiis, 1886, 3 vols. is for the use of Uniates and is not a true presentation of the original Nestorian text (for the Jacobites, see: A. Baumstark, *Festbrevier und Kirchenjahr der syrischen Jakobiten*, Paderborn, 1910; of course the rules were not the same there as among the Nestorians; they seem to have maintained seven hours).

The quotations of the Evening service that open the answer, see: *E.S.D.O.*, p. 2; the beginning of the present formulary was omitted.–Marmitha is a part of an Hulala. The Psalter of the Nestorians or Dawida is divided into 21 Hulala's and subdivided into 60 Marmitha's, containing from one to four Psalms. A very clear "Table of the Divisions of the Psalter" may be found in: *E.S.D.O.*, index i, p. 259, (the division is not the same as among the Greeks and Jacobites, cf. Budge, *B.G.* ii, p. 292, n. 6–293. The name is not found in: *B.G.* ii, p. 292, which uses the word "stations"; the first instance of it known to me is Abraham Bar Lipheh), with a survey of their use and the Daily Offices (index ii, p. 260); the *Expos.* i, p. 93–106 has the same. The first name (root: ܪܡܐ) does not seem to be found outside its technical use; its meaning is not quite clear; Hulala = Hallelujah. The origin of these names is obscure just as is their division. It is remarkable that the *Expos.* does not seem to connect it with Isho'yabh iii, cf. *Expos.* i, p. 160: "unaquaeque schola in re hullālarum adhibendorum suum exsequitur consilium. . . si (Isho'yabh) regulam imposuisset de hullālis, non potuissent *homines* regulam eius transgredi." It is not necessary to enter further into these questions; there is still a wide field here awaiting the scholar.

For the Night-service see: *E.S.D.O.*, p. 85 (beginning omitted): the answers and prayers "strengthen, Our Lord etc." p. 85, and "May the secret strength etc." p. 86 are omitted as is done also according to the notes in the Roman Catholic edition; one proceedes immediately to the Hullala's.

We have observed already that nothing is said about the Morning-Service. There the Lord's Prayer comes in: *E.S.D.O.*, p. 106, in its present form after a very long introduction, followed by the prayer: "O Compassionate one whose name is holy etc." This entry is the same for Festival as for Ferial services. It should be noted that our writer indicates the sequence of prayers that was rejected as inferior by the author of the *Expos.*, p. 123; he thinks it better to say first Lord's Prayer and after that the prayers of the priests.

Q. 107. The Lord's Prayer that was introduced by Timothy was not the ordinary one but farced, that is: the addition of our question, viz. the Trishagion (2×) and the Doxologia Minor (cf. P. Drews, *Liturgische Formeln*, and: *Trishagion*, in: *P.R.E.*[3], xi, S. 547–548, and: xx, S. 126–128), both occurring very often in all Eastern liturgies, were inserted into it. So we get the form given in: *L.E.W.*, p. 252, where it is placed within brackets as an addition not found in the MSS. but in practice = T., p. 1 begins with an ordinary L.P. = *E.S.D.O.*, p. 1–2. On the other hand the Lord's Prayer in: *L.E.W.*, p. 303 seems to be said without farcings. This addition is not mentioned *ipsimis verbis* in the *Expos.*; but it was well-known, though some people recited it without Canon; the author leaves it undecided, *Expos.* i, p. 153.

"Canon" is here the antiphonical singing (cf. ad Q. 4). According to the asteriks in Maclean's text, the changes are after: "Come"; before the full text of the Lord's Prayer and after it; after the Gloria; after the following, Amen, and before the last Trishagion. This happened also at the Marmitha's "after the first clause of the first Psalm of each Marmitha say, Hallelujah (2×), yea Hallelujah, and repeat the first clause. After each Marmitha Doxologia Minor. Then there are two choirs in the church who sing it in turns, though this does not take place on weekdays (*E.S.D.O.*, p. 2 and n. 3). Therefore we find here this comparison. It is not quite sure what is meant by the second "Canon"; whether it is the same as before or "Ecclesiastical rule"; the former is more probable though the latter is not impossible. "Of the Nestorians"– applied to themselves; this shows it was not considered as an invective of a heretical name as is said sometimes; so e.g. J. H. Petermann–K. Kessler, *Nestorianen*, in: *P.R.E.*[3], xiii, S. 727. It is not a particularity of our QQ., but it is also found, *Expos.* i, p. 86, 133 and cf. Isho'Barnun, *ad Macarium* 47, where the question is put: "If a Nestorian is sojourning in a country where they have no churches . . ."

Q. 108. After this deviation in the foregoing QQ. they come back to the original point.–The importance of prayer for the faithful is explained in various treatises dealing with this part of the Christian life, in some way or another (cf. Tertullian, Origen, Cyprian, *on Prayer;* Theodore Mops., *ad Baptizandos* ii; Isaac of Niniveh, Index in Wensinck's Translation, s.v. *Prayer*). But this does not offer an explanation of the "advantage" mentioned here, since it deals with the meaning of the Lord's Prayer. Nor can it be explained by pointing to a treasury which is augmented by the prayers even if it were possible to show that this thought is found among the Syrians, or to thoughtless praying because saying prayers has a worth in itself. The *Expos.* i, p. 125 says: "in his quae docuit eos verbis, Dominus totum evangelii canonem comprehendit" that it is: ܡܠܝܐ ܒܘܣܡܐ ܫܪܝܪܐ (this phrase is of doubtful interpretation; it means either: "which fills the true beatitude", or: "which is full of the true beatitude".

At any rate it is not quite clear what are the contents of this beatitude. In connection with the rest of the *Expos.* it means probably the eternal state of blessedness of which this prayer gives a glimpse and for which it asks). The ritual of Baptism was published in: T., 55–75. It was translated and examined by G. Diettrich, *Taufliturgie*, (cf. also the Review of this book by A. Baumstark, in: *O.C.*, 1903, S. 219-226). He pointed out that this liturgy was moulded upon that of Eucharist (p. xx–xxiii), though Baumstark showed that this was not particularly Nest. It may be that the latter author is right in his criticism. But the fact should not be overlooked that all Nestorian rituals seem to have the same effect (cf. ad Q. 3 and 92), and accordingly the same structure. We have found before and it is corroborated in this place that there should be a close parallel between the rituals. About the mysteries see Q. 89 sqq. The place of the *Questions on Baptism* in which he deals with this matter was already been referred to on p. 77–78. From this quotation it must be concluded that the first time it was omitted (because they did not want to follow the rule of Timothy i ?; cf. G. Diettrich, *a.a.O.*, S. 59).

Q. 109. As the remark in that place was somewhat vague they asked to give the precise places. They are found T., p. 55, 69, 73 (Badger ii, p. 195, 206, 210; G. Diettrich, *a.a.O.*, S. 4, 38 and 50) where also the Antiphons are found. "Holy oil" to sign with, see rubric T., p. 69 = Diettrich, *a.a.O.*, S. 37–38. The "power" of the Lord's Prayer means here "its meaning". About the beginning of Baptism, cf. Diettrich, S. 59 (his suggestion sub 4 is right). According T. the loosing of the water took place after the sealing (also *Expos.* ii, p. 103). The two alternative or accompanying prayers are not found in T. It gives on p. 74 two different forms of prayer plus an "alternative prayer" but not in the form supposed here. G. Diettrich, *a.a.O.*, S. 93 offers a survey of the different "sealings" in the MSS. he has examined; one of them, viz. that from Malabar, exhibits a text which is supposed in our Q.; the alternative prayer is "through Thine blessing, o our Lord and our God." Mr. Diettrich thought S. 91 that J mal. had preserved the original text in other places too). The text of "O Compassionate One etc." e.g. *E.S.D.O.*, p. 106. The *Expos.* is of no use here. "Alternative" not meaning: "taking the place of", but: "linked up with"; see e.g. Timothy ii, Ming. Syr. 13, fol. 134b, speaking about the prayer: "It is fitting, o my Lord etc." and its alternative prayer (*L.E.W.*, p. 302) styles it the two blessings of the Lord to His disciples. Nothing is known to me about further use of this word as a *terminus technicus* in Oriental Churches. "Sealing" and "seal": *E.S.D.O.*, p. 292, s.v. *Conclusions*, translates it simply by "Blessing". As a matter of fact this happens here, but what is the origin of this name? (cf. Apoc. vii: Sealing of the Tribes of Israel?) In Q. 116 occurs the phrase: "to seal the prayer", which cannot possibly be a blessing. The word is found at the end of almost every formulary to denote the end of the service. It seems as though these prayers and hymns had not yet been definitely selected when the Formularies were drawn up. Those in Eucharistic Formulary of Berol. 38 show a text which is different from that of T. and besides that it has more forms; T., p. 151–164 has a great number of ܚܘܬܡ̈ܐ ܕܟܠ ܐܪܙܐ, most of them are from a later date than our treatises (viz. of 'Abdisho' b. Berikha, 14th cent.); in *L.O.C.* they are not found. The same observation can be made in the various MSS.

of the Baptismal Rite, cf. G. Diettrich, *Tauflit.*, S. 93. About this late Nestorian kind of poetry see: A. Baumstark, *L.G.*, Index s.v. Ḥûttâmâ. The technical use of this word is not found in the other churches; cf. Diettrich, *a.a.O.*, S. 50, Ann. 3: "Die hier folgenden Ḥutâmē finden sich in keiner der verglichenen Taufliturgien" (Hanssens iii, p. 521 informs us that the same word is also found in the *Missale Sharfense*, p. 91–93; but this book cannot be considered as a witness of ancient liturgical practices. Besides this worthless remark Hanssens contains nothing of interest). Yet I think that it may go back to an ancient christian use. Timothy ii, Ming. Syr. 13, fol. 135a speaks of the last Lord's Prayer as "a seal of our prayers" i.e. a short summary and confirmation of them. Undoubtedly the same is meant here. Tertullian, *De Oratione* 18, in: *M.S.L.* 1, col. 1281, says that the kiss of peace is "the seal of prayer". It is the corroborating conclusion. We might also compare: *Testamentum Domini*, ed. Rahmani, Moguntiae, 1899, p. 44: "seal of thanksgiving", and: *Euphemia and the Goth*, ed. F. C. Burkitt, London, 1913, p. ܠ "... and sealing their prayer with tears". These places, show conclusively that the word was often used to denote the solemn ending of prayers. I do not know whether σφραγίζω is found in this sense. The *Expos.* mentions it in connection with baptism (see Index, s.v.) but that is not sufficient to make our point clear since "Seal" is there a common name for baptism from the earliest times of christianity (cf. W. Bauer, *Handwörterbuch zum N.T.* [2], Giessen, 1928, Sp. 1276, s.v. σφραγίς). At any rate it is worth while to notice that the *Expos.* does not mention it at the end of the Eucharist[1] and this poses the question, if this kind of ending a service was a speciality of a later age. Since the *Expos.* wants to explain the rules of I. iii it may be passing over the additions of a later age, but already existing in its time, without comment. In this connection we may observe that one of the most important Ḥutamâ's is ascribed in Berol. 38 to Elias of Nisibis (975–± 1050, cf. A. Baumstark, *L.G.*, S. 287–288; "anscheinend" on S. 288, Abt. 11 can be struck out; and if this statement is accepted, it is highly probable that this kind of ending was introduced by the reform of the liturgy in the High Monastery. It will not be out of place to quote a sentence of Prof. A. Baumstark, *L.G.*, S. 303 on this kind of ending; in dealing with the revival of religious poetry in the 11th and 12th cent. he says: "Freier ist in der Wahl des metrischen Aufbaues bei wenigstens vorherrschendem Gebrauche von alphabetischer Akrostichis und Endreim der als dichterische Weiterspinnung des priesterlichen Schlusssegens der eucharistischen Liturgie gedachte Ḥûttàma." This date is the same as that of our treatises! The Ḥ. is not only the end of the Euch. Lit.; the same question was discussed with regard to the Baptismal Ritual by G. Diettrich, *Tauflit.*, S. 93 who ascribed the introduction to Elias iii Abû Halîm (1176–1190, A. Baumstark, *L.G.*, S. 288–289), because this Elias is the only one who is known as a poet. As a matter of fact, he had been metropolitan of Nisibis, but the reason of Mr. Diettrich can also be applied to the former E. who is always called: of Nisibis and who is thought to be the author by Prof. Baumstark.

Q. 110–112. The question in regard to the formulary of marriage is once more repeated; for the answer see p. 113. For a right understanding of the following

(1) While *Expos.* uses the verb ܫܠܡ several times in the sense of "solemn ending" e.g. ii, p. 60.

Q.Q. it is necessary to give a brief summary of this rite (the laws concerning Marriage, see in: 'Abdisho', *Nomocanon*, ii. A translation of the formulary [ed. by the Arch-Bishop of Canterbury's Assyrian Mission, Urmia, which I know only by name] was given by Badger, ii, p. 244–276, cf. the chapter on "Marriage-Customs" in: Browne–Maclean, p. 142–159 [for the ancient rites, see: *D.C.A.*, s.v. *Marriage*, and: *D.A.C.L.*, s.v. *Mariage*, t. x, col. 1888–1899, but the data are not very old]). This blessing consists of the following parts: betrothal; marriage; blessing of the bridal attire; benediction of the colours and of the Crowns; coronation; setting up of the bridal chamber. The text of Badger contains a Lord's Prayer at the beginning of ii (p. 245); it seems that this was an addition of a later date, since otherwise Q. 114 would be without meaning. Here the question seems to have suggested the addition. Q. 111 *shows clearly that these Eastern Christians were very well conscious of the contents of the Lord's Prayer. They did not conceive it, as is often thought, as a dead or as a living but magically operative formula,*[1] which has power by being repeated. It is accentuated by the fact that the phrases used here, especially the verbs, do not agree with those found in the Peshita text, but replace them by synonyms. It is not obvious what suggested to the writer that this prayer is only to be said "by the mouth of the whole congregation". It is possible that it was said because it had been taught by the Lord to His disciples (Mt. vi, cf. v 1b; Lc. xi) and has the first person plural.

The writer hints at what is going on during this service. The betrothal consists of asking the man and woman if they are inclined to be married; if they want they are joined together and blessed by the priest. In the marriage-service prayers for help follow next, e.g. "Build up, O Lord, through Thy Word, and adorn with Thy hope, and establish in Thy mercy, this work which Thy servants have entered upon etc.", an anthem and new prayers of the same kind. Next the priest takes the chalice in his hand, prays for the espoused and prays over the ring. He makes a sign of the cross over the chalice with the ring and throws it into the cup, in glorifying the great power of the cross. A small cross and Ḥenana (p. 132, n. 2) is also thrown into it and then the cup is perfect (a similar formula as that of the sacramental elements, p. 253). Bridegroom and bride drink from the cup (we observe that in our treatise this blessing of the chalice seems to belong to the betrothal). The bridal attire is blessed during which the following prayer a.o. is said: "Let the right hand of Thy mercy, O Jesus our Lord, rest upon this bridegroom and bride in Thy grace and in Thy pity make them a blessed pair, and enrich their dwellings with wealth and all manner of possessions etc." followed by many biblical examples (p. 255–256). At the "crowning" (for this sign of victory, see: *D.C.A.*, s.v. *Crown; D.A.C.L.*, s.v. *Mariage*, t. x, col. 1889–1890; and the discussion of J. Rendel Harris–A. Mingana, *Odes and Psalms of Solomon*, ii, p. 207–214.) The hope is expressed upon a temporal and eternal crowning, it is accompanied by all sorts of glorifying of God's greatness and strength. After that the couple is blessed and God is asked to enrich them. The last part "setting up of the bridal chamber" is generally recited, as we are informed by Mr. Badger "in the evening, before the bridegroom and bride retire to rest for the night" (p. 271 n.). It consists

(1) The same observation can be made in reading the words of Timothy ii, quoted ad Q. 87 sqq., as in many other Eastern explanations of the meaning of the Liturgy.

once more of prayers for deliverance from the devil and of prayers for good faith: "Bless, O Lord, the bridal chamber of Thy servants, and keep the bridegroom and bride who dwell there in from the evil one," again followed by examples from the O.T. It will be seen that our writer brings to the fore the leading thoughts of this ritual. Again he paraphrases them in his own way as is seen in glancing through the pages. The second reason is less spiritual and has been spoken of before. The argument of our author himself is based upon history, curious enough, since it is only once or twice that he speaks in this way. Unfortunately he does not say what is exactly meant by "formerly". *D.C.A.*, ii, p. 1107 it is said that marriages were generally celebrated in the church in early times, but sometimes at home, especially in the East, referring to: Chrysostomus, *Hom.* xlviii *in Gen.* xxiv, in: *M.S.G.*, 54, col. 443. The latter practice was that of the writer's age in opposition to the general practice of the Nestorians. It is ordered in: 'Abdisho', *Nomocanon*, ii 2, that "Betrothal must be performed in the church." Our text agrees with the rubric of the present formulary (Badger ii, p. 244: "all shall assemble in the house of the damsel's father etc.") As far as I know the Nestorians are the only Christians who have this festival at home. This is the more striking, since they have a high idea of common worship (cf. *E.S.D.O.*, p. xviii). About the Lord's Prayer after the morning psalms see: *E.S.D.O.*, p. 167, referring to p. 106.

Q. 113 is the ordinary case. The present formulary does not provide the Lord's Prayer at the beginning, nor did it do so at the time of our writer. It was simply put before it. "To share," is possible. Yet the following ܠ is difficult to connect with it. I think it is the object-prefix and V. has preserved the better reading. In case the one of M. should be followed it must be remembered that an advantage (Q. 108) was contained in this prayer, of which one should avail oneself.

Q. 114. The unity of the two parts is also supposed in the formulary. The betrothal was the beginning of the married state (cf. *D.C.A.*, s.v. *Betrothal*, where some references to earlier times of the same effect are found). But I do not know whether there were special Canons about this point in the Eastern churchbooks; the *Synodicon Orientale* and other Nest. books which I consulted do not contain them. Again it appears (see: Q. 3 and 92) that all formularies were thought to be parallel and made up according to the same type. Mautᵉbha = Sessio: "an anthem at the nightservice, sung sitting" (*E.S.D.O.*, p. 296, where it is added that they vary and the books in which they are contained are mentioned. It is somewhat misleading to draw a parallel with the Greek Cathisma, because both words mean: sitting. For the Greek means a division of the Psalter, as Hulala among the Nestorians, and is different with regard to its contents from the Mautᵉbha. The part wich is said will be found: *E.S.D.O.*, p. 151–152 (since one M. is spoken of; this is better than referring to: *l.c.*, p. 85–96). The Hulala is mentioned p. 153. I did not find anywhere that this intermission of the service was allowed and practised.

Q. 115. The third point. Answer parallel to that of Q. 111: the contents of the service do not agree with those of the Lord's Prayer; therefore it is useless to say it here. "Return to the earth etc." cf. Gen. iii 19. To a right understanding of the first part we must remember that the Nestorians generally adhered to the doctrine of the "status intermedius" with regard to the dead i.e. that the dead after passing away are not judged immediately, but wait in a sleeping state till the day of the resurrection and the last judgment. Cf. Budge, *B.G.* ii, p. 307: "he departed this life of troubles and trials for the rest of those who sleep in Christ"; p. 265: "We shall both be buried until the day of the revelation of the Raiser of the dead"; p. 485: "Thus the blessed man departed from this laborious life . . . to the greatly desired chambers of Paradise"; very explicit is this word of *Expos.* ii, p. 124: "mortem enim somnium et dormitionem ostendimus esse". Often it was thought that after the death there was already a partial judgment, that the soul of the just goes to a better place viz. Paradise than that of the wicked. This Paradise is a place "dessen Wonne ihnen das letzte Pfand für ihre endgiltige Belohnung, die Anschauung Gottes, bittet" (A. Baumstark, *O.C.*, 1901, S. 341 and N. 3; cf. Salomon of Basra, *Book of the Bee*, ed. Budge, Oxford, 1886, p. 132). Some other places in Syrian writers who speak of this doctrine are mentioned by M. Jugie, *Theologia Dogmatica*, v, p. 336–340. This teaching is not confined to the Nestorian Church, but was found in many places and at an early date, see: J. N. Bakhuizen van den Brink, *Gegevens betreffende graf en eeuwig leven in de oud-christelijke Epigraphie*, in: *Nederlandsch archief voor Kerkgeschiedenis*, 1924–1925, blz. 81–94, and: F. Heiler, *Urkirche und Ostkirche*, S. 232–234. A fuller discussion than is given there is a desideratum. We may point out that this view tries to give an explanation of all the biblical data (see e.g. Ps. cxv 17); it reaches back to Jewish conceptions, see: H. L. Strack–P. Billerbeck, *Kommentar zum N.T. aus Talmud und Midrasch*, München, 1928, iv 2, S. 1016–1165.

The burial-service of the priests was translated, though not completely, by Badger ii, p. 282–321 (cf. p. 282 n. cf. Browne–Maclean, p. 279–289; I have not consulted the edition of the Archbishop of Canterbury's Mission (mentioned by A. Baumstark, *L.G.*, S. 111 and 357). In this case too the writer reproduces in his own words the tenor of the prayers though we observe that most of them as given by Mr. Badger speak in the first person plural and are not direct intercessions; about prayers for the dead see: M. Jugie, *Theol. Dogm.*, v, p. 341–344. Such a prayer is given e.g. p. 301–302. Those quoted by the author are verses of Ps. lxxxviii and xxxviii. Those mentioned first and last in: Badger ii, p. 283–284 where also the proper Antiphon is printed. Hymn = Madrasha, see: A. Baumstark, *L.G.*, S. 39, who gives some explanation of this doctrinal chant and those chants of the dead: *Register* s.v. (most of them are made after the time of our treatise) V. has extended the number of examples; for "Antiphons of the way" see Q. 117.

Q. 116. Mautᵉbha is used in a twofold sense: the first one is the sessio of the night-service (as in Q. 114), that is to say that the first part of the night-service was said together with the Lord's Prayer at the house of the dead man (*E.S.D.O.*, p. 151). The second is a hymn sung during the burial of which Mr. Badger gives some instances.

Nowhere else I found a remark expressing the command to the priest of saying such prayers; but on the other hand prayers should be said over the dead body as soon as possible (*D.C.A.*, s.v. *Obsequies*). The end however shows that fixed rules did not exist. In the morning the prayers of *E.S.D.O.*, p. 103–105 were said and the beginning of the burial-service (Badger ii, p. 283 sqq.) was added to it.

It is possible that the following part formed originally a separate *Q.* and *A.* (p. 71), the response beginning at: "We are not able." The village Niniveh is well known in history; it was situated opposite to Mosul. For long it had become an insignificant spot, which was quite superseded by Mosul. Bar Hebraeus mentioned it fairly often (also in the time of our treatise: *Chr. Eccl.* iii, col. 319, 325, 331, 335, 337, 339). It may be that this was done by Jacobite aversion against Mosul, which was a stronghold of Nestorianism. About its History cf. *B.O.*, iii 2, p. dcclxvi–dcclxvii, and: E. Sachau, *Zur Ausbreitung des Christentums in der Persis*, 1916, S. 48. Why it is called "House of the Ignorant" is not clear. Isho'yabh iii (*Epistulae*, ed. Duval, p. 55) said that it was a poor church. But this can hardly explain the expression in question. Possibly it was called so because the Jacobites who were ignorant by the mere fact of being heretics, had here a bishop's see.–Hazza, cf. Payne Smith, *Thesaurus Syr.*, Col. 1238, and: *Supplement*, p. 123 with various references (cf. also: *B.O.*, iii 2, p. dccx and dccxx). It was situated in the neighbourhood of Arbela, famous through its important Chronicle. For some time it was the Capitol of Adiabene. Interesting is the interpolation in: Gismondi ii, p. 32: a bishop "ex regimine Hazzae (nunc notae nomine Arbela)." It was at a distance from Mosul and far from the place where our writer probably lived (ch. iv). Therefore he says "I have heard etc." (cf. the Map in: J. Labourt, *Christianisme*).

The burial-service consists of washing the dead man at home (this was obligatory, cf. 'Abdisho', *Nomocanon*, vi 6, Mai, p. 280) while prayers and hymns are said (*D.A.C.L.*, s.v. *Funérailles*, t. v, col. 2705–2715 does not contain anything of interest for our Q.). After that the dead body (at least that of the clerics) is taken to the church, the "Antiphons of the way" (Q. 115 V., 117) being recited (the Greek use, cf. L. Petit, *D.A.C.L.*, s.v. *Antiphone*, t. i, col. 2484–2485). In the church there is reading of the Scriptures besides prayers and hymns and usually there is communion-service, if a priest is buried. This being done one goes to the grave and the body is interred, and earth is thrown in it in the form of a cross. Each of these acts is accompanied by proper prayers and hymns. In the churchyard the service is ended by "sealing". The next day follows a "consolation" or memorial service, see ad Q. 16. It will be seen that this formulary is of a very loose structure (cf. the remark in Q. 117). The writer did not know the tradition which furnished a solemn beginning and end. In Niniveh it was done in the church and there the question which formed the starting point of the discussion would be superfluous. Nevertheless this was apparently left to discretion of the priests. The expression "They ate" means the dinners after the burial at the house of the deceased which were usual in all places, cf. Browne–Maclean, p. 284. John Bar Abgare (in: 'Abdisho', *Nomocanon*, vi 6, Mai, p. 280) had ordered the priests not to take too much food or drink. We hear of various complaints about this institution, which seems to have often become more or less an orgy. Our author only states the fact. Some more about this as well as about the burial–services among the Jacobites may be found in: Kayser, S. 155, ad Q. 60. It is not out of place to observe that these meals are different from the "Agapes Funèbres", mentioned in: *L.O.O.*, p. 257–258, since they are simply a Eucharist at the grave.

Q. 117. The formulary does not give any rubric about the point that is under discussion here. It seems to be the intention there that the dead man will be buried on the same day on which he died. We must remember that the sequence of services was in the evening, at night and in the morning. The former group considered the Mautebha's of the evening as the beginning of a service that was interrupted for some time (cf. Q. 52) and carried on the next morning. The latter thought it to be a special service; hence it was ended in the usual way; the next day they began afresh. The end of the ordinary Evening-service which the author has in mind is found: *E.S.D.O.*, p. 20 sqq.: "The priest takes the cross in his hand, and turning to the people says: Bless O my Lord. By Your Command (*sc.* I will give the blessing). They answer, By the Command of Christ and glory to his holy Name and they bow their heads." The conclusion (= Sealing) follows during which the priest makes the sign of the cross over the people. This conclusion is in the form of an invocation for help (the form given by Dean Maclean ends with giving the kiss of peace and reciting the Nicene Creed. The editor remarks that "this appears to be the universal custom," but that the former is not to be found in the Roman Catholic edition and in that of Urmia, while the latter is not found in the R.C., p. 22, n. 2. In fact our author does not refer to it and therefore it is probably a later addition). That he is "a partaker of the signing" is the same thought that leads to putting the Host into the mouth of the dead as though they were living (*D.A.C.L.*, s.v. *Communion des morts*, t. iii, col. 2445–2446).

Q. 118–123. Together with these QQ. we must deal with Q. 97 and 103 since they are concerned with similar questions, viz. the place of Cross and Gospel at the beginning of the service. They were indispensable for a valid Eucharist (cf. ad Q. 35). The Cross and the Gospel are constantly mentioned together, not only in the Eucharist, but also in every solemn procession (though no mention is made of special processional crosses, cf. *D.A.C.L.*, s.v. *Croix et Crucifix*, t. iii, col. 3102–3103, and: Kaufmann, *Handbuch*, S. 575–576). In Q. 101 we saw what meaning these two objects had for the devote Nestorian. It is not out of place to summarize what is said in T. concerning this matter (*L.E.W.* is quoted): it is not said where the priest stands at the beginning, nor during the "anthem of the Sanctuary" (p. 253–254) nor during one of the following prayers and hymns until the lections (p. 255–256). It seems, though it is not expressed anywhere that it was the Bema (cf. ad Q. 97). For on p. 257 after the prayer before the apostle we read: "When the priest goes down from the Bema and reaches the door of the altar he and the deacon both incline . . ." "They all go down to the nave (temple) . . ."; p. 258 brings the rubric: "When the priest goes to make ready the Gospel . . ."; "when he takes up (the Gospel) to go out (of the altar)", followed by the other readings. On page 262 the censer is taken and the paten with the hosts prepared during the caruzutha. The following rubric bringing something about it is on p. 267 "the deacons enter the altar", while the priest places the mysteries upon the altar, "and going outside the Sanctuary the priest lades the deacons with the Cross and

Gospels (p. 268; is this still practised? Hanssens iii, p. 107 says: "Hodie utraque processio, evangelii scilicet et crucis, plane obsolevisse videtur.") The deacons are distinguished from those who remain inside the altar. It is described how the priest worships on the Bema (p. 269) after which he goes back to the altar giving peace (p. 269–271). During the rest of the liturgy he remains there.

The rubrics in: *L.O.C.*, and: Berol. 38 are somewhat different. But at any rate it is clear that these precepts, unless supplemented by indications from other sources, are not quite clear, though it must be admitted that this will be specially the case for those who are obliged to rely upon these rubrics and are not able to assist at a real Nestorian service. In passing it will be noticed that these entrances have nothing to do with the so-called Little Entrance of the Greek liturgy (cf. Hanssens iii, p. 100).

It will be useful to consult here the various expositions (a short summary in: Hanssens iii, p. 107, cf. p. 104–108). Narsai, *Hom.* xvii does not yield much evidence for he deals only with the Missa Fidelium. The only reference is the following: "the priests now come in procession into the midst of the Sanctuary" (Connolly, p. 4). The sequence in the exposition of Abraham Bar Lipheh (*Expos.* ii, p. 158–161) is clear: after the Anthem of the Sanctuary follows the "Egressus Crucis et Ascensus super Bema" (not found in: *L.E.W.*), accompanied by lights etc.; the Gospel is not mentioned. This comes after the reading of the Apostolos and a psalm: "egressio evangelii, crucisque cum eo," escorted by deacons. The Cross is held upon a long pole. After the reading of the Gospel that follows next comes the "sublatio crucis et evangelii de throno Bematis" (cf. Q. 104) by a deacon and priest without escort. The Cross is put in "superliminari porta sanctuarii" and the Gospel at the other side. This description is one of an ordinary service. Here in Q. 118 it is specially emphasized that the bishop or Metropolitan is present. Such a high service, which was not provided for in the ordinary service-books, is underlying the *Expos.* Its evidence is the following: The Anthem of the Sanctuary is sung, sub-deacons stand near the door of the altar carrying lamps and deacons carry tapers. They are preceded by two deacons without anything, while an arch-deacon is on the left hand of the bishop. Then the deacons go out, first the two without anything, the sub-deacons join in, next the rest of the deacons followed by him who carries the Cross "signum Regis victoriosi, et seriem mandatorum eius". They go from the Sanctuary to the Bema. The sub-deacons remain standing in a corridor. The two deacons stand on the Bema near the altar in honour of the altar and the bishop having the Cross and Gospel. Those who stand in the corridor go back to the sacristy, the others carrying censers descend from the Bema. Only those two remain there. The reading of Law and Prophets follows next. The reader comes from the sacristy, bows before the altar and comes to the Bema. After that the Apostolos is carried into the Bema (two practices regarding the door). After three verses the deacon of the order and some people with him go to the sacristy worshipping and a priest goes with him ("surgit sacerdos et adorat, et crucem osculatur et episcopum"). There they prepare the procession to bring out the Gospel while the Apostle is being read. A hymn is sung and every one prepares himself for the reception of the Gospel. It enters the Bema a priest going on the righthand-side; the Gospel is kissed by the bishop. While it is brought in it is received with all the splendor of Eastern ritual. The Gospel being read, the various members of the clergy are blessed by the Bishop, and the deacons draw near to the altar and the Cross and the Gospel. Then they go back to the altar, two deacons carrying the Cross and the Gospel and they go in to the throne and the veils that have been opened since the beginning are closed; "qui crucem et evangelium portant, non ponunt ea super altare donec vela ligentur" (cf. various places between p. 9–33). Timothy ii in his Exposition, Mingana Syr. 13, fol. 115b–121b, mentions the Anthem of the Sanctuary; the bringing out of the Cross and its being placed on the Bema; the veils are opened; the readings of the Scripture; the priest who reads the Gospel descends from the Bema, goes to the door of the altar and prays there; the priest puts a pure stole over his shoulder and takes the Gospel preceded by deacons with lights and incense, after which the Gospel is read; this reading is ended with an adoration; the priest gives Cross and Gospel to the deacons who carry them from the Bema without procession; at the altar-door the Cross is placed on the lefthand side and the Gospel on the righthand side.

It will be seen that there is some difference between these sketches; the *Expos.* has the fullest details which shows and is explained by the fact that it is a pontificale. It is interesting to notice that Timothy who is the latest expositor says exactly where Cross and Gospel must be placed in the end, while the others have no indication whatever. It may be that this point and others were decided under the influence of such questions as are discussed here.

We should remember in order to understand these questions well that the righthand-side has always been the side of most honour (cf. Mt. xxv 33, Marc x 37, and: Klostermann's comment, *Das Markusevangelium* [2], Tübingen, 1926, and: *Das Matthäusevangelium*, [2], Tübingen, 1927, on these places.–Jewish materials in: Strack–Billerbeck, *Kommentar zum NT.*, München, 1922, i, S. 835–836, 980–981.–*D.A.C.L.*, s.v. *Droit*, t. iv, col. 1547–1549: "la droite est le côté sacré, le côté de la vie et de la force; la gauche, le côté profane, de la mort, de la faiblesse," in almost every religion, cf. the use of "dexter" and "sinister"). For the exact places of right and left see ad Q. 98.

Q. 97: Deacons carrying it, cf. what was quoted from Abraham and *Expos.* This comparison shows a difference in which Timothy stands on the side of our Q. The moments of coming out and entering see before. "They" are the priests and deacons of the Sanctuary (*Expos.*). ܩܒܠ Pa. lit. = to receive–to go to meet, a meaning also of the Af. What is meant by the Bema? *E.S.D.O.*, p. 292 gives two explanations: 1) raised space between the Sanctuary-doors and the dwarf wall in the nave parallel to them; 2) rarely the Sanctuary. The same in: *L.E.W.*, p. 571 where the readers are referred to the word: *Ambon* (p. 569). The former use can be illustrated by a reference to: Budge, *B.G.* ii, p. 413 sketch; the latter is found in the quotation from: Badger ii, p. 325 (ad Q. 27). The use of the word in our Q.Q. supposes that there is a kind of procession going through the church. This agrees with the description given in the *Expos.* where the Bema is a place in the middle of the Church (besides the references given before, cf. i, p. 31 and the Sketch of Dom. Connolly i, p. 196 M.) on which the Gospel etc. is read and which correspond with the Ambo (in the Greek church formerly but now obsolete). Compare: *D.A.C.L.*, s.v. *Ambo*, t. i, col. 1330–1347; in the East its place was in the middle of the church.

Q. 103. A high mass as in *Expos.* It is illustrated by our quotations from the explanations. The kissing, a sign of devotion (Q. 22), is not found elsewhere. That "they" means here the congregation is apparent from the version of our Q. in

Q. 118–119. Probably the answer of Q. 103 was not sufficiently detailed. For there are no traces whatever that our treatise is composed from different parts of separate origin. At any rate the latter two are a more expanded form. None of the sources mentioned before shows that the priests go out during the said antiphon, or we must suppose synchronism instead of sequence of events. That the priest = Jesus, that he in spite of his humanity acts "vice Christi" is a supposition which is continually found in all the mystagogies. It is superfluous to give here texts to prove this since it is met everywhere (Nest.: Narsai, *Hom.* xvii, p. 4 Connolly; Isho'yabh i, *Canon* 1, in: O. Braun, *Synhados*, S. 240; *Expos.* ii, p. 7, 12, 18, 24 etc.). The quotations are to be found in: *Breviarium Chaldaicum*, ed. P. Bedjan, iii, the former, p. 304, cf. *Expos.* i, p. 122; the latter p. 302 quoted from Prayers in the Hebdomada of the Holy Cross. Nevertheless the reasons are dark why this way of arrangement is chosen as one would expect that "Jesus" would be right as in Q. 119. "Ancients" ch. vi. Palm-sunday, lit. Hosanna's, clearly borrowed from Mt. xxi 9 (cf. about it also *Expos.* i, p. 52–58 which does not say anything about the festival itself). A. Baumstark, *Festbrevier*, S. 230, mentions a Homily of Severus of Antioch with the same name in its title. Nevertheless it does not seem as if the name: "Hosanna's" was generally accepted. Among the Nestorians it is most common. To celebrate this day with a procession is already found in the first description of this festival in the Peregrinatio Silviae (see: P. Drews, *Woche, grosse*, in: *P.R.E.*[3], xxi, S. 416–419). It seems as though it was introduced among the Persians in the time of Babai ± 500 (Labourt, *Christianisme*, p. 154–160), cf. Gismondi i, p. 41: "Eius diebus celebratum est Nisibi et Madainae festum palmarum et Transfigurationis. Porro solemnitas palmarum apud graecos ex festis est celebrioribus" (*Expos.* i, p. 52–58; ii, p. 90 does not afford any help).

For the reasons in Q. 119 and 120 cf. the Comments of the Preface ch. vi. Their thoughts were clearly a presumption when we see how the Cross and Gospel are estimated by our author (Q. 101 and 123).

Q. 121. "Platform" is not a terminus technicus, cf. T., p. 10, l. 7; p. 145, l. 11. It is the same place called "Katastroma" elsewhere (cf. Connolly's Sketch, *Expos.* i, p. 196, G.G.; = now the Bema?); cf. *L.E.W.*, p. 586: "the footpace before the altar." The Cross facing the altar was thus probably expressing adoration of the altar and its Sacraments. East and West mentioned here are explained by the orientation of the whole cult (the same in the Baptismal Ritual, see: Diettrich, *Tauflit.*, S. 78). It is found everywhere in the Christian church from the oldest times (a good summary in: *D.A.C.L.*, s.v. *Orientation*, t. xii, col. 2665–2668 and add to the literature mentioned there: G. Graf, *Zur Gebetsostung*, in: *Jahrbuch f. Liturgiewissenschaft*, 1927, S. 153–159, specially from Christian Arabic sources). But this use is not specially Christian, but is very wide spread in various religions, cf. G. van der Leeuw, *Phänomenologie*, S. 372–377. The later Christian authors offer all sorts of mystagogical reasons. *Expos.* i, p. 87–90 are devoted to the question why the people must pray turned to the East and not to Jerusalem as the prophets did, a point of special interest for the Nestorians of course, since they were east of Jerusalem. The answer is: because in the East lies Paradise, the place of immortality and sanctity (these reasons mentioned in: Browne–Maclean, p. 235 are not only those of the modern Nestorians, as is thought by G. Diettrich, *Tauflit.*, S. 78, Anm. 1). 'Abdisho', *Nomocanon*, v 8 says that it is done because of the apostolic commandments and an (apocryphal) tradition, that Jesus blessed His disciples at the Ascension (Luke xxiv, 50) looking west, while the disciples looked east. These reasons seem to point back to a common Christian tradition since they occur in all the Eastern churches.

The answer is not extremely clear. The beginning seems to express that the Cross must stand as far East as possible. But the ambiguity of expression appears where the opinion of those who are mentioned in the Question, is summarized. Particularly doubtful is where the apodosis begins in the sentence ܠܡܕܢܚܐ-ܕܐܝܟ ܕܐܠܝܨ. Or in other terms must ܐܠܝܨ be explained as a modification of the following verb (Nöldeke, *Syrische Grammatik*, § 337) or is it verbum finitum; in the former case "they need not etc." is the apodosis, while in the latter it is a special sentence of its own. In both cases there seems to be a difference with what is said at the end of the question. It seems as though the teacher corrects the statement of the questioner. We have adopted the latter possibility taking "to come" to mean: the coming back of the Cross to the altar. Nevertheless I do not see the solution quite well.

Q. 122. ܟܣܝܗ cf. Q. 104. I have never heard that a gospel is mentioned connected with the Cross. It may mean that the Cross stands with one arm over the Gospel. Those people that are spoken of in the question placed it in the West of the Bema, for undoubtedly the altar here means: the altar in the Bema. The faithful are the officiating priests. The adoration is by bowing and metanoia's which are met several times in the rubrics where the priests worship before the altar and kiss it, cf. e.g. *L.E.W.*, p. 285, p. 272. For the setting see ch. vi, i.–About the end of the Q., see ad Q. 1.

Q. 123. Refers to Q. 119. It is a reflex of the dispute mentioned in Q. 101 (see there about the meaning of the Cross). It is worth while to draw here the attention to the sentence of the author, that without the Cross the Gospel would not have been known. Such a word shows sufficiently that for people like our author the ritual had not obscured the comprehension of the vital truths of Christianity; but that the ritual really conveyed them and made them tangible before the eyes of those who knew their interpretation; that the truth was living and was not superseded by magic and paganism.

# APPENDIX OF VARIOUS READINGS

(Cf. Ch. iii)

| *Folio and Line of Ming. Syr.* 566 | | *Vat. Syr.* 150 |
|---|---|---|
| | om. | in margine fol. 1*b* manu ܕܓܘܪܓܝܘܣ maronitica ܡܠܦܢܘܬܐ ܕܐܪܡܝܐ |
| 1*b* 7 | ܢܦܫܐ | om. |
| 9 | ܡܪܐܘܬ | ܡܟܪܐܬ |
| 10 post: | ܐܬܕܪܫܘ | add: ܒܩܢܝܐ |
| 11 | ܕܐܠܝ | om. |
| 13 | ܐܝܟ | ܡܢ |
| 16 | ܒܡܫܒܚܢܐ ܘܡܒܢܝܐ | ܒܢܝܐ ܘܒܡܫܒܚܢܐ |
| 17 | ܘܢܬܪܘܨ | ܘܢܬܪܨ |
| 18 | ܐܢܫ | om. |
| 2*a* 1 | ܫܦܬܐ | ܫܦܘܬܐ |
| 2 post: | ܐܡܪܝܢ | add: ܕܡܢ ܐܝܟܐ ܒܗ ܒܗܘܢܐ ܡܢܬܐ ܒܡܫܢܝܬܐ |
| 2 | ܐܘ ܗܘ | ܘܗܘ |
| 5 | ܒܗܕܐ | add: ܡܢܬܐ |
| 6 | ܕܣܗܕܘܬܐ | ܕܣܗܕܘܬܐ |
| 6 post: | ܕܣܗܕܘܬܐ | add: ܕܝܢ |
| 11 | ܢܗܘܐ | ܢܗܘ |
| 16 | ܡܫܬܪܐ | om. |
| 2*b* 1 | ܘܣܘܟܡ | ܡܢ ܣܘܟܡ |
| 14 | ܐܝܟ ܡܐ ܕ | ܐܝܟܢܐ ܐܝܟ ܕ |
| 15 | ܕܒܢܝܗܘܢ ܒܫܘܪܝܬܐ | om. |
| 18 | ܬܪܬܝܢ | ܟܠ ܬܪܬܝܢ |

| | | M. | V. |
|---|---|---|---|
| 3a | 1–2 | ܒܝ ܡܐܬܠܝ | om. |
| | 4 post: | ܠܚܘܫܬܐ | add: ܡܫܬܟܚܬܐ |
| | 5 | ܘܝܘܡܘܬܐ | ܘܕܟܝܪܘܬܗ |
| | 6–7 | ܘܫܒܩܬܝ ܟܠܝ ܒܒܝܬ | 2–3–1 |
| | 8 | ܐܓܒܪ ܐܝܟ ܥܡܝܪܐ | ܐܝܟ ܓܒܪܐ ܥܡܝܪܐ |
| | 12 | ܠܬܪܥܐ | add: ܗܢܐ |
| | 13 post: | ܒܫܬܝܩܘܬܐ | add: ܒܝ ܠܡܦܩ ܕܝܢ ܠܐ ܬܪܥܐ<br>ܪܘܚܐ ܠܟܢܗ ܒܟܝܢܘܬܐ . ܐܦ ܕܝܢ<br>ܐܫܬܐܠܬ ܡܢܗ ܠܗܝ |
| | 17 | ܕܚܠܝܘ | add: ܡܢ ܗܢܐ ܥܠܡܐ |
| 3b | 2 | ܫܒܩܬܝ | add: ܕܝܢ |
| | 8 | ܦܘܪܢܐ | ܕܦܘܪܢܐ |
| | 12 | ܘܡܫܬܪܪܐ ܘܡܫܬܟܠܠܗ ܐܢܬܝ | ܘܡܫܬܟܠܠܗ ܡܫܬܪܪܐ ܘܐܢܬܝ |
| | 15 | ܐܦܣܘܣܐ | om. |
| 4a | 3 | ܫܢ̈ܝܐ | ܠܫܢ̈ܝܐ |
| | 8 | ܡܫܝܚܐ | ܡܟܬܪ ܠܢܘܩܒܘܗܝ |
| 4b | 2 | ܠܡܫܡܠܝܘܬܗ | om. |
| | 6 | ܒܩܘܡܐ ܡܫܡܫܝ ܠܗ | 2–3–1 |
| | 14 pro: | ܡܫܡܫܢܝ | add: ܒܗܕܐ |
| | 15 | ܗܘ | ܗܝ |
| | 16 | ܕܟܝܢܐ | ܕܒܟܝܢܐ |
| | 17 | ܠܐܡܐ ܒܟܝܢܐ ܘܠܟܝܢܐ<br>ܒܐܡܐ | ܠܟܝܢܐ ܕܐܡܐ ܘܠܐܡܐ<br>ܒܟܝܢܐ |
| 5a | 3 post: | ܘܡܠܗܡܠܐ | add: ܠܒܪܘܫܬܐ |
| | 3 post: | ܒܡܫܝܗ | add: ܒܡܦܪܬܗ |
| | 9 | ܘܦܪܝܐ | ܦܪܝܫܐ ܘܡܟܝܢܐ ܢܣܒܬܐ ܒܥܡܐ ܐܦܐ<br>ܘܟܝܢܐ ܘܦܪܝܐ |

| | | M. | V. |
|---|---|---|---|
| | 9 | ܡܢ ܢܣܝܘܬܐ | add: ܟܠܐ ܡܢ ܡܕܒܪܢܐ |
| | 13 | ܘܡܪܚܐ | add: ܠܡܫܡܫܘܬܐ ܕܐܪܙܐ ܩܕܝܫܐ ܕܡܢܗܪܐ ܣܟܠܘܬܐ ܒܥܡܠ ܐܚܐ ܘܒܢܐ ܘܡܪܚܐ |
| 5b | 6 | ܐܘ | om. |
| | 6 post: | ܣܟܠܘܬܐ | add: ܐܝܟ ܟܠ ܡܫܟܚܘܬܗ |
| | 10–11 | ܐܟܘܬ ܘܡܢܗܪܐ | 2–1 |
| | 12 | ܘܡܢܗܪܐ | om: ܘ |
| | 13 | ܘܡܦܪܫ | om: ܘ |
| | 14 post: | ܣܟܠܘܬܐ | add: ܟܠ |
| | 15 post: | ܡܬܘܟܠܢܐ | add: ܕܐܘܣܦ ܒܗ |
| | 18 post: | ܟܘܪܗܢܐ | add: ܘܡܢܐ ܟܪܗܐ |
| 6a | 1 post: | ܡܕܒܪܢܐ | add: ܐܘ ܟܝܢܗ ܡܕܒܪܢܐ |
| | 3 | ܠܡܕܒܪܢܐ | om: ܠ |
| | 3 | ܘܐܦܢ ܢܗܘܐ ܣܓܝܐܐ | ܣܓܝܐܐ ܘܐܠܐ ܕܐܦܢ ܢܗܘܐ ܐܘ ܠܐ |
| | 7 | ܘܐܟܪܐ | om: ܘ |
| | 12 | ܘܣܓܝ ܠܗ ܠܐܦܐ | ܘܐܝܟ ܠܐܦܐ |
| | 17 | ܘܣܝ | ܘܐܣܝܪܐ |
| | 18 | ܡܫܡܫܢܐ | om. |
| 6b | 2 | ܒܡܕܒܪܢܐ | ܠܡܕܒܪܢܐ |
| | 2 | ܘܣܓܝܐ | ܟܡܐ ܣܓܝܐ |
| | 3 | ܡܢܐ ܡܠܟܝ ܠܗ | om. |
| | 4 post: | ܒܡܫܝܚܐ | add: ܒܫܘܡܠܝܐ |
| | 4 | ܘܣܓܝܐ | om: ܘ |
| | 5 | ܘܡܬܚܫܒ ܡܛܠ ܐܢܫܐ ܘܡܬܚܫܒܘܢ ܠܡܫܡܫܢܐ ܕܡܛܠܐ | ܘܡܫܡܫܢܐ ܢܩܦܝܢ ܡܢ ܕܟܠܐ ܐܢܫܐ ܡܢܐ ܕܟܠܗܝ ܢܦܫܗܝ ܟܠ ܣܓܝܐ ܕܠܐ ܐܝܟ ܡܠܟ ܠܗܘܢ |

| | M. | | V. |
|---|---|---|---|
| 7–8 | ܟܠ ܡܕܒܪܢܐ ܦ̈ܐܪܐ ܘܪܡܙܐ | 3–4–1–2 | |
| 11 | ܡܟܠ | | ܐܠܐ ܟܠ |
| 12 | ܘܟܠ | | ܐܘ ܟܠ |
| 14 | ܡܕܒܪܢܐ | om. | |
| 14–15 | ܬܡܟܠܘܬܐ ܠܡܕܒܪܢܐ | om. | |
| 15 | ܟܠ | | ܠ |
| 16 | ܘܡܬܐܡܪ | om: | ܘ |
| 7a 1 | ܒܗ | | ܠܗ |
| 14 | ܘܐܬܡܪܡ | om. | |
| 15 post: | ܪܘܫܡܐ | add: | ° ܐܣܝܐ |
| 15 post: | ܐܦܝܣ | add: | ܒܗ |
| 15 | ܐܘ | | ܘ |
| 16 | ܕܢܫܟܚ | | ܕܬܫܪܫ |
| 16 post: | ܠܗ | add: | ܗܠܝܢ |
| 18 | ܕܡܢܫܐ ܘܡܢ̈ܐ | | ܕܡܢ̈ܐ ܘܐܬܐ |
| 7b 5 | ܕܢܪܡܘܢ | | ܢܪܡܘܢ |
| 6 | ܐܢܘܢ | | ܐܢܝܢ |
| 9 post: | ܐܦܝܣܘ | add: | ܒܗ |
| 11 | ܡܛܝܐ | | ܡܛܐ |
| 14 post: | ܘܒܪܐ | add: | ܘܪܘܚܐ |
| 16 post: | ܒܗܐ | add: | ܕܡܫܝܚܐ ܢܬܬܪ ܒܡܠܟܘܬܐ ܡܢ̈ܐ ܘ |
| 17 | ܕܡܬܬܠܒܫ ܒܦܓܪܐ | | ܕܡܬܠܒܫ ܒܠܒܫܐ ܕܦܓܪܐ |
| 17–18 | ܒܗ ܡܢܝܚܐ | | ܒܡܢܝܚܐ |
| 18 post: | ܡܢܝܚܐ | add: | ܕܡܕܒܪܢܐ |

| | M. | V. |
|---|---|---|
| 8a 2 | ܒܦܪܨܘܦܘܬܐ | ܒܦܪܨܘܦܗ |
| 3 | ܠܟܝܢܗ ܕܒܣܡܐ | om. |
| 8–9 | ܠܒܝܬܐ ܗܘ | 2–1 |
| 10 | ܡܠܠ̈ܝܢ | ܡܠܠܬܐ |
| 10 | ܒܦܘܪܫܢܐ ܚܕ | 2–1 |
| 11 | ܐܠܐ ܢܗܘܘܢ ܐܝܠܝܢ<br>ܕܡܫܡܫܝܢ | ܟܕ ܦܩܘܕܐ ܗܘ ܗܢܐ ܚܪܝܐ<br>ܐܠܐ ܟܠܝܢ ܕܡܗܘܢܝܢ ܕܠܐ ܢܚܪܘܢ<br>ܠܗܘܢ ܗܢܐ ܚܪܝܐ ܡܚܪܙܢ |
| 13–14 | ܐܝܟ ܢܐܡܪ | 2–1 |
| 14 | ܕܬܐܡܪ | ܕܬܦܩܘܕ |
| 15 | ܕܬܫܬܐܠ | ܕܬܫܐܠ |
| 8b 3 post: | ܘܬܫܐܠ | add: ܘܬܬܪܥܐ ܐܦܫܝܗܘ |
| 6 post: | ܦܓܪܐ | add: ܡܓܠܐ |
| 14 | ܘܠܘܬ ܟܠܗܘܢ ܡܢܝܢܐ ܡܢ<br>ܡܐ ܕܦܩܕ | om. |
| 9a 3 | ܡܢܗܘܢ | add: ܕܝܢ |
| 4 | ܕܬܠܒܫܗ | add: ܠܐ ܙܕܩ ܠܦܫܝܛܐ ܕܢܬܟܫܦܘܢ<br>ܡܛܠ ܕܠܐ ܐܬܒܣܡܘ ܠܗ ܐܘ.<br>ܐܦ ܠܟܣܘ ܡܢܣܝ̈ ܕܢܬܟܫܦ ܡܛܠ<br>ܕܠܐ ܙܕܩ ܕܬܬܒܥ ܐܚܝ̈ܢ ܢܩܘܡ<br>ܐܝܟ ܡܘܕܐ ܘܕܡܫܡܫܝܢ ܠܒܣܡܐ<br>ܕܡܢܗ ܠܐ ܡܫܪܐ ܢܦܝܫܘܬܗ |
| 7 | ܢܬܬܠܗܘܢ | ܢܬܟܫܦܘܢ |
| 10 | ܐܬܠ | ܐܬܠܐ |
| 10 | ܐܘ ܬܫܐܠ | bis |
| 12 | ܕܒܠܒܟܘܢ ܘܠܐ ܐܡܬܝ | 2–3–1 |

| | M. | | V. |
|---|---|---|---|
| 13 | ܒܡܘܡܬ | | ܒܡܘܡܬܐ |
| 13 post: | ܢܒܥܘܢ | add: | ܠܗ |
| 9b 4 | ܕܦܪܦ | om: | ܕ |
| 14 | ܘܗܘܒ | | ܕܗܘܒ |
| 14 | ܒܒܒܡܬܐ | | ܒܒܡܬܐ |
| 15 post: | ܡܕܒܚܐ | add: | ܒܣܘܒܪܐ ܗܘܐ |
| 10a 7 | ܘܢܦܩܬ | | ܘܢܦܬ |
| 11 | ܠܗ | | ܠܗܠܗ |
| 14 post: | ܘܢܦܩܬܐ | add: | ܙܒܢܐ |
| 17 post: | ܒܗܘ | add: | ܕܝܢ |
| 10b 1 | ܢܦܩܬ | | ܢܦܬ |
| 3 | ܒܪܘܟܬܗ | | ܒܐܪܗ |
| 4 post: | ܒܒܡܬܐ | add: | ܕܡܟܢܐ ܒܒܗ |
| 5 | ܐܣܝܢܐ | om. | |
| 5 | ܘܢܦܫܘܗܝ | | ܘܢܦܠܘܗܝ |
| 12 | ܙܒܢܐ | om. | |
| 13 | ܕܦܩ | om: | ܕ |
| 15 | ܕܘܪܫܬܐ | om. | |
| 17–18 | ܒܪܐ ܘܦܪܟܐ | om. | |
| 11a 1–2 | ܘܒܗ ܟܝܢܐ ܕܗܝ ܒܟܠܗ | om. | |
| 8 | ܗܘ | om. | |
| 9 | ܒܒܗܢܐ | | ܒܡܫܡܫܐ |
| 10 | ܐܬܒܠܬ | om. | |
| 16 ante: | ܡܫܡܫܐ | add: | ܠ |
| 18 | ܡܢ ܚܙܘܗܝ | om. | |
| 18 | ܡܩܒܠ | | ܢܩܒܠ |

| | M. | | V. |
|---|---|---|---|
| 11b 1 | ܘܢܦܫܗ ܒܥܠܘܪܐ | | ܘܢܦܫܗܘܢ |
| 2 | ܟܠ ܐܪܥܐ | | ܒܐܪܥܐ |
| 3 | ܡܫܡܫܢܐ | | ܡܫܡܫܢ |
| 4 | ܘܟܐܢܐ ܐܠܗܢ | om. | |
| 4 | ܘܢܦܩܘܢܗܘܢ | | ܘܐܝܠܝ |
| 5 | ܐܦ | om. | |
| 6 | ܘܐܡܪ | om: | ܘ |
| 8 post: | ܘܟܠ | add: | ܡܢܗ |
| 11 | ܐܢܘܢ | | ܐܢܗܘ |
| 11 | ܘܟܬܒܘܗܝ | | ܘܟܬܒܘ |
| 11 post: | ܒܒܬܐ | add: | ܕܬܒܫܘܗܝ |
| 12 | ܐܠܗܢ | | ܕܐܠܗܢ |
| 15 | ܕܝܢ | om. | |
| 12a 8 | ܒܝܕ ܐܝܕܗ | om. | |
| 10 | ܘܐܡܪ | (prius scripsit: ܐܡܪ) | ܘܐܡܪܢ |
| 16 | ܘܫܡܫܘ | | ܘܫܡܫܘܗܝ |
| 18 | ܗܘܢܐ | om. | |
| 12b 1–2 | ܘܒܢܐ ܘܒܢܝܐ | om. | |
| 2 | ܐܝܟܢ | | ܗܟܢ |
| 7–8 | ܕܟܐܢܐ ܠ | | ܕܟܐܢܐ |
| 13a 5 | ܒܫܘܪܐ ܒܫܡܫܢܐ | | ܒܫܘܪܝ ܡܪܒܢܐ |
| 9 | ܡܢܐ | om. | |
| 11 | ܘ | | ܐܘ |
| 14 | ܒܪܘܚܐ | om. | |
| 18–13b 1 | ܡܪܚܡܢܘܬܐ ܘܪܚܡܘܬܐ | om. | |
| 13b 1 | ܕܟܠܬܐ | om. | |

| | M. | | V. |
|---|---|---|---|
| 2 | ܐܠܗܘܬܗ | | ܡܪܢܘܬܗ |
| 2 post: | ܐܠܗܘܬܗ | add: | ܘܦܪܨܘܦܗ ܠܡܫܝܚܐ |
| 2 | ܟܠ | | ܟܐܠ |
| 5–6 | ܢܦܫܐ ܒܣܘܟܠܐ | | ܠܢܦܫܐ ܣܘܟܠܐ |
| 9 post: | ܡܬܐܡܪ | add: | ܘܡܬܚܙܐ |
| 10 | ܘܒܪܐ ܘܪܘܚܐ | om. | |
| 12 | ܡܬܩܪܐ | | ܡܬܐܡܪ |
| 15 | ܟܠ | | ܟܠܝ |
| 15 | ܟܗ | | ܒܗ |
| 16 | ܟܠ | | ܟܠܝ |
| 14a 5 post: | ܒܬܘܪܐ | add: | ܕܐܝܬܘܗ |
| 5 | ܕܒܗ | | ܕܒܬܘܪܐ |
| 6 | ܗܘ | om. | |
| 7 | ܡܢ ܒܬܘܪܐ | om. | |
| 14 | ܢܟܘܠ | | ܢܗܘܐ |
| 14 | ܟܠ | | ܟܠ ܐܦܝ̈ |
| 14b 5 | ܡܘܕܐ | | ܘܠܐ ܡܘܕܐ |
| 18–15a 1 | ܒܬܘܪܐ — ܘܗܘܐ | om. | |
| 15a 2 | ܕܩܢܘ̈ܡܐ | | ܕܩܢܘܡܐ |
| 13 | ܐܘ ܡܢ | om. | |
| 14 | ܠܩܢܘܡܐ — ܢܘܡܐ | om. | |
| 16 | ܘܡܢ ܕܐܦ | om. | |
| 15b 6 | ܗܘ ܡܐ ܕܠܒܪ | | ܠܟܝܢܗ |
| 8 post: | ܡܪܢܘܬܗ | add. | ܒܫܡܗ |
| 9–10 | ܐܘ — ܢܩܡܬܐ | om. | |
| 11 | ܡܬܐܡܪ ܡܫܝܚܐ | 2–1 | |

| | M. | V. |
|---|---|---|
| 16*a* 1 | ܡܢ | om. |
| 3 | ܒܠܐ ܦܬܘܪܐ | ܒܦܬܘܪܐ |
| 4 | ܡܩܪܒܢܐ | ܠܡܩܪܒܘܬܐ |
| 5 post: | ܩܕܝܫ | add: ܒܗܘܢ |
| 5 | ܩܕܝܫ ܕܗܘ | ܡܬܩܕܫ ܗܘ |
| 6 | ܚܝܒܐ | ܕܚܝܒܐ |
| 6 | ܘܡܬܒܗ ܠܡܩܪܒܘܬܐ ܡܚܝܗ | ܘܡܬܬܠܐ ܡܚܝܗ ܠܡܩܪܒܘܬܐ |
| 7 | ܠܗܝ ܒܗ | ܡܬܠܗܝ |
| 9 | ܠ | om. |
| 11 | ܕܬܠܒܘܢ | ܕܬܠܐ |
| 12 | ܕܠܐ ܦܣܩܐ | om. |
| 16 | ܕܬܠܒܘܢ | om. |
| 18 post: | ܘܟܠܐ | add: ܡܟܠܐ |
| 16*b* 1 | ܡܕܒܚܐ | om. |
| 3 | ܦܫܬܐ | ܦܫܟܬܐ |
| 4 | ܡܢܐ ܣܝܡ ܡܕܒܚܐ ܕܬܪܝܨ | ܣܝܡ ܡܕܒܚܐ ܕܬܪܝܨ ܡܢܐ ܐܝܟ |
| 10 post: | ܐܟܠܗ | add: ܕܝܢ |
| 12 | ܡܬܚܡܬܐ | ܐܦܩܬܐ |
| 13 | ܕܫܡܫܝ | ܕܫܡܗܘܢ |
| 17*a* 8 | ܘܗܘܐ | om: ܘ |
| 8 | ܠܡܢܟܝܐ | om: ܠܐ |
| 12 | ܕܫܩܒܐ | ܕܡܩܪܒܐ |
| 12–13 | ܡܠܟ ܕܝܢ ܐܘ ܣܗܕ ܟܝܢܐ ܕܒܠܡܫܝܚܐ | ܡܠܟ ܣܗܕ ܟܝܢܐ ܕܝܢ ܕܡܕܒܚܢܘܬܐ |
| 15 | ܘܡܠܟ | om. |

| | M. | V. |
|---|---|---|
| 17 | ܐܝܟ ܕܠܐ ܓܫܡܢܘܬ | om. |
| 17*b* 3 | ܕܡܢܟܐ | om. |
| 4 | ܐܢ | om. |
| 6 | ܠܡܫ̈ܝܚܐ | om. |
| 10 | ܦܪ̈ܘܫܐ | ܦܪ̈ܘܫܐ |
| 11 | ܢܗܘܘܢ | ܐܢܘܢ |
| 17 | ܘܡܬܚܫܒܝܢ ܒܗ | om. |
| 18*a* 5 | ܘܐܪܕܐ | ܘܐܪܕܝܐ |
| 6–13 usque ad finem Responsionis | ܐܝܟܢ ܕܝܢ | ܒܟܠܝܢ ܕܝܢ ܗܢܐ ܡܠܘܐ ܕܟܠܗ ܓܒܪܐ ܟܠܝܢ ܕܡܫܡܫܘ ܡܢ ܪ̈ܡܫܐ ܠܫܢ ܘܐܦܢ ܠܗ ܠܟܠܝܐ |
| 16 | ܠܡܬܟܢܘ — ܢܟܝܢ | om. |
| 18*b* 1 | ܟܠܗ ܣܡܟܢܐ ܐܣܝܪܐ | om. |
| 6 | ܣܡܟܢܐ — ܠܡܬܓܠܐ | om. |
| 11 | ܠܐ | ܐܠܐ |
| 15–16 | ܡܢ ܒܬܪ — ܒܟܒܪܐ | om. |
| 17 | ܒܗ | om. |
| 18 | ܢܦܫܗܘܢ | ܢܦܫ |
| 19*a* 3 | ܟܠܝܘܪܬܐ | ܟܠܝܘܪܐ |
| 5 | ܕܐܝܠܐ | om. |
| 6 | ܘܡܠܟܬܐ ܓܪܐ | ܘܡܠܟܐ ܓܪܐ |
| 7 | ܕܒܠܒܘܢ | ܕܒܠܐ |
| 9 | ܡܟܡܘܗ̇ | ܡܟܡܢܗ̇ |
| 11–13 | ܠ — ܒܗ | om. |
| 14 | ܡܬ̈ܢܐ | om. |
| 15 | ܡܢ ܦܢܝܬܗ̇ | om. |

| | *M.* | *V.* | |
|---|---|---|---|
| 16 | ܚܟܡܬܗ̇ | om. | |
| 19*b* 1 | ܒܗ | om. | |
| 1 post: | ܓܒܐ | add: | ܕܠܐ ܟܠ ܡܕܝܢܐ ܢܦܩ |
| 3 | ܦܫܩܢܐ | om. | |
| 3 post: | ܒܒܘܒܪܐ | add: | ܒܝ ܡܠܐܟܐ |
| 6 | ܘܫܘܐܪܗ ܗܢ — Q. 61 | om. | |
| 11 post: | ܘܡܫܡܫܘܗܝ | add: | ܠܡܕܝܢܐ |
| 13 | ܩܝܡܐ ܠܡܕܘܗ | 2–1 | |
| 14–15 usque ad finem Quaestionis | ܐܘ ܓܝܪ ܒܥܠ | om. | |
| 16 | ܐܦ | om. | |
| 16–17 | ܐܦ ܡܕܝܢܐ | om. | |
| 18–20*a* 1 | ܗܘܬ — ܦܘܫܩ | | ܗܘܬ ܡܢܬܐ ܐܬܠܝܬܗ̇ ܕܡܫܡܫ |
| 20*a* 3 | ܘܡܫܡܫ | | ܕܡܫܡܫ |
| 6 post: | ܢܦܪܘܫ | add: | ܡܢܒܐ |
| 10 | ܗܕܐ | om. | |
| 10 | ܦܢܝܬܐ | | ܦܢܝܐ |
| 14 | ܢܫܡܫܘܢ | | ܡܫܡܫܝܢ |
| 16 | ܒܡܕܐ | om. | |
| 18 | ܟܠ ܒܒܢܝܢܬ | | ܠܡܫܡܫܘ |
| 20*b* 1 ante: | ܐܘ | add: | ܗܘܝ |
| 6 | ܡܢܟܠܝܢ | | ܡܗܘܦܟܝܢ |
| 8 | ܕܢܕܒܘܢ | | ܢܬܒܢܘܢ |
| 9 post: | ܒܒܢܝܬܗܘܢ | add: | ܕܦܠܚܬܐ |
| 11 | ܐܘ ܕܢܬܠܘܢ | | ܘܢܬܠܘܢ |
| 13 | ܠܡܕܝܢܐ | | ܟܠ ܡܕܝܢܐ |

| | *M.* | *V.* | |
|---|---|---|---|
| 21*a* 5 | ܒܗ | om. | |
| 7 | ܡܢܐ | om. | |
| 8 sqq. usque ad finem Quaestionis | ܘܐܡܪ | om. | |
| 21*b* 4 | ܒܡܐ ܕܟܠܐ ܕܡܘܫܐ | 3–1–2 | |
| 4 | ܠܗ | | ܠܝܡܐ |
| 4 | ܠܡܘܡܐ | om: | ܠܐ |
| 6 | ܡܪܡܝܬܐ | om. | |
| 7 | ܗܝ | om. | |
| 9 | ܘܡܫܡܫ | | ܘܐܫܡܫ |
| 12 | ܕܝܢ | om. | |
| 14 post: | ܪܘܚܐ | add: | ܘܐܬܩܝܡ |
| 15 | ܒܡܫܝܚܐ | om. | |
| 22*a* 3 | ܕܐܡܪ ܐܢܫܝ | om. | |
| 12 | ܒܥܒ̈ܕܐ | | ܦܘ̈ܪܫܢܐ |
| 12 | ܕܠܐ | om: | ܕ |
| 15–16 | ܕܢܗܘܐ — ܒܥܠܡܐ | om. | |
| 16 | ܐܦ | om. | |
| 18 | ܝܗܒ | | ܢܬܠ |
| 18 | ܡܢܬܐ | om. | |
| 22*b* 1 | ܘܣܡܟ ܠܗ ܘܢܬܠ | | ܘܦܩܘܣ |
| 2 | ܠܐ | | ܕܠܐ |
| 3 | ܠܦܘܪܫܢܐ | om: | ܠܐ |
| 5 | ܠܟܘ ܡܢ | om: | ܡܢ |
| 7–9 usque ad finem Solutionis | ܘܢܗܝܪ | om. | |

| | M. | V. | |
|---|---|---|---|
| 23a 2 | ܒܬܪܟܢ | om. | |
| 11 post: | ܟܠ ܗܕܐ | add: | ܘܟܠܠ |
| 11–12 | ܗܘ ܡܗܘܕܥܢܘܬܐ | 2–1 | |
| 12 | ܡܫܬܐ | om. | |
| 23b 5 | ܒܡܓܠܬܗ | | ܒܡܓܠܬܐ |
| 6 | ܒܡܦܩܬܗ | | ܒܡ̈ܦܩܬܗ |
| 8 | ܡܦܩܢܐ | | ܡܦܩܬܐ |
| 24a 1 | ܡܓܠܬܐ — ܐܠܗܘܬܗ | om. | |
| 6–7 | ܡܫܡܠܝܢ ܡܫܡܠܐ ܠܐܒܐ | | ܡܢܝܢ ܒܠܚܘܕܐ ܡܫܡܠܐ ܠܐܒܐ |
| | ܘܡܢܝܢ ܒܗ ܒܠܚܘܕܐ ܘܫܠܡܐ | | ܘܡܢܝܢ ܒܗ ܒܠܚܘܕܐ |
| 10 | ܕܢܬܓܠܐ | om. | |
| 15 post: | ܗܘ̇ | add: | ܒܦܓܪܐ |
| 24b 7 post: | ܒܟܠ ܐܦܝ | add: | ܒܟܠܗܘܢ |
| 7 | ܘܕܬܐܦܝ | | ܘܬܐܦܝܐ |
| 7 post: | ܡܫܡܫܝܢ | add: | ܚܢ |
| 8 | ܒܦܓܪܐ | om: | ܒ |
| 11 | ܕܐܠܗܘܬܗ | om. | |
| 25a 1 | ܡܥܕܪܐ | | ܡܥܕܪܗ |
| 4 | ܟܠ ܢܦܫܗ | om. | |
| 5 | ܡܢ | | ܘܐܣܝܪܐ |
| 5–6 | ܚܕ ܐܒܐ ܡܫܝܚܐ | 3–1–2 | |
| | ܚܕ ܒܪܐ ܡܫܝܚܐ | 3–1–2 | |
| 7 | ܕܥܠ ܟܠ | om: | ܥܠ |
| 25b 1 | ܘܡܢ | om: | ܘ |
| 8 | ܒܗܘܢ | om. | |
| 13 | ܡܬܚܫܚܫܝܢ | | ܡܬܚܫܚܝܢ |

| | M. | V. |
|---|---|---|
| 14 | ܐܘ ܐܚܝ̈ | om. |
| 14 | ܕܠܐ ܐܬܚܘܝ | ܕܐܬܚܘܝ |
| 26*a* 1–2 | ܡܢ — ܠܥܠܡܐ | om. |
| 3 | ܗܘܐ ܟܠܐ ܩܪܝܒܬ | om. |
| 16 | ܡܟܝܢ̈ܬܐ | ܡܟܝܢܬܐ |
| 17–18 | ܡܢ — ܒܝ | om. |
| 18 post: | ܡܛܘܪ | add: ܒܗܢܐ |
| 18 | ܡܛܠ ܕ | om. |
| 26*b* 2 inter: | ܗܘܐ et ܐܠܐ | add: ܐܡܪ. ܗܢܐ ܐܦ ܡܬܩܛܠܢܐ ܣܓܝ̈ܐܐ ܡܫܬܐܡܠܝܢ |
| 2–3 | ܗܠܝܢ ܐܡܪ | 2–1 |
| 9 | ܫܒܩܬܗ | ܫܒܩܗ |
| 9 | ܒܫܘܪܥܗܘܢ | ܒܫܘܪܗ |
| 12 | ܡܢ ܟܠܗ ܩܘܡܐ ܕܫܡܫ | ܡܢ ܩܪܝܒ ܕܫܡܫ |
| 16 | ܘܣܒ | ܘܐܣܝܐ |
| 27*a* 4 | ܐܘ | ܘ |
| 10 ante: | ܡܫܡܫܝܢ | add: ܘ |
| 11 post: | ܐܘ | add: ܠܐ |
| 14 | ܕܟܠܬ | om: ܕ |
| 27*b* 4 | ܕܡܢ ܡܫܡܫܢܐ | om. |
| 6 | ܕܫܡܫܐ | ܘܐܡܝ ܠܗܘܢ |
| 7 | ܒܕܫܝܢ | ܡܢ |
| 8 | ܡܟܝܢ̈ܬܐ | ܡܟܝܢܬܐ |
| 9 | ܡܫܡܫܢܗ ܘܫܡܫܬܗ | ܡܫܡܫܢܐ ܘܫܡܫܬܐ |
| 15 | ܠܐ | om. |

| | M. | | V. |
|---|---|---|---|
| 28*a* 6 | ܕܗܘܿܬܡܬܐ | | ܕܕܡܐ |
| 7 | ܗܕܐ | om. | |
| 7 | ܒܣܘܪ | | ܒܣܝܪ |
| 10 ante: | ܠܚܘܕ | add: | ܒ |
| 12 | ܒܓܦܐ | om. | |
| 12 | ܗܘܐ | om. | |
| 16 | ܠܡܢ | om. | |
| 28*b* 16 | ܡܥܝܢܐ | | ܡܣܩܢܐ ܕܒܢ̈ܝܐ |
| 16 | ܒܗܘܢ | | ܒܗܘ̈ܝ |
| 17 | ܡܠܠܝܢ | | ܡܠܠܝܢ |
| 29*a* 10 | ܠܥ̈ܘܠܬܐ | | ܠܥܘܠܬܐ |
| 11 | ܕܐܝܟ | | ܗܕܐ ܐܝܟ |
| 15 | ܕܝܢ | om. | |
| 18 | ܡܬܚܫܫܝܢ | | ܡܬܚܫܝܢ |
| 29*b* 4 | ܡܢ — ܐܢܫܗ | om. | |
| 7 | ܘܡܣܟܢܐ | om. | |
| 8 | ܠܦܘܩܕܐ ܕܪ̈ܘܚܗܘܢ | | ܘܦܘܩܕܐ ܠܪ̈ܘܚܗܘܢ |
| 12 | ܘܡܥܒܕܢܘܬܗܘܢ | om. | |
| 13 | ܒܢ̈ܝܟܘܬܐ | | ܒܢܝܟܘܬܐ |
| 18–30*a* 1 | ܐܢܬ — ܡܢܐ | om. | |
| 30*a* 12 | ܒܒܥܠܬܐ | | ܒܒܥܬܐ |
| 12 | ܡܬܬܐܘܦܝܢ | | ܡܬܐܘܦܝܢ |
| 30*b* 4 | ܘܠܐ | om: | ܘ |
| 4 post: | ܐܠܐ | add: | ܙܒܢܬܐ |
| 7 | ܠܗܿ | om. | |
| 12 | ܡܫܡܫܢ | om. | (ante ܡܫܡܫܢ) |

| | M. | V. |
|---|---|---|
| 31*a* 1 | ܕܦܘܪܩܢܢ | ܕܦܘܪܩܢ |
| 2 | ܟܠܢܫ | om. |
| 3 usque ad finem Responsionis | ܘܡܪܒܐ | ܡܕܡܐ ܠܐܦܠܐ ܘܟܝܢܐ ܐܝܟ ܟܬܒܐ ܘܡܕܢܚܐ ܗܟܢܐ ܘܟܠܡܬܠܬܐ ܒܗ ܒܪܚܡܐ . ܘܡܕܝܢܬܐ ܚܘܝܢܢ ܡܢܝ ܘܒܢܝܢܐ ܒܐܝܐ ܘܚܘܝܢܢ ܒܬܫܡܫܬܗ ܘܡܪܒܐ ܕܟܘܢܢܬܐ ܕܐܘܪܝܐ . |
| 6 | ܒܥܘܬܐ | om. |
| 8 | ܠܐܡܬܝܢ | ܠܐܡܬܝ |
| 14 | ܒܠܒ | om. |
| 15 | ܕܒܬܪ | om. |
| 31*b* 3 | ܕܢܦܩܬܐ | ܕܢܦܩܬܐ |
| 6 | ܕܐܦ | om. |
| 32*a* 3 | ܡܠܬܐ | ܒܝܕ |
| 12 | ܕܡܚܝܢ | ܕܠܡܚܝܢ |
| 15 | ܡܚܝܢܐ | om. |
| 16 | ܗܘ ܕܡܠܟ | ܡܠܟ |
| 17 | ܕܒܥܠܡܐ | om. |
| 18 post: | ܕܡܠܡܪܐ | add: ܐܘ |
| 32*b* 2 | ܕܡܢܒܐ | ܕܡܢ̈ܒܐ |
| 5 | ܒܫܡܗ | om. |
| 5 | ܘܡܪܒܐ | om. |
| 14 post: | ܐܝܟܗ | add: ܕܐܦܣܩܘܦܐ |
| 17 | ܕܐܦܣܩܘܦܐ — ܘܡܫܝܚܗ | om. |
| 33*a* 12 | ܡܢܒܐ | ܡܢ̈ܒܐ |

| | *M.* | | *V.* |
|---|---|---|---|
| 33b 1 | ܠܡܫܪܒܢܐ | | ܠܡܫܪܝܢܐ |
| 6 post: | ܐܝܬ | add. | ܕܝ |
| 7 | ܠܗ | om. | |
| 7 | ܫܡܫܝ | | ܫܡܫ |
| 9 | ܐܘܒ | om. | |
| 10 | ܡܢ | om. | |
| 11 | ܐܡܬܐ | | ܐܡܬܢܐ |
| 17 | ܕܩܫܫܐ | | ܕܐܦܣܩܘܦܐ |
| 34a 3 post: | ܐܝܬܘܗܝ | add: | ܕܟܢܬܐ |
| 4–6 | ܘܟܠܡܘ — ܘܡܘܟܢܐ | om. | |

## ERRATA:

p. 3, 147, read: 157.
p. 37 sqq., Bickel, read: Bickell.
p. 75, n. 1, cf. p. . ., delendum.
p. 78, n. 2, cf. p. , n. , read: p. 69.
p. 88, l. 2, Bishop, read: a Bishop.
p. 88, l. 4, correligionists, read: co-religionists.
p. 90, l. 23, solation, read: isolation.
p. 90, l. 27, have, read: has.
p. 109, l. 37, Untersuchingen, read: Untersuchungen.
p. 110, l. 41, of a scholar, read: or a scholar.
p. 152, l. 6–7, of S. Mari, dele.
p. 198, l. 38, 000, read: 152–153.
p. 226, l. 49, hould, read: should.
p. 258, 1.41, times of the Nupteries, read: time of the Mysteries (cf. p. 274).
p. 271, l. 27, *D.A.C.*, read: *D.C.A.*
Commentary in several places: Gemurtha, read: Gemurta.

FACSIMILE-REPRODUCTION

OF

# CODEX-MINGANA SYRIACUS

566, FOL. 1B–34A, 46B–48A

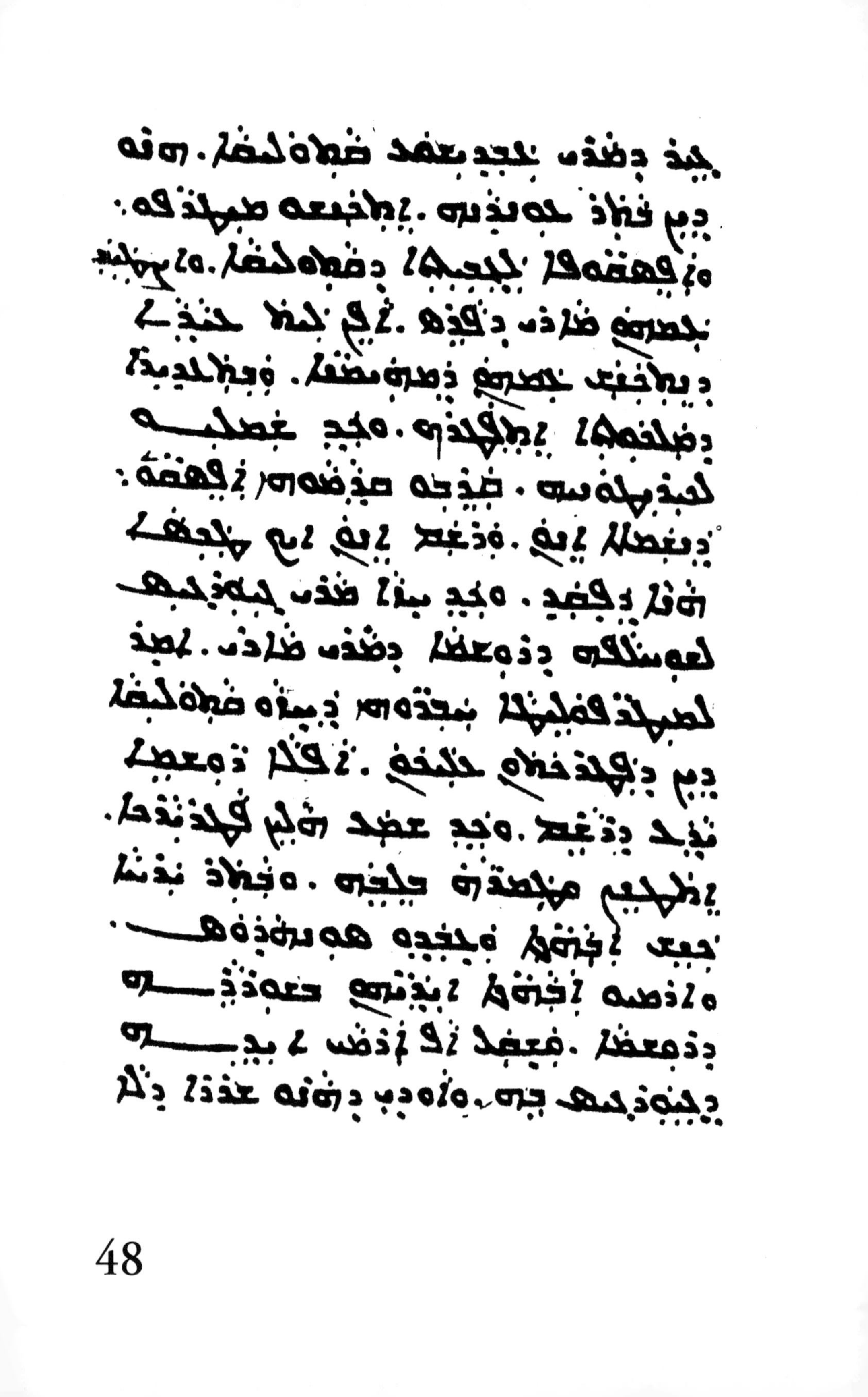

ܓ̈ܒܝܢܐ ܕܡܪܢ ܕܩܕܝܫ. ܘܐܡܪ ܕܒ̈ܢܝܢܐ
ܓ̈ܒܝܢܐ ܕܩܕܝܫ̈ܐ ܐܦܝܣܩܘܦ̈ܐ ܘܡܝܛܪܦܘܠܝܛ̈ܐ
ܘܠܐ ܡܒܠܓ ܐܢܐ ܟܠܗܘܢ. ܐܡܪܬ ܠܐ ܥܠܝܗܘܢ
ܠܗ. ܐܢܬܘܢ ܕܝܢ ܐܚ̈ܝܢܐ ܚܒܝܒ̈ܐ ܠܥܘܒܕ̈ܢܐ
ܕܩܕܝܫܐ ܗ̇ܘ. ܦܘܠܐ ܐܢܐ ܠܐ ܢܥܘܕ ܐܢܐ
ܐܚ̈ܝܢܐ ܡܢ ܩܕ̈ܝܫܐ ܕܒܝܬܐ. ܡܢ ܢܘܡ ܕܢܠܐ
ܠܫܡܫܐ ܕܒܝܬܐ ܘܕܝܢܘܬܐ. ܕܝܠܗ ܠ
ܠܒܢ̈ܝܢܗ. ܘܕܝܢܘܬܐ ܦܪܫ ܚܕܬܐ
ܒܝܬܐ. ܡܬܩܕܫ ܗ̇ܘ ܦܢܝܐ ܘܡܬܩܢܐ
ܒܡܕܒܪܐ ܕܢܨܚܢܐ. ܐܚܝ ܕܩܕܝܫܗ
ܕܡܪܝ ܒܢ̈ܝܢܗ ܚܢܢܐ ܕܩܕܝܫ ܗ̇ܘ.
ܘܐܡܪܝ ܒܢ̈ܝܢܗ ܦܪܫ ܒܨܘܡܐ ܕܒܝܬ
ܦܘܠܚܢܐ. ܥܒܕ ܠܢܦܫܐ ܕܒܛܠܝܢ ܗ̇ܘ
ܡܢܗ. ܕܐܚ̈ܝܢܐ ܚܒܝܒ̈ܐ ܠܢܦܫܐ ܘܠܠܘܩܒܠ
ܡܬܢܨܚܢܝܢ ܕܩܕܝܫ ܗ̇ܘ. ܘܦܘܫܘ ܠܗ
ܫܦܝܪ ܕܠܐ ܢܥܘܕܝܢ ܘܠܐ ܢܫܬܒܩܘܢ ܐܚ̈ܝܢܐ
ܕܩܕܝܫ ܗ̇ܘ. ܫܘܠܡ ܦܢܝܐ ܡܬܠܐ ܠܡܪܝ
ܡܪܝ ܚܕ ܗܘܐ ܫܘܠܡܐ. ܦܘܫܐ ܕܐܒܐ

ܦܓܪ

ܟܕܡܥܠܐ ܘܟܕܡܦܩܐ ܠܟܝܢܐ ܒܢܝܢܫܘܬܗ. ܘܡܢ
ܐܝܕܝܗ ܕܢܦܫܐ ܡܢܟ ܠܐܝܕܝܗ ܕܦܓܪܐ.
ܘܟܝܢܘܬܗ ܐܡܪ. ܕܡܢ ܟܝܢܐ ܒܢܝܢܫܘܬܗ
ܕܡܬܬܗܦܟܢܘܬܐ ܐܝܟ ܕܝܢܬܐ ܟܕܡܥܠܬܐ
ܘܟܕܡܦܩܐ ܠܟܝܢܬܗ. ܘܡܢ ܐܝܕܝܗ ܕܢܦܫܐ
ܠܦܓܪܐ. ܐܝܟ ܐܡܪ ܡܢ ܐܬܪܝܗ. ܘܐܟܢܐ
ܐܬܝܘܬܗ ܕܩܘܡܐ ܚܕܐ ܕܐܬܐ ܚܕ ܒܪܝܗ
ܕܡܫܝܚܐ ܠܗ ܐܬܝܠܕ. ܘܐܝܟܢܐ ܢܣܒ ܦܓܪܐ
ܠܗܠܝܢ ܕܡܩܒܠܝܢ ܕܐܬܩܪܝ ܗܘܐ ܘܒܪܐ
ܐܦ ܝܠܘܕܬܐ. ܡܛܠ ܕܟܕ ܢܣܒ ܗܘܐ ܡܪܢ
ܡܪܢ ܡܫܝܚܐ. ܕܐܬܩܪܝ ܗܘܐ ܐܠܗܐ
ܦܓܪܝܗ. ܘܡܛܠ ܕܝܢ ܕܐܬܩܪܝ ܐܠܗܐ
ܕܐܬܩܪܝ ܗܘܐ ܡܪܢ ܝܫܘܥ. ܘܟܕ ܐܬܐ ܠܡ
ܐܝܟ ܕܠܒܫܐ ܫܘܒܚܐ ܕܐܠܗܘܬܗ
ܘܫܘܒܚܗ ܕܝܠܗ. ܢܣܒ ܕܐܬܐ ܐܠܗܐ
ܡܫܘܚܬܐ ܕܚܝܠܐ ܗܘܐ ܗܘܐ. ܡܫܝܚܐ
ܩܕܝܫܐ ܕܡܪܢ ܝܫܘܥ ܐܬܝܠܕ. ܘܐܦ
ܗܘܐ ܡܫܝܚܐ ܕܗܘܐ ܡܪܢ ܢܣܒ ܐܝܟ ܐܡܪ

ܒܟܘܪ̈ܐ ܘܢܚܬ ܡܫܝܚܐ. ܢܦܪܘܩ ܡܫܝܚܐ
ܐܢܫܝܢ ܒܟܠܗ ܥܘܠܡܐ ܕܡܘܬܐ ܡܫܝܚܐ.
ܘܐܦ ܢܬܦܪܩ ܒܟܘܪ̈ܐ ܠܢܘܚܐ ܐܢܫܝܢ. ܘܐܝܟ
ܠܒܢܝܢ ܕܢܬܦܩܘܢ ܒܡܫܝܚܐ ܘܠܐ ܢܬܟܢܫܘܢ.
ܘܠܐ ܐܝܟ ܕܢܣܒܪ ܐܢܫ ܡܢ ܛܘܒܬܐ.
ܡܛܠ ܕܩܛܠܐ ܬܠܬܝܢ ܡܫܬܠܛܝܢ ܗܘ ܩܠܐ
ܕܦܪܫ ܡܢ ܠܒܝܢ. ܫܘܠܡܐ ܐ ܘܐܝܟ ܠܒܢܝܢ
ܕܢܦܩܘ ܩܕܡ ܒܡܠܟܘܬܐ ܟܕ ܡܥܢܝܢ
ܒܟܘܪ̈ܐ ܘܠܐ. ܦܘܫܐ ܥܠܝܗ ܠܗ ܩܪܝܢܐ.
ܕܡܫܢܐ ܗܘ ܟܕ ܕܫܡܥܬܗ ܕܢܦܩܝܢ ܡܢܚܡܢܐ.
ܐܠܗܐ ܩܢܝܢ ܢܘܪܐ ܘܐܝܟ ܠܗ ܕܢܬܦܠܓ
ܟܕ ܡܢܚܡܢ ܡܢ ܚܕ ܩܕܡܘܗܝ. ܫܘܠܡܐ ܕܫܒ
ܬܠܝܬܐ ܢܝܢ ܩܕܡ ܩܠܝܠ ܦܬܓܡܐ
ܠܩܕܡ ܢܒܘܪܟܗ ܡܬܪܦܣܝܢ ܕܡܘܢ.
ܡܛܠ ܕܥܒܕܐ ܕܡܫܡܫܢܐ. ܕܐܝܟ ܘܐܝܟ
ܕܢܬܒܥܘܢ ܟܠ ܪܥܝܐ ܕܡܬܬܦܩܢܐ.
ܡܢ ܩܕܡܝܢ ܘܟܕ ܗܘ ܠܛܘܒܬܐ. ܩܕܡ
ܩܛܪ ܐܩܕ. ܕܡܢ ܒܚܛܗ ܡܥܢܝܢܐ

ܒܪܥܡܬ

ܡܢܝܢ ܩܠܝܠ. ܕܐܬܢܨܚܘ ܡܢܗܘܢ ܡܢ ܡܠܟܐ. ܗܘ
ܢܕܚܘܢ ܕܝܠܗܘܢ ܡܠܟܘܬܐ ܠܐ ܕܢܥܒܕ ܬܘܒ ܐܬܢܨܚܘ.
ܘܡܠܟܐ ܥܕܡܐ. ܘܕܘܟܝܬܐ ܡܥܡܕܢܝܬܐ ܕܝܠܗܘܢ.
ܘܩܠܝܠ ܩܕܝܫܐ ܕܐܬܢܨܚܘ ܠܗ. ܫܠܡܘ ܕܝܠܗ
ܒܝܘܡܐ ܕܐܪܒܥܐ ܕܡܠܟܘ ܡܠܟܘ ܘܐܬܢܨܚܘ

ܥܘܕܪܢܐ

## ܗܘܒ ܫܘܐܠܐ ܕܥܠ ܚܘܫܒܐ

ܡܫܐܠܢܐ ܢܫܐܠ ܕܐܝܟܢܐ ܠܗ ܡܕܝܢܬܐ.
ܚܕܐ ܕܐܝܬܝܗ ܥܠ ܡܫܝܚܐ. ܘܚܕܐ
ܥܠ ܘܢܐ. ܘܚܕܐ ܥܠ ܢܡܘܣܐ. ܟܘܢܫܐ
ܕܠ ܠܟܢܫܐ ܘܫܘܒܚܐ ܕܡܠܟܐ
ܫܡܥܘܢ ܡܬܠܡܝܕܐ. ܡܢܗܘܢ ܐܠܦ
ܡܕܝܢܬܐ ܫܘܐܠܐ ܡܕܡܢܐ ܢܩܝܦܐ ܠܡܥܒܕ
ܡܛܠ ܫܘܒܚܐ ܕܟܠܗ ܕܡܠܟܐ. ܡܛܠ ܡܢܐ
ܕܐܡܕܝܢܐ ܫܘܒܚܐ ܕܟܢܘܫܬܐ. ܟܕ ܐܢܫ
ܡܢܗܘܢ ܡܢܐ ܠܗܘܢ ܕܢܥܒܕ ܫܘܠܡ ܡܢܐ
ܡܕܡܢܐ ܢܩܝܦܐ ܘܡܩܕܫܐ ܐܝܟ ܕܡܢܗܘܢ
ܗܘܐ ܕܝܠܗܘܢ ܠܐܠܗܐ ܘܢܩܦܘ

ܗܕܐ. ܠܡܕܝܢܬܐ ܕܒܝܬܐ ܢܦܩܘܢ ܕܡܫܟܚ ܕܝܢ
ܡܥܕܪܢܘܬܐ ܩܛܝܢ. ܚܠܦܝܗ ܕܐܠܗܐ ܕܒܝܬܐ
ܦܪܝܫ ܠܗ. ܠܐ ܗܝܡܢܝܢ ܕܡܬܩܛܠܝܢ
ܢܦܩܘ ܕܡܝܠܝܢ ܡܢ ܡܕܝܢܬܐ ܠܡܕܝܢܬܐ.
ܘܗܕܐ ܡܕܒܪܐ ܠܗܘܢ ܘܐܬܬ ܡܢ ܩܛܝܠܘܬܐ. ܘܐܬܡ
ܠܐ ܢܕܥܘܢ. ܥܡܐ ܐܠܗܐ ܐܬܬܢܝ ܕܒܕ ܡܫܝܚ
ܠܗ ܠܡܫܝܚܐ. ܡܫܡܫܝܢ ܠܗ ܒܒܝܬ. ܡܢܟܪܝܢ
ܦܩܘܕܝ ܠܡܕܝܢܬܐ. ܘܐܬܒܢܝܘ ܒܒܝܬܐ.
ܘܐܦܩܘܗܝ ܠܘܬ ܠܡܕܝܢܬܐ ܥܕܬܐ ܗ̇ܕܐ ܠܐ
ܫܪܝܪܐ ܘܠܐ ܐܬܚܙܝܬ ܠܝ ܡܢ ܩܕܡܝܐ. ܡܢ
ܐܢܫܐ ܕܡܬܬܩܢܝܢ ܡܫܝܚܐ ܘܐܬܒܢܝܘ
ܒܡܕܝܢܬܐ ܐܝܟ ܕܡܬܬܩܢܝܢ. ܕܝܢܘܦ
ܡܬܬܒܢܝܢ ܡܢ ܐܝܬܐ. ܘܩܡ ܕܡܫܬܡܥ
ܦܠܚ ܡܕܡ. ܫܠܡ ܡܢ ܥܕܬܐ ܕܒܝܬܗ.
ܥܘܬܐ ܘܗܘ ܗܘܐ ܕܐܬܒܢܝܬ ܕܒܐܦܪܝܡ
ܫܪܝܪ ܕܡܫܝܚܐ ܦܠܚ ܡܢ ܫܠܛܢܗ
ܕܡܫܝܚܐ. ܘܐܬܒܢܝܘ ܡܢ ܢܨܝܒܘ. ܠܐ ܐܝܬ
ܕܗ ܐܬܬܐܡܢ. ܥܕܬܐ ܗ̇ܕܐ ܡܫܬܡܥܢܘܬܐ
ܩܝܡ

ܕܗܢܘܢ ܡܕܐ. ܐܘ ܡܢ ܛܥܝܘܬܗ. ܐܘ ܡܢ
ܠܐ ܝܕܥܬ. ܥܘܠܐ ܕܐܝܟ ܐܢܫ ܥܒܕܐ ܒܗܘܢ
ܕܐܝܬ ܠܗ ܡܫܟܢܘܬܐ. ܕܗܘܝܘ ܐܝܟ ܕܐܝܬ
ܡܕܝܢܬܐ. ܡܬܠܒܫܝܢ ܥܠ ܟܠ. ܘܕܒܝܢ ܡܢ
ܛܠܝܐ ܘܐܬܐ ܢܦܩ. ܐܘ ܢܦܫܐ ܕܠܐ ܝܕܥܬ.
ܕܠܐ ܝܕܥܝܢ ܐܢܫ ܐܝܟ ܕܢܦܫܗ. ܘܐܬܐ ܠܘܩܒܠܗ
ܕܡܬܠܒܫ ܠܐܣܟܡܐ ܡܕܡ ܛܠܝܐ ܗܢܐ
ܝܕܥܬ ܫܪܪܐ. ܥܘܠܐ ܐܝܬ ܠܘܬ ܐܢܫ
ܡܢ ܡܕܝܢܬܐ. ܕܝܠܗ ܕܡܕܝܢܬܐ ܐܚܪܬܐ. ܫܡܥܝܢ
ܠܗ ܠܛܠܝܐ ܟܕ ܡܬܪܥܐ ܡܕܡ ܡܕܝܢܬܐ.
ܘܐܬܟܢܫ ܕܛܠܝܐ ܠܘܩܒܠ ܡܕܝܢܬܐ. ܘܐܬܟܢܫܘ
ܕܫܡܥܘ ܠܗ ܠܛܠܝܐ ܕܟܠܗܘܢ ܕܡܕܝܢܬܐ.
ܡܘܕܝܢ ܐܬܟܢܫ ܠܡܕܝܢܬܐ ܘܢܦܩܘ ܠܘܩܒܠܗ.
ܥܒܕܐ ܛܠܝܐ ܟܠ ܟܕ ܕܡܬܬܚܙܐ ܐܬܟܢܫ
ܠܡܕܝܢܬܐ ܢܦܩܘ. ܘܡܕܝܢܬܐ ܐܝܟ ܕܡܬܬܚܙܐ.
ܘܢܦܩܘ ܕܫܡܥܘ ܠܗ ܘܢܦܩܘ ܠܘܩܒܠܗ.
ܡܬܬܚܙܐ ܠܗ ܕܐܬܐ ܠܡܕܝܢܬܐ ܡܕܡ ܗܘ
ܕܛܠܝܐ. ܘܫܡܥܘ ܢܦܩܘ ܠܗ ܘܢܦܩܘ: ܫܠܡ

ܐܪܥܐ. ܘܢܦܩܘܢ ܥܡ ܡܠܟܐ ܕܪ̈ܗܘܡܝܐ
ܕܫܢܬܐ. ܐܝܟ ܐܢܫ ܕܢܥܘܪ ܡܠܟܐ ܡܢ
ܒܢܝܗܝ ܕܐܝܫܡܥܝܠ ܘܡܢ ܦܠܛܘܣ. ܥܪ̈ܒܝܐ
ܒܐܝܫܡܥܝܠ ܕܡܢ ܝܡܐ ܡܥܪܒܝܐ ܐܝܟ ܦܠܛܘܣ
ܥܠܝܗܘܢ. ܕܒܪ̈ܘܬܐ ܐܝܟ ܢܩܒܘ ܕܢܥܒܕ ܡܥܒܕܬܐ
ܘܡܠܟܐ ܢܣܒ ܕܐܪܥܗܘܢ. ܘܐܝܟ ܕܡܢ ܕܡܝܐ
ܥܕܡܝܢܐ. ܕܡܢ ܡܠܟܐ ܒܐܪܥܗ. ܡܢ ܩܕܡ
ܠܥܝܢܘ ܕܡܠܟܐ. ܩܕܡ ܡܠܟܐ ܡܢ ܒܢܝܗܝ
ܕܐܝܫܡܥܝܠ ܐܝܟ ܕܢܡܘܬ. ܡܛܠ ܒܢܝܗܘܢ
ܢܗܘܘܢ. ܘܡܠܟܐ ܡܬܠܗܒ ܒܚܡܬܐ. ܘܢܐܬܐ
ܠܐܝܫܡܥܝܠ. ܘܒܢ̈ܝܐ ܢܦܩܘܢ ܡܢܗ ܩܕܡܝܐ.
ܥܘܠܐ ܗܠܐ ܕܡܫܬܡܥܝܢ ܡܫܪܝܬܐ ܪܒܝܬܐ
ܕܗܢܕܝܐ. ܡܠܟܐ ܡܢ ܗܢܕܘ ܕܐܝܫܡܥܝܠ
ܦܝܡ ܘܠܐ ܢܥܢܐ ܐܝܕܗ ܡܬܠܗܒ ܘܢܐܟܘܠ ܠܡܠܟܐ
ܘܟܠ ܚܠܐ ܥܒܥܒܐ ܗܕܡܝܗ. ܟܕ ܐܬܩܕܡ ܚܘܪܒܐ
ܡܢܝܢܐ ܠܐܪܥܐ. ܡܠܟܐ ܡܢ ܗܢܕܘ
ܕܐܝܫܡܥܝܠ ܘܐܬܒܠܥܘ ܡܢ ܒܢܝܗܘܢ. ܥܪ̈ܒܝܐ
ܬܓܪܐ ܕܐܬܚܝܢ ܗܢܐ ܡܢ ܩܕܡܝܗ ܒܝܕܥܐ ܠܒܝܬ
ܕܗܢܕܝܐ

ܕܚܢܢܐ ܗܘܐ. ܕܟܕ ܡܫܬܡܥܝܢ ܠܟ ܫܠܝܚܐ.
ܐܦ ܡܫܡܠܝܢ ܦܘܩܕܢܐ ܚܕ ܬܠܬ ܚܕ. ܘܗܘ ܕܐܡܝܢ
ܟܘܢܫܐ ܕܥܘܕܪܢܐ. ܘܬܠܬܐ ܕܡܥܡܕܝܢ ܡܢܗ.
ܡܬܟܠܝܢ ܟܠܗ ܒܡܥܡܘܕܝܬܗ. ܘܗܘ ܕܐܡܝܢ
ܫܠܝܚܐ. ܘܫܡܥܝܢ ܠܗ ܠܦܘܩܕܢܐ ܗܘ ܕܪܡܫܐ.
ܥܕܬܐ ܕܩܢܘܡ ܕܝܠܕܐ. ܘܗܘܘ ܫܡܥܘܗ
ܕܦܓܪ ܟܠܗ ܥܘܕܪܢܐ ܫܠܝܚܐ. ܘܗܘܢ
ܕܫܠܝܚܐ ܚܕܕܐ ܕܡܫܐ. ܗܢܘܢ ܠܩܕܡ. ܕܫܘܥܬܐ
ܦܘܩܕܢܐ ܚܕ ܡܬܡܥܕܝܢ. ܘܫܠܝܚܐ ܐܬܢܘܗܝ
ܕܗܘܝܘ ܕܩܕܝܫܐ. ܘܟܠܗܘܢ ܫܠܝܚܐ ܕܩܕܝܫܐ.
ܘܠܡܫܝܚܐ ܡܫܒܚܝܢ ܒܬܫܒܚܬܗ ܕܥܘܕܪܢܐ. ܘܐܦ
ܡܫܡܫܝܢ ܗܘܘ ܕܢܘܪܐ ܚܕ ܗܘܝܘ ܕܩܕܝܫ.
ܚܕܘ ܕܩܪܝܢ ܘܫܠܝܚܝܢ ܠܟܠܗ ܕܒܝܬܐ.
ܕܟܠ ܒܥܠܕܒܒܐ ܕܟܠ ܟܘܪܗܢܐ ܘܕܡܫܠܡ ܕܦܬܓܡܐ
ܩܕܝܫܐ. ܘܡܫܘܕܥ ܟܕ ܡܫܝܚܐ ܘܐܦ ܠܡܫܝܚܐ.
ܐܝܟ ܗܘ ܕܥܡ ܕܫܪܟܐ ܟܪܝܟ ܚܕ ܐܝܬܘܗܝ.
ܡܢ ܕܡܫܠܡ ܕܦܬܓܡܐ ܗܢܘܢ. ܫܘܒܚ ܠܐܠܗ
ܢܦܫܐ ܕܡܫܠܡܢܐ ܬܫܥܝܬܐ ܘܐ ܡܦܩܢܬܐ ܕܦܛܪܘܣ

ܘܢܘܗܪ ܥܠܡܐ ܠܥܒ̈ܕܐ. ܘܡܫܬܠܡܢ ܐܘ̈ܪܚܬܢ
ܬܪ̈ܬܝܢ ܘܢܩܝܦܝܢ. ܘܪܕܝܢ ܢܦܫܝܢ ܠܚ̈ܝܠܘ
ܕܡܢܗ̇ ܘܐܬܝܢ ܫܠܡܘܬܐ. ܪܕܝܢ ܘܢܦܩܢ ܠ
ܗܘ ܝܠܕܐ ܕܐܬܐ ܕܫܡܝܐ. ܕܫܡܫܐ ܡܢ
ܚܘܒܐ ܕܫܡܝܐ. ܕܐܬܡܢܥܬ ܠܗ ܡܛܘܠ
ܕܗܘ ܒܐܬܪܐ ܕܢܗܘܐ ܡܫܡܫ ܚܘܒܐ ܐܝܟ
ܕܫܡܝܐ. ܚܙܝ ܕܝܢ ܕܢܬܝܠܕ ܡܫܝܚܐ
ܕܫܡܝܐ ܠܗ ܡܫܡܫܝܢ. ܐܝܟ ܕܝܢ ܐܡܪܐ ܕܫܒܩܐ
ܠܗ ܡܪܢ. ܫܡܥܬ ܐܝܟ ܫܘܡܗܐ ܐܬܪܐ ܡܢ
ܡܫܟܚܐ ܐܡܪܐ ܕܡܫܡܫܝܢ ܫܘܒܚܐ ܒܫܡܝܐ
ܥܠ ܡܢܗ ܕܡܫܬܠܡܢ ܐܘ̈ܪܚܬܢ ܬܪ̈ܬܝܢ ܠܡܥܒܕ. ܘܠܐ
ܢܛܪܝܢ ܝܠܕܗ. ܘܠܐ ܪܚܡܝܢ ܥܠ ܒܝܬܐ ܕܠܐ ܥܠ
ܡܢܗ. ܡܫܡܫܝܢ ܕܝܢ ܢܛܪܝܢ ܝܠܕܗ. ܘܪܚܡܝܢ
ܥܠ ܒܝܬܐ ܘܠܐ ܥܠ ܡܢܗ. ܦܪܫܘ ܒܝܬܗ
ܕܗܘܐ ܡܫܬܠܛܐ. ܘܐܝܟܐ ܒܝܬܗ ܐܝܢܘܢ ܗܠܝܢ
ܕܪܚܡܝܢ. ܘܐܝܟܐ ܕܐܫܬܡܥ ܦܛܪܝܢ ܗܠܝܢ ܕܠܐ
ܪܚܡܝܢ. ܡܫܝܚܐ ܗܠܝܢ ܕܠܐ ܪܚܡܝܢ. ܗܢܘ
ܡܫܡܫ. ܕܡܫܘܕܥܐ ܕܡܫܝܚܐ ܘܡܘܕܥܐ
ܕܫܡܝܐ

ܡܫܒܚܝܢ. ܐܝܟ ܗܘ ܕܡܪܝܐ ܐܠܗܐ ܕܦܘܪܩܢ-
ܘܗܘܐ ܠܡܫܝܚܐ. ܘܠܐ ܢܬܚܫܒܘܢ ܠܢܦܫܗܘܢ. ܡܪܝܐ
ܠܐ ܒܢܘܒܝܢܗ ܡܥܡܕܐ. ܡܕܘܪܝܬܗ ܘܡܦܪܩܢܐ
ܘܡܥܡܕܐ. ܫܘܠܡܐ ܘܢܐ ܕܝܢ ܐܣܛܘܠܐ ܩܕܝܫܐ.
ܥܡܗ ܐ ܣܒܝܢ ܐܢܐ ܟܬܒܐ ܕܢܡܘܣܐ
ܕܠܐ ܢܬܚܫܒܘܢ ܕܡܥܡܕܐ. ܐܝܟ ܡܘܗܒܬܐ
ܠܟܠܗܘܢ ܕܡܫܝܚܐ. ܘܡܫܡܫܝܢ ܟܠܗܘܢ
ܩܘܕܫܐ. ܘܗܘܐ ܐܬܚܙܝܬ ܐܝܟ ܕܡܫܡܫܢܐ.
ܡܢܗ ܢܦܩܐ ܟܠܗܘܢ ܩܘܪܒܢܐ ܕܢܦܩܐ
ܘܡܬܒܪܟ ܩܘܕܫܐ ܕܩܘܪܒܢܐ ܘܟܠܗ
ܡܫܡܫܢܘܬܗ. ܘܗܘܐ ܐܬܚܙܝ ܐܝܟ ܕܡܫܡܫܢܐ.
ܘܐܬܝܗܒ ܠܟܠܗܘܢ ܕܐܝܟ ܕܝܢܐ ܟܠ
ܩܢܘܢܐ. ܕܡܫܡܫܢܐ. ܕܐܝܟ ܕܡܫܡܫܢܐ. ܕܟܠܗ
ܒܢܝܢܐ ܡܫܡܫܢܐ ܒܝܬ ܩܘܕܫܐ ܡܢܗ ܘܐܢܫܐ.
ܘܡܢܗ ܠܡܫܡܫܢܐ ܕܟܠܗܘܢ ܕܩܕܝܫܐ ܕܡܫܡܫܢܐ
ܡܢܗ ܘܡܫܡܫܝܢ ܟܠܗܘܢ ܒܬܪ ܩܘܪܒܐ. ܘܡܩܪܒܝܢ
ܗܘܢ ܘܡܟܠܠ ܒܩܘܕܫܐ ܕܡܫܡܫܢܘܬܐ ܠܟܠܗܘܢ.
ܘܡܩܪܒܝܢ ܐܝܟ ܕܡܫܡܫܢܐ. ܘܡܫܡܫܝܢ ܟܠܗܘܢ

ܘܐܢܫ̈ܐ ܕܒܢܝ̈ܢ ܒܝܕܥܬܐ ܡܫܡܫܝܢ ܩܕܡܝܗ̇ܝ
ܒܝܕ ܟܠܝܠܐ ܒܝܬ ܕܡܫܚܐ. ܘܕܡܫܚ ܗܘܟܝܠܗ
ܕܟܠܠܐ ܘܩܢܘܡܝܢ ܕܢܗܪܝܬܗ ܕܟܠܠܐ ܡܫܠܡܝܢ
ܒܬܫܡܫܬܗ. ܘܠܐ ܐܦܪܝ ܐܝܟ ܕܢܒܝܘܬܐ. ܕܠܐ
ܡܢܬܝܢ ܡܫܠܡܝܢ ܡܫܠܡܐ. ܘܫܡܫܐ ܕܝܢ ܟܗܢܘܬܗ
ܟܠܝܠܐ. ܒܝܕ ܕܐܬܡܫܚܬ ܡܫܝܚܐ ܐܦ ܐܝܟܘ
ܕܢܒܝܘܬܐ. ܠܐ ܗܘܝܢ ܕܐܬܡܫܚܘ ܠܗ ܒܝܕܝ
ܫܘܠܡܐ ܕܫܡܫܐ ܗܘܝ ܒܝܬܐ ܕܠܐ ܐܦܪܝܡ ܟܗܢ
ܟܗܢܐ ܕܟܗܢܘܬܐ ܢܒܝܘܬܐ ܕܐܝܟ ܕܢܒܝܘܬܐ.
ܫܘܠܡܐ ܡܫܚܐ ܕܫܡܫܝܢ ܩܕܡܝ ܠܒܝܕܝܗ
ܡܫܚܐ. ܘܠܐ ܢܒܝܘܬܐ ܡܢܬܐ. ܘܠܐ ܡܫܡܫ
ܠܟܠܗ. ܘܠܐ ܡܫܡܫ ܡܫܡܫ ܠܟܗܢܗ. ܘܟܗܢ
ܠܟܠܗܘܢܗ. ܘܢܒܝܘܗ ܒܫܡܫܬ ܒܗ ܕܠܒܝܬܗ
ܗܢܝܢ. ܘܠܐ ܠܡܫܡܫܢܐ. ܘܠܐ ܠܟܗܢܐ ܡܫܡܫ.
ܡܢ ܒܢܝ̈ܐ ܕܟܗܢܐ ܕܐܬܡܫܚ. ܘܗܠܝܢ ܕܡܫܠܡ
ܫܡܫܘܗܝ ܟܠܝܢ ܕܡܫܡܫ ܡܢ ܩܕܡܘܗܝ. ܘܕܡܫܡܫܢ
ܠܗ ܒܟܘܠܗ ܟܠ ܡܫܡܫܢܘܗܝ. ܘܕܡܫܚܬܐ ܡܢ
ܫܘܟܠܗܘܢ. ܘܐܝܟ ܕܡܢ ܫܡܫܗ ܕܡܫܚܐ
ܡܫܡܫܝܢ

ܠܗܘܢ ܕܝܢ ܐܢܐ ܥܢܝܢܐ. ܒܩܘܕܫܐ ܐܝܠܐ ܐܡܪ ܩܢܐ
ܐܢܐ ܕܓܠܝܢ ܒܩܘܪܒܐ ܕܡܫܬܡܠܝܢ ܠܡܫܡܫܢܐ
ܟܝܢܐ ܟܝܢܝܐ ܕܝܘܬܐ ܡܫܬܡܠܝܢ ܗܘ ܐܘܣ.
ܘܡܫܬܡܠܝܢ ܒܦܘܪܫܢܐ ܕܡܫܡܫܢܐ
ܕܡܫܡܫܢܐ. ܘܐܝܟ ܕܡܫܡܫܢܘܬܐ ܕܡܫܝܚܐ ܕܫܡܫܐ
ܕܟܠܗܘܢ ܠܗ ܠܡܫܡܫܢܘܬܐ. ܕܡܢܝܢ ܡܫܡܫܢܐ
ܕܝܠܗ ܒܡܫܡܫܢܘܬܐ. ܘܒܬܪ ܩܘܪܒܢܐ ܕܡܫܡܫܢܐ
ܠܥܠܡ ܗܘܘ ܕܒܗ ܕܡܫܡܫܢܐ. ܘܡܫܬܠܡ ܗܘܐ
ܒܡܫܟܢܐ ܕܡܫܡܫܢܘܬܐ. ܘܗܘܐ ܐܝܠܐ ܠܡܫܡܫܢܐ
ܡܠܟܘܬܐ ܕܒܗ ܕܡܫܡܫܢܐ. ܥܘܢܝܬܐ ܕܡܫܡܫ
ܠܐ ܡܫܡܫܝܢ ܒܡܫܡܫܢܘܬܐ. ܘܐܝܠܝܢ ܡܫܡܫܝܢ
ܒܫܡܫܐ ܕܒܠܗ. ܐܡܪ ܡܫܬܡܠܝܢ ܠܡܠܟܘܬܐ
ܕܒܗ ܕܡܫܡܫܢܐ ܥܢܝܢܐ ܕܡܫܡܫܢܐ ܡܫܡܫ
ܒܗ ܕܡܫܡܫܢܐ. ܡܫܡܫܝܢ ܒܡܫܡܫܢܐ ܕܡܫܡܫܢܘܬܐ.
ܥܘܢܝܬܐ ܕܡܫܡܫ ܟܠܗ ܡܫܡܫܢܘܬܐ ܘܐ ܒܡܫܡܫ
ܡܫܬܡܠܝܢ ܒܡܠܟܘܬܐ ܕܡܫܡܫܝܢ ܡܫ
ܡܫܬܡܠܝܢ. ܕܒܗ ܕܡܫܡܫܢܐ. ܥܢܝܢܐ
ܡܫܡܫܢܘܬܐ ܘܡܫܡܫܢܘܬܐ ܟܠܗ ܡܫܬܐ ܐܝܟ ܡܠܟܘܬܐ.

ܢܬܠܝܒ ܥܠ ܐܪܥܐ. ܘܟܠܡܢ ܕܡܫܡܫ ܢܣܒ
ܡܫܡܫܢܘܬܐ ܐܠܗܝܬܐ. ܫܘܒܚܐ ܠܐܒܐ ܘܠܒܪܐ ܘܠܪܘܚܐ
ܠܗ. ܫܘܒܚܐ ܠܐܠܗܐ ܕܝܠܗ ܕܐܒܘܗܝ
ܕܫܡܝܐ. ܡܢ ܟܠܗܝܢ ܡܫܡܫܢܐ ܐܠܗܝܐ. ܘܡܢ
ܟܠܗܝܢ ܕܟܠܗܘܢ ܒܫܡܝܐ ܘܒܐܪܥܐ. ܟܕ ܡܕܡ
ܠܐܠܗܐ ܘܡܫܒܚܝܢ ܠܫܡܗ. ܘܡܩܪܒܝܢ
ܠܡܠܟܘܬܗ ܫܒܝܚܬܐ. ܡܫܠܡ ܫܘܒܚܐ
ܠܡܘܗܒܬܐ ܕܒܢܝ̈ܢܫܐ. ܘܕܒܫܘܒܚܗ ܡܢ ܕܫܡܝܐ.
ܫܡܝ̈ܢܐ ܕܝܢ ܘܫܠܘܬܐ ܕܟܠܗ ܡܠܘܐܝܬܐ
ܘܐܬܩܪܒܘܬܐ ܥܠ ܐܝܕܝ ܩܕܝܫܘܬܐ
ܐܠܗܐ. ܕܢܬܒܣܡ ܫܡܝ̈ܢܐ. ܘܢܬܩܕܫ
ܢܦܫܢ ܘܦܓܪܢ. ܘܢܬܡܠܐ ܟܠܢ
ܕܫܘܒܚܐ ܘܫܠܘܬܐ. ܕܢܬܒܪܟ ܚܠܒܢܐ.
ܘܢܬܡܠܐ ܒܪܘܚܐ. ܘܢܬܚܢܢ ܫܘܒܚܐ ܠܐܠܗܐ.
ܘܠܗ ܥܠ ܟܘܠܗܝܢ ܕܝܠܗܝܢ. ܘܡܘܕܝܢܢ
ܘܫܡܝܐ ܫܡܝܐ ܒܟܠ ܐܪܥܐ. ܐܡܝܢ ܕܝܢ
ܐܒܘܢ ܕܒܫܡܝܐ ܕܫܡܝܢ ܠܐ ܐܒܘܢ
ܡܠܟܘܬܐ ܕܐܒܘܢ ܕܫܡܝܐ ܫܘܒܚܐ ܐܝܟ ܕܝܢ
ܫܠܡ

ܡܠܟܘܬܐ ܕܐܒܘܗ̱ܝ ܕܒܫܡܝܐ. ܒܥܘܬܪܝ̈ܗ
ܘܒܦܘܪܥܢܗ ܘܒܡܘܠܟܢܗ. ܐܝܟ ܕܒܟܬܒܐ ܐܡܪ
ܕܪ̈ܐ ܗܠܝܢ ܕܒܢ̈ܝܐ. ܥܘܬܪܐ ܐܝܟܢ ܐܝܬ
ܗܠܝܢ ܕܒܢ̈ܝܐ. ܕܗܘܐ ܗܕܡܝܗ ܕܒܢ̈ܝ ܟܠܗܘܢ
ܡܢ ܐܢܫܐ ܗܟܢܐ ܐܝܬ ܠܝ. ܥܒܕܐ ܡܕܪܐ
ܘܒܢ̈ܝܐ ܒܥܘܕܪ ܒܫܡܝܐ. ܗܕܝܢܐ ܗܘܐ:
ܟܠܗ ܕܡܫܡܫ ܠܫܡܝܐ. ܘܕܡܐ ܠܗ
ܒܫܡܝܐ ܡܕܒܪܢܐ ܘܐܡܪ. ܢܬܐ ܠܝ ܡܪܝ
ܘܐܒܘܗ̱ܝ. ܡܢܟܘܢ ܐܒܘܗ̱ܝ ܕܒܫܡܝܐ. ܘܡܠܟܘܬܗ:
ܟܕ ܥܒܕ ܡܢܐ ܕܒܫܡܝܐ. ܐܡܪ ܠܗܘܢ ܒܢ̈ܝܐ
ܕܐܒܘܗ̱ܝ ܕܒܫܡܝܐ ܡܥܒܕܢܐ. ܘܡܫܡܫܝܢ ܒܢܘܗ̱ܝ
ܡܢܐ ܡܥܒܕܢܐ. ܢܫܠܡ ܠܡܠܟܘܬܐ ܕܐܒܘܗ̱ܝ
ܕܒܫܡܝܐ. ܒܗܠܝܢ ܕܐܬܡܠܝ ܒܗܘܢ ܡܢܗܝܢ
ܟܠܗ. ܘܐܢܫܘܬܐ ܠܥܠܡܐ ܡܫܘܕܪܐ ܕܗܠܝܢ
ܘܡܥܒܕܢܘܬܗ. ܕܡܢܗܠܝܢ ܕܝܢ ܟܠܗܘܢ ܡܢܟܘܢ
ܕܡܥܒܕ ܥܒܕܗ ܘܡܥܒܕܢܘܬܗ ܘܡܢܗܝܢ
ܥܘܬܪܐ ܒܠܚܘܕ. ܡܢܐ ܡܕܡ ܕܝܢ ܘܡܠܟܘܬܐ ܡܫܘܕܪܐ
ܕܠܐ ܡܫܬܥܝܢ ܒܚܘܕܪܐ ܡܠܟܘܬܐ. ܫܠܡܬ ܬܫܥܝܬܐ

ܒܪܐ ܝܚܝܕܗ ܕܐܒܘܢ ܕܒܫܡܝܐ. ܩܕܝܫܐ ܐܡܪܘ
ܗܘ ܫܘܒܚܐ ܩܕܡܝܐ ܗܘ ܝܚܝܕܐ ܡܢ ܐܒܐ
ܐܦ ܠܒܪܗ ܕܠܐ ܫܘܠܛܢܐ. ܐܝܟ ܕܐ ܡܢ ܝܚܝܕܐ
ܢܣܒܘܢܐ. ܘܥܡ ܡܠܐܟܐ ܡܪܝܐ ܫܒܚܘܗܝ ܘ
ܥܝܪ̈ܐ. ܐܡܪܘ ܗܘ ܩܕܝܫܐ ܐܒܐ. ܩܕܝܫ
ܩܕܝܫ ܩܕܝܫܐ ܐܒܐ ܕܒܫܡܝܐ. ܕܡܠܝܢ.
ܟܕ ܫܡܝܐ ܡܢ ܫܘܒܚܗ ܘܐܪܥܐ ܟܠܗܝܢ. ܘܡܢܗ
ܩܕܝܫܐ. ܘܫܘܒܚܗ ܕܝܚܝܕܐ ܐܡܪܘ
ܫܘܒܚܐ ܠܟܠ. ܡܢ ܟܠܗ. ܡܢ ܩܕܡ ܥܠܡܝܢ
ܥܠܡܐ ܩܕܡܝܐ. ܘܡܢܗ ܩܕܝܫܐ ܩܕܝܫ
ܩܕܝܫ. ܐܝܟ ܕܡܫܒܚܝܢ ܡܠܐܟܐ ܒܩܘܕܫܐ.
ܘܐܬܝܠܕ ܩܕܝܫܐ ܗܘܐ ܒܒܬܘܠܬܐ ܕܩܕܝܫܬܐ
ܕܝܠܕܬ ܐܠܗܐ. ܫܘܒܚܐ ܠܒܪܐ ܗܘ ܝܚܝܕܐ
ܗܘܐ ܕܒܒܬܘܠܬܐ ܒܐܘܢܓܠܝܘܢ ܐܬܝܠܕ. ܘܒܝܘܡܐ
ܕܟܠܐ ܐܬܝܠܕ. ܫܘܒܚܐ ܘܬܘܕܝܬܐ ܘܩܘܕܫܐ
ܘܣܓܕܬܐ. ܠܐܒܐ ܠܐ ܐܬܩܪܝ ܚܘܒܐ ܐܒܐ ܕܒܫܡ̈.
ܫܘܒܚܐ ܠܒܪܐ ܠܐܒܐ ܩܕܝܫܐ ܠܟܠܗܘܢ.
ܘܗܘܝܘ ܕܡܫܬܒܚ ܕܐܬܐ ܐܡܝܢ ܠܗ

ܫܠܡܬ ܡ.ܠ

ܟܗ

ܕܝܪܝܐ ܚܒܝܫܐ ܗܘ ܒܐܒܝܠܘܬܗ. ܟܕ ܡܢܣܟܝܢ
ܘܐܡܪ. ܕܐܝܬܘ ܒܡܫܬܘܕܝܢܐ ܚܠܦܝܗ ܗܘ ܒ
ܕܐܝܠܝܢ ܡܪ ܠܫܠܝܢܘܬܗ ܠܐ ܐܡܪ ܠܗܘ
ܒܥܘܠܡ ܐܡܪ ܠܗ ܕܡܛܠ ܐܝܟ. ܒܫܦܝܪܘܬܗ
ܒܫܡܝܢܐ. ܘܟܕ ܫܡܥ ܛܘܒܢܐ ܒܫܡܝܗ
ܕܗܘܐ ܡܫܟܢܐ. ܫܡܥ ܦܘܠܚܢܐ ܕܒܝܬ ܐܠܗܐ
ܚܠܦܝܗ ܗܘܐ ܕܐܝܟ ܕܒܪܝܢܐ ܒܥܘܕܪ
ܒܥܢܝܢܐ ܘܒܥܘܠܡܗܘܢ. ܘܐܬܚܫܒ ܕܢܠ
ܢܣܒ ܬܘܟܠܢܐ. ܘܟܕ ܕܗܒ ܒܥܘܠܡ ܒܫܡܝܢܐ ܗܘ
ܐܡܪ ܠܗ ܠܣܘܕ. ܥܘܕܠܐ ܘܡܕܡ ܕܠܐ ܝܕܥ
ܐܝܬܘܗܝ ܗܘܐ ܥܘܕܪ ܒܫܡܝܢܐ: ܟܕ ܡܫܚܠ
ܘܒܠܥܐ ܘܒܝܬܐ ܥܕܬܐ ܡܫܒܚ ܗܘܦܠ
ܡܫܡܫܢܐ ܥܠܡܐ. ܘܡܢܝܚ ܗܘܐ ܒܗܘܢ ܒܝܬܗ
ܕܡܫܚܐ. ܢܘܗܪܐ ܡܢܗ ܠܐ ܠܡܐܡܪ. ܘܡܫܟܚ ܗܘܐ
ܡܕܡ. ܘܒܠܥܐ ܐܡܪ ܗܘܐ ܡܫܡܫܢܐ.
ܢܡܘܬ ܠܝ ܠܗܘܢ ܒܝܬ ܥܠܡܐ ܢܚܡ. ܘܡܢܝܚ
ܗܘܐ ܚܘܬܐ. ܢܡܘܬ ܡܢܗ ܒܢܝܢܐ. ܘܡܫܟܚ
ܗܘܐ ܡܬܠܠ ܥܘܕܠܐ ܘܐܝܕܐ ܕܐܬܚܫܒ ܕܐܝܬ

ܐܝܕܥܬ ܡܪܢ ܡܫܝܚܐ ܕܒܟܠܗܘܢ ܕܒܘܪܗܢܐ
ܕܒܪܐ ܒܣܘܟܠܗ܁ ܘܦܩܕܗ ܕܡܫܝܚܐ ܕܒܝܬ
ܘܡܫܚܐ. ܘܒܟܠܗܘܢ ܕܚܫܚܝܗ ܕܡܫܝܚܐ. ܘܟܠܗ
ܕܥܡ ܡܫܝܚܐ. ܘܐܫܬܪܪܗ ܘܦܘܡܒܪܢܘܬܗ.
ܒܗܝܡܢܘܬܐ ܕܠܐ ܡܣܒ ܟܠܝܕܗ ܐܘܡܢܐ
ܕܥܘܠܢܐ. ܐܦ ܗܘܐ ܕܒܝܬ ܡܫܝܚܐ. ܕܗܘ ܡܢܐ
ܕܐܡܝܢ ܚܪܘܬܐ ܒܝܬ ܦܘܪܫܢ ܒܝܬ ܐܦܣܘܬܗ
ܕܝܕܥܟ. ܗܠܝܢ ܡܫܝܚܐ ܡܢ ܗܠܝܢ ܕܚܛܝܢ.
ܗܠܝܢ ܕܚܛܝܐ ܕܡܢ ܢܦܫܗ ܘܡܠܘܗ. ܥܘܠܐ
ܠܟܠܐ ܕܟܠܗܘܢ ܕܚܛܝܬܐ ܥܘܕܪܢܗܘܢ ܐܝܟ
ܕܚܛܝܐ. ܒܬܝܒܘܬܐ ܘܒܛܠܐ ܘܒܫܘܒܩܢܐ
ܕܚܛܗܐ. ܠܐ ܢܬܕܟܐ ܐܝܟ ܕܚܛܝܬܐ ܠܟ
ܒܬܝܒܘܬܐ ܘܠܐ ܒܥܘܠܢܐ. ܦܘܪܫܢܐ ܕܝܢ ܕܒܝܢܬ
ܕܟܪܘܒܐ ܦܘܪܫܢܐ ܠܐ ܢܬܕܟܐ ܦܘܫܩܗ ܡܠܟܘܬܐ
ܦܘܪܐ ܕܐܝܟ ܕܚܛܝܬܐ. ܠܐ ܒܥܘܕܪܢ ܒܚܛܝܬܐ
ܘܠܐ ܒܥܘܠܢܘܬܗܘܢ. ܘܐܫܬܡܫܬ ܐܢܬ
ܢܦܘܩܘܢܐ ܕܝܕܥܐ. ܡܛܠ ܕܝܕܥ ܢܦܫܟ
ܦܘܠܘܣ ܕܒܝܬ ܕܚܛܝܬܐ. ܘܚܠܦ ܗܢܘ
ܕܝܠܟ

ܙܩܝܦܐ ܕܦܘܚܡܐ ܡܫܠܡܢܐ ܗܘ ܠܡܠܬܐ ܘܠܐ
ܕܦܘܚܡܐ ܥܒܘܕܐ ܐܪܐ. ܡܥܒܕ ܚܙܘܢܐ
ܡܠܬܐ ܕܢܦܩܘ ܠܒܪ. ܐܢܫܐ ܗܢܘ ܚܙܘܢܐ
ܕܒܟܠܗ ܡܠܬܐ. ܫܘܐܠܐ ܕܡܫܬܐܠܐ ܐܘ ܕܡܫܡܠܐ.
ܥܠܝܐ ܕܦܘܚܡܐ ܗܢܘ ܡܢ ܩܕܡ ܦܘܫܩܐ
ܘܦܩܘܕܗ ܠܦܘܢܝܐ. ܘܡܠܬܐ ܫܘܐܠܐ ܕܡܫܬܐܠܐ
ܥܠ ܕܡܫܬܐܠܘ ܕܦܘܚܡܐ. ܘܡܠܬܐ ܕܦܘܩ
ܦܘܫܩܗ. ܘܐܦ ܡܠܬܐ ܡܫܠܡܐ ܘܗܘܝܐ
ܠܦܘܚܡܐ. ܗܢܘ ܕܫܘܐܠܐ ܕܡܫܬܐܠ
ܡܣܬܟܠ ܠܡܠܬܐ. ܚܕܐ ܡܢ ܗܠܝܢ ܕܒܪܢܫܐ
ܠܗܘ. ܐܘ ܡܢ ܟܠ ܕܝܠܗܝܢ ܩܪܝܢܐ ܗܘܝܐ. ܘܠܐ
ܫܒܝܠܐ ܥܘܗܕܢܐ ܕܠܦܘܢ ܕܗܘܐ ܡܢܗ ܕܒܪ
ܒܪ ܡܠܬܐ. ܥܘܕܠܐ ܕܢܐ ܠܗ ܦܩܕ ܡܫܬܒܚ
ܚܘܕܬܐ ܕܢܘܩܡܐ. ܐܘ ܕܫܘܒܚܐ ܡܠܬܗ ܠܐ.
ܘܡܬܩܪܝܐ ܦܩܘܕܐ ܕܡܠܬܗ. ܦܩܘܕܐ
ܚܘܕܬܐ ܕܢܘܩܡܐ ܐܝܟ ܕܒܐܘܠܨܐ ܗܘ ܕܒܪܗ
ܡܒܥܐ ܡܠܬܗ ܕܦܪܘܩ ܒܠܒܗ ܡܫܬܒܚ.
ܡܠܬܐ ܕܗܘܐ ܒܕܡܘܬܗ. ܦܩܘܕܐ ܕܟܠܗܘܢ

ܒܚܕܐ ܡܫܬܐܠܐ ܕܒܠ ܦܓܪܗ ܕܡܪܢ ܐܝܬܘܗܝ
ܗܘܐ. ܐܝܟ ܡܪܟܢܐ ܫܦܝܪܐ ܗܘܐ. ܐܠܐ ܗܘܠܝܢ
ܗܘܝܢ ܠܡܘܕܝܘ ܚܝܝܢ ܢܘܚܡ ܕܒܫܡܫܬܐ
ܕܡܕܒܪܢܐ ܘܕܒܪܘܬܐ ܕܡܫܝܚܐ. ܫܘܐܠܐ
ܡܢܘ ܟܢܫܐ ܕܒܢܝܢ. ܕܐܝܬܝܗ ܕܝܢ ܥܕܬܐ ܠܘ
ܩܝܡܬܗ. ܦܘܢܝܐ ܐܢܫܝܢ ܐܡܪܝܢ ܕܐܦ ܥܕܬܐ
ܕܒܝܬ ܩܝܡܬܗ. ܘܠܐ ܩܝܡܬܗ ܡܢ ܥܕܬܐ.
ܗܠܝܢܘܢ ܚܕ ܐܝܬܘ. ܥܕܬܐ ܕܘܟܬܐ ܡܫܡܫܢܝܬܐ
ܘܩܝܡܬܗ ܡܕܝܢܬܐ ܡܫܠܡܢܝܬܐ ܘܡܫܡܫܢܝܬܐ.
ܫܘܐܠܐ ܟܡܐ ܙܒܢܝܢ ܐܡܪ ܡܪܢ ܠܐܘܪܫܠܡ
ܫܠܡܐ ܠܟܘܢ. ܦܘܢܝܐ ܬܠܬ ܙܒܢܝܢ. ܚܕܐ
ܡܢ ܩܕܡ ܩܝܡܬܗ. ܐܚܪܬܐ ܡܢ ܒܬܪ
ܩܝܡܬܐ ܕܢܦܫ ܠܗ. ܘܕܬܠܬܐ ܡܢ ܩܕܡ
ܢܘܚܐ ܕܒܝܬ. ܘܥܢܝܢ ܗܘܘ ܫܠܡܐ
ܕܢܘܚܡܐ ܠܬܠܡܝܕܘܗܝ ܩܠܐ ܫܡܥܘܗܝ. ܚܕ
ܒܚܕܒܫܒܐ ܕܩܝܡܬܐ. ܘܚܕ ܒܚܕܒܫܒܐ
ܚܕܬܐ. ܫܘܐܠܐ ܚܕܐ ܒܗ̈ܘܢ ܕܡܬܒܥܝܐ.
ܟܕ ܐܡܪ ܡܪܢ ܕܫܠܡܐ ܥܡܟܘܢ. ܫܘܐܠܐ
ܦܘܢܝܐ

ܒܪ ܦܠܛ ܢܨܝܒܝܢ ܕܟܪܟܐ ܕܠܝܒܐ ܕܩܠܝܡ
ܐܦܩܘܗܝ ܠܗܘ ܓܢܒܐ . ܡܛܠ ܕܗܘ ܢܦܫ
ܡܕܝܢܬܗ. ܘܗܘ ܗܢܐ ܡܕܝܢܬܐ ܘܠܗ ܡܫܟܚܝܢ
ܡܫܟܚܝܢ. ܫܘܐܠܐ ܠܡܢܐ ܟܪܟܐ ܣܘܪܝܐ
ܩܪܝܬܐ ܟܪܟܐ ܕܗܘܠܐ ܩܐܡ ܘܠܗ ܟܪܟܐ
ܕܢܨܝܒܝܢ. ܦܢܝܬܐ ܡܛܠ ܕܩܪܝܬܐ ܡܢ ܢܨܝܒܝܢ
ܕܟܪܘܟܐ ܘܪܚ ܕܢܗܘܐ . ܘܗܘܝ ܡܫܟܚܝܢ
ܕܩܪܝܬܐ. ܘܠܐ ܢܫܬܪܐ ܕܡܘܬܢܐ ܘܕܟܪܘܟܐ
ܘܕܩܛܠܐ ܡܕܢܚܐ ܕܬܫܬܡܫ ܡܢ ܟܘܡܪܐ
ܒܗܢܐ. ܫܘܐܠܐ ܠܡܢܐ ܩܪܝܬܐ ܟܕ ܡܠܐܟܐ
ܟܠ ܡܕܝܢܬܐ ܟܪܟܐ ܕܗܘܠܐ ܡܠܐܟܐ.
ܘܟܦܪܐ ܟܪܟܐ ܕܢܨܝܒܝܢ ܡܠܐܟܐ. ܦܢܝܬܐ
ܡܛܠ ܕܟܕ ܡܬܩܪܐ ܐܦܩܘܗܝ ܟܪܘܟܐ ܠܡܕܝܢܬܐ
ܘܠܡܕܝܢܬܐ. ܐܝܟ ܕܟܪܘܟܐ ܡܫܟܚܐ ܠܩܪܝܬܐ
ܘܡܢܝܢܐ ܠܢܦܫܐ. ܫܘܐܠܐ ܡܢܐ ܗܘ ܟܘܟܒܐ
ܐܝܟ ܟܘܠܝܢ ܠܐܕܡ ܡܫܟܚܐ ܕܐܝܬ ܗܕܡ
ܡܫܟܚܐ ܣܓܝ ܡܕܝܢܬܐ. ܡܢ ܢܨܝܒܝܢ ܕܟܪܘܟܐ
ܡܢ ܗܢܘܢ ܟܕ ܡܫܟܚ. ܦܢܝܬܐ ܡܛܠ ܕܕܡܝܐ

ܢܚܝܬܗ ܡܢܗ ܥܒܝܕ ܠܗ. ܘܟܕ ܢܩܫ. ܡܢܬܐ
ܡܘܣܝܩܐ ܗܘܝܐ ܐܕܫܐ. ܗܘܝܐ ܡܬܬܩܢܢܘܬܐ
ܐܣܝܢ ܡܫܡܫܢܐ ܕܫܪܝܢ ܠܣܘܟܠܐ. ܟܕ ܠܐ
ܢܕܥܝܢ. ܥܠܬܐ ܫܪܝܐ ܐܝܬܝܗ̇ ܕܐܢܐ ܕܗܘܝܐ ܡܫܡܫܢܘܬܐ
ܡܘܣܝܩܐ ܐܝܬܝܗ. ܥܠܬܐ ܐܚܪܬܐ ܡܫܡܫܢܐ
ܒܟܠܗ ܐܢܫ. ܡܫܠܡܢ ܕܥܒܕ ܕܡܬܚܫܚܐ ܕܒܕܡܘܬܐ
ܕܟܠܗܘܢ ܗܘܝܐ ܥܠ ܒܢܘܗ. ܕܡܬܬܩܢܘܢ ܐܝܟ ܗܘܢ
ܒܥܠܡܐ. ܥܠܬܐ ܫܪܝܬܐ ܐܝܬܝܗܝܢ ܡܢ ܡܫܡܫܢܐ
ܐܝܟܢܐ ܕܫܡܠܝܢ ܠܣܘܟܠܐ. ܐܝܟ ܕܐܣܝܐ ܐܣܝܐ.
ܘܡܕܡ ܡܕܡ ܡܬܚܫܚ ܠܒܢܝܢܫܐ ܕܥܒܕܐ.
ܕܡܫܡܫ ܥܠ ܣܘܟܠܐ ܕܐܝܬܝܗ ܒܟܠܗ
ܥܠܬܐ ܕܝܠܗ. ܗܘܝܐ ܡܢܗܘܢ ܐܝܟ ܕܐܒܐ.
ܘܡܫܡܫܢܐ ܘܡܣܒܪܢܐ ܡܘܕܥܐ ܕܡܬܩܢܢܝܢ ܟܠ.
ܐܝܟ ܕܐܒܐ ܠܒܪܐ ܕܪܒܘܗ ܟܠ ܕܡܬܩܢܢ
ܠܟܠ ܕܡܬܟܠܐ. ܥܠܬܐ ܬܘܒ ܕܡܫܠܡܐ
ܡܫܡܫܢܐ ܡܢ ܚܕ ܚܕ ܡܫܠܡܝܢ ܠܣܘܟܠܐ
ܘܐܘܚܠܡܢܐ. ܟܐܢܐ ܟܕ ܟܐܢܐ ܗܘ ܕܡܫܠܡ
ܠܣܘܟܠܐ ܘܟܐܢܘܬܐ ܟܕ ܐܘܚܠܡܢܐ. ܥܠܬܐ ܗܝ
ܕܡܫܠܡ

ܡܘܪܝܐ. ܫܢܬܐ ܕܝܘܢܝܐ. ܫܢܬ ܐܠܦ ܐܒܠܝܡ ܐܒܘ
ܫܢܬܐ ܫܠܡ ܒܗ ܢܦܫܗ. ܘܫܠܡ ܒܗ ܦܛܪܝܪܟܐ
ܘܪܒܐ. ܘܫܠܡ ܒܗ ܒܫܢܬܐ. ܫܢܬ ܐܠܦ ܘܬܪܬܝܢ ܐܒܘ
ܠܗ. ܫܢܬܐ ܒܗ ܢܦܫܗ. ܚܕ ܡܢ ܗܠܝܢ.
ܘܚܕ ܒܝܕ ܕܝܢ ܠܩܘܪܝܐ. ܘܐܬܬܠܝܬ ܕܚܕ
ܐܬܐ ܦܪܘܫܐ ܚܕ ܡܢܐ ܦܪܘܫܐ. ܫܢܬ ܐܠܦ
ܘܬܠܬ ܕܢܚ ܡܘܪܝܐ ܒܕܠܝܡ ܐܒܘ ܕܝܘܠܝܘܣ
ܕܫܡܫܝܢ. ܘܬܠܬ ܕܢܚ ܒܫܢܬܐ ܐܒܠܝܡ ܐܒܘ
ܦܘܠܐ ܚܕ ܦܛܪܝܪܟܘܬܗ ܠܐܬܪܐ. ܕܫܡܫܢܐ
ܕܘܬܐ ܦܠܘ. ܘܬܠܬ ܒܗ ܢܦܫܗ ܕܫܡ. ܐܬܐ
ܐܒܗܬܗ ܩܕܡ ܠܟܠ ܕܒܗ ܒܫܢܬܐ ܒܕܫܡܫ
ܡܠܟܐ. ܘܐܦ ܗܘ ܒܫܢܬܐ ܡܠܟ ܕܝܠܗ ܠܡܫܒܘ
ܐܬܪܐ ܗܘܐ ܦܛܪܝܪܟܘܬܗ ܡܫܠܡ ܠܡܠܟܘܬܐ
ܕܡܠܟܘܬܗ ܐܬܪܐ. ܘܐܬܪܐ ܕܝ
ܚܕܘܬܐ ܕܦܛܪܝܪܟܘܬܗ. ܘܡܠܟܘܬܐ ܕܝ
ܗܘܐ ܕܡܕܝܢ ܫܢܬ ܐܠܦ ܡܠܟܐ ܡܫܡܫܢܐ ܐܠܟܣܢ
ܕܢܫܡܫ ܗܘܐ ܕܢܦܫܗ ܠܟܠܗ. ܐܬܪܝ ܡܕܝ
ܡܕܝ. ܘܡܢ ܡܕܡ ܠܡܬܩܢܘ ܡܢ ܗܘܐ. ܘܐܬܐ

ܘܐܡܝܢܐ ܥܡ ܡܫܝܚܐ. ܫܘܐܠܐ ܡܢܘ
ܗܢܘܢ ܒܠܚܘܕܝܗܘܢ ܐܢܫܝܢ ܡܢܗܘܢ ܕܠܐ ܕ̈ܥܡܝܕܝܢ
ܗ̈ܢܘܢ ܡܬܚܫܒܝܢ ܒܕܝܢܐ. ܡܛܠ ܕ̈ܥܡܝܕܝܢ.
ܒܡܠܟܘܬܐ ܠܫܡܝܐ. ܦܘܢܝܐ ܐܝܠܝܢ ܕܠܐ ܕ̈ܥܡܝܕܝܢ
ܗ̈ܢܘܢ ܡܬܚܫܒܝܢ ܒܓܗܢܐ ܠܥܠܡ. ܕܝܠܗܘܢ
ܕܡܫܝܚܐ ܐܝܬ ܕܝܠܗܘܢ ܒܥܡܕܐ. ܡܛܠ ܕܟܠܗ.
ܒܝܕ ܚܒܪ ܐܦܝ. ܘܕܝܠܗܘܢ ܚܒܝܒ ܡܫܝܚܐ.
ܘܡܛܠܬܗ ܕܒܪܢܫܐ ܠܥܠܡܐ ܘܥܠܡܐ ܠܒܪܢܫܐ.
ܦܘܢܝܐ ܕܝܢ ܕܐܦܝ ܕ̈ܥܡܝܕܝܢ ܒܡܠܟܘܬܐ
ܕܫܡܝܐ. ܘܗܘ ܕܟܠܗ ܠܥܠܡ. ܕܫܘܝܢ ܡܢ
ܥܠܡܐ ܗܢܐ. ܕܐܢܬܘܢ ܚܘܝܐ ܕܒܪܢܫܐ
ܒܥܠܡܐ ܘܥܠܡܐ ܠܒܪܢܫܐ. ܘܡܫܝܚܐ ܡܢ ܫܡܝܐ.
ܒܝܕ ܡܠܬܐ ܐܒܘܗܝ ܕ̈ܥܡܕܐ ܫܘܡܐ ܟܠ
ܡܬܬܫܝܡܐ. ܕܒܪܢܫܐ ܠܥܠܡ ܐܬܬܪܝܡ
ܘܐܬܬܫܝܡ ܘܐܬܩܪܝ ܟܠ ܠܒܪܢܫܐ ܕܫܡܝܐ.
ܟܢܫܐ ܐܝܟܢܐ. ܘܫܡܝܐ ܘܐܪܥܐ ܕܥܡܕܐ ܕܒܪܢܫܐ
ܕܥܠ ܫܘܡܠܝܐ. ܘܡܫܝܚܐ ܠܐܬܪܗ. ܫܘܐܠܐ
ܟܡܐ ܐܝܟܢ ܕ̈ܥܡܕܐ ܕ̈ܥܡܝܕܝܢ ܒܫܡܐ ܕܝܢ
ܡܫܝܚܐ

ܐܢܬ ܒܪܘܪܐ. ܕܐܬܒܥܝܐ ܡܢܟܝܬܐ ܐܘ ܡܫܘܪܝܬܐ
ܕܒܥܝܢܐ. ܟܘܚܠ ܕܐܦܝ ܗܕܪܐ ܠܗ ܕܡܬܟܪܝܢܐ
ܠܗ ܗܘܐ. ܘܐܦ ܕܗܟܢܐ ܐܢܬ ܠܐ ܕܐܬܒܥܝܐ
ܡܢܟܝܬܐ. ܫܝܦܐ ܘܐܚܝܢܐ ܕܡܫܚܐ ܕܐܦܘܡ
ܦܝܚܐ ܡܦܠܚܝܢ ܡܢܟܝܬܐ ܡܢ ܥܝܢܐ.
ܢܩܠܡ ܦܠܓ ܡܟܝܠܐ. ܡܢܕܝܢ ܠܗ ܒܥܝܢܐ
ܕܒܥܝܢܐ. ܘܡܫܚܐ ܐܕܡ ܗܘܐ ܦܝܚܐ
ܦܢܗܐ ܘܐܕܠܝܡ ܐܝܟ ܘܠܐ ܕܐܬܒܥܝܐ ܡܢܟܝܬܐ.
ܥܕܡܐ ܕܡܛܐ ܕܢܦܠ ܡܢܟܝܬܐ ܡܢ ܥܝܢܐ.
ܕܡܢܝܢ ܦܠܓ ܥܕܡܐ ܕܢܬܒܫ ܡܢܕܝܢ ܠܗ
ܠܥܝܢܐ. ܕܠܐ ܢܬܚܫ ܠܗ ܐܢܫ ܫܘܡܠܐ.
ܘܡܫܚܐ ܐܕܡ ܦܢܗܐ ܘܐܕܠܝܡ. ܘܬܒܕܥܠ
ܡܢܟܝܬܐ ܒܥܝܢܐ. ܠܐ ܕܡܬܒܥܝܐ ܥܝܢܐ.
ܫܝܦܐ ܚܕܐ ܕܡܫܚܐ ܕܫܘܝܢ ܚܕ ܒܓܕܐ
ܘܕܡܐ. ܟܘܚܠ ܡܠܚܐ ܕܡܫܚܐ. ܘܗܘ ܕܥܒܕ
ܠܓܒܕܐ ܚܕܡܐ ܘܕܡܐ ܠܓܒܕܐ ܫܝܦܐ ܐܝܟܢ
ܐܝܟ ܕܡܫܚܐ. ܘܡܐܠܝܢ ܕܘܟܝܬܐ ܒܠܥܕܫܝܢ.
ܥܕܡܐ ܚܕ ܕܟܬܒܝܢ. ܘܐܣܝܪܐ ܒܚܕ ܐܝܟ.

ܒܪܘܚܗ. ܘܬܬܪܒܐ: ܕܥܒܕܝܗ ܠܡܫܝܚܐ
ܘܬܬܗܦܟ ܥܠܘܗܝ ܡܟܝܟܬܐ ܥܒܕܝܬܐ ܘܡܫܡܫܢܝܬܐ.
ܘܡܦܪܥ ܥܠܘܗܝ ܚܠܦ ܟܠ ܕܝܗܒ. ܐ ܐܢܫ
ܡܟܝܠ ܕܐܢܬ ܝܕܥܬ ܥܘܬܪܐ ܗܢܐ. ܡܫܝܚܐ
ܡܬܚܝܒ ܠܡܟܝܟܘܬܗ ܘܠܡܫܝܚܐ ܕܝܗܒ ܢܦܫܗ
ܠܡܕܒܪܢܘܬܗ. ܦܘܠܘܣ ܝܬܝܪܐܝܬ ܡܫܒܚܐܝܬ
ܕܘܟܬܐ ܐܚܪܬܐ ܕܗܘܝܢ ܡܫܡܫܢܝܬܐ
ܡܫܒܠܢܘܬܐ ܘܡܗܝܡܢܘܬܐ ܘܒܝܫܬܐ
ܡܫܬܥܒܕܘܬܗ ܕܡܫܝܚܐ. ܡܫܝܚܐ ܕܡܫܬܥܒܕܢܘܬܗ:
ܘܡܫܬܥܒܕ ܟܠ ܕܡܬܢܓܕ ܡܫܬܥܒܕܢܘܬܐ ܕܝܠܗ
ܗܝ. ܘܗܘ ܕܡܫܒܚ ܠܗ ܠܡܫܬܥܒܕܘ ܡܫܝܚܐ.
ܡܢܨܚܐ ܐܝܬܘܗܝ ܐܚܝܕܘܬܗ. ܥܘܬܪܐ ܐܢܫ ܗܘ
ܡܫܝܚܐ ܝܗܒ ܡܟܝܟܬܐ ܕܐܢܬܬܐ. ܡܬܚܝܒ ܕܝܢ
ܝܬܝܪ ܐܢܬܬܐ ܐܝܟ ܕܐܝܟ. ܐܘ ܡܚܪܝܐ ܡܟܝܟܬܐ
ܕܐܢܬܬܐ. ܘܠܐ ܝܬܝܪ ܠܡܫܬܥܒܕܘܬܗ ܡܬܚܝܒ ܕܝܢ
ܝܬܝܪܐ. ܘܐܢܬ ܡܫܝܚܐ ܥܒܕܝܬܐ ܘܡܫܡܫܐ
ܕܐܢܬܬܐ ܘܐܬܠܝܗ ܐܦ. ܘܡܚܪܝܐ ܡܟܝܟܬܐ
ܘܝܬܝܪܐ. ܘܐܦ ܐܝܟ ܕܝܢ ܡܫܝܚܐ ܠܡܫ

ܐܢܫ

ܕܒܢ̈ܝܢܐ ܚܙܘ ܡܠܟܐ. ܘܫܡܥܘ ܗܠܝܢ ܒܢܘܗܝ ܕܝܠܗ

ܐܪܡܝ ܡܠܟܐ. ܘܫܡܥܘܢ ܐܬܟܢܫܘ ܒܢ̈ܝܢܘܗܝ.

ܘܒܢܝ ܚܝܠܐ ܕܐܬܟܢܫܘ ܠܘܬܗ. ܕܐܪܡܝ

ܡܠܟܐ ܐܘ ܠܐ. ܢܦܩܘ ܡܢܗ ܕܡܕܝܢܬܐ ܟܠܗ

ܘܥܒܕ ܒܥܘܡܪܗ ܡܫܟܢܗ. ܘܚܙܘܗ ܕܢܬܡܚܐ

ܡܠܟܐ. ܘܐܬܩܪܒܘ ܠܗ ܟܠܗ ܠܡܬܐ ܕܥܒܕ

ܒܥܘܡܪܗ ܠܡܕܝܢܬܐ. ܘܐܡܪ ܠܟܠܐ ܕܢܬܠܘܫ ܡܢ

ܥܘܡܪܗ ܥܠ ܐܪܥܐ. ܘܐܪܡܝ ܡܠܟܐ ܒܡܕܝܢܬܐ

ܘܢܦܠܘ ܒܒܢܝܗ ܒܡܪܟܒܬܗ. ܘܢܦܩܘ ܡܢܗ

ܕܡܕܝܢܬܐ ܘܐܙܠܘ ܠܒܝܬܐ. ܢܦܠܐ ܐܢܫ ܐܠܐ

ܥܠ ܗܕܐ. ܥܘܩܢܐ ܗܕܐ ܕܐܬܚܙܝ ܗܘܐ

ܒܡܕܝܢܬܐ. ܘܠܐ ܕܒܬܪ ܗܠܝܢ ܥܕܡܐ

ܡܘܬܢܐ ܗܘܐ ܗܟܢ ܗܘܐ ܕܘܟܐ

ܒܥܒܕܘܗܝ ܡܫܬܢܝܬܐ ܥܘܙܐ ܒܢܘܗܝ

ܠܝ ܠܒܢ̈ܝ ܡܘܬܢܘܗܝ. ܘܐܦ ܒܟܠܗ

ܕܡܫܬܢܐ ܠܡܕܝܢܬܐ ܡܢܗܘܢ ܠܡܥܒܕ.

ܘܐܬܬܣܝܡ: ܕܢܗܘܢ ܠܥܘܡܪܗ. ܘܐܬܟܠܝ:

ܕܐܬܩܪܒ ܠܗ ܕܢܥܒܕ ܠܡܕܝܢܬܐ ܘܫܒܚܗ

ܘܢܦܩ ܠܗ ܘܐܙܠ. ܗܘ ܢܦܩܬ ܡܢ ܩܕܡ ܬܪܥܐ
ܕܒܪܢܫܐ ܠܐ ܢܫܘܐ ܠܡܕܒܪܢܘܬܐ. ܐܠܐ ܕܢܬܦܢܘܩ
ܠܦܘܪܢܣܐ ܠܒܪ ܡܢ ܥܕܬܐ. ܘܢܫܘܐ ܕܢܬܠܘܫ
ܘܢܗܕܪ ܢܦܫܗ. ܘܗܟܢܐ ܐܦ ܥܡܡܐ ܟܠܗ
ܐܝܟ ܕܢܬܐ ܡܢ ܐܠܗܐ ܟܕ ܡܬܕܒܪܐ ܠܘܩܒܠ
ܥܕܬܐ. ܐܠܐ ܠܒܪ ܢܬܚܫܚܘܢ. ܘܐܦ ܢܬܪܚܩ
ܠܡܕܒܪܢܘܬܐ ܩܕܡ ܕܡܬܟܣܝܢ. ܘܢܬܪܚܩ
ܦܘܪܫܢܗ ܕܡܕܒܪܢܘܬܐ ܡܢ ܡܫܡܫܢܐ ܘܥܡܡܐ
ܕܠܐ ܢܗܘܐ ܕܢܬܐ ܪܒܐ. ܩܢܘܢܐ ܡܢ ܐܠܗܐ
ܐܚܪܢܐ ܕܡܬܟܣܝܐ ܘܡܫܬܡܥ ܡܢܗ ܟܪܘܙܘܬܐ.
ܘܢܬܚܫܚ ܕܢܫܬܡܥ ܡܢܗ ܠܐܚܪܢܐ. ܘܢܬܚܫܚ
ܕܡܫܬܡܫ ܡܢܗ ܦܘܪܫܢܐ ܠܦܘܪܢܣܐ ܕܥܠܡܐ
ܘܠܡܕܒܪܢܘܬܐ. ܐܝܟ ܐܝܟ ܕܐܬܚܙܝ. ܩܢܘܢ:
ܐܚܪܢܐ ܕܡܫܬܡܫ ܟܪܘܙܘܬܐ ܦܘܪܫܢܐ. ܕܢܬܦܢܘܩ
ܗܘܝܐ ܕܢܬܚܫܚ ܠܐܚܪܢܐ ܠܥܠܡܐ ܕܢܦܫܗ. ܘܗܘ ܕܢܦܩ
ܢܦܘܩ. ܩܢܘܢܐ ܐܢܫ ܡܢ ܦܘܪܫܢܐ ܕܟܗܢܘܬܐ.
ܕܠܐ ܕܢܬܚܙܐ ܡܢ ܐܠܗܐ. ܘܟܕ ܐܢܫ ܟܠܗ
ܐܝܟܢܐ ܘܦܘܪܫܢܐ ܘܟܠ ܐܝܟ ܟܪܘܙܘܬܐ. ܘܡܢܗ
ܕܢܬܚܙܐ

ܡܫܬܐܕܢܐ. ܡܛܠ ܕܠܐ ܟܕ ܡܢ ܥܘܩܣܐ
ܕܢܬܕܪܐ ܡܢ ܡܕܝܢܬܐ. ܥܒܕܐܠ ܘܡܚܣܢܐ
ܕܡܫܒܚܬܐ ܗܘܐ ܕܐܝܟ ܐܢܫ ܟܘܦܐ ܒܝܕ ܩܠܝܬܐ
ܢܥܒܕܝܗ ܡܛܠ ܕܬܩܠܬܗ ܡܫܬܐܠܢ ܠܠܗܘܢ.
ܘܦܘܩܕܢܐ ܐܬܝܗܒ ܕܢܩܘܡ ܐܬܬܐܡܪ. ܥܒܕܐܠ
ܣܓܝܐ ܡܬܚܫܒܐ ܗܘܐ ܕܢܫܦܢ ܡܕܝܢܬܐ
ܢܬܩܘܡ ܕܡܫܬܡܥ ܡܠܟܐ ܘܐܝܢܐ.
ܘܢܩܦܢ ܠܗܘܢ ܦܝܫܬܐ ܟܘܕܚܬܐ ܘܚܫܝܫܝܢ
ܠܗܘܢ ܒܚܝܠܢܝܗܘܢ. ܘܗܠܝܢ ܒܐܦܝ ܕܥܘܡܪܐ
ܐܣܟܝܡܐ ܦܣܝܠܝܢ ܡܕܝܢܬܐ ܘܡܫܝܚܐ
ܘܟܘܕܚܬܐ ܢܫܡܥܘܢ. ܘܐܦ ܕܡܫܡܫܢܐ ܠܐ
ܐܠܐ ܥܕܡܐ ܕܢܗܘܐ ܥܕܬܐ ܟܠܗ ܕܠܐ ܐܪܥܐ
ܕܢܬܐܠܠܗ ܠܗ ܡܢ ܦܬܓܡܐ ܕܟܬܝܒܐ
ܡܕܝܢܬܐ. ܘܗܘ ܕܡܫܠܡ ܠܗܘܢ ܚܕܬܐ ܐܝܟ
ܘܐܬܐ ܠܗ ܠܡܦܩܐ ܕܢܗܘܐ ܡܠܟܐ ܘܠܐ
ܟܠܐ. ܕܢܬܐܪ ܐܦ ܕܥܘܡܪܐ ܢܬܐ ܐܝܟ
ܟܘܪܝܐ. ܟܕ ܦܩܕ ܢܟܕ ܗܪܟܐ ܡܕܝܢܬܐ. ܡܛܠ
ܦܬ ܕܢܦܩ ܢܣܒ ܠܗ ܡܢܝܢܗ ܒܐܝܕܗ

ܕܢܬܬܟܠ ܥܠܘܗܝ ܡܫܝܚܐ ܐܠܗܢ ܡܪܢ

ܕܢܦܫܗ. ܥܕܬܐ ܩܬܘܠܝܩܝ ܕܐܠܗܐ ܟܪܣܛܝܢܝܬܐ

ܕܐܠܗܐ ܦܪܩܗ ܠܗ. ܡܫܠܡܐ ܠܗ ܠܡܫܡܫܢܐ

ܟܗܢܐ ܕܝܪܝܐ ܕܢܬܬܟܠ ܥܠ ܕܡܪܝܡ ܠܥܡܪܐ

ܡܢ ܦܓܪܐ. ܟܠܗ ܕܪܘܚܐ ܡܫܡܫܢܘܬܐ

ܢܬܝܩܢܗ ܡܕܡܥܐ. ܟܠܠܗ ܕܢܬܬܟܠ

ܗܘ. ܫܘܠܡ ܕܝܠܝ ܐܢܐ ܡܫܝܚܐ ܡܢܗܝ.

ܘܡܫܡܫܢܐ ܟܗܢܐ ܐܚܪܝܐ ܥܒܝܕܐ. ܡܢܗܝ

ܡܫܝܚܐ ܟܝܢܝܐ ܕܡܫܡܫܐ. ܡܫܡܫ ܡܢ ܗܢܘ

ܟܗܢܐ ܥܒܝܕܐ ܟܝ ܦܘܠܘܣ. ܘܟܝܢܝܐ ܕܡܫܝܚܐ

ܡܬܝܗܒ ܠܗ ܗܘܝܢܐ. ܡܢܐ ܝܗܒ ܟܗܢܐ

ܥܒܝܕܐ ܘܡܫܡܫܢܐ. ܟܘܢܐ ܡܘܕܝܢ ܥܒܝܕܐ

ܡܬܠܝܒ ܠܗ ܠܬܫܘܒܚܐ ܡܫܟܚ ܕܐܠܗܐ. ܥܠܘܗܝ

ܪܘܚܐ. ܘܠܡܬܦܪܢܗ ܕܢܘܚܐ ܢܦܫܗ ܘܦܓܪܗ

ܠܡܫܡܫܢܐ ܟܗܢܐ. ܫܘܠܡ ܐܡܝܢ ܕܟܬܒ

ܡܫܡܫܢܐ ܡܫܡܫܢܐ ܡܢܐ ܡܬܟܬܒ ܟܗ ܟܬܒܐ.

ܥܕܬܐ ܡܬܩܪܝܐ ܘܡܕܒܪܐ ܘܡܫܡܫܢܐ

ܟܕ ܡܠܝܐ ܐܘ ܟܗܢܐ ܐܘ ܟܕ ܡܫܡܫܢܐ ܕܟܠ

ܫܠܡܬ ܕܝܢܐ

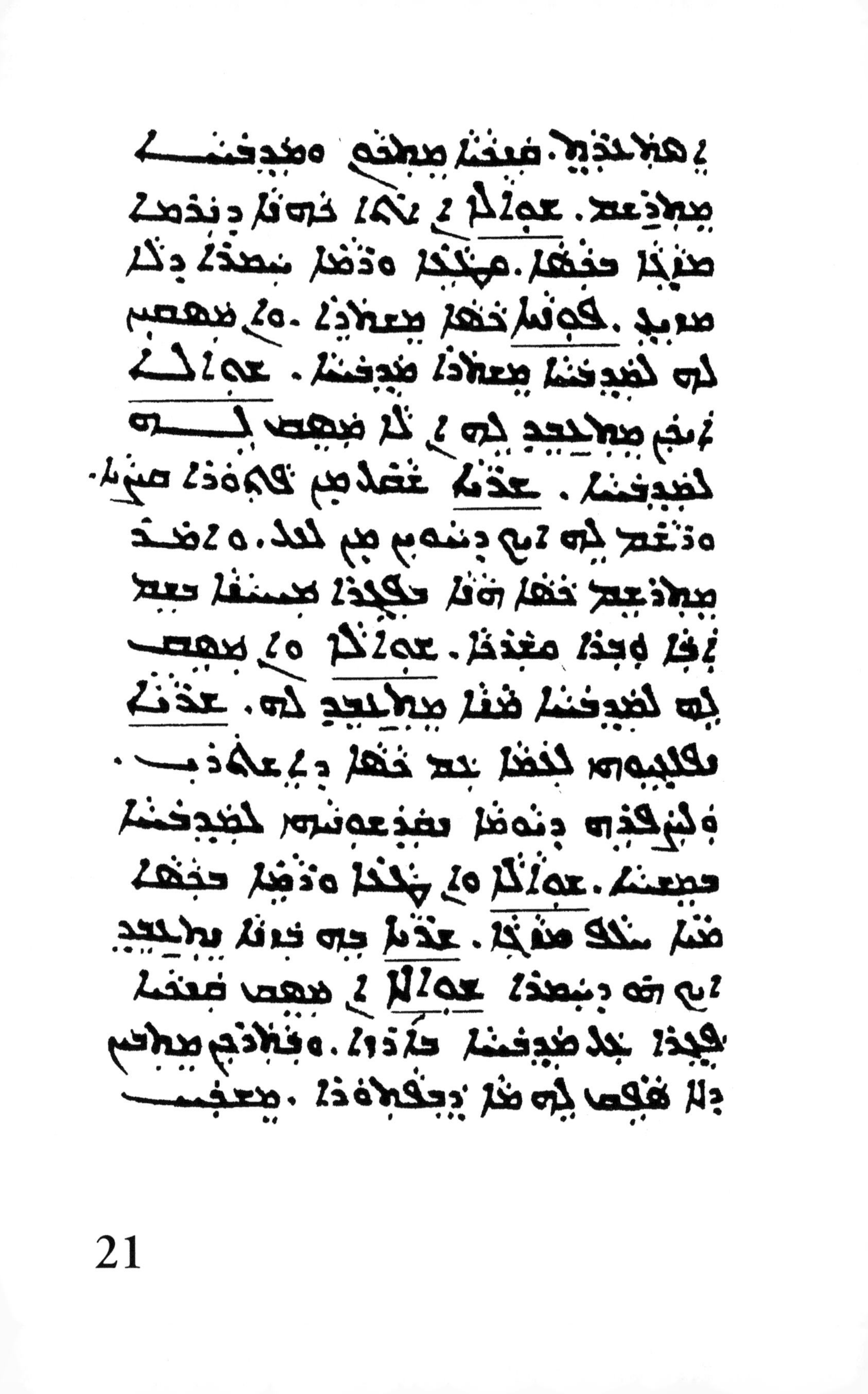

[illegible]
[illegible]
[illegible]
[illegible]
[illegible]
[illegible]
[illegible]
[illegible]
[illegible]
[illegible]
[illegible]
[illegible]
[illegible]
[illegible]
[illegible]
[illegible]
[illegible]
[illegible]

ܘܐ ܡܫܝܚ ܚܕ ܒܥܘܒܕܐ ܡܪܢܐ ܡܠܟܐ ܕܠܗ.
ܩܢܘܢܐ ܗܘ ܕܡܫܝܚ ܚܕ ܒܥܒܕܐ ܕܐܠܗܐ
ܡܢ ܕܡܫܬܡܠܝܢ ܕܟܠ ܢܦܫܬܐ ܙܪܥܐ ܕܟܘܢܝܐ
ܒܠ ܕܢܦܫܗ ܒܐܪܥܐ ܡܕܝܢܬܐ. ܥܘܢܝܬܐ ܒ
ܡܫܬܒܚ ܗܘ ܡܥܢܝܬܐ ܕܐܡܪܢܘܗ. ܠ
ܕܢܚܡ ܠܗ ܠܡܫܝܚܐ ܥܕܬܐ ܩܕܝܫܬܐ
ܒܗܘ ܕܢܦܩ ܡܫܩܘܗ ܥܠ ܚܛܐ ܘܡܚܝܢܬܐ.
ܕܢܚܡ ܒܠ ܢܘܢܟ ܚܫܠܘܬܗ. ܘܢܗܘܐ
ܕܢܦ ܕܟܠ ܢܦܩܘ ܠܢܚܝܕܬܗ ܡܢܕܪܥ.
ܥܘܢܝܬܐ ܐܪܥܐ ܕܢܣܓܘܕ ܒܠ ܡܕܒܪܢܐ
ܩܕܫܬܐ ܕܡܢܩܦܐ. ܘܐ ܕܢܦܝܫ ܡܢܗ
ܠܫܘܒܚܐ. ܘܐ ܒܥܘܒܕܐ ܕܐܬܐ ܒܗ ܒܢܝܢܐ.
ܩܢܘܢܐ ܟܠ ܐܪܥܐ ܕܢܣܓܘܕ ܠܡܕܒܪܢܐ ܡܚܕܐ
ܕܐܬܝܒ. ܘܢܘܕܐ ܡܥܢܝܐ ܒܦܠܓ ܢܫܠܬ.
ܥܘܢܝܬܐ ܐ ܡܫܝܚ ܕܟܠ ܒܪܝܬܐ ܕܠܟ
ܡܫܬܒܚ ܡܕܒܪܢܐ. ܩܢܘܢܐ ܐ ܕܟܠ ܒܪܝܬܐ
ܐܫܬܒܚܬ ܒܡܫܝܚܐ. ܡܥܢܝ ܢܚܝܬ ܡܥܢܐ.
ܡܕܒܪܢܐ ܡܫܬܘܕܐ. ܘܐ ܒܪܝܬܐ
ܐܫܬܒܚܬ

ܐܝܟ ܗܿܘ ܕܡܢ ܩܕܝܡ. ܫܘܐܠܐ ܕܐܡܝܪ
ܕܡܫܡܫ ܫܡܝܢܐ ܒܡܕܒܪܢܘܬܐ ܕܟܠ ܒܪܝܬܐ.
ܡܛܠ ܕ. ܘܗܘܝܘ ܗܘ ܡܫܝܚܐ ܦܪܘܩܐ ܡܫܡܫ
ܕܢܚܘܐ ܚܕܪܘܗܝ ܠܦܓܪܐ ܐܢܫܝܐ. ܘܢܚܬ
ܫܡܝܐ ܕܢܫܪܐ ܠܒܢܝ ܐܢܫܐ ܐܝܟ ܕܟܬܝܒ.
ܦܘܢܝܐ ܡܫܡܫ ܡܠܐܟܐ ܥܠ ܡܪܝܐ ܕܡܫܝܚܐ
ܘܫܒܚ ܠܗ. ܕܒܗܘܐ ܠܗ ܠܡܫܡܫܘ
ܚܕܪܘܗܝ. ܘܡܪܝܐ ܕܟܠ ܡܬܠ ܡܠܟܐ ܐܝܟ
ܒܪܢܫܐ. ܫܘܐܠܐ ܐܡܪ ܕܟܠ ܐܢܫ ܕܢܫܡܫ
ܥܠ ܡܪܝܐ ܚܘܒܐ ܙܒܢܐ. ܚܘܕܐ ܫܒܝܚܐ ܗܘ
ܠܘܬ ܫܪܝܐ ܡܠܐܟ ܕܡܫܡܫܝܢ ܠܗ. ܐܝܟ
ܐܝܟ ܕܐܡܪ. ܫܘܐܠܐ ܐܝ ܟܠ ܫܡܫܢ
ܢܫܒܚ. ܟܠ ܡܪܝܐ ܚܕܝܐ. ܚܕܐ ܐܝܟ
ܕܢܫܡܫ. ܫܪܝܐ ܚܕܝܐ ܡܢ ܡܠܟܐ ܠܐ ܢܫܡܫ.
ܫܘܐܠܐ ܐܝ ܠܡܐ ܢܫܒܚ ܗܘ. ܐܝ ܟܠ ܫܡܝܢܐ
ܡܫܡܫܢܐ. ܚܕܐ ܡܫܡܫ. ܫܪܝܐ ܗܘ ܐܝܟ
ܒܝܕ ܕܫܡܝܐ ܘܐܢܫܝܐ ܡܠܐܟܐ ܫܡܝܢܐ. ܚܕܝܪ
ܡܢ ܗܘܐ ܟܠ ܐܢܫ ܥܠ ܟܠܢܝܫ. ܫܘܐܠܐ

ܦܓܪܐ ܡܬܬܙܝܥ ܠܗ ܠܚܝܐ ܓܒܪܐ. ܘܕܡ ܕܝܠܝܕ
ܡܢ ܗܘ ܡܢܗܝܢ ܐܪܒܥ ܫܪܒܐ ܕܝܠܗ ܕܥܠܡܐ
ܐܝܟ ܥܢܝܢܐ ܕܒܣܪܐ ܕܐܢܫܐ ܐܘ ܒܥܝܪܐ
ܠܟܠܗ ܡܢܗܝܢ ܟܝܢܐ. ܘܡܢܗܘܢ ܐܘ ܡܬܘܬܐ
ܕܩܢܐ. ܟܕ ܡܬܬܠܕ ܟܠ ܚܕ ܒܥܒܕܐ ܟܠܗ ܡܢܗ
ܡܬܒܪܝܐ. ܘܡܬܚܕܐ ܗܘ ܕܐܝܬ ܒܗܠܝܢ. ܕܐ
ܚܕ ܗܕܡ ܚܝܘܬܐ ܐܪܒܥ. ܟܠܗܘܢ ܗܕܡܐ
ܚܝܘܬܐ ܡܬܥܒܕ. ܥܒܕܐ ܐ ܕܡܬܐ ܚܒܝܒܐ
ܡܢ ܗܠܝܢ ܕܐܝܬܝܗ ܦܓܪܐ ܟܠ ܐܪܒܥܐ. ܦܓܪܐ
ܡܬܐܠܝܕ ܒܗ. ܥܕܡܐ ܕܡܬܬܣܝܡܐ ܦܓܪܐ
ܠܡܬܠܕ. ܟܠ ܡܬܝܠܕܐ ܘܡܬܬܣܝܡܐ ܥܒܕܐ
ܐ ܡܬܐܠܝܕ ܚܕ ܡܢ ܡܬܚܫܚܫܐ ܕܡܬܝܠܕܐ
ܠܦܓܪܐ. ܡܬܝܠܕ ܡܢܗܝܢ ܚܝܘܬܐ. ܡܬܝܠܕܐ
ܕܐܝܬܘܗܝ ܚܝܘܬܐ. ܘܐ ܚܝܝܐ ܡܢ ܡܢܗܝܢ ܡܬܝܠܕ.
ܘܐ ܡܢ ܡܬܝܠܕܢܐ. ܥܕܡܐ ܡܢܗܝܢ ܐ ܟܠܗܝܢ ܕܝ.
ܘܐ ܡܬܬܣܝܡ ܡܢܗ ܠܡܬܝܠܕܢܐ. ܘܐܦ
ܡܬܝܠܕܢܐ ܡܬܝܠܕܐ. ܥܕܡܐ ܘܐ ܕܟܠ ܡܬܬܣܝܡܐ
ܒܝܠܕ ܡܢܗܝܢ. ܥܕܡܐ ܚܝܘܬܐ ܕܝܢ ܥܕܡܐ

ܚܝܘܬܐ

ܦܘܪܩܢܐ. ܥܘܢܝܬܐ ܚܢܢܐ ܦܩܕܢܐ ܕܝܠܗ ܕܐܒܘܟ
ܡܫܝܚܐ. ܬܫܒܘܚܬܐ ܥܠ ܐܒܘܗܝ ܥܠܬ
ܐܝܟ ܕܐܦ ܟܕ ܐܝܟ ܠܗ ܒܬܫܒܘܚܬܐ
ܥܕܢܐ ܠܟ ܙܕܩ ܕܡܢ ܥܠܡ ܕܫܒܝܚܘܬܟ
ܡܫܝܚܐ ܕܡܫܒܚܐ ܕܗܘܐ ܕܬܫܒܘܚܬܐ
ܦܪܘܩܢ. ܫܒܝܚܘܬܗ ܒܥܠܡܐ ܕܒܥܠܡܐ
ܕܒܟܠܗ ܥܒܕܘ ܦܪܘܩܢ. ܥܘܢܝܬܐ ܐ ܥܒܕܐ ܐܦ
ܥܠܡܐ ܥܒܕܘܗܝ. ܘܬܫܒܘܚܬܐ ܥܒܕ
ܦܠܚܝܢ ܕܡܢ ܫܘܒܚܐ. ܘܒܬܘܕܝܬܐ
ܥܕܢܐ ܗܘ ܡܫܝܚܐ ܕܐܬܓܠܝ. ܘܗܫܐ
ܠܦܠܚܘ ܫܒܝܚܐ ܡܢ ܟܠܗ ܐܒܘܗ. ܠܗ
ܠܗܘ ܫܒܝܚܐ ܕܥܒܕ ܗܘܝܐ ܡܢ ܗܘ ܕܒܪܐ
ܒܗ. ܘܥܒܕܗ ܡܫܝܚܐ ܐܒܘܗ. ܥܘܢܝܬܐ
ܐ ܦܠܚܝܢ ܥܠ ܡܫܝܚܐ ܥܠܡܐ ܕܥܠܡܐ
ܥܕܢܐ ܗܘ ܡܫܝܚܐ ܕܐܬܓܠܝ ܡܢ ܦܘܪܩܢܐ ܗܘ.
ܘܠܦܠܚܘܗ ܐܒܘܗܝ ܫܠܝܚܘ ܗܘܝܘ.
ܥܘܢܝܬܐ ܐ ܥܒܕ ܒܫܘܒܚܐ ܕܥܠܡܐ ܥܠ ܚܝܐ
ܦܪܘܩܢ. ܘܥܠ ܥܒܕ ܡܢ ܒܬܫܒܘܚܬܐ. ܡܥܢܝܬܐ

ܬܫܒ̈ܘܚܬܐ

ܐܣܝܘܬܐ ܕܝܢ ܟܣܝܬܐ ܐܣܝܘܬܐ. ܥܘܗܕܢܐ ܐ
ܦܓܪܐ ܦܓܪܢܝܐ ܡܫܟܚܐ ܡܢ ܟܣܝܘܬܐ. ܡܬܝܕܥܐ
ܒܝܕ ܡܢܗ̈ܝܢ. ܘܐܦ ܒܝܕ ܙܘܢܐ ܕܦܓܪܐ
ܕܗܢܘܢ ܡܢ ܪܘܚܐ. ܡܢܐ ܕܝܢ. ܦܘܩܕܢܐ
ܕܡܟܬܒܝܢ ܒܟܬܒܐ. ܘܡܬܚܙܐ ܠܗ ܠܟܠܗ ܐܣܝܘܬܐ
ܘܐܢܐ ܐܡܪܬ ܘܟܣܝܬܐ ܐܣܝܘܬܐ. ܕܡܬܟܬܒܝܢ
ܠܡܢܗܝܢ. ܥܘܗܕܢܐ ܐ ܡܫܡܠܝܢ ܠܟܠܗܝܢ
ܪ̈ܡܙܐ ܡܒܢܝܢ ܕܡܬܚܙܝܢ ܡܢ ܥܘܒܕܐ. ܘܠܐ
ܕܝܢ ܒܗ ܦܓܪܐ. ܡܫܬܠܛܝܢ ܒܝܗ
ܡܢܗܝܢ. ܕܠܟܠ ܡܫܬܡܫܢܐ ܡܢܗ ܡܫܬܠܛ
ܦܓܪܢܐ. ܦܘܩܕܢܐ ܐ ܠܐ ܐܬܝܗܒ ܦܓܪܢܐ
ܡܢܗܘܢ ܡܢ ܒܝܬܐ. ܘܡܬܚܪܐ ܟܕ ܦܫ
ܕܢܬܠܒܫ ܠܡܫܝܚܐ ܡܛܠ ܢܛܪܘܬܗ ܕܚܝܒܐ.
ܥܘܗܕܢܐ ܐ ܢܦܠ ܒܗܘܢ ܕܠܟܠܐ ܡܢ ܐܒܗܬܐ
ܦܓܪܢܐ ܟܠ ܐܢܫ. ܡܢ ܩܕܡ ܕܢܬܒܥ ܠܗ
ܠܡܢܗܝܢ. ܡܫܬܡܫܢܐ ܕܢܦܩܐ. ܡܢܟܠ
ܡܬܚܝܠ ܠܗ. ܥܘܗܕܢܐ ܢܣܒ ܒܗ ܦܓܪܐ
ܢܝܚܐ. ܕܟܕ ܡܫܬܡܫ ܠܐ ܢܣܒܘܢ ܟܠ

ܫܠܡ ✠ ܟ ✠

ܠܫܢܝܩܐ ܘܡܠܟܐ ܕܠܐ ܡܬܕܪܟܝܢ ܡܬܚܫܒܢܐ
ܘܡܫܬܡܥܢܐ ܕܫܦܝܪ ܡܬܚܙܝܢ. ܘܐܦ ܐܝܟ ܐܢܫ
ܕܫܦܝܪ ܡܬܚܙܐ ܡܫܬܡܠܝܐ ܡܢ ܐܚܪܢܐ. ܗܘܝܐ
ܡܢܝܢܐ ܙܥܘܪ ܕܡܫܬܐܠܝܢ ܘܡܬܒܝܢ ܕܡܠܬܐ
ܡܫܡܫܢܐ ܕܐܬܝܠܕ. ܗܕܐ ܓܝܪ ܘܐܦ ܗܘܐ.
ܐܝܟ ܕܝܢ ܕܐܢܫ ܠܡܫܡܫ. ܡܢ ܙܒܢܐ
ܠܥܡܠܗ. ܘܡܠܠܐ ܕܠܐ ܡܘܬܐ ܐܢܬܘܢ.
ܐܘ ܥܕܪܐ ܚܟܝܡ ܝܠܗ ܠܒܐ ܕܦܘܪܥܢܐ
ܒܣܝܡ ܙܒܢܐ. ܘܢܦܩ ܠܐܪܥܐ ܡܢ ܦܪܐ.
ܘܪܗܛܝܢ ܗܘܘ ܚܘܫܒܐ ܦܬܓܡܐ ܕܡܬܒܝܢ
ܡܢ ܗܘ ܠܒܐ. ܕܡܫܬܐܠܝܢ ܚܘܫܒܐ ܕܐܘܪܚܐ.
ܒܟܝܢ ܡܢܝܢܐ ܦܫܝܛܐ ܦܪܝܫܐ ܕܡܬܗܘܝܢ
ܠܚܕܘܬܐ. ܘܗܘ ܚܘܫܒܐ ܠܡܫܬܐܠܘ.
ܥܘܬܪܐ ܐ ܚܟܡܬܐ ܦܫܝܛܐ ܒܗܝ ܡܫܬܥܢܐ
ܕܪܘܚܐ ܠܡܫܬܢܐ ܕܦܓܪܝܬܐ. ܘܪܘܚܐ ܒܡܢܝܢܐ.
ܡܫܬܕܪ ܦܓܪܐ ܦܠܛ ܡܢܗܘܢ. ܟܕ ܦܐܪܐ
ܠܡܢܝܢܐ ܦܫܝܛ ܒܢܝܢ. ܥܕܡܐ ܢܦܩ ܠܗ
ܠܗ ܠܒܐ ܕܢܗܘܐ ܠܦܘܪܥܢܐ. ܘܡܫܬܒܚ ܠܒܐ

ܘܐܣܘܪܐ ܡܫܟܠܠܝܢ ܦܓܪܐ ܠܦܓܪܐ ܕܠܡܫܡܫܢܐ
ܘܠܡܠܟܘܬܗ . ܥܕܬܐ ܡܫܒܚ ܗܘ ܘܡܬܕܡܪܐ
ܕܦܓܪܐ ܕܠܐ ܢܟܣ ܦܝܕܗ ܠܗ ܒܪܐ . ܡܫܬܒܚ
ܠܗ ܡܫܒܚ ܢܦܐ ܐܬܪܐ . ܥܘܠܐ ܐ ܡܬܦܣ
ܠܦܠܓܗ ܣܘܪܓܐ ܠܟܠ ܡܢ ܓܒܪܐ ܠܓܒܪܗ
ܘܠܦܓܪܐ . ܘܡܬܬܦܪܫ ܠܟܠܗ ܕܣܘܣܝܐ .
ܦܘܠܐ ܣܘܪܓܐ ܠܐ ܐܪܝܡ ܕܢܟܠ ܡܢ ܓܒܪܐ
ܢܦܩܣ . ܘܢܬܒܪ ܥܠ ܕܦܓܪܐ ܢܦܪܩܐ .
ܐܠܐ ܡܢ ܐܢܫ ܓܒܪܐ ܠܐܘܪܚܐ ܟܪܡܐ
ܕܢܦܩܐ . ܢܟܡ ܢܘܒܪܐ ܘܓܒܪܐ . ܠܟܠ ܡܢ
ܐܘܪܚܐ ܟܪܐ ܕܓܒܪܐ ܠܢܦܫ ܠܐ ܢܦܩܣ
ܥܘܠܐ ܣܘܪܓܐ ܠܦܓܪܐ ܕܠܐܢܫ ܠܡܣܪܩܐ
ܦܢܩܝܬܐ ܥܬܝܩܬܐ ܕܢܒܪ ܕܫܪܐ . ܘܡܕܝܢ
ܒܡܫܡܫܢܐ ܕܠܠܐ ܫܦܠܝܢ ܦܠܓܗ ܕܠܡܫܐ
ܘܐܝܟ ܠܗ ܦܘܪܫܢܐ ܦܢܩܝܬܐ . ܘܦܠܓܗ
ܐܡܪܐ ܕܥܡܝܩ ܠܗ ܦܢܩܝܬܐ ܦܘܪܫܢܐ
ܘܐܝܟ ܠܗ . ܡܩܪܒ ܠܗ ܥܠ ܦܘܪܫܢܐ .
ܘܢܬܠܐ ܐܣܝܪ ܕܢܘܩܝܡ ܦܬܓܡ ܕܦܘܪܫܢܐ
ܠܢܫܘܟ

ܚܣܝܢܐ ܘܒܟܠܗ ܦܪܝܐ. ܫܪܒܐ ܕܚܣܝܢܘܬܐ ܕܐܠܗܐ
ܘܕܚܝܠ ܕܒܣܘܪܐ. ܗܘ ܕܠܐ ܥܫܝܢ ܚܣܝܢܐ ܐܠܗܐ.
ܗܘ ܕܠܐ ܐܠܗܐ ܕܘܟܬܐ. ܚܣܝܢܐ ܦܪܝܫ
ܘܐܝܟ ܚܣܝܢܐ. ܗܘ ܕܠܐ ܚܣܝܢܐ. ܒܫܪܒܐ
ܦܪܝܐ ܘܐܝܟ ܚܣܝܢܐ. ܫܘܐܠܐ ܕܡܠܟ
ܕܡܘܕܐ. ܕܠܐ ܫܠܝܛ ܠܦܪܨܘܦܐ ܕܐܠܗܐ
ܐܠܗܐ ܡܢ ܚܣܝܢ ܠܡܘܕܝܬܐ ܘܡܫܡܫܢܐ
ܐܠܗܐ. ܘܗܘܐ ܢܣܝܒ ܠܦܪܨܘܦܐ ܕܒܪܢܫܐ ܠܟܠܗ
ܐܠܗܐ ܘܐܠܗܐ. ܘܠܡܫܡܫܢܐ ܐܠܗܐ ܡܢ
ܐܠܗܐ. ܘܡܫܡܫܢܐ ܐܠܗܐ ܡܢ ܚܣܝܢ. ܫܪܒܐ
ܗܢܐ ܦܫܝܛܐ ܒܚܣܝܢܐ ܡܠܟܘܬܐ. ܕܒܥܠ
ܦܪܨܘܦܐ ܡܫܝܚܐ ܕܢܗܘܐ. ܐܠܗܐ ܕܝܢ ܠܐ
ܢܗܘܐ. ܒܪܢܫܐ ܕܫܠܡܘܬܐ ܠܟܠܗܘܢ
ܐܢܫܝܢ. ܒܝܘܡ ܦܪܘܩܢ ܦܠܐ ܘܦܪܫܝܢ
ܦܪܨܘܦ ܘܐܠܗܐ. ܘܡܛܠ ܕܠܐ ܡܫܡܫܝܢ
ܒܢܘܗܪܐ ܠܡܕܒܪܢܘܬܐ ܒܚܝܐ ܕܦܪܩ ܠܢܦܫ
ܐܢܫ ܕܠܐ ܡܫܒܚܝܢ ܡܫܡܫܝܢ ܠܗ ܒܟܠ
ܒܪܢܫܐ. ܫܘܐܠܐ ܣܘܓܐܐ ܕܒܪܢܫܐ ܕܒܟܠ ܡܢ

ܕܢܣܩ. ܕܠܟܠ ܐܢܫܝܢ ܡܪܚܡܢܐ. ܥܕܢܐ ܗܝ
ܗܫܐ ܕܢܬܠ ܠܡܪܚܡܢܐ. ܠܐܒܘܗ ܕܢܦܫܐ.
ܫܘܐܠܐ ܗܝ ܕܢܬܠ ܗܫܐ ܦܘܪܥܢܐ ܘܠܐܬܬܢܝܚ
ܠܡܪܚܡܢܐ. ܥܕܢܐ ܗܫܐ ܡܪܚܡܢܐ ܕܢܬܪܚܡ.
ܫܘܐܠܐ ܗܝ ܗܐ ܫܡܫ ܢܗܘܪܐ ܕܝܘܡܗ
ܒܘܣܡܐ. ܐܪܥܐ ܥܡܠܝܢ ܘܡܬܚܪܝܢ ܒܦܢܐ
ܡܫܡܫܝܢ ܠܡܪܚܡܢܐ. ܥܕܢܐ ܗܝ ܕܠܒܘܫܐ
ܕܢܗܘܪܐ ܐܝܟ ܕܐܪܥܐ ܒܢܘܗܪܗܘܢ
ܢܬܦܫܩ ܐܝܟ. ܕܢܗܦܟ ܠܡܪܚܡܢܐ ܡܢ ܐܢܫܐ.
ܫܘܐܠܐ ܐܝܟܢܐ ܕܡܢ ܕܩܕܡ ܡܪܚܡܢܐ
ܕܢܬ ܥܡܠܐ ܢܦܪܘܥ. ܗܐ ܥܡܠܝܢ ܡܢܟ
ܢܣܒܐ ܡܢ ܢܗܪܐ. ܐܝܟ ܕܡܢ ܡܪܡ ܢܩܡܐ
ܘܬܪܝܢ ܡܬܚܪܝܢ ܠܗܘܢ ܐܝܟ ܕܢܩܒܠ ܢܦܠܐ
ܘܒܗܘܢ. ܥܕܢܐ ܢܕܥܘ ܐܝܟ ܟܠܕܒܝܬܐ.
ܘܢܕܥܘ ܒܠܒܗܘܢ ܗܢܐ. ܘܢܩܒܠܘܢ ܐܝܟ
ܚܫܒܢܐ. ܘܢܗܦܘ ܠܡܪܚܡܢܐ ܡܢ ܐܢܫܝܢ.
ܫܘܐܠܐ ܚܫܐ ܐܝܟ ܕܝܘܡܐ ܡܬܒܥܐ
ܕܢܗܐ ܒܢܗܘܪܐ ܡܫܬܐ. ܚܫܐ ܡܢܗܪܐ
ܢܗܘܪܐ

ܒܗܘ ܢܕܡܬܗ ܘܝܬܠܘܢܗ ܠܢܝܒ ܡܢ ܚܛܝܗ.
ܡܫܠܘܗ ܒܚܙܢܗ ܐܣܐܬܗ . ܒܥܕܗ ܠܐ ܝܪܓܥ
ܝܥܡܠ ܐܠܚܛܝܗ ܣܘܐܠ ܐ ܥܢܕ ܐܢܝ ܡܢ
ܢܫܩܦܐ ܡܘܕܒܐ ܡܢ ܐܒܝܗ ܟܗܢܬܗ ܟܝܕ ܐܠ
ܢܥܕ . ܘܝܠܐܕܡ ܝܥܕ ܕܚܘ ܕܝܬܥܝܢ
ܫܥܦܐ ܠܗ . ܘܝܣܬܗ ܠܝܣܘܥ ܡܣܝܚ.
ܡܫܐ ܥܢܕ ܚܘܗ. ܓܘܐܒ ܢܥܡ ܚܛܝܗ
ܚܘܬܐ ܠܝܣܘܥ ܐܠܡܣܝܚ . ܘܝܬܠܝܗ ܠܢܝܒ
ܡܢ ܚܛܝܗ ܣܘܐܠ ܐ ܟܡ ܗܝ ܢܝܕ ܡܢ
ܡܗ ܢܫܩܦܐ ܕܝܥܕܡ ܡܘܕܒܐ . ܘܐ ܥܢܝܫ
ܠܚܛܐܝܐ ܕܝܥܡܠ ܠܝܦܥܠܗ . ܘܟܝܦ ܕܡܐ
ܝܕܥܘܗ ܕܠܐ ܦܝܥܠܗ . ܐܘ ܕܝܬܠܘܗ ܠܗ
ܕܡܐ ܝܕܥܘܗ ܕܠܐ ܦܝܥܠܗ . ܓܘܐܒ ܐ ܢܥܡ
ܠܟܦܐܪܗ ܚܛܝܗ . ܘܝܟܕ ܥܩܘܒܬܗ ܚܛܝܗ.
ܐܘ ܕܝܬܠܘܗ ܠܗ ܠܝܥܩܘܒܗ . ܘܕܠܐ ܥܩܘܒܬܗ
ܚܛܝܗ ܟܠܗܘܢ ܠܐ ܐܘ ܕܝܬܠܘܗ . ܣܘܐܠ
ܐ ܡܢ ܐܠܡܥܡܘܕܝܗ ܡܥܡܕܐ ܗܘ ܟܡ . ܘܦܝܗ
ܡܪܐ ܗܘ ܟܡ . ܘܟܠܝܕ ܠܡܥܡܕܐ ܘܠܟܝܦ

ܐ̈ܢܫܐ. ܗܘܘ ܒܝܘܡܬܐ ܕܢܘܚ. ܫܘܐܠܐ ܡܢܘ ܩܕܡܝܐ
ܡܠܟ ܡܢ ܒܬܪ ܡܒܘܠܐ ܘܐܬܦܠܓ ܠܫ̈ܢܐ
ܢܡܪܘܕ ܓܢܒܪܐ. ܘܐܝܟܢܐ ܐܬܩܪܝ ܠܡܘܬܒܐ
ܕܡܠܟܘܬܗ. ܒܒܒܠ ܟܪܟܐ ܡܫܒܚܬܐ.
ܘܠܐ ܐܬܟܬܒ ܠܗ. ܐܝܟ ܐܚܪ̈ܢܐ ܟܠ
ܫܢܝ̈ܐ ܕܚܝܘܗܝ. ܐܠܐ ܕܡܠܟ ܒܐܪܥܐ.
ܦܘܢܝܐ ܡܕܒܪܢܐ ܡܬܩܪܐ. ܘܒܬܪܗ ܐܚܪ̈ܢܐ
ܟܠ ܡܕܡ ܕܝܠܗ. ܫܘܐܠܐ ܡܢܘ ܐܬܚܙܝ ܩܕܡܝܐ
ܕܒܢܐ ܡܕܝܢܬܐ ܘܡܬܩܪܐ ܒܫܡܗ. ܐܬܘܪ
ܢܘܟܪܝܐ. ܡܠܟܐ ܡܫܡܫ ܠܗ ܠܡܕܝܢܬܐ. ܦܘܢܝܐ
ܡܬܩܪܐ ܡܕܝܢܬܐ. ܫܘܐܠܐ ܡܢܘ ܐܬܚܙܝ ܩܕܡܝܐ
ܟܠܗ ܕܢܚܬ ܠܗ ܡܕܒܪܐ. ܦܘܪܫܢܐ ܘܡܠܝܘ
ܟܠ ܐܪܥܐ. ܐܝܟ ܢܘܟܪܝܐ ܠܡܕܝܢܬܐ ܟܠ
ܟܠ ܐܪܥܐ ܡܠܘ. ܦܘܢܝܐ ܠܐ ܐܬܚܙܝ
ܕܢܘܟܪܝܐ ܟܠ ܐܪܥܐ ܗܘ. ܐܠܐ ܟܠ ܕܐܝܬ
ܕܡܬܚܫܚܝܢ ܟܠܗ ܘܟܠܗ. ܫܘܐܠܐ
ܟܠܗܘܢ ܕܢܦܩܘ ܡܢ ܓܘܫܡܐ ܕܟܠ
ܡܕܝܢܬܐ ܗܟܢܐ ܡܫܬܡܥܐ ܠܗ. ܦܘܢܝܐ ܒܫܠܡܘܬܗ
ܫܪܝܪܬܐ

ܐܬܪܘܗܝ. ܘܥܒܕܝ̈ܢ ܡܢ ܐܢܫܝܢ ܡܫܡܠܝܐ
ܕܝܕܥܬܐ ܘܠܐ ܡܫܬܥܒܕܐ ܕܡܠܟܘܬܐ. ܥܡ ܗܠܝܢ
ܣܘܓܐܐ ܗܢܐ ܕܐܢܫܐ ܡܢ ܥܡܐ ܕܝܗܘܕܝܐ.
ܦܬܓܡܐ ܕܡܫܬܒܚܝܢ ܒܟܬܒܘܗܝ ܘܟܠܗ ܒܟܬܒܐ
ܒܠܐ ܡܟܣܐ ܕܢܦܘܩ ܕܥܠܝܢܐ ܘܕܠܒܪ.
ܘܡܬܟܠܠܝܢ ܒܗܘܢ ܠܐܬܪܐ ܐܝܟ ܚܙܘܗܝ ܠܐ
ܘܗܝܕܐ ܠܡܫܠܡܘ. ܘܢܩܘܕ ܠܒܢܝܐ ܟܠܗ ܢܡܘܣܐ.
ܘܚܙܝ ܕܡܫܡܫܐ ܢܩܕ ܦܬܓܡܐ ܡܢ ܟܬܒܐ
ܗܘܐ ܕܡܫܬܡܥܐ ܠܗ. ܘܡܬܝܕܥ ܠܢܦܫܗ
ܡܫܪܐ ܠܗ. ܘܡܫܡܫ ܕܩܪܐ ܒܟܬܒܐ ܗܢܐ
ܠܗ ܠܝܘܡܢܐ. ܘܠܐ ܢܦܩܘܢ ܕܢܩܫ ܐܪܥܐ
ܩܢܘܡܐ ܡܫܡܫ ܕܩܪܐ ܘܡܬܟܠܠ ܠܢܦܫܗ.
ܦܘܪܫܢܐ ܐܘܗܝ ܡܢ ܗܘܢܐ ܡܕܝܢܬܐ. ܠܒܟܠܗ ܦܘ
ܙܝܦ ܗܘܐ ܠܗ ܠܡܫܬܐ ܠܟܠܢ. ܠܥܘܠܡ
ܢܘܡܐ ܕܟܬܒܘܗܝ ܠܟܬܒܐ ܕܟܬܒܐ.
ܡܫܡܫ ܕܩܪܐ ܒܟܬܒܘܗܝ. ܕܢܘܡܐ ܡܝܬܘ
ܠܡܪܐ ܠܐ ܟܬܒܐ. ܣܘܓܐܐ ܐܢܫ ܕܢܩܕ
ܦܘܕܡܐ ܚܕܐ ܘܚܢ. ܡܫܡܫܐ ܡܝܬܘ ܠܢܘܡܐ

ܕܢܦܫܗ ܐܘ ܒܪܘܚܗ. ܥܘܠܐ ܣܢܝܐ ܕܡܪܕܘܬܐ
ܕܐܝܬ ܥܠܝܗܘܢ ܙܕܝܩܘܬܗ. ܘܠܝܬ ܥܠܝܗܘܢ
ܘܠܒܢܝܐ. ܡܛܠ ܕܡܬܪܥܝܢ ܥܠܝܗܘܢ ܡܡܕܥܝܐ.
ܥܘܠܐ ܕܝܢ ܐܚܪܢ ܕܡܬܚܫܒܐ ܡܢ ܡܕܒܪܢܐ
ܘܠܒܢܝܐ ܘܙܕܝܩܘܬܗ. ܘܠܐ ܡܛܠ ܕܡܬܪܥܝܢ ܡܘܕܝܢ
ܕܠܐ ܡܬܒܥܝܢ ܕܠܒܢܝܐ ܘܙܕܝܩܘܬܗܘܢ.
ܥܘܠܐ ܗܟܝܠ ܕܡܬܚܫܒܐ ܕܢܝܚܐ. ܐܝܟܢ
ܕܡܬܚܫܒ ܡܘܕܥܐ. ܟܕ ܝܕܥܐ ܡܫܠܡ
ܠܗ ܚܝܠܐ ܗܘ ܕܡܬܚܫܒ ܒܟܠܗܘܢ
ܘܡܫܬܠܛ ܢܦܫܗ ܒܕܡܘܬܐ ܠܐܠܗܐ. ܘܫܪܝܪ
ܡܛܠ ܗܢܐ ܠܗ ܚܘܒܐ ܠܡܪܝܐ. ܥܘܠܐ ܗܘܐ
ܡܬܬܢܝܚܐ ܒܟܠܗ ܐܝܠܝܢ ܡܢ ܥܘܠܐ.
ܘܡܛܠ ܗܢܐ ܐܚܪܢܐ ܒܥܘܠܢܐ ܕܢܦܫܐ
ܟܕ ܡܛܠ ܕܡܬܒܥܐ ܒܐܠܗܐ ܐܘ ܒܐܠܗܐ
ܥܘܠܢܐ. ܘܗܘܐ ܕܝܢܐ ܗܝܡܢܘܬܐ ܕܡܫܝܚܐ.
ܐܝܟ ܕܝܢ ܕܝܠܗ ܡܫܡܫܢܐ ܒܦܓܪܐ.
ܡܬܒܥܐ ܟܠܗ ܦܓܪܐ ܡܫܬܠܛ ܠܗ
ܒܪܘܚܐ ܘܢܦܫܐ. ܘܗܘܐ ܠܡܪܝܐ ܕܡܫܝܚܐ
ܐܡܝܢ

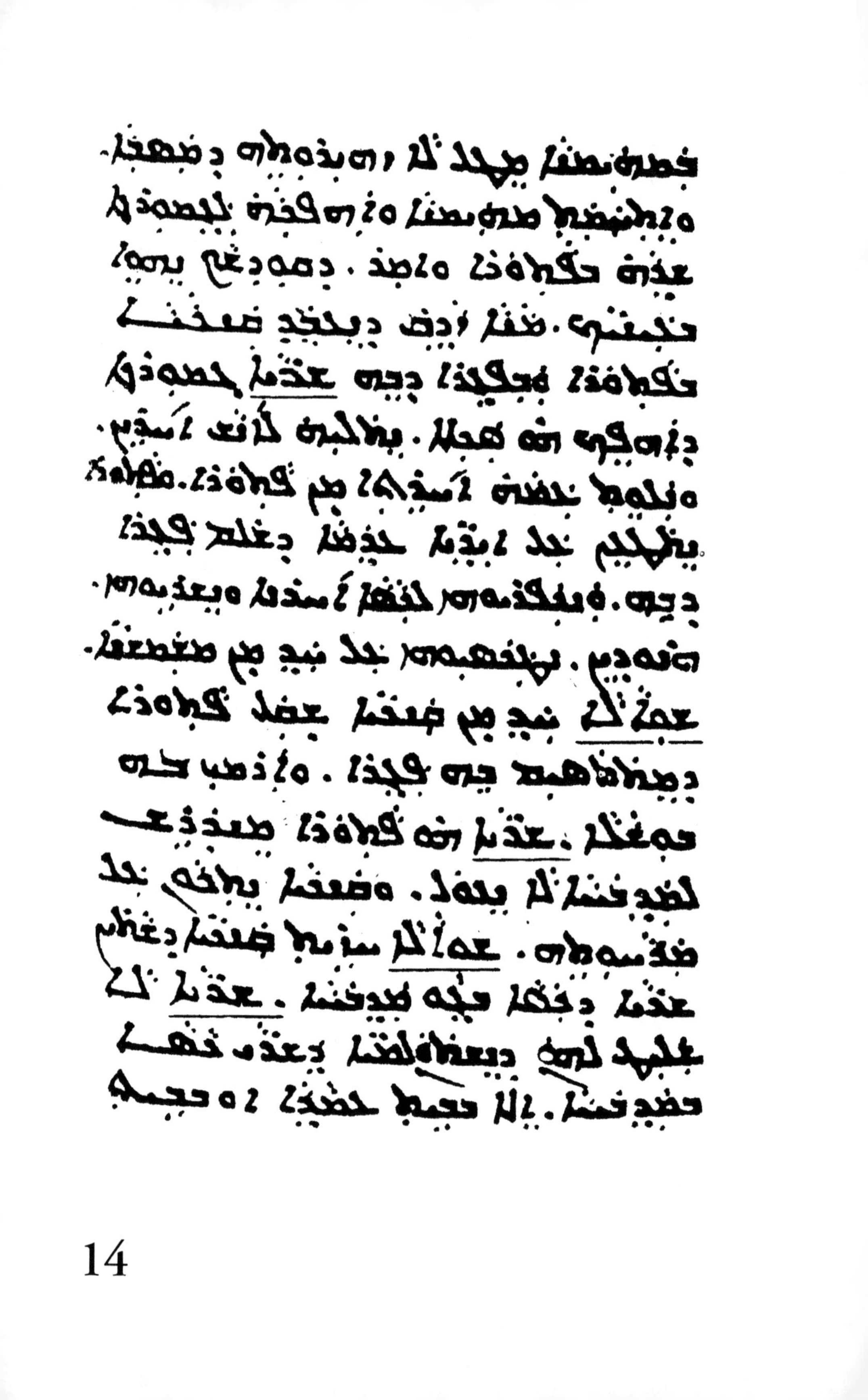

ܘܪܡܫܐ. ܢܦܩܘ ܡܢ ܬܪܥܐ ܕܒܝܬܣܗܕܐ ܥܕ
ܬܪܥܐ ܕܗܝܟܠܐ. ܥܘܢܝܬܐ ܕ ܥܠ ܢܦܩܬܢ
ܠܡܕܒܪܐ ܗܘܠܝܬܐ ܐܚܪܬܐ. ܕܠܚܡܐ ܡܫܝܚܐ
ܡܕܒܪܐ. ܥܩܒܬܐ ܐܦܪܝܡ ܕܡܢ ܢܦܩܬܢ ܠܟ
ܡܫܝܚܐ ܡܕܒܪܐ. ܟܕ ܡܫܚܐ ܕ ܠܐ ܝܕܥܝܢ
ܥܡ ܟܕܢܐ. ܢܣܒܘܗܝ ܕܐܬܘ ܡܕܒܪܐ
ܦܨܝܚܘܬܗ ܕܡܕܒܪܐ. ܠܐܝܠܝܢ ܡܕܒܪܝܢ
ܡܢ ܐܘܪܫܠܡ. ܟܕ ܚܠܝܢ ܗܘܘ ܢܦܫܐ. ܘܒܬܪ
ܡܠܬܐ ܡܫܠܡܢܐ ܡܕܒܪܐ ܗܘܬ ܟܝܬ
ܐܬܐ ܘܒܬܐ ܡܥܕܐ. ܥܘܢܝܬܐ ܕ ܚܙܘ ܠܟܘ
ܡܢ ܗܘܐ ܢܦܫܐ ܘܢܦܩܘ ܠܡܕܒܪܐ. ܣܘܓܝܬܐ
ܡܫܠܡܢܐ ܡܕܒܪܐ ܕܥܡܐ. ܥܘܢܝܬܐ ܕ ܦܬ
ܚܙܘ ܚܕ ܡܢ ܫܠܝܚܐ ܕܒܣܘܓܝܐ ܥܒܕܘ
ܕܠܒܝܬ ܐܒܘܗܝ. ܘܠܐ ܗܘܐ ܟܠܗܘܢ
ܟܠ ܥܕܬܐ ܠܒܝܬ ܐܒܘܟܘܢ ܡܫܚܐ ܕܠܒܝܬܗ
ܒܢܝܢܐ. ܘܠܐ ܗܘܐ ܟܠܗܘܢ ܟܠ ܥܘܢܝܬܐ
ܣܘܓܝܐ ܠܟܠ ܡܢ ܡܕܒܪܐ. ܕܢܦܩ ܗܘܐ ܕܢ
ܠܟܠ ܡܢ ܗܘ ܣܘܓܝܐ. ܘܒܬܪ ܗܘ ܡܕܒܪܐ

ܦܘܫܩ ܫܡܥܐ

ܒܪ ܠܡܕܒܪܢܐ ܘܬܐܙܠ ܡܬܠܐ. ܒܡܫܡܫܢܘܬܐ

ܐܢ ܢܬܒܪ. ܡܛܠ ܕܡܕܒܪ ܠܡܕܒܪܢܐ. ܥܘܕܠܐ

ܠܐ ܚܕܐ ܠܡܕܒܪܘܬܐ ܕܡܨܛܒܝܢܘܗܝ ܕܡܕܒܪܢܐ

ܥܡ ܠܗܘ ܥܠ ܐܝܟܢ. ܕܢܬܒܥܐ ܠܗ ܥܠ

ܡܕܒܪܘܬܐ. ܗܟܢ ܠܡܘܕܥܘ ܕܡܫܡܫܢܐ. ܥܘܠܐ

ܠܐ ܬܐܙܠ ܡܫܡܫܐ ܘܡܫܡܫܢܐ ܠܡܕܒܪܢܐ.

ܘܐܡܪ ܠܗ. ܘܗܟܢܐ ܘܟܠܗܘܢ ܕܠܡܐ ܡܬܬܠܐ

ܡܕܒܪܢܐ. ܒܬܠܬܐ ܠܗ. ܘܡܫܡܫܢܐ ܐܬܬܠܐ

ܕܐܙܠ ܠܐ ܥܘܕܠܐ. ܠܗ ܕܡܬܒܥܝܢ ܡܛܠ

ܘܡܛܠ ܢܦܩ ܢܒܥܐ ܠܝ. ܠܢܦܫܗ ܒܪܢܫܐ

ܕܫܡܫܬܐ ܠܗ ܥܘܕܠܐ. ܐܬܕܒܪ ܘܐܙܠܐ ܫܡܥܘܗܝ.

ܘܡܠܟܐ ܠܐ ܒܥܠܕܒܒܘܗܝ ܡܢ ܡܕܒܪܢܘܗܝ ܢܦܩ.

ܘܡܫܡܫܢܘܗܝ ܠܗܘܢ. ܒܥܠܕܒܒܐ ܢܦܫܗ ܘܢܬܕܒܪ

ܕܐܬܐ ܡܕܒܪܢܐ. ܘܢܦܫܗ ܡܢ ܡܕܒܪܢܐ.

ܥܠ ܠܗ. ܘܫܡܫܬܗ ܠܡܕܒܪܢܐ ܘܡܫܡܫ

ܡܕܒܪܢܐ ܕܒܥܠܕܒܒܘܗܝ ܠܡܕܒܪܘܬܐ ܚܕܐ.

ܡܫܡܫܢܐ ܕܡܬܒܥܐ ܡܕܒܪܢܐ ܗܟܢ.

ܐܡܪ ܠܗ ܡܫܡܫܢܐ ܠܗ ܕܡܬܬܠܐ ܥܘ

ܗ̇ܘܐ ܒܥܠܡܐ ܡܪܝܡܐ. ܒܝܘܡ ܐܬܐ ܘܒܪܐ
ܡܫܝܚܐ. ܒܪܝܫ ܫܢܬ ܐܠܦ ܕܡܪܝܡ ܒܗ.
ܝܥܩܘܒܘܗܝ ܠܒܪܗ ܝܠܕܗ ܡܢ ܝܘܣܦ ܐ
ܕܡܫܝܚܐ. ܘܝܘܣܦ ܘܒܪܬܗ. ܘܝܠܕܬ
ܠܒܪܗ ܒܒܝܬܗ ܘܢܘܟܪܝܘܗܝ ܠܡܠܟܐ ܡܫܝܚܐ.
ܘܝܕܥܘܗܝ ܡܓܘܫܐ ܕܒܥܠܡܐ ܘܣܓܕܘܗܝ
ܠܡܫܝܚܐ. ܗܪܘܕܣ ܐܬܚܙܝ ܐܡܪܘ ܕܒܥܠܡܐ
ܐ ܢܘܟܪܝܘܗܝ ܒܣܘܪܝܘܗܝ ܥܠ ܡܫܝܚܐ.
ܕܡܠܟܐ ܡܫܝܚܐ ܘܒܥܠܡܐ ܥܘܬܪܐ. ܘܫܢܐ
ܐܡܪ ܐܝܟ ܕܝܕܥܘܗܝ ܡܓܘܫܐ
ܘܣܓܕܘܗܝ ܠܡܫܝܚܐ. ܥܠ ܗ̇ܘ ܫܢܐ
ܡܠܟܐ ܐܘܠ ܡܫܝܚܐ. ܗܘܦܐ ܫܢܐ
ܐܝܟ ܕܡܠܟܐ ܡܠܟܘܬܗ ܒܥܠܡܐ
ܘܗܦܟ ܠܡܕܝܢܬܗ. ܘܒܥܠܡܐ ܐܝܟ
ܕܡܠܟܐ ܟܠ ܡܠܟܘܬܗ ܥܕܡܐ. ܘܐ
ܡܪ ܠܡܫܝܚܐ ܥܠ ܡܠܟܐ ܘܫܢܬ ܠܡܫܝܚܐ
ܢܟܐ. ܗܪܘܕܣ ܐ ܝܕܥ ܠܝܠܕܗ ܡܫܝܚܐ
ܐܘ ܡܫܡܫܢܐ. ܕܢܗܘܐ ܒܫܠܡܐ ܥܕܡܐ
ܫܠܡܬ

ܕܡܫܝܚܐ. ܘܢܦܩܘܢ ܡܢܗܘܢ ܥܘܒܕܐ ܟܠ
ܡܫܬܘܬܦܘ. ܥܕܡܐ ܫܦܪܐ ܕܗܘܐ ܠܗܘܢ
ܠܡܗܝܡܢܐ ܘܠܐ ܠܡܫܬܠܛܢܐ. ܘܠܐ ܢܬܒܝܨܘܢ
ܢܦܩܘܢ ܡܢ ܐܝܕܝܗܘܢ ܐܠܐ ܢܬܚܪܐ ܘܠܐ ܚܘܝܕܪܐ.
ܥܘܠܐ ܚܛܝܬܐ ܐܘ ܡܓܫܫܢܐ ܕܩܛܠ
ܢܦܫܐ ܘܢܬܩܠ ܘܢܬܒܗ ܒܬܚܘܡܐ. ܐܘ ܒܝܕ
ܒܚܪܒܐ ܐܘ ܒܚܒܝܫܬܐ. ܐܝܢܐ ܗܢܐ ܘܢܬܘܗ
ܒܚܒܫܬܐ ܟܡܝܢܐ ܐܝܢܘ ܐܠܐ ܡܢ ܦܪܨ.
ܘܕܒܗܘܢ ܠܢܦܫܐ ܠܚܒܫܬܐ ܠܐ ܡܥܒܕ.
ܡܢܐ ܒܡܓܒܝ ܗܘ ܕܩܛܠ ܢܦܫܐ. ܘܐܢ ܟܝ
ܢܬܕܘܢ ܠܗܘܒܕܢܐ. ܐܝܟ
ܒܡܩܛܠ ܐܘ ܒܚܝܠ ܒܚܒܫܐ ܢܦܠ
ܘܢܬܗ ܕܗܘ ܕܩܛܠ ܢܦܫܐ. ܐܘ ܡܢܕܥܡ
ܡܥܒܕܐ ܐܘ ܡܬܚܫܒܢܐ. ܢܬܠܒܘܢ ܠܢܦܫܐ
ܠܐܝܕܘ ܢܦܩܘܬ ܒܕܘܟܝܬܗ. ܘܐܢ ܗܟܢ
ܘܢܬܗ ܘܝܬܩܛܠ ܠܢܦܫܐ ܠܡܕܝܢܬܐ
ܕܡܕܝܢܬܐ. ܘܢܬܩܛܠܘܢ ܠܢܦܫܐ ܒܢܕ ܡܢ
ܡܢܬܐ. ܘܡܚܝܠܐ ܐܡܪ. ܒܐܠܕܝܢ ܢܦܫܐ

ܕܓܪܒܝܐ ܐܝܟܢ ܢܫܬܟܚܘܢ. ܘܕܢܫܒܘܢ ܠܦܘܬܗ̇
ܥܠ ܐܪܥܐ ܟܠܗ̇ ܝܩܢܐ. ܘܕܢܘܫܒܘܗܝ
ܠܡܕܢܚܐ ܟܠ ܡܥܪܒܐ ܕܢܫܒܘܢ ܕܠܐ ܙܘܥܐ.
ܘܓܪܒܝܐ ܕܐܬܝܐ. ܘܕܢܘܫܒܘܗܝ ܠܡܕܢܚܐ
ܡܥܪܒܝܐ ܐܠܡܕܢܚܐ. ܫܡܐ ܕܝܢ ܠܓܪܒܝܐ
ܘܠܡܕܢܚܐ. ܘܐܝܟ ܕܥܠܘܗܝ. ܟܘܢܫܐ
ܗܘ ܕܚܠܡܐ ܠܦܠܘܬܐ ܥܠ ܡܥܠܝܐ ܘܕܝܢܗ
ܘܢܦܠ ܐ. ܗܕܒܪ ܠܗ ܗܢܐ ܐܘ ܡܫܡܫܢܐ.
ܢܗܘܘܢ ܘܢܦܠ ܠܗ ܚܙܐ ܘܢܫܡܫ
ܘܕܝܢܗ ܘܢܗܠܟܘܢ ܠܦܠܘܬܐ ܕܐܠ
ܐܪܥܘܗܝ ܘܢܩܠܒܘܢܗ ܠܚܙܐ. ܡܛܠ
ܕܓܪܒܝܐ ܗܘ ܐܬܝܐ. ܘܠܡܕܢܚܐ ܟܠ
ܢܘܫܒܘܗܝ ܕܠܐ ܢܦܠܝܐ ܡܕܢܚܐ. ܘܠܟܠ
ܡܢ ܡܕܢܚܐ ܢܦܩܘܢܗܘܢ ܚܕܝܐ ܚܙܝܐ.
ܘܐ ܚܘܫܒܢܐ. ܚܠܦ ܕܝܢ ܕܡܦܩܝܢ ܡܕܢܚܐ
ܘܢܦܠܘܢ ܐܟ ܢܘܗܪܐ ܕܠܐ ܢܗܘܐ ܢܚܫܐ ܥܠ
ܡܕܢܚܐ. ܫܠܡ ܣܪܝܢܐ ܕܡܥܒܕܢܘܬܐ ܕܐܦܝܗ
ܕܢܗܫܡ ܣܘܪܚܐ ܠܐ ܢܥܒܕ ܕܚܠܡܘܢ
ܕܚܘܫܒܢܗ

ܦܘܠܚܢܗܘܢ ܕܒܥܘܬܗ ܡܢ ܐܢܫܐ . ܘܢܒܥܐ
ܠܒܢܝܐ ܕܒܪܐ ܚܕܬܐ . ܥܘܠܐ ܣܓܝܐ
ܡܫܡܫܢܐ ܕܐܪܙܐ ܕܢܦܩܘܢ ܩܘܕܫܐ
ܡܫܠܡܝܢ ܠܟܗܢܘܬܐ . ܘܫܡܫܐ ܐܝܕܗܘܢ
ܕܟܗܢܘܬܐ . ܡܩܕܫܝܢ ܩܘܪܒܢܐ ܘܠܐ ܟܐܢܝܢ
ܒܥܘܠ . ܘܠܐ ܢܬܚܫܒ ܩܢܝܢܐ ܗܢܐ ܕܟܗܢܘܬܐ
ܕܐܠܗܐ . ܥܘܠܐ ܠܐ ܫܠܝܛܝܢ ܡܫܡܫܢܐ
ܕܢܬܩܢܘܢ ܕܟܗܢܘܬܐ ܗܘ . ܘܐܦ ܠܗ
ܠܐܢܫ ܕܡܛܝܢ ܠܟܗܢܘܬܐ . ܕܒܪܘܚܐ ܕܗ
ܘܢܬܠܒܘܢ ܠܟܗܢܘܬܐ ܒܡܫܡܫܢܐ ܕܫܪܝܪܐ
ܡܢ ܚܕ ܚܒܪܗܘܢ ܐܚܪܢܐ ܕܟܠ ܕܠܐ ܝܗܒܐ ܡܢܗ
ܡܢܗ ܕܢܗܘܐ . ܘܡܫܠܡܝܢ ܠܡܫܡܫܢܐ . ܘܠܗ
ܠܟܗܢܘܬܐ . ܐܝܟ ܕܠܐ ܡܢ ܕܘܟܝܐ ܕܟܗܢܘܬܐ .
ܘܢܬܦܠܓ ܡܫܡܫܢܐ ܕܟܗܢܘܬܐ . ܡܬܚܫܒܐ
ܟܕ ܥܘܠܐ ܡܬܥܒܕ . ܘܡܫܡܫܢܐ ܡܢܗܘܢ
ܡܢ ܟܕܘ . ܥܘܠܐ ܩܢܝܐ ܘܡܫܡܫܢܐ
ܕܡܛܝܢ ܟܗܢܘܬܐ ܕܒܟܠܗ ܠܥܠܡܐ . ܘܟܕܒ
ܘܡܫܠܡܝܢ ܘܢܩܒܠ ܡܢ ܚܕܐ . ܘܠܐ ܡܫܟܚ

ܐܪܡܝܘ ܘܐܝܟܘ ܕܫܠܝܛܝܢ ܒܡܠܟܘܬܐ. ܣܘܦ
ܡܠܟܐ. ܠܐ ܢܘܟܝܘܗܝ ܠܡܠܟܘܬܐ ܠܡܕܝܢܬܐ.
ܐܠܐ ܒܪܘܚܗܘܢ ܢܣܒܠܘܢ. ܒܪܡܫܐ ܕܫܩܠܝܢ ܗܘܘ
ܠܢܫܐ ܕܡܕܝܢܬܐ. ܘܫܒܩܘܗܝ ܒܟܦ̈ܐ
ܐܣܓܝܘ. ܘܝܩܪܘܗܝ ܠܢܫܐ ܟܠ ܚܕ ܡܢ
ܡܫܡܫܢ̈ܐ ܠܟܪ ܡܢ ܡܕܝܢܬܐ. ܥܘܠܐ
ܢܦܠ ܐܢܫܐ ܕܢܘܚܡ ܠܗܘܢ ܟܢܫܐ. ܕܠܐܢܫܐ
ܕܠܐ ܢܬܐܢܬܘܢ. ܘܐܬܚܝ ܠܗ ܠܢܫܐ ܒܬܠܬܐ ܝܘܡܝܢ
ܐܢܘܢ ܘܢܦܩܘ. ܗܘܐ ܠܗ ܐܠܝܦ ܟܢܫܐ
ܘܪܕܘ ܕܢܘܟܝܘܗܝ ܟܠ ܡܕܝܢܬܐ. ܦܘܩܐ
ܐܬܚܠܠ ܕܢܬܚܫܒ ܟܢܫܐ ܡܢ ܐܢܫܐ ܥܢܝܫܐ.
ܕܢܫܐ ܕܝܢ ܚܙܐ ܠܟܠܗܘܢ ܕܠܐ ܦܘܠܓ. ܘܐܡܪ
ܕܢܘܐ ܒܟܢܫܐ. ܘܕܚܠ ܠܗ ܠܟܢܘܫܐ ܕܡܢ ܡܕܡ
ܕܢܘܟܝܘܗܝ ܠܢܫܐ ܠܡܕܝܢܬܐ. ܢܦܩ ܟܪܘܙܐ
ܡܢ ܡܠܟܘܬܐ ܡܢܝܢܐ ܕܪܡܫܐ. ܘܢܬܚܫܒܘܢ
ܒܟܪܡܝܢ ܕܡܫܡܫܢ̈ܐ. ܘܐܝܢܐ ܕܢܬܚܫܒ
ܟܢܫܐ ܗܘܢܐ ܡܠܟܐ ܡܕܝܢܬܐ ܟܢܫ ܐܢܫܐ ܘܡܪܐ
ܘܢܦܩܘ. ܘܐ ܠܐ ܡܕܝܢ ܟܪܘܙܐ. ܡܫܡܫܢ̈ܐ

ܫܠܡܬ ܕܗܘܐ

ܡܕܢܚܐ ܕܪܘܚܐ ܡܢܗ ܡܕܢܚܐܝܬ ܐܬܝܗܒ
ܠܡܫܝܚܐ ܠܒܪܢܫܘܬܗ. ܘܐܬܕܪܫܗ ܥܡ
ܚܕܘ ܟܝܢܐ. ܠܐ ܗܘ ܕܫܐ ܕܝܢ ܗܘ ܡܕܢܚܐ
ܘܠܐ ܗܘܝܘ ܡܬܕܪܫܝܢ ܥܠ ܕܡܫܚܐ. ܡܘܠܕܐ
ܡܫܝܚܐ ܓܒܪ ܐܠܗܘܬܐ ܕܝܠܗ ܠܟܠܢܫ
ܘܒܗܿ ܗܝ ܡܢ ܡܢܫܡܬܐ. ܘܐܪܫܡ ܘܐܘܪܐ
ܐܠܗܘܬܐ. ܘܫܠܡܘܬܐ ܐܝܬܘ ܠܡܫܝܚܐ ܕܐܠܗܘܬܐ.
ܡܢ ܡܕܘܡ ܕܒܗܘܢ ܟܘܪܐ ܐܪܫܝ
ܡܚܒܬܗ. ܘܐܪܫܝܗ ܠܐܠܗܘܬܐ ܠܡܬܚܙܝܢܐ.
ܡܢܐ ܠܐ ܝܗܒܗ ܕܡܫܝܚܐ ܘܝܗܒܗ ܕܡܬܚܙܝܢܐ.
ܡܛܠ ܐܝܟ ܕܝܗܒ ܠܗ ܠܐܠܗܘܬܐ
ܘܠܡܬܚܙܝܢܐ ܠܗܢܐ ܗܘܟܢܐ ܕܡܫܝܚܐ ܝܗܒ
ܠܗܘ ܗܘܢ. ܘܡܢ ܡܕܒܪܢܘܬܗ ܒܪܘܚܢܝܬܐ
ܡܫܡܫܝܢ ܡܢ ܗܘܢܢܘܗܝ. ܘܝܗܒܐ ܘܡܫܡܗܐ
ܕܢܩܠ ܡܫܝܚ ܕܪܘܚܢܐ. ܐܝܟ ܐܝܟ ܠܗ
ܠܡܫܝܚܐ ܕܝܠܗ ܗܘܝܐ. ܘܝܠܕܝܢ ܫܠܝܚܘܗܝ
ܡܢܗ ܘܐܪܫܡ ܒܐܠܗܘܬܐ. ܐ ܡܢ ܪܘܡܐ
ܐܪܫܝܗ ܠܫܠܝܚܘܗܝ ܝܗܒܐ. ܘܐܦ ܒܡܘܪܒܐ

ܚܘܪܒܗ. ܘܒܣܘܦܐ ܠܡܕܡ ܕܐܝܬ ܒܝܬ ܐܒܗܬܗ.
ܘܗ̈ܘܝܢ ܝܗܒܝܢ ܢܫ̈ܐ ܠܒܢ̈ܘܗܝ. ܘܡܢ ܒܢ̈ܬܗ
ܠܢܫ̈ܐ ܚܢܦ̈ܐ ܘܒܥܠܘܬܗܘܢ ܠܥܒܕܐ ܗܘ
ܕܒܝܬ ܐܒܗ̈ܬܗ. ܥܘܠܐ ܩܥܝܬܐ ܕܩܕܝܫ
ܡܘܕܥܐ. ܘܡܢ ܡܕܡ ܕܝܕܥܘܡ ܕܡܥܒܕܐ
ܐܣܓܝܐ. ܕܒܝܬܐ ܠܒܝܬܐ ܘܕܡܐ ܠܟܝܢܐ.
ܢܫܐ ܩܥܝܬܐ ܣܗܘܪܘܬܐ. ܒܝܕ ܐܝܟ ܒܨܒܝܗ
ܩܠܝܕܐ. ܡܥܒܕ ܣܘܟܠܐ ܡܢ ܩܠܝܕܐ
ܕܒܝܬ ܩܕܝܫܐ. ܘܡܢ ܝܘܡ ܣܩܠܝܕܐ
ܐܣܓܝܐ ܕܒܝܬܗ. ܘܐܡܪܝܢ ܩܥܝܬܐ ܗܘ
ܕܩܕܝܫ ܕܚܕܝܬܐ ܠܐ ܕܥܒܕܗ. ܘܐܦܠܘ
ܐܝܟ ܠܡܫܝܚܐ ܠܩܠܝܕܐ ܕܐܝܬܝܗ ܒܝܬܐ.
ܘܕܥܡܘܗܝ ܠܟܝܢܐ. ܘܗܘܝܢ ܗܘܦܟܐ
ܥܡܐ ܡܥܒܕ ܡܨܝܐ ܘܒܝܕ ܠܢܠܡܐ. ܐܡܪ
ܠܝ ܝܠܝܕ ܩܕܝܫܐ ܐܘ ܠܐ ܩܘܝܐ ܐ ܡܢ
ܡܕܡ ܡܕܡܝܐ ܕܪܘܚܐ ܥܡܗ ܣܘܒܪܐ
ܘܡܢ ܐܘܡ ܣܩܠܝܕܐ ܐܣܓܝ.
ܗܘܪܢܫܐ ܪܒܐ ܒܥܒܕܗ. ܝܗܒܝܢ ܫܘܒܚܐ
ܡܪܝܐ

ܡܫܝܚܐ ܫܠܝܚܐ ܕܒܗ ܡܕܒܪܢܐ. ܘܠܐ ܢܕܚܠ
ܡܢܗ. ܘܠܒܝܫ ܒܡܘܬܗ ܟܠ ܡܕܒܪܢܘܬܐ.
ܢܘܗܪܐ ܡܢ ܩܕܡ ܕܢܬܚܙܐ ܘܢܬܓܠܐ. ܘܡܛܠ ܐܝܟ
ܕܢܦܩ ܒܡܘܬܗ. ܘܠܡܘܬܐ ܕܠܥܠܡ.
ܘܐܝܟ ܐܝܟ ܕܐܬܚܙܝ. ܢܬܠܘܢ ܠܗ ܟܠܗ
ܦܓܪܐ ܢܒܗܬ. ܘܠܐ ܢܬܪܘܡ ܠܗ ܠܥܠ ܡܢ
ܟܠܗ. ܒܟܠܗ ܗܘܐ ܕܢܗܘܐ ܠܗ ܒܗܘܢ
ܒܡܠܟܘܬܗ. ܘܐܦܠܐ ܠܐ ܣܒܪܐ ܘܠܐ ܢܦܫܐ
ܡܢ ܩܠܝܠ ܕܡܕܒܪ. ܟܕ ܐܝܟ ܢܗܘܐ
ܐܦܪܐ ܐܢܐ. ܘܐ ܠܐ ܢܘܗܪܐ ܢܬܦܫ.
ܡܬܚܫܒܢܐ ܠܗ ܡܘܕܝܢܐ. ܘܡܢ ܡܕܡ
ܕܢܦܩ ܠܡܚܫܒܗ. ܢܦܫܗ ܠܡܕܝܢܬܐ ܚܕܬܐ.
ܘܢܦܩ ܐܪܥܐ ܘܗܢܘܢ ܗܘ ܦܓܪܗ
ܠܟܠܗܘܢ. ܘܢܬܠ ܟܠܗ ܡܢܗܘܢ ܡܢ ܟܠ
ܕܢܦܩ. ܘܢܬܠܘܢ ܠܐܝܢ ܡܢ ܡܢܗ ܢܦܫܐ.
ܘܢܬܠ ܠܗ ܠܢܦܫܐ ܒܥܘܠܡܐ. ܐܝܟ ܕܡܢ ܗܕܡ
ܢܘܗܪܐ ܘܐ ܠܐ ܘܢܬܒܪ. ܗܘܢ ܕܢܦܩ
ܕܝܢ ܡܢ ܟܠ ܦܓܪܗ ܐܝܟ ܕܢܬܠܘܢ

ܠܥܠܡ ܥܠܡܝܢ

ܠܝܕܥܬܐ ܕܒܥܝܢܐ . ܫܘܐܠܐ ܕܬܪܝܢ ܡܢ
ܠܡܥܢܝܐ ܘܒܓܠܝܢܗ ܕܡܕܒܪܢܘܬܗ ܕܚܕܪܐ
ܠܝܠܕܐ . ܘܐܬܡܫܚܬ ܠܝܠܕܗ ܕܢܘܗܪܐ
ܚܕܝܘܬܐ ܕܥܡܡ̈ܐ ܘܐܘܡܘܬܐ . ܘܦܠܓܐ ܚܝܕ
ܡܢ ܡܥܢܝ̈ܐ ܕܢܦܩܝܢ ܐܪ̈ܒܥܐ . ܘܠܐ ܝܕܥ
ܕܟܝܢܐ ܐܝܬܝܗ ܟܢܫܬܐ ܬܪܬܐ ܡܢ ܐܬܩܛܠ . ܫܢܬܐ
ܠܗ ܕܐܬܝܠܕ ܡܫܝܚܐ ܘܝܫܘܥ ܥܠ ܡܘܪܥܐ .
ܘܠܐ ܐܬܝܠܕ . ܦܘܢܝܐ ܠܗ ܕܒܥܬܐ ܚܕܝܘܬܗ
ܗܘܬ . ܠܐ ܚܕܝܘܬܐ ܡܢ ܐܬܝܠܕܘܬܗ . ܡܛܠ
ܕܠܐ ܐܝܟ ܕܐܬܐ ܦܠܓܘܬ ܥܠ ܚܘܪܒܐ ܚܕ
ܢܦܫܗ . ܠܐ ܢܗܘܪܘ ܐܬܝܢ ܕܡܥܡܕܝܢ
ܡܫܝܚܐ . ܘܠܐ ܗܘܝܘ ܡܫܝܚܐ ܕܢܬܚܙܐ
ܡܛܠ ܕܠܗ ܡܢܗ ܢܘܚܪܐ ܗܘ . ܐܝܢܝܢ ܐܦܝ
ܠܗ ܡܢ ܕܗܘܝܘ ܡܫܝܚܐ ܕܢܬܐܙܝܥ . ܠܐ
ܡܬܚܙܝܢ ܠܥܡܠܗ . ܕܢܬܚܙܐ ܠܗܘܢ ܕܡܬܐ
ܘܗܕܡܘܗܝ . ܫܘܐܠܐ ܐ ܕܬܠܬܐ ܘܡܛܠ ܡܢ
ܥܠܬܐ ܥܠ ܡܫܝܚܐ ܠܡܦܩܬܐ . ܘܐ ܡܢܗܝܢ
ܐܘܡܘܬܐ ܡܬܚܙܝܢ . ܘܡܛܠ ܕܐܝܟܢܐ ܗܘܦܟܐ

ܕܐܬܒܪܝ ܘܐܬܩܢ ܒܡܠܬܗ ܕܡܪܝܐ. ܥܠܡܐ
ܐܝܟ ܕܢܚܙܘܢ ܠܥܒܕܐ. ܘܕܗܘܝܢܐ ܡܢ
ܟܝܢܐ. ܥܒܕܐ ܕܒܪܐ ܠܐ ܕܐܬܩܢ ܒܡܠܬܗ
ܕܡܪܝܐ. ܥܒܕܐ ܕܐܬܚܙܝ ܐܝܟ ܗܘܦܟܐ ܠܗܘܢ ܠܚܡܝܢ.
ܘܡܕܡ ܕܒܟܝܢܐ ܘܡܕܡ ܕܠܐ ܡܬܚܙܐ. ܕܝܢܘܗܝ
ܐܝܟ ܒܗܝܡܢܘܬܐ ܕܡܬܬܠܝܢ ܠܡܬܚܙܝܢܘ.
ܘܡܕܝܢܐ ܕܐܬܒܪܝ ܒܗܝܡܢܘܬܐ. ܕܝܢ
ܕܐܬܩܢ ܒܡܠܬܗ ܕܡܪܝܐ. ܘܢܒܝܐ ܕܡܥܡܕܐ
ܐܡܪܝܢ. ܒܫܬܐ ܝܘܡܝܢ ܐܬܒܪܝ. ܕܡܢ
ܡܢ ܫܡܝܐ ܘܐܪܥܐ. ܘܒܝܘܡܐ ܫܒܝܥܝܐ ܕܫܒܬ
ܠܐ ܕܟܠܗܘܢ. ܘܢܝܚܬܗ ܠܟܠܗ
ܡܢ ܟܠܗܘܢ ܥܒܕܘܗܝ. ܘܐܝܬܝܗ ܕܡܪܐ.
ܡܠܟܘܬܗ ܟܠܗ ܗܘܬ ܠܥܒܕܐ ܕܫܒܬ.
ܘܐܦ ܥܒܕܐ. ܘܣܘܟܠܗܘܢ ܠܟܠܗ ܟܠ
ܥܒܕܘܗܝ. ܘܫܡܠܝ ܐܪܥܐ. ܘܝܗܒ ܠܟܠܗ
ܐܝܟ ܓܒܝܐ. ܘܗܘ ܟܠܗ ܕܐܬܚܙܝ
ܕܡܬܬܠܝܢ ܒܫܡܝܐ. ܘܠܐ ܢܕܥܘܢ ܟܠ
ܥܒܕܐ. ܠܡܬܚܙܝܘ ܕܝܢ ܕܡܫܚܐ. ܢܥܒܕܘܢܗܘܢ
ܠܥܒܕܝܗ

ܡܢܐ ܕܠܐ ܡܬܕܟܪܢܐ. ܐܡܪ ܡܫܡܫܢܐ ܟܝ ܗܘ.
ܥܕܡܐ ܠܐ ܢܕܥܘܢ ܡܢܐ. ܐܠܐ ܟܕ ܢܚܘܢ
ܕܡܫܡܫܢܐ ܟܗܢܐ ܘܡܩܕܫܢܘܬܐ ܠܕܘܟܬܐ
ܘܗܘܕܐ ܒܗ. ܟܕ ܠܐ ܡܕܡ ܠܥܠܡܐ ܡܬܕܟܪܢܐ.
ܥܘܠܐ ܠ ܕܡܫܡܫܢܐ ܗܟܝܠ ܡܬܚܙܐ ܡܬܕܟܪܢܐ.
ܥܕܡܐ ܕܡܫܡܫܢܐ ܡܩܕܫܢܘܬܐ ܠܕܘܟܬܐ ܗܝ
ܘܗܘܕܐ ܒܗ. ܥܘܠܐ ܠ ܡܫܡܫܢܐ ܕܡܢܐ ܡܢ ܟܗܢܐ
ܟܕ ܡܫܡܫ ܟܗܢܐ. ܕܠܟܠ ܡܫܡܫܢܐ ܡܬܕܟܪܢܐ.
ܥܕܡܐ ܠܐ ܡܫܡܫܢܐ ܡܬܕܟܪܢܐ ܡܢ ܗܘ ܕܐܬܡܫܚ.
ܐܠܐ ܡܩܕܫܢܘܬܐ ܠܕܘܟܬܐ ܕܡܫܡܫܢܐ. ܥܘܠܐ
ܕܢܚܬ ܒܗ ܠܟܠ ܡܢ ܫܡܝܐ ܕܝܠܗ
ܢܦܫܐ ܡܢܐ ܟܗܢܐ. ܡܫܝܚܐ ܘܐܝܟ ܚܠܦ
ܢܦܫܐ ܡܫܝܚܐ ܕܝܠܗ. ܘܫܡܫܐ ܗܘܐ ܡܢܐ
ܠܡܫܡܫܢܐ. ܘܐܬܡܫܚ ܘܡܫܡܫ ܟܠܗ ܗܘ
ܡܫܝܚܐ. ܘܟܝܢܐ ܕܡܫܡܫ ܐܝܟ. ܘܐ ܡܢ
ܡܕܡ ܕܢܦܫ. ܡܠܐ ܠܗ ܡܫܡܫܢܘܬܗ ܠܗ.
ܠ ܕܡܢ ܠܐ ܕܐܬܡܫܚ ܡܢܐ ܡܫܡܫܢܐ ܟܝ ܗܘ
ܚܠܝܐ. ܘܡܫܡܫ ܟܗܢܐ ܕܡܫܝܚܐ ܘܡܢܐ. ܘܐ

ܢܘܗܪܐ ܗܘ ܕܐܝܬܘܗܝ ܡܪܝܐ. ܡܛܠ ܕܒܝܕܝܗ
ܒܡܕܢܚܐ. ܘܫܡܫܐ ܗܘ ܕܙܕܝܩܘܬܐ ܠܟܠܗܘܢ.
ܡܢܗ ܡܬܝܠܕ ܝܘܡܐ. ܩܘܢܐ ܡܕܢܚܐ
ܡܬܩܪܐ ܒܫܡܝܐ. ܘܫܡܫܐ ܗܘ ܕܡܬܦܠܓ
ܠܟܘܟܒܐ ܐܝܟ ܒܘܟܪܐ. ܘܢܚܫܘܢ ܡܢܗ
ܢܘܗܪܐ. ܘܢܫܬܘܬܦܘܢ ܠܫܘܒܚܐ ܕܟܘܟܒܐ.
ܥܘܕܐ ܐ ܢܛܪܐ ܡܬܚܫܒ ܥܠ ܡܕܢܚܐ
ܩܪܝܐ ܘܕܢܚܐ. ܡܛܠ ܕܐܝܬ ܢܗܝܪ ܥܠ ܡܕܢܚܐ
ܡܢ ܡܕܡ ܕܡܬܩܪܐ. ܕܠܘܬܗ ܡܛܠ ܕܝܠܗ
ܡܕܢܚܐ. ܩܘܢܐ ܐ ܡܬܩܪܐ ܒܫܡܗ
ܕܡܛܠ ܕܟܠ ܢܦܩܘ ܒܡܕܢܚܐ. ܡܛܠ
ܗܘܦܟܐ ܡܛܠ ܡܛܠ ܡܪܐ. ܡܢ ܟܠ
ܡܬܡܨܝܐ ܕܐܠܗܘܬܐ ܠܡܕܢܚܐ. ܠܐ ܡܬܝܠܕܐ
ܡܕܢܚܐ. ܐܝܟ ܡܬܡܨܝܢܐ ܕܐܠܗܘܬܐ
ܠܡܕܢܚܐ. ܗܟܢ ܥܠ ܡܘܕܐ ܡܫܝܚܐ.
ܥܘܕܐ ܐ ܢܛܪܐ ܘܡܛܠ ܢܦܩ. ܘܢܦܠ
ܠܗܘܦܟܐ ܣܓܝ ܡܕܢܚܐ. ܘܢܚܟܡ ܕܢܕܥܘܢ
ܚܝܠܗ ܡܪܐ. ܘܢܛܪ ܘܢܦܠ ܡܢ ܕܗܒܐ
ܡܪܐ

ܢܦܫܐ . ܦܓܪܐ ܚܙܐ ܠܓܒܪ ܡܢ ܥܒܕܝ̈ܢܐ .
ܐܘ ܚܒܝܒ ܕܢܦܫܗ . ܓܠܝܐ ܠܗ ܕܝܚܝܕ
ܠܥܒܕܝ̈ܢܐ ܘܒܬܪ ܢܦܫܐ ܝܚܝܕܝܐ . ܗܘܢܐ
ܠܐ ܓܠܝܐ ܠܗ ܕܝܚܝܕ ܠܥܒܕܝ̈ܢܐ ܠܓܡܪ .
ܐܠܐ ܡܣܬܟܠ ܐܢܫ ܕܝܗܒ ܘܡܬܐܠ
ܡܬܝܗܒ ܠܗ ܠܪ̈ܘܚܐ ܢܦܫܐ . ܥܘܐܠܐ ܐܝܕܝܢ ܠܐ
ܡܣܬܟܠ ܐܢܫ ܕܝܗܒ . ܘܐܠܐ ܠܗ
ܠܡܫܝ̈ܚܐ ܕܝܚܝܕ ܠܡܫܝܚܐ . ܐ ܓܦܪ ܙܘܡܢܐ
ܐܘ ܡܥܢܐ ܘܡܬܝܗܒ ܠܗ ܠܪ̈ܘܚܐ ܢܦܫܐ . ܡܟܝܠ
ܠܗ ܕܝܚܝܕ ܐܘܠܐ . ܗܘܢܐ ܐܝܕܝܢ ܠܓܒܪ ܡܢ
ܠܐܕܡ ܕܡܥܒܕ ܦܓܪ ܘܟܠܝܕܗ ܡܥܢܐ ܐܘ
ܙܘܡܢܐ ܘܡܬܝܗܒ ܠܗ ܠܪ̈ܘܚܐ ܢܦܫܐ ܓܠܝܐ
ܠܗ . ܕܝܚܝܕ ܕܝܢ ܠܝܬܘܗܝ ܡܢ ܐܘܣܝܐ ܠܐ
ܓܠܝܐ . ܘܝܕܝܥ ܕܠܐ ܡܬܚܙܐ ܙܘܡܢܐ
ܕܟܠܝܕܗ ܠܥܒܕܝ̈ܢܐ ܘܡܠܟܐ ܝܗܒܐ . ܥܘܐܠܐ
ܣܘܟܠܐ ܢܝܕ ܡܢ ܡܥܢܐ ܕܡܢܝܢ ܠܐܕܡ ܢܦܫܐ
ܢܝܕ ܢܦܓܪܐ ܡܫܬܐ . ܘܢܝܕ ܦܓܪܐ ܠܢܦܫ .
ܘܝܠܕ ܗܘܕܥܐ ܡܟܠ ܡܫܡܫܢܐ . ܘܐܗܦܟ

ܠܒܗ ܡܠܐ ܠܟܠ. ܘܡܢ ܗܪܟܐ ܠܡܫܒܚܢܐ
ܠܐܠܗܐ ܡܫܒܚܐ ܕܡܢ ܟܠܗܘܢ ܕܡܫܒܚܢܐ.
ܘܡܢܗ ܢܬܦܢܐ ܠܡܫܒܚܢܘܬܐ. ܘܡܫܒܚ
ܐܒܘܗܝ ܟܐܪܐ ܘܫܡܝܐ ܕܐܬܦܩܕܘ ܘܒܪܝܬܐ. ܫܘ̈ܒ:
ܡܪܝܐ ܐܠܗܢ ܕܫܘܒܚܐ ܟܠܗ ܒܟܠܙܒܢ
ܕܒܪܐ ܥܠܡܐ. ܐܘ ܡܪܝܐ ܐܠܗܐ ܚܝܠܬܢܐ.
ܡܠܟܐ ܗܘ ܡܪܝܐ ܐܠܗܐ ܫܒܝܚܐ. ܘܒܟܠ ܐܬܪܘܬ.
ܐܠ ܐܬܪ ܕܒܫܠܝܬ ܐܘܠܐ ܫܡܝܐ ܟܠ
ܡܘܫܟܐ ܕܐܒܐ ܕܒܪܐ ܘܒܪܐ ܘܪܘܚܐ ܕܩܘܕܫܐ
ܘܫܡܝܐ ܘܐܪܥܐ. ܟܠܗ ܒܪܝܬܐ. ܐܠܗܐ
ܡܪܝܐ ܐܒܘܗܝ ܫܘܒܚܗ. ܘܗܘܝܐ ܒܪܝܬܐ
ܕܒܪܐ ܥܠܡܐ. ܠܡܐ ܚܝ ܐܠܗܐ ܡܪܝܐ.
ܡܫܒܚ ܒܫܡܗ ܠܐܠܗܘܬܐ ܗܘܝܐ. ܕܠܗ
ܡܪܝܐ ܐܠܗܐ ܚܝܠܬܢܐ ܕܒܪܐ ܥܠܡܐ. ܡܪܝ
ܒܟܠܙܒܢ ܫܘܒܚܐ ܠܐܠܗܐ. ܘܐܡܝܢ ܕܗܘܒܐ
ܒܐܠܗܐ. ܕܠܐ ܡܬܒܪܝܢܐ ܡܢ ܚܝܐ ܐܠܗܐ
ܘܡܪܝܐ. ܫܘ̈ܒ: ܐ ܒܪܝܟ ܠܡܫܒܚܐ ܒܪ
ܡܫܒܚܘ ܠܥܘܠܡܐ. ܡܫܒܚܐ ܕܝܠܗ ܠܟ:
ܫܠܡ

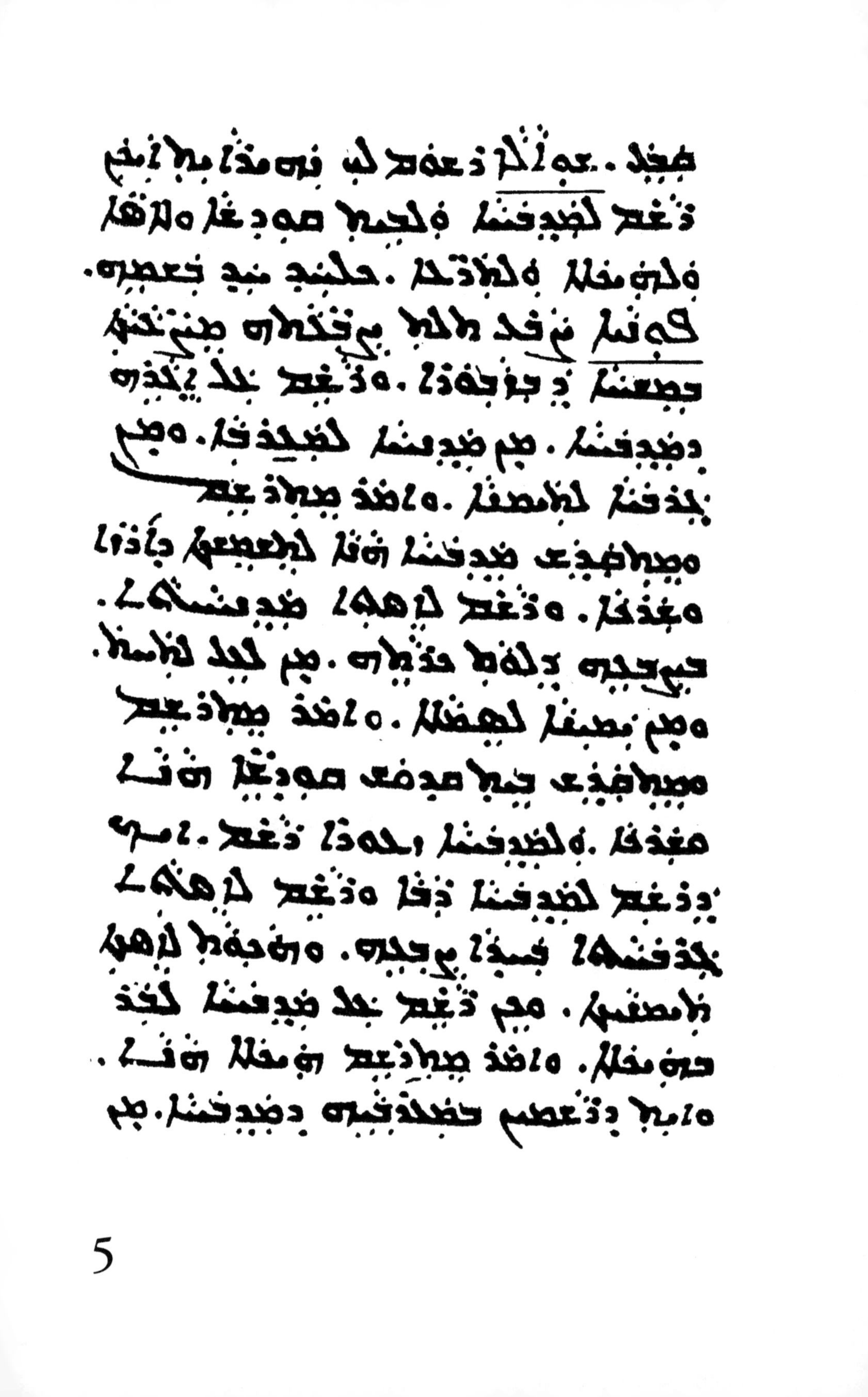

ܗܠܝܢ ܒܥܘ̈ܬܗ. ܗܘ ܕܡܕܒܚܐ ܐܝܠܝܢ
ܫܒܥܐ ܐܠܦܐ ܡܠܐܟ̈ܐ ܗܢܘܢ ܠܡܫܠܡܢܘܬܗ.
ܢܠܦܬܐ ܕܡܢܗ ܡܕܒܚܐ ܐܝܠܝܢ. ܡܛܠ
ܡܫܘܡܫܘ ܩܕܡ ܡܫܡܫܢܐ. ܟܕ ܚܙܐ
ܫܡܫܝܢ ܐܪ̈ܒܥܐ ܕܡܫܝܚܐ ܥܠ ܡܕܒܚܐ.
ܕܥܡܝܩܐ ܡܢܗܝܢ ܠܗ. ܘܚܝܠܘܬܐ ܡܕܒܚܐ
ܥܠ ܡܫܘܡܫܘ ܩܕܡ. ܘܬܠܬܐ ܡܫܡܫ
ܐܕܡܢܫܐ ܥܠܡܐ. ܘܐܬܐ ܠܡܫܡܫܘ.
ܘܩܕܡ ܥܠ ܡܫܝܚܐ. ܘܠܗܘܢ ܗܠܝܢ ܫܒܥ
ܒܫܡܐ ܗܝܡܢܘܬܐ. ܘܒܡܘܠܕܗ ܩܕܡ
ܗܠܝܢ. ܘܗܠܝܢ ܚܕܐ ܥܡܝܩܐ. ܘܒܡܠܟ
ܫܘܒܚܗ ܩܕܡ ܗܠܝܢ. ܘܫܝܪܝܢ ܩܕܡ
ܡܢ ܕܥܝܪ ܒܗܠܝܢ ܢܦܫܬܗ ܕܡܫܡܫܐ
ܕܒܝܬܐ. ܘܡܫܡܫܝܢ ܗܠܝܢ ܥܠ ܗܢܘܢ
ܕܒܝܬܐ. ܗܘ ܕܟܝܢܐ ܘܪܘܚܐ. ܟܕ ܗܠܝܢ
ܐܢܫܐ ܕܩܕܡ ܠܗ. ܡܢܕܥ ܢܩܕܡ
ܠܪܘܚܐ ܕܟܝܢܐ. ܘܠܟܝܢܐ ܕܪܘܚܐ. ܘܡܠܟܘܬܐ
ܠܐ ܡܬܡܫܡܫܢ ܠܗ ܡܫܠܡܘ. ܐܡܪܐ ܕܫܒܚܬܐ ܠܝ

ܫܠܡ

ܡܢ ܕܒܬܪܟܢ. ܥܠ ܗܠܝܢ ܕܡܬܩܪܝܢ ܗܫܐ.
ܐܬ̈ܘ / ܘܗܠܝܢ ܐܬ̈ܘܬܐ ܕܡܬܩܪܝܢ: ܪܘܟܟܐ ܣܘܡܟܐ
ܘܚܕܐ ܕܡܬܒܥܝܢ ܡܢܗܿ. ܗܝ ܕܝܢ
ܐܝܟܢܐ ܠܗܘܢ. ܐܬ̈ܘܬܐ ܕܒܓܕܟܦܬ ܟܠܗܘܢ
ܕܡܬܩܪܝܢ ܗܠܝܢ ܐܬ̈ܘܬܐ. ܩܘܫܝܐ ܗܘܝܘ
ܕܣܝܡܐ ܒܐܬ̈ܘܬܐ ܗܠܝܢ. ܦܘܪܫܢܐ ܐܚܪܝܢ
ܠܐܬ̈ܘܬܗ ܕܦܘܡ. ܘܡܬܩܪܝܢ ܘܩܢܝܢ ܚܕܐ.
ܗܘ ܕܝܢ ܐܝܟ ܣܝܡܢܐ. ܘܡܬܩܪܐ ܦܘܩܕܢܐ
ܐܡܪ ܕܡܬܩܪܐ ܠܐܬ̈ܘܬܐ. ܘܡܢ ܕܐܡܪ ܠܗ
ܠܐܬ̈ܘܬܐ ܒܗܠܝܢ ܕܐܬܘܬܗ ܒܩܠܗ ܕܐܬܘܬܗ
ܘܐܦ ܡܬܩܪܝܢ. ܡܬܦܫܩܝܢ ܡܫܡܠܝܢ
ܗܘܐ ܦܘܩܕܢܐ ܟܠܗܘܢ ܕܒܦܬܓܡܐ ܫܡܫܐ
ܘܡܫܡܠܝܢ. ܕܗܘܐ ܠܕܡܝܢ ܕܡܬܩܪܐ
ܕܦܘܩܕܢܐ ܗܘܐ. ܗܘ ܐܢ̈ܫܐ ܘܒܗܠܝܢ ܘܐܬܘܬܐ
ܕܡܬܩܪܐ. ܘܗܘܐ ܐܬܟܠܗܘܢ ܗܠܝܢ ܕܡܬܩܪܝܢ.
ܪܘܟܟܐ ܘܗܠܝܢ ܕܡܬܩܪܝܢ ܡܢܟܝܢ ܘܐܬܝܢ
ܗܠܝܢ ܐܬ̈ܘܬܐ. ܐܝܟܢܐ ܕܡܬܩܪܝܢ ܘܡܬܩܢܝܢ
ܕܐܬ̈ܘܬܐ ܕܡܬܩܪܝܢ. ܩܘܫܝܐ ܗܘܝܘ ܕܐܬܝܢ

ܡܫܬܡܠܝܐ. ܡܠܐ ܗܘܐ ܓܝܪ ܟܠ ܐܬܪ̈ܐ.
ܘܫܒܚܘ ܠܗ ܠܡܫܝܚܐ ܘܠܐܠܗܗ. ܫܘܠܡܐ
ܣܘܪܓܐ ܘܫܠܡܐ ܕܐܣܝܪܘܬܐ ܕܡܪܝ ܣܒܪܝܫܘܥ
ܠܡܪܒܢܐ. ܘܡܪܝ ܦܘܣܝ ܘܡܪܝ ܡܟܣܝܪܐ
ܒܡܘܪܝܗ ܘܒܪܘܡܦܘܗܝ. ܚܕܝܐ ܚܠܝܢ
ܠܟܘܠ ܒܪ̈ܢܝܗ. ܘܐܪܝ ܡܣܠܡܢܗ ܘܐܪܝ
ܚܝܠܗ ܘܫܠܡܢܗ ܗܢܐ ܕܚܘܐ ܐܚܪܐ
ܕܡܪܝ. ܘܗܘܐ ܡܘܪܒܐ ܚܢܢܐ ܢܗܘܘܢܗ
ܡܬܡܢܝܢ. ܘܐܠܗ ܢܠܡܘܢ ܢܨܠܝܢ ܕܢܫܡ
ܡܪܐ ܟܠܗܘܢ ܕܡܪܝܢܐ ܡܬܡܢܝܢ ܡܪܐ.
ܐܚܕܐ ܕܝܢ ܕܟܠܬܗ ܐܡܪ. ܕܢܬܠܐ ܐܝܬܘ:
ܡܪܝܢܐ ܘܡܫܬܐܠܐ. ܘܟܠܬܗ ܐܡܘܢ
ܕܡܫܬܐܝܠ ܡܢ ܐܝܟ ܘܡܬܡܢܝܢ ܡܪܝܢܐ.
ܫܘܠܡܐ ܚܕܐ ܕܡܫܚܐ ܡܬܕܟܪ ܡܫܝܚܐ
ܕܡܢܝܢ ܐܝܟܢܐ ܠܡܢܝܢ ܕܡܪܝܢܐ.
ܘܥܒܕܐ ܕܘܟܪܢܐ. ܟܘܪܐ ܚܕ ܡܘܪܒܐ ܕܐܒܐ.
ܐܡܝܢܐ ܕܡܪܝܢܐ. ܘܐܡܝܢ ܕܢܟܪܐ ܘܕܡܢ.
ܐܡܝܢ ܕܚܢܢܐ. ܘܐܡܝܢ ܕܗܡܝܢܘܬܐ. ܘܐܡܝܢ ܕܡܫܡܫܢܐ.
ܘܐܡܝܢ

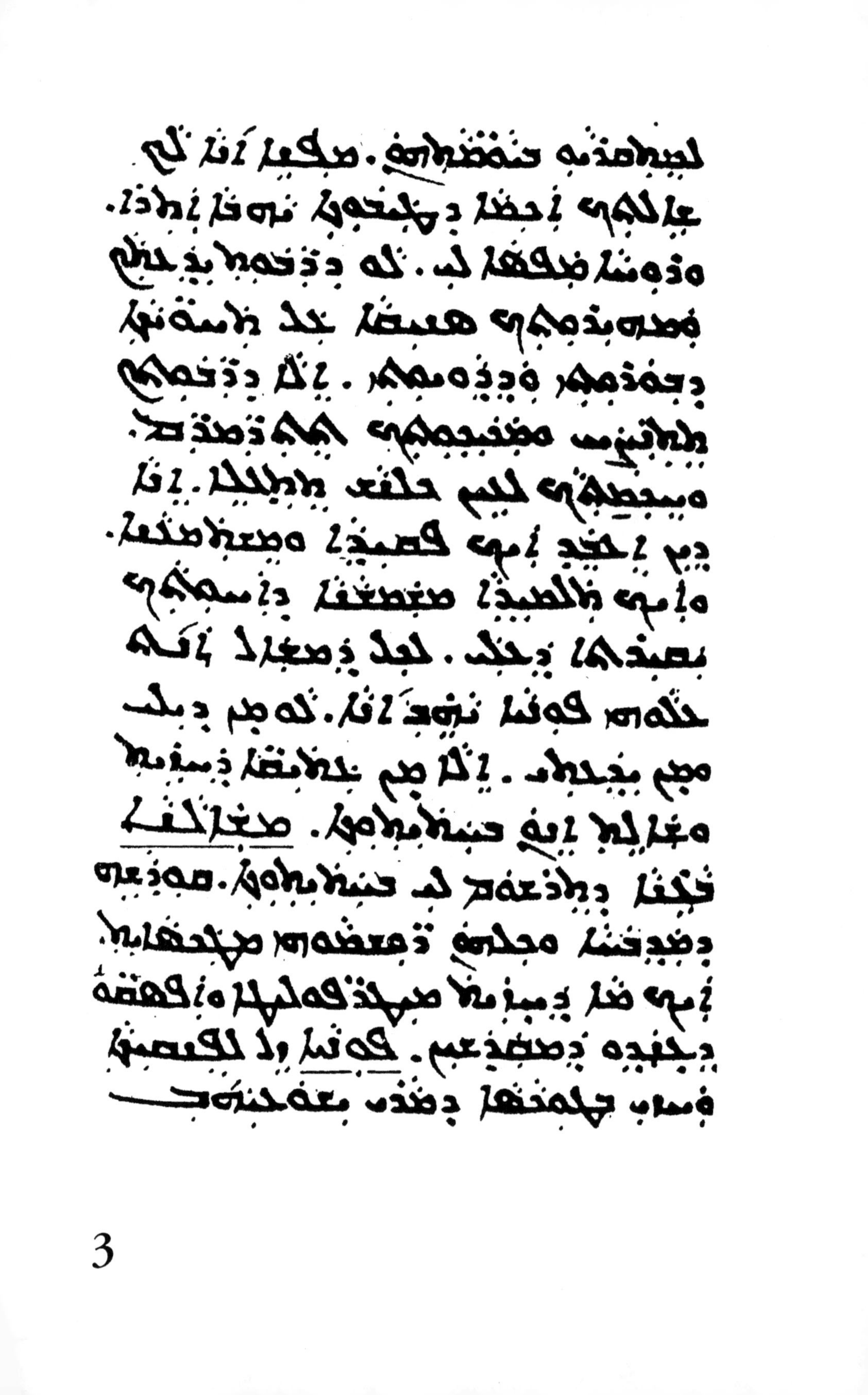

ܘܕܐܘܪܚܝ ܒܢܗܘܢ ܘܣܘܥܪܢܝ ܡܬܒܥܐ ܐܢܐ.
ܘܕܐܬܒܠܥܘ ܠܠܡܣܟܢܘ ܡܬܒܥܐ ܒܝܬ ܕܝܢܐ
ܐܢܐ. ܘܗܘܐ ܩܐܡ ܐܢܐ ܕܡܣܝܒܪܐ ܢܦܫܐ.
ܘܡܫܬܥܐܠ ܡܢ ܟܠ ܚܕ ܚܕ ܥܠ ܚܘܒܝ.
ܘܕܐܡܪܘ ܒܩܘܠ ܕܝܢܐ ܐܢܐ ܕܟܠ ܒܥܒܕ
ܢܦܫܐ. ܘܠܐ ܚܕܐ ܡܫܬܒܩܐ ܐܦ ܠܐ.
ܘܕܐܥܠܬ ܡܢ ܕܐܡܪܘ ܒܥܡܡܐ ܚܒܪܝ
ܐܢܐ ܐܝܟ ܐܪܥܐ ܟܕ ܡܛܝܐ ܒܚܝܠܐ. ܘܠܡܪܝܐ
ܡܪܐ ܐܢܐ ܠܕܝܢܐ. ܕܐܣܘܪ ܟܐܒܝ ܘܕܐܚܘܣ
ܡܢ ܢܦܫܐ ܕܡܫܬܥܐܠ. ܘܠܠܫܐ ܕܥܢܝܐ
ܒܥܒܪܢ. ܕܠܡܘܥܪܝ ܐܝܬܘܗܝ ܡܫܬܡܠܝܐ.
ܘܕܠܐ ܒܟܘܡܪܐ ܗܦܟܢܝ ܕܚܒ. ܠܗ ܟܕ ܐܢܬ
ܡܬܡܪܐ ܒܕܝܢܐ. ܘܠܐ ܒܠܝܫܐ ܕܒܥܡܝܢ
ܒܕܝܢܗܘܢ. ܐܠܐ ܐܝܟ ܡܐ ܕܢܗܘܐ ܘܚܝܐ
ܡܢ ܗܟܐ ܒܛܝܒܘܬܐ. ܘܒܪܚܡܘܗܝ ܠܒܘܪܟܬܐ.
ܕܡܪܚܡܢܘܬܐ ܥܠܝܢܐ ܘܠܐܒܘܟ ܒܪܚܡܘܗܝ
ܘܒܠܥܡܝܢ ܒܕܝܢܗܘܢ. ܐܠܐ ܕܐܦܠܐ
ܠܐܢܫܐ ܕܒܛܝܒܘܬܗ ܡܠܟܘܬܐ ܫܘܒܚܐ
ܠܥܠܡܝܢ.

ܘܡܢܗ ܠܗܘܢ. ܦܠܚܝܢܢ ܗܠܝܢ ܡܢܗ ܠܟܠܗܘܢ ܐܢܫܐ

ܐܦܢܝܡ. ܐܘ ܒܪܝ ܐܣܬܟܠ ܕܒܗ ܐܣܬܟܠܘ

ܚܠܡ ܕܠܐ ܘܡܥܒܕܐ ܘܕܝܢܐ. ܘܐܣܬܟܠ ܒܢܗܘܢ

ܣܢܐ ܗܘܐ ܒܫܢܝܗܘܢ. ܘܚܙܐ ܚܝܕܘܬܐ

ܒܕܝܠܗ ܘܠܐ ܡܬܕܥܝܢ ܚܘܒܝܐ. ܡܢ ܐܢܐ

ܗܘܕܥܬܐ ܕܗܢܝܢ ܒܟܠܝܘܡ ܐܣܝܪ ܟܐܒܐ.

ܕܡܝܬܝܢ ܢܦܫ ܐܦܠ ܘܠܐ ܐܝܟܢܐ ܕܐܝܬ. ܐܝܟ

ܗܘܕܥܬܐ ܦܘܪܫܢܐ. ܕܗܘܕܥܬܗ ܕܐܠܗܐ

ܒܝܕܥ ܥܒܕܐ ܗܝ. ܦܩܕ ܟܠܐ ܠܗ ܒܠ ܚܠ

ܥܘܐܠ ܕܐܚܪܢܐ ܢܦܫܗ. ܒܠ ܚܕ ܚܕ

ܦܠܚܢܐ. ܐܝܟ ܗܘ ܕܕܘܠܐ ܡܕܒܪܐ ܗܘܐ

ܠܗ. ܘܗܘ ܕܘܟܐ ܡܢ ܡܢܟܘܢ ܠܗ ܘܡܥܕܪܐ

ܠܦܠܚܘ. ܐܝܟ ܕܡܚܡܣܢ ܐܡܕܝܢܬܐ ܕܐܠܗܐ.

ܠܘܬ ܦܘܩܕ ܚܕܘܬܐ ܕܗܢܐ ܠܟܠ

ܐܗܘܕܥܬܐ. ܕܐܦ ܗܘ ܦܘܠܚܢܐ ܢܬܒܕܩ ܐܝܬܝܗ

ܕܐܕܡܝܐ ܠܟܠ ܘܠܐ ܐܝܟ ܡܢܗܘܢ. ܡܢܗܘܢ

ܠܗ ܡܢ ܟܠܗܘܢ ܡܢܦܫܬܐ ܕܐܢܫܝܢ

ܘܒܢܝܫܬܐ. ܘܠܐ ܡܬܚܫܒ ܐܢܐ ܠܗܘܢ.

ܥܠ ܚܝܠܗ ܕܡܪܢ ܢܦܩ ܡܫܒܚܢܐ ܡܬܩܪܝܢ
ܠܝܘܠܦܢ ܥܘܠܡܐ ܘܠܘܬܗ ܕܡܫܝܚܘܬܐ
ܕܡܕܒܪܢܐ ܕܒܠܚܘܕ ܒܕܘܟܬܗ ܀ ܫܘ
ܢܒܕܘܚ ܠܡܫܒܚܘܬܐ ܐܡܝܢ ܀

ܡܕܪܫܐ

ܦܢܩܝܬܐ ܕܡܫܬܠܡܢܐ. ܡܫܠܡܐ ܐܢܐ ܠܐܚܘܢ
ܠܘ ܗܢܐ ܢܒܥܐ. ܕܒܝܢ ܗܢܐ ܕܐܬܒܪܝ ܡܢ
ܗܢܐ ܒܠܚܘܕ ܢܦܫܐ. ܘܒܠܚܘܕ ܡܫܝܚܐ
ܡܬܩܪܝܢ ܥܘܠܡܐ ܐܝܬ ܐܚܪܢ ܠܒܪܝܬܐ ܘܠܐ
ܐܬܒܪܝܘ. ܡܢ ܡܫܬܘܬܐ ܡܫܬܢܐ
ܕܡܫܝܚܘܬܐ ܕܡܕܒܪܢܐ. ܘܒܪܢܫܐ ܕܐܬܝܠܕ
ܡܫܬܡܠܝܢ ܠܗܘܢ ܒܕܝܢ ܐܝܟ. ܡܢ ܒܬܪܟܢ
ܘܚܕܐ. ܘܥܠ ܚܕ ܐܢܘܢ ܢܕܒܪܘܢ ܡܫܬܡܠܝܢ
ܠܒܢܝܐ ܕܡܫܬܡܠܝܢ. ܘܐܝܬ ܐܢܫܐ ܕܡܢ
ܡܫܬܡܫܝܢ ܢܦܫܐ ܘܠܐ ܡܫܬܡܫܝܢ
ܡܬܒܪܝܬܐ. ܘܠܐ ܡܫܬܘܐ ܠܡܕܒܪܢܐ ܘܠܒܢܝܐ
ܕܢܦܫܐ. ܘܡܬܕܒܪ ܠܒܢܝܐ ܘܠܒܢܝܬܐ
ܕܡܫܬܡܠܝܢ. ܘܐܢܬ ܐܝܟ ܒܢܝܐ ܡܫܒܚܘ
ܡܫܒܚܘ

# FACSIMILE-REPRODUCTION

OF

# CODEX-MINGANA SYRIACUS

566, FOL. 1B–34A, 46B–48A